MOTOCOURSE™

THE WORLD'S LEADING GRAND PRIX & SUPERBIKE ANNUAL

icon
PUBLISHING LIMITED

THE CHOICE
OF CHAMPIONS
LEON HASLAM
2018 BRITISH
SUPERBIKE CHAMPION
JONATHAN REA
2015 / 2016 / 2017 / 2018
WORLD SUPERBIKE CHAMPION
ANA CARRASCO
2018 SSP300
WORLD CHAMPION

CONTENTS

MOTOCOURSE
2018–2019
is published by:
Icon Publishing Limited
16 Imperial Square
Cheltenham
Gloucestershire
GL50 1QZ
United Kingdom

Tel: +44 (0)1242 269154

Email: info@motocourse.com
Website: www.motocourse.com

Printed in Italy by
L.E.G.O. S.p.A.
Viale dell'Industria, 2,
I-36100 Vicenza
Email: info@legogroup.com

ISBN: 978-1910584-32-3

DISTRIBUTORS
Gardners Books
1 Whittle Drive, Eastbourne,
East Sussex BN23 6QH
Tel: +44 (0)1323 521555
email: sales@gardners.com

Bertram Books
1 Broadland Business Park, Norwich,
Norfolk, NR7 0WF
Tel: +44 (0)871 803 6709
email: books@bertrams.com

Chaters Wholesale Ltd
25/26 Murrell Green Business Park,
Hook, Hampshire RG27 9GR
Telephone: +44 (0)1256 765443
Fax: +44 (0)1256 769900
email: books@chaters.co.uk

NORTH AMERICA
Quayside Publishing Group
400 First Avenue North, Suite 300,
Minneapolis, MN 55401, USA
Telephone: (612) 344 8100
Fax: (612) 344 8691

publisher
STEVE SMALL
steve.small@iconpublishinglimited.com

commercial director
BRYN WILLIAMS
bryn.williams@iconpublishinglimited.com

editor
MICHAEL SCOTT

text editor
IAN PENBERTHY

results and statistics
PETER McLAREN

chief photographers
GOLD & GOOSE
David Goldman
Gareth Harford
Brian J. Nelson
David 'Chippy' Wood
www.goldandgoose.com
tel +44 (0)20 8444 2448

MotoGP bike and circuit illustrations
ADRIAN DEAN
f1artwork@blueyonder.co.uk

Acknowledgements

The Editor and staff of MOTOCOURSE wish to thank the following for their assistance in compiling the 2018–2019 edition: Pepe Aznar, Matt Birt, Majo Botella, Alex Briggs, Peter Clifford, Simon Crafar, Steve Day, Matt Dunn, Federica De Zottis, William Favero, Neil Morrison, Mat Oxley, Simon Patterson, David Pato, Elisa Pavan, Ignacio Sagnier, Julian Thomas, Frine Vellila, Tim Walpole, Mike Webb, Ian Wheeler, Gunther Wiesinger and Colin Young; as well as numerous others, including riders and technicians. A special thanks to Marlboro and HRC hospitality staff, and to colleagues and friends for advice freely given, but only grudgingly taken.

Photographs published in MOTOCOURSE 2018–2019 have been contributed by:
Chief photographers: Gold & Goose.
Other photographs contributed by: Whit Bazemore, Gavan Caldwell, Clive Challinor, Dave Collister, Ducati Corse, ECSTAR Suzuki, Bernd Fischer, HRC/Repsol Honda, John Morris/MPix, Monster Energy, MotoAmerica – Brian J. Nelson, Movistar Yamaha, Dave Purves, Neil Spalding, Mark Walters.

Dust jacket: Honda's Marc Marquez secured a classic fifth MotoGP title to equal the legendary Mick Doohan.
Photo: Repsol Honda

Title page: Superbike superstar Jonathan Rea claimed a record fourth championship in a row, completely dominant on the Kawasaki Ninja.
Photo: Gold & Goose

MOTOCOURSE
www.motocourse.com

MXGP /
FREESTYLE /
RALLIES /
SPEEDWAY /
ICE GLADIATORS
FIM-LIVE.COM
THE OFFICIAL WEBSITE
TRIAL / XTRIAL
SUPERENDURO /
ENDURO /
ENDURANCE /
MotoGP / SUPERBIKE /
AND MUCH MORE...
FIM
GET CONNECTED
LATEST RESULTS AND INSIGHTS

FOREWORD by MARC MARQUEZ

Photo: Repsol Honda

BECOMING World Champion for the seventh time makes me very proud. On top of that, it makes me very grateful to all the people who have been important to me throughout my career. My family, my team, who are like my second family, Honda.

Always when we lose, we all lose, but if we win, we also win together.

The season is never easy, I have very good rivals, we have great battles on the track, and I also try that people enjoy the races, giving always my best.

This year has been a very good season because I have been able to finish on the podium consistently, but in 2014, I had more wins – 13 races. I'm satisfied, we have worked well throughout and have managed to hold on in difficult times, and to take advantage when we were in good shape.

This annual, with its high-quality reporting and spectacular photographs, has been a celebrated part of the grand prix since before I was born.

In writing this foreword again, I am one of a long list of the world's greatest riders who have done so before me. It is a great pleasure to be part of that company.

Now I look forward to getting home to Cervera and celebrating with friends and family. And coming back in 2019 to do it all again!

Above: New heights. Jets over the grid at Mugello.
Photo: Gold & Goose

Right: Record-breaker Rea became the benchmark rider at World Superbikes.
Photo: Monster Energy

Bottom right: Marquez and the Repsol Honda family celebrate a year of being almost unbeatable.
Photo: Repsol Honda

EDITOR'S INTRODUCTION

FLYING HIGH

IT'S seamless. One year runs into the next. Two days after the last race of 2018, tests began for the following year. It had been the same at the end of 2017.

Grand prix racing has always been intense. Quite rightly.

Yet it seems to become more so, year by year. The rules are increasingly restrictive, but the technology doesn't slow down. The level is eternally rising, and the riders are taking it with them.

We are fresh from a fascinating season. Marquez was sublime, his talent blatant, almost unbelievable. Nobody could begrudge his fifth title in six years.

But it wasn't all about Marquez. Lorenzo transformed himself. Dovizioso steadfastly sought the maximum. Rossi refused to succumb to age or circumstances. Crutchlow kept on fighting.

Machine-wise, it was a year of Honda getting it righter than ever, and Yamaha wronger; of Suzuki making something beautiful go beautifully fast, of Ducati learning new things, of KTM lucking in to a first podium.

The smaller classes brought forth stunning new talent: Bagnaia and Oliveira illuminated Moto2; Martin and Bezzecchi did the same for Moto3.

And Jonathan Rea was simply historic on his Kawasaki Superbike.

In 2019, if the above is true, it will be even better!

Michael Scott

Forest Hills, KwaZulu Natal
November, 2018

FIM WORLD CHAMPIONSHIP 2018

TOP TEN RIDERS

THE EDITOR'S CHOICE

Rider Portraits by Gold & Goose

1 MARC MARQUEZ

THE image of Marquez from 2018 is not so much flashing past another chequered flag. It is of his Repsol Honda at an absurd angle of lean, the front wheel pointing inwards and the rear sliding sideways; the rider with one foot in the air, knee and elbow on the tarmac. A split second later, he will be back in control, throttle open, stopwatch ticking once more.

Marquez led a charmed life in 2018. On all but four occasions, he finished on the podium, most usually on the top step. While dismayed Rossi fans booed and sneered, he showed a choirboy smile imbued with a new maturity.

There can be no doubt. He is a giant of the sport. Boundless natural talent is backed by fearsome determination, underpinned by intelligence and supported by a team whose unity and effectiveness owes everything to its central figure.

What must it be like to race against Marquez?

Ask everybody else. Those close enough to give a worthwhile answer must be very exceptional riders.

2 ANDREA DOVIZIOSO

THOSE in search of an updated nickname for Desmo Dovi called him The Professor. It fitted well in 2018. He was calm and thoughtful, studious and precise. He stood back from emotion and reserved his passion. He measured out what was possible, then got as close to it as was achievable.

Almost every time.

If it weren't for Marquez, he would be outstanding. But if it weren't for Marquez, who would have given him the standard to aim for? The same is true for Ducati and their pursuit of Honda.

His own depth of understanding and ability to communicate with Ducati's engineers have helped to bring the Desmosedici to an unprecedented level. He has not been the only beneficiary, but he made the most of it.

He had to threaten to leave, however, before the Italian factory proved that they appreciated him more than the much more highly paid Lorenzo.

Dovi (32) wasn't perfect in 2018. He made uncharacteristic errors, falling at Le Mans and in Catalunya, but he was better than almost everybody else.

3 JORGE LORENZO

LORENZO'S compelling combination of talents had carried him to greater heights than in 2018. But in the years when he won the title, he had started from a more elevated position.

In 2018, he showed something quite new: adaptability. He had to change his technique 180 degrees.

On the Yamaha, he used skills he'd polished on a 250: smooth, sweeping lines and high corner speed. He generally won from the front.

The Ducati required a completely different approach: hard braking, quick turning, savage acceleration. Where he once caressed his way around a track, now he had to use muscle instead.

It took the 31-year-old more than a year to become thrice unbeatable. Luck conspired against him. He took three poles in a row, only for the first race (Silverstone) to be cancelled, the next two (Misano and Aragon) to end in crashes, and then injury to ruin the rest of his year.

He'd proved his point. Now he is off to Honda to do it again.

4 VALENTINO ROSSI

THE disastrous two years of Ducati aside, 2018 was measurably Valentino's worst season since he had won his first 125 race in 1996. Not one win, and not even a top-three since the German GP in July.

Yet, at 39, the oldest rider on the grid, he not only finished third overall, but also he never lost his capacity to surprise. After all these years and in all sorts of circumstances, you could never, ever rule him out.

He was hampered by his motorcycle. The Yamaha wasn't actually bad, but the Ducati and Honda were conspicuously better in several important areas. With racing closer than it had ever been, at Assen (admittedly, a somewhat extreme example), just over two seconds made the difference between second and seventh places.

What impressed more than the results was his unquenchable need to compete. It led him to crashes in the last two races, but he was leading one of them and second in the other.

Is he unstoppable?

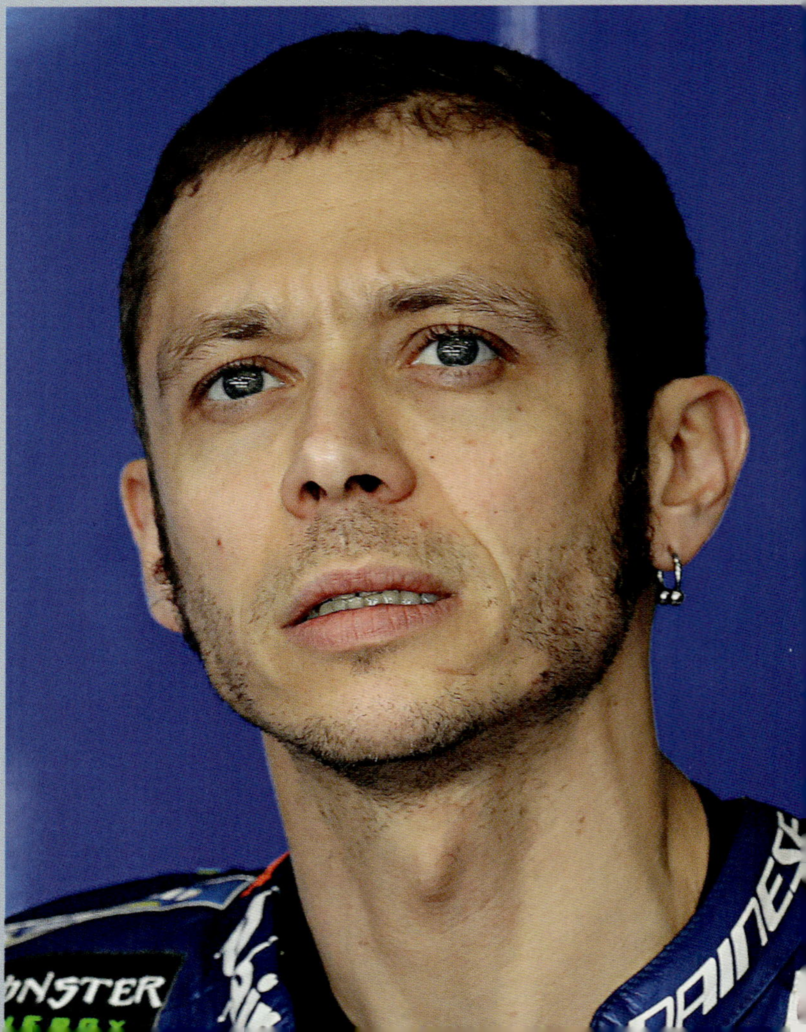

5 CAL CRUTCHLOW

"I KNOW I'm a crasher." In his own words, Crutchlow highlighted his weak point. Generally, however, his strong points outweighed this to such an extent that he was second only to Marquez on the hard-to-ride factory Honda, and obviously ahead of the experienced Pedrosa.

Sadly, his conspicuous courage and willingness to push cost him not only four race finishes earlier in the season, but also the last three races, and a clear lead in the independent-team riders' championship, after a bad ankle injury in a very fast crash in Australia.

Before then, Crutchlow's status had become ever higher, highlighted with a perfectly judged win in Argentina and acknowledged by HRC with an early contract extension. The 32-year-old's forceful riding style makes him an excellent foil for the similar Marquez, allowing him to provide valuable information to the factory engineers.

He was twice more on the podium, but the year ended in too much pain, and with too many might-have-beens.

6 ALEX RINS

NOTHING leaves a better impression than ending the season well; and nobody ended it better than Rins. Over the flyaways and the European finale, from Thailand to Valencia, the 22-year-old scored more points even than Marquez.

This was partly proof of how much the Suzuki had improved, but then you must compare him with team-mate Iannone. Rins wasn't necessarily always faster, but he was classier, and certainly more reliable, at least by the end of the season.

He did have five race crashes in the early stages, but it was only his second season in the premier class, after finishing second in both Moto3 and Moto2. He seemed to have learned the big bikes pretty well by the end of the year.

He had also visibly gained in confidence, off the track as well as on.

Rins won the backing of his team, and in 2019 would be the undisputed senior rider. He gave every sign of being ready the job.

7 MAVERICK VINALES

WHEN he was good, he was very, very good. But when he was bad...

Maverick (23) at least won a race in 2018, and by the end of the year had cheered up a lot and was fully competitive. Small changes to the Yamaha had made a big difference to him.

Up to that point, as well as the wheelspin and acceleration difficulties shared with team-mate Rossi, there were other puzzling problems – in particular a tendency to take half the race to get up to speed, by which time it was too late to make much impact.

His discomfort until the latter stages of the season was easy to understand, and it was easy to sympathise. Even when he was a little too public in his willingness to lay blame on his team, and particularly his respected crew chief, Ramon Forcada.

But at this level, a rider is expected to show more resilience, not to mention loyalty. Vinales's fragility did not do his image any good in 2018.

8 PECCO BAGNAIA

MOTO2 can be an austere class. Overtaking is difficult with identically underpowered bikes. The championship statistics in 2018 were no different. Bagnaia and Oliveira seldom clashed on track, but were close throughout on points. Pecco's winning margin was just seven.

Yet he never looked as though he didn't deserve to win, and it was one of the best seasons in the short history of the Honda-powered class.

Bagnaia not only took eight race victories, but also added a solid record of scoring points in every race of the season and for the final 12 of 2017. That shows strength in depth. He could fight, and he could finish.

Closely mentored by Rossi, Bagnaia has been impressive throughout his career, and he was the only rider to win in Moto3 on a Mahindra. Now he moves into MotoGP on a Ducati. Much is expected of the 21-year-old.

9 JORGE MARTIN

IS it possible to compare a 20-year-old Moto3 rider with the likes of Marquez and Rossi? It might be too early, but the way Martin rose head and shoulders above a maelstrom of rivals in a series of epically close races suggests an exceptional talent.

One measure was 11 poles, bringing his class total to a record 20. He achieved them not by following and drafting, as is the Moto3 norm, but almost always alone. This ability for extra speed was often displayed in races, where he would win by biding his time and then galloping away.

He won seven races in 2018, and had two race crashes through his own mistakes. Two others were as innocent victim of other riders. And he displayed exceptional courage in fighting for victory in Austria, a week after breaking his wrist.

Martin moves to Moto2 for 2019. His speed, tactics and racecraft give every indication that, like previous tiny-class tigers Rossi and Vinales, he could go all the way.

10 MIGUEL OLIVEIRA

IT hurts to be number two, and Portugal's first bike racing star has tasted it a couple of times now, finishing close runner-up to Kent in Moto3 in 2015 (six points) and now close to Bagnaia in Moto2 (seven points).

If sportsmanlike behaviour is any criterion, he has excelled on both occasions. But in 2018, he was more clearly beaten than in the smaller class, with Bagnaia's last-corner defeat in Austria particularly instructive.

Oliveira (23) is articulate and multi-lingual, and for the present he has suspended his medical studies (dentistry) in a quest for the chequered flag. He won three Moto2 races in 2017 and another three in 2018, backed with solid podiums at another nine races, without a single no-score. It took a very good rider to beat him.

He follows Bagnaia to MotoGP for 2019, riding a KTM – the first to benefit from the Austrian marque's newly-made ladder through the classes. He will, in the politest possible way, be seeking revenge.

THE STATE OF RACING

MORE OF THE SAME, BETTER THAN EVER

Racing was closer than ever in 2018, and there was plenty of it. Michael Scott reports...

Above: Donner and blitzen! But only figuratively. The MotoGP pack thunders off the grid at the Sachsenring.
Photo: Gold & Goose

Top right and above right: And just rain, but literally. Zarco looks anxious as chaos rules on the Silverstone grid; Rossi at least has someone to hold his umbrella.
Photos: Monster Energy

Right: And where do you think you're going? A different kind of chaos in Argentina as Marquez manhandles his stalled Honda on a grid where almost everyone was officially on the back row.
Photo: Gold & Goose

WITH the addition of the Thai Grand Prix, the 19-round season was the longest ever. And exceptional in other ways. The number of 'closest ever' MotoGP records broken during 2018 became almost monotonous. But that was just statistics. What really mattered was the racing. And that was arguably – indeed measurably – as good as it had ever been in the 70 years since the championship had begun.

Six different manufacturers were lined up on the MotoGP grid, and five of them made it to the podium at least once.

Since it was only six years after Dorna had introduced production-based CRT bikes to the premier class to boost the dwindling grid numbers, this was a significant improvement.

The other reason for bringing in the souped-up street bikes was tactical. Dorna CEO Carmelo Ezpeleta was bullish in his insistence that if the factories didn't find a means of reducing costs, increasing numbers and supplying competitive machinery to non-factory teams, "we will go racing without the factories".

Looking back, it is clear that the tub-thumping worked. The last so-called Golden Age had come about because of a confluence of talented riders on a group of 500cc two-strokes, which were all too powerful for their tyres. The current Golden Age has come about through deliberate design.

This is not to say that everything was perfect. Problems still cropped up, sticking-plaster solutions had to be found, and the evolution of regulations continued.

What a pity, however, that Dorna can't control the climate. In a year with a record-breaking dry European summer, rain caused the biggest problems.

The first of two major disruptions occurred at only the second round, in the Argentine. Jack Miller had already claimed a fine pole position, having braved slicks on a damp track, and he opted for the same gamble on a damp race-day. After the sighting lap, the rest of the grid decided to follow suit, pulling into the pits to change from wet tyres. That raised the dangerous spectre of a mass pit-lane start; and the on-the-spot solution was to put everyone except Miller on the back row of the grid. Which in effect meant just moving them back a few yards.

This meant, said a subsequent official statement announcing a rules rethink, that Miller's well-earned advantage had been rendered negligible; and a new plan was put in place should these rare circumstances prevail in the future. The long and the short was that riders who change to different tyres after the sighting lap will line up on their previous grid places, but will have to serve a ride-through penalty, the equivalent of stopping to change tyres during the race. If they decide to change after the warm-up lap, it's a pit-lane start and a ride-through. And if at any time there are more than ten riders making a pit-lane start, the race will be red-flagged and started all over again.

The second was completely out of MotoGP's control and happened at Silverstone, where the fully resurfaced circuit proved disgracefully unfit for purpose. After interminable delays all Sunday, the whole event had to be cancelled. Manager Stuart Higgs promised a full independent investigation, but as MOTOCOURSE went to press, three months later, no further information was forthcoming; while the future of the British GP hung in the balance.

The puddles at the badly drained track caused the worst injury of the season, when Tito Rabat was put out for the

RAMAC

MOTUL
MOTUL

Above: **Wet weather wonder-worker Dovizioso took victory during a deluge at Valencia.**

Top right: **Exciting new blood. The Turkish Oncu twins, Can (*centre*) and Deniz, with their father before Can's historic debut GP win.**
Photos: Whit Bazemore Photgraphy

Above right: **Jonathan Rea was even more dominant in World Superbikes than Marquez in MotoGP.**

Centre row, from left: **Even Dorna couldn't halt the incoming weather at Silverstone; Andrea Iannone lost out at Suzuki in MotoGP's game of thrones; running the show, Dorna's Carmelo Ezpeleta chats with Yamaha's Lin Jarvis.**
Photos: Gold & Goose

Bottom: **Who's next? Young riders in the British Talent Cup line up at Silverstone with GP winners *(standing, from left)*, Scott Redding, Cal Crutchlow, Sam Lowes, John McPhee, Danny Kent and Bradley Smith.**
Photo: Clive Challinor Motorsport Photography

remainder of the year after being hit by another machine in a multi-bike aquaplaning accident. For the rest, safety provisions and improving equipment made it a merciful season. One contribution was that airbag leathers had become compulsory in all classes. At year's end, a new homologation for crash helmets was introduced.

The winning arrival of 15-year-old Can Oncu at Valencia was the high point of a year of boosted efforts seeking the next generations of racers. As well as the well-established Red Bull Rookies Cup and its maturing equivalent, the Shell Advance Asia Talent Cup, the British Talent Cup got under way. The Dorna-backed British Talent Team was withdrawn, with the organisers easing rider John McPhee's place in the CIP team, and financial support was switched to the CEV Junior World Championship. Britain is several steps behind Europe (especially Spain and Italy) and Asia, but at least has a chance to catch up.

At the other end of riders' careers, the plights of Alvaro Bautista and Andrea Iannone gave rise to thoughts of the introduction of a football-style transfer window, banning the signing of new riders until later in the season. In 2018, it had all started in January, with Vinales signing his 2019–2020 Yamaha contract, followed soon after by Rossi and Marquez. That set a frantic pace, and Iannone lost his place at Suzuki in June to Joan Mir, as the factory jumped in to avoid missing the boat. Iannone's subsequent performance suggested that this might have been premature. Bautista also performed strongly in the latter part of the year, but by then the game of musical chairs was over, and he was without a seat. So too Bradley Smith and Scott Redding. Unfair? Possibly not. It just shows that there is more talent available than there are rides, in spite of the full grids.

Moto2's final Honda year was the best yet, but it was time for the Cinderella class to take a step forward. Tests of the sonorous new Triumph triple were highly encouraging, with riders praising the increased torque and rideability, as well as the considerably more sophisticated electronics package. One less happy consequence of the change stems from the fact that there are no equivalent national championships, as there were for the original Honda-powered 600cc version, so there will be no wild-cards in the class in 2019.

Moto3 enjoyed a blinding season, but new harsher sanctions were only partially successful in taming the practice of cruising at low speed during qualifying, waiting for a tow from a faster rider. The worst case occurred at Aragon, where 13 riders were penalised. The new sanctions, introduced late in 2017, ranged from a 12-place grid penalty for a first offence via back of the grid for a second to a pit-lane start for a third. Any rider who carried on offending risked being suspended for a race.

At the end of 2018, a different approach was decided upon: from 2019, both Moto3 and Moto2 will follow MotoGP practice, with aggregate times from three free practices determining which riders will go straight through to Q2. In MotoGP, the top ten are chosen; in the smaller classes, it will be the top 14. In the bigger class, the top two in Q1 go through to Q2; in Motos 2 and 3, it will be the top four.

Whether this will prevent Moto3 riders from following to pick up a tow remains to be seen. It does address a curious phenomenon in Moto2, though, where almost invariably the fastest qualifying times were set in the first two or three laps, when the track still had freshly-laid Michelin rubber from MotoGP. Once the Dunlops had put a layer on top, times became slower.

Cost control remained on the GP agenda, with tighter regulations for aerodynamics introduced. The 2018 rules allowed modifications to homologated bodywork, which gave rise to a great variety of 'not-wings' as manufacturers (particularly Ducati) exercised the right to remove sections of their original bodywork. In July, new 'aero-body design guidelines' were released by the technical director, whose word, in the absence of specific regulations, is law. The present designs will be allowed, but without the removal of sections as permitted in 2018 – one aero body only (and one standard), with no variations. Another change was a further reduction in testing, with one less European test.

Significantly, a unified inertial platform (a crucial element of the ECU package) will be introduced for the 2019 season.

This is to curb potentially runaway costs, with increasingly sophisticated units giving an electronic advantage to the bigger spenders.

The 2019 MotoE bike made an appearance at the GPs, with sundry celebrity riders, including in Australia Mick Doohan, performing demonstration laps at very varied speeds. If the experience was underwhelming, it might be different at the five races scheduled (at Jerez, Le Mans, Sachsenring, Red Bull Ring and Misano), when there will be 18 of the silent sportsters jostling for position. The entry list was announced at the end of the year, the biggest surprise being the presence of erstwhile Rossi rival and 500cc/MotoGP race winner Sete Gibernau, who had retired in 2009 and was returning at the age of 46. The 18 riders are a mixture of old and new, including several ex-GP riders of various levels, among them Alex de Angelis, former 125 champions Nico Terol and Mike di Meglio, woman GP racer Maria Herrera, and 2018 MotoGP riders Xavier Simeon and Bradley Smith.

All told, with strong attendances, good industry support and lively racing in all three classes, MotoGP was in booming good health in 2018.

If the same could not be said of World Superbikes, the still relatively new series owners, Dorna, might yet be able to engender a similar turnaround for the production series, and there were encouraging signs at the end of the year. Honda were set for a factory-level return, BMW likewise, with hopes for increased involvement by Suzuki.

Dorna also addressed the unpopular format they introduced of splitting the traditional two-race programme over two days. In 2019, race one will still be held on Saturday and race two on Sunday, but a third sprint race on Sunday morning will give spectators another reason to attend.

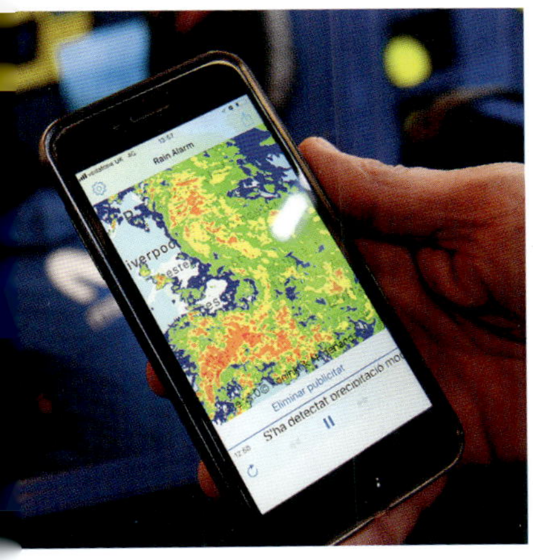

THE HEADMASTER

High in the control tower, surrounded by screens and assistants, one man is in control of every grand prix. MAT OXLEY examines the role of Race Director Mike Webb...

Above: Webb centre. The race director is master in the control tower.
Photo: Andrew Northcott

Top right: Webb explains his decision to award three penalty points to Rossi after his clash with Marquez in Malaysia in 2015. The result was a back-of-the-grid start and the end of his fading title hopes.

Above right: At the same event, Rossi is on his way to see the headmaster.

Right: The cancellation of Silverstone's British GP put Webb and his colleagues in the spotlight.
Photos: Gold & Goose

Far right: In touch and in control. Webb surveys the grid from on high.
Photo: Courtesy MotoGP

BACK in the 1980s, when MOTOCOURSE was in its infancy and motorcycle grand prix racing advancing beyond the age of 30, the way the sport was run was – to riders and press alike – a cause of much concern.

Individual race promoters had a free hand in many aspects, particularly in accepting entries and negotiating payments; detailed management was very erratic. It was run under the auspices of the Swiss-based Fédération Internationale de Motocyclisme, the FIM, and national race stewards frequently made unpredictable decisions on the spot. On occasion, long after the event, these were reversed.

How different is MotoGP today. The federation still plays a role, but within a unified and rationalised management structure. And the man at the top, as far as the racing itself is concerned, is a friendly and thoughtful New Zealander.

Mike Webb took over from MotoGP's first race director, Paul Butler, in 2012. Since that time, there have been very few MotoGP stars who haven't been summoned to his office. Like schoolboys in front of the headmaster, they would have been lucky to escape with a good telling-off.

Punishing errant riders is the most public aspect of Webb's job. He has sent both Marc Marquez and Valentino Rossi to the back of the grid at various times. But this isn't what the job is all about – as the addition, in 2016, of a panel of stewards to decide punishments underlined. Webb chaired this panel, but at the end of 2018, it was announced that former triple champion Freddie Spencer would take over the role. Because being the race director involves so much more: nothing less than the smooth running of every detail of every event.

A task at 2018's cancelled British GP, for example, required the proverbial patience of Job, the wisdom of Solomon and the courage of leonine convictions.

The book of regulations describes his duties thus:

The Race Director is responsible for ensuring proper observance of the regulations and efficient running of practice and races...
The Race Director shall have overriding authority in the following matters:

a) *The control of practice and races*
b) *The stopping of practice or races if he deems it unsafe to continue*
c) *The starting procedure*
d) *The use of medical cars/fast interventions vehicles.*

Before becoming race director, Webb spent ten years as MotoGP technical director, dealing with the arrival of new bikes and the explosion of four-stroke racing technology. Prior to that, he was chief engineer for Carlos Checa, Simon Crafar, Niall Mackenzie, Neil Hodgson and Peter Goddard.

20ポスト
T12
場内共聴
FLC-7

ENEOS
movistar
YAMAHA

SHOWSEC
FIAMM
PRAMAC
9

Above: Webb and Carlos Checa on the grid at Valencia in 2001.
Photo: Gold & Goose

Top right: First GP years – as a crewman for Peter Goddard's 500cc ROC Yamaha in 1992.
Photo: Courtesy Mike Webb

Above right: Webb in 2003, now technical director for the new four-stroke class.

Above centre right: Webb had great respect for Wayne Rainey.

Above far right: Erratic talent Norick Abe. Webb took over as crew chief for the Japanese rider in 1997.

Right: On the front row in Argentina with Neil Hodgson, 1995.
Photos: Gold & Goose

And before that, he was twice New Zealand 250cc road-racing champion.

Webb grew up in the rural hinterland of New Zealand's north island. He gained a taste for two wheels by riding a bike around his godfather's farm. His family hated motorcycles, but he didn't let that stop him. While studying geology at university, he got a job at a bike shop owned by Ginger Molloy, recently back from finishing a heroic second to Giacomo Agostini in the 1970 500cc world championship, riding an air-cooled Kawasaki H1-R triple and an overbored Bultaco 350 single against the factory MV Agusta.

"I was surrounded by racing people and thought, 'This looks fun'," recalled Webb. In 1982, he bought a second-hand RD250LC. By the late 1980s, he was dominating the national championship on a TZ250. "In 1989, I won every race, so I thought I was quite good. I got a wild-card entry for the first Australian GP at Phillip Island, borrowed a bike off an Aussie bloke and didn't even qualify. That was a light-bulb moment: these guys are serious, I'm just having fun."

He returned the next year and did qualify, but was lapped by 250 GP winner John Kocinski. He retired at the end of 1991. "I started noticing things that I'd never even seen before – 'Hey, that wall looks close' – so I realised it was time to stop."

On his way home, he stopped to visit former racer and MOTOCOURSE editor Peter Clifford, who was setting up a 500cc grand prix team, backed by American enthusiast Bob MacLean. "Peter said, 'Great, perfect timing! We could do with a hand.'"

In 1992, Webb travelled to Europe to fettle Goddard's ROC Yamaha YZR500 for the WCM team. "We did okay and finished the season as top privateers. The bike was good and Peter was great. He was quite a technical rider, so he taught us a lot, but my plan was only to do a year, then go back to New Zealand, where I owned three motorcycle shops. I sold the shops and never went home..."

Mackenzie joined MacLean's team in 1993, and Webb became crew chief. After two years with the Scot, he did a year with Hodgson, then switched to World Superbikes with Crafar: "But I wanted to be back in the grand prix paddock. World Superbikes was owned by the Flamminis at the time, and I found it an unfriendly place."

Webb joined Wayne Rainey's factory Yamaha team for 1997, wielding the spanners for Norick Abe, but when the rider's crew chief failed to show, Webb got the job. "Abe was probably the most talented rider I've worked with, but he had no idea what was going on, so it was really difficult for him to repeat his good performances. We would look at his data traces – what he was doing with the brake and the throttle was spooky. He had a supernatural talent, but one day he was awesome, and the next day, no way.

"Working for Wayne was great. He was like a god to us and such a nice bloke, with so much knowledge. It was the best team atmosphere I ever had, like a family. But there was a lot of frustration for Wayne, because he knew he could win the race, so he tried his heart out, explaining to Abe what to do, but Abe's talent was based on feeling, not on logic."

Webb joined the Marlboro-backed factory Yamaha squad in 1999, as crew chief to Carlos Checa. "Carlos was another version of talent and frustration. He wasn't as mercurial as Abe, but he was another of those talents which was difficult to nail down. He had unbelievable feel, plus total commitment and bravery. It didn't matter how many times he crashed, he always went faster."

Both Abe and Checa, said Webb, were at a disadvantage on Yamahas that had been developed for Dunlop tyres, but had been switched to Michelins. "They both struggled with confidence from the front tyre. Abe would always say, 'Scary front feeling.'"

In 2002, Webb became MotoGP technical director, taking over from veteran Continental Circus rider Jack Findlay. At first, he wasn't sure it was the right job for him.

"What I knew of technical control with the 500 two-strokes was literally this: has it got the right fuel in it and does it weigh the right amount? That was it. Then suddenly the job of technical director got huge because of the four-strokes.

21
Valvoline
DUNLOP

TEAM
SHOEI
YAMAHA

25
DUNLOP
SUZUKI

Above: "A bunch of dickheads." Moto3 riders give Webb more work than the other classes combined.

Top right: Hear no evil, see no evil, speak no evil. The triumvirate of Webb, Capirossi and Uncini.

Above right: Work before the race. Webb conducts a track inspection in Argentina in 2014.
Photos: Gold & Goose

Right: A bank of closed-circuit monitors gives the race director visual access to every part of every circuit.
Photo: Courtesy IMG

Now we've got a big fat rules book, and the IRTA [International Road-Racing Teams Association] technical department has its own truck and trailer, with people everywhere.

"In the early years of MotoGP, the job was very challenging. It was really hard to keep up, trying to have an understanding of what the factory engineers might try next. Back in the days of 500s, it was the factory race departments that went racing; with MotoGP, it was the factories themselves, with loads more serious engineers involved and the factories caring more deeply about what was going on because of the bigger investment."

Today, MotoGP's rule-makers spend most of their time working to restrict performance, but it was the opposite at the dawn of bike racing's second four-stroke era.

"The brief was this: these things must be faster than the 500s and they must sound good." Faster was not a problem. Webb and Checa had already proved that with a race simulation at Brno on a very underdeveloped Yamaha prototype in 2001, 20 seconds better than the race record. "From that day, I knew a 500 would never win another race. The four-strokes had power everywhere. Carlos was only using three gears around Brno. The key was how the four-strokes used the rear tyre; you could fit a well-used tyre and the four-stroke would still be very fast, but the 500 would be unrideable."

Yet when Honda's five-cylinder RC211V was unleashed, Yamaha's first MotoGP bike proved a dud. "The RC211V was beautifully thought out, and Honda were very clever when they proposed that five-cylinder bikes should have the same weight limit as four-cylinder bikes. When Honda suggested that, they already knew what kind of bike they were going to build, so the people making the first MotoGP regulations were a bit naive!"

The rate of development was such that many riders and teams called for a reduction in horsepower. At that time, the Motorcycle Sports Manufacturers Association (MSMA) was writing most of the rules and proposed 2007's disastrous switch to 800s. They were no slower than the 990s and triggered a boom in electronics technology. A further attempt, by restricting fuel from 24 litres to 22 and then 20, created its own problems, making the bikes trickier to ride, especially into corners.

These were troubled times. Global financial meltdown and the end of tobacco sponsorship brought MotoGP almost to its knees. The recovery was tortuous: CRT bikes, the return to 1000s and the introduction of restricted electronics.

"Today, the grid is full and the racing is the best it's ever been. It's been a long road to get here, but this has always been the target. We made some technical rule decisions that made it look like we didn't know what we were doing, but we always knew where we wanted to be."

The hard-fought Moto3 class gives Race Direction the most headaches: "It takes more Race Direction man-hours to manage Moto3 than the other two classes put together. A hell of a lot of work goes into trying to stop them being dickheads!

"The biggest nightmare is riders exceeding track limits. We are developing a new camera and software system to police track limits, using image-recognition software. It's getting very good. These are the lengths we have to go to, because we took the artificial grass away from the side of the tracks, which has saved a bunch of crashes.

"The real work in my job is done in the weeks and months before each race: making sure everything is in place, making sure the local people are doing what they need to do, making sure the track is up to scratch and that everyone knows what they're doing way ahead of time. Then I turn up before the race weekend to make sure everything is okay. Once the bikes are on track, I'm in race control staring at the screens, dishing out penalties.

"We are quite proud of where MotoGP is now, especially the racing itself, but this brings downsides: all the squabbling and people doing anything to get an advantage and misbehaving, which is a factor of the racing being so competitive. It's like the penalties for jumping the start. When I go back to New Zealand, I sometimes visit Hugh Anderson [a four-times

world champion in the 1960s], who tells me that if he won a race after jumping the start, it didn't matter because he was winning races by 30 seconds!"

What is the best aspect of the job? "The best bit is that me and everyone else in Race Direction are all fans. We appreciate the skills and a good performance. We all sit there watching, going, 'Wow, how did he do that? Isn't that amazing?' We aren't fans of one rider or another, so we've a different way of looking at it from many fans. Like most people in the paddock, I grew up being a racer and an enthusiast, so I've got that real grounding in racing. Being an insider and watching every little thing is great."

Webb's full-time Race Direction colleagues are safety officer Franco Uncini and Carlos Ezpeleta, son of Dorna CEO Carmelo. Riders' representative Loris Capirossi and MotoGP director of technology Corrado Cecchinelli are heavily involved as well.

The low points of Webb's tenure, of course, are the deaths of Shoya Tomizawa, Marco Simoncelli and Luis Salom. Otherwise, his worst memory is of the hullabaloo that dominated the end of the 2015 MotoGP championship – Rossi accusing Marquez of unfair tactics, slowing and causing him to crash in Malaysia, and the subsequent fallout.

"Safety things are always the worst, but from a nastiness point of view, the 2015 episode was easily the worst. I was quite shocked, even though I've been around this for a long time, especially by some of the media and the public, who were out to sensationalise things and take sides. To me, it didn't seem like part of our sport. I was naively thinking that kind of nastiness doesn't exist in motorcycle racing, but it's obviously there. I was disappointed and surprised. My job is trying to see both sides of everything, so I was surprised to see people being completely one-eyed in their points of view."

SIZE MATTERS, TALENT MATTERS MORE

Weighing in at just over 110 pounds and barely five feet tall, Dani Pedrosa repeatedly delivered giant-killing performances. He had to. MICHAEL SCOTT pays tribute...

Above: Giant killer. Little Dani on the big Honda.
Photo: Repsol Honda

Right: Fast company. On the podium as 250 champion, Pedrosa is flanked by a young Lorenzo (*left*) and Stoner.
Photo: Gold & Goose

WHEN the word first went out about Spain's new talent-spotting series for 1999, the well-sponsored brainchild of former 500 GP winner Alberto Puig, there were said to be something like 6,000 applicants. Never one to do anything by halves, Puig – in 2018, the new manager of the triumphant Repsol Honda team – whittled the numbers of 14- to 16-year-olds down to the most promising 400. Each had a riding test, then a personal interview. Puig picked the 25 best and sent them racing.

One of the successful applicants was a tiny, shy youth. But the former Minimoto star made a big impression on the man who was just beginning to take on the role of racing Svengali, nurturing talent and steering it towards GP racing. The 14-year-old wasn't the fastest, Puig remembered, but "he was hardly up to my waist and he was so determined."

It was, of course, Dani Pedrosa, and his progress through Puig's three-year programme, starting with the 1999 Movistar Aktiva Cup, was the start of something remarkable.

Something that finally came to an end in 2018, after 16 record-breaking winning years. Pedrosa had grown a bit during that time. Three inches to be precise – to five foot three (160cm). Now he could look down at Puig's waistline. His tiny size, like that of a pre-teen boy, makes his list of achievements on the world's most powerful racing motorcycles all the more impressive.

Perhaps not so much on a 125. Those bikes were also light, the distance to the ground not so great. Dani joined the junior class in 2001, along with fellow Akativa Cup graduates Joan Olive and Toni Elias. Elias was the most experienced and won two races in his first season. His successful career continues in the USA and includes a MotoGP win, the inaugural Moto2 championship and the MotoAmerica Superbike title. But of the three, Dani would go on to the greatest glory.

In his first year on the blue Telefonica MoviStar Honda 125, Dani made the podium three times. In 2002, he took three wins, the first at Assen, and finished third overall. Then in 2003, he was dominant, with five wins and a clear title win ahead of Alex de Angelis. Dani was on the move...

To where? Alas, to hospital. The wins were one aspect of his career path. Success interrupted by pain and injury another.

Dani was already confirmed champion when at the second-last race, he slid off at Phillip Island's MG Corner, feet first into the barrier, breaking both ankles. He wouldn't often crash, being a rider of neatness and precision, of focus and control. But when he did fall, all too often something would break – a wrist here, a collarbone there, a knee somewhere else. This was the

Above: Dani on his way to the third of seven wins at Valencia. This was in 2005, after winning his second 250 title.

Top left: Dwarfed by the trophy for his second win, 125 rider Dani at the 2002 Pacific GP.

Above left: Cheer up. A typically sombre Pedrosa in 2003.

Top: At the Dutch TT, in his 125 title year of 2003.

Above centre: Up a class and double champion. Dani waits on the grid at Estoril with his mentor, Alberto Puig (*left*).

Photo: Gold & Goose

Above: Pedrosa was all but unbeatable on a 250, taking 15 wins in 2004 and 2005.

Top centre right: On his way to a second straight 250 title in 2005.

Above right: The 800cc MotoGP Honda was flawed. Here at Catalunya, Dani took one of his two wins in 2008.

Top right: Pedrosa's first MotoGP win was in his fourth race, on the 990cc Honda in China. He leads team-mate and eventual 2006 champion Nicky Hayden.

Right: Laguna Seca, and Pedrosa is heading for his first of two wins in 2009.

Photos: Gold & Goose

price he would pay for his physical delicacy. Nor was there a positive. His spell as the fastest starter on a MotoGP bike had less to do with his low weight than his accurate technique.

Most of the injuries would come in the future. Patched up over the winter, he moved straight into 250s in 2004 and was brilliant, winning his first race.

His two seasons on the Honda 250 would be his best years. The size and weight were manageable, the power perfectly suited to his accurate style. Dovizioso, following a year or so behind, recalled, "Even on a 250, he was picking up the bike to accelerate out of the corners."

Dani, still a teenager, won the 250 championship at his first attempt, and again the following year, with seven wins in 2004, eight in 2005. This second title was tougher. He was up against another Puig protégé, Casey Stoner, who took five wins. Lorenzo had also joined the class. It was a good time to move on.

Stoner went to the satellite LCR Honda team, and would have to wait another year before moving to Ducati and powering straight to the MotoGP title.

Dani, with his powerful patronage and Spanish sponsorship, went straight into the Repsol Honda team, alongside eventual 2006 champion Nicky Hayden.

Conventional paddock wisdom was far from sure that this was the right thing. The first-generation MotoGP bikes were 990cc bruisers, Honda's sonorous V5 about as far as you could get from a narrow and nimble two-stroke 250 V-twin. One doubter was Rossi's renowned crew chief, Jeremy Burgess. Dani would never get to grips with the 990, he believed. He was far from alone in this view. I recall hearing the phrase "like a rat on a greyhound".

Pedrosa, speaking at the end of 2018, also said that he had had major reservations: "When I got on for the first time, the bike was very big, and I knew I wasn't able to do as well as in the lower class. But I was immediately fast. I knew there would be times I would struggle, like in the rain and at very fast tracks, but I was good overall. I was really surprised. I felt I could cross that border that I didn't expect."

In a way, however, the doubters were proved right. Dani's stature was always a drawback, most obviously during his final season, exaggerated by the nature of the Michelin control tyres. These needed to be used hard to get them up to working temperature. Dani just didn't have the heft to do it. As a result, 2018 was his worst ever season in MotoGP. Indeed it was the first year since his second season on a 125, in 2002, when he didn't win a single race. He didn't even make the podium.

That was atypical. Less so his injury record. At round two in the Argentine, he was knocked down by Zarco, who mystifyingly went unpunished, and broke his wrist. He had it fixed, then suffered a painful hip injury in the three-bike tangle with the Ducatis at Jerez. Only towards the end of his last year was he completely free from pain.

In the meantime, however, Dani had done far better than expected. He was only four races in to his first season when he took his first win in China, from a first pole position. After Freddie Spencer, he was the youngest premier-class winner, by 31 days.

From 2006 to 2009, he would take two race wins every year. This was mildly disappointing after his good start, because if the 990s had been too big for him, surely the 800s that were introduced in 2007 would have suited him more? Before the season began, he told me, "For me, this bike is better. The other one was too big and sometimes difficult to manage, because my arm length was short, and everything … I couldn't cover the bike. The bike was covering me."

This turned out to be beside the point, however. Honda's switch from V5 to V4 was not sure-footed. Stoner's Ducati won the 2007 title; Dani was second, one point ahead of Rossi. But between 2007 and 2009, the 800cc V4 won only seven races, six for Dani and one for Dovizioso, while Yamaha won 24 and Ducati 21. The RC212V was a significant failure after the class-defining RC211V.

Dani would take that runner-up spot three times altogether, and finish third three times as well: "Sometimes I wasn't there, sometimes the bike wasn't there, sometimes I was injured, sometimes another rider was faster than me." But his title

movistar
SAMSUNG
HONDA

REPSOL
69
26

REPSOL
2

Red Bull
REPSOL
3
HONDA
GAS

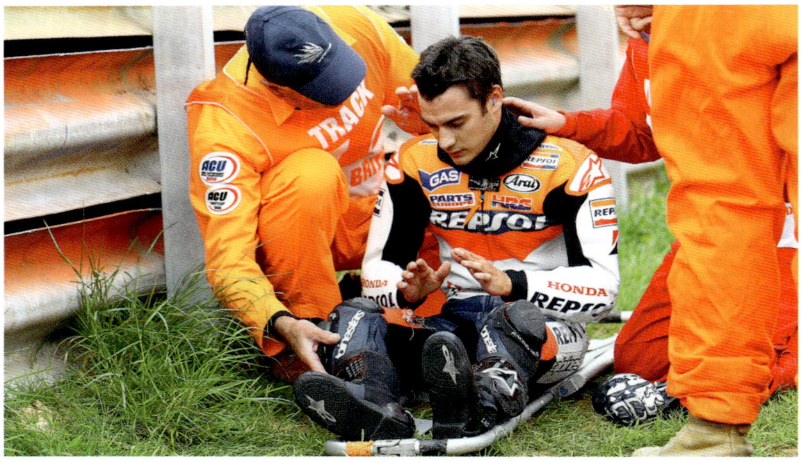

hopes would be repeatedly thwarted, more by his propensity to injury than his size or any other factor.

His fifth season was his first near miss. It was 2010, and halfway through the year HRC had finally started to make sense of the 800. Dani won four races and got to Motegi 56 points adrift of eventual Yamaha champion Lorenzo. It was a significant gap, but not insurmountable. There were five races to go, and over the last three, Dani and the improving RCV had reclaimed 21 points. One slip by Lorenzo, and the target was definitely within reach.

The slip, however, came on Pedrosa's side, blamed on a mechanic's error. During practice for the Japanese GP, his throttle jammed open. He crashed, and snap went his collarbone. His championship hopes were over.

The next year started well. After the first three races, he was narrowly behind to Lorenzo, 61 points to 65. At round four, the French GP at Le Mans, he was lying second to Stoner and about to take the title lead when a headlong Marco Simoncelli attacked. They collided, Dani fell, and broke his collarbone.

He missed four races, and when he returned, he publicly snubbed Simoncelli, who was under a lot of pressure for what his rivals considered to be reckless riding. The Italian took his first podium later that year, then crashed fatally in Malaysia a week later. Dani looked back on his snub: "I have learned that perhaps life is too short to have enemies. But in that moment, when these things happen, I was right, because I was angry. Because of that, I had to go through two surgeries and I lost my championship chances. It was very, very personal for me."

His most wins – seven – came in 2012, and his narrowest miss in the championship too – only 18 points adrift of Lorenzo in that first 1000cc year. Again, Honda took time to get the bike right, and in 2013 came what would turn out to be the biggest block yet to his title hopes – his new team-mate, Marc Marquez.

It didn't happen immediately, however. After the first seven of 18 rounds, with two wins and three second places, Pedrosa was leading on points when they arrived at the Sachsenring. What transpired was all too typical for Dani. On his first flying lap on Saturday morning, going into the first corner and "not even pushing", the bike suddenly slewed sideways and pitched him skyward. He clutched at his left shoulder; soon afterwards, in the medical centre, his blood pressure dropped dramatically. He was airlifted to hospital, but only a partial fracture to his left collarbone was found. He was passed fit for morning warm-up, but another giddy spell revealed that his blood pressure was bottoming out once more, and he was out.

There was some friction concerning Marquez's ruthless tactics as the younger rider went on to claim a rookie title, but no jealousy, and by the end, the two got on well, with plenty of obvious laughs. Dani has a different personality from the sombre, humourless reputation he gained, especially in his earlier years, and by comparison to the flamboyant Rossi. Where the latter would treat every TV interview or press conference as a chance to deliver a sound bite, Dani was always determinedly matter of fact.

Here is how he described his tactics for the coming week-

Left: Jerez in 2013, and Dani has won again.

Far left: This victory in Japan followed three consecutive second places in 2011.

Below left: En route to victory at Brno in 2012, one of seven wins. He was second overall for a third time.

Centre row, far left and centre left: Dani didn't crash often, but he was prone to getting hurt. Here, he receives treatment at Donington Park in 2010; and hits the road in Japan in 2013.

Below left: Enjoying the final accolades of his peers at the 2018 FIM awards ceremony.

Bottom left: Braking into the Museum, Dani leads Dovi at Le Mans in 2013, his second win of the year.

Below: Dani's 31st MotoGP win at Valencia in 2017 was the last of a 16-year run of victories.

Photos: Gold & Goose

end, at Brno a couple of years ago: "Have a good practice, good qualifying, a good start and a good race." He did crack a smile on the podium when he won it, but when it comes to crowd-pleasing displays and quotable quotes, Pedrosa is not one to oblige. No showing off.

"It's not my style. I care more about being concentrated and focused, and do the racing as best I can. I care less about making show. I don't feel it is natural for me. Because when I am in the public, I am racing, and it's my concentration. Nothing disturbs me. I am always looking straight ahead."

The record beats any pantomimes. Over the following years, there were more wins, at least one a year, and two in 2015 and 2017. Sixteen years of wins, a record not even Agostini could match. A total of 112 premier-class podiums secures Pedrosa's place among the greats.

Does size matter? Not according to a legion of fans, nor a paddock full of admirers of Dani's dedication, concentration, quiet nature and – behind an often glum expression – a well-developed sense of humour.

His farewell announcement, at the Sachsenring, was typically straight-faced and matter of fact as he described the difficult decision, adding, "I'd like to express how fortunate I feel to have this opportunity. It's been an amazing life to be racing for such an important team, in front of all the fans. I achieved way more than I expected, and I am very, very proud of all that I have done. I fulfilled my dream of becoming a racer, which I didn't think was possible when I was very young."

Tears emerged only briefly when he was asked to pick a special moment from his career. There were many, he said, but the day he caught Puig's eye at the Jarama tests stood out: "I was very small, and I didn't imagine with so many riders that I would be picked. From that moment to here … is amazing."

The emotion came more from others in the paddock, and showed just how much respect he had earned. Riders including Marquez and Vinales spoke of his importance not only to Spanish racing, but also to the championship. Long-time rival Rossi was eloquent: "His style was really technical and clean. He was also one of the first to pick up the bike in acceleration. It is a great shame that he never won the World Championship. I think he deserved at least one." Dovizioso spoke also of how he had learned to prepare for a racing weekend by studying Dani, but perhaps Jack Miller put his finger on it best: "With his size in MotoGP, he had to have a lot of talent to cope with the difficulties."

MOTO2 – THE HONDA YEARS

GP racing has seen and heard the last of the shrieking four-cylinder Moto2 bikes. In 2019, Triumph takes over from Honda. PETER McLAREN and MICHAEL SCOTT look back over the class that changed racing...

Above: **Pecco Bagnaia leads Quartararo and the pack at Motegi; 2018 was the closest-fought Moto2 championship.**

Top right: **The Kalex breaks cover at the end-of-season 2009 Valencia tests. Eventually, it would become the most successful chassis.**

Above centre right: **With 16 wins Marc Marquez won the most Moto2 races. He was also the last champion to ride a Suter.**

Above right: **The experienced Toni Elias took the first championship on the long-since departed Moriwaki.**

Right: **Mass-produced engine, handmade chassis. This is the Technomag Suter at Jerez tests in 2012.**

Photos: Gold & Goose

IF MotoGP is technically the most exotic grand prix class, the championship that fed it has been the least. In the words of MotoGP Director of Technology Corrado Cecchinelli, if Moto3 is zero in terms of technology and MotoGP 100, the 600cc Moto2 class was minus ten.

This was the case from 2010 to 2018. In 2019, the intermediate class will grow to 765cc, with three-cylinder Triumph engines fitted with considerably upgraded control electronics. That will put Moto2 up to 50 on Cecchinello's technology scale, equidistant between Moto3 and MotoGP.

Introduced in 2010, in the aftermath of the global financial crisis, Moto2 was the antidote to the final years of the 250 two-stroke class it replaced. This had become all but a one-make series, dominated by Aprilia. The Italian factory not only could decide their own costs, but also had a huge influence on results, able to supply favoured riders or well-heeled teams with a higher level of technology.

For 2010, an official one-make philosophy was adopted for engines (and tyres), with costs strictly controlled. Chassis were free within limits; exotica such as carbon brakes were banned. But for the rest, teams ran identical race-tuned Honda CBR600 engines, with the simplest of electronics.

Engines were supplied to the teams under Dorna's control on a random basis and to a fixed maintenance schedule. For the first three years, Geo Technology, an independent company, handled the task, working with Honda. From 2013, a Dorna subsidiary, ExternPro, based at the Aragon circuit, took over.

The term 'race-tuned' was somewhat relative. In the interests of costs and longevity, the motors were less powerful than those in the nominally production-based Supersport 600 class in the World Superbike paddock.

Diehards mourned – indeed, continue to mourn – the loss of the pure bred 250 racers, but sadly two-strokes had dropped firmly out of fashion. Their replacements were pure bred racing chassis on control Dunlop tyres, but with chubby production engines driving through road-based gear ratios.

The notion was that it would make for closer, more evenly matched racing, and in some ways that was the case. But it wasn't closely fought racing, in terms of the action. Near identical performance and no fiddle-room for different gearing or electronic solutions made overtaking very difficult, even by slipstreaming. Races, especially up front, were more often processional than exciting.

Ironically, the 2018 season was one of the best, with seven different winners and the closest ever championship, just nine points between winner Pecco Bagnaia and Miguel Oliveira.

Over the nine years, there have been eight different champions. Only Johann Zarco (2015, 2016) successfully defended his title, while all but the first champion, former MotoGP race winner Toni Elias, moved up to MotoGP. Of them, only Marc Marquez (2012 champion) went on to win the premier-class title, but several other current riders, including Pol Espargaro (2013) and Franco Morbidelli (2017), are past champions; while Scott Redding, Alex Rins and Maverick Vinales are among former Moto2 race winners.

Opinions vary as to the value of Moto2 as training for the

top class, although only one of the current riders actually gave the intermediate class a miss. Jack Miller vaulted directly to MotoGP from Moto3, where he had narrowly lost the 2014 title to Alex Marquez.

Did he think he had missed anything? Would he have gone to Moto2 had there been more powerful engines and a more sophisticated ECU back in 2015? "No. The goal was always to go to MotoGP, and as soon as I got the option, I grabbed it. I think, no matter the bike, whether it was 250 or Moto2, I wanted to skip the class. I wanted to be like Garry McCoy or those guys who just jumped straight into MotoGP."

Vinales spent just a year in Moto2 and learned some valuable lessons, in spite of the humble power unit: "The engine has nothing to do with it. Everything is different in Moto2. But I learned about when there is a tough moment, because in Moto2, if you just have one bad day, you are 19th. So you have to be always there, always there. This makes you learn a lot for MotoGP."

Technically, the training offered by Moto2 was severely lacking for Hafizh Syahrin, who unexpectedly was thrust into the premier class to take the place of Jonas Folger on the Monster Yamaha in 2018.

"When you jump, it's quite difficult to understand MotoGP electronics," Syahrin said. "In Moto2, you control only by hand. Now with Triumph and electronics similar to MotoGP, it will be good for the riders. When they jump to MotoGP, they just need to learn the power of the bike, the tyres."

Double Moto2 champion Zarco had a typically thoughtful response: "For some riders, you learn good things in Moto2, but for some others it is not a good preparation. It depends how you think.

"For me, it was so good to work on myself, and also understand a big bike and how to control rear grip when it is spinning, how to control a bike to turn in the entry. Even with different tyres and different types of bikes, you learn to rely on yourself, and that is a key in life, not only in MotoGP."

The Frenchman was not convinced that a higher level of electronics in 2019 would be that valuable, "because there is not enough power [in Moto2]. It is better to learn the electronics when you have real power. For Moto2, they will be a good help for some situations, but then maybe it will be more information for the riders and just more trouble."

Earlier champion Pol Espargaro spoke about the extreme accuracy that had come as Moto2 climbed to higher levels: "It is so 'controlled' with engine, electronics, chassis, front forks. Everything is so on the limit that they are talking about being faster in one sector by 20 milliseconds! So it is difficult to do epic races, or go from the back to the front. This is not nice any more. The new change is a challenge for the teams and the manufacturers.

"Change is beautiful for the sport, and I think it needs to happen every X amount of years, a big change and reset to start from zero."

But Moto2 was an important transition for riders. "I think the guys that skip the class or just do one year are missing an important part of the process," said Espargaro. "For me, I learned a lot, and it was important to win the championship and be a solid rider in Moto2 to be fast in MotoGP. The problems I had in the third year and with managing the tyre in stressful situations helped me so much for MotoGP.

"I had to change completely my riding style and feelings, and use harder tyre compounds where I was good with the soft ones. Just changing the mentality and fighting the problems. It was super-hard. My best year, and the one I enjoyed the most, was 2012, fighting with Marquez until the last races of the season. I expected a bit better in 2013, but found it even harder! Still, I got the trophy at the end."

Bradley Smith is another graduate: "The best thing about Moto2 has been the performance that Honda achieved, with so few technical breakdowns. That's allowed for really close racing. I hope that Triumph can keep that same level of performance and reliability. One of the key things that ruins championships is technical problems."

Above and top: Pol Espargaro won out as 2013 champion over Scott Redding (*top*) in a sustained battle. Both rode Kalex.

Above right: The QMMF Speed Up chassis in 2014. Anthony West took it to a wet win at Assen that year.

Top right: While the Honda engine was ultra-reliable, it was lacking in sophistication.

Top far right: KTM's unique steel-tube chassis joined the class in 2017, and challenged for the title in 2018.

Above centre right: Johann Zarco was the only double champion of the Honda era.

Above far right: Taller, slimmer, torquier – the Triumph 765 engine takes over from Honda in 2019.

Right: Danny Kent's bike at Brno in 2016. Kalexes like this took the top nine championship positions, and almost all the rest.

Photos: Gold & Goose

And what did Moto2 teach him? He laughed, "I learned how to suffer in Moto2!"

He continued, "I learned some bits and pieces, but when you get on a MotoGP bike, it's a completely different ball game. But I don't think it's been a bad stepping-stone. A lot of riders have adapted quickly to MotoGP, and I think that the new regulations could help even more. With more horsepower and more electronics, it can only help riders to adapt even better to MotoGP."

The restrictions also meant that crew chiefs had to find a new way to work, to an extent with one hand tied behind their backs. One of the most successful is New Zealander Pete Benson, who joined the new class after several years at high level in the Repsol Honda team, with riders including Doohan and Rossi, and 2006 champion Nicky Hayden. He went to the new Marc VDS team, with rider Scott Redding. Among his charges have been champions Tito Rabat (2014) and Franco Morbidelli (2017), and in 2018 he was crew chief to star rookie Joan Mir.

At first, Benson was not a great fan of the production-powered class: "I've always liked the prototype thing." But the Honda engine had done a great job: "It's been super reliable. It's been very cheap racing from the point of view of the engine. For me, what's lacking was electronics, to help the guys that make the jump to MotoGP. Moto3 had more electronics than Moto2.

"Also not being able to change gearbox ratios." The Honda's wide power band helped, "but there are a few places where you have to use first gear a couple of times, like Texas. There is quite a big gap between first and second, and the backshift into first was hard on the engine and the gearbox."

After a few early teething troubles, the CBR600s had been rock solid: "It was closely monitored by Honda, who have a super-high standard for safety and reliability. It proved to be really good. I don't think they got much value out of it, but it's been a good thing for them as well."

There was little advantage to be found in terms of power. With a standard airbox and filter, only the exhaust could be changed. "You just make sure that you are not losing anything. Everything else is in the chassis and the rider."

There were different chassis options, with Kalex becoming the most popular, KTM making a huge investment for their own successful version and the Speed Up showing particularly well at some tracks, he said. Engineers had to work hard to find any edge: "Any advantage you can find is a big advantage. If you can make half a tenth a lap in 20 laps…

"But you sort of find everybody always ends up with something similar in the end. You can be as secretive as you want, but when you've got a suspension, tyre or exhaust supplier, if three-quarters of the paddock have the same supplier and you're winning, they're just watching you. They want to know what you're doing."

The rider was the key, said Benson: "When you get a rider that wins seven-eight-nine races in a year, he's really stepped up to the plate." Looking back on his time with Redding, with three race wins and second overall in 2013, "we probably should have spent more time worrying about Scott than worrying about the bike."

Compared with Moto3, the actual riding had more in common with MotoGP, said Benson: "It's stopping the bike, getting it turned, getting it picked up and using the drive part of the tyre. If you see these guys that come from Moto3 and don't adapt, and they keep doing the big sweeping, classic lines, they just go backwards in the race.

"For me, the first guy who really showed it up the most was Tito Rabat. When he came to us, he had a really good understanding of the tyres and everything because he'd done a million laps on a Moto2 bike. And to me, he kind of changed the way Moto2 was ridden. Then Zarco took it to another level in getting things stopped and turned and picked up, and using the drive to get the speed. The lap time comes in the acceleration and speed, because you spend so much more time than

Moto2 Facts: The Honda Years

- **158 races**
- **204 riders**
- **101,969 racing laps**
- **476,753km raced**
- **21 race tracks**
- **30 constructors**
- **36 race winners**
- **Most wins – Marc Marquez (16)**
- **54 riders on podium**
- **Most podiums – Thomas Luthi (45)**

(With thanks to Steve English)

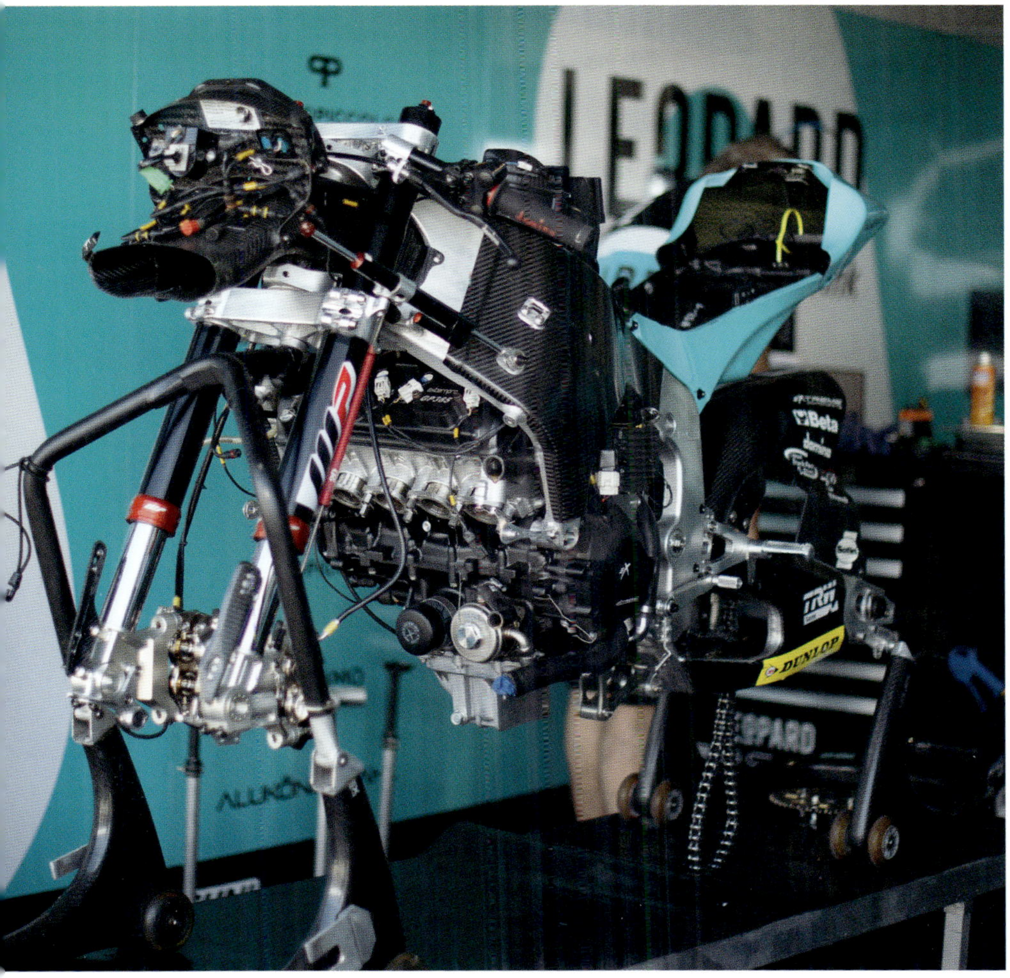

you do on the brakes, or on the side of the tyre being slow. This also is something you need to do in MotoGP."

The new electronics, he thought, "are a step in the right direction. But it's a very basic package. You can't write your own software. It's basically a number of settings to choose from. It's not like MotoGP where you have almost infinite adjustment. But it sounds like it works quite well. It's more MotoGP style than what we've had in Moto2."

After two years of development and a handful of encouraging tests, the Triumph era began with group tests at Jerez as MOTOCOURSE went to press. Early reports were positive: the engine not only being physically smaller and lighter than the earlier-generation CBR600, but also having more torque, as is the nature of a three-cylinder, longer-stroke engine compared with a four, even before taking account of the extra 165cc.

The engine is based on Triumph's 765cc Street Triple RS engine, which was derived from the Daytona Supersport 675. Race modifications include improved porting, a higher compression ratio, lighter inlet valves and revised cam timing, plus higher-flow fuel injectors and a low-inertia alternator. Importantly, first and second gear ratios have also been revised, for more of a close-ratio box. There's an adjustable slipper clutch, plus the Magneti Marelli ECU. Power is quoted at 140PS.

Although at present it is without traction or wheelie control, the new ride-by-wire system is predicated on that used in MotoGP, and it shares the inertial platform that is to be standardised in the senior class from 2019. Along with more electronic adjustability comes engine braking control, meaning a probable end to the exaggerated sideways corner entry used in Moto2 until now. In every other respect, the racing world is hoping for improvement.

But Honda have set the bar high in terms of predictability and reliability. According to ExternPro's figures, in racing and practice – and excluding testing – the CBR engines have covered more than 1.7 million miles at racing speeds. And that's enough to go to the moon and back more than three times.

THE YEAR OF LIVING DIFFERENTLY

Jorge Lorenzo undertook a massive task when he joined Ducati, changing his whole approach to riding. He got it right just in time to have to do the same thing again in 2019. NEIL MORRISON discovers why…

Main: **Redemption – three wins in 2018 restored Lorenzo's reputation. But he knew he had been right all along.**

Photo: Gold & Goose

Below right: **Jorge hugs the line. He changed his style for Ducati, and they changed the bike for him.**

Photo: Monster Energy

THE make-up of a champion goes far beyond the ability to amass more points than a rival across a particular season. Among other traits, an unerring belief in oneself and one's abilities is a requisite. Of this, Jorge Lorenzo is clear.

'The difference between champions and just normal sportsmen is that champions know that [if] they're in a bad situation, the future will change," he said.

Lorenzo spoke from experience. There were more highs and lows for the 31-year-old in 2018 than in any of his other 14 seasons on the world stage. His legend in grand prix racing had long been established before a high-risk switch to Ducati at the end of 2016. While three podiums and the gradual gaining of momentum outlined a promising first year, his sophomore season in red began abysmally. Flailing between set-ups and bike specs through pre-season, he could only score a single point in Argentina, the second race of the year. Two weeks on in Austin, he suffered the indignity of finishing behind not one satellite Ducati, but *two*.

Anyone watching knew that these showings weren't befitting of a rider of his stature. But, as so often during his days spent sharing a garage with Valentino Rossi, that unerring self-belief carried him through. "You always need to be positive," he said. "You always need to keep working, or work even harder to solve the situation. I always believed in myself. In Austin, it was very tough, but I knew inside we were closer than a lot of people thought. I was telling Gigi [Dall'Igna, Ducati chief] and some of the bosses that we just needed the last thing, the last piece. We were very close."

The rest, as they say, was history. A new seat/dummy tank unit revised the ergonomics of Ducati's wonderfully designed Desmosedeci GP18 ahead of the Italian Grand Prix. Dominant back-to-back wins at Mugello and Montmelo followed. And while injury scuppered the autumn of 2018, the year will be remembered, in part, for Lorenzo's return and evolution. Don't let the championship fool you. Yes, a final position of ninth was his worst in any category since 2003. But he proved capable of winning aboard a Ducati, something former foe Rossi couldn't do.

He was also capable of adapting a riding style that had become synonymous with the YZR-M1 after a nine-year stay with Yamaha, while adding an aggressive, combative streak to his skill-set. Even Marquez had to yield to his attack in a breathless final-lap showdown in Austria. That others – notably Ducati CEO Claudio Domenicali – appeared to doubt that very skill-set early in the season only served to hasten his exit from Ducati at the year's end, a judgement on the factory's part that appeared increasingly senseless as the season ticked through the long summer days.

The rider from Palma de Mallorca said it himself: he is a more complete rider for his experience with Ducati. "For sure, I'm much better now," he told MOTOCOURSE. "I'm older. I have more experience. I am more conscious about many more things. I needed to change the way I ride, to use different kinds of skills." Thanks to his input, the GP18 had become widely regarded as the grid's best bike by the autumn months. There was reason to believe eventual champion Marc Marquez when he labelled the Majorcan as "the rider that impressed me most" in 2018. "There were many races where people didn't believe in him," he said. "But in the end, he was one of the leaders."

And that's before we even mention Lorenzo's plans for 2019. Two days on from breaking his 19-month winning drought at the Italian Grand Prix, HRC spectacularly announced that Dani Pedrosa, loyal servant of 13 years, would be making way for his countryman. There he would embrace the clinical outlines of Repsol Honda, the most successful, well-resourced team on the grid.

He will race alongside reigning champion Marquez, one of an all-Spanish 'Dream Team' that boasts each of the past seven MotoGP rider's titles, and sparks are bound to fly. Few, if anyone, saw it coming. Even in his quiet days, it seemed as though Lorenzo wasn't shy of hogging 2018's headlines.

In that respect, not a great deal had changed since his premier-class debut in 2008, a year when this publication described the then 21-year-old as "more earnest, more grandiose, more theatrical" than Rossi, a figure whose success he sought to emulate.

More recent times have hinted at a different character, even if occasionally he has regressed to the norm. Complimenting Rossi and Marquez, rivals of the past, only to react angrily to the goading of team-mate Andrea Dovizioso; relaxed and humble in the face of defeat, as he was at Assen and the Sachsenring, before delivering a spiky riposte to Marquez's role in his own downfall at Aragon; calm and contemplative discussing the successes and failures of his career, yet manically headstrong mid-session, caught on camera berating his engineers.

In conversation, Lorenzo, a resident of the Swiss city of Lugano, is thoughtful and considered. The sense that racing is never far from his thoughts is clear. "I understood by experience that life is a roller coaster: to enjoy the joy of good moments, you have to go through bad moments," he reflected.

Above: At a low ebb. Gabarrini and Lorenzo on the grid in Argentina. He scraped a single point for 15th.

Top right: His third win in Austria was accomplished with a bold last-lap attack that turned the tables on rival Marquez.
Photos: Monster Energy

Above right: The intensity – Lorenzo was always thinking about how he could become better.
Photo: Gold & Goose

Above far right: Visor down and ready for action.

Right: Full chat in the wet during practice at the Red Bull Ring.
Photos: Monster Energy

"So it's a matter of time and it's a matter of keeping believing, keeping working harder when you go through a difficult time. I am the kind of person that is this way.

"Normally, I live my life to be living with more people. You speak about that and they give you their opinion. You try to find also motivation with some books or some movies or something, some information on the internet that can help you. I'm always a curious guy and always try to find the why of the things."

It was this curiosity that stoked his interest in riding elsewhere early in 2016. Despite his brilliance in dramatically clinching the world crown at the very last race in the previous year, he had gained a reputation, somewhat unfairly, as something of a one-trick pony. Certainly, he was fast, and he was unflappable once ahead, having led all 178 laps during his seven victories in 2015. But could he fight? And that silky-smooth riding style, with high corner speeds and wide, arcing lines was great on Yamaha's M1. But was it really applicable elsewhere?

Addressing these issues was a reason for joining Ducati for a reported base salary of 12 million euros a year. "With Yamaha, I already demonstrated everything," Lorenzo said of the decision to leave the manufacturer with whom he had won all three of his premier-class crowns. "Mainly, I decided to change because I needed more of a challenge. I needed to work with different people or to use a different bike to demonstrate to myself that I could be also competitive.

"I believe it was like changing category, because to change from Yamaha, a very smooth bike, very friendly for the rider, to a Ducati, this is the opposite kind of bike. I needed to change completely my riding style. So it was easier to swap from a 250 to a Yamaha than Yamaha to Ducati in the same category, after having experience of about nine years in the category. We underestimated this thing, Ducati and myself."

As Lorenzo's results in 2017 testify, that adaptation didn't come all at once. But by May, 2018, he was coming round to the GP18, with which he had floundered in the early races. Adaptation was always going to come, however, such was the seriousness with which Jorge addressed the task. "He's unbelievable," said Cristian Gabarrini, his crew chief at Ducati. "During his sleeping, he's thinking about something to improve. Sometimes when I'm at home, he texts me because he had an idea. Or he'll call me [and say], 'Did you check this or that?' You're not losing time when working with him because every second of his life, he's thinking about how he can improve his performance."

Complaints after the French Grand Prix centred on the physical demands the powerful Ducati placed on his forearms when braking. Mid-race fatigue regularly set in. But that redesigned dummy fuel tank at Mugello provided greater comfort from then on. From an altered riding position, his on-bike technique became more natural. "You have to make all the time on braking," Lorenzo said of his change in riding style in 2018. "Braking hard, braking late, using the rear brake to make the slide for this Ducati to turn – you cannot lean so much with this bike; and to take profit of all the power."

It was even a trend team-mate Dovizioso noted at Misano. "Jorge brakes a little bit softer at the beginning and much hard-

SHARK
FLEX-BOX
Unibat
DUCATI
NetApp
REPSOL
93

DUCATI

MONSTER
ENERGY

riello
FLEX-BOX
ADVANCE
CUPRA
DUCATI
SHARK
Reflexallen
AKRAPOVIC
PittaRosso

Above: *Lorenzo was back on top at Mugello, and even old rival Rossi seemed happy to applaud his come-back on home turf.*
Photo: Monster Energy

Right: Getting to know you. Lorenzo rides the Honda for the first time in the end-of-season tests in Valencia.

Centre right: The crutches told their own story after a mechanical failure in Thailand effectively brought an end to his season.

Far right: Lorenzo looked as fresh as the dawn after his brilliant defeat of Marquez at the Red Bull Ring. Team-mate Dovizioso was exhausted after battling to keep up.
Photos: Gold & Goose

er in the last part of braking," he said. "This is why it's very difficult to overtake him. He stays very close to the corners. When he enters, he stays [on the] inside. It's the opposite way to his normal style from last year and with the Yamaha."

Another startling detail: after brilliant wins at Mugello and the Red Bull Ring, Lorenzo explained how he had studied his weak points from free practice overnight. A revised riding style, with different lines in certain sectors, was adopted in warm-up. "It's one of the most difficult parts of racing," he said. "In about an hour, you need to change your natural way of riding that you've been doing through your life to a different one very quickly." That these late changes were pivotal in those successes is surely a sign of greatness.

The 2018 season did feature a new experience, however: the fear of being left out. In the midst of an ever-maddening silly season a comprehensive defeat by Danilo Petrucci at Le Mans shifted Ducati's focus for 2019 to the Italian. CEO Domenicali even questioned Lorenzo's abilities to adapt – treatment that bordered on the intolerable for the 31-year-old. Then Suzuki, another possibility feted for several weeks, agreed a deal with Moto2 hotshot Joan Mir. Suddenly, Lorenzo was short of options. "There were some days when things got quite dark," he admitted. "I don't need to be here for the money or to improve my life, because I have already achieved so many things. So probably if the final possibility didn't arrive, I will compete anyway in another team because I wanted to keep going at least some more years."

That the "final possibility" was Repsol Honda was of some comfort. A phone call to team boss Alberto Puig was enough to convince the ex-500cc Grand Prix winner to sign him up for 2019 and 2020. "For sure, this experience [with Ducati] will help me to be able to adapt a little bit faster to the next project," he said.

In the recent golden age, it's easy to overlook Lorenzo's place among the greats. Only Rossi, Agostini and Doohan have won more premier-class races. And he was fully aware of it. When it was put to him that only a handful of riders had taken the chequered flag with three different manufacturers, he quickly interjected, "I think it's four." He was correct. They are Hailwood (Norton, MV, Honda), Lawson (Yamaha, Honda, Cagiva), Mamola (Suzuki, Honda, Yamaha) and Capirossi (Yamaha, Honda, Ducati).

So another motivation for joining Honda then? "If I'm able to do it in the next years, I will be the fifth," he said. "But the first one in four-stroke era. I know about history. I actually have a good museum about letters and helmets of the champions of MotoGP and also Formula 1. I am very good at numbers and the statistics of the history. Obviously, it will be a nice challenge to be the first one in four-stroke to be able to win with three bikes."

From a young age, Lorenzo had always been destined to reach his current status. His father, Jose Manuel (better known as 'Chicho'), was strict and implemented rigorous methods when training his son on and off the bike. This included "thousands of hours" riding around a local water park. It also included psychological training techniques borrowed from Mossad, Israel's secret security service, which aimed to instill unflinching focus in moments of chaos.

Lorenzo admitted that this had come at the cost of a normal upbringing. But subsequently he was thankful to his father for introducing a work ethic and rigour into his early life. "It's not only essential, it's the only way in most of the sports," he said. "Most of the sports, especially gymnastics, from when they are kids, they go through eight hours, ten hours a day of very hard training. Swimmers, also golfers, tennis or soccer. We've been lucky, the riders, because it's only now, they are starting having new methods of training. It's not a very sophisticated method in the motorcycle world. So that's why my always very intense preparation I had from when I was a kid to now, it has really paid off."

But comments on how he would spend the early days of retirement offer a glimpse of the sacrifice he had undergone through his 31 years: "I've been very lucky in my life to achieve what I achieved, to do what I like to do. But it's also true that I have to go through a lot of sacrifices in my life: a lot of injuries, a lot of moments of hard training, every day, every year, a lot of years.

"Some things that normal people do, I couldn't do. I couldn't go so many times on holiday. I couldn't eat whatever I want. I could not wake up without alarm, usually. Even if now I try to. So these kind of things I would like to do. At least at the first years after I retire. Then maybe I will get bored. Maybe not. But I think I will try to enjoy as much as possible life, and the things I didn't do during my career."

TECHNICAL ESSAY

THE TIDES OF WINNING AND LOSING

What happens when fossilised management opts for cheap computer science in place of experienced human beings? KEVIN CAMERON examines the ebb and flow of racing success...

Above: Maverick Vinales finally broke Yamaha's longest ever winless streak in Australia. But was this serendipity?
Photos: Monster Energy

Top right and above centre right: Casey Stoner took the title for Ducati in 2007, but by 2009 (*lower pic*), a 'logical' chassis rethink left them struggling.

Above right: Even the combined pit-box talents of ex-Kawasaki Andrea Dosoli, former world champion Marco Melandri and current Rossi crew chief Silvano Galbusera couldn't overcome BMW's built-in Superbike problems.

Right: The BMW Superbike at Jerez in 2012: what worked in F1 cars didn't apply to racing motorcycles.
Photos: Gold & Goose

WHEN Maverick Vinales won at Phillip Island, Yamaha's 409-day victory drought came to an end (for the moment at least), but it raised two questions. How can this and other such slumps occur in the first place? How are they brought to an end? Consider the following impressive list:

a) Honda's low-performance period, 2004 to the middle of 2010, broken only by the late Nicky Hayden's single 2006 championship. In mid-2010, something changed at Honda: Pedrosa stopped looking like he was trying to stay on an electric bar-bull and at last could display his own grace. On that fast-improving bike in 2011, Stoner took ten wins and the championship.

b) Yamaha's inability to break Mick Doohan's five-year run of world titles, 1994–1999, continuing through their indecisive first two years of MotoGP, 2002–2003. There were wins in those ten years, but no championships.

c) Ducati's 'era of reverse development', during which Casey Stoner took his stunning 2007 world title, then scored fewer points in each of the three following years. This was followed by their 'time in the wilderness', from Stoner's last race win at Phillip Island in 2010 to the 2016 wins by Iannone (Austria) and Dovizioso (Malaysia). That one was severe – three years of decline, followed by five winless seasons.

d) The standout in World Superbike was BMW's brave, but unavailing assault with their powerful, though out-of-character S1000RR. This manufacturer, best known for touring and adventure-tour bikes, placed Marco Melandri third in the 2012 championship, then fourth a year later. The bikes were impressively fast, but riders could not keep tyres on them. Five years of hard work, but no championships.

e) Yamaha's level in MotoGP declined to fourth in 2018, behind Honda, Ducati and the increasingly strong Suzuki. Riders Rossi and Vinales were outspoken, yet vague in their criticisms of the bike. Vinales's win at Phillip Island was the first for Yamaha in over a year. He said, "Our problems start in the braking zone..." and "Acceleration, for example, is not consistent..." Rossi, less optimistic, said at Motegi, "I keep saying the same things during those meetings [with Yamaha]. I might as well leave a recording and a photo of myself on the table, rather than [attending] myself."

All of these manufacturers – Honda, Yamaha, Ducati, BMW – have powerful R&D resources and long histories of racing success. How could they allow themselves to fail over multiple seasons?

Breaking out of a slump has almost always required a decisive change of personnel. Resources are important to the realisation of ideas, but resources don't have new ideas.

The management of racing programmes is not taught at business college. It requires intense and expensive concentration of resources and talent that would not be tolerated in any other department. After 1965, when Honda decided it had established its name worldwide through grand prix road-racing, it moved resources and talent away from racing to acceler-

ate its entry into car manufacturing. Tiny MV Agusta and rider Giacomo Agostini were then able to defeat Honda and Mike Hailwood for the 500cc championship twice: 1966 and '67.

Racing isn't cheap, but cheeseparing has serious consequences. In the winter of 1970–71, when a sharp-eyed cost accountant at Kawasaki spotted an item for unusually expensive bearing rollers, he flagged it for possible cancellation. Those con-rod big-end rollers were made of special low-defects vacuum-remelted 52100 steel, and when they were replaced by ordinary penny-a-dozen rollers, the crankshafts of the company's H1-RA road racers failed at between 50 and 150 miles – a small fraction of the 1000-mile life they'd given in 1970. This kind of thing is why 'Mr Superbike', Rob Muzzy, once said, "Do everything possible in your own shop. That way, you have complete control over it." When, in 1973, 750 H2-R pistons, which had been reliable in 1972, began to crack and then break up, the team was told, "Piston, new-type, maybe six months." We continued to shake piston fragments, wrist pins and bearing cages out of our exhaust pipes.

Another leading cause of programme failure is corporate 'internal friction'. At Harley-Davidson during the years of effort to make their VR1000 Superbike win AMA national races, a tense struggle for control was waged between the company's engineering department and the separate racing group under Steve Scheibe. That classic turf war consumed energy that neither side could afford to waste, and it showed.

Further complicating poor management is the easy confusion of greater horsepower with quicker lap times, a common assumption of engineers without trackside experience. Honda took this route when upstart Ducati brought a very fast bike to MotoGP in 2003. The Japanese manufacturer's reply in 2004 was to cripple the handling of their bike by dumping extra power into it. Handling is as much a property of engines as of chassis, for the way in which power is delivered determines how much can actually be used. As Muzzy also observed, "The more you tune a four-stroke, the more it acts like a two-stroke." Honda's original RC30 Superbike had defeated Ducati chiefly by acceleration – its pulling range beginning as low as 6,500rpm. As more and more power was required to win races, the RC30's engine was tuned higher and higher, narrowing its range. At the end, power came in hard at 10,500rpm, and the RC30's day was done.

How could Honda allow world titles to slip through their fingers **(a)**? We can't know the details, but I suspect the company became enamoured with analytical methods coming into use in Formula 1. There, extensive computer-based data gathering is combined with advanced vehicle dynamics models to predict what ought to work. Any time a new methodology is applied, managers are told, "Give it time." Success may require years of sustained effort. Such persistence had worked for Honda in F1. Why should it have been any different on two wheels? On they went, patiently accepting not only dominance by Yamaha, but also even by minor producer Ducati (Casey Stoner's 2007 championship).

There is a parallel here with the BMW experience **(d)**. BMW made exhaustive preparations before returning to F1 with Williams in 2000, building a reported 100+ different V10 test engines. Similar preparations preceded their entry into World Supers in 2009, when the very experienced two-times series champion Troy Corser came a lowly 13th in the championship. The bikes were powerful, and with steady development were soon able to lead early laps. This was followed by rapid tyre fatigue and falling to low finishing positions. Like Honda, BMW seemed sure that its methods must soon succeed.

To a degree, a corner was turned when Marco Melandri succeeded in putting over this idea: in F1, you can work to data, but on two wheels you must work to rider confidence, which is difficult to simulate by computer. Without confidence, a rider on a technically advanced motorcycle achieves nothing. Melandri was third in the 2012 series. After one more non-championship season, BMW's team was withdrawn (perhaps they get all the exposure they want from providing the MotoGP safety car).

Above: Winning streak. Rossi's 2008 campaign took him to the third of four titles on the Yamaha M1.

Top right: Right man, right time. AMA Superbike champ Mat Mladin on his Yoshimura Suzuki.

Above right: Yamaha guru Masao Furusawa.

Above far right: Kel Carruthers and Kenny Roberts.

Right and below right: HRC's Shuhei Nakamoto and (*lower pic*) Takeo Fukui, former HRC chief and later Honda Motor CEO.

Far right: Rainey, who could be fast on anything, leads Doohan in 1992.

Photos: Gold & Goose

Honda persisted in BMW/F1 fashion until someone – possibly a very senior engineer, such as Takeo Fukui – decided that their long and growing drought in MotoGP must be ended. MotoGP tech journalist/photographer Neil Spalding believes that the decisive change was the appointment of Shuhei Nakamoto to manage Honda's MotoGP work. Nakamoto had experience with the poor turning ability of the slow-maturing RC45 Superbike and with the progressive chassis-softening programme that had made the RC51 V-twin Superbike a Bayliss-beater. Others feel that Nakamoto was given special authority, as he was thought to have a highly-placed protector in Honda management. Either way, changes were made, and by mid-2010, Dani Pedrosa began to achieve consistent results, winning at Sachsenring, Indianapolis and Misano. Honda's slump was over. Their dominance was about to begin.

How did Yamaha, whose two-stroke 500s were noted for their torque-based turning ability in fast corners, lose out in the 1990s to the front-end problems and torque-less revs of Doohan's NSR500 Hondas? Before his unfortunate 1993 accident, Wayne Rainey had brought Yamaha three consecutive titles in 1990, '91 and '92.

In Yamaha's Hamamatsu Media Centre (Museum) in 2003, I encountered a Yamaha engineer, who said, "We lost our way because Wayne Rainey was too good. He could ride anything we gave him. He could not say, 'This way is better', because he was always able to find his own way to go fast."

Another way to fail is through a lack of full co-operation between factory racing and a top rider. Yamaha trusted Kenny Roberts and his veteran crew chief Kel-san (Carruthers). Suzuki's long 1990s drought in US AMA Superbike came to an end when new boys Mat Mladin and data engineer (originally climate scientist!) Ammar Bazazz proved that they could reliably turn hardware developments they requested from the factory into race victories and championships won.

It's hard to justify big R&D if a race team is sitting back, hoping some quick-wrist messiah will stagger in from the desert and somehow miraculously ride the bike that others called "the light-switch" (because of its weak acceleration and tyre-spinning top-end power). Mladin won seven AMA Superbike championships in an era when other manufacturers were subcontracting their racing (Kawasaki) or ducking the high cost of HRC race bikes by running homebuilts (American Honda).

In MotoGP, Yamaha recovered in 2004 because someone in upper management rejected their weak half-measures and failure – their first MotoGP entries had streetbike-style chain-driven cams, warmed-over two-stroke chassis and compromise-ridden carburettors instead of fuel injection. It was decided to put in their one-man R&D 'tiger team', Masao Furusawa (If he fails, he gets the blame, but if he succeeds…).

Furusawa quickly eliminated the 'traction gap' to the V-engines by giving Yamaha's in-line a 90-degree crankshaft, then replaced the slow-burning five-valve cylinder head with best Duckworth-style four-valve practice. New rider Valentino Rossi, strongly backed by Furusawa personally, took championships in 2004, '05, '08, and '09. Like Roberts-Carruthers-Yamaha, that was a strong relationship based on mutual trust.

And Yamaha's more recent drought? The only race department personality to stand out is MotoGP manager Kouji Tsuya, who in mid-2018 was made to apologise publicly to the race team for non-optimal engine power delivery. Rossi's response was, "Apologies are all very well, but what we need is improved performance."

How had Yamaha failed for so long to give Maverick Vinales the engine and chassis qualities that had enabled him to win three of the first five GPs of 2017? Paddock opinion was that Yamaha higher management regarded racing as just another corporate activity, such as employee pensions or scrap recycling. This parallelled the view of former US Secretary of Defense Robert McNamara, who regarded military commissioned officers as middle managers. Because all had received identical training, they had to be functionally interchangeable, right? That being so, the position of a retiring successful leader

Above: Working to the rider's feel helped Lorenzo win on the Ducati. Here the crew celebrates in Catalunya in 2018.
Photo: Ducati Corse

Top right: People matter. Ducati's Dall'Igna makes a point to renowned crew chief Cristian Gabarrini.

Above right: Stoner left Ducati to win again on a Honda in 2011, proving that the rider had not been the cause of deterioration.

Right: Not even Rossi, his experienced crew and a new aluminium chassis could overcome Ducati's difficulties in 2012.
Photos: Gold & Goose

(such as Masao Furusawa) might have been filled by Human Resources sending a generic Bill or Bob with the usual university degree and a firm handshake.

A racing enthusiast friend in investment banking in past years was often in the Far East and once sought out Yamaha's long retired 1960s GP engineer known as 'Big Naito'. When he asked him about the difference between then and now, the engineer replied, "In those years, lights on late at night in the factory, maybe all night. But now? I can look down from my house and see the factory. No lights."

As to Ducati's long drought **(c)**, the initial shock was the failure of their revolutionary and extremely stiff 2009 frameless construction. Because the previous steel-tube 'trellis' frame had become too flexible for the grip of the latest Bridgestone tyres (in 2008, it had weaved vigorously off corners), Ducati leapt to the opposite extreme – a super-rigid box structure of carbon fibre, joining the steering-head to the engine's cylinder heads and incorporating the intake airbox.

By making so radical a change, Ducati engineers revealed just how little they knew of how chassis stiffness affects tyre grip. Yamaha had done something similar, but to a lesser degree, when they adopted a very stiff extruded-side-beam chassis in 1993, causing rider Rainey to tell the Eastern Creek, Australia press conference, "We have chatter, we have hop and we have skating." In 2009, Casey Stoner said, "On that thing [the new carbon frame], one moment you're doing exactly the same thing that worked the last three laps, and the next you're in the gravel – no warning." They had followed the tradition established by Honda's RC30 and RC45 Superbikes – making the front chassis so stiff that front grip could disappear without warning. On the carbon bike and chronically losing the front, Stoner won fewer races each year until he went to Honda in 2011, where he won ten GPs and another championship.

That left Ducati with no chassis insight at all, perhaps tempting them to seek answers from 'on high' – via theoretical/numerical methods rather than through the old process of track testing, identifying trends of improvement and then following them to peak. The arrival of Valentino Rossi in 2011–12 did nothing to illuminate the mystery. Yet, as in Honda's case, it appeared that at some high level, the company's entrenched methods or possibly a favoured manager were dearer to their hearts than races and championships won. This kind of thing is familiar in US industries, desperate to cut costs by phasing out expensive product testing and replacing it with 'concept-to-production' computer modelling. By putting lower-paid 28-year-olds in front of computer work stations, higher-paid experienced staff can be cleared out by offering them early re-

tirement. But what if software alone isn't ready to do the job? What if the video-gamers fall off the drop-down menus of their $30,000 software packages?

In the resulting hectic meetings, someone says, "We need somebody who actually knows something. Al could fix this. We gotta get Al in here."

"Al's retired, remember? Hitting little white balls in Florida."

"Never mind. Call him. Get him up here. Give him whatever he wants."

In similar fashion, Ducati tried to lure Gianluigi Dall'Igna away from Aprilia to lead their MotoGP team, but reportedly quailed when he demanded a free hand in management and personnel. As their pulse rates thudded to new heights, they tried again, this time giving him the free hand.

Under Dall'igna's direction, Ducati have become competitive again. Is he a brilliant engineer? We don't need to know. Maybe, like Louis Coatalen at Sunbeam 100 years ago, or Gary Mathers at American Honda 30 years ago, he finds capable people for key jobs and acts decisively to back their work.

What so often makes remote fossilised management prefer continuing failure to the quite real risks of innovation? Their mandate is to fix the problem without changing anything or spending money. As in politics, inaction is always cheaper and more comfortable than action.

TECHNICAL REVIEW

BACK TO THE FUTURE

Regulations restricting engine numbers and a freeze on development were intended to cut costs. Among other consequences, they triggered a return to a pre-war engine feature – the external flywheel. NEIL SPALDING explains...

Above: Rossi's Ducati at Sepang in late 2012. The small flywheel on the crankshaft end is clearly visible.

Above right: The original 2007 Desmosedici 800 engine had no external flywheel.

Above far right: The arrival of the Magneti Marelli control ECU and its simpler unified software meant that the basic motorcycle design had to be better.

Photos: Gold & Goose

Top right: At Brno in 2016, Honda's MotoGP project leader, Takeo Yokoyama, ponders the changes needed to cure the RC213V's wayward tendencies.

Right: By 2014, the external flywheel had become standard for Ducati. This is test-rider Pirro's development bike at Mugello. It is much more substantial than the first version from 2012.

Photos: Neil Spalding

WHEN it was decided to limit the number of engines available to each rider during a season, and subsequently also to freeze engine design, the goal was a reduction in costs.

In a world where it wasn't uncommon for a rider to get through 20 engines in a 16- or 17-round season, the sudden drop to a mere six engines a year in 2010 came as a major shock. Engine longevity became a key design aim, peak revs dropped, and the quality of materials and internal engine coatings soared.

But the design freeze of 2014 had the greatest effect on actual competition. When the rule was first introduced, each MSMA member factory had engine design frozen at the start of the first MotoGP of the year.

Ducati, with newly appointed chief Gigi Dall'Igna, decided that the ability to develop engine design was critical to becoming competitive again, so they renegotiated the rule book to allow less successful factories more leeway. By the time the 2014 race season started, Ducati were the beneficiaries of a revised set of rules that, as they had not been successful in the dry since the start of 2013, allowed them to use 12 rather than six engines, and to redesign those engines through the year. Even better, they could use 24 rather than 20 litres of fuel per race, and benefit from the softer tyres available to the non-factory Open Class bikes.

Over the years, the amount of fuel and the number of engines have changed. Under current regulations, it is seven engines for successful factories and nine for those still benefiting from the concession, which also allows them to modify their designs during the racing year; everyone gets 22 litres of fuel. There is a precise points system to define when a struggling factory might become eligible for concessions, and when they should lose them, if they achieve (or regain) competitiveness.

The effect of the design freeze has also been altered as a side effect of other rule changes, mainly the adoption of control ECUs (2014) and control software (2017). With open electronics, it was possible to control the engine's reaction to throttle movements very accurately. This meant that if a crankshaft design was a little too light, the throttle response could still be adequately controlled. Now, however, the significantly dumber compulsory unified software does not have the range or accuracy to do that. High-quality electronics could mask quite a few design problems. Without them, the motorcycle requires a significantly better basic design from the start.

With crankshaft design, however, finding the right compromise isn't easy. Crankshaft weight, direction of rotation and inertia all have a big effect on the way a racing motorcycle works. The crankshaft and all the items in the power train need to be light enough so as not to affect the bike's ability to accelerate or hold a line in a corner. But those same components must also be heavy enough, or at least have enough inertia, to dampen the engine's throttle response, to a point where the throttle can be applied safely and smoothly early in a corner, when the bike is at a high lean angle. Relatively small changes can make a big difference. In the years before sealed engines, Honda had several different alternator 'flywheels' that could be used to change crankshaft inertia, allowing a bike to be tailored to its rider.

For years, Ducati had a crankshaft that was effectively too light. The throttle response was very quick, and modulating the reaction to opening the throttle was very difficult. The 990s were quite abrupt, but the shorter-stroke 800 was particularly tricky. Only Casey Stoner ever really mastered it. During Rossi's time at Ducati, however, the lack of flywheel effect became an issue.

Ducati used an L4 engine layout through most of the first decade of MotoGP, with an air-cooled alternator on the left, and the rotor was modified to work as an additional external

flywheel. The following year, the external flywheel became bigger. That would have required a redesign of that side of the crankcase, with a larger and stronger main bearing journal, and a bigger supporting bearing.

Over subsequent years, Ducati experimented a lot with flywheels of different mass. Most weighed around 4–5kg, while different levels of inertia were also tried, some using heavy metal inserts in the outer edge of the flywheel.

Most observers expected that once sufficient data had been obtained to make a final choice, later engines would have the flywheel mass back inside the crankcase. However, the latest engines still have a very substantial external flywheel. That represents a change in priorities. Until now, keeping the mass of a racing motorcycle on the centre-line has been considered the most advantageous. The closer all the mass is to the centre, the quicker the bike can turn. But now it seems that the smallest possible crankcases, which enable the engine position to be moved, and the ability to modify the crankshaft inertia are at least as important.

Changing the weight positioning on a modern MotoGP bike can make a major difference to how it works. Control tyres mean that the bike must be adjusted to get the best from them; no longer can the tyre design be changed to suit the bike. Put the weight in the right place, and the rider can load pressure on to the tyres in a fashion that maximises their performance.

This strategy will have had side effects. A 4–5kg flywheel spinning at up to 19,000rpm will exert some gyroscopic forces, and they will be off the centre-line. This makes a significant difference. (A search of YouTube for gyroscopic effect will be educational. Add the name 'Eric Laithwaite' to the search terms for additional Britishness.) These asymmetrical effects probably would be small, only just enough to be felt by the rider, but one has to hope that the feeling wouldn't be too unsettling.

Then there is the braking. A high-inertia flywheel isn't easy to slow down as the bike is braked into corners; the brakes have to slow the crankshaft as well as the whole machine. This in itself is not new, but substantial reductions in internal engine friction have made the problem more severe. At the same time as the flywheel mass increased, Ducati also fitted butterfly valves in the exhausts, similar to those employed on the street for noise control. This 'corking' was an attempt to generate more engine braking. In early experiments, a few engines became overly warm, and there was at least one failure, so the effectiveness of this strategy is not apparent.

There would appear to have been some additional developments in this direction. The latest Ducati flywheels, seen on customer bikes that are a year old, appear to be heavily scored on the outer edge. Careful scrutiny of photographs reveals two redundant electrical connections right next to the flywheel. It appears that something has been removed. I think it is highly likely that Ducati have fitted some sort of physical brake on the flywheels of their factory bikes, giving computerised physical control of the level of engine braking. It would probably be easy to use the ECU channel supposedly dedicated to the butterfly valves to control it.

Honda, and probably also KTM, have some method of adjusting crankshaft inertia. These are V4 engines, thus narrow enough to have an alternator on the crankshaft. Using a dry alternator mounted outside the engine cases would allow some level of adjustment without breaking the engine seals. Given Honda's predeliction for centralised mass, however, the main crankshaft mass is likely to be still as close to the centre-line as possible.

But what about the two in-line four-cylinder bikes – Suzuki and Yamaha? Such engines, whether with 180-degree or cross-plane cranks, have a lot more flywheel effect in their basic design. Each cylinder has two crank 'cheeks' per connecting rod, where a modern V4 typically has two rods per pair. An in-line four is obviously wider and has greater resistance to initial lean when turning in to a corner.

Right: The first Yamaha M1 engine of 2002, complete with carburettors. It had a reverse-rotating crankshaft with an alternator on the jackshaft, which achieved the directional shift. Adjusting the mass of the alternator rotor would offer Yamaha (and Suzuki) some chance of tailoring crankshaft inertia.

Below: Before the days of sealed engines, the 2006 990cc Honda RC211V had a choice of three different alternator rotors to adjust crankshaft inertia.

Top right: Crutchlow's Ducati at the 2014 Catalunya test. It features a high-inertia flywheel with heavy metal inserts.

Photos: Neil Spalding

Above right: Dovizioso's bike at the Czech GP in the same year has a slightly different version.

Photo: Gold & Goose

Right: Alvaro Bautista's Desmosedici GP17. The flywheel is now easily 4–5kg, spinning at up to 19,000rpm.

Photo: Neil Spalding

Top far right: Model F Manx Norton. The external flywheel is inboard of the clutch.

Photo: Courtesy Sammy Miller Museum

Visit: www.sammymiller.co.uk

Above far right: The author's 1954 Moto Guzzi Falcone 500.

Photo: Neil Spalding

Yamaha pioneered reverse crankshaft rotation in the modern MotoGP era. All of their M1 engines have spun backwards, with the jackshaft that reverses rotation taking the power from the centre of the crankshaft to minimise the twisting effect of a high power output. What initially was seen as a side effect of this packaging has taken on a life of its own, however. The reduction of the overall 'gyroscopic stability' brought about by turning the crank in the opposite direction to the wheels means that the Yamahas can turn in quite effectively, compensating for the additional mass.

The gyroscopic and torque-reaction effects of a reverse-rotating crank are now well documented. As well as the reduced overall gyroscopic effect, the torque reaction that encourages the bike to run wide mid-corner also helps to hold the front down under corner exit acceleration.

If the crankshaft is too heavy, these effects are amplified. Acceleration and cornering can be affected adversely. That was Honda's experience in 2016, and Suzuki's in 2017. Yamaha went into 2018 searching for improved acceleration, and went too light, suffering as a result with a pair of works bikes that were hard to control at the initial touch of throttle. Crankshaft flywheel inertia increases proportionally with engine revs and at the square of the radius, so bigger-diameter and/or higher revving flywheels are most effective. Yamaha tried all the usual fixes, including a heavier clutch, in an attempt to improve matters, to little effect. The clutch was on the wrong end of the primary gears so didn't rotate quickly enough to make a sufficient difference.

Where Honda could add a dry alternator to the end of their crankshaft, and Ducati a flywheel, it would be much harder for Yamaha and Suzuki, and we can assume that neither currently has an adjustable flywheel. Nevertheless, it must be possible to redesign the engine to have a small external flywheel outboard of the gear-driven jackshaft behind the cylinder block, rotating at engine speed. It couldn't be very big, but at least it would allow a little adjustability.

There are other possible strategies to smooth throttle response at first opening.

Following a difficult 2016 with a too-heavy crankshaft, Honda not only lightened the crank for 2017, but also redesigned their engine to fire all four cylinders in one revolution, with no combustion for the next revolution. That evacuated the airbox and made it inefficient at low rpm, coincidentally smoothing throttle response.

KTM introduced a different firing sequence during their first year, but their 'big bang' was different from Honda's. In the latter half of 2018, KTM began race developing their reverse-spin engine, and now it seems to have the same combustion sequence as the Honda. This doesn't overtake the need for accurate crankshaft inertia, but it might allow the use of a slightly lighter crankshaft.

Supposedly, the 'frozen engine' rule was brought in to lower costs. Yet it has been the cause of three factories having had ridiculously bad years. Given that three of the competitors now have external crank mass adjustment, however, I don't think it will be possible to change the rule.

HISTORY REPEATS

THERE'S nothing new. External flywheels have been seen before, both on and off the track.

In 1918, Carlo Guzzi designed his first motorcycle, now known as the Guzzi-Parodi (GP for short). It was an unusual design for its time, a laid-down single cylinder with an integral gearbox and gear primary drive. The crankshaft rotated backwards, and the first prototype had four valves per cylinder.

The crankcases were notably small. This was possible because there was a large external flywheel that provided all the inertia a 500cc single could possibly need.

Moto Guzzi fettled and modified this design for nearly 50 years. All the top-of-the range Guzzi singles followed the same basic DNA, until the final Falcone rolled out of the Mandello del Lario factory in 1967.

For a long time, Guzzi had the reputation of having experimented with more different engine concepts than any other marque. As well as the long-serving singles, there were in-line fours; triples, with and without superchargers; and twins, in both parallel and 120-degree vee versions. There was the legendary 500cc V8 race bike, and finally their current staple longitudinal 90-degree V-twin. Guzzi singles dominated the 250 GP class in the early 1950s and, when stretched to 350cc, that class as well, from 1953 to the factory's withdrawal from racing in 1957.

Most Moto Guzzi engines had external flywheels until the mid-1950s. If a different inertia was required, a different flywheel could be fitted. The civilian Falcone models had flywheels of 280mm diameter; the 'all road' military version, the Superalce, had a 270mm flywheel with a thicker 'high-inertia' edge, all the better for a flow of seamless power.

The large flywheels smoothed the power output, and kept the crankcases small – a real benefit when Guzzi adopted rear swing-arm suspension and decided to encase the springs in a box under the engine, linked to the front of the swing-arm's underslung bracing.

Such was Moto Guzzi's GP racing prowess that other factories followed. Norton's last official works Manx racers in 1954, both 350 and 500 versions had nine-inch flywheels. However, they were soundly criticised by some for not having increased their crankshaft diameter sufficiently to handle the loads created by the external flywheel, and because it did not have a similar 'high-inertia' section to that of the Moto Guzzi.

One intriguing aspect of riding a bike with such a large flywheel is the effect it has on braking. From personal experience, there is definitely a feeling that these bikes stop more quickly with the clutch lever pulled in; the big flywheel really doesn't want to slow down.

2018 MOTOGP · BIKE BY BIKE by Neil Spalding

GET IT RIGHT FIRST TIME

HONDA RC213V

IT soon became clear that Honda had built a very good motorcycle from the start. It made excellent power and had a throttle response that the riders were happy with, plus it handled in a way that Marquez liked. It was still a very focused and particular bike; one that demanded the rider push it hard, just as Marquez does, for it to work as its designers had intended.

Honda had taken several years to get their MotoGP V4 bike working as they wanted it, reacting very well to precise changes in its centre of gravity. They had managed to maintain that focus through four major design or rule changes, first from 800cc to 1000cc, then from Bridgestone tyres to Michelins, and now from forward-rotating to backward-rotating crankshaft, as well as the introduction of control electronics.

The Honda was designed to arrive in a corner hard on the brakes, having been pitched on to its nose. This compressed the front tyre sufficiently to spread the contact patch and allow additional braking pressure to be added. To maintain that pressure, the height of the centre of gravity had to be kept the same, so the rear wheel was allowed to rise as the front dived. Once the initial phase was over, the rider had to lower the centre of gravity to bring the rear tyre back down. He did that by lowering his shoulders, dropping his foot off the foot-peg and slightly tilting the bike to one side. If the rate at which the bike slowed was maintained, the rear tyre came down and allowed the rider to bring the rear brake into play just as the bike reached the apex. It could then be part turned and part slid into a position where it could be fired back out of the corner.

Marquez could be seen regularly 'feeling' for the limit of grip through the apex of a corner. His bike control was surreal, but the machine let him do it, if it was treated appropriately.

Marquez could use the Honda as it was intended to be used; that wasn't as easy for other riders, though, and Honda knew it. They realised that this would leave them in a precarious position should they lose his services. At the same time, Jorge Lorenzo's achievement in both understanding the Ducati and helping to change its nature wasn't lost on HRC. Their decision to sign him was a clear message that they wanted to change their development focus, and that future versions of the Honda would be more usable to riders not called Marquez.

Honda designed a carbon swing-arm that looked very similar to the aluminium unit they had used over the previous few years – the same section and the same basic shape. It shouldn't have worked, but clearly it did, allowing Marquez to regularly use a very hard front tyre with a soft rear. Initially, only three were built; Pedrosa had one, but destroyed it in the massive crash with the works Ducatis at Jerez. Marquez had two, but usually they were only brought out for FP4 and thereafter, once he had had his 'where is the limit?' crashes. The lead times for replacements were very long, which indicated that the necessary construction techniques were very unusual.

Carbon-fibre swing-arms in MotoGP weren't new – Ducati had used them for years – but those that worked had always employed very different construction and sections to aluminium designs. Carbon fibre typically vibrates at a different frequency from aluminium, so even if the carbon swing-arm works identically to the aluminium version, it may suffer less from chatter.

Honda took a while to commit to their 'aero fairing' design for 2018. At the test at Jerez, on the Monday after the race, new fairings were tried with a selection of winglets. Pedrosa simply ran his new fairing with and without the small fenced wings he preferred. Marquez, however, opted for winglets that looked similar to the new-for-2018 Yamaha examples.

Above: **Honda's new plug-in starter allowed better clutch set-up. Marquez was still able to push-start in an emergency.**

Above right: **Yamaha tested a chassis with a stiffer headstock at Jerez, but it never raced. Note the reduced cutaway section.**

Photos: Neil Spalding

Right: **Yamaha's 2018 bike, here at the pre-season Sepang test, married an upgraded engine with an earlier chassis concept.**

Photo: Gold & Goose

Above: The Marc VDS Honda shows its bones.

Above right: Rossi's late-season Yamaha at the Thai GP.
Photos: Gold & Goose

Left: Honda's pipes were shorter, with a bigger diameter, and had two cylindrical Helmholtz resonators as well as a stone-guarded exit vent.
Photo: Neil Spalding

Far left: Marquez's bike being prepped during qualifying at the Sachsenring. Note the carbon-fibre swing-arm.
Photo: Repsol Honda

YAMAHA YZR-M1

DURING the Lorenzo/Bridgestone era, Yamaha had concentrated on building a bike that would work at up to 63 degrees of lean in long sweeping arcs. That was fine while the edge grip of the Bridgestones lasted to the end of the race, but Yamaha quickly discovered that the same wasn't true of the Michelins. A new strategy was needed.

The only real option was to slow down more for corners, have the bike over on its side for a shorter time and accelerate harder on to the next straight. That meant the bike needed more power and better aero. It also required a chassis that worked better with the new stiffer-carcase Michelin front. The mid-season 2016 chassis was seen as a new starting point for development, and that is what Yamaha used for the first few races of 2018.

At Qatar, it was obvious that the works team had engines with a higher state of tune, or at least more compression, than the Tech 3 bikes. The sound they made during warm-up was very different from the independent team's machines, which were of 2017 spec. It soon became clear that the older engine made less power, but was much more controllable than the 2018 edition.

The works Yamahas quickly proved very difficult to ride, and the riders criticised the factory for not investing enough effort in making the control electronics more usable. The real issue, however, was a difficulty in controlling the initial response on throttle opening. This is typically caused by a crankshaft with inertia that is too low for the state of tune of the engine, making initial response too aggressive. That, in turn, affects how early and accurately the throttle can be opened, which is critical at full lean. Timing and accuracy also affect how the bike pitches on to its rear tyre, and therefore how much grip it has available at that point of the corner.

The best solution would be to use a heavier crankshaft, but Yamaha were one of the top factories, so their engines were 'frozen' from the start of the season; no internal changes were possible. In the short term, Yamaha tried to slow the engine's throttle response by increasing the rotational inertia of the clutch.

Another answer would be to improve the accuracy of the programming of the control electronics, to smooth the transition from neutral throttle to slightly open. As the season wore on, Yamaha were working hard on improving their electronics package.

At the start of the year, tyre wear was also an issue for the factory riders: for some reason, their rear tyres wore out faster than on the older bike used by Zarco. Some of this might have been down to the extraordinarily smooth way that Zarco rode the bike, but some was due to its less aggressive power delivery. Since the advent of the control electronics, it had become far more important for the basic motorcycle to be 'right'; the electronics could no longer be relied upon to fix major issues.

In 2018, the works team started the year with what appeared to be a copy of their 2016 'B' chassis, as used by Folger in 2017. It had a 'sculpted' headstock area, with the front section of the main beam resembling a big I-beam, while the back appeared more like the conventional rectangular box section. This allowed more lateral flex in that area while also having a reinforced front engine mount and side beam to maintain the best possible stiffness under braking. It was designed to work well in long high-lean-angle corners.

Yamaha had new rear suspension links at Mugello, most probably designed to be less progressive and abuse the rear tyre less. All MotoGP rear suspension systems are progressive – the rear suspension becomes stiffer as it is compressed. Some of that might come from acceleration, but some might also be caused by the load on the tyres increasing as the bike is leaned over. It is quite possible that the links did not provide as much ultimate grip at either end of the bike, but may have been conceived to retain as much grip as possible for as long as possible during the race.

More new chassis were tried, one with a stiffer headstock at the Jerez test, which was rejected. A chassis with a softer headstock was tried at the Catalunya race. Slowly Yamaha improved their bike. Its initial preference for cooler racetracks declined, and it became more competitive in the hotter conditions usually experienced in the afternoons, which was helpful on race-day.

DUCATI DESMOSEDICI

DUCATI started 2018 as well as they could possibly have hoped, with a win in Qatar. For the first two races, Dovizioso raced with the non-aero version of the bike. But after that, he tended to change from a normal fairing to the version with the large wings after the first few practice sessions.

There is no doubt that Dovi was quicker with the aero fairing, although he appeared to prefer running without wings if at all possible. The most likely reason seemed to be that it calmed some high-speed instability. In 2017, he had hardly ever used the aero fairing, so the sudden change indicated that the new chassis must have been less stable.

The main chassis, let's call it the 2018A, was issued to Lorenzo and Petrucci. It had revised beams and a cut-away steering head that appeared similar to the version Dovi had used for his wins in 2017. This steering head design appeared to allow more flex when leaned right over, putting less lateral pressure on the tyre.

Dovizioso had another design, though; let's call this the 2018B. On this, the front part of the main beam had an I-beam section, very similar to that used by Yamaha. This was hidden by tape at the first few rounds. At Le Mans, Lorenzo received a chassis with a similar front beam construction, and by the start of practice at Mugello, he had a second. The two chassis certainly looked similar to Dovi's, but there was a clue that suggested they might have been slightly different – the wings. Compared to the massive biplanes used by Lorenzo to date, they were much smaller, similar to those employed by Honda and Yamaha.

The tail section was new, a bigger box to hide the mass damper in the tail. Ducati did a good job of keeping the actual contents of the tail out of sight, but it became increasingly apparent that the main advantage of the Ducati system was that it could be adjusted easily to change the frequency. It might be that weight had to be moved around, and a bigger box would have allowed more room for that.

At Mugello, it all came together. Lorenzo received new bodywork that let him brace himself for stability on braking, while also being wide enough for him to use his body weight to manoeuvre the bike. Perhaps understandably, the shape of this spacer was quite close to that of a Yamaha dummy fuel tank. I suspect that the new chassis carried its weight slightly further forward to replace some of the downforce previously provided by the wings. At the same time, the additional padding behind the dummy tank moved some of Lorenzo's weight further back. But it was the combination of the three that was important.

First there was a little less downforce from the wings, and consequently less effort required to change direction. Then there was a chassis that flexed more at the front at full lean, improving front-end grip and tyre life; and finally a seating position that supported Lorenzo under braking and also allowed easier weight transfer as the tyres wore, to maximise their performance.

Lorenzo made good use of all these aspects in his run to a dominant victory at Mugello. He won by six seconds, yet was only 15th fastest in the top-speed table, 10km/h slower than Dovi. The Spaniard's old team-mate, Rossi, was third, having pushed his Yamaha to the limit. Lorenzo did it again in Catalunya two weeks later.

Development didn't stop. At Brno, yet another wing system was introduced, and testing was under way on a quicker-shifting gearbox. The new aero system worked well enough to become almost the standard fitment.

Then came Lorenzo's mystery crash in Thailand. It looked as though the rear wheel had locked, and for a modern rider that would have been quite a shock. Very few now cover the clutch lever, as was the case in the days of the two-stroke race bike. However, simply pulling in the clutch lever would only have worked if the engine had seized; if it had been the gearbox, then nothing would have solved the problem.

Right: The Suzuki early in the season. This is Iannone's bike in Catalunya.

Far left: Two Ducatis at Brno. Lorenzo's is closest, Dovizioso's beyond. Note the different pads on the seats and dummy fuel tanks.

Above left: Ducati's carbon-fibre swing-arm. They had been using the material for some years.

Left: Rear-brake thumb lever on Lorenzo's bike.
Photos: Gold & Goose

Below left: At Mugello, Lorenzo had a new dummy tank extension (*top pic*) and new chin pad (*lower pic*).
Photo: Neil Spalding

SUZUKI GSX-RR

THE bike Suzuki had on track in 2018 was quite familiar. It looked very like the machine Aleix Espargaro had ridden 18 months before. It had a new aero fairing and a slightly stronger chassis around the swing-arm pivot, but the rest really didn't appear to have changed much.

That assumption would have done the engine and electronics groups a disservice, however. In 2017, Suzuki had had to deal with a 'frozen' engine design and a limit of only seven engines; and something wasn't right in the specification they chose. Crankshaft inertia was too great, and this led to sub-standard acceleration and understeer.

With poor results that year, Suzuki regained their concession team status for 2018. Thus their engine design was free of constraints, and each rider was allowed nine engines for the year.

A new-specification engine was delivered at Assen, giving them decent power, with the correct crankshaft weight for good handling.

It was the same story with electronics. Suzuki had appointed Shinichi Sahara to run the team after it became obvious that there were problems early in 2017. He had been the chief trackside engineer when Suzuki had run their V4 GSV-R racer before the 2010 withdrawal. One of his first moves was to expand the electronics team, and that seemed to have paid off.

Aerodynamics received attention, too, with a new set of wings designed to take advantage of the allowance for areas of wing to be removed. The full-size wing was almost as big as that on the Ducati, but the somewhat smaller 'normal' version was similar to those of Yamaha and Honda.

Changes arrived through the year. From Mugello onwards, there was a reinforced chassis with an additional bonded-on carbon-fibre skin. This stiffened the chassis, which seemed to suit Rins's hard-turning style more than Iannone's preferred more sweeping cornering technique. At Brno, there was a new sub-frame, which raised the seat more elegantly than the 50mm thick carbon-fibre pad that had been used previously.

Suzuki had also decided to change their rider line-up, and the combination of this and a bike that was genuinely better led to some impressive results from both riders. Rins matured superbly, while Iannone was far more competitive than he had been in 2017. By the end of the year, however, Rins had the upper hand more often than not.

Above: Carbon-fibre reinforcement was bonded to Suzuki's aluminium chassis to increase stiffness.

Above far left: The Silverstone version of Lorenzo's Ducati had a revised dummy tank pad and the new aero bodywork.
Photos: Neil Spalding

Left: Suzuki's new frame was designed to carry a torque sensor when required. Note the mounting points by the swing-arm pivot.

Right: Rins's Suzuki had a carbon 'modesty cover' to hide details of the thin and carefully machined top triple-clamp.

Left: The 2018 Suzuki chassis was thicker in section at the swing-arm pivot than the 2017 version.
Photos: Gold & Goose

APRILIA RS-GP

AT the Sepang test, Aprilia debuted a new chassis. This had been subjected to a radical change of weight distribution, the engine having been moved up and back, and the fuel down and back – so far back that the tank had to be refuelled through a hole in the back of the seat pad.

Thus the bike ran with substantially more weight on the rear than before. That was great for acceleration, but not so good for the front. When this suited the tyres, it could be a good thing, but if it did not, it became an issue over full race distance.

Things really didn't go to plan for Aprilia in 2018. The bike was fast and, with Aleix Espargaro on it, quite competitive. The new, more powerful engine tune initially used too much fuel, however, resulting in one DNF and one 'slow' finish on the initial flyaways. On the return to Europe at Jerez, Aleix's brand-new engine lasted just five corners before it developed a problem with the pneumatic valve-spring system and the bike stopped.

Although it soon became obvious that the power delivery was simply too aggressive, it took a long time for Aprilia to achieve some sort of balance between throttle response, power and fuelling. It seemed that with a bit more reliability, and a sensible trade-off between power output, power delivery and fuel use, the Aprilia could have been capable of top-ten finishes, and probably top-sixes on a regular basis.

It took until Silverstone for a new engine set-up to be available, a higher-inertia crankshaft and more progressive power delivery winning immediate favour with the riders. Unfortunately, only two of the new engines were available initially, one for each rider, and by Phillip Island they must have been getting quite long in the tooth.

A new chassis arrived for Aragon, although only Espargaro appeared to have use of it. This had smaller-section main beams and seemed to make a difference at that track, where he finished sixth, but the advantage didn't seem to last. At Motegi, there was some confusion with the fault-warning programme, which led to him pulling in after just a few laps.

There was a late-season test at Misano, where Espargaro had an outing on the 2017 chassis. This was quite successful, such that a 2017 chassis and running gear were shipped to Phillip Island in the hope that he could duplicate some of the speed he had demonstrated at that circuit a year before.

KTM RC16

AFTER a dizzying programme of change in the first half of 2017, KTM didn't make many visible changes during the first half of 2018. There were some new wings, and also two designs of swing-arm for the riders to choose from. But while fine-tuning the set-up and electronics seemed beneficial, it did not have a scintillating effect.

The main reason was that the early-2018 KTM differed from the rest of the grid in one very important aspect: its crankshaft rotated forwards. Most MotoGP crankshafts weigh over 8kg, to smooth out the all-important initial throttle response. An 8kg lump of steel rotating at up to 18,000rpm also creates a very powerful gyroscope, especially when acting in concert with the forward-rotating wheels, tyres and brakes. It most certainly won't want to change direction, and if it is forced to do so, it will have some ideas of its own as to where it wants to go. Thus in a bike with a forward-rotating crank, the crankshaft tends to be as light as possible to minimise the effect.

KTM tested engines fitted with the necessary additional gear in the primary drive to allow the crankshaft to turn backwards. They let test rider Mika Kallio race the new engine at Jerez and Catalunya, and he clearly enjoyed it. Unfortunately, he crashed in practice at the Sachsenring, which ended his testing for the year.

Pol Espargaro had several opportunities to try the new engine at Monday tests, and he was clearly very pleased with the new-found ability to change direction. By Catalunya, the KTM test bike also had a chassis that was more capable of working with the lines a reverse-rotating engine would use. Typically, a 'reverse rotator' is leaned over for longer and employs a chassis with less lateral rigidity. The latest version of the chassis had swing-arm side plates that had been reduced in size even further.

It isn't easy to make sudden major changes like this to an engine. Once you know it works, the new crankcases need to be cast and machined. Theoretically, the crank can stay the same, but it makes more sense to build crankshafts with more inertia to obtain the full benefit of the change. In KTM's case, their early-season engine was basically the same as the 'big bang' engine that had been introduced at Jerez in 2017. The new 'reverse rotator' had a different combustion sequence, one that seemed to be very similar to the Honda.

Following Kallio's crash, Bradley Smith was given the job of testing the first generation of reverse-rotating engines. He had two at Brno, but didn't use them in the race, or at the following Red Bull Ring or Silverstone rounds. Since then, however, he used them all the time, with a third arriving for Motegi. Given the changes in feel and response, the clear difference was in the racing lines used. Undoubtedly, some major set-up changes were required, but by Motegi, a new base set-up had begun to take shape.

WINGS, NOT-WINGS AND NO WINGS AT ALL

Aerodynamics after the ban

Left: Espargaro tried a chassis with a carbon-reinforced headstock.

Below left: The new frame allowed the engine to be mounted higher and further back. It helped in some corners, reducing front-wheel crashes.

Below: Kallio's bike at Catalunya tests. He had the job of testing KTM's reverse-rotating-crank engine and more flexible chassis.

Photos: Neil Spalding

Panel, clockwise from top left: Iannone's Suzuki fairing at Qatar; prototype Honda wings that didn't get to race; from Brno on, there were new wings on the Ducati, which seemed the most effective; Rossi's Yamaha at Le Mans; new wings for Espagaro's KTM; Dovizioso's Ducati at Assen.

Photos: Gold & Goose and Neil Spalding

THE 2018 rules on aerodynamics didn't really do what had been intended. The rule makers wanted to keep the restrictions on the designs – nothing sticking out that could injure a rider – but also wanted to limit the number of different designs allowed during the year.

It had already been decided that no more than two 'aero bodies' per rider would be sanctioned. That seemed to be quite restrictive. However, the rule allowing changes to the shape of the approved parts remained for 2018 and specified that "Material may be removed from Aero Body Parts without affecting the Approval, but Material may not be added."

The original homologation drawings remained confidential between each manufacturer and the technical director, so outside observers had to wait to see what was used on track and then to speculate as to what had been homologated originally.

Ducati clearly had homologated a very large structure and then supplied differing combinations of that structure as the year progressed. Lorenzo and Dovizioso tried large and small wing sets early in the year. Then Lorenzo received a Yamaha-style set for Mugello. The smaller wings allowed him to manoeuvre the bike as he wished, but produced just enough downforce to permit hard acceleration.

Each new shape had to be approved by Danny Aldridge, the FIM technical director, who required proof that the shape being proposed could be hewn from the original homologation.

At Brno it all changed again. Ducati debuted a box-section wing lower down on the fairing flank, with a pair of small wings higher up and forward on the nose.

KTM, Honda and Yamaha tried wing sets in testing that never got as far as a race. Some of these weren't homologated due to their shape or sharp edges; some were rejected due to rider preference. Most factories started 2018 with new aero solutions, but as before, only Ducati really pushed the envelope in terms of wing size and shape.

The rules were revised yet again for 2019. Permission to modify homologated designs was deleted. It would no longer be possible to remove or swap significant aerodynamic parts. The intention was to maintain an element of competition in the aerodynamic field while keeping costs under tighter control.

MONSTER
ENERGY
YAMAHA
FACTORY RACING
PESCAO
TECH3
BARRACUDA
FACOM
MONSTER
ENERGY
YAMAHA
MOTUL
FACOM
MONSTER
ENERGY
BARRACUDA
FACOM
MOTUL

TEAM-BY-TEAM

2018 MOTOGP REVIEW

Teams and Riders
MATTHEW BIRT

Bike Illustrations
ADRIAN DEAN

Bike Specifications
NEIL SPALDING

Photo: Monster Energy

REPSOL HONDA TEAM

TEAM STAFF

Tetsuhiro KUWATA: HRC Director

Alberto PUIG: Team Manager

Takeo YOKOYAMA: HRC Technical Manager

MARC MARQUEZ PIT CREW

Santi HERNANDEZ: Race Engineer

Carlo LUZZI: Fuel Injection Engineer

Gerold BUCHER: Data Engineer

Carlos LINAN: Chief Mechanic

Roberto CLERICI, Jordi CASTELLA,
Javier ORTIZ, Kochi UJINO: Mechanics

DANI PEDROSA PIT CREW

Giacomo GUIDOTTI: Race Engineer

Jose Manuel ALLENDE: Fuel Injection Engineer

David GARCIA: Data Engineer

Masashi OGO: Chief Mechanic

Emanuel BUCHNER, Pedro CALVET,
Denis PAZZAGLINI, Jorg HORNIG: Mechanics

DANI PEDROSA

Born: 29 September, 1985 – Sabadell, Spain

GP Starts: 295 (217 MotoGP, 32 250cc, 46 125cc)

GP Wins: 54 (31 MotoGP, 15 250cc, 8 125cc)

World Championships: 3 (2 250cc, 1 125cc)

MARC MARQUEZ

Born: 17 February, 1993 – Cervera, Spain

GP Starts: 186 (108 MotoGP, 32 Moto2, 46 125cc)

GP Wins: 70 (44 MotoGP, 16 Moto2, 10 125cc)

World Championships: 7 (5 MotoGP, 1 Moto2, 1 125cc)

IT was another season when the mercurial Marc Marquez came, saw and ultimately conquered the MotoGP World Championship – for the fifth time at only his sixth attempt. Records crashed almost as often as he did, but at the final reckoning, he comfortably walked away with the individual glory, while he almost single-handedly helped Repsol Honda retain the constructor and team awards to complete yet another triple crown.

Marquez wrapped up the title with three rounds to spare, but to suggest that the season had been a casual canter would be to belittle his achievement, as he stood firm in the face of a renewed onslaught from Ducati.

The Spaniard effectively fought a one-man crusade for Honda, and his value to HRC was incalculable when you consider that his personal points tally of 321 was not far short of the combined 348 that the other five Honda riders could muster.

The first of many smart moves occurred on 26th February, when he announced that he'd signed a new two-year deal to remain with Repsol Honda until the end of 2020. That instantly freed him from the potentially constant grilling about his future by the media, allowing him to focus solely on maintaining his and Honda's roles as the man and machine to beat.

Then, in early July, quite predictably, Repsol confirmed that they would remain as title sponsor of HRC

HONDA RC213V – Repsol

Engine: 1000cc 90-degree V4, reverse-rotating 360-degree crank, pneumatic valve return system, DOHC, 4 valves per cylinder
Power: More than 270bhp, revs up to 18,000rpm

Ancillaries: Magneti Marelli electronics and ride-by-wire throttle and fuel-injection system with torque sensor, NGK sparking plugs • *Lubrication:* Repsol

Transmission: Gear primary drive, multi-plate dry slipper clutch, six-speed seamless-shift cassette-type gearbox, RK chain

Suspension: Front, Ohlins TRBSP 25/30 48mm 'through-rod-bleed solid-piston' 46mm forks
Rear, Ohlins TRSP 44-Lightweight 'through-rod' shock with linkage; carbon-fibre swing-arm

Wheels: OZ Racing, 17in front and rear • *Tyres:* Michelin • *Brakes:* Brembo 320 or 340mm carbon-carbon front; Yutaka 218mm steel rear

Marquez and his crew celebrate their victory at Aragon

Stefan Bradl

Alberto Puig

Photos: Gold & Goose and Repsol Honda

Marc Marquez and Dani Pedrosa were paired at Repsol Honda for a sixth season

until the end of 2020. Repsol and HRC had enjoyed unrivalled success since they had joined forces in 1995; the 2020 campaign would be their 24th.

At Qatar, Marquez again suffered a last-corner defeat by Dovizioso. He went rogue at round two in Argentina with a cavalier and chaotic ride, being given a ride-through penalty for his U-turn on the grid. He'd already clouted Espargaro's Aprilia, then barged into Rossi, who fell, earning another penalty.

This reopened the wounds of their acrimonious title duel in 2015, and the backlash against Marquez was barbarous, Rossi accusing him of "destroying our sport". Marquez weathered the storm, and normal service was resumed when he extended his undefeated run in the USA, the first of nine victories. Undoubted highlights were his win in Assen's 200mph bar-room brawl, his ninth straight win from a ninth pole at Sachsenring, and a nail-biting last-corner win over Dovizioso in Thailand, where he'd become the first rider to pass through Q1 and take pole.

The Spaniard's riding may have been put under the microscope after Argentina, but following the turmoil of Termas, he only finished off the podium once in the final 16 races.

Marquez marched to glory with an unchanged support network behind him, managed in minute detail by long-term mentor and manager Emilio Alzamora.

The shop floor of the Repsol Honda garage was run like clockwork by crew chief Santi Hernandez, ably supported by chief mechanic Carlos Linan, electronics engineer Carlo Luzzi, data engineer Gerard Bucher, and mechanics Roberto Clerici, Koichi Ujino, Jordi Castella and Javi Ortiz.

Further credit for success has to go to HRC technical director Takeo Yokoyama. A major winter overhaul of the RC213V motor produced crucial horsepower and top speed that slashed the clear advantage held by Ducati in the top three gears. A new carbon-fibre swing-arm to help rear tyre life was also a key change.

Overall responsibility for Honda's effort fell once again to Tetsuhiro Kuwata, one of three HRC directors. His official title was General Manager Race Operations Management Division. A director role was also retained by Shinichi Kokubu, as general manager of the technology development division. The third director was Shigehisa Fujita, general manager of the business support division.

The major change in the upper echelons of HRC came when Alberto Puig was installed as the new team manager in mid-January, taking over from Livio Suppo, who had served in the position for the previous five years. Puig's arrival considerably altered the landscape within HRC. Suppo was more of a marketing man and schmoozer, while Puig was a no-nonsense character, who was only interested in winning.

Puig immediately improved the chain of communication between the track and HRC in Japan, and his previous experience as a rider of some distinction made him perfectly qualified to understand the importance of constant dialogue between box and base.

His arrival also created an interesting dynamic within the HRC garage. He had locked horns in the past with Alzamora, whom Marquez trusted implicitly; and he had discovered and nurtured Pedrosa from the start. Their close relationship had cooled and they had split at the end of 2013, and it was well known that during 2017, as a pundit for Spanish TV, he had heavily criticised his former protégé.

Pedrosa's crew was unchanged from 2017, with Giacomo Guidotti his crew chief, and electronics and data duties in the hands of David Garcia and Jose Manuel Allende respectively. Emanuel Buchner, Pedro Calvet, Denis Pazzaglini and Jorg Hornig stayed on as mechanics.

Hopes that Pedrosa could capture an elusive premier-class title at his 18th attempt all but vanished after just three rounds. A disappointing seventh in Qatar was followed by a first-lap crash in Argentina, after an aggressive, but unpunished move from Johann Zarco. Anxious to get back in the saddle, with speculation rife that HRC was sharpening the axe, he had surgery on a fractured right wrist, but fell heavily again in a three-rider pile-up at Jerez while scrapping for the podium.

Two days after the worst qualifying of his premier-class career, 20th at Mugello, which resulted in a first-lap tangle with Takaaki Nakagami, it was announced that Pedrosa's distinguished career with HRC was over. His contract would not be renewed.

This was not such a shock. What astonished the paddock was the news that Jorge Lorenzo would take his place, after a major transfer coup by Puig.

Pedrosa's exit from HRC was a mutual decision, and it was clear that he was on the brink of calling time on his illustrious career. An announcement was anticipated at his home race in Catalunya, but by then, he'd been approached by the new Petronas SIC Yamaha satellite team, eager for a marquee signing to spearhead the project.

Only Pedrosa was not sold on the idea, and he appeared to engage in talks more out of courtesy and curiosity than anything, before politely declining. Then, on the eve of the German GP, he confirmed that 2018 would be his final season. He was no longer willing to make the mental and physical sacrifices necessary to race at the elite level.

Pedrosa completely cut his ties with HRC and signed as test rider with KTM, which would reunite him with his former crew chief, Mike Leitner.

Sadly, there would be no fairy-tale ending for the career of the most successful rider never to have won the MotoGP crown. For the first time since his 125 rookie season in 2001, he not only didn't take at least one victory, but didn't even make the podium. He managed just six top-six finishes, and it was difficult to find anyone who felt his retirement, at the age of 33, had been too hasty.

As well as continuing to run Marquez and Pedrosa, HRC recruited former Moto2 world champion Stefan Bradl to the role of test rider. His deal included wild-card appearances in Brno and Misano, but he finished neither outing. He also took out Maverick Viñales and Bradley Smith after just three corners in the Czech Republic.

YAMAHA FACTORY RACING

FACTORY STAFF

Kouichi TSUJI: General Manager Motorsport Development
Kouji TSUYA: Yamaha M1 Project Leader

TEAM STAFF

Lin JARVIS: Managing Director, Yamaha Motor Racing
Massimo MEREGALLI: Team Director
William FAVERO: Communications Manager
Alen BOLLINI: Media Manager
Maider BARTHE: Press Officer
Marc CANELA: Team Co-ordinator
Takehiro SUZUKI: Parts Co-ordinator
Raffaella PASQUINO: Marketing Co-ordinator
Maria COLLECCHIA: Racing Event Assistant
Paolo GIANNOTTA: Driver/Helper
Leonardo GENNA: Driver/Helper

MAVERICK VINALES PIT CREW

Ramon FORCADA: Crew Chief
Yoichi NAKAYAMA: YMC Engineer
Davide MARELLI: Data Engineer
Wilco ZEELENBERG: Rider Performance Analyst
Javier ULLATE, Jurij PELLEGRINI, Ian GILPIN,
Juan MADURGA REVILLA: Mechanics

VALENTINO ROSSI PIT CREW

Silvano GALBUSERA: Crew Chief
Ooshi MASATO: Yamaha Engineer
Matteo FLAMIGNI: Data Technician
Luca CADALORA: Rider Performance Analyst
Alex BRIGGS, Bernard ANSIAU, Brent STEPHENS,
Mark ELDER: Mechanics

MAVERICK VINALES

Born: 12 January, 1995 – Figueres, Spain
GP Starts: 139 (72 MotoGP, 18 Moto2, 49 Moto3/125cc)
GP Wins: 21 (5 MotoGP, 4 Moto2, 12 Moto3/125cc)
World Championships: 1 Moto3

VALENTINO ROSSI

Born: 16 February, 1979 – Urbino, Italy
GP Starts: 383 (323 MotoGP/500cc, 30 250cc, 30 125cc)
GP Wins: 115 (89 MotoGP/500cc, 14 250cc, 12 125cc)
World Championships: 9 (6 MotoGP, 1 500cc, 1 250cc, 1 125cc)

EVER since Valentino Rossi had dragged Yamaha out of the doldrums in 2004, his iconic number 46 had been synonymous with success at the Iwata factory. But it became associated with abject failure in 2018, when Yamaha slumped to its worst losing streak since Chas Mortimer had delivered its first premier-class triumph at Montjuich 46 years earlier in 1972.

Maverick Vinales's dominant win in Australia brought massive relief, ending Yamaha's worst ever winless streak. The total stood at 25, with talk of a full-blown crisis hardly an exaggeration, considering that the respected factory's last win had been registered by Rossi at Assen in the middle of 2017.

On examination, it was easy to pinpoint the source of Yamaha's slump. Bitter rivals Honda and Ducati had made a better fist of marrying the control Magneti Marelli electronics with the Michelin tyres when sweeping technical changes had been implemented for 2016.

Progress was practically non-existent in 2018, with Rossi and Vinales frequently blaming poor acceleration and tyre endurance issues for their failure to arrest Yamaha's bewildering decline. Their constant complaints and the lack of race-winning silverware piled pressure on Yamaha's senior management, led by Yamaha Motor Racing (YMR) President and Motorsport Develop-

YAMAHA YZR-M1

Engine: 1000cc transverse in-line 4; reverse-rotating cross-plane crankshaft, DOHC, 4 valves per cylinder, pneumatic valve return system
Power: Around 270bhp, revs up to 18,000rpm

Ancillaries: Magneti Marelli electronics, full electronic ride-by-wire throttle, NGK sparking plugs • *Lubrication:* Yamalube

Transmission: Gear primary drive, multi-plate dry slipper clutch, six-speed seamless-shift cassette-style gearbox, DID chain

Suspension: Front, Ohlins TSB46 'Blackfisken' 46mm forks (Rossi – TSB46 CF carbon outer upper tubes)
Rear, Ohlins TRSP 44 'through-rod' shock with linkage

Wheels: MFR, 17in front and rear • *Tyres:* Michelin • *Brakes:* Brembo 340mm carbon-carbon front; Yamaha steel rear

Rossi rode harder than ever in 2018

Kouichi Tsuji

Kouji Tsuya

Lin Jarvis

Massimo Meregalli

ment Division General Manager Kouichi Tsuji and YMR Managing Director Lin Jarvis.

Both were repeatedly in the firing line, but arguably the man under the most scrutiny was YZR-M1 project leader Kouji Tsuya, who was most accountable for machine development, or lack of it as the case appeared to be. Another prominent position in the camp was occupied by team director Massimo Meregalli.

Yamaha's senior figures had good reason to be pleased with pre-season business, with Vinales quickly ruling himself out of the silly-season speculation when he signed a new two-year deal at the team's official launch in Madrid in late January. Rossi didn't wait too long to end the speculation about his own future: his two-year extension was confirmed at the opening round in Qatar, as was his previous renewal in 2016.

All was well off track at that stage, and when the action began, there was little indication of the bleak season ahead, Rossi finishing within a second of Andrea Dovizioso in an enthralling curtain-raiser in Qatar. That extended Valentino's incredible sequence of podium finishes to a 23rd consecutive season, the 19th in the premier class. Then he rolled back the years in Mugello, where he powered to a first pole position since the Twin Ring Motegi round in Japan in 2016, the oldest rider to do so since Jack Findlay in 1974. He celebrated that with third place.

Then Rossi and Vinales played a pivotal role in the classic that unfolded in Assen, with the Spaniard third in a mesmerising race, and Rossi a close fifth from the front row. And they stood on the podium together in Germany, Yamaha's first double rostrum of the year. Up to that stage of the season, thanks also to Zarco, Yamaha had been the only manufacturer to have at least one bike on every podium.

Rossi was close to the podium before the old Achilles heel of fading rear grip struck again in Brno, but the wheels came off well and truly in Austria. Rossi slumped to 14th on the grid, while Vinales was only three places better off, and both men admitted to feeling bereft of motivation and expectation.

What followed was extraordinary, with project leader Tsuya trotted out in front of the world's media to make a grovelling public apology for Yamaha's poor performance. If ever there was a scapegoat, then Tsuya was it. The entire business was a humiliating experience for a proud Japanese engineer.

Worse was to follow, with Rossi's 18th on the Aragon grid, his worst since the Dutch TT of 2006, when he had ridden injured. He limped home a lowly eighth, Yamaha's worst 'best finish' since 2007 in Valencia, where Sylvain Guintoli had been 11th.

By then, Tsuya and his fellows had already set the wheels in motion to solve some of the YZR-M1's electronics deficiencies. The most obvious change was the growing influence of Pata Yamaha World Superbike

Maverick Vinales's Phillip Island win finally ended Yamaha's slump

Photos: Gold & Goose

electronics guru Michele Gadda, who began to make fleeting appearances in the paddock.

Vinales swept to his first podium in five races in the close Thai GP, two races before his breakthrough win. Rossi was behind him in fourth, his first time in 13 Yamaha years that he had been outside the top three for five successive races.

Rossi's crew featured just one change for 2018, with YMC engineer responsibility falling to Ooishi Masato, who had replaced devoted Rossi team member Hiroya Atsumi.

Silvano Galbusera worked closely with data engineer Matteo Flamigni as crew chief, while ex-250cc world champion Luca Cadalora was retained as rider performance analyst. His tight-knit quartet of mechanics again comprised Bernard Ansiau, Alex Briggs, Brent Stephens and Mark Elder.

Vinales's problems were not just restricted to the limitations of his YZR-M1. In Brno, it was finally confirmed, after weeks of gossip, that he would be splitting from crew chief Ramon Forcada at the end of the season. An increasingly frosty relationship had gone past the point of being salvaged, and Vinales turned to an old and trusted ally for 2019. Esteban Garcia, with KTM as Bradley Smith's crew chief in 2018, had been influential in Vinales's 2013 Moto3 title, and they would be reunited in 2019.

It was Forcada who lit the blue touch paper, declaring on Spanish TV that Vinales had not been courteous enough to inform him of his imminent dismissal. Held in high regard, Forcada had joined Yamaha in 2008 and had been instrumental in helping Jorge Lorenzo capture three world titles. Reluctant to lose him, Yamaha quickly found him fresh employment as Franco Morbidelli's crew chief in the new Petronas SIC Yamaha squad.

Yamaha was keen to offer the new Malaysian project as much experience and knowledge as possible, and Vinales's rider performance analyst, Wilco Zeelenberg, was also ceded to them as team manager.

Yamaha's quest to end Honda and Ducati's iron grip on the top step of the podium caused them to commit to the formation of a new European-based test team. With the full blessing of Rossi and Vinales, the important riding role was assigned to former Monster Yamaha Tech 3 star Jonas Folger, who had quit racing at the start of 2018 due to ongoing health issues.

Another significant change to Yamaha's factory effort in 2019 would be the identity of its title sponsorship. Spanish communications giant Movistar had decided not to renew the five-year deal that expired at the end of the 2018 season, the void being plugged immediately by Monster Energy. It was the perfect fit, Monster Energy having been seeking a new team to display its famous 'M' claw after long-term partner Tech 3 Racing had quit Yamaha to form an alliance with KTM, closely associated with rival brand Red Bull. Monster Energy had been an associate sponsor of the official factory Yamaha team since 2013, and both Rossi and Vinales were established Monster Energy athletes.

DUCATI TEAM

TEAM STAFF

Luigi DALL'IGNA: Ducati Corse General Manager
Paolo CIABATTI: Ducati Corse Sporting Director
Davide TARDOZZI: Team Manager
Riccardo SAVIN: Vehicle Dynamics Engineer
Fabiano STERLACCHINI: Track Technical Co-ordinator
Gabriele CONTI: Software and Strategies Manager
Massimo BARTOLINI: Track Engineer
Michele MUZZI: Data Analyst
Francesco RAPISARDA: Communications Director
Julian THOMAS: Press Manager
Artur VILALTA: Press Officer
Mauro GRASSAILLI: Sponsorship Manager
Yuri DE CASSAN: Sponsor Account & Hospitality
Paola BRAIATO: Operations Manager
Silvio SANGALLI: Crew Co-ordinator
Davide BARALDINI: Warehouse & Components

ANDREA DOVIZIOSO PIT CREW

Alberto GIRIBUOLA: Track Engineer
Dario MASSARIN: Electronics Engineer
Michele PERUGINI: Chief Mechanic
Enrico SAMPERI, Fabio ROVELLI, Giuliano POLETTI, Pedro RIVERA CRESPO: Mechanics
Peter BERGVALL: Ohlins Suspension Engineer

JORGE LORENZO PIT CREW

Cristian GABARRINI: Track Engineer
Tommaso PAGANO: Electronics Engineer
Marco VENTURA: Chief Mechanic
Ivan BRANDI, Juan Llansa HERNANDEZ, Massimo TOGNACCI, Lorenzo CANESTRARI: Mechanics
Giacomo MASSAROTTO: Ohlins Suspension Engineer

ANDREA DOVIZIOSO

Born: 23 March, 1986 – Forlimpopoli, Forli, Italy
GP Starts: 294 (196 MotoGP, 49 250cc, 49 125cc)
GP Wins: 20 (11 MotoGP, 4 250cc, 5 125cc)
World Championships: 1 125cc

JORGE LORENZO

Born: 4 May, 1987 – Palma de Mallorca, Spain
GP Starts: 282 (188 MotoGP, 48 250cc, 46 125cc)
GP Wins: 68 (47 MotoGP, 17 250cc, 4 125cc)
World Championships: 5 (3 MotoGP, 2 250cc)

DUCATI may well reflect on the 2018 MotoGP World Championship as a year in which it lost far more than it gained, despite the Bologna factory having recorded its highest tally of wins in a single season since Casey Stoner's unforgettable romp to glory over a decade before.

The final total of seven wins was three more than it had achieved during an outstanding 2017 campaign, when Andrea Dovizioso had pushed Marc Marquez all the way to a final-round title decider in Valencia. However, the greater success in 2018 didn't translate into a second successive title tilt.

Uncharacteristic unforced errors spiked Dovizioso's challenge, while Jorge Lorenzo paid the price for a sluggish start and a disastrous spell in the final third of the season.

There was plenty to admire about Ducati's technical improvement in 2018, but could the season be declared a resounding success in the light of the asset stripping that unfolded? By the end of the year, Ducati had lost two of the fastest riders in the history of MotoGP.

After just one top-six in the opening five races, Lorenzo correctly perceived that Ducati was preparing to cut him loose, forcing him to instigate whirlwind negotiations with HRC. How ironic then that the Spaniard won his first Ducati race in Ducati's backyard at Mugello, on the very day that Danilo Petrucci

DUCATI Desmosedici GP18

Engine: 1000cc 90-degree V4, reverse-rotating 180-degree crank, DOHC, 4-valves per cylinder, desmodromic valve gear, variable-length inlet tracts
Power: Around 290bhp, revs up to 18,500rpm

Ancillaries: Magneti Marelli electronics, full electronic ride-by-wire throttle, NGK sparking plugs • *Lubrication:* Shell Advance

Transmission: Gear primary drive, Xtrac six-speed seamless-shift cassette-type gearbox

Suspension: Front, Ohlins TSB 46 CF 'Blackfisken' 46mm forks, carbon outer upper tubes
Rear, Ohlins TRSP 44-12 Lightweight 'through-rod' shock with linkage

Wheels: Marchesini, 17in front and rear • *Tyres:* Michelin • *Brakes:* Brembo 340mm carbon-carbon front; 200mm steel rear

MICHELE PIRRO

Born: 5 July, 1986 – San Giovanni Rotondo, Italy

GP Starts: 99 (52 MotoGP, 18 Moto2, 29 125cc)

GP Wins: 1 Moto2

ALVARO BAUTISTA

Born: 21 November, 1984 – Talavera de la Reina, Spain

GP Starts: 274 (158 MotoGP, 49 250cc, 67 125cc)

GP Wins: 16 (8 250cc, 8 125cc)

World Championships: 1 125cc

Andrea Dovizioso

was informed that he would be given Lorenzo's prized Desmosedici seat in 2019.

Lorenzo's jaw-dropping move to Repsol Honda in early June blindsided everyone, as it had appeared that his only MotoGP option would be on a satellite Yamaha in the new Petronas SIC squad.

The bombshell was followed by another later in the year, when Casey Stoner announced that he was unwilling to continue as Ducati test rider and ambassador. Ducati's sole champion's discontent surfaced in early September, when he declared frustration that his feedback and development direction was being largely ignored. There was even speculation that the Australian was contemplating a shock switch back to HRC as test rider, thus reuniting with Repsol Honda's Alberto Puig, so influential in helping Stoner on to the world stage.

The loss of such talent, in the space of a few months, raised questions about how Ducati CEO Claudio Domenicali, Ducati Corse general manager Gigi Dall'Igna, sporting director Paolo Ciabatti and team manager Davide Tardozzi could let such a situation materialise.

Davide Tardozzi

Gigi Dall'Igna

Claudio Domenicali

Celebrating a Ducati 1-2 finish at Brno

Photos: Gold & Goose & Ducati Corse

Ducati's counter would be that its star performer in 2017 and 2018 had been Dovizioso, and that they were still well equipped to challenge with him in 2019.

Dovizioso and his manager, Simone Batistella, played hardball during early-season negotiations with some justification, chasing a big pay hike, given his outstanding performances in 2017. A new two-year deal was finally nailed and announced at Le Mans, but on the same weekend, the first big crack appeared in Dovizioso's 2018 title bid.

Dovi had made the perfect start to the season with a brilliant last-corner defeat of Marquez in Qatar. He had been the innocent victim of a collision between Lorenzo and Pedrosa in Jerez, but then came the costly Le Mans blunder, when inexplicably he crashed just seconds after sweeping into the lead.

He tumbled out of third in Catalunya, another unforced error and his third DNF in four races. He would never threaten to recover the deficit to Marquez, and a crash while lying second to the Spaniard at Japan's Twin Ring Motegi was the final nail in the coffin.

In between, a clinically executed win in Brno, in his 100th Ducati appearance, came from a first dry pole position since the opening round of 2015. Then there was more glory in Misano, making up for double disappointment at the Red Bull Ring, where he had lost pole to Marquez in the closest qualifying gap in 15 years, and then wilted under an onslaught from Lorenzo and Marquez in the race. A golden run of four successive podium finishes from Brno to Aragon was the best in his premier-class career.

That spell of the season was also golden for Ducati, with three victories in successive races for the first time since 2008. Only the genius of Marquez at Aragon ended hopes of a first fourth win in a row.

Dovizioso worked with track engineer Alberto Giribuola again, and given his breakthrough season in 2017, it was no surprise that he didn't tamper with a successful formula. His entire staff, including electronics engineer Dario Massarin and chief mechanic Michele Perugini, remained identical.

A large portion of credit for Ducati's excellent season must go to the technical team under the influential Dall'Igna. That select group included vehicle dynamics engineer Ricardo Savin, track technical coordinator Fabiano Sterlacchini, software and strategies manager Gabriele Conti, track engineer Massimo Bartolini and data analyst Michele Muzzi.

Lorenzo may have toiled through a humbling first season on the Ducati, but his 2017 crew was also unchanged, with Cristian Gabarrini filling the role of track engineer once more.

Ergononomic body-position modifications that Lorenzo had been requesting for months finally arrived in Mugello, where the modest tweaks (including an enlarged dummy fuel tank) instantly transformed him from no-hoper to winner. His victory over Dovizioso in Italy was Ducati's first 1-2 on home soil since the Monza 125cc race in 1958. He followed that up with another success in Catalunya, becoming only the fourth rider in history to reach 150 podiums. Then he maintained Ducati's unblemished record in Austria to take Spain's 150th premier-class victory, after an engrossing race-long duel with Marquez.

Lorenzo's challenge for a top-three finish overall came apart, however, when he fell from second in Misano, then crashed at the first corner at Aragon, after a fourth successive pole position. Subsequently, he courted controversy by blaming a bemused Marquez for the resulting injuries to his right foot.

A brave return for the following race in Thailand ended in another bone-jarring crash after a mechanical failure. He was out of that race, withdrew from the next in Japan and missed the Australian GP. His place went to Alvaro Bautista, who did a sterling job as substitute, battling for the podium in Phillip Island before finishing a season-best fourth.

Lorenzo withdrew after the opening day of practice in Malaysia. Test rider Michele Pirro, who was already in Kuala Lumpur on standby, took his seat.

Once again, Pirro played a pivotal role behind the scenes, which earned him three wild-card rides. He was scheduled to make his 50th premier-class appearance at Mugello, but a shocking high-speed crash at Turn One in FP2 prevented that milestone from being accomplished until his second outing in Misano, where he finished 15th.

TEAM SUZUKI ECSTAR

TEAM STAFF

Shinichi SAHARA: MotoGP Project Leader
Davide BRIVIO: Team Manager
Ken KAWAUCHI: Technical Manager
Tetsuya SASAKI: Chassis Engineer
Motohiko TONO: Vehicle Development
Tom O'KANE: Consultant
Russell JORDAN: Parts Manager
Roberto BRIVIO, Mitia DOTTA: Co-ordinators
Alberto GOMEZ: Marketing & Communication
Federico TONDELLI: Press Office & Social Media Manager
Hatsumi TSUKAMOTO: Marketing Relations & Operations
Massimo TOMASONI, Emanuele MAZZINI: Logistics

Akira YAMAJUKU: Engine Development
Elvio DEGANELLO, Francisco VENTURATO, Roverto COSTA, Elena DE CIA, Francisco MUNZONE: Performance Analysts

ANDREA IANNONE PIT CREW

Marco RIGAMONTI: Crew Chief:
Claudio RAINATO: Data Engineer
Sadayuki TSUJIMURA: Engine Management Engineer
Raymond HUGHES, Tsutomu MATSUGANO, Jacques ROCA, Fernando Mendez PICON: Mechanics

ALEX RINS CREW

Jose Manuel CAZEAUX: Crew Chief
Elvio DEGANELLO: Data Engineer
Yuta SHIMABUKURO: Engine Management Engineer
Davide MANFREDI, Massimo MIRANO, Paco NOQUEIRA, Marco Rosa GASTALDO: Mechanics

ANDREA IANNONE

Born: 9 August, 1989 – Vasto, Italy

GP Starts: 229 (101 MotoGP, 51 Moto2, 77 125cc)

GP Wins: 13 (1 MotoGP, 8 Moto2, 4 125cc)

ALEX RINS

Born: 8 December, 1995 – Barcelona, Spain

GP Starts: 119 (31 MotoGP, 36 Moto2, 52 Moto3)

GP Wins: 12 (4 Moto2, 8 Moto3)

SUZUKI may have ended 2018 without a win, but there was ample reason for the team to reflect on its fourth year back in MotoGP as one of success and progress. The loss of performance enhancing concessions was the most discernible barometer of its competitiveness.

Andrea Iannone's third place at MotorLand Aragon in late September took the much-improved GSX-RR to the six concession points (three for a win, two for second and one for third), stripping the team of the benefits of additional engines, unlimited private testing and the exemption from the in-season engine development freeze for 2019.

After a miserable failure to capitalise on the 2016 success of Maverick Vinales during 2017, Suzuki's off-season improvements reaped instant rewards, with Alex Rins a close third to Cal Crutchlow and Johann Zarco in round two in Argentina. That concluded a dismal run without a podium that had stretched back 22 races to the end of 2016.

A fortnight later in Texas, Andrea Iannone became only the eighth rider to claim a MotoGP podium for Suzuki; and he pounced on the chaotic crash that collected Pedrosa, Lorenzo and Dovizioso in Jerez to sweep Suzuki to rostrum finishes in three races in suc-

SUZUKI GSX-RR

Engine: 1000cc transverse in-line 4, reverse-rotating 90-degree cross-plane crankshaft, DOHC, 4 valves per cylinder, pneumatic valve return system

Power: Approximately 275bhp, revs to approximately 18,000rpm

Ancillaries: Magneti Marelli electronics, full electronic ride-by-wire throttle, NGK sparking plugs • *Lubrication:* Motul

Transmission: Gear primary drive, multi-plate dry slipper clutch, six-speed constant-mesh seamless-shift cassette-style gearbox, RK chain

Suspension: Front, Ohlins TSB 46 CF 'Blackfisken' 46mm forks, carbon outer upper tubes; Rear, Ohlins TRSP 44-12 'through-rod' shock with linkage

Wheels: MFR, 17in front and rear • *Tyres:* Michelin

Brakes: Brembo 340mm carbon-carbon front; steel rear

SYLVAIN GUINTOLI

Born: 24 June, 1982 – Montélimar, France

GP Starts: 124 (44 MotoGP, 80 250cc)

World Championships: 1 World Superbike

Celebrating Alex Rins's second place at Assen

cession for the first time in ten years. A first-lap tumble at Le Mans ended hopes of four successive podiums for the first time since 1994!

Much of Suzuki's transformation was down to the influence of Shinichi Sahara, who had replaced team director Satoru Terada in the middle of 2017. Sahara had intimate knowledge of Suzuki's race department, having been at the helm of the MotoGP project when the global economic crisis had forced the manufacturer into a three-year sabbatical at the end of 2011.

Although predominantly based in Hamamatsu Sahara worked closely with technical manager Ken Kawauchi on development of all aspects of the GSX-RR, while the trio of senior management was completed once again by team manager Davide Brivio.

Other prominent technical roles were occupied by Motohiko Tono, who was responsible for vehicle development, and Tetsutya Sasaki, who was employed as chassis engineer.

A major contribution to Suzuki's success came from temperamental Italian firebrand Iannone, who at the end of the European season had outscored studious Spaniard Alex Rins by three podium finishes to two. Iannone married occasional blistering speed with improved consistency, scoring top-ten finishes in more than half the races.

He worked again with loyal crew chief Marco Rigamonti, who had followed him from Ducati; with data engineer Claudio Rainato, and mechanics Raymond Hughes, Tsutomu Matsugano and Jacques Roca all having been with Suzuki since its return in 2015.

Iannone's 2018 contribution may have been noteworthy, but nothing would save him from the axe. With contract talks and deals agreed earlier and earlier each season, he paid dearly for a wayward 2017. It was obvious that he had dropped off Suzuki's radar at Le Mans when a two-year extension was agreed with Rins, despite the fact that he'd crashed out of three of the four opening races.

Conversely, Iannone's podiums in Austin and Jerez were his first in back-to-back races since 2011, when he had been in Moto2; his vulnerability was obvious.

Suzuki were strongly linked to a swoop for Jorge Lorenzo, but that trail went cold, and ultimately Brivio decided not to deviate from a tried-and-tested formula, combining proven talent with an emerging young gun from the unforgiving proving ground of Moto2.

That thrust 2017 Moto3 World Champion Joan Mir into the limelight. He had taken just five races in Moto2 to find his way to the podium at Le Mans.

Mir had made no secret that he was not willing to hang around in Moto2 for longer than necessary, and his fierce ambition meant that he was determined to follow a career path already successfully negotiated by Vinales: win the Moto3 title, enhance reputation with explosive performances in Moto2, earn full factory MotoGP ride in just a few months.

Davide Brivio

Andrea Iannone

Alex Rins

Iannone pre-empted an official announcement during his home round in Mugello by declaring that Suzuki were dispensing with his services.

That made Mir's signing a mere formality, and the capture of the prodigiously talented Spaniard was confirmed during the build-up to the Catalunya round in mid-June. The burden of leading a factory team's development would then fall on the shoulders of Rins, in only his third season in the premier class in 2019.

Rins operated with an unchanged support team in 2018: Jose Manuel Cazeaux working as crew chief, with lead roles taken by Suzuki's engine management engineer Yuta Shimabukuro as data engineer as well as Elvio Deganello.

One highlight of the year for Rins was his stunning contribution to the Race of the Century in Assen, where he finished second to Marc Marquez. What made that even more remarkable was the fact that Rins's participation had been in serious doubt, after he had woken on race-day morning with a severe bout of food poisoning.

He scored three top-six finishes in a row for the first time in his premier-class career in Misano, Aragon and Buriram. A third and two more seconds meant more podiums than Iannone, and fifth overall.

Rins and Suzuki at least would be able to count on the vast experience of test rider Sylvain Guintoli to help with development of the GSX-RR for 2019. The Frenchman appeared three times in 2018 as a wildcard: in Catalunya, Brno and Twin Ring Motegi. He failed to score points, but his ride to 19th in Brno was courageous in the extreme, since he learned during the weekend that a spill at the Suzuka 8 Hours endurance race the previous weekend had broken two ribs.

Photos: Gold & Goose & www.suzuki-racing.com

ALMA PRAMAC RACING

TEAM STAFF

Paolo CAMPINOTI: Team Principal
Francesco GUIDOTTI: Team Manager
Felix RODRIGUEZ: Team Co-ordinator
Jacopo MENGHETTI: Pramac Marketing
Federico CAPELLI: Press Officer
Alex GHINI: Hospitality & PR
Andrea DENARO: Warehouse Spare Parts

DANILO PETRUCCI PIT CREW

Daniele ROMAGNOLI: Crew Chief

Cristian BATTAGLIA: Electronics Engineer

Federico PECCI, Fabrizio MALAGUTI, Gianluca PERETTI, Simone ZERBONIA: Mechanics

Morris GRAZZI: Tyres & Fuel

JACK MILLER PIT CREW

Cristian PUPULIN: Crew Chief

Nicola MANNA: Chief Mechanic

Marco FRIGERIO: Data Engineer

David GALACHO, Francesco GALINDO, Marco POLASTRI: Mechanics

Tommaso PELI: Tyres & Fuel

DANILO PETRUCCI

Born: 24 October, 1990 – Terni, Italy

GP Starts: 118 MotoGP

JACK MILLER

Born: 18 January, 1995 – Townsville, Queensland, Australia

GP Starts: 121 (66 MotoGP, 55 Moto3/125cc)

GP Wins: 7 (1 MotoGP, 6 Moto3)

NO independent team in the 2018 MotoGP World Championship appeared more closely affiliated to its factory supplier than Pramac Racing to Ducati.

Danilo Petrucci effectively functioned with factory-rider status, like Dovizioso and Lorenzo, while both he and new team-mate Jack Miller were directly contracted to the Bologna marque.

Technically, Petrucci's side of Pramac Racing was undeniably a full works effort, the Italian being equipped and trusted with a GP18 machine that was identical in specification to those of the factory riders. As had become traditional policy in Ducati's central independent team, one rider had the latest-spec model, while the other was given a year-old version; thus Miller had a Desmosedici GP17.

The most obvious alteration for 2018 was a name change, with Italian employment agency and human resources specialist, Alma, taking over title sponsorship rights from previous incumbent Octo. Alma logos had first appeared on Petrucci and Scott Redding's bikes halfway through 2017, but the new title sponsorship agreement, signed in mid-January, was for three years, up for renewal at the end of 2020.

Aside from the name tweak, Pramac Racing had a very familiar appearance. Paolo Campinoti was the charismatic team principal, while Francesco Guidotti continued in the role of team manager.

Eager to build on a breakthrough season in 2017, during which he had become Ducati's most successful independent team rider for a decade, Petrucci continued working with crew chief Daniele Romagnoli. Electronics engineer Cristian Battaglia also played a

DUCATI Desmosedici GP18 – Pramac

Engine: 1000cc 90-degree V4, 360-degree reverse-rotating crankshaft, DOHC, 4 valves per cylinder, desmodromic valve gear, variable-length inlet tracts
Power: Around 290bhp, revs to 18,500rpm

Ancillaries: Magneti Marelli electronics, full electronic ride-by-wire throttle, NGK sparking plugs • *Lubrication:* Shell

Transmission: Xtrac six-speed seamless-shift cassette-type gearbox

Suspension: Front, Ohlins TSB 46 CF 'Blackfisken' 46mm forks, carbon outer upper tubes
Rear, Ohlins TRSP44-12 Lightweight 'through-rod' shock with linkage

Wheels: Marchesini, 17in front and rear • *Tyres:* Michelin • *Brakes:* Brembo 340mm carbon-carbon front; 200mm steel rear

It was a season of two halves for Jack Miller

Petrucci sported a livery change for the race at Mugello

Francesco Guidotti and Paolo Campinoti

Pole for Miller in Argentina

Petrucci took second place at Le Mans

key role, with mechanic Gianluca Peretti the only revision to his crew from the previous season.

A wheel had not even been turned in anger, however, on the eve of the first official test in Sepang, when Petrucci publicly revealed that 2018 would be his last with Pramac Racing. Due to have turned 28 by the end of the season, he felt the time was right to seek a factory team slot for 2019. It was an amicable decision, fully supported by Pramac's management, themselves eager to blood fresh young talent after a four-year relationship.

The rider's early declaration allowed the team to cherry-pick from a rich seam of talent in Moto2. Pecco Bagnaia, Miguel Oliveira and Joan Mir quickly emerged as outstanding candidates. It was in late February, during a live announcement on Sky TV in Italy, that it was confirmed that Bagnaia, a leading light in Valentino Rossi's expanding VR46 Academy, had penned a two-year deal.

Anxious to prove himself worthy of a top factory berth, Petrucci adopted desperate measures during the pre-season, arriving for the season-opener in Qatar 4kg lighter after a brutal winter training regime.

An excellent start to the season helped him fulfil his factory team aspiration. Fifth from the front row in Qatar was followed by fourth at Jerez and a stellar ride to a close second behind Marc Marquez at Le Mans. Petrucci was informed immediately after finishing seventh at Ducati's home round in Mugello that a prized seat alongside Dovizioso was his, and it was made public just a few days later.

Petrucci's worthiness to replace Lorenzo was frequently questioned as the year evolved, however, with Le Mans his only visit to the podium all season. How do you measure success though? He had scored three more podiums in 2017, but 2018 yielded a record personal points tally of 144.

He had already surpassed his 2017 record with four races remaining, and engaged in a close contest with Cal Crutchlow and Johann Zarco for the top independent team rider award, which was only decided in favour of Zarco at Valencia.

Petrucci's switch to the factory team was also good news for Bagnaia, who discovered that he would be under the stewardship of Jorge Lorenzo's 2018 crew chief, Cristian Gabbarini. The Italian had previously helped Casey Stoner capture world titles at Ducati and Honda, but had to leave the factory garage when Petrucci was permitted to bring Romagnoli with him.

For his first season on a Ducati, Miller joined a crew that was blessed with immense insider knowledge of how the Bologna factory functions. Cristian Pupulin had been a mainstay of Ducati's MotoGP project since its inception in 2003 and was crew chief, with Nicola Manna and Marco Frigerio continuing to serve as chief mechanic and electronics engineer respectively. The only alteration to the crew that had been at Redding's side was the promotion off Marco Polastri from fuel and tyres technician to mechanic, after Jerome Galland had moved with the Briton to Aprilia.

Miller's year was peppered with flashes of brilliance. That was never better demonstrated than by his astonishing and fearless attack using a Michelin slick tyre on a damp track to take pole in Argentina. It made him the first Australian on a MotoGP pole since Casey Stoner in 2012, and also the first independent Ducati rider to do so.

Five top-tens in the opening five races, including brilliant fourth-place finishes in Argentina and Le Mans, ensured that Miller's seat at Pramac Racing was never in jeopardy. So it came as no surprise that by mid-June, Ducati had exercised an option on him for 2019.

The crucial aspect of that extension was that he would get a GP19 machine, on the same technical level as the official factory squad.

After his outstanding surge to a close fourth behind Valentino Rossi in France, however, Miller had an alarming lull, during which he finished no higher than ninth for the next nine races, and he never returned to the top six.

Photos: Gold & Goose

MONSTER YAMAHA TECH 3

TEAM STAFF

Herve PONCHARAL: Team Manager

Gerard VALLEE: Team Co-ordinator

Laurence COTTIN: Team Assistant

Fabien ROPERS: Parts Manager

Thomas RUBANTEL: Fuel & Tyres

Mathilde PONCHARAL, Maria POHLMANN: Press & Communications

JOHANN ZARCO PIT CREW

Guy COULON: Crew Chief

Alexandre MERHAND: Data Engineer

Steve BLACKBURN, Jerome PONCHARAL,

Brice GROSSIN: Mechanics

Pierre-Laurent BEGHIN Fuel & Tyres

HAFIZH SYAHRIN PIT CREW

Nicolas GOYON: Crew Chief

Maxime REYSZ: Data Engineer

Eric LABORIE, David LIEBERT,

Thomas RUBANTEL: Mechanics

Nicolas GUICHARD: Fuel & Tyres

JOHANN ZARCO

Born: 16 July, 1990 – Cannes, France

GP Starts: 174 (36 MotoGP, 88 Moto2, 50 125cc)

GP Wins: 16 (15 Moto2; 1 125cc)

World Championships: 2 Moto2

HAFIZH SYAHRIN

Born: 5 May, 1994 – Selangor, Malaysia

GP Starts: 96 (18 MotoGP, 78 Moto2)

THE old cliché about all good things coming to an end certainly applied to the Monster Yamaha Tech 3 squad in 2018. A wheel had not turned in anger when the bombshell news surfaced in late February that Tech 3's 20-year partnership with Yamaha was to come to an end. And just days later, in early March, it was confirmed that team owner and manager, Herve Poncharal, had inked a three-year agreement to become a full factory-supported independent team for KTM's rapidly expanding empire.

What swayed the deal in favour of KTM appeared to be motorsport director Pit Beirer's concrete assurance that the RC16 machinery supplied to Tech 3 would be identical to the bikes run by the official factory team. That had not been the case with Yamaha, who had offered little additional technical support to Tech 3, despite Johann Zarco's standout performances throughout his rookie season in 2017.

Tech 3's KTM deal came with ready-made title sponsorship, as there was no way that the French-based squad could continue its collaboration with US energy drink giant Monster. The Austrian manufacturer is intrinsically linked with Monster's closest competitor, Red Bull. And Tech 3 would not have to seek fresh investment now that they too were under the Red Bull umbrella.

YAMAHA YZR-M1 – Tech 3

Engine: 1000cc transverse in-line 4, reverse-rotating cross-plane crankshaft, DOHC, 4 valves per cylinder, pneumatic valve return system

Power: Approximately 270bhp, revs to approximately 17,000rpm

Ancillaries: Magneti Marelli electronics, full electronic ride-by-wire throttle, NGK sparking plugs • *Lubrication:* Motul

Transmission: Gear primary drive, multi-plate dry slipper clutch, six-speed constant-mesh floating-dog-ring cassette-style gearbox, RK chain

Suspension: Front, Ohlins TRSP 25 48mm forks; Rear, Ohlins TRSP 44 shock with linkage

Wheels: MFR, 17in front and rear • *Tyres:* Michelin

Brakes: Brembo 340mm carbon-carbon front; Yamaha steel rear

Johann Zarco

Hafizh Syahrin

Poncharal's deal also meant the demise of his home-made Mistral 610 chassis project in Moto2. The Red Bull-KTM alliance covered Moto2 as well, and Tech 3 would line up in the new Triumph triple era with a KTM chassis, ridden by highly rated Italian Marco Bezzecchi and KTM favourite Philipp Oettl.

News of Tech 3's move from Yamaha to KTM was a bolt out of the blue, but these were not the team's first shock headlines of the year. In 2017, German Jonas Folger had distinguished himself as a hot rookie with great potential. But his campaign had been ended prematurely as a result of chronic fatigue caused by a mystery illness, subsequently diagnosed as the debilitating genetic disorder Gilbert's Syndrome.

Apparently, he had been convalescing well during the winter break and was eager to show the world that his health issues were under control, but then the racing world was rocked on 17th January, when Tech 3 announced that Folger had ruled himself out of any competitive action for the entire season. It prompted concern that Gilbert's Syndrome had not been the only reason why Folger had gone into self-imposed exile, and his withdrawal brought into sharp focus the stresses and strains that both brain and body endure to reach and remain at the pinnacle of MotoGP.

Crew chief Guy Coulon (*centre*) with Johann Zarco

Photos: Gold & Goose and Monster Energy

Folger's eleventh-hour withdrawal left Tech 3, Yamaha and their backers in a major predicament. Any rider with world championship pedigree is generally already under contract by mid-January. Poncharal was inundated by approaches from interested parties, but was reluctant to poach a rider who was already engaged elsewhere.

Colombian Yonny Hernandez auditioned at the opening winter test in Sepang, but no deal was struck. Salvation came in historic fashion, when Hafizh Syahrin was released from a commitment to race for the new Petronas Sprinta Racing squad in Moto2 to become the first Malaysian in the premier class.

His signing was confirmed on 21st February, but was overshadowed less than 24 hours later by the news that Tech 3 was quitting Yamaha at the end of the season.

The racing started with Zarco maintaining the momentum built up during a dazzling 2017. He took a stunning pole position in Qatar, which astonishingly made him the first French rider since 1954 to kick off a premier-class campaign from the front of the grid. He led the opening race for 17 laps, before dropping to eighth.

A close second to Crutchlow in Argentina was followed by another second in Jerez, as he was one of the chief benefactors of the three-bike crash that wiped out both factory Ducatis and Pedrosa.

Incredibly, Zarco would only score one more podium, as an early crash from a first home French pole position in 30 years at Le Mans seemed to knock him completely out of kilter. The hangover from that

Herve Poncharal

blunder lingered way longer than anybody could have anticipated, and it wasn't until nine races later, in the inaugural Thai GP, that he returned to the top six.

And there was no escaping the harsh reality that a two-decade partnership between Tech 3 and Yamaha hadn't yielded a single victory, despite having the likes of Olivier Jacque, Shinya Nakano, Norick Abe, Alex Barros, Colin Edwards, Andrea Dovizioso, Ben Spies, Cal Crutchlow and Zarco on the team's books.

There was only one change to Zarco's crew, with mechanic Brice Grossin joining legendary crew chief Guy Coulon, data engineer Alexandre Merhand, and mechanics Steve Blackburn and Jerome Poncharal.

Zarco's blazing start to 2018 reinforced his status as hot property in the rider market. Manager Laurent Fellon confirmed that both Repsol Honda and Ducati had been sniffing around at the start of the season, but KTM's long-term admiration of Zarco was one of the paddock's worst kept secrets, and Beirer was adamant that the Frenchman could take the RC16 to another level. His recruitment was announced on the eve of the Spanish GP at Jerez. Zarco's journey to MotoGP had begun with KTM and Red Bull, when he had triumphed in the first Rookies Cup in 2007.

Syharin's late arrival put him on the back foot compared to the four other rookies who had earned promotion from Moto2, but a hugely experienced crew gave him a leg up on the tough learning curve.

Expecting to link up with a fully recovered and revitalised Folger in 2018, the staff on that side of the garage were unchanged. Nicolas Goyon was crew chief again, with support coming from data engineer Maxime Reysz, and mechanics Eric Laborie, David Liebert and Thomas Rubantel.

Syharin's 14th place in the season-opener in Qatar allowed him to seize a slice of history by becoming the first Malaysian to score points in MotoGP. A memorable ride to ninth in just his second outing in Argentina showed he was quickly repaying the faith shown in him by Tech 3 and Yamaha, but he had to wait until the Japanese GP at the far end of the season to get back into the top ten.

His performances, though, rightfully earned him a new contract for 2019, which was announced in early June in a deal that would certainly give KTM and Red Bull key exposure in the MotoGP-mad Southeast Asia region. Joining Syharin in the new KTM Tech 3 partnership would be Portugal's Miguel Oliveira, who narrowly failed to defeat Pecco Bagnaia in 2018's Moto2 title chase. This was announced at Jerez, just 48 hours after Zarco's transfer was confirmed. It meant that Oliveira would have appeared in all three current world championship classes for the Austrian factory and sponsor.

LCR HONDA

TEAM STAFF

Lucio CECCHINELLO: CEO
Martine FELLONI: Administration & Legal
Oscar HARO: Public Relations
Elisa PAVAN: Press Officer & Logistic Resp.
Elena CECCHINELLO: Hospitality Manager & Workshop Manager
Fabio ALBERTI, Fabio MAZZONI, Elisabetta BONETTI: Commercial & Marketing

CAL CRUTCHLOW PIT CREW

Christophe BOURGIGNON: Chief Engineer
Marco BARBIANI: Data Recording
Arlan HOLTERMAN: Engine Management
Yuji KIKUCHI: HRC Supervisor Engineer
Andrew ROCHE: Rider's Assistant
Joan CASAS, Xavier CASANOVAS,
Chris RICHARDSON: Mechanics
Michele ANDREINI: Tyres

TAKAAKI NAKAGAMI PIT CREW

Ramon AURIN: Chief Engineer
Eric PEREZ: Data Recording
Alessandro DAMIA: Engine Management
Katsuhiko IMAI: HRC Supervisor Engineer
Momoyo NAKAGAMI: Rider's Assistant
Carlos FABREGAS, Federico VICINO,
Filippo BRUNETTI: Mechanics
Willibrord KLEINE: Tyres

CAL CRUTCHLOW

Born: 29 October, 1985 – Coventry, England
GP Starts: 138 MotoGP
GP Wins: 3 MotoGP
World Championships: 1 World Supersport

TAKAAKI NAKAGAMI

Born: 9 February, 1992 – Chiba, Japan
GP Starts: 157 (18 MotoGP, 105 Moto2, 34 125cc)
GP Wins: 2 Moto2

WHEN LCR team owner Lucio Cecchinello finally completed his long-term mission to expand to a two-rider MotoGP effort in 2015, it was both short lived and turbulent. Caught in a storm of negative publicity when the title sponsor ran into scandal, LCR Honda downsized to focus on only Cal Crutchlow in 2016 and 2017.

Cecchinello had not wavered from his desire to restore his Monaco-based project to a fully-fledged two-rider effort, however, and his perseverance paid off handsomely in 2018, when Japanese rookie Takaaki Nakagami joined.

Crutchlow was entered under the LCR Honda Castrol banner in every race, but 2018 was yet another season when Cecchinello conducted a system of rotation for the lead sponsorship of the Briton's RC213V machine. As well as full Castrol livery in selected races, Crutchlow's Honda was emblazoned with the logos of associate backers Givi, Rizoma, Beta and Flex-Box at several others.

Honda took a leaf out of Ducati's book for 2018, bringing Crutchlow closer under the umbrella of the factory, much as the Bologna brand had done with Danilo Petrucci at Pramac Racing. His contract was now directly with HRC, and with that elevated status came such trappings as a much greater presence of Honda technical staff in the garage.

Stability had been the backbone of Crutchlow's

HONDA RC213V – LCR

Engine: 1000cc 90-degree V4, reverse-rotating 360-degree crankshaft, pneumatic valve return system, DOHC, 4 valves per cylinder
Power: More than 280bhp, revs to 18,500rpm

Ancillaries: Magneti Marelli electronics, ride-by-wire throttle and fuel injection system, Denso sparking plugs • *Lubrication:* Castrol Power 1

Transmission: Gear primary drive, multi-plate dry slipper clutch, six-speed seamless-shift cassette-style gearbox, DID chain

Suspension: Front, Ohlins TRBSP 25/30 'through-rod-bleed solid-piston' 46mm forks • Rear, TRSP 44-12 Lightweight 'through-rod' shock with linkage

Wheels: OZ Racing, 17in front and rear • *Tyres:* Michelin • *Brakes:* Nissin/Brembo 320 or 340mm carbon-carbon front; HRC 218mm steel rear

STEFAN BRADL

Born: 29 November, 1989 – Augsburg, Germany

GP Starts: 178 (91 MotoGP, 33 Moto2, 54 125cc)

GP Wins: 7 (5 Moto2, 2 125cc)

Crutchlow took a brilliantly judged win in Argentina

success with LCR in the past, and it was no surprise that for 2018, he returned with a completely unrevised technical crew. Christophe 'Beefy' Bourguignon was his trusty sidekick as chief engineer, while data recording and engine mapping roles were filled by Marco Barbiani and Arlan Holterman respectively.

Long-serving LCR mechanics Xavier Casanovas, Chris Richardson and Joan Casas all remained on board, and Yuji Kikuchi was the HRC supervisor engineer again.

Crutchlow made notable contributions to the Honda cause. A brilliantly executed win in Argentina put him in the rare position of being an independent team rider leading the points standing, which had not happened since Sete Gibernau had ridden the Gresini Honda in 2004. In addition, he was the first Briton to hold that position, albeit briefly, since Barry Sheene in 1979.

He also took pole at Jerez and a fortuitous podium in Misano, after Lorenzo jumped off his Ducati when lying second halfway around the penultimate lap.

Once again, Crutchlow firmly established himself as a consistent menace in the top six in both qualifying and races, and he might comfortably have been top independent had old habits not died hard, with costly crashes at CoTA, Jerez, Sachsenring and Aragon, then a season-ending injury in Australia.

His value to Honda was confirmed when he was given a one-year extension to his contract, meaning that he would be an official factory HRC rider until the end of 2020 at least. He had already been signed up for 2019, but was anxious to come into line with most of the grid, who'd penned new two-year deals. It was announced at Silverstone, but actually had been finalised during the Catalunya round in early June.

Nakagami's close relationship with Honda meant that he was the only one of five rookies who graduated from Moto2 to be directly under contract to his manufacturer. Jack Miller's defection from the Marc VDS squad to Ducati had effectively freed up the position and the factory technical support.

Nakagami's side of the LCR garage ran different branding, with Japan's petroleum giant Idemitsu as title sponsor, and his livery didn't deviate from that all season.

Vastly experienced crew chief Ramon Aurin, a direct employee of HRC, rather than Marc VDS, during his time with Miller, was immediately installed as Nakagami's senior technical man. Mechanic Filippo Brunetti and gearbox technician Katsuhiko Imai also moved over to work with Nakagami.

However, his close connections to HRC did not come with the benefit of the latest-spec RC213V for his maiden MotoGP season. Like fellow Honda-mounted rookies Franco Morbidelli and Tom Luthi, he'd have to learn his craft on a 2017-spec machine.

Nakagami made frequent visits to the points, with a season best of sixth at Valencia, his only top-ten, but he was never a serious challenger for the coveted Rookie of the Year prize, remaining on the periphery of a season-long battle between Morbidelli and Tech 3 Yamaha's Hafizh Syharin.

Honda's unfaltering determination to nurture home-grown Japanese talent on the biggest stage of all meant that Nakagami's place on the 2019 grid was never under serious threat. However, he did have to wait until just before his home race at the Twin Ring Motegi in mid-October before it was confirmed by HRC.

One significant change would be the need to adjust to a new crew chief. Aurin had first joined the paddock in 1990 as telemetry engineer for legendary Spanish engineer Antonio Cobas, who at the time was running Jorge Martinez in the 125cc class, and Sito Pons in the 500cc arena. Highly regarded by HRC, he had filled the same role with Nicky Hayden for his 2006 title year, followed by stints at Repsol Honda as crew chief to both Dovizioso and Pedrosa. Now he had landed the golden ticket of Jorge Lorenzo's new crew chief at Repsol Honda for 2019.

Nakagami was scheduled to work with Dani Pedrosa's ex-Repsol Honda crew chief, Giacomo Guidotti, in 2019.

MotoGP rookie Takaagi Nakagami ran with Idemitsu livery

Photos: Gold & Goose

ANGEL NIETO TEAM

TEAM STAFF

Jorge MARTINEZ: Team Owner
Angel NIETO Jr: Team Principal
Gino BORSOI: Sporting Director
Jose Maria IBANEZ, Sylvia PELUFO: General Managers
Maria Jose BOTELLA: Media & Logistics
Vicente VILA: Communications & Social Media
Roger MARCACCINI, Andrea ORLANDI: Spare Parts

KAREL ABRAHAM PIT CREW

Francesco CARCHEDI: Chief Mechanic
Luca CONTI: Data Technician
Daniel VILLAR, Antonio HABA,
Oscar GRAU: Mechanics

ALVARO BAUTISTA PIT CREW

Alessandro TOGNELLI: Track Engineer
Davide TAGLIATESTA: Data Engineer
Miguel Angel GALLEGO, Simone FALCINI,
Adrian VILA AGUSTI, Salvador MORALEDA: Mechanics

KAREL ABRAHAM

Born: 2 January, 1990 – Brno, Czech Republic

GP Starts: 195 (103 MotoGP, 61 Moto2/250cc, 31 125cc)

GP Wins: 1 Moto2

ALVARO BAUTISTA

Born: 21 November, 1984 – Talavera de la Reina, Spain

GP Starts: 274 (158 MotoGP, 49 250cc, 67 125cc)

GP Wins: 16 (8 250cc, 8 125cc)

World Championships: 1 125cc

OF all the moving tributes to Spanish racing legend Angel Nieto, who had died in a traffic accident in August, 2017, the decision by Jorge 'Aspar' Martinez to rename his Ducati MotoGP squad was one of the most poignant.

Nieto and Aspar had enjoyed a unique and unbreakable bond, forged over decades, because of their mutual love of motorcycle racing and admiration for each other's accomplishments both on and off track. When Aspar announced in late December, 2017 that his team would be rebranded as the Angel Nieto Team, it was greeted with universal commendation. Further cementing his close ties, Aspar confirmed that Angel's eldest son, Gelete, who had raced for the Valencia-based team from 1993 to 1997, would take up the new role of team principal.

The name change presaged a dramatic change in circumstances for Martinez and his MotoGP team, which had competed in the premier class since 2010 with Ducati, Honda and Aprilia machinery.

At the start of the European season, long-serving sporting director Gino Borsoi was supremely confident of a quick renegotiation for the continued lease of Ducati machinery for a two-rider effort beyond 2018. That confidence soon began to erode, however, when it emerged that a key piece of the jigsaw in an ambitious new Malaysian project directly impacted on the future of the Angel Nieto Team.

Dorna had rewarded the loyalty of the independent teams that had supported MotoGP through the bleak times of thin grids and the global economic crisis by signing long-term contracts, preventing a new team

DUCATI Desmosedici GP17

Engine: 1000cc 90-degree V4, 180-degree reverse-rotating crankshaft, DOHC, 4 valves per cylinder, desmodromic valve gear, variable-length inlet tracts
Power: Around 290bhp, revs to 18,500rpm

Ancillaries: Magneti Marelli electronics, full electronic ride-by-wire throttle, NGK sparking plugs • *Lubrication:* Shell Advance

Transmission: Xtrac six-speed seamless-shift cassette-type gearbox

Suspension: Front, Ohlins TSB 46 CF 'Blackfisken' 46mm forks; Rear, Ohlins TRSP 44-12 Lightweight 'through-rod' shock with linkage

Wheels: Marchesini, 17in front and rear • *Tyres:* Michelin • *Brakes:* Brembo 340mm carbon-carbon front; 200mm steel rear

MIKE JONES

Born: 25 February, 1984 – Brisbane, Australia

GP Starts: 3 (3 MotoGP)

Bautista riding to fifth place at Motegi

from waltzing in at the expense of an existing competitor. A new team could join forces with an existing team, however, or come to an amicable agreement to take over its grid slots.

After weeks of speculation, it was confirmed in early July that in 2019, the Aspar MotoGP project would be taken over by the new Petronas SIC Yamaha squad, with Aspar retained as sporting advisor. Just minutes later, Yamaha announced "a memorandum of understanding", with SIC to succeed Tech 3 as its satellite team for 2019, 2020 and 2021. That completed a meteoric rise for SIC, which only four years before had formed its own Moto3 team, and in 2018 entered Moto2. The magnitude of Malaysia's influence was abundantly clear at the official launch at the British GP, where top-table dignitaries included the Malaysian government's Minister of Youth and Sport, and the President and Group CEO of Petronas, as well as top SIC management.

Already committed to continuing his KTM-backed Moto3 project with Albert Arenas and new signing Raul Fernandez for 2019, Martinez seized the opportunity to align himself with the Austrian factory for a first return to Moto2 since 2013. Aspar rider Julian Simon had finished runner-up to Toni Elias in the inaugural series in 2010, and the team had won four races with Nico Terol and Jordi Torres in 2013. The Moto2 entries would be BSB runner-up Jake Dixon and Xavi Cardelus.

The Dixon deal was eased because his manager was Briton Francesco Carchedi, on the Aspar payroll as Karel Abraham's crew chief. Carchedi had also landed himself a plum deal as Joan Mir's new crew chief in Suzuki's factory squad for 2019.

That left riders Alvaro Bautista and Abraham looking for new employment for 2019. Once Lorenzo and Pedrosa had politely rejected SIC's advances to join alongside the signed Morbidelli, Bautista and his manager, Simone Batistella, went into hard-sell mode, convinced that his experience and an impressive run of form that had carried him to seven top-ten finishes between Jerez and the Red Bull Ring would make him a valuable asset.

It was to no avail, however, and with all avenues having reached dead ends, Bautista reluctantly conceded that his 16-year grand prix career was over. He hardly had to accept a wooden spoon, though, since at Silverstone he confirmed that he would join Chaz Davies in Ducati's official factory World Superbike team to spearhead the challenge of the new Panigale V4. Later, Abraham was signed up by Avintia Ducati.

Many of Bautista's 2018 performances on the year-old Ducati GP17 strongly suggested that he still had plenty to offer in MotoGP, with a pair of fifth places and then a strong fourth on the factory bike in Australia, his best results since 2013.

Crew chief duty again fell to Alessandro Tognelli, while data engineer Davide Tagliatesta, and mechanics Miguel Gallego, Salvador Moraleda and Adrian Vila all continued in an unchanged line-up from 2017.

A run of six consecutive top-ten finishes was Bautista's best in five years, but that excellent sequence was abruptly ended by a second-lap spill in MotorLand Aragon.

Toiling on a two-year-old Ducati GP16 made for a season of considerable frustration for Czech rider Abraham, who collected points in just five races and didn't trouble the top ten once, his best result 11th in Australia on Bautista's GP17.

Like Bautista, Abraham worked with the same crew that had been at his side during the 2017 campaign, led by Carchedi. Data engineer duty went to Luca Conti, while Spanish trio Oscar Grau, Antonio Haba and Daniel Villar remained as mechanics. The mechanics' quartet was completed by Bruno Leoni, who had world titles with Casey Stoner at Honda and Ducati on his CV.

Jorge Martinez

Karel Abraham

Photos: Gold & Goose

RED BULL KTM

TEAM STAFF

Pit BEIRER: Motorsport Director
Kurt TRIEB: Head of Technology Road Racing
Mike LEITNER: Team Manager
Sebastian RISSE: Technical Director
Luca FASO: Strategy Engineer Manager
Tobias GRUBER: Electronics
Giovanni PIRAS: Vehicle Dynamics
Richard ASPODINGER: Engine & Fuel Injection
Philipp GRUENBERGER: Press/PR & Marketing
Jeremy WILSON, Beatriz AMODEO: Team Co-ordinators
Thomas ROCKENMEYER: Spare Parts

POL ESPARGARO PIT CREW

Paul TREVATHAN: Crew Chief
Jenny ANDERSON: Electronic Strategy Engineer
Peter SCHLAEGER: Data Recording Engineer
Niklas WINKLER: Mapping Engineer
Christophe LEONCE (Chief), Xavi QUEIXALOS,
Andreas RIEGER: Mechanics
Mark BARNETT: Gearbox Craig BURTON: Tyres/Truck
Manuel OLIVENCIA: WP Suspension Technician

BRADLEY SMITH PIT CREW

Esteban GARCIA: Crew Chief
Riccardo SANCASSINI: Electronic Strategy Engineer
Tex GEISSLER: Data Recording Engineer
Niklas WINKLER: Mapping Engineer
Mark LLOYD (Chief), Jonny EYRE,
Daniel PETAK: Mechanics
Florian FERRACCI: Gearbox
Michele BUBBOLINI: Tyres/Truck
Gerald PERDON: WP Suspension Technician

BRADLEY SMITH

Born: 28 November, 1990 – Oxford, England

GP Starts: 217 (104 MotoGP, 33 Moto2, 80 125cc)

GP Wins: 3 125cc

POL ESPARGARO

Born: 10 June, 1991 – Granollers, Spain

GP Starts: 208 (86 MotoGP, 51 Moto2, 71 125cc)

GP Wins: 10 Moto2; 5 125cc

World Championships: 1 Moto2

KTM'S unrelenting attempt to transfer its astonishing success in a variety of off-road disciplines to elite-level road-racing showed no sign of halting in 2018. If ambition and the will to win guarantee success, then KTM's ascent towards the top step of the podium is a foregone conclusion. If only it were as easy as that. The Austrian company's second season demonstrated how the road to the top is peppered with pitfalls.

The impression was of a musician attempting to produce new material off the back of a critically acclaimed debut album. But if there was a sense that KTM had stalled, rather than made significant progress in 2018, the time sheets painted a completely different picture.

At almost every race, the gap to the race winner was slashed dramatically. The gain at Austin was 45 seconds; at Mugello, 30 seconds; at Jerez, 28; Le Mans, 20. In simple terms, KTM improved in 2018, but not substantially enough to mount the consistent top-ten assault of the latter part of 2017, although it did take a first podium at the last race.

The effort was under the overall control of fiercely determined and ambitious CEO Stefan Pierer, while day-to-day running of the MotoGP project fell under the jurisdiction of motorsport director Pit Beirer, team manager Mike Leitner and technical director Sebastien Risse, with Jeremy Wilson moving into the role of team co-ordinator.

The RC16's debut season had raised a few eyebrows, with Pol Espargaro and Bradley Smith amass-

KTM RC16

Engine: 1000cc 90-degree V4, 180-degree forward-rotating crankshaft (from San Marino onwards), DOHC, 4 valves per cylinder, Del West pneumatic valve return system; *Power:* Approximately 270bhp, revs to 18,000rpm

Ancillaries: Magneti Marelli electronics, full ride-by-wire throttle • *Lubrication:* Motorex

Transmission: Gear primary drive, KTM six-speed seamless-shift cassette-type gearbox

Suspension: Front, WP MotoGP 48mm 135mm-travel forks (with the option of carbon outer tubes from Aragon); Rear, WP MotoGP twin-tube shock with linkage

Wheels: Marchesini, 17in front and rear • *Tyres:* Michelin • *Brakes:* Brembo 340mm carbon-carbon; 200mm steel rear

MIKA KALLIO

Born: 8 November, 1982 – Valkeakoski, Finland

GP Starts: 240 (39 MotoGP, 119 Moto2/250cc, 82 125cc)

GP Wins: 9 Moto2/250cc, 7 125cc

Pol Espargaro

Pit Beirer

Mike Leitner

Bradley Smith

Photos: Gold & Goose

ing 19 points-scoring finishes, six inside the top ten; and between them seven trips through to Q2.

Success on that scale proved impossible in 2018, although thanks to Valencia's podium and eighth in the rain, the points tally equalled the first year's 95, and the top-ten count swelled to five compared with seven in the previous season.

The hiatus could be blamed on bad luck, as Espargaro endured a brutal year for injury. On just the second day of winter testing at Sepang, he suffered a shocking 250km/h crash. A hernia in his L4 vertebrae required surgery back in Barcelona that ruled him out of the three-day test in Thailand. His absence at a phase of the year when vital development decisions were being taken severely hampered KTM.

Worse was to follow. A shocking crash at Brno, "the worst in my career", rendered Espargaro unconscious, and the gruesome sounding outcome was severe inflammation of the spinal cord and a fractured left collarbone. That ruled him out of KTM's crunch home round at the Red Bull Ring and Silverstone. Former Avintia Ducati rider Loris Baz was briefly released by the Gulf Althea BMW World Superbike squad to replace him in Britain, but the calamitous cancellation of that race meant he didn't ride the RC16.

Espargaro's spinal-cord issue ruled out routine surgery to pin and plate the damaged collarbone, and that came back to haunt him. At Aragon, he fell in FP3 and broke it again. Valencia's break-through podium after a year-long dearth of top-tens underlined how tough his season had been.

His crew was largely unchanged. Kiwi crew chief Paul Trevathan was at the helm, with Peter Schlaeger as data recording engineer and Jenny Anderson as strategy engineer. Craig Burton was drafted in from Team Estrella Galicia 0,0 to take on tyre duty.

KTM's much publicised pursuit of Johann Zarco made it clear from an early stage that Espargaro and Smith were fighting for just one 2019 seat. Then came a flurry of announcements at Jerez. Espargaro had signed a new two-year deal on the eve of the Spanish GP, and the next day speculation about the swoop on Zarco was abruptly ended when his two-year deal was announced.

Smith was out, despite good results. At first, he was contemplating retirement if he could not secure a MotoGP seat. Ever since his formative days on a 125cc two-stroke, he had only competed on pure racing bikes, and a possible shift to production-based Superbikes didn't appeal. After some soul searching, though, he decided he wanted to ride on.

With his manager, Bob Moore, he pushed hard for a berth alongside Morbidelli in the new Petronas SIC Yamaha squad. The team was enthusiastic, but Yamaha dealt him two savage blows. He'd been on a Tech 3 YZR-M1 between 2013 and 2016, and Yamaha didn't want to cover old ground, preferring an emerging talent from Moto2. Then he was overlooked in his attempt to spearhead a new European-based Yamaha test team. His future was finally decided in Misano, where Aprilia pounced on the chance to sign him as their new official test rider. Fast, ultra-reliable and highly motivated to try to earn his place back on the grid, he ticked all their boxes.

Smith teamed up once more with crew chief Esteban Garcia, who had been seconded from the test team to join the Briton when Tom Jojic was moved out halfway through the 2017 season. Familiar faces included data engineer Tex Geissler, and mechanics Mark Lloyd, John Eyre and Daniel Petak, who could boast a wealth of factory team experience at HRC and Kawasaki.

KTM's injury woes weren't limited to Espargaro. Highly valued test rider Mika Kallio was also a lengthy absentee. The Finn was taking the third of five scheduled wild-card rides in Germany when he suffered a high-speed crash in FP2 that shredded ligaments and tendons in his right knee. The intricate operation to reconstruct the joint took seven hours, and the Finn was ruled out for the rest of the year.

That was a body blow to KTM. Not only was Kallio a tireless workhorse, but also he fed back clear, concise information, while still lapping at a pace that was fast enough to finish comfortably in the points – he was a brilliant tenth at Jerez, riding a prototype 2019 RC16.

With a factory full of new parts to evaluate, KTM recruited an old ally in Randy de Puniet to take over testing duties. He'd helped in the early development phase of the RC16 and also had been influential in developing Suzuki's GSX-RR.

Kallio was retained as test rider for 2019. Then, in a late-season coup, Dani Pedrosa was signed for two years to the same role. But there would be no more wild-card rides, because the management felt that too much emphasis was being placed on race preparation, rather than the priority of testing and developing new components.

APRILIA RACING TEAM GRESINI

TEAM STAFF

Romano ALBESIANO: Aprilia Racing Manager
Dario RAIMONDI: Sports Manager
Fausto GRESINI: Team Manager
Carlo MERLINI: Marketing & Commercial Director
Michele MASINI: Team Co-ordinator
Paolo BONORA: Project Manager
Giovanni MATTAROLLO: Frame Manager
Giuseppe BUSATO, Marco GRIFFONI, Mario MANGANELLI, Walter SCATTOLIN: Engine
Luigi ZUCCHI: Data Engineer
Massimo MENEGHIN: Spare Parts Manager
Paolo PEZZINI: Press Manager

ALEIX ESPARGARO PIT CREW

Marcus ESCHENBACHER/Pietro CAPRARA: Crew Chief
Erkki SIUKOLA: Track Engineer
Guido FONTANA: Telemetry Engineer
Oscar BOLZONELLA: Suspension
Carlo TOCCAFONDI: Chief Mechanic
Antonio MIR MORANGUES, Salvador Franco BORJA, Jerome GALLAND: Mechanics
Eddy BOSI: Pit Assistant

SCOTT REDDING PIT CREW

Giulio NAVA: Crew Chief
Stefano FERRO: Track Engineer
Gianluca GIORGINI: Telemetry Engineer
Ivano MANCURTI: Chief Mechanic
Alberto PRESUTTI, Maurizio VISANI, Roberto MARINONI: Mechanics
Lino ZAMENGO: Pit Assistant

ALEIX ESPARGARO

Born: 30 July, 1989 – Granollers, Spain

GP Starts: 230 (146 MotoGP, 61 Moto2/250cc, 23 125cc)

SCOTT REDDING

Born: 4 January, 1993 – Quedgeley, England

GP Starts: 189 (90 MotoGP, 66 Moto2 33 125cc)

GP Wins: 4 (3 Moto2, 1 125cc)

IT'S a measure of just how much the Aprilia factory team's fortunes floundered in 2018 that by its conclusion, the Noale brand had mustered just three top-ten finishes all season.

When Aprilia rejoined MotoGP in 2015, racing manager Romano Albesiano had confidently predicted that the RS-GP machine would be consistently giving the big hitters a run for their money in the top five by 2018.

In truth, Aprilia appeared to be even further from its ambitious goals than ever.

Albesiano was still very much the public figurehead of the Aprilia project, with Fausto Gresini tasked with team manager responsibility once again. Various job titles had been altered, with Paolo Bonora designated project manager after being electric and electronics manager in 2017. Giovanni Mattarollo's title changed from vehicle engineer to frame manager.

The dearth of attention-grabbing results was a reflection on just how much development of the RS-GP had stagnated.

Aleix Espargaro rode the bike into the top ten in Austin and Le Mans, and again with a stunning surge from 13th to sixth in Aragon, which equalled Aprilia's best ever MotoGP result. The RS-GP's one-lap pace was hardly more impressive than in race trim, although Espargaro managed to force his way into Q2 five times.

For much of the season, the Spaniard was a demoralised and frustrated figure, but his faith in Aprilia survived, and he signed a two-year contract extension as early as round five in France.

APRILIA RS-GP

Engine: 1000cc 75-degree V4, 180-degree reverse-rotating crankshaft, DOHC, 4 valves per cylinder, pneumatic valve return system

Power: Approximately 275bhp, revs to 18,000rpm

Ancillaries: Magneti Marelli electronics, full electronic ride-by-wire throttle, NGK sparking plugs • *Lubrication:* Motul

Transmission: Gear primary drive, Zeroshift six-speed seamless-shift cassette-type gearbox, Regina chain

Suspension: Front, Ohlins TSB 46 CF 'Blackfisken' 46mm forks, carbon outer upper tubes; Rear, Ohlins TRSP 44-12 Lightweight 'through-rod' shock with linkage

Wheels: Marchesini, 17in front and rear • *Tyres:* Michelin • *Brakes:* Brembo 320 or 340mm carbon-carbon front; 200mm steel rear

Aleix Espargaro

Romano Albesiano

Aprilia, top independent team at Aragon

Espargaro started the season with largely the same crew from 2017, with key positions filled by crew chief Marcus Eschenbacher, track engineer Erkki Siukola and telemetry engineer Guido Fontana. It became common knowledge relatively early in the season that Eschenbacher would switch to KTM in 2019, unable to resist the temptation of teaming up with Johann Zarco.

With Aprilia throwing new parts at the RS-GP like confetti at a wedding later in the season, and given that KTM were close rivals, it was felt that Eschenbacher would have been privy to too much insider information. He was relieved of his duties prior to Aprilia's home race in Misano, although Espargaro indicated that his imminent switch to KTM was not the sole reason. He was replaced for the last seven rounds by Pietro Caprara, whose most recent engagement had been as technical director and crew chief at SKY VR46 in Moto3.

This was a stopgap appointment, however, and it was confirmed at Aragon that Antonio Jimenez would take over in 2019, having most recently worked with Xavi Vierge in Moto2. His last senior technical job in MotoGP had been with Gresini in 2014, working with Alvaro Bautista. He had also been crew chief to Carlos Checa in the factory Yamaha squad.

Scott Redding

Photos: Gold & Goose

If Espargaro thought he was treading water on the RS-GP, then team-mate Scott Redding was in danger of sinking without trace. He scored points in only six races without a single top-ten, and never escaped from Q1.

Redding worked with many of the crew who had endured a wretched 2017 season with Sam Lowes. Giulio Nava was crew chief, and Gianluca Giorgini continued as telemetry engineer; Sander Donkers had been replaced by Stefano Ferro as track engineer.

The season had barely hit Europe when it emerged that Aprilia was already contemplating ditching Redding. After six races, it was confirmed that Andrea Iannone would be taking his place, on a two-year deal.

Riled by a lack of results and the lack of any other MotoGP opportunities, Redding was still locked in talks with Aprilia about a test-rider vacancy when he committed career suicide with an expletive-laden rant after another bitterly frustrating performance in Austria. His outburst not only forced him into a grovelling apology, but also put a big dent in his wallet, after Aprilia hit him with a fine that was rumoured to be around 50,000 euros. It also ended any hopes of a test-rider role.

The Briton toyed with the idea of switching back to Moto2, undaunted by the difficulties this had caused for the likes of Toni Elias, Lowes, Yonny Hernandez and Hector Barbera. He hoped to join the Dynavolt intact GP squad, but Tom Luthi bagged that.

With no competitive World Superbike options, it transpired that grand prix racing's youngest ever winner, and Britain's brightest prospect in a generation, was resigned to leaving the world stage. In early October, he finally revealed that his destiny in 2019 would be in the British Superbike series, where he would ride Ducati's new V4 Panigale for the successful Paul Bird Motorsport outfit.

Stung into action by its results, Aprilia committed to a new concerted effort behind the scenes with a fully-fledged testing team created for 2019. With no test-rider option to stay at KTM, Bradley Smith had sought the opportunity to return to Yamaha when it became clear that the Iwata brand would form a European-based testing team in 2019. That avenue was shut at Silverstone, however, and just a fortnight later, Smith inked a deal to be Aprilia's test rider, with an assurance of five wild-cards, which included an outing at the opening round in Qatar.

ESTRELLA GALICIA 0,0 MARC VDS

TEAM STAFF

Marc VAN DER STRATEN: Team President
Marina ROSSI: Team Co-ordinator
Patrick KRAMER: Logistics/Technical Co-ordinator
Stefan PREIN: Rider Coach
Mike WATT: Ohlins Technician
Lou ACEDO Marketing & Communications Manager
Sarah COLSON: Travel Co-ordinator
Delphine LEMAITRE: Team Secretary

FRANCO MORBIDELLI PIT CREW

Diego GUBELLINI: Chief Mechanic
Stefano GUIDI: Fuel Injection
Pablo GUILLEM: Data Engineer
Mori YUJI: Gearbox Mechanic
Francesco FAVA: Fuel Injection Engineer
Ignacio CABEZA, Matt LLOYD,
Sergi SANGRA: Mechanics
Martin ZABALA: Tyres & Fuel

TOM LUTHI PIT CREW

Gilles BIGOT: Chief Mechanic
Enrico PELLIZZARI: Fuel Injection
Andrew: GRIFFITH: Data Engineer
Kazuhiku IMAI: Gearbox Mechanic
Achim KARINGER, Daniele GRELLI,
Olivier BOUTRON: Mechanics
Ignacio LORENZANA: Tyres & Fuel

FRANCO MORBIDELLI

Born: 4 December, 1994 – Rome, Italy
GP Starts: 87 (16 MotoGP, 71 Moto2)
GP Wins: 8 Moto2

TOM LUTHI

Born: 6 September, 1986 – Oberdiessbach, Switzerland
GP Starts: 267 (18 MotoGP, 182 Moto2/250cc, 67 125cc)
GP Wins: 16 (11 Moto2, 5 125cc)
World Championships: 1 125cc

A BITTER power struggle and rancorous infighting, which led to the shock early-season departure of talisman team principal Michael Bartholemy, plunged the Marc VDS Racing project into murky and troubled waters for the first time since its formation in 2010.

Given the enormous personal wealth of tycoon and team president Marc van der Straten, it would be unjust to say that the Marc VDS Racing story had been a rags-to-riches fairy-tale. But it is indisputable that the Belgian-based team quickly became an all-conquering powerhouse and reference for success in Moto2, and one of the highest-profile and most respected independent teams in MotoGP.

However, it was reduced to a crumbling ruin before the season had even reached the halfway stage. In the space of a few short weeks, Marc VDS went from the unique position of being courted by Honda, Yamaha and Suzuki with lucrative leasing deals for 2019 to a full-blown crisis. And if there was one burning question at the end of a turbulent 2018 season, it would surely be: "Where did it all go wrong?"

The scandal erupted at the Spanish Grand Prix in Jerez, with Bartholemy accused of financial impropriety following an alleged breakdown in relations between the former Kawasaki MotoGP team boss and Marc VDS team co-ordinator Marina Rossi. Bartholemy unreservedly refuted all the allegations and launched a robust defence, while remaining determined to weather the storm and continue at the helm of the project.

Too many bridges had been burned, however, and by the time the paddock arrived at Le Mans, the acrimonious feud had resulted in Bartholemy's contract being terminated. That wasn't the end of it, though.

HONDA RC213V – EG-VDS

Engine: 1000cc 90-degree V4, 360-degree reverse-rotating crankshaft, pneumatic valve return system, DOHC, four valves per cylinder
Power: More than 275bhp, revs to 18,000rpm

Ancillaries: Magneti Marelli electronics and ride-by-wire throttle and fuel injection system, NGK sparking plugs • *Lubrication:* Elf

Transmission: Gear primary drive, multi-plate dry slipper clutch, six-speed seamless-shift constant-mesh cassette-style gearbox, RK chain

Suspension: Front, Ohlins TRBSP 25/30 'through-rod-bleed solid-piston' 46mm forks ; Rear, Ohlins TRSP 44-12 'through-rod' shock with linkage

Wheels: OZ Racing, 17in front and rear • *Tyres:* Michelin • *Brakes:* Brembo 320 or 340mm carbon-carbon front; HRC 218mm steel rear

STEFAN BRADL

Born: 29 November, 1989 – Augsburg, Germany

GP Starts: 178 (91 MotoGP, 33 Moto2, 54 125cc)

GP Wins: 9 250cc

Tom Luthi

Stefan Bradl

Marc van der Straten with Tom Luthi

Franco Morbidelli

Photos: Gold & Goose

Bartholemy threatened legal action unless he was completely exonerated by van der Straten. A resolution to the damaging affair was finally reached in early June, with a statement from van der Straten declaring that a mutual agreement had been reached "to end their association, which is solely due to differing strategic approaches". It added that Bartholemy had been "entirely vindicated" of any allegations of "supposed embezzlement".

Former JiR MotoGP team boss Gianluca Montiron was plucked from obscurity to steer the rudderless ship, but his tenure was brief, and *de facto* management responsibility passed to 1999 125cc World Champion Emilio Alzamora from Mugello onwards. Alzamora was already firmly ensconced in the Estrella Galicia set-up, as manager of the Moto3 team, and he also acted as personal manager to Moto2 star Alex Marquez.

Marc VDS was contracted to participate in MotoGP until the end of 2021, but at the end of the season, the premier-class squad was disbanded, despite a concerted push from Alzamora to prolong its existence as a one-man team for the younger Marquez. The common belief was that Dorna would reserve the two vacant grid slots for an inevitable future foray into MotoGP management by Valentino Rossi.

While the MotoGP team would cease trading, the crisis didn't precipitate the extinction of the entire endeavour, as some had feared. Instead, Marc VDS would return to its roots and field an all-Spanish squad with Marquez and Xavi Vierge in Moto2 for the 2019 season.

The year had started full of confidence and optimism, with the team welcoming two exciting rookie prospects for its fourth MotoGP season: Moto2 World Champion Franco Morbidelli and runner-up Tom Luthi. That optimism appeared well placed when Morbidelli finished 12th on his debut in Qatar, less than two seconds outside the top ten, while Luthi missed the points by less than a second in 16th.

Morbidelli was paired with hugely experienced crew chief Diego Gubellini, which aided his tough transition to the Honda RC213V, given that they could communicate in their native tongue. The Italian hit the ground running and scored points in all but two of the races he started, which included two top-ten finishes; and he took the top rookie award.

Unfortunately, he also hit the ground hard following a high-speed crash at Assen, and he missed the Dutch TT with a third metarcarpal fracture in his left hand. Bravely, he tried to ride in Germany just 12 days later, but pain and lack of strength in his left hand at the predominately left-handed Sachsenring forced his withdrawal at the end of an uncomfortable FP1. His place in Germany went to 2011 Moto2 World Champion Stefan Bradl, who for 2018 had become an HRC staffer as official test rider for Marc Marquez and Dani Pedrosa. Bradl was already on site at Sachsenring, as an expert analyst for Austrian Servus TV. He finished 16th, but over ten seconds ahead of full-time rider Luthi.

The Swiss former 125 champion had waited patiently until way beyond his 30th birthday to achieve his big break in MotoGP, but the season turned out to be a chastening experience, and he didn't score a single point all year. He had graduated to the premier class with a familiar face in tow, former Moto2 crew chief Gilles Bigot.

The team's demise unexpectedly threw Morbidelli and Luthi back on to the rider market, although the Italian didn't remain a free agent for very long. A buddy of mentor Valentino Rossi, he was soon signed up for the Petronas SIC Yamaha project. At the launch of the new team at Silverstone, it was confirmed that he would ride a YZR-M1, identical in specification to those with which Rossi and Vinales would start the 2019 season.

Luthi spoke briefly with Reale Avintia Ducati, but decided to beat a hasty retreat to Moto2 with the Dynavolt Intact GP squad.

REALE AVINTIA DUCATI

TEAM STAFF

Raul ROMERO: General Manager

Augustin ESCOBAR: Team Manager

Luca FERRACCIOLI: Ducati Race Engineer

Marc VIDAL: Logistics

Jose MAROTO: Press Manager

Luca BELLOSI: Spare Parts

TITO RABAT PIT CREW

Jarno POLASTRI: Chief Mechanic

Renato PENNACCHIO: Data Engineer

Alex CIONNA, Jordi PRADES, Davide CASTANEDA, Jesus MORENO: Mechanics

XAVIER SIMEON PIT CREW

Paolo ZAVALLONI: Chief Mechanic

Eric CHIARVESTO: Ducati Data Engineer

Rafael LOPEZ, Joan TORTOSA, Oscar MARTINEZ, Angel PINA: Mechanics

TITO RABAT

Born: 25 May, 1989 – Barcelona, Spain

GP Starts: 205 (46 MotoGP, 83 Moto2, 76 125cc)

GP Wins: 13 Moto2

XAVIER SIMEON

Born: 31 August, 1989 – Etterbeek, Belgium

GP Starts: 144 (17 MotoGP, 127 Moto2)

GP Wins: 1 Moto2

A SEVERE and season-ending injury for number-one rider Tito Rabat at Silverstone, and the subsequent controversy over the criteria for replacement riders in MotoGP, gained Reale Avintia Ducati column inches for the wrong reasons in 2018.

When the paddock convened for the British GP in August, former Moto2 champion Rabat had already put behind him two nightmare years on a Honda RC213V with a series of eye-catching performances on the hand-me-down Ducati GP17. He'd scored points seven times, with a best of seventh from an outstanding fourth on the grid in Argentina, where he'd advanced into Q2 for only the second time.

The Spaniard inherited almost the entire crew that had worked with Hector Barbera, including crew chief Jarno Polastri and Ducati data engineer Renato Pennacchio. The only new arrival was mechanic David Castenada, who replaced Marc Argemi.

Rabat's impressive season ended in excruciatingly painful fashion during a weather-disrupted FP4 at Silverstone. He was one of several riders to aquaplane at high speed on standing water as they approached Stowe corner. Seconds after he fell, Morbidelli did the same, and his Honda was launched on a trajectory towards Rabat, who had got to his feet, but was totally oblivious. In a sickening collision, Rabat's right leg took the brunt of the impact. His screams of pain were so ear-piercing that they could be heard on trackside cameras. Later, the worst fears were confirmed in the University Hospital Coventry, where he was diagnosed with a triple fracture of his femur, with severe breaks to the tibia and fibula as well.

DUCATI Desmosedici GP17

Engine: 1000cc 90-degree V4, 180-degree reverse-rotating crankshaft, DOHC, 4 valves per cylinder, desmodromic valve gear, variable-length inlet tracts

Power: Around 290bhp, revs to 18,500rpm

Ancillaries: Magneti Marelli electronics, full electronic ride-by-wire throttle, NGK sparking plugs • *Lubrication:* Shell Advance

Transmission: Gear primary drive, Xtrac six-speed seamless-shift cassette-type gearbox

Suspension: Front, TSB 46 CF 'Blackfisken' 46mm forks, carbon outer upper tubes; Rear, Ohlins TRSP 44-12 Lightweight 'through-rod' shock with linkage

Wheels: Marchesini, 17in front and rear • *Tyres:* Michelin • *Brakes:* Brembo 340mm carbon-carbon front; 200mm steel rear

Jordi Torres

CHRISTOPHE PONSSON

Born: 23 December, 1995 – Lyon, France

GP Starts: 1 MotoGP

JORDI TORRES

Born: 27 August, 1987 – Rubi, Spain

GP Starts: 60 (5 MotoGP, 55 250cc)

GP Wins: 1 Moto2

Tito Rabat

Xavier Simeon

Photos: Gold & Goose

Rabat was pictured miraculously walking in the hospital barely 24 hours after the crash, and like any racer reduced to the role of frustrated spectator, he set himself an ambitious target – to return in five weeks for the Thai GP in early October. This proved impossible, however, and he did not race again in 2018, although he did attempt post-season tests.

It was difficult to foresee the fallout of his crash, with the complexity of replacing a top-level MotoGP racer when absent through injury brought into sharp focus. Regulations permit only one race to be missed, and the team sought a replacement for Misano and the foreseeable future.

Former Reale Avintia Ducati rider Loris Baz was quickly ruled out. While his knowledge of the team, machine, electronics and tyres made him the ideal candidate, powerful figures at Spanish insurance company Reale had not forgiven his very public criticism of bullfighting in Spain, which had cost him the ride in 2018 in the first place.

Running out of options, general manager Raul Romero and team manager Agustin Escobar signed the little-known Christophe Ponsson, who had been plying his trade in the FIM CEV Superbike Championship in Spain. The 22-year-old Frenchman was thrown into the lion's den without an opportunity to test the Ducati GP16, and his selection drew fierce criticism, mostly aimed at Reale Avintia's management.

The affair proved so divisive that the powerful Grand Prix Commission swiftly modified the regulations concerning rider replacements to ensure better-quality substitutes in future. Henceforth, nominated replacement riders would be vetted by the same MotoGP selection committee that approved full-time riders.

As quickly as he arrived, Ponsson reluctantly departed, having finished 23rd in Misano, his entry in the next three races vetoed.

Eager to calm the storm, Reale Avintia drafted in the considerably more experienced and streetwise Jordi Torres for the final six races of the season. Shortly before his second appearance in Thailand, the MV Agusta World Superbike squad announced an early termination of his contract with them, so that he could focus exclusively on his new commitments in MotoGP.

Meanwhile, the GP17 that Rabat had been campaigning with distinction was handed over to his Belgian team-mate, Xavier Simeon. However, the upgrade didn't spark any drastic improvement in performance from the former Moto2 race winner, who consistently finished inside the top 20 without ever troubling the points.

Simeon worked with the majority of Baz's 2017 crew. Paolo Zavalloni continued as crew chief, while Rafa Lopez, Joan Tortosa, Oscar Martinez and Angel Pina remained as mechanics. The only change from the previous season was the introduction of Eric Chiarvesio as Ducati data engineer.

Simeon's points drought threw doubt on what had been reported as a two-year contract, although with obvious performance related clauses that permitted the team to cancel year two. Brief talks took place with Alex Marquez around the middle of the season, but never gained any serious impetus.

It was no secret that both Reale Avintia seats came with a price tag, nor that Karel Abraham had always been supported by serious financial clout. He was seeking to continue his MotoGP career after the termination of the Angel Nieto Team. The consequent reduction in the number of customers meant that Ducati no longer needed to keep two-year-old bikes running to supply them all, and the promise of a GP18 Desmosedici fuelled Abraham's determination to strike a deal with Avintia.

A two-year contract with the Czech rider was confirmed shortly before the San Marino round in early September, and in the same announcement, it was revealed that Reale Avintia had agreed a two-year extension to remain a Ducati customer team for 2019 and 2020.

FIM MOTO2 WORLD CHAMPIONSHIP

2018 TEAMS AND RIDERS

By PETER McLAREN

FRANCESCO BAGNAIA won his and the VR46 team's first world championship in 2018, as Kalex repelled the KTM challenge during the final season of Honda engines.

Three successive KTM victories at the end of 2017 had prompted predictions that the Kalex era was over. But, spurred on by some stark warnings from its top teams, the German manufacturer faced down the only major factory in the class to take a sixth consecutive championship.

While the world championship was a straight fight between the top Kalex and KTM riders, the arrival of NTS alongside Speed Up, Suter and Tech 3 meant a total of six chassis manufacturers. Half of them won races and featured on the podium. A new championship for teams was also added.

Franco Morbidelli, 2017 Moto2 champion, plus Thomas Luthi (second), Hafizh Syahrin (tenth) and Xavier Simeon (23rd) left the class to form the annual sink-or-swim intake of MotoGP hopefuls. By contrast, Sam Lowes and Hector Barbera tried a Toni Elias-style career relaunch by returning from MotoGP to the intermediate class.

Miguel Oliveira was the highest ranked rider (third) to remain in Moto2. He began the new season tied with Lowes and Alex Marquez for most class wins on the current grid (three).

Bagnaia, Lorenzo Baldassarri and Dominque Aegerter (one win each) were the only other proven Moto2 winners, while Barbera had taken four victories in the previous 250cc two-stroke class, where he had raced from 2005 to 2009.

Reigning Moto3 world champion Joan Mir headed the Rookie of the Year entry alongside Romano Fenati, Joe Roberts, Federico Fuligni, Eric Granado, Zulfahmi Khairuddin, Bo Bendsneyder and Jules Danilo. Interestingly, only half of them had stepped up directly from the Moto3 class (Mir, Fenati, Bendsneyder and Danilo).

The 32-rider grid may have been numerically dominated by Italian (nine) and Spanish (seven) riders, but 12 other countries also featured. South Africa, France, Britain and Malaysia had two riders apiece, with a single entry each for the United States, Germany, Portugal, Japan, Brazil, the Netherlands, Switzerland and Australia.

Iker Lecuona was the youngest full-time rider and one of three 18-year-olds on the Qatar grid alongside Fabio Quartararo and Stefano Manzi. The oldest was 32-year-old Mattia Pasini, with Barbera and Simone Corsi the only others over the age of 30.

Unsurprisingly, in the ninth and final season of 600cc Honda engines, the technical regulations were unchanged, teams and chassis manufacturers devoting any spare resources to preparation for the debut of the new 765cc Triumph three-cylinder engines.

In 2019, a new ECU, made by Magneti Marelli, would be introduced, bringing some of MotoGP's electronics to Moto2. Launch control, adjustable ride-by-wire torque management, plus new engine-braking controls (including automatic throttle 'blipping' for downshifts) are expected – but perhaps not traction control, at least not in year one.

Likewise, Dunlop is expected to revamp its tyre supply for the new machinery.

Triumph wouldn't be the only famous brand joining the Moto2 grid in 2019, with MV Agusta launching a chassis project in partnership with the Forward team. The Tech3 chassis would depart, however, as the French team moved to KTM for both its MotoGP and Moto2 projects.

Bagnaia, Oliveira, Mir and Quartararo would move from Moto2 to MotoGP for 2019.

KALEX

Kalex may have defended its rider and constructor titles with ease in 2017, but KTM's late victory run spooked its leading teams.

"In the last three races of 2017, KTM made a big step forward, and this year there will be even more of their bikes on the grid," said Michael Bartholemy, erstwhile team manager of defending champions Marc VDS. He also highlighted the difference in scale between the two leading chassis suppliers: "It's never easy to fight against a factory [KTM], but that's exactly what we intend to do this year."

Some also expressed concern that the necessary investment in the 2019 Triumph project would take a bigger toll on Kalex than KTM. On the other hand, Kalex didn't have MotoGP and Moto3 projects to simultaneously support.

Ultimately, there was only one defection from Kalex to KTM over the winter, CGBM, title runner-up under the Interwetten banner with Swiss rider Thomas Luthi. The other teams that switched from Kalex elected for Suter (Forward Racing) and NTS (RW Racing), while Petronas Raceline Malaysia dropped from the grid. In their places came new Kalex entries run by Dynavolt Intact (two), Marinelli Snipers, Tasca and the Sepang International Circuit (one apiece).

The new season started with a Kalex top-four in Qatar, suggesting that talk of its decline had been greatly exaggerated.

Meanwhile, Kalex called on Jonas Folger to help develop its 2019 chassis, giving him the opportunity to return to the racetrack after quitting MotoGP.

Francesco 'Pecco' Bagnaia (21) had been named as a 2019 Pramac Ducati MotoGP rider long before the new Moto2 season began. That soon appeared to be a wise decision, with the Italian – Rookie of the Year with four podiums in 2017 – taking his and the SKY VR46 team's debut Moto2 victory in the dusk at the opening Qatar race.

If his rivals had been hoping for inconsistency, the chances were remote: Bagnaia had finished every Moto2 race in 2017. The addition of winning speed and further experience made the Torino native a formidable opponent, and ultimately only Oliveira could challenge him.

Luca Marini (20) had switched from Forward Racing to half-brother Valentino Rossi's team for his third Moto2 season. He had been 15th overall in 2017's standings, and few would have predicted podium, pole and victory performances from him, especially after struggling with shoulder dislocations in the early part of the season. But a front row at Assen would light the touch paper.

Marini was set to become VR46 team leader in 2019, with countryman Nicolo Bulega sent up from Moto3 to replace Bagnaia.

Fourth overall after claiming overdue debut Moto2 victories in 2017, **Alex Marquez** (21), on paper at least, was a serious title candidate. The goal was clear: continue the momentum, become the latest in a long line of Marc VDS champions (to add to his 2014 Moto3 crown) and then step up with the team to MotoGP, joining brother Marc.

Marc had watched when Alex took part in a MotoGP test for VDS at Jerez in late 2017, and the Belgian team was understood to have reserved a 2019 MotoGP seat for him. But neither Alex nor Marc VDS would be in MotoGP for that season, following a management rift that severed the title-winning partnership of Bartholemy and team owner Michael van der Straten early in 2018.

Bartholemy and several close associates departed, leaving Marc VDS without an official team manager for the rest of the year. While the future of the Moto2 team was at least secured, the disruption was obvious, and it soon became clear that the VDS MotoGP project would cease to exist at the end of 2018.

To make matters worse for Marquez, he appeared to have been forgotten as several MotoGP factories fought over the signature of rookie team-mate Mir.So, for the third time in as many years, Marquez would wave a team-mate off to MotoGP (after Tito Rabat and Franco Morbidelli) while remaining in the intermediate class. The Spaniard would be joined at Marc VDS by countryman Xavi Vierge for 2019.

On track, Marquez's 2018 season began with a rear brake disc glowing in the Qatar night, having jammed on during the race. He still salvaged a podium, and more would follow, but he couldn't hold the level of Bagnaia and Oliveira. A fumble at the final turn in Austria effectively ended any title chances.

Moto3 champion **Joan Mir** (20) arrived at the start of the European season in the dream situation of having three race-winning MotoGP factories courting his services for 2019. The feeding frenzy increased when he took a debut podium at Le Mans, then a repeat rostrum at Mugello. By then, Suzuki had seen enough and signed him to be its next Maverick Vinales.

Plenty wondered whether a MotoGP deal after only a pair of Moto3 seasons and six Moto2 starts was not a little premature. But Suzuki had been stung by the Iannone experience and wanted a rising, rather than established star. Meanwhile, Mir and his manager were eager to move up due to the uncertainty of the Triumph Moto2 era and two-year nature of top MotoGP contracts.

In other words, if Mir didn't go to MotoGP in 2019, it would mean staying for two more years in Moto2, during which the balance of power among the teams and chassis manufacturers would be difficult to predict due to the new engine and electronics.

Time would tell if the timing was right. Either way, Mir blitzed the Rookie of the Year title, despite having lost some momentum during the middle of his only Moto2 season.

After three seasons and one victory at Forward Racing, **Lorenzo Baldassarri** (21) switched to Pons HP 40. Neither rider nor team had won in 2017, but it proved an inspired partnership, the Italian enjoying his best grand prix season to date, despite some shocking luck – such as a flat tyre at Assen.

There was an early-season dismissal on the other side of the garage. Big-name signing **Hector Barbera** (31) – 250cc runner-up with Pons in 2009, before spending the next eight years in MotoGP – made an underwhelming return to the class, and then was sacked after failing a drink-drive test.

Sito Pons, who had taken Pol Espargaro to the 2013 title, called up **Augusto Fernandez** (21) to take over Barbera's ride. He soon exceeded Barbera's points and would be retained by Pons, alongside Baldassarri, for 2019.

Alex Marquez

Luca Marini

Pecco Bagnaia

Joan Mir

Hector Barbera

Andrea Locatelli

Lorenzo Baldassarri

Augusto Fernandez

Tetsuta Nagashima

Marcel Schrotter

Khairul Idham Pawi

Mattia Pasini

Zulfahmi Khairuddin

Jorge Navarro

Xavi Vierge

Niki Tuuli

IDEMITSU Honda Team Asia held on to **Khairul Idham Pawi** (19) for a second season, as well as signing **Tetsuta Nagashima** (25) from SAG to replace MotoGP-bound Takaaki Nakagami. Former 250cc world champion Hiroshi Aoyama was team manager. But the podiums and victories of previous seasons with Nakagami became a distant memory.

Nagashima's second full grand prix campaign was interrupted by a finger injury at Assen, while Pawi again appeared far removed from the rider who had made history for Malaysia with Moto3 wins in 2016. However, his passport helped secure a Moto2 ride with the Sepang Team in 2019.

Italtrans kept the same mix of home-grown youth and experience, retaining **Mattia Pasini** (32) alongside **Andrea Locatelli** (21). After some heroic rides, most notably a last-lap first Moto2 victory at home in Mugello, Pasini, who has both a front brake and clutch lever on the left handlebar due to motocross injuries in his youth, pledged to add consistency to his armoury in pursuit of a 2018 title challenge. True to his word, he was second in the standings as the series headed to Europe, with a race win already in the bag.

Things didn't go to plan thereafter, despite impressive speed in qualifying, but many were surprised when it became clear that Pasini would be out of the Italtrans door at the end of the season. Moto3 race winner Enea Bastianini would replace him for the 2019 season, with Locatelli keeping his seat after building steadily on his rookie form.

Federal Oil Gresini Moto2 again fielded **Jorge Navarro** (21) as its sole Moto2 rider, for a solid, if unspectacular, season. Gresini, having been inaugural Moto2 champions (with Toni Elias on a Moriwaki), clearly had higher expectations and would be reunited with Sam Lowes in 2019. Former Moto3 race winner Navarro would switch to Speed Up.

Dynavolt Intact GP split with long-time rider Sandro Cortese in favour of Tech3 podium finisher **Xavi Vierge** (20) as team-mate to **Marcel Schrotter** (25). Expecting to stay with Suter, Intact was forced into a late deal with Kalex when the Swiss manufacturer announced that it would be withdrawing from Moto2, if only temporarily.

An early podium and pole set up Vierge as a potential title contender, although the Spaniard had slipped down the order by the time he suffered a hand injury in a dramatic incident with Steven Odendaal during qualifying in Austria. As Vierge recovered, Schrotter rose, the German fighting back from an early-season shoulder injury to claim his debut grand prix podium, after ten years and 151 race starts.

Double Moto2 title runner-up Thomas Luthi was set to drop back from MotoGP to replace the departing Vierge for 2019.

The SIC Racing Team had been formed to run Hafizh Syahrin in the 2018 Moto2 World Championship, but when the Malaysian received a dream MotoGP call-up in February, the Moto2 spotlight fell on a surprised **Zulfahmi Khairuddin** (26).

A past home Sepang master in Moto3 and WorldSSP, Khairuddin hadn't expected to be racing in 2018 and was dedicating his time to helping the next generation of Malaysian riders. Feeling duty bound to help his local team, he accepted the challenge, but bowed out after spending four races at the back of the field. He was replaced by Niki Tuuli.

The Finn, a star in World Supersport on Yamaha machinery, was in the midst of a difficult WorldSSP campaign with Honda when he gambled on the change of championship.

But Moto2 proved an even tougher and more painful prospect. Tuuli lost most of a finger during qualifying at Assen (the race before Petronas added its sponsorship to the bike), then missed Phillip Island after suffering another punishing fall. He would not be with the team in 2019, SIC having signed up Malaysian Pawi.

The SAG Team took on rookie **Jules Danilo** (22) in place of Nagashima, with **Isaac Vinales** (25) staying for a second full season. Or at least that was the plan; the Spaniard split with the team before Brno and later surfaced at Forward Racing. Fellow Spaniard **Alejandro Medina** (21) and later 2018 European Moto2 Champion **Jesko Raffin** (22, from Switzerland) took over his SAG seat.

With Xavier Simeon having switched to the premier class, Tasca Racing hired feisty Italian veteran **Simone Corsi** (30) from Speed Up. They also added a second machine for rookie countryman **Federico Fuligni** (22).

Corsi made the headlines for the wrong reasons by carelessly ramming into Oliveira after the chequered flag in Catalunya, earning a back-of-the-grid start. Later he suffered a hand injury at the Austrian GP. One of the few remaining active riders to have won a 125cc race, he would be back with Tasca in 2019.

The Marinelli Snipers Team had tapped into the talent of **Romano Fenati** (22) in 2017, picking up the Italian after his split with VR46 and surging to second place in the Moto3 World Championship. That success prompted the team to set up a Moto2 project for him in 2018, but it was a dark year on and off track.

In May, the team was rocked by the death of main sponsor Andrea Marinelli, while Fenati's actions at Misano brought worldwide condemnation. After petulantly grabbing Manzi's front brake lever on the straight, initially he was handed a two-race ban by the FIM stewards. Then he was sacked by both Snipers and his 2019 employer, MV Agusta. Later he had his license suspended until the end of the season by the FIM.

By that time, Fenati had said that he might quit racing altogether. But had it been a bluff? By the end of the year, rumours were growing that he would make a comeback in 2019. Time would tell...

Xavi Cardelus (20) – who had made wild-card appearances and a surprise Avintia MotoGP debut during post-race testing at Jerez – took over from Fenati for the remainder of the season.

KTM

Having won the final three races of its rookie campaign with Miguel Oliveira, KTM was tipped as the manufacturer to beat from the start of 2018. Instead, it was a slow-burning season, the Austrian factory not winning until round six, then reaching the top of the Moto2 World Championship – for the first time, but not for long – at Brno.

Again, KTM ran its own factory team for Oliveira and Brad Binder, while adding new satellite entries from CGBM (Swiss Innovative Investors) and Kiefer Racing.

Miguel Oliveira (23) was again at the controls of the orange steel-framed racer, with its ubiquitous WP suspension, for its belated first victory of 2018. The Portuguese rider maintained the momentum to pursue a breakaway title duel with Bagnaia from mid-season, by which time he had also been confirmed as a KTM MotoGP rider with Tech3 for 2019.

Olivera had been left just short of Danny Kent after hunting down the Englishman in their 2015 Moto3 title battle, and he hadn't led a world championship before the 2018 season. But his hopes of beating Bagnaia were complicated by poor qualifying performances, partly attributed to the KTM's easy-on-the-tyre character.

Having backed up his team-mate's 2017 victories with podiums in the closing rounds of his rookie campaign, **Brad Binder** (21) was expecting wins sooner rather than later in 2018. However, it was a frustrating start for the South African, who had to wait nearly half the season before finally breaking his win drought – and claiming his first podium of the season – on the weekend of a KTM contract renewal. More success would follow.

With both the familiar Interwetten branding and crew chief Gilles Bigot having followed 2017 title runner-up Thomas Luthi to MotoGP, it was a case of rider, sponsor and chassis changes for CGBM Evolution.

Iker Lecuona (18) remained on strength, while **Sam Lowes** (27) joined from MotoGP as the team switched from Kalex to KTM machinery with new title backing from Swiss Innovative Investors.

Lowes, a former race winner for Speed Up and title contender with Kalex, was aiming for a title victory, which would clear the way for a return to the premier class on a KTM, after a miserable MotoGP season with Aprilia. The reality would be much more modest, however. KTM's early-season difficulties were magnified for its satellite teams, with CGBM's chances further eroded by rumoured funding troubles.

Sensing that there would be no upturn in fortunes, Lowes opted for a return to Gresini, Kalex and Ohlins for 2019. Nonetheless, Lecuona claimed his best grand prix finish and would stay for 2019, when he would be joined by Joe Roberts.

Rocked by the death of team principal Stefan Kiefer in the closing stages of the 2017 season, Kiefer Racing then faced ownership turmoil as a planned takeover hit the rocks during the winter. A salvage operation resulted in a slimmed-down, single-rider entry for former race winner **Dominique Aegerter** (27), present in Moto2 since its debut 2010 season, the team switching from Suter to KTM.

The Swiss rider – who had been stripped of his 2017 Misano victory due to non-compliant oil – broke his pelvis in an enduro accident after Austin, which ruled him out of Jerez and Le Mans. German **Lukas Tulovic** (18) took his place at those races.

SPEED UP

Speed Up again ran its own factory team, headed by former racer Luca Boscoscuro, but with an all-new rider line-up of **Fabio Quartararo** (18) and **Danny Kent** (24), in place of Simone Corsi and Axel Bassani.

The team tried WP, Kayaba and finally Ohlins suspension during winter testing, which left them playing catch-up during the opening rounds, while also trying carbon-fibre and aluminium swing-arms. Perhaps aptly, the Speed Up also lacked some straight-line performance.

While both riders were announced on two-year contracts, neither would be with the team in 2019.

Quartararo had arrived after a reasonable rookie season at Pons. His shock mid-season surge, which claimed Speed Up's first win since 2015 and made him the youngest ever French rider to win in the intermediate class, launched him into MotoGP with Sepang Yamaha for 2019.

The contrast couldn't have been greater on the other side of the garage, where Kent appeared lost at sea and endured the worst run of his grand prix career, with three successive falls. The Englishman was sacked by the team, in favour of 23-year-old **Edgar Pons**, on the eve of the flyaway rounds.

Having previously struggled on Tech3, Kalex and Suter Moto2 machinery – including walking out on Kiefer early in 2017 – Kent's Speed Up deal had been likened to pulling a rabbit out of a hat. With that chance lost, the former Moto3 world champion appeared at the final round of BSB.

Jorge Navarro and Moto3's Fabio Di Giannantonio would move from Gresini to headline Speed Up's Moto2 challenge during the new Triumph era.

SUTER

Suter had intended to withdraw from the Moto2 World Championship in 2018 due to a lack of entries, after Kiefer's switch to KTM had left only Dynavolt Intact planning to run the Swiss chassis. "From a strategic point of view, participation in the Moto2 World Championship can no longer be justified," owner and founder Eskil Suter had said.

That news prompted Intact to ink a hasty deal with Kalex, only for Forward Racing (previously with Kalex) to convince Suter to stay! "Since we had already virtually finished the 2018 material anyway, we have now agreed to enter into the co-operation with Forward Racing," Suter said.

Stefano Manzi (18), from VR46, and **Eric Granado** (21), returning to grands prix, were the only Forward/Suter riders, although Granado was dumped in favour of Isaac Vinales from the Austrian round.

Forward announced that Granado was leading the Brazilian Superbike Championship and "from our point of view, this double effort does not allow him to be fully focused on the World Championship."

The only table Manzi was in contention of leading was for most falls in the season, although the feud with Fenati at Misano provided media coverage way beyond his rare points finishes. He also missed several races due to injury, while Vinales was ruled out of Aragon because of a wrist fracture that he had sustained at Silverstone.

Forward announced its 2019 MV Agusta partnership early in the season. Former World Superbike race winner Lorenzo Lanzi was helping with testing, but the severing of the Fenati contract forced a change of plans as far as rider line-up was concerned.

Having lost its only team, Suter's 2019 Moto2 programme was unclear, although the Swiss manufacturer was rumoured to be assisting in the MV project.

TECH 3

The 2018 season would be the last year for the once race-winning Tech3 chassis, the French team's future KTM MotoGP deal including a simultaneous switch to the Austrian brand in Moto2.

Remy Gardner (20), son of Wayne, continued for a second season, joined by Dutch rookie **Bo Bendsneyder** (19). Unfortunately, neither was able to send the Mistral 610 into retirement on a high.

Gardner's early season showed promise, with a career-best sixth in Argentina, but multiple leg and ankle fractures suffered in a motocross training accident put him out of action for Jerez, Le Mans and Mugello. Wild-card Hector Garzo was called up again to replace the Australian, whose luck was probably summed up when he claimed a first front-row start at Silverstone – for a race that never happened.

Bendsneyder, a factory KTM Ajo rider in Moto3, struggled to make an impact on the points and suffered surely the unluckiest injury of the year when an exploding alternator fractured his tibia on the last lap in Japan. Bryan Staring, Dimas Ekky Pratama and then Garzo featured as his replacements.

The team signed Moto3 starts Marco Bezzecchi and Philipp Oettl for 2019's switch to KTM.

NTS

Japanese manufacturer NTS committed to a full Moto2 season following previous CEV and wild-card grand prix appearances. The Dutch-based RW Racing squad, owned by Roelof Waninge and managed by former racer Jarno Janssen, switched from Kalex to become the sole NTS team, running **Steven Odendaal** (25) and American **Joe Roberts** (20).

South African Odendaal was competing in his first full Moto2 season since 2013, while Roberts was technically classed as a rookie, despite having spent the tail end of 2017 racing for AGR. The pair switched crew chiefs early in the year, and both earned points for NTS.

The chassis constructer would stay with RW Racing for 2019, and the team signed Dutch rider Bo Bendsneyder to replace the departing Roberts.

Miguel Oliveira

Fabio Quartararo

Brad Binder

Iker Lecuona

Dominique Aegerter

Simone Corsi

Hector Garzo

Jules Danilo

Jesko Raffin

Steven Odendaal

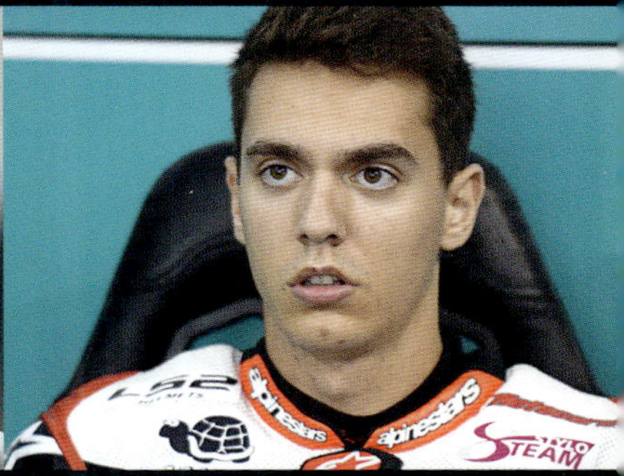
Xavi Cardelus

Bo Bendsneyder

Romano Fenati

Sam Lowes

Isaac Vinales

Edgar Pons

Federico Fuligni

Lukas Tulovic

Eric Granado

Stefano Manzi

Danny Kent

Remy Gardner

Joe Roberts

FIM MOTO3 WORLD CHAMPIONSHIP

2018 TEAMS AND RIDERS

By PETER McLAREN

The 2018 Moto3 World Championship came down to a duel between Jorge Martin and Marco Bezzecchi, after a roller-coaster season put the pair almost equal with three rounds to go. But Martin would only need two of them to take his and the Gresini team's first Moto3 title.

Honda's fourth riders' crown in five seasons also put it ahead of KTM for the first time since the four-stroke class replaced 125cc in 2012.

The departure of Mahindra left the reduced 28-rider field divided 15–13 between KTM and Honda respectively. Hopes of a third manufacturer entering in the near future increased when TM made its Moto3 debut as a wild-card at Misano.

For the second year, Moto3 engines and gearboxes were leased rather than sold. The price of the package was again set at a maximum 60,000 euros per rider – for six engines, two throttle bodies and two complete gearboxes. The engines, limited to 13,500rpm, were randomly distributed by the technical director. Each manufacturer was allowed two different specifications per season, but had to supply them to all its riders.

Any manufacturer wishing to enter Moto3 needs to support a minimum of six riders. Established brands must be prepared to supply up to 14, a rule designed to limit expensive technology.

Five rookies – Jaume Masia, Dennis Foggia, Kazuki Masaki, Alonso Lopez and Makar Yurchenko – joined the class. Sixteen-year-old Lopez was the youngest on the grid. The oldest was Jakub Kornfeil, at 24.

With new champion Joan Mir and nearest rival Romano Fenati having gone to Moto2, Aron Canet was the highest-ranked rider to remain in the class. He and Niccolo Antonelli also had the most wins under their belts (3), but with Enea Bastianini (2), Jorge Martin (1), Livio Loi (1), Andrea Migno (1) and John McPhee (1) also proven winners.

Italy (9) and Spain (6) formed most of the grid, albeit with one less rider than in 2017. Japan rose to four, with one rider each from Malaysia, Belgium, Great Britain, Argentina, South Africa, Thailand, Germany, Kazakhstan and the Czech Republic.

The previous season's harsh penalties for slow riding while in search of a tow during qualifying had a noticeable impact – until Aragon anyway, where a raft of punishments meant only two riders started where they had qualified. More such instances would follow.

During the season, it was announced that the winner of the Red Bull Rookies Cup would join the winner of the Moto3 Junior World Championship in being allowed to race in GPs from the age of 15 (rather than 16). The exemption applied from the moment a rider had won the championship.

HONDA

Honda may have enjoyed its most dominant 125cc/Moto3 season since 1993 in 2017 and was still considered the best all-round package, but the NSF250R was no longer the bike of numerical choice in 2018 The swing towards KTM was down to the departure of two Honda seats (British Talent Team and Snipers), with no new additions, while all the ex-Mahindra teams joined KTM.

Former racer Fausto Gresini had competed as a team owner in GPs since 1997, winning titles with Daijiro Kato (2001) and Toni Elias (2010) in the intermediate class. After finally taking his maiden grand prix win with Gresini in the final round of 2017, it seemed the bottle had been uncorked for **Jorge Martin** (20), who would win the opening round of 2018.

Despite a tyre gamble in Argentina, the Spaniard was back on top of the world for the start of the European season – when the wipe-outs, mistakes and injuries that would taunt his title campaign began.

During his worst run, Martin – who had more Moto3 pole positions than any other rider – failed to finish three out of four races and later missed Brno with a broken wrist. But a victory challenge on his return just a week later impressed even the toughest of racers.

In a further twist, Martin suffered a bizarre hand injury while having a massage in Thailand that prevented him from operating the clutch properly. He used a specially modified glove and would be glad he didn't miss the race. But joy turned to heartbreak a week later at Motegi, setting up the duel with Bezzecchi.

After podiums in both previous grand prix seasons, team-mate **Fabio Di Giannantonio** (19) finally took his first GP win at Le Mans. Or so he thought; the Italian left devastated by a post-race penalty. Official victory eventually came after the summer break, in a race where 2.8s covered the top 15 – by which time Di Giannantonio was in some tense negotiations with Gresini over 2019. The rapidly-growing Roman (1.75m and rising) desperately wanted – and felt he had been assured of – a move to Moto2, but Gresini had signed Sam Lowes to its only entry.

Di Giannantonio confirmed a Speed Up deal on the eve of the flyaways, and promptly won another race to briefly create a three-way title fight, until a double Gresini disaster in Japan. Martin's Moto2 future had been decided much earlier in the season, and the Spaniard would join the factory Red Bull Ajo KTM squad for 2019, in place of Miguel Oliveira. Taking their places at Gresini would be Gabriel Rodrigo and rookie Riccardo Rossi.

After dominating 2017 with Joan Mir, Leopard Racing fielded an all-new line-up of **Enea Bastianini** (20), from Gresini, and **Lorenzo Dalla Porta** (20), from Aspar.

Championship runner-up in 2016, Bastianini had gone off the boil slightly in 2017, suffering a winless season. He returned to the top step with Leopard, then switched to Moto2 for 2019 with Italtrans.

Countryman Dalla Porta began his second grand prix season in style with a debut podium. His return to the rostrum would be as a GP winner, on the weekend of his contract extension with Leopard.

Marcos Ramirez would switch from Bester Capital Dubai and return to Leopard, the team he raced for in the 2016 CEV Moto3 Junior World Championship, alongside Dalla Porta in 2019.

Having set up a Moto2 project for Romano Fenati, the Marinelli Snipers Team signed up **Tony Arbolino** (17), from the SIC58 squad, for its slimmed-down Moto3 project.

The young Italian earned a first pole position and comfortably eclipsed the meagre two-points of his rookie season. He would remain on board for 2019, when Snipers (CBC Corse) would return to a two-strong line-up with the addition of Makar Yurchenko, who made a wild-card entry at Sepang.

An irate **Aron Canet** (18) sent Yurchenko unceremoniously to the ground during practice in Argentina. That wasn't the only dubious move by the Spaniard, who began his second GP season with the Estrella Galicia 0,0 team by taking podiums in the opening rounds, before causing carnage at Jerez.

Canet received a back-of-the-grid start for his actions, while rookie team-mate **Alonso Lopez** (16), who seemed to have benefited from the chaos for a first podium, was also hit with a post-race penalty!

A triple race winner in 2017, Canet's career flatlined in 2018, with rumours of a 2019 split from Emilio Alzamora's Monlau team confirmed prior to Buriram, which he missed due to a collarbone injury. He was replaced by Estrella's CEV Junior World Championship rider Jeremy Alcoba in Thailand, and by Alcoba's team-mate, Sergio Garcia, for 2019.

Lopez, meanwhile, produced some inspiring rides, including a charge up the order in Catalunya, although his early grip on the Rookie of the Year title soon slipped away. Nonetheless, he would be back with the team in 2019.

The only Moto3/Moto2 team with 'Honda' in its title, Honda Team Asia ran an unchanged line-up of **Kaito Toba** (17) and **Nakarin Atiratphuvapat** (21). The Thai rider had had the upper hand over Toba in 2017, but the Japanese struck back in year two. They got a little too close at Aragon, where Toba clipped Atiratphuvapat into a qualifying high-side. Toba would stay with the team in 2019, alongside rookie countryman Ai Ogura.

The Sepang team, retitled Petronas Sprinta Racing, also stuck with the same rider line-up of **Ayumu Sasaki** (17) and **Adam Norrodin** (19). But only one would return in 2019, and it wouldn't be the 'home' Malaysian rider. Set-up to help promote home-grown talent, the Sepang Circuit proved that results trumped nationality by retaining Sasaki, moving Norrodin to the CEV Moto2 class to make way for the experienced John McPhee.

Sasaki – 2017's top rookie – came off worst in a dramatic five-rider Misano pile-up, fracturing his left wrist, which ruled him out of Aragon, but he was top of the practice time sheets on his return in Thailand.

Norrodin suffered the ignominy of a pit-lane start at his home round, but made amends with a stunning ride through the field – only for his podium hopes, and Moto3 career, to reach a premature end.

SIC58 Squadra Corse, headed by Marco Simoncelli's father, Paolo, swapped Arbolino for **Niccolo Antonelli** (22) while retaining **Tatsuki Suzuki** (20).

Antonelli arrived after a season of soul searching, having taken only a single podium for the title-winning Red Bull KTM Ajo team. It was a feat he struggled to match, despite pole position for his SIC58 debut. The Italian, who had competed in every Moto3 season, missed Catalunya with a shoulder dislocation, then Phillip Island due to back and foot injuries; he was replaced by Yari Montella.

Suzuki's season was also interrupted by injury, before it had barely begun. The Japanese, who made his first front-row grid appearances in 2018, broke his right wrist during practice in Qatar, but was gamely on track again in Argentina.

The SIC riders collided in Thailand, shortly after Suzuki had been confirmed as staying for 2019.

Enea Bastianini

Jorge Martin

Fabio Di Giannantonio

Adam Norrodin

Jeremy Alcoba

Nakarin Atiratphuvapat

Kaito Toba

Ayumu Sasaki

Tatsuki Suzuki

Alonso Lopez

Tony Arbolino

Lorenzo Dalla Porta

Niccolo Antonelli

Aron Canet

Jakub Kornfeil

Dennis Foggia

Marco Bezzecchi

Ai Ogura

Livio Loi

Somkiat Chantra

Vincente Perez

Marcos Ramirez

Albert Arenas

Darryn Binder

KTM

Thrashed by Honda in 2017's championship, KTM overcame some early struggles to take the lead of the riders' standings at Jerez and manufacturers' standings at Le Mans. Incidents and penalties had played a part, and the Honda riders soon retalliated, but the RC250 GP continued to hold a visible straight-line advantage for much of the season.

Ajo may still be KTM's clear factory team in Moto2, but the company has increasingly spread its support in Moto3, where the ranks were boosted by the former Mahindra/Peugeot teams – PruestelGP, Angel Nieto and CIP – all switching to the Austrian machines.

One of those teams – and an ex-Mahindra rider – led KTM's challenge in 2018, as surprise of the season **Marco Bezzecchi** (19) turned a single podium from his rookie campaign with CIP into a title attack for Redox PruestelGP. The Italian soon became a race winner, the first for KTM since Mugello 2017, and led more laps than any other rider in the season.

But Bezzecchi's inexperience relative to Martin – a rider with twice as many race starts – showed in the form of some costly accidents, although he was clearly the innocent victim in Thailand and Phillip Island.

At the other end of the experience scale was teammate **Jakub Kornfeil** (24), who had raced in every Moto3 GP since the class was founded. The Czech rider had only been rewarded with three podiums prior to 2018, a tally he would add to over the season, while taking a first ever pole position.

Kornfeil also provided some of the images of the year when he jumped over Bastianini's fallen machine at Le Mans. It would take until Aragon for the 2009 Red Bull Rookies Cup champion to actually hit the deck, making him the last rider in any class to fall.

Kornfeil would stay and be joined by countryman and Red Bull Rookies Cup front-runner, Filip Salac in 2019, Bezzecchi moving to Moto2 with Tech3 KTM.

Darryn Binder (20) was the sole focus for the Red Bull KTM Ajo team, still reeling from a single podium with Niccolo Antonelli and Bo Bendsneyder in 2017.

No doubt the South African, starting his fourth Moto3 campaign, wanted to add his name to the list of Ajo's 125cc/Moto3 champions: Mike di Meglio (2008), Marc Marquez (2010), Sandro Cortese (2012) and older brother Brad Binder (2016). But he and Ajo were forced to lower their sights, with a debut podium out of reach for much of the year. It looked like he might do it in Thailand, until he tangled with Arenas, expressing his displeasure with a single-digit hand gesture as he slid across the asphalt.

Binder's final rostrum debut came too late to save his Ajo seat, the team signing Red Bull Rookies champion Can Oncu for 2019, and Binder switching over to CIP.

Binder suffered a collarbone fracture while training on a Supermoto bike earlier in the season, prompting Angel Nieto wild-card Raul Fernandez to appear in his place at Sachsenring.

Having dispensed with its only 2017 race winner, Andrea Migno, Sky Racing VR46 went into the new year with reigning CEV Moto3 champion **Dennis Foggia** (17) promoted alongside **Nicolo Bulega** (18).

Bulega had underlined his raw speed with five front-row starts in 2017, but finished that year without a podium – and with a broken ankle, after tangling with Antonelli in practice at Valencia. The biggest rider in the class at 1.81m and 65kg, he had long felt handicapped by his size in the junior class – KTM confirming he is outside the ideal working range of its machine – but few would have predicted it would take until Assen for him even to score a point in 2018.

He would finally get his wish of more horsepower in 2019 with a place in the VR46 Moto2 team.

Foggia made steady progress, building to a debut podium from 25th on the grid and laying the groundwork for Moto3 team leadership in 2019. But he could have a fight on his hands. Joining him would be the next young rider on the VR46 production line, Celestino Vietti Ramus, who stepped up from the CEV.

Photos: Gold & Goose

abriel Rodrigo

Jaume Masia

Philipp Oettl

azuki Masaki

Raul Fernandez

Makur Yurchenko

Celestino Vietti

ohn McPhee

Nicolo Bulega

Andrea Migno

Vietti had an early GP debut after Bulega injured his hand at home playing with his dog. The youngster made an immediate impact on the world stage.

After he had grabbed headlines with a pair of podiums during his first full season, **Marcos Ramirez** (20) not surprisingly was retained by the retitled Bester Capital Dubai team for 2018. They added rookie **Jaume Masia** (17) in place of Darryn Binder after some impressive wild-card rides.

While Ramirez celebrated early podiums, Masia emerged as the rider to beat for Rookie of the Year, setting fastest race laps and front-row starts – but also suffering some big accidents, notably at Misano.

Masia showed his grit by fighting through the pain of a shoulder injury at Aragon and should be one to watch during the second year of his contract.

Gabriel Rodrigo (21) became a podium finisher in his fifth year of Moto3, all of which had been spent with RBA Racing, the Argentinean leaping up the standings each season since waiting 27 races to score his first point. His rise didn't go unnoticed, with a call from Gresini meaning a Honda debut in 2019.

Alongside Rodrigo was Japanese **Kazuki Masaki** (17), current Red Bull Rookies Cup champion.

Philipp Oettl (21) and Schedl GP had also worked their way up the results sheets together since the German joined the team in 2015. An emotional first victory came in 2018, in Oettl's 91st race start. It put the Oettls on the father-and-son grand prix winners' list, team manager Peter having celebrated victories in the former 80 and 125cc classes.

Oettl was forced to sit out the Misano race due to a concussion, by which time he had been announced as a Tech3 KTM Moto2 rider for 2019. Aron Canet would take over his Moto3 seat.

Having lost Bezzecchi to PruestlGP, CIP also parted with Manuel Pagliani as they put together a mix of youth and experience with rookie **Makar Yurchenko** (19) and former race winner **John McPhee** (23).

McPhee's arrival had been expedited by Dorna, after it had closed the British Talent Team following a single season. The Scotsman, who had made his GP debut in 2010, took his first KTM podium just before the summer break and made a strong ride from the back of the grid in Austria, by which time he had been linked with a return to Honda via the Sepang team. That was made official at Silverstone.

Rookie countryman Tom Booth-Amos would take McPhee's place in 2019, alongside fellow new CIP signing Binder.

Kazakhstani Yurchenko had made good progress into the points by the start of the European season, but was replaced (apparently for financial reasons) by Italian Stefano Nepa from Assen. Fortunately, he had done enough to secure a Snipers seat in 2019, while Nepa's biggest impact was an oil spill at Phillip Island, for which he was banned from riding in FP2.

A new Moto3 entry came from the Reale Avintia Academy team, which ran a single KTM for ex-Leopard rider and 2013 Indianapolis winner **Livio Loi** (20). But the Belgian was dropped after posting just eight points in eight races, with Vicente Perez promoted from Avintia's CEV team to take over the GP ride.

Perez – who cracked the top six – raced with the No. 77 of former team-mate Andreas Perez, 14, who had lost his life at the Catalunya CEV round.

Former factory Mahindra team Aspar switched to KTM machinery and was rebranded as the Angel Nieto Team for 2018.

Albert Arenas (21) remained, with race winner **Andrea Migno** (22) arriving from VR46 to replace Lorenzo Dalla Porta. Arenas got off to a nightmare start, suffering a fractured collarbone during warm-up in Qatar. But fortune swung radically the other way with a shock debut victory (and podium) at Le Mans, after a penalty for Di Giannantonio. He also won later in the year. Migno took his maiden rostrum at the same Le Mans race, but struggled to repeat the feat.

Arenas would stay on for a fourth season at Aspar in 2019, with wild-card Raul Fernandez given Migno's seat. The Italian was tipped to join Bester Capital.

Photo: Repsol Honda

MOTOGP · MOTO2 · MOTO3

GRANDS PRIX 2018

Reports by MICHAEL SCOTT

Statistics compiled by PETER McLAREN

FIM WORLD CHAMPIONSHIP · ROUND 1

QATAR GRAND PRIX

LOSAIL INTERNATIONAL CIRCUIT

Inset, left: Forza! Winner Dovi and third-placed Rossi celebrate.

Inset, far left: No quarter for Desmo Dovi and Marquez. Rossi awaits possible developments.

Main: Repeat performance. As in 2017, Zarco led early on, from Rossi, Petrucci, Crutchlow and Dovizioso, until a treacherous tyre forced a drop in his pace.

Photos: Gold & Goose

Above: Zarco and his Tech 3 squad celebrate the year's first pole.

Above right: Committed. Marquez was as determined as ever to find the limit.

Right: New wings for the new year, restrictive rules notwithstanding.

Far right: Understandably apprehensive, ex-Moto2 rider Hafizh Syahrin was a late, but effective replacement for Jonas Folger at Tech 3.

Below right: Ducati Sporting Director Davide Tardozzi, CEO Claudio Domenicali and test rider Michele Pirro are glued to the monitors.
Photos: Gold & Goose

THE year started well – at least as close and exciting as any of the vintage 2017 season. And the finish was a literal replay of the best of the previous year: Marquez made a desperate last-corner lunge past Dovi; the Italian calmly let him by, and then regained the lead by the flag. It was *déjà vu*. All over again.

This was in line with a general lack of major change, especially at the higher levels. The Honda, Yamaha and Ducati factory teams had the same line-ups, as did KTM. A minor shuffle resulted in Scott Redding switching from Ducati to Aprilia alongside the elder Espargaro; while satellite Honda riders Miller and Rabat shifted to the Duke – this move bearing fruit from the start.

The silly season began early. Marquez was already signed up with Repsol Honda for 2019 and 2020, ditto Movistar Yamaha's Vinales and (on race eve) Rossi. Yamaha seemed also to have preserved their wheelspin problems from 2017, in spite of a switch to a '2016-style' chassis, with Rossi and Vinales qualifying a downbeat eighth and 12th. Meanwhile, Zarco had elected to remain with the real 2016 chassis he'd used so effectively the previous year. He'd outpaced the factory men in testing and now qualified on pole.

With Rossi's signature confirming that there could be no Yamaha factory ride for the Frenchman, the effect was to make him a hot property for other teams. Speculation linked him to Repsol Honda, and it would intensify in the coming months. It looked as though Yamaha's early retention of their current stars had been something of an own goal. In fact, KTM had already scooped the pool, including also the Tech 3 satellite team.

There was little change also in rubberwear, the Michelins having been updated slightly. The alteration came in a fresh Dorna standardisation diktat. Tyre allocation was limited to three compounds front and rear, the specifications pre-set at the start of the year, with no development allowed. This elicited mixed feelings from riders: Rossi loyally approved and remarked on the similarity to the Bridgestone years; Marquez lamented that more variety potentially would be more productive.

One complaint was shared by many and would run through the coming season: a lack of consistency. The game of rubber roulette was continuing, with Michelin promising greater efforts in quality control, while riders railed against an unpredictable inability to achieve the same lap times on supposedly identical tyres.

All the same, the top three qualifiers broke a ten-year-old record, the last survivor from the era of supersoft qualifying tyres. Two of them – Zarco and Petrucci – were not even in factory teams; they were split by Marquez. The 2008 record had been set by Lorenzo, on a Yamaha; the times came in an explosive Q2, with the top 11 inside one second, at one of the longer tracks of the season.

One significant change was in scheduling, the previous four-day weekend having been cut to the conventional three, thanks to earlier starts to the first practice sessions each day. Previously, the action on Thursday, Friday and Saturday had started at 18:00 (dusk), while Moto3 'race warm-up' had taken place the day before. Now a more conventional agenda got proceedings under way in clear daylight between 12:40 and 13:40.

This was generally popular, not least because it meant that practice, qualifying and racing (the MotoGP race two hours earlier, at 19:00) could easily be completed before the crucial dew point, around 21:00, made the track treacherously slippery. But there was a downside: the afternoon track temperature was sky high for FP1, FP3 and race warm-up. "With the temperature so much higher, there is no grip ... lap times are at least one second slower," said Ducati manager Davide Tardozzi; while Marquez commented, "Sure, it's not ideal. You can't set the bike up in the afternoon at 15:00 for the race at 19:00. In reality, we have only two useful practices – FP2 and FP4. But we tested here three nights two weeks ago. Anyway, Qatar is a special weekend, with the night GP."

The spectre of rain remained spectral, which was just as well because trials on an artificially wet track at the preceding pre-season tests had left Dorna safety officer Loris Capirossi still in doubt. Although some riders, including Marquez and Zarco, had pronounced themselves ready to race under the lights in the wet, Capirossi had said, "I think we need

another test on race weekend before we can be sure. The reflections were not too bad, but we need to understand what would happen in proper rain, and also with 20 bikes together."

In 2009, a heavy rainstorm just before the start of the MotoGP race had caused its postponement by 24 hours; in 2017, rain had washed out qualifying and delayed a shortened MotoGP race by 40 minutes.

New aero bodywork (formerly known as 'winglets') had been homologated all round before the race, although several designs sailed very close to the wind, testing the deliberately vague regulations. These banned sharp-edged projections, but Yamaha in particular, and to an extent Suzuki, had pin-sharp outer edges to their closed loops. As usual, there was no consensus, but most discarded the drag-inducing protuberances, including usual fan Lorenzo, but not Rossi and Marquez.

The Honda riders had decided on which configuration of new engine to use late in tests; the last new unit to arrive was Aprilia's, and still only for Espargaro, who welcomed the improved performance, but whose race was spoilt when he ran short of fuel.

Lorenzo's struggle to adapt to the Duke continued, with little help from the equipment – a worrying brake failure in the race obliged him to bail out at speed. Brembo kept the details under wraps, promising that it would never happen again – but it emerged that at least one of the pads had been shed in the course of the crash.

Hafizh Syahrin, last-ditch Tech 3 replacement after Jonas Folger's unexpected withdrawal and the first Malaysian in the premier class, made an impressive debut, in the points.

Less exciting was the first appearance of the Energica E-bike, demonstrated by former GP winner and new TV pit-lane reporter Simon Crafar. The production-based machine will be used by 11 teams for the electric series starting in 2019, with a first joint meeting of teams and Dorna's project chief, ex-Michelin boss Nicolas Goubert, during the weekend.

MOTOGP RACE – 22 laps

With Zarco taking his third pole, ahead of Marquez and Petrucci, Crutchlow led the second row from Dovizioso and Rins, then Pedrosa, Rossi and Lorenzo. Ducati first-timer Miller and Vinales – both through from Q1 – sandwiched Iannone on row four.

Rear tyre choice was universal: soft. Up front, only the factory Honda riders went hard, while Petrucci was among eight to choose the soft.

Zarco had leapt away in the lead, and although Marquez pushed ahead the first time over the line, the Frenchman took it back directly, and stayed there for the next 16 laps.

Rossi had also made a great start and took third off Pedrosa on lap three. By then, Petrucci was fifth, followed by Crutchlow and Dovi, who'd lost places on the run to Turn One after a near collision with Rins.

The Suzuki rider was close behind by lap three, having got ahead of team-mate Iannone, who would soon lose another place to Miller. All the while, slow-starting Lorenzo was gradually catching this pair; he would get past Miller by half-distance, now a couple of seconds adrift of a desperately close lead group of eight.

Zarco headed Marquez, Dovi, Rossi, Crutchlow, Petrucci, Rins and Pedrosa – all covered by just over 1.2 seconds. As Dovi explained later, the early pace had been relatively slow, with everyone saving tyres.

Now a couple of changes. Rins was on the move, and he had just got ahead of Crutchlow for fifth when he ran wide, lost the front and slid off. Later the same lap, Lorenzo had his frightening front brake failure.

The changes up front came all of a sudden at the start of lap 18. As Dovi firmly took the lead into the first corner, Marquez followed him, close to crashing as he was sucked along in the slipstream.

By the end of the lap, Rossi was also ahead: Zarco was starting to lose ground steadily, experiencing unexpected grip problems: "When the other guys overtook me, I really understood I couldn't use the front tyre correctly on right-hand corners. I couldn't fight … a few times I almost crashed." Pedrosa and Miller also complained of tyre problems.

Up front, Dovi started his final run, and it looked as though he might escape. But Marquez was not giving up. On the final lap, he closed right up. Then into the final corner, he lunged inside. He did get ahead briefly, but once again, with trademark calm, Dovi waited until inevitably he ran wide on the exit, then cut inside and unleashed his Ducati to lead over the line by 0.027 of a second.

"I'm really happy, because we confirmed Ducati's hard work of the winter," he said, after following up three second places in a row. "We were competitive here in the past, but not like this. I could make a bad start, but still save the tyre and race to win."

Marquez was hugely amused by his final corner: "The show goes on. When Dovi pushed in the last four laps, I was extra on the limit, closing the front and losing the rear. But I arrived close at the last corner, so I try. I thought he could overtake me before the finish line, but some day I will do it."

Rossi was still close. Some overnight changes had improved his bike's balance, but not enough. "Dovi and Marc are the faster riders now, so I was so happy to stay with them," he said, having silenced any critics of his contract renewal.

The first three were a couple of seconds clear of Crutchlow, with a small gap to Petrucci.

Vinales was a belated sixth. He'd finished lap one 14th and had been a distant 12th at half-distance, but unobtrusively he had started picking up places, passing Pedrosa with two laps to go. He credited a setting change he'd been requesting "for a long time".

Zarco was two seconds adrift,

Another five seconds away, Iannone had regained ninth from Miller. Fighting a sliding front, the Australian was left to defend tenth from former team-mate Tito Rabat, also a Ducati first-timer, barely half a second adrift over the line. Aleix Espargaro had been between them until the Aprilia began spluttering on the last lap; he dropped out of the points.

A second behind Rabat, top rookie Morbidelli made a strong debut, comfortably clear of Bautista in 13th, who had taken the place off another impressive rookie, Syahrin, on the penultimate lap. The last point went to Abraham; rookie Luthi was less than a second behind. Nakagami and Smith also passed Espargaro, with Redding and Simeon trailing. Pol Espargaro, still battered from a heavy testing crash, retired.

MOTO2 RACE – 20 laps

The pre-season promise of close Moto2 racing was fulfilled – qualifying had the first dozen riders within one second. While rich in tension, however, the middle-class race remained processional.

Marquez took pole from flatmates and rivals Baldassarri and Bagnaia, with Kalex taking first front-row honours ahead of KTM's winner of the last three races of 2017, Oliveira. He led row two, from rookie Romano Fenati and the returned Danny Kent, back after most of a season's absence, now on a Speed Up.

Bagnaia, taking a first win, didn't quite lead from start to finish, but he was only headed once, very briefly, on the final lap, when Baldassarri nosed in front, only to be pushed back immediately on the subsequent change of direction.

"I knew he was faster on the straight, so I had to try, but it was not enough," said the former winner, just over a tenth adrift over the line.

For Bagnaia, top rookie in 2017, "it was a long, long race. I was watching the gap every lap; it was difficult to remain concentrated." It was an ominous display of his powers.

It had been a three-bike affair and might have ended more dramatically, had Marquez not slowed suddenly at the start of lap 15, after moving past Baldassarri to close on Bagnaia four laps earlier. It took him time to notice what the TV cameras had picked up: that his rear brake disc was glowing red hot. "I'd been saving the rear tyre, everything under control – then it felt like the engine broke," he said. Whatever had jammed it on (he suspected perhaps a chunked piece of tyre) prevented him from using the rear brake for the rest of the race, so it was a good effort to stay just over a second clear of the pursuing Pasini's Italtrans Kalex.

The veteran, in turn, had outpaced a gang of four; and by the end, the Red Bull KTMs had taken control of it, Oliveira ahead of team-mate Binder. The former had been lucky to survive a collision with Marquez's back wheel as they accelerated off the line, which dropped him to eighth at the end of lap one.

Schrotter's Kalex and Vierge's Tech 3 were still close at the finish.

Above: The sun goes down as Moto2 gets up: Bagnaia (42) leading Baldassarri and the gang.
Photo: Monster Energy

Above left: Crutchlow liked the 2018 Honda and took it to a fourth.

Left: Contrasting emotions in Moto3. Aron Canet, pipped to the post, was dismayed; winner Jorge Martin jubilant; third-placed Lorenzo Dalla Porta slightly surprised.

Below left: Second place and fastest lap for Lorenzo Baldassarri.

Below: Jorge Martin held his line over the looming Aron Canet.
Photos: Gold & Goose

Almost ten seconds behind, Marini finally won out after a long battle with Navarro. Moto3 champion Joan Mir was top rookie in 11th, through from 24th on the grid.

Another gap, then Gardner prevailed for 12th over a group that had become six strong by the finish, with returned MotoGP rider Hector Barbera, veteran Corsi (both Kalex) and Dominique Aegerter (making his KTM debut) wrapping up the last points, ahead of Isaac Vinales and Kent.

Sam Lowes, having returned from his MotoGP misadventures and now on a KTM, finished the first lap 17th, but he had battled through into the top ten when he fell just after half-distance.

Fenati's strong qualifying had flattered to deceive, and he fell back throughout to 24th – one place ahead of American rookie Joe Roberts, on the new Japanese NTS chassis.

MOTO3 RACE – 18 laps

The first race of the year was fought start-to-finish between two of 2017's race winners, Spaniards Martin and Canet, with a third former winner and fellow Honda rider Bastianini, who crashed out of the front battle after five of the 18 laps.

There was seldom much of the late afternoon daylight between the remaining two, but it was Martin ahead by just over two-tenths of a second, Canet's final slipstreaming attack having fallen just a metre or so short.

The battle was absorbing. Even more so the fight for the final rostrum position. At half-distance, there were six in the group; as they started the last lap, it had swelled to 13 riders, all elbows and paint-scraping over the final 5.380km.

Two erstwhile leaders didn't make it. KTM riders Bezzecchi and McPhee (a late arrival) slipped off. That left 11, across the line within a whisker over two seconds.

Narrowly in front for a first top-three, Dalla Porta completed another Honda podium lockout, barely four-hundredths ahead of pole-qualifier Antonelli, Rodrigo on the first KTM. Then came three more Hondas – Di Giannantonio, Toba and Sasaki ahead of the KTMs of Kornfeil and Migno.

The huge group was so far ahead of the rest that Bezzecchi was able to remount and claim points in 14th. There were 19 finishers, Oettl and Binder being the first of several to crash out, followed by Bastianini, Bulega, Lopez, Bezzecchi and McPhee.

Tatsuki Suzuki didn't make the race, an arm fractured in practice making him the first injury victim of the season.

OFFICIAL TIMEKEEPER

GRAND PRIX OF QATAR

LOSAIL INTERNATIONAL CIRCUIT

Race: 22 laps
Length: 5.380 km / 3.343 miles
Width: 12m

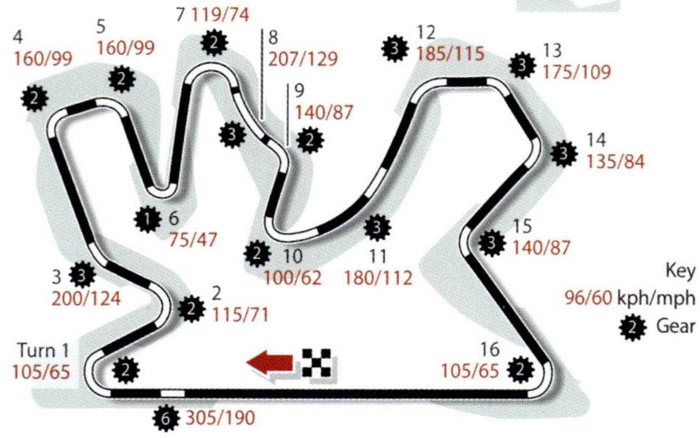

MotoGP

RACE DISTANCE: 22 laps, 73.545 miles/118.360km · RACE WEATHER: Dry (air 21°C, humidity 46%, track 23°C)

Pos.	Rider	Nat.	No.	Entrant	Machine	Tyres	Race tyre choice	Laps	Time & speed
1	**Andrea Dovizioso**	ITA	4	Ducati Team	Ducati Desmosedici	M	F: Medium/R: Soft	22	42m 34.654s 103.6mph/ 166.7km/h
2	**Marc Marquez**	SPA	93	Repsol Honda Team	Honda RC213V	M	F: Hard/R: Soft	22	42m 34.681s
3	**Valentino Rossi**	ITA	46	Movistar Yamaha MotoGP	Yamaha YZR-M1	M	F: Medium/R: Soft	22	42m 35.451s
4	**Cal Crutchlow**	GBR	35	LCR Honda CASTROL	Honda RC213V	M	F: Medium/R: Soft	22	42m 37.535s
5	**Danilo Petrucci**	ITA	9	Alma Pramac Racing	Ducati Desmosedici	M	F: Soft/R: Soft	22	42m 38.475s
6	**Maverick Vinales**	SPA	25	Movistar Yamaha MotoGP	Yamaha YZR-M1	M	F: Medium/R: Soft	22	42m 38.542s
7	**Dani Pedrosa**	SPA	26	Repsol Honda Team	Honda RC213V	M	F: Hard/R: Soft	22	42m 39.275s
8	**Johann Zarco**	FRA	5	Monster Yamaha Tech 3	Yamaha YZR-M1	M	F: Medium/R: Soft	22	42m 41.766s
9	**Andrea Iannone**	ITA	29	Team SUZUKI ECSTAR	Suzuki GSX-RR	M	F: Medium/R: Soft	22	42m 47.611s
10	**Jack Miller**	AUS	43	Alma Pramac Racing	Ducati Desmosedici	M	F: Medium/R: Soft	22	42m 49.248s
11	**Tito Rabat**	SPA	53	Reale Avintia Racing	Ducati Desmosedici	M	F: Soft/R: Soft	22	42m 49.835s
12	**Franco Morbidelli**	ITA	21	EG 0,0 Marc VDS	Honda RC213V	M	F: Medium/R: Soft	22	42m 50.928s
13	**Alvaro Bautista**	SPA	19	Angel Nieto Team	Ducati Desmosedici	M	F: Soft/R: Soft	22	42m 54.442s
14	**Hafizh Syahrin**	MAL	55	Monster Yamaha Tech 3	Yamaha YZR-M1	M	F: Medium/R: Soft	22	42m 54.953s
15	**Karel Abraham**	CZE	17	Angel Nieto Team	Ducati Desmosedici	M	F: Medium/R: Soft	22	42m 57.941s
16	Thomas Luthi	SWI	12	EG 0,0 Marc VDS	Honda RC213V	M	F: Medium/R: Soft	22	42m 58.843s
17	Takaaki Nakagami	JPN	30	LCR Honda IDEMITSU	Honda RC213V	M	F: Medium/R: Soft	22	42m 59.208s
18	Bradley Smith	GBR	38	Red Bull KTM Factory Racing	KTM RC16	M	F: Soft/R: Soft	22	43m 06.358s
19	Aleix Espargaro	SPA	41	Aprilia Racing Team Gresini	Aprilia RS-GP	M	F: Soft/R: Soft	22	43m 09.366s
20	Scott Redding	GBR	45	Aprilia Racing Team Gresini	Aprilia RS-GP	M	F: Soft/R: Soft	22	43m 12.295s
21	Xavier Simeon	BEL	10	Reale Avintia Racing	Ducati Desmosedici	M	F: Soft/R: Soft	22	43m 21.360s
	Pol Espargaro	SPA	44	Red Bull KTM Factory Racing	KTM RC16	M	F: Soft/R: Soft	15	DNF-technical
	Alex Rins	SPA	42	Team SUZUKI ECSTAR	Suzuki GSX-RR	M	F: Medium/R: Soft	12	DNF-crash
	Jorge Lorenzo	SPA	99	Ducati Team	Ducati Desmosedici	M	F: Medium/R: Soft	12	DNF-crash

Fastest lap: Andrea Dovizioso, on lap 19, 1m 55.242s, 104.4mph/168.0km/h.
Lap record: Jorge Lorenzo, 1m 54.927s, 104.7mph/168.5km/h (2016).
Event maximum speed: Danilo Petrucci, 218.7mph/351.9km/h (race).

Qualifying

Weather: Dry
Air Temp: 24° **Track Temp:** 25°
Humidity: 58%

1	Zarco	1m 53.680s
2	Marquez	1m 53.882s
3	Petrucci	1m 53.887s
4	Crutchlow	1m 54.072s
5	Dovizioso	1m 54.074s
6	Rins	1m 54.339s
7	Pedrosa	1m 54.368s
8	Rossi	1m 54.389s
9	Lorenzo	1m 54.431s
10	Miller	1m 54.449s
11	Iannone	1m 54.619s
12	Vinales	1m 54.707s
13	A. Espargaro	1m 55.140s
14	Morbidelli	1m 55.169s
15	Syahrin	1m 55.258s
16	Rabat	1m 55.273s
17	Redding	1m 55.380s
18	Luthi	1m 55.381s
19	Abraham	1m 55.392s
20	Smith	1m 55.553s
21	Bautista	1m 55.638s
22	P. Espargaro	1m 55.706s
23	Nakagami	1m 56.401s
24	Simeon	1m 56.545s

Fastest race laps

1	Dovizioso	1m 55.242s
2	Marquez	1m 55.272s
3	Rossi	1m 55.315s
4	Rins	1m 55.333s
5	Vinales	1m 55.450s
6	Crutchlow	1m 55.505s
7	Iannone	1m 55.586s
8	Miller	1m 55.617s
9	Petrucci	1m 55.630s
10	Zarco	1m 55.678s
11	Pedrosa	1m 55.680s
12	Lorenzo	1m 55.767s
13	Morbidelli	1m 55.894s
14	Rabat	1m 55.896s
15	Abraham	1m 56.028s
16	A. Espargaro	1m 56.042s
17	Syahrin	1m 56.051s
18	Luthi	1m 56.069s
19	Nakagami	1m 56.136s
20	Bautista	1m 56.178s
21	P. Espargaro	1m 56.283s
22	Smith	1m 56.590s
23	Redding	1m 56.644s
24	Simeon	1m 57.303s

Grid order		1	2	3	4	5	6	7	8	9	10	11	12	13	14	15	16	17	18	19	20	21	22	·
5	ZARCO	93	5	5	5	5	5	5	5	5	5	5	5	5	5	5	5	5	4	4	4	4	4	1
93	MARQUEZ	5	93	93	93	93	46	46	46	46	46	93	4	93	93	4	4	4	93	93	93	93	93	2
9	PETRUCCI	26	26	46	46	46	93	93	93	93	93	4	93	4	4	93	93	93	46	46	46	46	46	3
35	CRUTCHLOW	46	46	26	9	9	9	9	4	4	4	46	46	46	46	46	46	46	5	35	35	35	35	4
4	DOVIZIOSO	9	9	9	35	35	35	35	35	35	35	35	35	35	35	35	35	35	35	5	5	9	9	5
42	RINS	35	35	35	4	4	4	4	9	9	9	9	42	9	9	26	26	26	26	9	9	25	25	6
26	PEDROSA	4	4	4	26	42	42	42	42	42	42	42	9	26	26	9	9	9	9	26	26	26	26	7
46	ROSSI	29	29	42	42	26	26	26	26	26	26	26	26	29	29	25	25	25	25	25	25	5	5	8
99	LORENZO	42	42	29	29	43	43	43	43	43	29	29	29	43	25	29	43	43	43	43	29	29	29	9
43	MILLER	41	43	43	43	29	29	29	29	29	43	99	99	25	43	43	29	29	29	29	43	43	43	10
29	IANNONE	43	99	99	99	99	99	99	99	99	99	43	43	41	41	41	41	41	41	41	41	41	53	11
25	VINALES	21	41	21	21	21	21	21	25	25	25	25	25	21	21	21	21	21	21	21	53	53	21	12
41	A. ESPARGARO	99	21	41	41	25	25	25	21	21	21	21	21	53	53	53	53	53	53	53	21	21	19	13
21	MORBIDELLI	25	38	25	25	41	41	41	41	41	41	41	41	55	55	55	55	55	55	55	55	19	55	14
55	SYAHRIN	38	25	38	38	38	38	53	53	53	53	53	53	44	44	19	19	19	19	19	19	55	17	15
53	RABAT	45	45	45	55	55	55	55	55	55	55	55	55	19	19	44	17	17	17	17	17	17	12	
45	REDDING	55	55	55	53	53	53	38	38	38	38	44	44	17	17	17	12	12	12	12	12	12	30	
12	LUTHI	12	17	53	44	44	44	44	44	44	44	38	19	38	38	12	38	30	30	30	30	30	38	
17	ABRAHAM	44	53	17	17	19	19	19	19	19	19	19	17	12	12	38	30	38	38	38	38	38	41	
38	SMITH	17	44	44	45	17	17	17	17	17	17	17	38	30	30	30	45	45	45	45	45	45	45	
19	BAUTISTA	53	12	12	19	12	12	12	12	12	12	12	12	45	45	45	10	10	10	10	10	10	10	
44	P. ESPARGARO	19	19	19	12	45	30	30	30	30	30	30	30	10	10	10								
30	NAKAGAMI	10	10	30	30	30	45	45	45	45	45	45	45											
10	SIMEON	30	30	10	10	10	10	10	10	10	10	10	10											

44 Pit stop

Championship Points

1	Dovizioso	25
2	Marquez	20
3	Rossi	16
4	Crutchlow	13
5	Petrucci	11
6	Vinales	10
7	Pedrosa	9
8	Zarco	8
9	Iannone	7
10	Miller	6
11	Rabat	5
12	Morbidelli	4
13	Bautista	3
14	Syahrin	2
15	Abraham	1

Constructor Points

1	Ducati	25
2	Honda	20
3	Yamaha	16
4	Suzuki	7

Moto2 RACE DISTANCE: 20 laps, 66.860 miles/107.600km · RACE WEATHER: Dry (air 22°C, humidity 38%, track 24°C)

Pos.	Rider	Nat.	No.	Entrant	Machine	Laps	Time & Speed
1	**Francesco Bagnaia**	ITA	42	SKY Racing Team VR46	Kalex	20	40m 19.802s 99.4mph/ 160.0km/h
2	**Lorenzo Baldassarri**	ITA	7	Pons HP40	Kalex	20	40m 19.914s
3	**Alex Marquez**	SPA	73	EG 0,0 Marc VDS	Kalex	20	40m 25.427s
4	**Mattia Pasini**	ITA	54	Italtrans Racing Team	Kalex	20	40m 26.459s
5	**Miguel Oliveira**	POR	44	Red Bull KTM Ajo	KTM	20	40m 30.098s
6	**Brad Binder**	RSA	41	Red Bull KTM Ajo	KTM	20	40m 30.146s
7	**Marcel Schrotter**	GER	23	Dynavolt Intact GP	Kalex	20	40m 31.221s
8	**Xavi Vierge**	SPA	97	Dynavolt Intact GP	Kalex	20	40m 31.318s
9	**Luca Marini**	ITA	10	SKY Racing Team VR46	Kalex	20	40m 40.492s
10	**Jorge Navarro**	SPA	9	Federal Oil Gresini Moto2	Kalex	20	40m 40.763s
11	**Joan Mir**	SPA	36	EG 0,0 Marc VDS	Kalex	20	40m 42.827s
12	**Remy Gardner**	AUS	87	Tech 3 Racing	Tech 3	20	40m 50.094s
13	**Hector Barbera**	SPA	40	Pons HP40	Kalex	20	40m 50.101s
14	**Simone Corsi**	ITA	24	Tasca Racing Scuderia Moto2	Kalex	20	40m 50.534s
15	**Dominique Aegerter**	SWI	77	Kiefer Racing	KTM	20	40m 50.672s
16	Isaac Vinales	SPA	32	SAG Team	Kalex	20	40m 50.854s
17	Danny Kent	GBR	52	Beta Tools - Speed Up Racing	Speed Up	20	40m 51.760s
18	Bo Bendsneyder	NED	64	Tech 3 Racing	Tech 3	20	40m 52.184s
19	Andrea Locatelli	ITA	5	Italtrans Racing Team	Kalex	20	40m 55.030s
20	Fabio Quartararo	FRA	20	Beta Tools - Speed Up Racing	Speed Up	20	40m 55.159s
21	Tetsuta Nagashima	JPN	45	IDEMITSU Honda Team Asia	Kalex	20	40m 55.771s
22	Steven Odendaal	RSA	4	NTS RW Racing GP	NTS	20	41m 02.347s
23	Khairul Idham Pawi	MAL	89	IDEMITSU Honda Team Asia	Kalex	20	41m 02.578s
24	Romano Fenati	ITA	13	Marinelli Snipers Team	Kalex	20	41m 04.364s
25	Joe Roberts	USA	16	NTS RW Racing GP	NTS	20	41m 15.879s
26	Stefano Manzi	ITA	62	Forward Racing Team	Suter	20	41m 21.383s
27	Jules Danilo	FRA	95	Nashi Argan SAG Team	Kalex	20	41m 21.655s
28	Zulfahmi Khairuddin	MAL	63	SIC Racing Team	Kalex	20	41m 31.420s
29	Federico Fuligni	ITA	21	Tasca Racing Scuderia Moto2	Kalex	20	41m 39.950s
30	Eric Granado	BRA	51	Forward Racing Team	Suter	20	41m 45.994s
	Sam Lowes	GBR	22	Swiss Innovative Investors	KTM	10	DNF
	Iker Lecuona	SPA	27	Swiss Innovative Investors	KTM	7	DNF

Fastest lap: Lorenzo Baldassarri, on lap 4, 2m 0.303s, 100.0mph/160.9km/h.
Lap record: Sam Lowes, 1m 59.421s, 100.7mph/162.1km/h (2016).
Event maximum speed: Joan Mir, 177.5mph/285.6km/h (free practice).

Qualifying

Weather: Dry
Air Temp: 28° **Track Temp:** 29°
Humidity: 37%

1	Marquez	2m 00.299s
2	Baldassarri	2m 00.607s
3	Bagnaia	2m 00.843s
4	Oliveira	2m 00.846s
5	Fenati	2m 00.899s
6	Kent	2m 00.965s
7	Navarro	2m 01.038s
8	Pasini	2m 01.062s
9	Schrotter	2m 01.129s
10	Lowes	2m 01.167s
11	Vierge	2m 01.176s
12	Gardner	2m 01.252s
13	Binder	2m 01.338s
14	Corsi	2m 01.351s
15	Lecuona	2m 01.355s
16	Quartararo	2m 01.404s
17	Marini	2m 01.420s
18	Vinales	2m 01.421s
19	Barbera	2m 01.482s
20	Bendsneyder	2m 01.562s
21	Aegerter	2m 01.745s
22	Odendaal	2m 01.936s
23	Locatelli	2m 01.954s
24	Mir	2m 02.324s
25	Pawi	2m 02.433s
26	Nagashima	2m 02.568s
27	Roberts	2m 03.233s
28	Manzi	2m 03.263s
29	Danilo	2m 03.453s
30	Granado	2m 03.516s
31	Fuligni	2m 04.078s
32	Khairuddin	2m 04.780s

Fastest race laps

1	Baldassarri	2m 00.303s
2	Marquez	2m 00.326s
3	Bagnaia	2m 00.472s
4	Pasini	2m 00.587s
5	Oliveira	2m 00.698s
6	Schrotter	2m 00.711s
7	Binder	2m 00.804s
8	Vierge	2m 00.813s
9	Lowes	2m 01.136s
10	Marini	2m 01.146s
11	Kent	2m 01.160s
12	Navarro	2m 01.217s
13	Barbera	2m 01.378s
14	Mir	2m 01.400s
15	Vinales	2m 01.453s
16	Gardner	2m 01.478s
17	Bendsneyder	2m 01.535s
18	Lecuona	2m 01.570s
19	Aegerter	2m 01.587s
20	Quartararo	2m 01.602s
21	Corsi	2m 01.632s
22	Locatelli	2m 01.682s
23	Nagashima	2m 01.748s
24	Pawi	2m 01.834s
25	Fenati	2m 01.893s
26	Manzi	2m 02.121s
27	Odendaal	2m 02.130s
28	Roberts	2m 02.892s
29	Danilo	2m 03.072s
30	Khairuddin	2m 03.236s
31	Granado	2m 03.472s
32	Fuligni	2m 03.958s

Championship Points

1	Bagnaia	25
2	Baldassarri	20
3	Marquez	16
4	Pasini	13
5	Oliveira	11
6	Binder	10
7	Schrotter	9
8	Vierge	8
9	Marini	7
10	Navarro	6
11	Mir	5
12	Gardner	4
13	Barbera	3
14	Corsi	2
15	Aegerter	1

Constructor Points

1	Kalex	25
2	KTM	11
3	Tech 3	4

Moto3 RACE DISTANCE: 18 laps, 60.174 miles/96.840km · RACE WEATHER: Dry (air 25°C, humidity 30%, track 33°C)

Pos.	Rider	Nat.	No.	Entrant	Machine	Laps	Time & Speed
1	**Jorge Martin**	SPA	88	Del Conca Gresini Moto3	Honda	18	38m 18.207s 94.2mph/ 151.6km/h
2	**Aron Canet**	SPA	44	Estrella Galicia 0,0	Honda	18	38m 18.230s
3	**Lorenzo Dalla Porta**	ITA	48	Leopard Racing	Honda	18	38m 24.953s
4	**Niccolo Antonelli**	ITA	23	SIC58 Squadra Corse	Honda	18	38m 24.998s
5	**Gabriel Rodrigo**	ARG	19	RBA BOE Skull Rider	KTM	18	38m 25.057s
6	**Fabio Di Giannantonio**	ITA	21	Del Conca Gresini Moto3	Honda	18	38m 25.123s
7	**Kaito Toba**	JPN	27	Honda Team Asia	Honda	18	38m 25.153s
8	**Ayumu Sasaki**	JPN	71	Petronas Sprinta Racing	Honda	18	38m 25.205s
9	**Jakub Kornfeil**	CZE	84	Redox PruestelGP	KTM	18	38m 25.363s
10	**Andrea Migno**	ITA	16	Angel Nieto Team Moto3	KTM	18	38m 25.906s
11	**Adam Norrodin**	MAL	7	Petronas Sprinta Racing	Honda	18	38m 25.960s
12	**Jaume Masia**	SPA	5	Bester Capital Dubai	KTM	18	38m 26.233s
13	**Kazuki Masaki**	JPN	22	RBA BOE Skull Rider	KTM	18	38m 27.036s
14	**Marco Bezzecchi**	ITA	12	Redox PruestelGP	KTM	18	38m 40.045s
15	**Marcos Ramirez**	SPA	42	Bester Capital Dubai	KTM	18	38m 45.119s
16	Dennis Foggia	ITA	10	SKY Racing Team VR46	KTM	18	38m 45.188s
17	Tony Arbolino	ITA	14	Marinelli Snipers Team	Honda	18	38m 51 608s
18	Nakarin Atiratphuvapat	THA	41	Honda Team Asia	Honda	18	38m 51.653s
19	Makar Yurchenko	KAZ	76	CIP - Green Power	KTM	18	38m 51.829s
	John McPhee	GBR	17	CIP - Green Power	KTM	17	DNF
	Alonso Lopez	SPA	72	Estrella Galicia 0,0	Honda	11	DNF
	Livio Loi	BEL	11	Reale Avintia Academy	KTM	11	DNF
	Nicolo Bulega	ITA	8	SKY Racing Team VR46	KTM	10	DNF
	Enea Bastianini	ITA	33	Leopard Racing	Honda	5	DNF
	Philipp Oettl	GER	65	Sudmetal Schedl GP Racing	KTM	3	DNF
	Darryn Binder	RSA	40	Red Bull KTM Ajo	KTM	3	DNF

Fastest lap: Aron Canet, on lap 4, 2m 6.373s, 95.2mph/153.2km/h.
Lap record: Alexis Masbou, 2m 5.862s, 95.6mph/153.8km/h (2014).
Event maximum speed: Gabriel Rodrigo, 147.8mph/237.9km/h (free practice).

Qualifying

Weather: Dry
Air Temp: 28° **Track Temp:** 30°
Humidity: 38%

1	Antonelli	2m 06.364s
2	Martin	2m 06.365s
3	Rodrigo	2m 06.848s
4	Sasaki	2m 07.043s
5	Toba	2m 07.048s
6	Bezzecchi	2m 07.058s
7	Canet	2m 07.059s
8	Oettl	2m 07.187s
9	Dalla Porta	2m 07.320s
10	Bastianini	2m 07.324s
11	Kornfeil	2m 07.326s
12	McPhee	2m 07.407s
13	Masia	2m 07.462s
14	Migno	2m 07.586s
15	Ramirez	2m 07.607s
16	Di Giannantonio	2m 07.634s
17	Norrodin	2m 07.758s
18	Loi	2m 07.901s
19	Masaki	2m 08.108s
20	Binder	2m 08.202s
21	Lopez	2m 08.280s
22	Bulega	2m 08.364s
23	Arenas	2m 08.480s
24	Yurchenko	2m 08.547s
25	Foggia	2m 08.785s
26	Arbolino	2m 08.795s
27	Atiratphuvapat	2m 08.936s
	Suzuki	No Time

Fastest race laps

1	Canet	2m 06.373s
2	Bastianini	2m 06.427s
3	Dalla Porta	2m 06.486s
4	Kornfeil	2m 06.573s
5	Di Giannantonio	2m 06.608s
6	Martin	2m 06.644s
7	Binder	2m 06.665s
8	Bezzecchi	2m 06.714s
9	Rodrigo	2m 06.717s
10	Norrodin	2m 06.729s
11	Masaki	2m 06.843s
12	McPhee	2m 06.911s
13	Migno	2m 06.935s
14	Antonelli	2m 06.960s
15	Sasaki	2m 06.974s
16	Toba	2m 06.993s
17	Masia	2m 07.018s
18	Lopez	2m 07.115s
19	Oettl	2m 07.155s
20	Bulega	2m 07.427s
21	Ramirez	2m 07.519s
22	Foggia	2m 07.723s
23	Arbolino	2m 07.889s
24	Yurchenko	2m 08.052s
25	Loi	2m 08.294s
26	Atiratphuvapat	2m 08.378s

Championship Points

1	Martin	25
2	Canet	20
3	Dalla Porta	16
4	Antonelli	13
5	Rodrigo	11
6	Di Giannantonio	10
7	Toba	9
8	Sasaki	8
9	Kornfeil	7
10	Migno	6
11	Norrodin	5
12	Masia	4
13	Masaki	3
14	Bezzecchi	2
15	Ramirez	1

Constructor Points

1	Honda	25
2	KTM	11

FIM WORLD CHAMPIONSHIP · ROUND 2

ARGENTINE GRAND PRIX

TERMAS DE RIO HONDO CIRCUIT

Inset, right: "At the slowest possible speed." Winner Crutchlow celebrated a perfectly judged ride.
Photo: Gold & Goose

Inset, far right: Suzuki, Ducati, Yamaha, Honda – Alex Rins heads Miller, Zarco and Crutchlow en route to a first MotoGP podium.
Photo: Team Ecstar Suzuki

Main: Chaos reigns as Marquez manhandles his stricken Honda on the extraordinary reassembled grid.
Photo: Repsol Honda Team

MOTUL
DE LA REPÚBLICA

Above: Every which way but right – pit-lane pandemonium as all call in to change to slicks.

Top right: Looking harassed, Race Director Mike Webb attempts to explain the inexplicable to MotoGP team chiefs.

Above right: "What did I say?" Miller, the only rider to risk slicks from before the sighting lap, was left high and dry on pole.

Above far right: Lorenzo's miserable start to the season continued as he trailed home 15th.

Right and below right: Racing incident, or attempted assassination? Marquez and Rossi had different interpretations.

Photos: Gold & Goose

IS racing too predictable? Seldom so in the Argentine. This was doubly true in 2018, when extraordinary events just kept becoming weirder. The Rio de Termas Hondo race was far out, figuratively as well as literally.

The outcome was far reaching, triggering disappointment for deserving tyre-gambler Jack Miller, criticism of hard-pressed race officials, an impromptu redrawing of the grid, a subsequent revision of the rules, a surprise British title leader (the first since Barry Sheene in 1979) and the noisy revival of the Marquez-Rossi feud after an accumulation of penalties for the rampant Spaniard.

All because of a smattering of rain.

As always, smatterings are bad. Better properly wet, or properly dry. This rain started with little effect on Friday, but became more disruptive over the next two days. For it was a very difficult kind of rain, coming and going unpredictably. As pole first-timer Miller said, after an ultra-daring qualifying flyer on slicks, "It wasn't nice to ride. It could be raining at one corner, then two laps later, it would be raining somewhere else."

Come race day, Moto3 served warning of difficulty to come, with tricky mixed conditions that turned against Qatar winner Jorge Martin's bold tyre gamble. Moto2 just got away with it. Then came MotoGP, after lunch – and things went seriously haywire.

As they formed up on the grid, it looked as though it would be dry, then wet, then dry again. The race was declared wet 15 minutes before the scheduled start, even as dry patches began to appear. By then, at least one rider, Petrucci, had called in to change to wets in time to run a second sighting lap. There was just one rider on slicks: pole-man Miller.

And there he stayed, pretty soon in glorious isolation. Morbidelli had been the first to leave the grid to return to the pits for slicks, but soon all but one had followed suit, Lorenzo the last.

The rules didn't cater for this specifically: only for riders leaving the grid if unable to start their engines. So by default, it seemed that Miller should have started from the grid, everyone else from the pit lane. But something similar had happened at the Sachsenring in 2014, where a gang of 14 had lined up at the pit exit, officials struggling to get them in qualifying order, before they departed jostling and rubbing elbows on the narrow exit road. It had been unfair, but more importantly desperately dangerous. Race Direction had decreed that it must never happen again.

Cue confusion: the start delayed by 15 minutes, riders lining up at the pit exit, then returning to their boxes. Then a summit meeting between Race Director Mike Webb and team representatives on the grid. All riders except for Miller would have to start from the back of the grid, in qualifying order. But they couldn't all be at the back, so a compromise was devised – five empty rows behind Miller, with the tail end not even on painted grid slots.

Unfair to Miller, but at least practical.

The next curve ball came when Marquez stalled on the grid. It was, he explained later, an electronic glitch: "something on the gearbox, on the dash, something electronic. The same thing happened to Cal in practice. It was a pity it happened on the grid."

Under the rules, he was required to raise his hand and await guidance back to the pit lane. He did raise his hand, for a couple of seconds "that felt like more than four", then took his own decision, most impressively succeeding in bump-starting his Honda. At that point, two IRTA officials ordered him back to the pit lane, but he effected to have misunderstood, made a U-turn and rode back to his grid slot.

Not surprisingly, this earned a ride-through penalty, nominally for riding in reverse direction. It was the first of three sanctions that meant eventually he scored no points. The second was for a rough overtake of Aleix Espargaro, to lose one position – he dropped back two to be sure. The third came after he'd caused Rossi to crash with yet another rough pass. Thirty seconds added to his time dropped him from fifth to 18th.

Then came the aftermath.

Marquez, his manager Alzamora and Honda team manager Puig went straight to the Yamaha pit after the race to apologise. They were brusquely dismissed by Rossi's right-

hand man, Uccio Salucci. Yamaha Racing boss Lin Jarvis kept out of it, but later joined Rossi in a trip to Race Direction to complain, and he publicly echoed Rossi's statement that Marquez "destroys our sport" and that he (Rossi) was "scared" to be on the same track with him. "He goes between your leg and the bike. He does it purposely, because he knows he won't crash, but he hopes you will. I don't have fun when I race with him, because he don't play clean."

Marquez explained, "My biggest mistake was with Aleix, because I arrived so fast. I tried to not hit him. With Valentino, I didn't think I did anything crazy. You need to understand the track condition. The line was dry, but I took a wet patch and locked the front. I had to release the brake. But if you check, look at Zarco with Dani, Petrucci with Aleix – it was quite difficult today. They were mistakes for the track condition."

But did Rossi need to crash? Did Marquez really take him by surprise? When the Honda rider had pulled similar moves on Dovizioso, the Ducati rider had been ready for them, let him through and then passed him back. Rossi could have been warned, and surely could have let him go.

Equally and much more reprehensibly, Marquez didn't need to pass so aggressively. He was much quicker than Rossi – indeed had been blisteringly faster than everybody all weekend, in all conditions. He could have blown by on the subsequent straight.

And if Marquez had earned the 30-second penalty that dropped him out of the points, why was Zarco not punished for doing almost exactly the same to Pedrosa on the first lap? Particularly since Pedrosa had been injured.

The Argentine GP reflected well on almost nobody, Miller and winner Crutchlow excepted.

But it was a brilliant and thrilling race all the same.

MOTOGP RACE – 24 laps (shortened)

Marquez had been head and shoulders clear in free practice, but the track had damp patches in qualifying, and though he was the first to risk slicks, he (along with Crutchlow) pulled straight in again for wets. Only Miller persisted, and all but crashed more than once. "My mother always said, 'You never listen.' I guess the bike was telling me something, but I wasn't listening," he laughed.

Pedrosa and Zarco were alongside him, the Frenchman's sixth front row in succession; with a surprise second-row start for Rabat, ahead of Rins and Marquez.

Aleix Espargaro was seventh, from Dovizioso, both of them through from Q1; Lorenzo hadn't made the cut and was on row five.

The line-up on the grid was chaotic, with all but Miller pitting as the track dried quickly. Eventually, 15 minutes late, they formed up five rows back, Miller alone. Still joking, he said later, "It was like I farted on the grid and everyone disappeared." His reward for the tyre gamble was at least a clear hole shot.

The fine, intermittent drizzle was in abeyance, but there were damp patches, notably a stripe just off the racing line on the tight right-hander just before the final left. This would play a crucial role.

Miller set off in a clear lead, with Pedrosa heading the pursuit, the chase taken over by Marquez before the end of the lap.

Pedrosa never made the start of the second – pushed wide by a typically aggressive Zarco overtake into the penultimate corner and on to the stripe. He walked away from the consequent high-sider, but had sustained fractures to his right wrist.

Marquez took over the lead and forged away rapidly until lap five, when he was given the signal for his ride-through. He finished lap six 19th.

Up front once more, Miller was gradually being pegged back by Rins, heading for his first MotoGP podium. Zarco was on his back wheel, and Crutchlow shadowing. The quar-

Above: Crutchlow waited until the end to stamp his authority. Zarco and Rins were close, Miller finally out of touch.

Top right: Best yet. A revitalised Rabat was seventh; even more impressively, Syahrin (55) was ninth.
Photos: Gold & Goose

Above centre right: Eyes on the prize. A jubilant Bezzecchi celebrates his first Moto3 win.
Photo: Monster Energy

Above centre far right: Rins was overjoyed with his first MotoGP podium.

Above right: Mattia Pasini prevailed over Xavi Vierge and Miguel Oliveira in Moto2.
Photos: Gold & Goose

Right: Marco Bezzecchi (12) led from the first corner to the last. On his right, Rodrigo (19) and Bastianini (33, obscured); to his left, Norrodin (7), Di Giannantonio (21, obscured), pole-starter Arbolino (14), Migno (16), Canet (44), Antonelli (23) and Suzuki (24).
Photo: Monster Energy

tet pulled rapidly clear of Rabat and was some five seconds ahead when Dovizioso passed the Spaniard on lap six.

The front four made all the running. Rins got ahead of Miller several times on laps 13–17; but Crutchlow was strongest, up to second when Miller had his own big moment on that wet stripe at the end of the lap, dropping to fourth and losing touch.

Now there were three. Zarco led three laps, but Crutchlow was in control and able to stay clear of Zarco's final attack. It had been easy, he said, "I took no risks. I just stayed calm. I knew I was the fastest of the four guys by far – I was second fastest to Marc, wet or dry, and I won at the slowest possible speed. I was even taking different lines so that if any of them crashed, I wouldn't be mixed up in it."

As for Zarco, so narrowly beaten, and on the podium for the previous four races: "I know the win will come soon."

The factory Yamahas, having a difficult weekend, had been moving forward gradually, Vinales ahead of Rossi on lap eight as they passed Iannone's Suzuki. Vinales also led Dovi, in fifth, on lap 14, Rossi following him past next time around.

But all eyes were on Marquez, fastest on the track, as he forged through, setting one fastest lap after another and chewing up the competition.

His overtake of Aleix Espargaro was brutal, almost punting the Aprilia off the track and earning him a 'drop one place' penalty. But that barely slowed his progress, and as they were about to finish lap 20, he was ready to pass Rossi.

He did it with a crazy inside lunge at the slow penultimate corner, colliding with the Yamaha. Both ran wide. Marquez stayed on the asphalt, Rossi went on to the wet grass and crashed, by then almost stationary.

This was the start of a scandal, and of frantic action by the officials. They hit Marquez with another ride-through, but with the race now over, it became a 30-second penalty, which dropped him out of the points.

That put his last victim, Vinales, back to fifth, with Dovi sixth, half a second clear of Rabat, who was under pressure from Iannone and impressive top rookie Hafizh Syahrin.

Two seconds down, Petrucci completed the top ten. Pol Espargaro, Redding, Nakagami, Morbidelli and a desperately out-of-sorts Lorenzo wrapped up the points. Rossi remounted for 19th.

Aleix Espargaro retired; Smith crashed out, making just three non-finishers.

MOTO2 RACE – 21 laps

Mercifully settled conditions and an absence of the fine misty drizzle ensured that the second race of the day was declared officially dry, and it remained so, amid the crackling tension of a second successive fierce fight for full distance.

Qualifying had been enlivened, in spite of increasingly heavy rain in the closing minutes, by a stunning lap by Xavi Vierge, for his first pole. Baldassarri had seemed safe, having set his time before the weather got worse. But in a display of brinkmanship on the now sodden surface, Vierge displaced him by less than three-tenths.

Kent was third; Navarro forged through to fifth, to start between Pasini and Lowes. Oliveira and Marques led Remy Gardner, fastest in the wet FP3, on row three; rookie Roberts was tenth, Bagnaia languished in 15th.

There were still damp patches, including a slight stream across the corner before the long back straight. It was a wobble over this that gave Pasini his biggest scare, and Oliveira his first chance to take the lead at the other end of the straight.

That occasion and the next, Pasini grabbed it straight back, the veteran holding on to the finish, by which time Vierge had pushed Oliveira to third, the trio crossing the line within just over a second.

Pasini's determination had won the day. "I didn't think about the other riders – only myself, corner by corner, lap by lap, to not make any mistakes. I felt quite comfortable," he said.

Vierge had led away, but Baldassarri took over into the first corner and held on for two laps. He stayed in the podium mix almost throughout, just losing touch by the end.

By then, Marquez had recovered from a couple of misadventures, twice running wide, and he was fifth, barely two-tenths behind.

Remy Gardner, son of Wayne, had a strong race. By half-distance, he had pushed through to lead and then escape from a group going for sixth; and he was comfortably there to the finish, the best of his career.

A couple of seconds adrift, class rookie Mir managed to regain seventh from Aegerter by less than a tenth.

Qatar winner Bagnaia was mired in the next group, but managed to recapture tenth from Lecuona with two laps to go, then get past Schrotter for ninth.

Kent had lost touch with this group, but narrowly held on to 12th from pursuing early front-runner Lowes, who'd had a couple of moments that dropped him back to 14th before half-distance. Another six seconds away, Isaac Vinales and Locatelli took the last points, Marini missing out by just half a second.

There were only three non-finishers. Binder crashed out on lap two after hitting the back end of Navarro when the Spaniard braked unexpectedly early. Navarro also retired, his Kalex damaged. Jules Danilo burned his clutch off the start.

MOTO3 RACE – 21 laps

The gamblers came up short in the first race of the day, while rising Italian star Marco Bezzecchi laid on a display of consistent speed, with wet tyres on a drying track, to claim his first win, and the first for KTM since the Italian GP in 2017.

The start was damp and tyre choice vexed. First-time pole-starter Tony Arbolino started on slicks; likewise Bulega, Atiratphuvapat and Ramirez at the back of the grid.

Then Martin and Oettl also gambled, fitting slicks after the warm-up lap to start from the pit lane.

Bezzecchi and Co proved them wrong. The 19-year-old led into the first corner and was never challenged, at one stage almost eight seconds ahead. After the race, he was hugged by mentor Rossi. "I am so happy I have already forgotten everything," he told the TV cameras.

A group of five vigorously disputed second in his wake. At half-distance, Di Giannantonio led from Canet, rookie Masia, Argentine hope Rodrigo and Norrodin. Massia fell after colliding with Di Giannantonio's back wheel, and Rodrigo faded; while Bastianini had come through to take fourth well clear of Norrodin.

Five seconds back, the remnants of a tussle had Spanish rookie Alonso Lopez an impressive sixth ahead of Dalla Porta, Antonelli and the slowing Rodrigo.

The slick-tyre runners had gained speed throughout, but only moved into the points in the closing stages, helped by a number of crashes: Arbolino tenth; Martin (who set one fastest lap after another) up to 11th, picking up six places in the last two laps.

Ramirez, Migno, Kornfeil and Loi closed out the points, survivors of a massive battle. Binder, Arenas and Foggia had crashed out of it, while McPhee had also been knocked out of contention.

GRAN PREMIO MOTUL DE LA REPÚBLICA ARGENTINA

8–9 APRIL, 2018

AUTÓDROMO TERMAS DE RÍO HONDO

24 laps
Length: 4.806km / 2.986 miles
Width: 16m

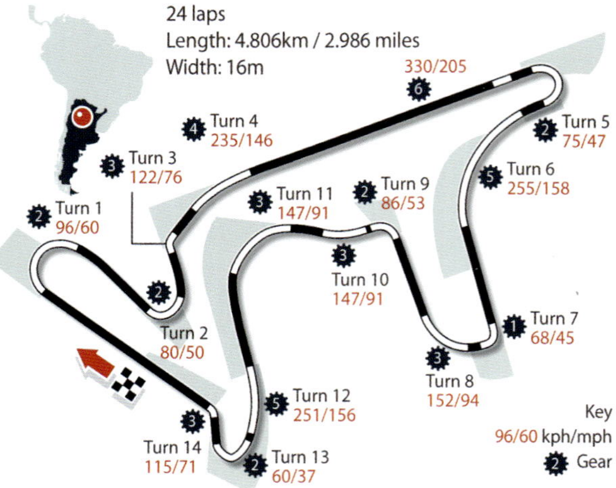

MotoGP

RACE DISTANCE: 24 laps, 71.671 miles/115.344km · RACE WEATHER: Wet (air 22°C, humidity 94%, track 23°C)

Pos.	Rider	Nat.	No.	Entrant	Machine	Tyres	Race tyre choice	Laps	Time & speed
1	**Cal Crutchlow**	GBR	35	LCR Honda CASTROL	Honda RC213V	M	F: Medium/R: Medium	24	40m 36.342s 105.9mph/ 170.4km/h
2	**Johann Zarco**	FRA	5	Monster Yamaha Tech 3	Yamaha YZR-M1	M	F: Soft/R: Medium	24	40m 36.593s
3	**Alex Rins**	SPA	42	Team SUZUKI ECSTAR	Suzuki GSX-RR	M	F: Medium/R: Medium	24	40m 38.843s
4	**Jack Miller**	AUS	43	Alma Pramac Racing	Ducati Desmosedici	M	F: Medium/R: Medium	24	40m 40.732s
5	**Maverick Vinales**	SPA	25	Movistar Yamaha MotoGP	Yamaha YZR-M1	M	F: Medium/R: Medium	24	40m 51.283s
6	**Andrea Dovizioso**	ITA	4	Ducati Team	Ducati Desmosedici	M	F: Medium/R: Medium	24	40m 58.875s
7	**Tito Rabat**	SPA	53	Reale Avintia Racing	Ducati Desmosedici	M	F: Medium/R: Medium	24	40m 59.368s
8	**Andrea Iannone**	ITA	29	Team SUZUKI ECSTAR	Suzuki GSX-RR	M	F: Soft/R: Medium	24	41m 00.263s
9	**Hafizh Syahrin**	MAL	55	Monster Yamaha Tech 3	Yamaha YZR-M1	M	F: Soft/R: Medium	24	41m 00.653s
10	**Danilo Petrucci**	ITA	9	Alma Pramac Racing	Ducati Desmosedici	M	F: Medium/R: Medium	24	41m 02.345s
11	**Pol Espargaro**	SPA	44	Red Bull KTM Factory Racing	KTM RC16	M	F: Medium/R: Medium	24	41m 07.364s
12	**Scott Redding**	GBR	45	Aprilia Racing Team Gresini	Aprilia RS-GP	M	F: Soft/R: Medium	24	41m 08.233s
13	**Takaaki Nakagami**	JPN	30	LCR Honda IDEMITSU	Honda RC213V	M	F: Medium/R: Medium	24	41m 08.794s
14	**Franco Morbidelli**	ITA	21	EG 0,0 Marc VDS	Honda RC213V	M	F: Medium/R: Medium	24	41m 18.403s
15	**Jorge Lorenzo**	SPA	99	Ducati Team	Ducati Desmosedici	M	F: Medium/R: Medium	24	41m 18.616s
16	Alvaro Bautista	SPA	19	Angel Nieto Team	Ducati Desmosedici	M	F: Medium/R: Medium	24	41m 18.967s
17	Thomas Luthi	SWI	12	EG 0,0 Marc VDS	Honda RC213V	M	F: Medium/R: Medium	24	41m 19.692s
18	Marc Marquez	SPA	93	Repsol Honda Team	Honda RC213V	M	F: Medium/R: Medium	24	41m 20.202s
19	Valentino Rossi	ITA	46	Movistar Yamaha MotoGP	Yamaha YZR-M1	M	F: Medium/R: Medium	24	41m 28.424s
20	Karel Abraham	CZE	17	Angel Nieto Team	Ducati Desmosedici	M	F: Medium/R: Medium	24	41m 40.286s
21	Xavier Simeon	BEL	10	Reale Avintia Racing	Ducati Desmosedici	M	F: Soft/R: Medium	24	41m 46.486s
	Bradley Smith	GBR	38	Red Bull KTM Factory Racing	KTM RC16	M	F: Medium/R: Medium	17	DNF-crash
	Aleix Espargaro	SPA	41	Aprilia Racing Team Gresini	Aprilia RS-GP	M	F: Medium/R: Medium	13	DNF-technical
	Dani Pedrosa	SPA	26	Repsol Honda Team	Honda RC213V	M	F: Medium/R: Medium	0	DNF-crash

Fastest lap: Marc Marquez, on lap 22, 1m 39.902s, 107.6mph/173.1km/h.
Lap record: Valentino Rossi, 1m 39.019s, 108.6mph/174.7km/h (2015).
Event maximum speed: Marc Marquez, 206.9mph/333.0km/h (free practice).

Qualifying

Weather: Wet
Air Temp: 20° **Track Temp:** 22°
Humidity: 99%

1	Miller	1m 47.153s
2	Pedrosa	1m 47.330s
3	Zarco	1m 47.365s
4	Rabat	1m 47.681s
5	Rins	1m 47.743s
6	Marquez	1m 47.754s
7	A. Espargaro	1m 47.845s
8	Dovizioso	1m 48.247s
9	Vinales	1m 49.044s
10	Crutchlow	1m 49.304s
11	Rossi	1m 49.326s
12	Iannone	1m 49.975s
13	Abraham	1m 49.878s
14	Lorenzo	1m 50.063s
15	Redding	1m 50.175s
16	P. Espargaro	1m 50.324s
17	Simeon	1m 50.364s
18	Petrucci	1m 50.449s
19	Bautista	1m 50.606s
20	Luthi	1m 50.833s
21	Smith	1m 51.007s
22	Morbidelli	1m 51.012s
23	Syahrin	1m 51.142s
24	Nakagami	1m 51.387s

Fastest race laps

1	Marquez	1m 39.902s
2	Crutchlow	1m 40.386s
3	Zarco	1m 40.425s
4	Vinales	1m 40.614s
5	Iannone	1m 40.647s
6	Rins	1m 40.756s
7	Miller	1m 40.840s
8	Rossi	1m 40.895s
9	Lorenzo	1m 41.060s
10	Syahrin	1m 41.091s
11	Nakagami	1m 41.093s
12	Dovizioso	1m 41.148s
13	Rabat	1m 41.160s
14	Petrucci	1m 41.167s
15	Smith	1m 41.203s
16	Bautista	1m 41.284s
17	P. Espargaro	1m 41.622s
18	A. Espargaro	1m 41.667s
19	Morbidelli	1m 41.668s
20	Redding	1m 41.707s
21	Luthi	1m 41.962s
22	Abraham	1m 42.312s
23	Simeon	1m 42.445s

Championship Points

1	Crutchlow	38
2	Dovizioso	35
3	Zarco	28
4	Vinales	21
5	Marquez	20
6	Miller	19
7	Petrucci	17
8	Rossi	16
9	Rins	16
10	Iannone	15
11	Rabat	14
12	Pedrosa	9
13	Syahrin	9
14	Morbidelli	6
15	P. Espargaro	5
16	Redding	4
17	Bautista	3
18	Nakagami	3
19	Abraham	1
20	Lorenzo	1

Constructor Points

1	Honda	45
2	Ducati	38
3	Yamaha	36
4	Suzuki	23
5	KTM	5
6	Aprilia	4

Grid order		1	2	3	4	5	6	7	8	9	10	11	12	13	14	15	16	17	18	19	20	21	22	23	24	
43	MILLER	43	93	93	93	93	93	43	43	43	43	43	43	43	43	43	42	43	35	35	5	5	5	35	35	1
26	PEDROSA	93	43	43	43	43	43	42	42	42	42	42	42	42	42	42	43	35	5	5	35	35	35	5	5	2
5	ZARCO	42	42	42	42	42	42	5	5	5	5	5	5	5	5	5	5	5	42	42	42	42	42	42	42	3
53	RABAT	5	5	5	5	5	5	35	35	35	35	35	35	35	35	35	35	42	43	43	43	43	43	43	43	4
42	RINS	35	35	35	35	35	35	4	4	4	4	4	4	4	25	25	25	25	25	25	25	25	25	25	93	
93	MARQUEZ	53	53	53	53	53	4	53	53	53	53	25	25	25	4	46	46	46	46	46	93	93	93	93	25	5
41	A. ESPARGARO	4	4	4	4	4	53	29	25	25	25	46	46	46	46	4	4	4	93	93	4	4	4	4	4	6
4	DOVIZIOSO	46	46	46	46	29	29	25	46	46	46	53	53	53	53	53	93	93	4	4	53	53	53	53	53	7
25	VINALES	38	38	29	29	46	25	46	29	55	55	55	55	55	55	55	53	53	53	53	55	9	9	29	29	8
35	CRUTCHLOW	29	29	38	38	25	46	55	55	29	29	29	29	29	29	93	55	55	55	55	9	55	55	55	55	9
46	ROSSI	45	45	45	45	38	45	45	45	45	9	9	9	9	9	29	9	9	9	9	29	29	29	9	9	10
29	IANNONE	25	41	41	25	45	55	9	9	9	45	45	45	45	93	9	29	29	29	29	44	44	44	44	44	11
17	ABRAHAM	41	25	25	41	55	9	12	12	44	44	44	44	44	45	44	44	44	44	44	45	45	45	45	45	12
99	LORENZO	9	9	9	9	44	44	44	44	12	38	38	93	93	44	45	45	45	45	45	30	30	30	30	30	13
45	REDDING	55	55	55	55	9	12	38	38	38	21	21	21	21	21	21	30	30	30	30	21	21	12	21	21	14
44	P. ESPARGARO	44	44	44	44	12	38	21	21	21	93	93	38	38	30	30	21	38	21	12	12	12	21	12	99	15
10	SIMEON	17	17	12	12	30	30	41	30	30	12	12	30	30	38	38	38	21	12	21	99	99	99	99	19	
9	PETRUCCI	12	12	30	30	41	21	30	41	93	30	30	12	12	12	12	12	12	99	99	19	19	19	19	12	
19	BAUTISTA	30	30	21	21	21	41	93	93	41	41	41	41	41	99	99	99	99	19	19	46	46	46	46	46	
12	LUTHI	10	10	10	10	10	19	19	19	19	19	19	19	19	19	19	19	19	17	17	17	17	17	17	17	
38	SMITH	19	21	19	19	19	99	99	99	99	99	99	99	99	17	17	17	17	10	10	10	10	10	10	10	
21	MORBIDELLI	21	19	99	99	99	10	10	10	10	10	10	17	17	10	10	10	10								
55	SYAHRIN	99	99	17	17	17	17	17	17	17	17	17	10	10												
30	NAKAGAMI																									

93 Ride-through penalty

Moto2

RACE DISTANCE: 23 laps, 68.685 miles/110.538km · RACE WEATHER: Dry (air 22°C, humidity 91%, track 23°C)

Pos.	Rider	Nat.	No.	Entrant	Machine	Laps	Time & Speed
1	**Mattia Pasini**	ITA	54	Italtrans Racing Team	Kalex	23	40m 37.538s 101.4mph/163.2km/h
2	**Xavi Vierge**	SPA	97	Dynavolt Intact GP	Kalex	23	40m 38.388s
3	**Miguel Oliveira**	POR	44	Red Bull KTM Ajo	KTM	23	40m 38.952s
4	**Lorenzo Baldassarri**	ITA	7	Pons HP40	Kalex	23	40m 42.716s
5	**Alex Marquez**	SPA	73	EG 0,0 Marc VDS	Kalex	23	40m 42.969s
6	**Remy Gardner**	AUS	87	Tech 3 Racing	Tech 3	23	40m 47.963s
7	**Joan Mir**	SPA	36	EG 0,0 Marc VDS	Kalex	23	40m 50.917s
8	**Dominique Aegerter**	SWI	77	Kiefer Racing	KTM	23	40m 50.998s
9	**Francesco Bagnaia**	ITA	42	SKY Racing Team VR46	Kalex	23	40m 59.576s
10	**Marcel Schrotter**	GER	23	Dynavolt Intact GP	Kalex	23	41m 00.405s
11	**Iker Lecuona**	SPA	27	Swiss Innovative Investors	KTM	23	41m 01.640s
12	**Danny Kent**	GBR	52	MB Conveyors - Speed Up Racing	Speed Up	23	41m 03.510s
13	**Sam Lowes**	GBR	22	Swiss Innovative Investors	KTM	23	41m 03.548s
14	**Isaac Vinales**	SPA	32	SAG Team	Kalex	23	41m 09.307s
15	**Andrea Locatelli**	ITA	5	Italtrans Racing Team	Kalex	23	41m 10.802s
16	Luca Marini	ITA	10	SKY Racing Team VR46	Kalex	23	41m 11.366s
17	Tetsuta Nagashima	JPN	45	IDEMITSU Honda Team Asia	Kalex	23	41m 26.141s
18	Steven Odendaal	RSA	4	NTS RW Racing GP	NTS	23	41m 28.189s
19	Romano Fenati	ITA	13	Marinelli Snipers Team	Kalex	23	41m 29.132s
20	Hector Barbera	SPA	40	Pons HP40	Kalex	23	41m 30.608s
21	Stefano Manzi	ITA	62	Forward Racing Team	Suter	23	41m 30.798s
22	Fabio Quartararo	FRA	20	MB Conveyors - Speed Up Racing	Speed Up	23	41m 34.517s
23	Simone Corsi	ITA	24	Tasca Racing Scuderia Moto2	Kalex	23	41m 36.804s
24	Khairul Idham Pawi	MAL	89	IDEMITSU Honda Team Asia	Kalex	23	41m 47.659s
25	Joe Roberts	USA	16	NTS RW Racing GP	NTS	23	41m 49.589s
26	Zulfahmi Khairuddin	MAL	63	SIC Racing Team	Kalex	23	42m 10.531s
27	Federico Fuligni	ITA	21	Tasca Racing Scuderia Moto2	Kalex	23	42m 10.756s
28	Bo Bendsneyder	NED	64	Tech 3 Racing	Tech 3	23	42m 13.616s
29	Eric Granado	BRA	51	Forward Racing Team	Suter	23	42m 16.489s
	Jorge Navarro	SPA	9	Federal Oil Gresini Moto2	Kalex	3	DNF
	Brad Binder	RSA	41	Red Bull KTM Ajo	KTM	1	DNF
	Jules Danilo	FRA	95	Nashi Argan SAG Team	Kalex	1	DNF

Fastest lap: Xavi Vierge, on lap 21, 1m 44.329s, 103.0mph/165.8km/h.

Lap record: Jonas Folger, 1m 43.001s, 104.3mph/167.9km/h (2015).

Event maximum speed: Joan Mir, 169.2mph/272.3km/h (free practice .

Qualifying

Weather: Wet

Air Temp: 20° **Track Temp:** 21°

Humidity: 96%

1	Vierge	1m 56.137s
2	Baldassarri	1m 56.408s
3	Kent	1m 56.536s
4	Pasini	1m 56.591s
5	Navarro	1m 56.679s
6	Lowes	1m 56.830s
7	Oliveira	1m 57.006s
8	Marquez	1m 57.070s
9	Gardner	1m 57.166s
10	Roberts	1m 57.263s
11	Aegerter	1m 57.582s
12	Marini	1m 57.621s
13	Vinales	1m 57.677s
14	Odendaal	1m 57.813s
15	Bagnaia	1m 57.891s
16	Binder	1m 57.898s
17	Mir	1m 58.058s
18	Barbera	1m 58.342s
19	Fenati	1m 58.534s
20	Schrotter	1m 58.585s
21	Lecuona	1m 58.614s
22	Corsi	1m 58.673s
23	Nagashima	1m 58.813s
24	Granado	1m 58.991s
25	Bendsneyder	1m 59.630s
26	Locatelli	1m 59.677s
27	Pawi	2m 00.166s
28	Quartararo	2m 00.295s
29	Danilo	2m 00.428s
30	Fuligni	2m 00.438s
31	Khairuddin	2m 01.770s
32	Manzi	2m 02.644s

Fastest race laps

1	Vierge	1m 44.329s
2	Pasini	1m 44.368s
3	Oliveira	1m 44.517s
4	Marquez	1m 44.830s
5	Baldassarri	1m 45.098s
6	Kent	1m 45.175s
7	Gardner	1m 45.185s
8	Lowes	1m 45.200s
9	Aegerter	1m 45.206s
10	Bagnaia	1m 45.263s
11	Schrotter	1m 45.279s
12	Mir	1m 45.365s
13	Lecuona	1m 45.389s
14	Vinales	1m 45.490s
15	Fenati	1m 45.746s
16	Quartararo	1m 45.835s
17	Marini	1m 45.899s
18	Locatelli	1m 45.917s
19	Nagashima	1m 46.023s
20	Barbera	1m 46.105s
21	Corsi	1m 46.128s
22	Odendaal	1m 46.304s
23	Manzi	1m 46.506s
24	Roberts	1m 46.740s
25	Pawi	1m 47.081s
26	Bendsneyder	1m 47.504s
27	Khairuddin	1m 47.988s
28	Granado	1m 48.073s
29	Fuligni	1m 48.182s
30	Navarro	1m 50.179s

Championship Points

1	Pasini	38
2	Baldassarri	33
3	Bagnaia	32
4	Vierge	28
5	Oliveira	27
6	Marquez	27
7	Schrotter	15
8	Gardner	14
9	Mir	14
10	Binder	10
11	Aegerter	9
12	Marini	7
13	Navarro	6
14	Lecuona	5
15	Kent	4
16	Barbera	3
17	Lowes	3
18	Vinales	2
19	Corsi	2
20	Locatelli	1

Constructor Points

1	Kalex	50
2	KTM	27
3	Tech 3	14
4	Speed Up	4

Moto3

RACE DISTANCE: 21 laps, 62.713 miles/100.926km · RACE WEATHER: Wet (air 22°C, humidity 92%, track 23°C)

Pos.	Rider	Nat.	No.	Entrant	Machine	Laps	Time & Speed
1	**Marco Bezzecchi**	ITA	12	Redox PruestelGP	KTM	21	41m 43.822s 90.2mph/145.1km/h
2	**Aron Canet**	SPA	44	Estrella Galicia 0,0	Honda	21	41m 48.511s
3	**Fabio Di Giannantonio**	ITA	21	Del Conca Gresini Moto3	Honda	21	41m 48.785s
4	**Enea Bastianini**	ITA	33	Leopard Racing	Honda	21	41m 49.640s
5	**Adam Norrodin**	MAL	7	Petronas Sprinta Racing	Honda	21	41m 52.934s
6	**Alonso Lopez**	SPA	72	Estrella Galicia 0,0	Honda	21	41m 57.171s
7	**Lorenzo Dalla Porta**	ITA	48	Leopard Racing	Honda	21	41m 57.747s
8	**Niccolo Antonelli**	ITA	23	SIC58 Squadra Corse	Honda	21	41m 58.185s
9	**Gabriel Rodrigo**	ARG	19	RBA BOE Skull Rider	KTM	21	42m 00.395s
10	**Tony Arbolino**	ITA	14	Marinelli Snipers Team	Honda	21	42m 08.121s
11	**Jorge Martin**	SPA	88	Del Conca Gresini Moto3	Honda	21	42m 09.195s
12	**Marcos Ramirez**	SPA	42	Bester Capital Dubai	KTM	21	42m 09.882s
13	**Andrea Migno**	ITA	16	Angel Nieto Team Moto3	KTM	21	42m 10.198s
14	**Jakub Kornfeil**	CZE	84	Redox PruestelGP	KTM	21	42m 10.310s
15	**Livio Loi**	BEL	11	Reale Avintia Academy	KTM	21	42m 10.359s
16	Ayumu Sasaki	JPN	71	Petronas Sprinta Racing	Honda	21	42m 13.074s
17	John McPhee	GBR	17	CIP - Green Power	KTM	21	42m 16.759s
18	Nakarin Atiratphuvapat	THA	41	Honda Team Asia	Honda	21	42m 17.714s
19	Kaito Toba	JPN	27	Honda Team Asia	Honda	21	42m 21.487s
20	Kazuki Masaki	JPN	22	RBA BOE Skull Rider	KTM	21	42m 22.024s
21	Tatsuki Suzuki	JPN	24	SIC58 Squadra Corse	Honda	21	42m 46.127s
22	Darryn Binder	RSA	40	Red Bull KTM Ajo	KTM	21	43m 01.206s
23	Philipp Oettl	GER	65	Sudmetal Schedl GP Racing	KTM	21	43m 20.808s
24	Makar Yurchenko	KAZ	76	CIP - Green Power	KTM	20	42m 10.992s
	Jaume Masia	SPA	5	Bester Capital Dubai	KTM	19	DNF
	Dennis Foggia	ITA	10	SKY Racing Team VR46	KTM	18	DNF
	Albert Arenas	SPA	75	Angel Nieto Team Moto3	KTM	17	DNF
	Nicolo Bulega	ITA	8	SKY Racing Team VR46	KTM	16	DNF

Fastest lap: Jorge Martin, on lap 18, 1m 55.968s, 92.6mph/149.1km/h.

Lap record: Miguel Oliveira, 1m 48.977s, 98.6mph/158.7km/h (2015).

Event maximum speed: Jorge Martin, 142.9mph/230.0km/h (free practice).

Qualifying:

Weather: Dry

Air Temp: 18° **Track Temp:** 20°

Humidity: 100%

1	Arbolino	1m 53.782s
2	Bezzecchi	1m 54.088s
3	Rodrigo	1m 54.330s
4	Norrodin	1m 54.346s
5	Bastianini	1m 54.361s
6	Di Giannantonio	1m 54.363s
7	Antonelli	1m 54.366s
8	Canet	1m 54.380s
9	Martin	1m 54.388s
10	Migno	1m 54.562s
11	Masia	1m 54.568s
12	Arenas	1m 54.649s
13	Sasaki	1m 54.799s
14	Foggia	1m 54.988s
15	Dalla Porta	1m 55.323s
16	Loi	1m 55.458s
17	Masaki	1m 55.514s
18	Kornfeil	1m 55.516s
19	Suzuki	1m 55.604s
20	Oettl	1m 55.800s
21	Lopez	1m 55.982s
22	McPhee	1m 56.107s
23	Atiratphuvapat	1m 56.176s
24	Toba	1m 56.222s
25	Binder	1m 56.333s
26	Ramirez	1m 56.478s
27	Bulega	1m 57.976s
28	Yurchenko	2m 00.087s

Fastest race laps

1	Martin	1m 55.968s
2	Yurchenko	1m 55.987s
3	Arbolino	1m 56.621s
4	Ramirez	1m 57.118s
5	Di Giannantonio	1m 57.679s
6	Bastianini	1m 57.820s
7	Atiratphuvapat	1m 57.847s
8	Kornfeil	1m 58.065s
9	Canet	1m 58.077s
10	Foggia	1m 58.186s
11	Masia	1m 58.295s
12	Migno	1m 58.320s
13	Loi	1m 58.329s
14	Bulega	1m 58.564s
15	Dalla Porta	1m 58.590s
16	Norrodin	1m 58.597s
17	Lopez	1m 58.688s
18	Bezzecchi	1m 58.803s
19	Antonelli	1m 58.925s
20	Rodrigo	1m 58.969s
21	Suzuki	1m 59.040s
22	Sasaki	1m 59.458s
23	Arenas	1m 59.461s
24	McPhee	1m 59.500s
25	Oettl	1m 59.591s
26	Toba	1m 59.614s
27	Binder	1m 59.752s
28	Masaki	2m 00.038s

Championship Points

1	Canet	40
2	Martin	30
3	Bezzecchi	27
4	Di Giannantonio	26
5	Dalla Porta	25
6	Antonelli	21
7	Rodrigo	18
8	Norrodin	16
9	Bastianini	13
10	Lopez	10
11	Toba	9
12	Kornfeil	9
13	Migno	9
14	Sasaki	8
15	Arbolino	6
16	Ramirez	5
17	Masia	4
18	Masaki	3
19	Loi	1

Constructor Points

1	Honda	45
2	KTM	36

Main: King of the Hill. Marquez leads Iannone, Vinales, Rossi (hidden) and Crutchlow.
Photo: Repsol Honda

Inset: Unbeaten. Unbeatable.
Photo: Whit Bazemore Photography

FIM WORLD CHAMPIONSHIP · ROUND 3

GRAND PRIX OF THE AMERICAS

CIRCUIT OF THE AMERICAS

Above: **Riding for his job, Iannone took a first Suzuki podium. It would not be enough.**
Photo: www.suzuki-racing.com

Top right: **Bravery on ice: Pedrosa looked forlorn, rode like a hero.**
Photo: Repsol Honda

Above centre right: **Well deserved. Randy Mamola ran the emotional gamut as he was inducted into the MotoGP Hall of Fame.**
Photo: Whit Bazemore Photography

Above right: **Three world champions – Ben Spies and Colin Edwards (SBK), and Kenny Roberts Jr (MotoGP).**

Right: **Miller, Rabat and Aleix Espargaro were still this close at the finish, Rabat in front by barely a bike length.**
Photos: Gold & Goose

NOTHING could stop Marquez in Texas. Not lingering controversy from Argentina. Not another penalty denying him pole position. Not his dislike of leading from the first lap. Not a series of bumps that some called dangerous. Nor the booing of an unappreciative podium crowd.

And especially not any of his rivals. For a sixth Texas win in a row, his tenth straight US MotoGP win (including Indianapolis and Laguna Seca) and his 12th successive American win, counting Moto2, he was simply imperious. And if not back in the lead of the championship, he was only adrift by one point.

But it had been a long race. He explained that his usual preference was to follow other riders, then attack at the end. But under the circumstances, this would have been to court controversy: "After Argentina, my strategy was clear. We worked all weekend for this kind of race. I didn't have the confidence to battle, so I pushed to get away." More important, he continued, "is my feeling with the bike. It is sweet. Now it is important to see if we can have the same feeling in the European races." It was the first time in two years that he'd been able to say that.

The Argentine mish-mash was still very fresh in the mind, with neither Marquez nor Rossi repenting. The latter said that he'd replayed the incident on TV, and "I confirm all my words". But he received an oblique rebuke at a pre-race conference from Jack Miller, who recalled the 2011 feud between Dani Pedrosa (and more vocally, Jorge Lorenzo) and Marco Simoncelli, which was abruptly silenced by Simoncelli's fatal accident. "Riders need to be careful what they say," the Australian said. Journalists would ask provocative questions, and words could be twisted. "You have to remember life is short and we are risking our lives here."

The incident was thoroughly rehashed at the Riders Safety Commission meeting on Friday, a lively and well-attended affair, with Dorna chief Carmelo Ezpeleta joining in. No further sanctions resulted, but for the promise of stricter invigilation of and punishment for dangerous or obstructive riding.

Sure enough, the next day, Marquez and Pol Espargaro felt the force, each penalised three grid places for riding slowly on the racing line in qualifying to disrupt other riders. Marquez's victim was an angrily gesturing Vinales, who next time around set second fastest time and was promoted to pole. That improved his mood, on a weekend when he reported some relief from his troubles. This was thanks to cutting back on traction-control electronics. "I am controlling more with my hand … I feel better with the bike when I ride more aggressively," he said.

No more was said, at least publicly, about Zarco's Argentine attack on Pedrosa, and the Spanish veteran returned to racing 12 days after it had fractured his right wrist. He'd flown home for surgery and wasn't sure he would be able to start, given the high physical stress of multiple direction changes in the early part of the lap, and the hard braking, from almost 340km/h to less than 60 at the end of the straight. He admitted that he was struggling, with strength as much as the predictable pain, but he earned much respect

by racing to an impressive seventh, only dropping out of the battle for fifth (with Zarco and Dovizioso) in the closing laps.

The complex layout of the third longest track of the year makes it popular with the riders, but the fact that it is shared with F1, and that there are at least two areas of very heavy braking, count against it, with the problem of rippling bumps. Similar concerns at Silverstone and Catalunya were addressed in 2018 with full resurfacing, but this was beyond CotA's means, so a novel alternative was tried: the track surface was shaved in an attempt to smooth it out. This proved unsuccessful and unpopular, however, with some riders suggesting that actually it had made the bumps worse. Rossi: "For me, it's the worst situation of the whole season. The bike is moving around at top speed. Three or four bumps are very big." And at Turn 18, the bike was grounding out over another whoop.

Another result was to leave the surface dirty. The bikes were leaving such dust trails, especially on Friday, that it looked as though it was wet. "Something will have to be done," opined Vinales, echoing the general concern.

One result was to bring out the aero bodywork, even for Dovizioso, who hitherto had preferred not to use it. Adding front-end downforce helped to stabilise the bike over the bumps, and even the KTMs – which had eschewed wings in 2017 – were running with 'box-kites' on the fairing flanks. The reduction in top speed was a price worth paying for less buffeting by the bumps. This was the first time this aspect of aerodynamic aids had surfaced, an interesting aside with possible relevance to street motorcycles.

Memories of America's last champion were kept alive, most notably by the freshly designated Hayden Hill, with a giant painted number 69 beneath the track's trademark tower overlooking Turn 18.

And there was honour for Randy Mamola, named the latest MotoGP Legend at a ceremony both tearful and good humoured. Mamola is the only one of 27 Legends not to have won a championship. However, he was not only massively popular, but also four times runner-up during a very competitive era. His 13 premier-class wins far outrank previous US inductees Kenny Roberts Jr (eight wins) and Nicky Hayden (three). His own view on never quite winning was clear: "I am one of the best riders to have thrown his leg over the screaming 500s." He is also a tireless worker for charity, as a prime mover of Riders for Health, using motorcycles to

provide health care in rural Africa: "We are reaching 15 million people, but to me that is still small, because my dream is to make it more."

MOTOGP RACE – 20 laps

Marquez was fastest in qualifying, but the penalty dropped him back to lead the second row, with Vinales heading Iannone and Zarco, the Frenchman's seventh successive front-row start, in spite of placing fourth.

Marquez had Rossi and Lorenzo alongside; Crutchlow led row three from Dovi and the heroic Pedrosa, riding with a specially reinforced right glove. Petrucci and Pol Espargaro were behind, both through from Q1 and flanking Rins.

Marquez's pace made for a somewhat processional race, once he had seized the lead from Iannone at the end of the main straight. In fact, Iannone did nose ahead briefly at the same place on lap three, but it was only for a few yards. Thereafter, the Repsol Honda simply motored away, in an uneventful afternoon for the dominant force. He set fastest lap fifth time around, a second short of his own record.

Nor was it a race of much variety for the rest. Tyre selection was not significant, with little to choose between the three compounds. Only the two Aprilia riders selected the hard front; and only Abraham and Bautista the soft rear, with the rest almost equally divided between medium and hard rears, both factory and both Pramac Ducati riders, Iannone, Crutchlow and Marquez among the latter. Front tyre wear problems of recent years were not mentioned.

Vinales had started well, but had to fend off Rossi in the early laps, after the Italian had got by Crutchlow on lap two. But when he settled into his pace, the Spaniard was able to get clear, then ahead of Iannone by lap seven. This brief respite of encouragement, his first podium since the Australian GP of 2017, was notably cheering. "We are coming," he said after the race.

In this way, the first three positions were set early on.

A first ever podium on a Suzuki was even more important for Iannone, who was under pressure to keep his job with the factory team. "I struggled a lot in 2017, but always I believed in me," he said. But a second successive podium for Suzuki would cost them dear, and in 2019 they would lose their 'concession team' privileges of extra testing and extra engines.

Rossi was some two seconds adrift of Iannone, taking a lone fourth.

That had left Crutchlow engaged with Zarco and Dovizioso. The Englishman had been fighting back between the pair when he slipped off on lap eight, remounting to finish out the points and thereby losing his short-lived title lead.

The other two battled on, joined by Pedrosa, who was enjoying an amazing ride and who only lost touch in the last laps, finishing some four seconds down.

By then, with four laps left, the ever-patient Dovizioso used his Ducati horsepower to get ahead of Zarco for fifth, and to stay there by just over half a second.

Team-mate Lorenzo had yet another disappointing day. He'd been holding a distant eighth for most of the race, but gradually came under pressure from a three-bike scrap between independent Ducati riders Miller and Rabat, and Aleix Espargaro's Aprilia.

Rabat got ahead, then the other two also barged past Lorenzo into the tight Turn One as they started lap 15, leaving him shaking his head and losing further ground to finish 11th, more than two seconds behind the trio. Some chassis changes had improved his feel for the bike, but his problem was simply fatigue in the latter part of the race, because changed ergonomics robbed him of physical support during hard braking.

The other three continued fighting to the end, Rabat ahead and Espargaro tenth, covered by less than half a second.

A further three seconds away, Petrucci had another downbeat and lonely ride to 12th, comfortably clear of Pol Espargaro and top rookie Nakagami. Bautista took the final point.

Smith led Redding and Luthi over the line; Crutchlow

Above: Moto3's fight for third. Bezzecchi (12) pips Migno (16) and Di Giannantonio.

Right: Bagnaia vs Marquez in Moto2.
Photos: Gold & Goose

Top left: Vinales started from pole, finished second. But claims of a comeback proved premature.
Photo: Monster Energy

Top right: A second win apiece: Bagnaia (above) dominated the Moto2 race; Martin (below) was masterful in Moto3.
Photos: Gold & Goose

was a dismayed 19th, having passed rookie Simeon on the penultimate lap. Rins had run wide in the early laps and dropped behind Pedrosa, only to tumble just after half-distance. Syahrin also crashed out, while Abraham retired.

With the first far-away races completed and the start of the European season two weeks away, Dovizioso took a narrow points lead over Marquez, while Vinales was just a few points behind.

MOTO2 RACE – 18 laps

It had rained overnight, but stayed dry for Saturday's qualifying, returning shortly after Moto2 qualifying had been finished. Marquez was on pole (a family affair), having snatched it from former Austin winner Sam Lowes by less than two-tenths in the closing minutes. Pasini completed the front row; Bagnaia – bruised by a heavy Friday crash – led the second from rookie Mir and team-mate Marini.

Times were close, with 18 riders in the first second; and free practice leader Oliveira barely eight-tenths slower, but on the fourth row of the grid.

Marquez galloped away from the start, drawing steadily clear of Pasini in convincing style. But the latter had gambled on a hard rear tyre, and when Bagnaia took second on lap two, Marquez's comfort zone was cut to nothing.

Later, Bagnaia said, "It was easy to go at his pace." Marquez explained that a change in the wind conditions had left him struggling. All the same, it was only at half-distance that Bagnaia had moved past him, and Marquez fought straight back to regain the lead.

For the next three laps, they tussled, changing places several times, but on lap 13, Bagnaia led over the line for the first time. Marquez would nose ahead briefly once more, but the job was done – and from there to the end, the black and blue Kalex pulled steadily away to win by better than two seconds.

"That was much better than my first win in Qatar," said Bagnaia, "because I had a big crash on Friday, and this is always a difficult track for me."

If Marquez was disappointed, he didn't show it. "The podium was always my target this weekend, and we made it," he said.

Argentine GP star Vierge was the next to pass Pasini, taking third on lap three and holding it until lap 11. By then, however, Oliveira had made his way through and was challenging strongly, soon past and moving clear. He would close to within a second of Marquez by the end, counting himself lucky "to avoid any contact in the first laps."

Now Vierge found himself at the head of a group of ten, and on lap 13, the pressure got to him. He crashed out

The man to take over, remarkably, was rookie Mir, through from 19th on lap one after almost crashing at the first corner following a clash with Marini.

By the finish, he was better than a second clear of Lecuona, who narrowly won a long tussle with second Red Bull KTM rider Binder.

Pasini was now almost three seconds down, but he saved seventh, ahead of Navarro. The Spaniard narrowly stayed ahead of Aegerter, who had charged through in the closing laps. His last victim had been Baldassarri, who completed the top ten.

Class returnee Lowes crashed on the first lap, remounting to finish out of the points. Schrotter was another victim. The German had been heading the big group disputing fourth when he crashed heavily on lap seven, suffering a suspected broken collarbone. Kent and Manzi also crashed out.

Joe Roberts, the only US rider in any class, finished 23rd, two places down on NTS team-mate Steven Odendaal.

Thus Bagnaia regained a lead he would stretch over the coming races.

MOTO3 RACE – 17 laps

Qualifying started damp, but ended dry. In the dying seconds, Martin took his tenth career pole, deposing fellow Honda rider Canet by almost half a second; McPhee sneaked into third, top KTM.

Sunny skies and a first-corner melee marked the start of the first race of the day; a masterful display by Martin the finish. With the front group throughout, he timed his run perfectly with five of the long laps to go, taking the win by just over a second.

The front group was still 12 strong at half-distance, with early one-lap leader Foggia soon off the back of it, as Bezzecchi and Di Giannantonio squabbled up front.

Bastianini and Oettl were right there, with Migno coming through from behind, and Canet – the only rider to risk a soft tyre – battling to stay with them.

Positions changed constantly, especially at the end of the long straight and the subsequent swerves.

As Martin escaped on lap 12, Bastianini also got away from the gang. Behind him, battle intensified for the final lap, with Oettl making a convincing attack at the end of the back straight only to be blocked when an over-enthusiastic move by Di Giannantonio pushed him wide.

That let Bezzecchi take third, by inches from Migno, then Di Giannantonio and Oettl, third to sixth within less than three-tenths.

Moto3 veteran Kornfeil was off the back by a second for seventh place, while Canet was well out of touch in a disappointed eighth, having held off Suzuki and Loi in a still intense top ten.

Antonelli crashed out on the first lap; while Rodrigo recovered to 12th, having been mixed up in a first-corner melee involving Ramirez, Toba, Norrodin and Masia.

Martin had regained the title lead for the journey home to Spain.

RED BULL GRAND PRIX OF THE AMERICAS

20-22 APRIL, 2018

CIRCUIT OF THE AMERICAS

Circuit: 5.513km / 3.426 miles
20 laps
Width: 15m

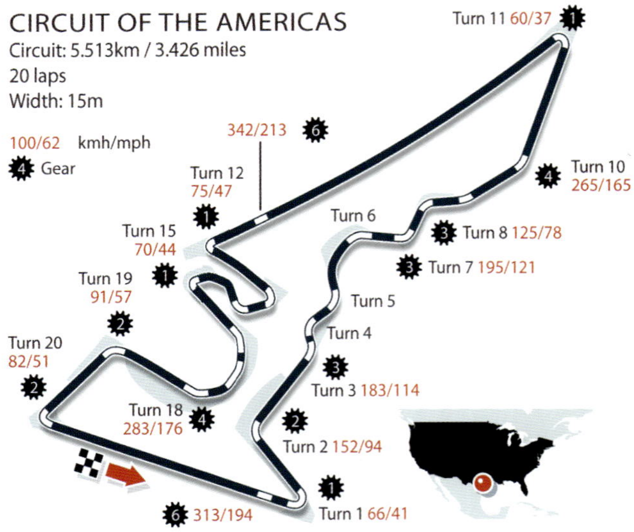

MotoGP

RACE DISTANCE: 20 laps, 68.512 miles/110.260km · RACE WEATHER: Dry (air 22°C, humidity 45%, track 35°C)

Pos.	Rider	Nat.	No.	Entrant	Machine	Tyres	Race tyre choice	Laps	Time & speed
1	**Marc Marquez**	SPA	93	Repsol Honda Team	Honda RC213V	M	F: Medium/R: Hard	20	41m 52.002s 98.2mph/ 158.0km/h
2	**Maverick Vinales**	SPA	25	Movistar Yamaha MotoGP	Yamaha YZR-M1	M	F: Medium/R: Medium	20	41m 55.562s
3	**Andrea Iannone**	ITA	29	Team SUZUKI ECSTAR	Suzuki GSX-RR	M	F: Medium/R: Hard	20	41m 58.706s
4	**Valentino Rossi**	ITA	46	Movistar Yamaha MotoGP	Yamaha YZR-M1	M	F: Medium/R: Medium	20	42m 01.589s
5	**Andrea Dovizioso**	ITA	4	Ducati Team	Ducati Desmosedici	M	F: Medium/R: Hard	20	42m 05.572s
6	**Johann Zarco**	FRA	5	Monster Yamaha Tech 3	Yamaha YZR-M1	M	F: Medium/R: Medium	20	42m 06.233s
7	**Dani Pedrosa**	SPA	26	Repsol Honda Team	Honda RC213V	M	F: Medium/R: Medium	20	42m 10.203s
8	**Tito Rabat**	SPA	53	Reale Avintia Racing	Ducati Desmosedici	M	F: Medium/R: Hard	20	42m 20.539s
9	**Jack Miller**	AUS	43	Alma Pramac Racing	Ducati Desmosedici	M	F: Medium/R: Hard	20	42m 20.673s
10	**Aleix Espargaro**	SPA	41	Aprilia Racing Team Gresini	Aprilia RS-GP	M	F: Hard/R: Medium	20	42m 20.877s
11	**Jorge Lorenzo**	SPA	99	Ducati Team	Ducati Desmosedici	M	F: Medium/R: Hard	20	42m 23.357s
12	**Danilo Petrucci**	ITA	9	Alma Pramac Racing	Ducati Desmosedici	M	F: Medium/R: Hard	20	42m 26.995s
13	**Pol Espargaro**	SPA	44	Red Bull KTM Factory Racing	KTM RC16	M	F: Soft/R: Medium	20	42m 29.266s
14	**Takaaki Nakagami**	JPN	30	LCR Honda IDEMITSU	Honda RC213V	M	F: Soft/R: Medium	20	42m 31.337s
15	**Alvaro Bautista**	SPA	19	Angel Nieto Team	Ducati Desmosedici	M	F: Medium/R: Soft	20	42m 32.889s
16	Bradley Smith	GBR	38	Red Bull KTM Factory Racing	KTM RC16	M	F: Medium/R: Medium	20	42m 40.477s
17	Scott Redding	GBR	45	Aprilia Racing Team Gresini	Aprilia RS-GP	M	F: Hard/R: Hard	20	42m 41.997s
18	Thomas Luthi	SWI	12	EG 0,0 Marc VDS	Honda RC213V	M	F: Medium/R: Medium	20	42m 43.117s
19	Cal Crutchlow	GBR	35	LCR Honda CASTROL	Honda RC213V	M	F: Medium/R: Hard	20	42m 51.057s
20	Xavier Simeon	BEL	10	Reale Avintia Racing	Ducati Desmosedici	M	F: Soft/R: Medium	20	42m 51.749s
21	Franco Morbidelli	ITA	21	EG 0,0 Marc VDS	Honda RC213V	M	F: Medium/R: Medium	20	42m 52.515s
	Alex Rins	SPA	42	Team SUZUKI ECSTAR	Suzuki GSX-RR	M	F: Medium/R: Hard	10	DNF-crash
	Hafizh Syahrin	MAL	55	Monster Yamaha Tech 3	Yamaha YZR-M1	M	F: Medium/R: Medium	8	DNF-crash
	Karel Abraham	CZE	17	Angel Nieto Team	Ducati Desmosedici	M	F: Medium/R: Soft	8	DNF-injured

Fastest lap: Marc Marquez, on lap 5, 2m 4.605s, 98.9mph/159.2km/h.
Lap record: Marc Marquez, 2m 3.575s, 99.8mph/160.6km/h (2014).
Event maximum speed: Danilo Petrucci, 216.2mph/347.9km/h (free practice).

Qualifying

Weather: Dry
Air Temp: 22° **Track Temp:** 23°
Humidity: 87%

1	Marquez	2m 03.658s
2	Vinales	2m 04.064s
3	Iannone	2m 04.209s
4	Zarco	2m 04.210s
5	Rossi	2m 04.229s
6	Lorenzo	2m 04.294s
7	Crutchlow	2m 04.456s
8	Dovizioso	2m 04.865s
9	Pedrosa	2m 04.963s
10	Petrucci	2m 05.058s
11	Rins	2m 05.260s
12	P. Espargaro	2m 05.829s
13	Nakagami	2m 05.457s
14	Rabat	2m 05.686s
15	Smith	2m 05.761s
16	Syahrin	2m 05.873s
17	Morbidelli	2m 05.943s
18	Miller	2m 05.966s
19	A. Espargaro	2m 06.035s
20	Luthi	2m 06.222s
21	Bautista	2m 06.296s
22	Redding	2m 06.370s
23	Abraham	2m 06.537s
24	Simeon	2m 06.726s

Fastest race laps

1	Marquez	2m 04.605s
2	Iannone	2m 05.096s
3	Vinales	2m 05.179s
4	Rossi	2m 05.404s
5	Crutchlow	2m 05.636s
6	Zarco	2m 05.652s
7	Dovizioso	2m 05.721s
8	Rins	2m 05.732s
9	Pedrosa	2m 05.753s
10	A. Espargaro	2m 06.175s
11	Rabat	2m 06.209s
12	Miller	2m 06.230s
13	Lorenzo	2m 06.326s
14	Syahrin	2m 06.357s
15	Smith	2m 06.454s
16	Petrucci	2m 06.556s
17	P. Espargaro	2m 06.615s
18	Bautista	2m 06.710s
19	Nakagami	2m 06.768s
20	Morbidelli	2m 06.900s
21	Redding	2m 07.167s
22	Luthi	2m 07.326s
23	Simeon	2m 07.461s
24	Abraham	2m 10.253s

Grid order		1	2	3	4	5	6	7	8	9	10	11	12	13	14	15	16	17	18	19	20	·
25	VINALES	93	93	93	93	93	93	93	93	93	93	93	93	93	93	93	93	93	93	93	93	1
29	IANNONE	29	29	29	29	29	29	25	25	25	25	25	25	25	25	25	25	25	25	25	25	2
5	ZARCO	25	25	25	25	25	25	29	29	29	29	29	29	29	29	29	29	29	29	29	29	3
93	MARQUEZ	35	46	46	46	46	46	46	46	46	46	46	46	46	46	46	46	46	46	46	46	4
46	ROSSI	46	5	5	5	5	5	5	5	5	5	5	5	5	5	5	5	4	4	4	4	5
99	LORENZO	5	35	35	4	4	4	35	4	4	4	4	4	4	4	4	4	5	5	5	5	6
35	CRUTCHLOW	4	4	4	35	35	35	4	26	26	26	26	26	26	26	26	26	26	26	26	26	7
4	DOVIZIOSO	26	26	26	26	26	26	26	42	42	42	99	99	99	53	53	53	53	43	43	53	8
26	PEDROSA	42	99	99	99	42	42	42	99	99	99	53	43	43	99	99	43	43	53	53	43	9
9	PETRUCCI	99	38	42	42	99	99	99	53	53	53	43	53	53	43	43	41	41	41	41	41	10
42	RINS	38	42	38	55	53	53	53	43	43	43	41	41	41	41	41	99	99	99	99	99	11
30	NAKAGAMI	55	55	55	53	55	55	43	55	41	41	9	9	9	9	9	9	9	9	9	9	12
53	RABAT	53	53	53	38	43	43	55	41	9	9	44	44	44	44	44	44	44	44	44	44	13
38	SMITH	43	43	43	43	38	41	41	9	44	44	38	38	38	38	30	30	30	30	30	30	14
44	P. ESPARGARO	44	41	41	41	41	38	38	44	38	38	30	30	30	30	19	19	19	19	19	19	15
55	SYAHRIN	41	44	9	9	9	9	9	38	30	30	19	19	19	19	38	38	38	38	38	38	
21	MORBIDELLI	9	9	44	44	44	44	44	21	19	19	21	45	45	45	45	45	45	45	45	45	
43	MILLER	45	45	30	30	30	30	30	30	21	21	45	12	12	12	12	12	12	12	12	12	
41	A. ESPARGARO	30	30	45	45	21	21	21	19	12	12	12	21	21	21	10	10	10	10	35	35	
12	LUTHI	21	19	21	21	45	19	19	12	45	45	10	10	10	10	21	21	21	21	10	10	
19	BAUTISTA	10	12	19	19	19	45	12	45	10	10	35	35	35	35	35	35	35	35	21	21	
45	REDDING	19	21	12	12	12	12	45	10	35	35											
17	ABRAHAM	12	10	10	10	10	10	10	35													
10	SIMEON	17	17	17	17	17	17	17	17													

17 Pit stop

Championship Points

1	Dovizioso	46
2	Marquez	45
3	Vinales	41
4	Crutchlow	38
5	Zarco	38
6	Iannone	31
7	Rossi	29
8	Miller	26
9	Rabat	22
10	Petrucci	21
11	Pedrosa	18
12	Rins	16
13	Syahrin	9
14	P. Espargaro	8
15	A. Espargaro	6
16	Lorenzo	6
17	Morbidelli	6
18	Nakagami	5
19	Redding	4
20	Bautista	4
21	Abraham	1

Constructor Points

1	Honda	70
2	Yamaha	56
3	Ducati	49
4	Suzuki	39
5	Aprilia	10
6	KTM	8

Moto2

RACE DISTANCE: 18 laps, 61.661 miles/99.234km · RACE WEATHER: Dry (air 21°C, humidity 50%, track 33°C)

Pos.	Rider	Nat.	No.	Entrant	Machine	Laps	Time & Speed
1	**Francesco Bagnaia**	ITA	42	SKY Racing Team VR46	Kalex	18	39m 30.016s 93.6mph/ 150.7km/h
2	**Alex Marquez**	SPA	73	EG 0,0 Marc VDS	Kalex	18	39m 32.480s
3	**Miguel Oliveira**	POR	44	Red Bull KTM Ajo	KTM	18	39m 33.720s
4	**Joan Mir**	SPA	36	EG 0,0 Marc VDS	Kalex	18	39m 35.392s
5	**Iker Lecuona**	SPA	27	Swiss Innovative Investors	KTM	18	39m 36.883s
6	**Brad Binder**	RSA	41	Red Bull KTM Ajo	KTM	18	39m 36.892s
7	**Mattia Pasini**	ITA	54	Italtrans Racing Team	Kalex	18	39m 39.324s
8	**Jorge Navarro**	SPA	9	Federal Oil Gresini Moto2	Kalex	18	39m 40.526s
9	**Dominique Aegerter**	SWI	77	Kiefer Racing	KTM	18	39m 40.611s
10	**Lorenzo Baldassarri**	ITA	7	Pons HP40	Kalex	18	39m 41.513s
11	**Isaac Vinales**	SPA	32	SAG Team	Kalex	18	39m 42.355s
12	**Simone Corsi**	ITA	24	Tasca Racing Scuderia Moto2	Kalex	18	39m 43.474s
13	**Luca Marini**	ITA	10	SKY Racing Team VR46	Kalex	18	39m 44.298s
14	**Andrea Locatelli**	ITA	5	Italtrans Racing Team	Kalex	18	39m 44.564s
15	**Fabio Quartararo**	FRA	20	MB Conveyors - Speed Up Racing	Speed Up	18	39m 47.185s
16	Romano Fenati	ITA	13	Marinelli Snipers Team	Kalex	18	39m 50.625s
17	Remy Gardner	AUS	87	Tech 3 Racing	Tech 3	18	39m 50.837s
18	Hector Barbera	SPA	40	Pons HP40	Kalex	18	39m 57.084s
19	Tetsuta Nagashima	JPN	45	IDEMITSU Honda Team Asia	Kalex	18	39m 57.261s
20	Bo Bendsneyder	NED	64	Tech 3 Racing	Tech 3	18	40m 02.160s
21	Steven Odendaal	RSA	4	NTS RW Racing GP	NTS	18	40m 08.366s
22	Eric Granado	BRA	51	Forward Racing Team	Suter	18	40m 08.595s
23	Joe Roberts	USA	16	NTS RW Racing GP	NTS	18	40m 14.273s
24	Sam Lowes	GBR	22	Swiss Innovative Investors	KTM	18	40m 15.305s
25	Khairul Idham Pawi	MAL	89	IDEMITSU Honda Team Asia	Kalex	18	40m 16.982s
26	Jules Danilo	FRA	95	Nashi Argan SAG Team	Kalex	13	40m 40.380s
27	Zulfahmi Khairuddin	MAL	63	SIC Racing Team	Kalex	13	40m 57.115s
28	Federico Fuligni	ITA	21	Tasca Racing Scuderia Moto2	Kalex	13	40m 57.273s
	Xavi Vierge	SPA	97	Dynavolt Intact GP	Kalex	13	DNF
	Stefano Manzi	ITA	62	Forward Racing Team	Suter	11	DNF
	Marcel Schrotter	GER	23	Dynavolt Intact GP	Kalex	6	DNF
	Danny Kent	GBR	52	MB Conveyors - Speed Up Racing	Speed Up	3	DNF

Fastest lap: Francesco Bagnaia, on lap 6, 2m 11.020s, 94.1mph/151.4km/h.

Lap record: Franco Morbidelli, 2m 9.948s, 94.9mph/152.7km/h (2017).

Event maximum speed: Brad Binder, 177.0mph/284.8km/h (free practice).

Qualifying

Weather: Dry

Air Temp: 22° **Track Temp:** 22°

Humidity: 89%

1	Marquez	2m 10.588s
2	Lowes	2m 10.744s
3	Pasini	2m 10.993s
4	Bagnaia	2m 11.009s
5	Mir	2m 11.124s
6	Marini	2m 11.199s
7	Vierge	2m 11.257s
8	Schrotter	2m 11.276s
9	Quartararo	2m 11.282s
10	Vinales	2m 11.283s
11	Aegerter	2m 11.309s
12	Oliveira	2m 11.321s
13	Lecuona	2m 11.421s
14	Corsi	2m 11.513s
15	Fenati	2m 11.548s
16	Binder	2m 11.566s
17	Baldassarri	2m 11.588s
18	Gardner	2m 11.593s
19	Navarro	2m 11.594s
20	Barbera	2m 11.649s
21	Locatelli	2m 11.699s
22	Kent	2m 11.905s
23	Bendsneyder	2m 12.189s
24	Granado	2m 12.278s
25	Pawi	2m 12.348s
26	Nagashima	2m 12.457s
27	Roberts	2m 12.518s
28	Manzi	2m 12.729s
29	Odendaal	2m 13.213s
30	Danilo	2m 13.340s
31	Khairuddin	2m 13.944s
32	Fuligni	2m 15.296s

Fastest race laps

1	Bagnaia	2m 11.020s
2	Marquez	2m 11.191s
3	Oliveira	2m 11.225s
4	Mir	2m 11.261s
5	Binder	2m 11.283s
6	Pasini	2m 11.283s
7	Lecuona	2m 11.365s
8	Vierge	2m 11.374s
9	Navarro	2m 11.444s
10	Aegerter	2m 11.475s
11	Lowes	2m 11.629s
12	Baldassarri	2m 11.648s
13	Manzi	2m 11.653s
14	Marini	2m 11.663s
15	Vinales	2m 11.676s
16	Schrotter	2m 11.688s
17	Corsi	2m 11.691s
18	Locatelli	2m 11.727s
19	Quartararo	2m 11.727s
20	Gardner	2m 11.807s
21	Fenati	2m 11.920s
22	Nagashima	2m 12.078s
23	Barbera	2m 12.117s
24	Bendsneyder	2m 12.606s
25	Roberts	2m 12.896s
26	Odendaal	2m 13.062s
27	Granado	2m 13.072s
28	Pawi	2m 13.090s
29	Kent	2m 14.002s
30	Danilo	2m 14.177s
31	Fuligni	2m 15.001s
32	Khairuddin	2m 15.387s

Championship Points

1	Bagnaia	57
2	Pasini	47
3	Marquez	47
4	Oliveira	43
5	Baldassarri	39
6	Vierge	28
7	Mir	27
8	Binder	20
9	Lecuona	16
10	Aegerter	16
11	Schrotter	15
12	Gardner	14
13	Navarro	14
14	Marini	10
15	Vinales	7
16	Corsi	6
17	Kent	4
18	Barbera	3
19	Lowes	3
20	Locatelli	3
21	Quartararo	1

Constructor Points

1	Kalex	75
2	KTM	43
3	Tech 3	14
4	Speed Up	5

Moto3

RACE DISTANCE: 17 laps, 58.236 miles/93.721km · RACE WEATHER: Dry (air 17°C, humidity 66%, track 22°C)

Pos.	Rider	Nat.	No.	Entrant	Machine	Laps	Time & Speed
1	**Jorge Martin**	SPA	88	Del Conca Gresini Moto3	Honda	17	39m 12.869s 89.0mph/ 143.3km/h
2	**Enea Bastianini**	ITA	33	Leopard Racing	Honda	17	39m 14.320s
3	**Marco Bezzecchi**	ITA	12	Redox PruestelGP	KTM	17	39m 16.981s
4	**Andrea Migno**	ITA	16	Angel Nieto Team Moto3	KTM	17	39m 17.041s
5	**Fabio Di Giannantonio**	ITA	21	Del Conca Gresini Moto3	Honda	17	39m 17.055s
6	**Philipp Oettl**	GER	65	Sudmetal Schedl GP Racing	KTM	17	39m 17.243s
7	**Jakub Kornfeil**	CZE	84	Redox PruestelGP	KTM	17	39m 18.321s
8	**Aron Canet**	SPA	44	Estrella Galicia 0,0	Honda	17	39m 20.840s
9	**Tatsuki Suzuki**	JPN	24	SIC58 Squadra Corse	Honda	17	39m 21.156s
10	**Livio Loi**	BEL	11	Reale Avintia Academy	KTM	17	39m 21.580s
11	**Ayumu Sasaki**	JPN	71	Petronas Sprinta Racing	Honda	17	39m 23.778s
12	**Gabriel Rodrigo**	ARG	19	RBA BOE Skull Rider	KTM	17	39m 26.614s
13	**Darryn Binder**	RSA	40	Red Bull KTM Ajo	KTM	17	39m 27.401s
14	**John McPhee**	GBR	17	CIP - Green Power	KTM	17	39m 28.940s
15	**Albert Arenas**	SPA	75	Angel Nieto Team Moto3	KTM	17	39m 29.050s
16	Dennis Foggia	ITA	10	SKY Racing Team VR46	KTM	17	39m 32.764s
17	Alonso Lopez	SPA	72	Estrella Galicia 0,0	Honda	17	39m 36.385s
18	Lorenzo Dalla Porta	ITA	48	Leopard Racing	Honda	17	39m 36.626s
19	Makar Yurchenko	KAZ	76	CIP - Green Power	KTM	17	39m 38.293s
20	Tony Arbolino	ITA	14	Marinelli Snipers Team	Honda	17	39m 38.308s
21	Jaume Masia	SPA	5	Bester Capital Dubai	KTM	17	39m 46.766s
22	Kazuki Masaki	JPN	22	RBA BOE Skull Rider	KTM	17	39m 51.221s
23	Nakarin Atiratphuvapat	THA	41	Honda Team Asia	Honda	17	39m 51.231s
24	Niccolo Antonelli	ITA	23	SIC58 Squadra Corse	Honda	17	40m 11.947s
	Marcos Ramirez	SPA	42	Bester Capital Dubai	KTM	12	DNF
	Nicolo Bulega	ITA	8	SKY Racing Team VR46	KTM	5	DNF
	Adam Norrodin	MAL	7	Petronas Sprinta Racing	Honda	2	DNF
	Kaito Toba	JPN	27	Honda Team Asia	Honda	1	DNF

Fastest lap: Enea Bastianini, on lap 14, 2m 17.496s, 89.7mph/144.3km/h.

Lap record: Aron Canet, 2m 15.583s, 90.9mph/146.3km/h (2017).

Event maximum speed: Tony Arbolino, 148.3mph/238.7km/h (free practice).

Qualifying:

Weather: Wet

Air Temp: 19° **Track Temp:** 20°

Humidity: 98%

1	Martin	2m 18.629s
2	Canet	2m 19.125s
3	McPhee	2m 19.421s
4	Suzuki	2m 19.428s
5	Di Giannantonio	2m 19.497s
6	Bastianini	2m 19.577s
7	Foggia	2m 19.588s
8	Sasaki	2m 19.640s
9	Bezzecchi	2m 19.684s
10	Masia	2m 19.808s
11	Oettl	2m 19.816s
12	Rodrigo	2m 19.850s
13	Atiratphuvapat	2m 19.970s
14	Ramirez	2m 20.002s
15	Binder	2m 20.027s
16	Migno	2m 20.257s
17	Dalla Porta	2m 20.323s
18	Yurchenko	2m 20.366s
19	Antonelli	2m 20.380s
20	Arbolino	2m 20.485s
21	Kornfeil	2m 20.824s
22	Lopez	2m 20.917s
23	Bulega	2m 20.965s
24	Arenas	2m 21.021s
25	Norrodin	2m 21.167s
26	Loi	2m 21.279s
27	Masaki	2m 22.820s
28	Toba	2m 23.083s

Fastest race laps

1	Bastianini	2m 17.496s
2	Martin	2m 17.512s
3	Bezzecchi	2m 17.594s
4	Kornfeil	2m 17.769s
5	Migno	2m 17.779s
6	Oettl	2m 17.812s
7	Di Giannantonio	2m 17.876s
8	Binder	2m 18.040s
9	Rodrigo	2m 18.076s
10	Foggia	2m 18.092s
11	Canet	2m 18.117s
12	Suzuki	2m 18.128s
13	Dalla Porta	2m 18.143s
14	Loi	2m 18.240s
15	Antonelli	2m 18.254s
16	McPhee	2m 18.271s
17	Arenas	2m 18.311s
18	Sasaki	2m 18.383s
19	Arbolino	2m 18.488s
20	Lopez	2m 18.691s
21	Masia	2m 18.810s
22	Yurchenko	2m 18.889s
23	Masaki	2m 19.023s
24	Ramirez	2m 19.137s
25	Atiratphuvapat	2m 19.303s
26	Bulega	2m 19.532s

Championship Points

1	Martin	55
2	Canet	48
3	Bezzecchi	43
4	Di Giannantonio	37
5	Bastianini	33
6	Dalla Porta	25
7	Migno	22
8	Rodrigo	22
9	Antonelli	21
10	Kornfeil	18
11	Norrodin	16
12	Sasaki	13
13	Lopez	10
14	Oettl	10
15	Toba	9
16	Suzuki	7
17	Loi	7
18	Arbolino	6
19	Ramirez	5
20	Masia	4
21	Masaki	3
22	Binder	3
23	McPhee	2
24	Arenas	1

Constructor Points

1	Honda	70
2	KTM	52

Main: Marquez in control; Lorenzo, Pedrosa and Dovizioso chase, heading for disaster.
Photo: Repsol Honda

Insets, clockwise from top: Serial winner Marquez lifts the Angel Nieto trophy; first-timer Oettl and second-timer Baldassarri savour victory.
Photos: Gold & Goose

FIM WORLD CHAMPIONSHIP · ROUND 4

SPANISH GRAND PRIX

JEREZ-ANGEL NIETO CIRCUIT

Above: Iannone saw off Miller and Rossi for a second rostrum in a row.
Photo: Team Ecstar Suzuki

Top right: Hot property. Johann Zarco announced that he was switching to KTM for 2019.

Above right: Michael Bartholemy was at the centre of accusations of corruption.
Photos: Gold & Goose

Above far right: Vinales was back to complaining about handling issues.
Photo: Monster Energy

Right: The KTMs play trains. Espargaro, Kallio and Smith, and the pursuing Nakagami would shuffle order by the end.

Below right: Cal Crutchlow was another front-runner to crash out.
Photos: Gold & Goose

THE European season opened the floodgates. News breaks aplenty kept the twitterati hash-tagging, while a whiff of financial scandal mingled with the traditional Jerez firecrackers. Overseeing it all, a new bronze statue of Angel Nieto, at a fully resurfaced circuit that henceforth would bear his name. Nieto, 12-plus-one-times champion, who had died in 2017, was uniquely remembered as the 68,000-strong crowd rose in orchestrated cheers on the 13th lap of each race.

It was a quirky touch to a busy weekend, during which KTM grabbed most of the banner headlines.

Firstly these concerned the hottest unsold property in the rider market, Johann Zarco. With no place at the factory Yamaha team, he revealed that he had rejected advances by Repsol Honda. In fact, these had come too late. Even before the first race, he had been pledged to KTM.

"It's a great challenge: a European bike with a European rider. The way KTM improved last year makes me think something is possible," he said. As for the thought of Honda: "I was talking with my coach, that if you are with Marquez and if you want to win races, you would have to improve your riding level a lot, so I thought with that level, I could be fast also with KTM. We were thinking, if you put Marc on the KTM, where would it be?"

Zarco had been signed up for two years, alongside current teamster Pol Espargaro. Bradley Smith appeared to be headed into the cold: the role of test rider was already well occupied by Mika Kallio.

According to a beaming KTM Motorsports Director Pit Beirer, Zarco had not been lured with extravagant promises of future developments, but by "the spirit of the team". At the same time, Kallio's performance, wild-card on a 2019 prototype, would certainly have inspired confidence.

The new bike had the direction of crankshaft rotation reversed, bringing it into line with all the other MotoGP bikes, and offering different (and most thought better) corner entry and exit characteristics. Kallio took it to the top ten, beating both full-time riders, albeit by the narrowest of margins.

The Austrian manufacturer had made another capture: the French Tech 3 squad, directly associated with Yamaha since 1998, first with 250s and then as the satellite 500/MotoGP team. Lured by the promise of full factory status and equipment, team owner (and IRTA president) Herve Poncharal had switched allegiance.

Further KTM news was that current Moto2 star Miguel Oliveira had been the first signing for the revised Tech 3 effort, where he would inherit Zarco's full pit crew, headed by the redoubtable Guy Coulon. This was a first demonstration of KTM's unique ladder of talent, able to guide riders class by class all the way from Moto3 to MotoGP.

Yamaha was now to be bereft of a long-term partner, which in the past had served as a transit camp for factory-team riders (Edwards and Spies), and a way to extend the service life of otherwise redundant racing machines. And more recently as something of an embarrassment, as their own technical direction faltered while Zarco made hay on a 2016 bike. This happened again at Jerez, with familiar problems for Rossi and especially Vinales in high-heat/low-grip conditions, in spite of their own reversion to a '2016-type' chassis design. Zarco explained a lack of edge grip at the high lean angles that were the M-1's stock in trade, having been made for fast sweeping corner lines, unlike the stop-and-go Hondas and point-and-squirt Ducatis.

With MotoGP entries frozen at least until 2021, one way or another, a new Yamaha partner would have to be found among the existing teams. Until that point, the search had focused on the Marc VDS team, where Belgian brewing billionaire owner Marc van der Straten had been hoping for something better than the B-grade Hondas they'd used since moving to the big class in 2015. But Yamaha were not the only suitors. Suzuki were also seriously considering adding their own first satellite team, and it was widely believed that they were about to sign a contract with VDS at Jerez.

The first fly in the ointment was that Suzuki race boss Shinichi Sahara, suffering back pain and unable to travel, had cancelled his trip. By the end of the weekend, however, all previous plans had been blown sky high and the Belgian-based team was engulfed in scandal.

The murky story surfaced on German-language website Speedweek.com, which reported on allegations by a disaffected former team member of wholesale corruption and large-scale embezzlement by team principal Michael Bartholemy. The Belgian vehemently protested his innocence amid threats of legal action, and the affair would play out over the next two races, after which an amicable settlement was reached, with Bartholemy out, but no further action. The immediate future of the team, fielding Morbidelli and Luthi in MotoGP, and Marquez and Mir in Moto2, seemed secure, and van der Straten pledged to see out the contract until 2021 – but events certainly put a hold on any plans with Suzuki or Yamaha.

For a second race in succession, Dovizioso used the aero bodywork, citing better front-end grip in the track's relatively few fast corners, notably the two right-handers at the end of the lap. Team-mate Lorenzo was encouraged with new chassis settings that settled the bike better in the fast bends, playing to his style. Now openly admitting that he was riding for his future with Ducati, he had "a little bit of happiness". The race came to an abrupt end for both of them, along with Pedrosa, with a spectacular three-bike tangle. Afterwards, Dovi ran to try to restart, only to discover he'd picked up Lorenzo's bike instead of his own.

This sort of scary crash is a corollary of very close racing, and there was another at the same spot in Moto3. In each case, they were potentially very influential in each championship, while mercifully there were no major injuries.

The GP Commission met and, in response to the many layers of confusion in the Argentine, revised the start-line rules, specifically that a rider who stalls on the grid would now be allowed to switch to another machine. Existing rules were clarified, specifying that "attempting to restart the motorcycle on the grid is not permitted."

MOTOGP RACE – 25 laps

Erstwhile championship leader Crutchlow employed a two-stop qualifying strategy to claim his fourth pole position, ahead of Pedrosa and Zarco (his eighth front row in succession). Likewise, Lorenzo took advantage of the short track, missing the front row by barely a hundredth, to head Marquez and Rins on the second.

Dovi, through from Q1, was in the middle of row three; Vinales also came through, but could do no better than 11th, one down on team-mate Rossi.

Thanks to the full resurface, pole was a new record.

Marquez fell twice in practice and again in warm-up, but was confident. "On this track, anyone can do one quick lap. But the race is long and you have to manage many things – tyres and the way the bike changes through the race."

Lorenzo led away and for the first seven laps. Pedrosa, Zarco, Marquez and Crutchlow had followed, but the last-named lasted for only seven laps before losing the front at Turn One.

Marquez took two laps to dispose of Zarco and Pedrosa, but then "it was almost impossible to pass Lorenzo. He was like the old Lorenzo, really late on the brakes and fast out of the corners. Then I saw his tyres were going a bit, and it was the time to attack."

He drew steadily clear, the gap beyond two seconds on lap 16. His only big scare was a lurid slide after Luthi crashed and scattered gravel on the ultra-rapid Turn 11. "When I saw the stones, I was too late. So I said, 'We'll see what happens.' I don't know how I stayed on the bike," he laughed. "After that, I thought I would have to win, because somebody was looking after me."

Thus he took the title lead.

Lorenzo was blocking. The only rider to choose the soft front, he was becoming slower mid-corner. But Dovizioso also found him hard to pass, helping Marquez escape.

This indirectly caused the crucial crash, Dovi thought, blaming both Pedrosa and Lorenzo. "Somebody made a mis-

Above: Zarco was second again, thanks to the big crash that took place ahead of him.

Top right: Baldassarri heads Oliveira and early leader Marquez en route to his second Moto2 win.

Top far right: A penalty denied rookie Lopez a podium in his fourth grand prix.

Above right: Italian flatmates Baldassarri and Bagnaia exchange post-race congratulations.
Photos: Monster Energy

Above far right: Canet, Martin and Arbolino on the deck. Bastianini was a fourth victim; Canet was penalised for his error.

Right: Philipp Oettl celebrates his first grand prix victory.
Photos: Gold & Goose

take." In fact, it wasn't really anybody's fault. A racing incident. Dovi went inside Lorenzo at the hairpin, but ran wide. Lorenzo cut back just as Pedrosa was diving up the inside to try to pass both. They touched, and all three went looping and tumbling. It was spectacular.

At this point, Zarco was less than three seconds adrift, and hoping to catch the group and fight for the podium, having lost places with a slide in the early laps. "Then I could not believe when I saw all those bikes were down. You need some luck sometimes. When the chance comes to you, you must catch it."

Early on, he'd dropped to seventh, behind Rins. But the Suzuki rider lasted only one more lap before his third crash in four races.

Team-mate Iannone was now chasing, but by half-distance the gap was two seconds and stretching, and the Italian needed to pay more attention to those behind.

Petrucci had caught and passed fast-starting Rossi; and now second Pramac rider Miller was catching them both, the trio closing on Iannone.

With five laps to go, Petrucci passed the Suzuki at the same time as Miller took Rossi; and the four stayed locked together to the finish – by which time Iannone had got back ahead of Petrucci, and Rossi of Miller.

Iannone admitted that he had been lucky after switching from a medium to a hard rear on the grid, and struggling with acceleration: "I think it was not a good decision." It was Suzuki's third podium in a row, for the first time since 2007.

Petrucci's plan had been to repass him on the last lap, but "he had something more than me on traction." Rossi simply said, "We were lucky for sixth ... we didn't have the pace and we need to work." Miller said he'd destroyed his front tyre regaining places after a bad start from the fourth row.

Almost four seconds behind, the unhappy Vinales finally got in front of Bautista's Ducati for seventh. Rookie Morbidelli had been ahead of them both until fading front grip dropped him behind, but he still took a first top-ten.

There was another small gap, then Kallio held off permanent Red Bull KTM rider Espargaro for tenth. Nakagami, in 12th, had passed Smith's KTM on the last lap. Rabat also had caught right up to Smith by the end; miles behind, Redding took the last point.

As well as the six crashers, Aleix Espargaro (Aprilia) retired with pneumatic-valve-spring failure on the first lap.

MOTO2 RACE – 23 laps

Training crashes had eliminated two strong riders during the gap following the US GP. Remy Gardner had suffered a double leg fracture in an awkward landing while motocrossing at Montmelo; Domi Aegerter also required surgery after a fall while enduro training fractured his pelvis. Gardner's place for the upcoming races was taken by Spaniard Hector Garzo, who had replaced him on the Tech 3 at the German GP in 2017; while rising German teenager Lukas Tulovic took over the Kiefer Team KTM.

Baldassarri set a new best lap on Saturday morning and (going slightly slower) a career first pole in the afternoon, heading a close time sheet with 20 riders inside less than a second.

Marquez's late bid was enough for second, with Bagnaia completing the front row; Navarro headed the second, from Binder and the ever impressive Mir. Oliveira, only six-tenths from pole, crashed on his last run and ended up 14th.

Again, the race was processional, after Marquez crashed out of third place on lap 11. Winner in 2017, he had led

the first two laps, before dropping back behind Baldassarri and Binder.

Oliveira, meanwhile, was on strong form once again and cutting through rapidly. On lap five, he took second from Binder and began pushing on to attack the leader. He was just over a tenth of a second adrift on lap eight, but Baldassarri, who had already set the only new lap record of the day, kicked again, and by lap 14, he was a full second clear.

There was nobody threatening the KTM, and the Portuguese rider settled for second.

Bagnaia had taken fourth off the slowly fading Binder on lap eight, then inherited third when Marquez fell at a slow corner, knocking off a footpeg so he couldn't restart. Bagnaia was too far behind to improve on that, and over the final laps had his hands full fending off Argentine GP runner-up Vierge.

Pasini was never close enough to make a difference, but successfully dropped Binder. Earlier, the Italian veteran had clashed with class rookie Fenati, pushing the Marinelli Kalex rider into a crash, which left him shaking his fist angrily.

Austin injury victim Marcel Schrotter was a fighting seventh, having got the better of Lowes. A little way back, Lecuona had held off Quartararo to round out the top ten.

Mir took 11th, ahead of Corsi by a couple of tenths; then came a gang of four: Nagashima, Barbera, Locatelli and Bendsneyder, the last out of the points by less than a quarter of a second.

There were a number of crashes, with Marini sanctioned by six grid places at the next race for his part in knocking down Navarro on the first lap. Navarro remounted, but finished out of the points.

Others to fall included Manzi and both NTS riders, Joe Roberts and Steven Odendaal; Tulovic and Garzo were never in real contention.

MOTO3 RACE – 22 laps

Philipp Oettl joined the ranks of father-and-son GP winners with a narrow (0.059 of a second) victory in a topsy-turvy Moto3 race, during which four of the lead pack crashed out with four laps to go and KTM inherited a first podium lock-out in years.

Oettl deserved his first win after 91 starts. He'd led across the line several times and was always well placed in a pack that had only dropped from 18 riders to six in the closing stages. He had to hold off a pushing Bezzecchi, with just two left up front after a kamikaze move by Canet had knocked out fellow Honda riders Martin, Bastianini and Arbolino, all erstwhile leaders.

It had been a massive indiscretion, but perhaps also an accident waiting to happen. The pack was so huge, the proximity breathless. On the first lap, Dalla Porta, wild-card Alcoba, Foggia and McPhee had tangled (McPhee's fault: for a six-place grid penalty), and it was surprising that there were not more incidents.

Pole qualifier Martin led away; then Bastianini and Bezzecchi. But it was all notional, Moto3 style. At half-distance, the top 18 were covered by 2.5 seconds.

Canet had come from 14th on the grid, and his fateful lunge at the Dry Sack hairpin did nothing for his reputation. It earned him a back-of-the-grid start at the next race.

The remaining pack grappled for the final podium position. Rookie Lopez crossed the line at the front, but was dropped one position for exceeding track limits, which gave a first podium to Marcos Ramirez.

All up close, third to 12th inside just half a second, with Masia fifth, while Suzuki, Di Giannantonio, Kornfeil, Toba and Rodrigo completed the top ten.

GRAN PREMIO RED BULL DE ESPAÑA

4-6 MAY, 2018

CIRCUITO DE JEREZ

25 laps
Length: 4.423 km. / 2.748 miles
Width: 11m

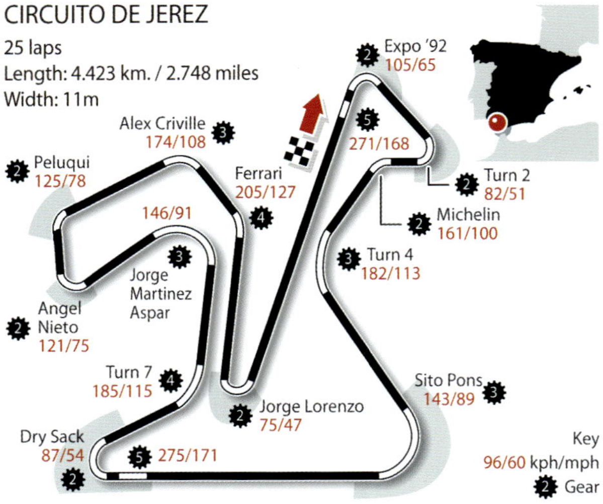

MotoGP

RACE DISTANCE: 25 laps, 68.708 miles/110.575km · RACE WEATHER: Dry (air 25°C, humidity 41%, track 40°C)

Pos.	Rider	Nat.	No.	Entrant	Machine	Tyres	Race tyre choice	Laps	Time & speed
1	**Marc Marquez**	SPA	93	Repsol Honda Team	Honda RC213V	M	F: Hard/R: Medium	25	41m 39.678s 98.9mph/ 159.2km/h
2	**Johann Zarco**	FRA	5	Monster Yamaha Tech 3	Yamaha YZR-M1	M	F: Medium/R: Medium	25	41m 44.919s
3	**Andrea Iannone**	ITA	29	Team SUZUKI ECSTAR	Suzuki GSX-RR	M	F: Medium/R: Hard	25	41m 47.892s
4	**Danilo Petrucci**	ITA	9	Alma Pramac Racing	Ducati Desmosedici	M	F: Medium/R: Medium	25	41m 48.295s
5	**Valentino Rossi**	ITA	46	Movistar Yamaha MotoGP	Yamaha YZR-M1	M	F: Medium/R: Medium	25	41m 48.421s
6	**Jack Miller**	AUS	43	Alma Pramac Racing	Ducati Desmosedici	M	F: Hard/R: Hard	25	41m 49.446s
7	**Maverick Vinales**	SPA	25	Movistar Yamaha MotoGP	Yamaha YZR-M1	M	F: Medium/R: Medium	25	41m 53.221s
8	**Alvaro Bautista**	SPA	19	Angel Nieto Team	Ducati Desmosedici	M	F: Medium/R: Medium	25	41m 53.754s
9	**Franco Morbidelli**	ITA	21	EG 0,0 Marc VDS	Honda RC213V	M	F: Hard/R: Medium	25	41m 56.500s
10	**Mika Kallio**	FIN	36	Red Bull KTM Factory Racing	KTM RC16	M	F: Medium/R: Medium	25	41m 59.083s
11	**Pol Espargaro**	SPA	44	Red Bull KTM Factory Racing	KTM RC16	M	F: Medium/R: Medium	25	42m 00.827s
12	**Takaaki Nakagami**	JPN	30	LCR Honda IDEMITSU	Honda RC213V	M	F: Hard/R: Medium	25	42m 00.852s
13	**Bradley Smith**	GBR	38	Red Bull KTM Factory Racing	KTM RC16	M	F: Medium/R: Medium	25	42m 01.443s
14	**Tito Rabat**	SPA	53	Reale Avintia Racing	Ducati Desmosedici	M	F: Medium/R: Medium	25	42m 01.781s
15	**Scott Redding**	GBR	45	Aprilia Racing Team Gresini	Aprilia RS-GP	M	F: Hard/R: Hard	25	42m 16.433s
16	Hafizh Syahrin	MAL	55	Monster Yamaha Tech 3	Yamaha YZR-M1	M	F: Medium/R: Medium	25	42m 21.539s
17	Xavier Simeon	BEL	10	Reale Avintia Racing	Ducati Desmosedici	M	F: Medium/R: Medium	25	42m 28.919s
18	Karel Abraham	CZE	17	Angel Nieto Team	Ducati Desmosedici	M	F: Medium/R: Medium	24	42m 22.308s
	Jorge Lorenzo	SPA	99	Ducati Team	Ducati Desmosedici	M	F: Soft/R: Medium	17	DNF-crash
	Andrea Dovizioso	ITA	4	Ducati Team	Ducati Desmosedici	M	F: Hard/R: Medium	17	DNF-crash
	Dani Pedrosa	SPA	26	Repsol Honda Team	Honda RC213V	M	F: Hard/R: Medium	17	DNF-crash
	Cal Crutchlow	GBR	35	LCR Honda CASTROL	Honda RC213V	M	F: Hard/R: Medium	16	DNF-crash
	Thomas Luthi	SWI	12	EG 0,0 Marc VDS	Honda RC213V	M	F: Medium/R: Medium	11	DNF-crash
	Alex Rins	SPA	42	Team SUZUKI ECSTAR	Suzuki GSX-RR	M	F: Hard/R: Hard	5	DNF-crash
	Aleix Espargaro	SPA	41	Aprilia Racing Team Gresini	Aprilia RS-GP	M	F: Hard/R: Medium	0	DNF-technical

Fastest lap: Marc Marquez, on lap 16, 1m 39.159s, 99.7mph/160.5km/h.
Lap record: Jorge Lorenzo, 1m 38.735s, 100.2mph/161.2km/h (2015).
Event maximum speed: Andrea Dovizioso, 182.7mph/294.1km/h (race).

Qualifying

Weather: Dry
Air Temp: 24° **Humidity:** 45%
Track Temp: 44°

1	Crutchlow	1m 37.653s
2	Pedrosa	1m 37.912s
3	Zarco	1m 37.956s
4	Lorenzo	1m 37.969s
5	Marquez	1m 37.977s
6	Rins	1m 37.984s
7	Iannone	1m 37.987s
8	Dovizioso	1m 38.029s
9	Petrucci	1m 38.086s
10	Rossi	1m 38.267s
11	Vinales	1m 38.281s
12	Miller	1m 38.522s
13	A. Espargaro	1m 38.389s
14	Nakagami	1m 38.481s
15	Morbidelli	1m 38.544s
16	P. Espargaro	1m 38.598s
17	Rabat	1m 38.610s
18	Luthi	1m 38.752s
19	Kallio	1m 38.759s
20	Bautista	1m 38.838s
21	Smith	1m 38.961s
22	Syahrin	1m 39.135s
23	Abraham	1m 39.146s
24	Simeon	1m 39.708s
25	Redding	1m 39.918s

Fastest race laps

1	Marquez	1m 39.159s
2	Dovizioso	1m 39.208s
3	Lorenzo	1m 39.274s
4	Rins	1m 39.276s
5	Crutchlow	1m 39.299s
6	Pedrosa	1m 39.314s
7	Zarco	1m 39.317s
8	Iannone	1m 39.347s
9	Petrucci	1m 39.530s
10	Rossi	1m 39.616s
11	Miller	1m 39.620s
12	Morbidelli	1m 39.754s
13	Bautista	1m 39.839s
14	Vinales	1m 39.843s
15	Abraham	1m 40.026s
16	Nakagami	1m 40.027s
17	Smith	1m 40.050s
18	Kallio	1m 40.117s
19	Rabat	1m 40.180s
20	P. Espargaro	1m 40.194s
21	Luthi	1m 40.217s
22	Redding	1m 40.455s
23	Syahrin	1m 40.709s
24	Simeon	1m 40.856s

Championship Points

1	Marquez	70
2	Zarco	58
3	Viñales	50
4	Iannone	47
5	Dovizioso	46
6	Rossi	40
7	Crutchlow	38
8	Miller	36
9	Petrucci	34
10	Rabat	24
11	Pedrosa	18
12	Rins	16
13	Morbidelli	13
14	P. Espargaro	13
15	Bautista	12
16	Syahrin	9
17	Nakagami	9
18	A. Espargaro	6
19	Kallio	6
20	Lorenzo	6
21	Redding	5
22	Smith	3
23	Abraham	1

Constructor Points

1	Honda	95
2	Yamaha	76
3	Ducati	62
4	Suzuki	55
5	KTM	14
6	Aprilia	11

Grid order	1	2	3	4	5	6	7	8	9	10	11	12	13	14	15	16	17	18	19	20	21	22	23	24	25	
35 CRUTCHLOW	99	99	99	99	99	99	99	93	93	93	93	93	93	93	93	93	93	93	93	93	93	93	93	93	93	1
26 PEDROSA	26	26	93	93	93	93	93	99	99	99	99	99	99	99	99	99	99	5	5	5	5	5	5	5	5	2
5 ZARCO	5	93	26	26	26	26	26	26	4	4	4	4	4	4	26	4	4	29	29	9	9	9	9	29	29	3
99 LORENZO	93	5	5	5	35	35	35	4	26	26	26	26	26	26	4	26	26	9	9	29	29	29	29	9	9	4
93 MARQUEZ	35	35	35	35	42	4	4	5	5	5	5	5	5	5	5	5	5	46	46	43	43	43	46	46	46	5
42 RINS	42	42	42	4	4	5	5	29	29	29	29	29	29	29	29	29	29	43	43	46	46	46	43	43	43	6
29 IANNONE	29	4	4	42	5	29	29	9	9	9	9	9	9	9	9	9	9	19	19	19	19	19	19	25	25	7
4 DOVIZIOSO	4	29	29	29	29	46	46	46	46	46	46	46	46	46	46	46	46	21	21	25	25	25	25	19	19	8
9 PETRUCCI	46	46	46	46	46	9	9	43	43	43	43	43	43	43	43	43	43	25	25	21	21	21	21	21	21	9
46 ROSSI	25	9	9	9	9	43	43	21	21	21	21	21	21	21	21	21	21	44	44	44	44	36	36	36	36	10
25 VINALES	9	25	21	43	43	21	21	19	19	19	19	19	19	19	19	19	19	36	36	36	36	38	38	38	44	11
43 MILLER	21	21	25	21	21	25	19	25	25	25	25	25	25	25	25	25	25	38	38	38	38	44	44	44	30	12
41 A. ESPARGARO	43	43	43	25	25	19	25	38	38	38	38	38	38	38	38	38	38	30	30	30	30	30	30	30	38	13
30 NAKAGAMI	38	38	38	19	19	38	38	44	44	44	44	44	44	44	44	44	44	53	53	53	53	53	53	53	53	14
21 MORBIDELLI	44	44	19	38	38	44	44	36	36	36	36	36	36	36	36	36	36	45	45	45	45	45	45	45	45	15
44 P. ESPARGARO	30	19	44	44	44	36	36	17	17	17	30	30	30	30	30	30	30	55	55	55	55	55	55	55	55	
53 RABAT	36	30	30	36	36	17	17	30	30	30	12	53	53	53	53	53	53	10	10	10	10	10	10	10	10	
12 LUTHI	19	36	36	17	17	30	30	53	53	53	53	55	45	45	45	45	45	17	17	17	17	17	17	17		
36 KALLIO	17	17	17	30	30	53	53	12	12	12	55	45	55	55	55	55	55									
19 BAUTISTA	53	53	53	53	53	12	12	45	55	55	45	10	10	10	10	10	10									
38 SMITH	12	12	12	12	12	45	45	55	45	45	10	35	35	35	35	35	17									
55 SYAHRIN	45	45	45	45	45	55	55	10	10	10	35	17	17	17	17	17										
17 ABRAHAM	55	55	55	55	55	10	10	35	35	35	17															
10 SIMEON	10	10	10	10	10																					
45 REDDING																										

17 Lapped rider

Moto2

RACE DISTANCE: 23 laps, 63.210 miles/101.729km · RACE WEATHER: Dry (air 23°C, humidity 45%, track 36°C)

Pos.	Rider	Nat.	No.	Entrant	Machine	Laps	Time & Speed
1	**Lorenzo Baldassarri**	ITA	7	Pons HP40	Kalex	23	39m 33.889s 95.8mph/ 154.2km/h
2	**Miguel Oliveira**	POR	44	Red Bull KTM Ajo	KTM	23	39m 36.740s
3	**Francesco Bagnaia**	ITA	42	SKY Racing Team VR46	Kalex	23	39m 40.139s
4	**Xavi Vierge**	SPA	97	Dynavolt Intact GP	Kalex	23	39m 40.842s
5	**Mattia Pasini**	ITA	54	Italtrans Racing Team	Kalex	23	39m 44.027s
6	**Brad Binder**	RSA	41	Red Bull KTM Ajo	KTM	23	39m 45.620s
7	**Marcel Schrotter**	GER	23	Dynavolt Intact GP	Kalex	23	39m 52.027s
8	**Sam Lowes**	GBR	22	Swiss Innovative Investors	KTM	23	39m 52.566s
9	**Iker Lecuona**	SPA	27	Swiss Innovative Investors	KTM	23	39m 54.632s
10	**Fabio Quartararo**	FRA	20	Beta Tools - Speed Up Racing	Speed Up	23	39m 54.676s
11	**Joan Mir**	SPA	36	EG 0,0 Marc VDS	Kalex	23	39m 57.091s
12	**Simone Corsi**	ITA	24	Tasca Racing Scuderia Moto2	Kalex	23	39m 57.308s
13	**Tetsuta Nagashima**	JPN	45	IDEMITSU Honda Team Asia	Kalex	23	40m 00.021s
14	**Hector Barbera**	SPA	40	Pons HP40	Kalex	23	40m 00.840s
15	**Andrea Locatelli**	ITA	5	Italtrans Racing Team	Kalex	23	40m 01.010s
16	Bo Bendsneyder	NED	64	Tech 3 Racing	Tech 3	23	40m 01.266s
17	Jorge Navarro	SPA	9	Federal Oil Gresini Moto2	Kalex	23	40m 07.082s
18	Khairul Idham Pawi	MAL	89	IDEMITSU Honda Team Asia	Kalex	23	40m 07.723s
19	Isaac Vinales	SPA	32	SAG Team	Kalex	23	40m 18.540s
20	Lukas Tulovic	GER	3	Kiefer Racing	KTM	23	40m 22.937s
21	Federico Fuligni	ITA	21	Tasca Racing Scuderia Moto2	Kalex	23	40m 24.222s
22	Xavi Cardelus	AND	18	Team Stylobike	Kalex	23	40m 26.905s
23	Hector Garzo	SPA	14	Tech 3 Racing	Tech 3	23	40m 33.378s
24	Jules Danilo	FRA	95	Nashi Argan SAG Team	Kalex	22	40m 11.543s
	Steven Odendaal	RSA	4	NTS RW Racing GP	NTS	21	DNF
	Joe Roberts	USA	16	NTS RW Racing GP	NTS	13	DNF
	Alex Marquez	SPA	73	EG 0,0 Marc VDS	Kalex	10	DNF
	Danny Kent	GBR	52	Beta Tools - Speed Up Racing	Speed Up	10	DNF
	Zulfahmi Khairuddin	MAL	63	SIC Racing Team	Kalex	9	DNF
	Stefano Manzi	ITA	62	Forward Racing Team	Suter	8	DNF
	Romano Fenati	ITA	13	Marinelli Snipers Team	Kalex	6	DNF
	Eric Granado	BRA	51	Forward Racing Team	Suter	2	DNF
	Luca Marini	ITA	10	SKY Racing Team VR46	Kalex	0	DNF

Fastest lap: Lorenzo Baldassarri, on lap 6, 1m 42.480s, 96.5mph/155.3km/h.

Lap record: Franco Morbidelli, 1m 42.596s, 96.4mph/155.1km/h (2017).

Event maximum speed: Brad Binder, 177.0mph/284.8km/h (free practice).

Qualifying

Weather: Dry

Air: 28° **Track:** 46°

Humidity: 38%

1	Baldassarri	1m 41.925s
2	Marquez	1m 41.996s
3	Bagnaia	1m 42.064s
4	Navarro	1m 42.324s
5	Binder	1m 42.362s
6	Mir	1m 42.367s
7	Vierge	1m 42.404s
8	Lowes	1m 42.408s
9	Fenati	1m 42.437s
10	Pasini	1m 42.439s
11	Kent	1m 42.480s
12	Marini	1m 42.513s
13	Corsi	1m 42.567s
14	Oliveira	1m 42.573s
15	Barbera	1m 42.590s
16	Nagashima	1m 42.660s
17	Schrotter	1m 42.772s
18	Quartararo	1m 42.797s
19	Lecuona	1m 42.798s
20	Locatelli	1m 42.896s
21	Vinales	1m 43.029s
22	Manzi	1m 43.064s
23	Bendsneyder	1m 43.085s
24	Tulovic	1m 43.256s
25	Pawi	1m 43.334s
26	Odendaal	1m 43.600s
27	Roberts	1m 43.613s
28	Granado	1m 43.943s
29	Danilo	1m 44.179s
30	Garzo	1m 44.327s
31	Cardelus	1m 44.382s
32	Fuligni	1m 44.626s
33	Khairuddin	1m 44.855s

Fastest race laps

1	Baldassarri	1m 42.480s
2	Oliveira	1m 42.510s
3	Marquez	1m 42.526s
4	Bagnaia	1m 42.598s
5	Binder	1m 42.742s
6	Navarro	1m 42.758s
7	Fenati	1m 42.853s
8	Pasini	1m 42.870s
9	Vierge	1m 42.897s
10	Schrotter	1m 43.028s
11	Lowes	1m 43.235s
12	Mir	1m 43.236s
13	Corsi	1m 43.253s
14	Lecuona	1m 43.268s
15	Quartararo	1m 43.281s
16	Kent	1m 43.313s
17	Locatelli	1m 43.485s
18	Bendsneyder	1m 43.504s
19	Odendaal	1m 43.520s
20	Pawi	1m 43.541s
21	Barbera	1m 43.543s
22	Nagashima	1m 43.578s
23	Roberts	1m 43.614s
24	Manzi	1m 43.654s
25	Vinales	1m 43.713s
26	Tulovic	1m 44.167s
27	Fuligni	1m 44.189s
28	Cardelus	1m 44.263s
29	Garzo	1m 44.301s
30	Danilo	1m 44.643s
31	Khairuddin	1m 45.197s
32	Granado	2m 13.306s

Championship Points

1	Bagnaia	73
2	Baldassarri	64
3	Oliveira	63
4	Pasini	58
5	Marquez	47
6	Vierge	41
7	Mir	32
8	Binder	30
9	Schrotter	24
10	Lecuona	23
11	Aegerter	16
12	Gardner	14
13	Navarro	14
14	Lowes	11
15	Marini	10
16	Corsi	10
17	Quartararo	7
18	Vinales	7
19	Barbera	5
20	Kent	4
21	Locatelli	4
22	Nagashima	3

Constructor Points

1	Kalex	100
2	KTM	63
3	Tech 3	14
4	Speed Up	11

Moto3

RACE DISTANCE: 22 laps, 60.460 miles/97.306km · RACE WEATHER: Dry (air 22°C, humidity 47%, track 19°C)

Pos.	Rider	Nat.	No.	Entrant	Machine	Laps	Time & Speed
1	**Philipp Oettl**	GER	65	Sudmetal Schedl GP Racing	KTM	22	39m 39.799s 91.4mph/ 147.1km/h
2	**Marco Bezzecchi**	ITA	12	Redox PruestelGP	KTM	22	39m 39.858s
3	**Marcos Ramirez**	SPA	42	Bester Capital Dubai	KTM	22	39m 43.532s
4	**Alonso Lopez**	SPA	72	Estrella Galicia 0,0	Honda	22	39m 43.314s
5	**Jaume Masia**	SPA	5	Bester Capital Dubai	KTM	22	39m 43.757s
6	**Tatsuki Suzuki**	JPN	24	SIC58 Squadra Corse	Honda	22	39m 43.799s
7	**Fabio Di Giannantonio**	ITA	21	Del Conca Gresini Moto3	Honda	22	39m 43.832s
8	**Jakub Kornfeil**	CZE	84	Redox PruestelGP	KTM	22	39m 43.960s
9	**Kaito Toba**	JPN	27	Honda Team Asia	Honda	22	39m 43.970s
10	**Gabriel Rodrigo**	ARG	19	RBA BOE Skull Rider	KTM	22	39m 44.015s
11	**Niccolo Antonelli**	ITA	23	SIC58 Squadra Corse	Honda	22	39m 43.975s
12	**Ayumu Sasaki**	JPN	71	Petronas Sprinta Racing	Honda	22	39m 44.063s
13	**Andrea Migno**	ITA	16	Angel Nieto Team Moto3	KTM	22	39m 47.965s
14	**Makar Yurchenko**	KAZ	76	CIP - Green Power	KTM	22	39m 48.181s
15	**Ai Ogura**	JPN	32	Asia Talent Team	Honda	22	40m 07.096s
16	Adam Norrodin	MAL	7	Petronas Sprinta Racing	Honda	22	40m 07.145s
17	Nicolo Bulega	ITA	8	SKY Racing Team VR46	KTM	22	40m 07.373s
18	Livio Loi	BEL	11	Reale Avintia Academy	KTM	22	40m 07.398s
19	Nakarin Atiratphuvapat	THA	41	Honda Team Asia	Honda	22	40m 07.594s
20	Kazuki Masaki	JPN	22	RBA BOE Skull Rider	KTM	22	40m 16.841s
	Enea Bastianini	ITA	33	Leopard Racing	Honda	18	DNF
	Tony Arbolino	ITA	14	Marinelli Snipers Team	Honda	18	DNF
	Jorge Martin	SPA	88	Del Conca Gresini Moto3	Honda	18	DNF
	Aron Canet	SPA	44	Estrella Galicia 0,0	Honda	18	DNF
	Albert Arenas	SPA	75	Angel Nieto Team Moto3	KTM	13	DNF
	Lorenzo Dalla Porta	ITA	48	Leopard Racing	Honda	0	DNF
	Dennis Foggia	ITA	10	SKY Racing Team VR46	KTM	0	DNF
	John McPhee	GBR	17	CIP - Green Power	KTM	0	DNF
	Jeremy Alcoba	SPA	52	Junior Team Estrella Galicia 0,0	Honda	0	DNF

Fastest lap: Alonso Lopez, on lap 2, 1m 46.730s, 92.7mph/149.1km/h.

Lap record: Brad Binder, 1m 46.723s, 90.9mph/149.1km/h (2015).

Event maximum speed: Tony Arbolino, 148.3mph/238.7km/h (free practice).

Qualifying:

Weather: Dry

Air: 25° **Track:** 39°

Humidity: 46%

1	Martin	1m 46.193s
2	Oettl	1m 46.346s
3	Di Giannantonio	1m 46.599s
4	Antonelli	1m 46.614s
5	Bezzecchi	1m 46.739s
6	Migno	1m 46.770s
7	Lopez	1m 46.820s
8	Bastianini	1m 46.894s
9	Dalla Porta	1m 46.898s
10	Suzuki	1m 46.905s
11	Toba	1m 46.931s
12	Foggia	1m 46.955s
13	Yurchenko	1m 46.967s
14	Masaki	1m 46.969s
15	Canet	1m 47.037s
16	Kornfeil	1m 47.042s
17	McPhee	1m 47.105s
18	Ramirez	1m 47.181s
19	Ogura	1m 47.215s
20	Rodrigo	1m 47.218s
21	Arbolino	1m 47.230s
22	Bulega	1m 47.253s
23	Sasaki	1m 47.261s
24	Arenas	1m 47.282s
25	Masia	1m 47.450s
26	Alcoba	1m 47.484s
27	Norrodin	1m 47.632s
28	Loi	1m 47.763s
29	Atiratphuvapat	1m 48.180s
30	Binder	1m 58.297s

Fastest race laps

1	Lopez	1m 46.730s
2	Canet	1m 46.878s
3	Arbolino	1m 46.893s
4	Bezzecchi	1m 46.957s
5	Bastianini	1m 46.999s
6	Suzuki	1m 47.103s
7	Yurchenko	1m 47.142s
8	Toba	1m 47.165s
9	Ramirez	1m 47.171s
10	Oettl	1m 47.179s
11	Di Giannantonio	1m 47.183s
12	Kornfeil	1m 47.216s
13	Masia	1m 47.225s
14	Rodrigo	1m 47.269s
15	Antonelli	1m 47.322s
16	Sasaki	1m 47.333s
17	Martin	1m 47.411s
18	Migno	1m 47.436s
19	Norrodin	1m 48.032s
20	Bulega	1m 48.127s
21	Loi	1m 48.204s
22	Atiratphuvapat	1m 48.270s
23	Ogura	1m 48.319s
24	Arenas	1m 48.526s
25	Masaki	1m 48.547s

Championship Points

1	Bezzecchi	63
2	Martin	55
3	Canet	48
4	Di Giannantonio	46
5	Oettl	35
6	Bastianini	33
7	Rodrigo	28
8	Antonelli	26
9	Kornfeil	26
10	Dalla Porta	25
11	Migno	25
12	Lopez	23
13	Ramirez	21
14	Suzuki	17
15	Sasaki	17
16	Norrodin	16
17	Toba	16
18	Masia	15
19	Loi	7
20	Arbolino	6
21	Masaki	3
22	Binder	3
23	McPhee	2
24	Yurchenko	2
25	Arenas	1
26	Ogura	1

Constructor Points

1	Honda	83
2	KTM	77

FIM WORLD CHAMPIONSHIP · ROUND 5

FRENCH GRAND PRIX

LE MANS CIRCUIT

Main: Before the fall. Zarco leads from Marquez, Petrucci and Rossi.
Photo: Gold & Goose

Inset, left: Zarcolepsy sufferers seek the healing touch of their hero.
Photo: Monster Energy

Above: Zarco looked composed on pole, but his race and season were about to unravel.
Photo: Monster Energy

Top right: With his contract renewal finally signed, Dovi's weekend ended on a low.

Above right: Marc van der Straten jetted in to stop the disintegration of his VDS team.

Centre, from left: Close to the wind – new 'not-wings' for Red Bull KTM, Movistar Yamaha and Repsol Honda.

Right: Hit by his bike, but ignored by Race Direction, Crutchlow was left unimpressed by the lack of safety measures after his massive qualifying crash.
Photos: Gold & Goose

A PARTICULAR mania seized the French fans at Le Mans. It was Zarcolepsy. The only cure, for many of the race-day record 105,000, was to arrive in force even while the MotoGP paddock was unpacking and to stay, becoming ever louder, until the bitter end.

And bitter it was, when the coolest customer in the top ten of any class let it all get to him. Zarco made the rarest of hothead errors, trying too hard too early and crashing out after just seven of 27 laps. He had too much fuel in the tank, both literally and figuratively.

The Gallic enthusiasm was inspiring in other ways. As at every other race, there was a demonstration lap of 2019's MotoE series bike, here ridden by Randy de Puniet. As usual, the noisiest thing was the sound of the rider's knee-scrapers. The Le Mans spectators, however, were in no mood to be underwhelmed, so with one voice they provided the missing engine noise.

This was a remarkable weekend in many ways, not least because of balmy weather throughout, a rarity at this historic venue. More puzzling, given such fine conditions, was the huge number of crashes – 109 over the weekend, with 28 on race day. Given the full resurfacing in 2017, the explanation was difficult to discover. Nor could impetuous youth take the blame: the smallest number (28) came in Moto3, while MotoGP counted 32 and Moto2 the most, at 49.

One possible culprit was the cool breeze, suggesting that the tyres were having trouble getting up to temperature, and then dropping off unexpectedly quickly. Marquez had another theory: "Here you have a lot of grip, then when the tyre starts to slide, it slides very aggressively."

High-profile MotoGP fallers included Marquez and Rossi, while Bradley Smith was lucky to escape unhurt from a big high-side on day one; and Aleix Espargaro from a very fast slide-off at well over 240km/h at Turn One during qualifying. In Moto2, Stefano Manzi fell four times, twice during qualifying, every time at the same place, Museum corner.

The unluckiest victim was Cal Crutchlow, with a soaring high-side at the corner before the back straight in Q1. He'd fallen shortly before in FP4 and hadn't had time to put on new leathers, which meant his airbags were inactive, and that made the impact worse. He did not lose consciousness, but was stretchered off and taken to hospital for observation. Having escaped fractures, the Briton reinforced his reputation for courage by discharging himself on Sunday morning and returning to race to a strong top-ten finish.

His crash was controversial. Having also been thumped by his bike, he was supine and immobile, struggling to breathe, and right beside the track. Normally this would mean an immediate red flag. Not this time. With a little less than two minutes of qualifying remaining, they were allowed to run their course, and only then was the session stopped, rather than allowing riders who had already started a lap to complete it. "There were bikes going past my head and the marshals were in danger. They couldn't attend to me because they were watching for other bikes. I'm really upset," Crutchlow said. But when the press asked Race Direction for an explanation, none was forthcoming.

More criticism followed a series of seemingly unfair decisions after a hectic Moto3 race, where several riders were given time penalties for "exceeding track limits", when in reality the chicane cutting was more usually the result of a collision or an attempt to avoid one. The greatest sufferer was Di Giannantonio, who crossed the line first and was celebrating a long-awaited win, only to be demoted to fourth. He was, said his Gresini team, "the moral victor".

The expected news of Dovizioso's future finally came, after a well-reported, but surely only semi-serious flirtation with Repsol Honda. This at least would have served to readjust his fee to something closer to the big money (some 24 million euros) paid to Lorenzo; and Sporting Director Paolo Ciabatti did say that negotiations had been "very difficult".

Dovi was on for the next two years; Lorenzo more exposed than ever. Ducati had brought him a new chassis, although with only one, he was finding settings progress problematic. Again, he would lead the early laps, before dropping back, again complaining of fatigue caused by a lack of physical support under the hard braking, which is such a feature of the stop-and-go Bugatti circuit. Ciabatti had a crusty comment about him as well, saying, "There is a big gulf between our budget and Lorenzo's fee."

Suzuki confirmed that they had renewed Rins's contract for another couple of years; and Iannone's insecurity was boosted by rumours that they were treating with Moto3 champion and top Moto2 rookie Joan Mir. This rather overlooked the fact that Mir had another year of his contract to run with the Marc VDS team, but the meltdown at the Belgian team was still much in progress.

Team principal Bartholemy was at the track and defiant, having again protested his innocence, rather surprisingly in an official team press release. But team owner van der Straten was en route in his private jet, accompanied by replacement team head Luca Montiron (formerly with JiR Racing), and on the second day Bartholemy was gone, along with team press officer Ian Wheeler and (temporarily) rider coach Stefan Prein. Bartholemy's parting shot, this time not on the team letterhead, but still protesting innocence, presented a further surprise, as he explained how he had generously decided not to exercise his legal right to withdraw both the Moto2 and MotoGP teams from the grand prix forthwith. Which doubtless was just as well for all concerned.

The Repsol Hondas had a new set of wings, developed in private tests at Mugello in the break, representing their one aerodynamic update for the season rather early. "We've played our Joker," said Marquez, adding that by combining the new Yamaha-like closed-loop protuberances with their existing bodywork, they expected to have options to suit all the upcoming tracks.

MOTOGP RACE – 27 laps

Zarco took his fourth pole and ninth straight front row by a tenth from Marquez, with a new track record. Petrucci (through from Q1) was third. Iannone led the factory Ducatis on row two; Miller the factory Yamahas on the next. He was the first Frenchman on pole at home since Christian Sarron in 1998, and he promised to "enjoy this moment, because these feelings don't come very often in your life."

The dream ended in the gravel at the double-right Garage Vert before the back straight. "I think I was too fast, went a bit wider and the front closed. I didn't expect it because my feeling was good. Maybe I should have waited until there was less fuel in the bike."

He was not the only early victim.

The two factory Ducatis took off in the lead, Lorenzo in front. Mindful of how he'd been held up at Jerez, Dovizioso made haste to get past, into the chicane at the start of lap five. At the next corner, La Chapelle, he lost the front under braking and was down, shaking his head in bafflement. "I was only pushing 80 per cent," he said.

Long before, on only the third corner, Iannone had also gone flying.

That left the stage clear for another Marquez/Honda demonstration. He'd finished lap one fifth, watched the mayhem, and had just passed Zarco when the Yamaha rider tried to fight back and fell. Now there was just Lorenzo ahead. Marquez, the only rider to have chosen the hard rear, waited until lap ten for the tyre to come in. Then, when Lorenzo ran slightly wide, he cut inside.

Lorenzo was now becoming tired and losing momentum. It was Petrucci who took up the chase and was pushing hard. But Marquez was in control, and with ten to go he set fastest lap to break free, finally winning by 2.3 seconds.

"The race was tough – everyone had the same pace," he said. But he claimed he could have gone faster at the end.

"This victory is important at a track where normally we struggle." The difference was that the 2018 RCV had eliminated earlier acceleration problems, and now he didn't have to push so hard under braking and in the corners.

It was his first three-in-a-row since his dominant 2014, and his 38th in the premier class, moving him ahead of Mike Hailwood and equal with Casey Stoner, with only Lorenzo (44), Doohan (54), Agostini (68) and Rossi (89) ahead.

With the field depleted, Rossi was poised to profit. He'd gone from ninth to sixth on lap one and now was pursuing Petrucci; while Miller and, a little further back, Pedrosa were chasing him.

Rossi passed Lorenzo just before half-distance; Miller did the same one lap later. The Australian was less than a second behind, and while the gap stretched to more than two seconds, he was closing again at the flag, to within less than a second, for a best dry-weather finish. "That's the first time I've ever wished a race would be a bit longer," he laughed. "I could still see Marquez at the end."

Rossi was equally pleased with a second podium: "We've improved a bit, and I made the right tyre choice."

Pedrosa, still nursing shoulder injuries from Jerez, had been shadowing Lorenzo. He finally got by with seven laps

Above: The VDS Moto2 squad celebrates second place for Alex Marquez and third for top rookie Mir.

Top right: From pole to flag, Bagnaia had the measure of Marquez.

Top far right: Vierge rode a stormer from the back of the grid to fifth.

Above right: Surprise Moto3 winner, Spaniard Albert Arenas.

Above far right: Arenas (75) and team-mate Andre Migno (16) took first and second for the Angel Nieto Moto3 squad.

Right: Bezzecchi flies over the top after his last-lap collision with Martin; Di Giannantonio speeds towards his moral victory.

Bottom right and far right: Jakub Kornfeil flies to YouTube stardom, using Bastianini's fallen Honda as a ramp. Amazingly, he landed wheels-down for a lucky sixth.

Photos: Gold & Goose

remaining, and in turn closed to within a second of Miller. Lorenzo was another three seconds away; the rest almost 15 seconds.

The early leader of that group had been Aleix Espargaro, who had deposed Rins. Morbidelli had followed him by, but after one-third-distance, Rins had got back, while Vinales had picked up speed after dropping to 13th on lap four. By lap 20, he had got past Rins and then took one more to pass the Aprilia.

By now, it was a lively fight, with a heroic Cal Crutchlow joining in: "For the first 15 laps, I wasn't willing to push, because if I'd crashed again, I'd really have been in trouble." Now he had passed both Aprilia and Suzuki and was closing on Vinales.

Pol Espargaro was five seconds down in 11th; Syahrin 12th, after coming off better in a battle with Morbidelli, who in turn narrowly stayed ahead of Smith.

Takaaki Nakagami was a lone 15th, the LCR Honda rider still hurting after a heavy crash on Friday.

Redding, Rabat and Bautista also crashed out.

With Zarco and Dovi not scoring, Vinales now held a surprising second place overall. But Marquez had extended his lead to a valuable 36 points.

MOTO2 RACE – 25 laps

Points leader Pecco Bagnaia claimed his first Moto2 pole by a couple of tenths from Vierge, who crashed in the closing minutes trying to get back. Baldassarri completed the front row; Mir led the second from Schrotter and Marquez; Lowes the third from Binder. Oliveira was tenth, ahead of Pasini, still within a second of pole.

The race conformed to type: processional, but tense, with start-to-finish leader Bagnaia's accuracy and consistency truly impressive.

He'd had a perfect launch off the line, but while it was a dominant performance, he couldn't slacken his pace or lose focus for a second: "The race was tough. I tried to impose my pace, but also to avoid using up the rear tyre in the first laps, to be competitive in the last laps." This was the Rossi protégé's third win in five races.

He was chased all the way by a remorseless Marquez. The Spaniard only slackened off in the final laps, to finish less than three seconds adrift. "Overall, it was a good weekend," he said, trying to contain his disappointment at being unable to attack.

The pair had outdistanced the rest, although Marquez's slowing pace had allowed the third-placed rider to close to within three seconds at the end. It was his team-mate – amazing rookie Mir. He had pushed past both Red Bull KTMs after finishing the first lap sixth, then patiently tailed Schrotter's Kalex before moving past firmly on lap 15. That gave him a clear first podium, leaving the still battered Schrotter an untroubled fourth.

"With a better start, I think I could have been fighting the top two guys," the 20-year-old threatened.

But perhaps the best ride of the race was to fifth by Vierge. Stricken by fuel-pump trouble on the warm-up lap, he'd had to start from the back of the grid. He came storming through, gaining 18 places in the first lap alone, and proving that although it doesn't happen very often with the bikes' identical performance, overtaking is possible in Moto2 if you are aggressive enough.

Vierge fended off a strong fight-back by Oliveira on the last lap.

Another rookie, Romano Fenati, had been ahead of both and was a close seventh. Quartararo led the next loose group, from Binder and Manzi at the head of a good battle. Barbera was just clear of Locatelli. Less than two seconds down, Lowes got the better of Corsi; with Pawi just off the back of it for the final point.

American Joe Roberts had been in the gang for his first dry points, but fell in the closing laps, rejoining to finish 19th, one place down on Pasini, who also had remounted after an early slip-off.

Baldassarri had been in the leading group when he crashed out on lap eight. Lecuona and Navarro were among several others to fall.

First-timer Niki Tuuli was 22nd. He had taken over from Zulfahmi Khairuddin after the Malaysian withdrew from the SIC team, saying he was finding it impossible to get up to speed after two years away.

MOTO3 RACE – 22 laps

The race was close, and then went properly mad. Crashes, lucky escapes and post-race penalties shuffled the results, leaving Di Giannantonio heartbroken, but handing a career-first win to Albert Arenas, who headed the first all-KTM podium since 2016.

Martin was on pole again, and the majority of the race was between him and Bezzecchi, with early leader Kornfeil breathing down their necks, until a chicane run-off dropped him back.

Now Di Giannantonio and Bastianini posed the biggest threat, with Antonelli and Migno also prominent.

Kornfeil (later penalised for another short cut) was back at the end of the penultimate lap, when Bastianini fell in the final corners. Kornfeil hit the fallen Honda, executed a spectacular high jump and was lucky to land wheels-down in the gravel. Amazingly, he regained control to rejoin the chase.

The final drama was played out through the same double-right corners.

Bezzecchi had been in front, but Di Giannantonio cut inside both his rivals. Bezzecchi made a desperate swerve to get back inside for the second apex, only to swing sideways and go flying. Martin was unable to avoid his bike and also fell, innocent victim for a second race.

As Di Giannantonio celebrated, Arenas crossed the line, narrowly ahead of Migno, with Antonelli close behind, from Ramirez and Kornfeil.

Then came the penalties: 1.3 seconds for Kornfeil, 1.8 for Antonelli and three for Di Giannantonio.

Thus the KTM podium, Ramirez promoted to third, Di Giannantonio fourth, then Antonelli; Kornfeil hung on to sixth, ahead of Arbolino.

Less than five seconds behind, Canet led a furious battle for eighth, after coming through from the back of the grid, penalised for causing a crash at the previous round. Eighth to 16th was covered by some 1.6 seconds.

HJC HELMETS GRAND PRIX DE FRANCE

18-20 MAY, 2018

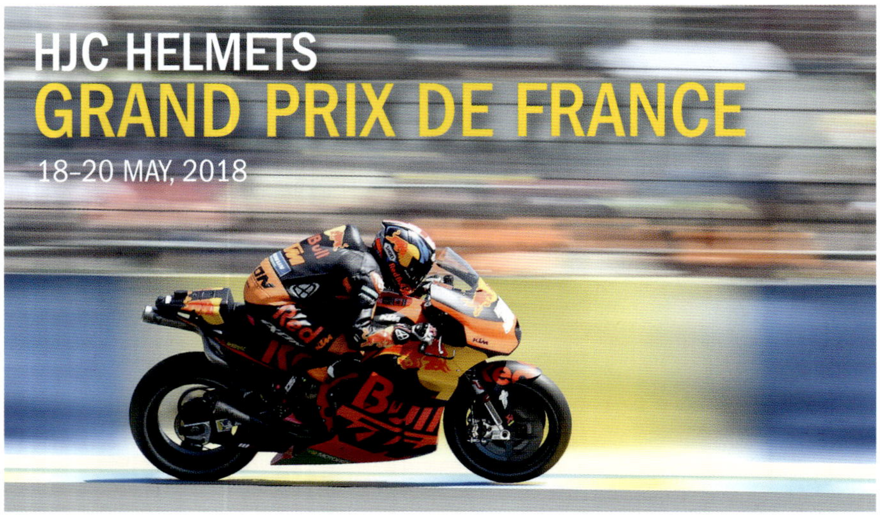

LE MANS – BUGATTI

27 laps
Length: 4.185 km / 2.600 miles
Width: 13m

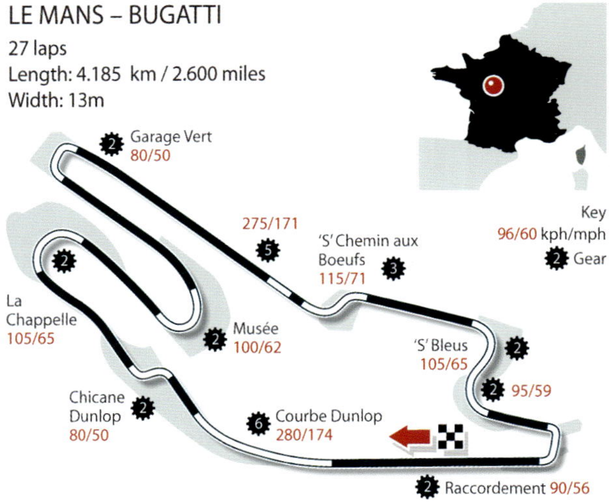

MotoGP

RACE DISTANCE: 27 laps, 70.212 miles/112.995km · RACE WEATHER: Dry (air 24°C, humidity 41%, track 45°C)

Pos.	Rider	Nat.	No.	Entrant	Machine	Tyres	Race tyre choice	Laps	Time & speed
1	**Marc Marquez**	SPA	93	Repsol Honda Team	Honda RC213V	M	F: Medium/R: Hard	27	41m 49.773s 100.7mph/ 162.0km/h
2	**Danilo Petrucci**	ITA	9	Alma Pramac Racing	Ducati Desmosedici	M	F: Soft/R: Soft	27	41m 52.083s
3	**Valentino Rossi**	ITA	46	Movistar Yamaha MotoGP	Yamaha YZR-M1	M	F: Medium/R: Soft	27	41m 55.123s
4	**Jack Miller**	AUS	43	Alma Pramac Racing	Ducati Desmosedici	M	F: Soft/R: Soft	27	41m 56.087s
5	**Dani Pedrosa**	SPA	26	Repsol Honda Team	Honda RC213V	M	F: Medium/R: Soft	27	41m 57.192s
6	**Jorge Lorenzo**	SPA	99	Ducati Team	Ducati Desmosedici	M	F: Soft/R: Soft	27	42m 00.128s
7	**Maverick Vinales**	SPA	25	Movistar Yamaha MotoGP	Yamaha YZR-M1	M	F: Soft/R: Soft	27	42m 13.531s
8	**Cal Crutchlow**	GBR	35	LCR Honda CASTROL	Honda RC213V	M	F: Medium/R: Soft	27	42m 15.568s
9	**Aleix Espargaro**	SPA	41	Aprilia Racing Team Gresini	Aprilia RS-GP	M	F: Medium/R: Soft	27	42m 15.979s
10	**Alex Rins**	SPA	42	Team SUZUKI ECSTAR	Suzuki GSX-RR	M	F: Medium/R: Soft	27	42m 17.710s
11	**Pol Espargaro**	SPA	44	Red Bull KTM Factory Racing	KTM RC16	M	F: Soft/R: Soft	27	42m 22.077s
12	**Hafizh Syahrin**	MAL	55	Monster Yamaha Tech 3	Yamaha YZR-M1	M	F: Soft/R: Soft	27	42m 24.735s
13	**Franco Morbidelli**	ITA	21	EG 0,0 Marc VDS	Honda RC213V	M	F: Medium/R: Soft	27	42m 27.654s
14	**Bradley Smith**	GBR	38	Red Bull KTM Factory Racing	KTM RC16	M	F: Soft/R: Soft	27	42m 28.072s
15	**Takaaki Nakagami**	JPN	30	LCR Honda IDEMITSU	Honda RC213V	M	F: Medium/R: Soft	27	42m 31.759s
16	Thomas Luthi	SWI	12	EG 0,0 Marc VDS	Honda RC213V	M	F: Medium/R: Soft	27	42m 35.033s
17	Karel Abraham	CZE	17	Angel Nieto Team	Ducati Desmosedici	M	F: Soft/R: Soft	27	42m 46.645s
18	Xavier Simeon	BEL	10	Reale Avintia Racing	Ducati Desmosedici	M	F: Soft/R: Soft	24	43m 01.890s
	Scott Redding	GBR	45	Aprilia Racing Team Gresini	Aprilia RS-GP	M	F: Soft/R: Soft	10	DNF-crash
	Tito Rabat	SPA	53	Reale Avintia Racing	Ducati Desmosedici	M	F: Soft/R: Soft	10	DNF-crash
	Johann Zarco	FRA	5	Monster Yamaha Tech 3	Yamaha YZR-M1	M	F: Medium/R: Soft	8	DNF-crash
	Andrea Dovizioso	ITA	4	Ducati Team	Ducati Desmosedici	M	F: Medium/R: Soft	4	DNF-crash
	Alvaro Bautista	SPA	19	Angel Nieto Team	Ducati Desmosedici	M	F: Soft/R: Soft	1	DNF-crash
	Andrea Iannone	ITA	29	Team SUZUKI ECSTAR	Suzuki GSX-RR	M	F: Medium/R: Soft	0	DNF-crash

Fastest lap: Marc Marquez, on lap 17, 1m 32.312s, 101.4mph/163.2km/h.
Lap record: Maverick Vinales, 1m 32.309s, 101.4mph/163.2km/h (2017).
Event maximum speed: Cal Crutchlow, 193.5mph/311.4km/h (race).

Qualifying

Weather: Dry
Air Temp: 22° **Track Temp:** 44°
Humidity: 34%

1	Zarco	1m 31.185s
2	Marquez	1m 31.293s
3	Petrucci	1m 31.381s
4	Iannone	1m 31.454s
5	Dovizioso	1m 31.553s
6	Lorenzo	1m 31.590s
7	Miller	1m 31.683s
8	Vinales	1m 31.784s
9	Rossi	1m 31.900s
10	Pedrosa	1m 32.024s
11	Rabat	1m 32.049s
12	A. Espargaro	1m 32.455s
13	Crutchlow	1m 32.315s
14	Syahrin	1m 32.397s
15	Rins	1m 32.401s
16	Morbidelli	1m 32.770s
17	Smith	1m 32.795s
18	P. Espargaro	1m 32.988s
19	Nakagami	1m 33.062s
20	Bautista	1m 33.324s
21	Luthi	1m 33.439s
22	Redding	1m 33.676s
23	Simeon	1m 33.802s
24	Abraham	1m 33.839s

Fastest race laps

1	Marquez	1m 32.312s
2	Rossi	1m 32.383s
3	Miller	1m 32.390s
4	Petrucci	1m 32.415s
5	Pedrosa	1m 32.666s
6	Dovizioso	1m 32.688s
7	Zarco	1m 32.783s
8	Lorenzo	1m 32.823s
9	Vinales	1m 32.871s
10	Crutchlow	1m 32.921s
11	A. Espargaro	1m 33.168s
12	Syahrin	1m 33.265s
13	Rins	1m 33.291s
14	Morbidelli	1m 33.456s
15	P. Espargaro	1m 33.506s
16	Rabat	1m 33.634s
17	Luthi	1m 33.664s
18	Nakagami	1m 33.674s
19	Smith	1m 33.726s
20	Redding	1m 33.923s
21	Abraham	1m 34.314s
22	Simeon	1m 34.693s

Championship Points

1	Marquez	95
2	Vinales	59
3	Zarco	58
4	Rossi	56
5	Petrucci	54
6	Miller	49
7	Iannone	47
8	Crutchlow	46
9	Dovizioso	46
10	Pedrosa	29
11	Rabat	24
12	Rins	22
13	P. Espargaro	18
14	Lorenzo	16
15	Morbidelli	16
16	A. Espargaro	13
17	Syahrin	13
18	Bautista	12
19	Nakagami	10
20	Kallio	6
21	Redding	5
22	Smith	5
23	Abraham	1

Constructor Points

1	Honda	120
2	Yamaha	92
3	Ducati	82
4	Suzuki	61
5	KTM	19
6	Aprilia	18

Grid order	1	2	3	4	5	6	7	8	9	10	11	12	13	14	15	16	17	18	19	20	21	22	23	24	25	26	27	
5 ZARCO	99	99	99	99	99	99	99	99	99	93	93	93	93	93	93	93	93	93	93	93	93	93	93	93	93	93	93	1
93 MARQUEZ	5	5	4	4	5	5	93	93	93	99	9	9	9	9	9	9	9	9	9	9	9	9	9	9	9	9	9	2
9 PETRUCCI	4	4	5	5	93	93	5	9	9	9	99	99	46	46	46	46	46	46	46	46	46	46	46	46	46	46	46	3
29 IANNONE	9	93	93	93	9	9	9	46	46	46	46	46	99	43	43	43	43	43	43	43	43	43	43	43	43	43	43	4
4 DOVIZIOSO	93	9	9	9	46	46	46	43	43	43	43	43	43	99	99	99	99	99	99	99	26	26	26	26	26	26	26	5
99 LORENZO	46	46	46	46	43	43	43	26	26	26	26	26	26	26	26	26	26	26	26	26	99	99	99	99	99	99	99	6
43 MILLER	43	43	43	43	26	26	26	41	41	41	41	41	41	41	41	41	41	41	41	41	25	25	25	25	25	25	25	7
25 VINALES	42	26	26	26	41	41	41	21	21	21	42	42	42	42	42	42	42	42	42	25	42	42	42	41	41	41	35	8
46 ROSSI	26	25	42	42	21	21	21	42	42	42	21	21	21	25	25	25	25	25	25	42	41	41	41	42	35	35	41	9
26 PEDROSA	53	42	41	41	42	42	42	44	44	44	25	25	25	44	44	44	44	35	35	35	35	35	35	35	42	42	42	10
53 RABAT	25	41	21	21	44	44	44	25	25	25	44	44	44	21	21	35	35	44	44	44	44	44	44	44	44	44	44	11
41 A. ESPARGARO	44	21	44	44	25	25	25	35	35	35	35	35	35	35	35	21	21	55	21	21	21	55	55	55	55	55	55	12
35 CRUTCHLOW	35	44	25	25	35	35	35	30	30	30	30	30	30	55	55	55	55	21	55	55	55	21	21	21	21	21	21	13
55 SYAHRIN	41	35	35	35	30	30	30	55	55	55	55	55	55	30	30	30	30	30	38	38	38	38	38	38	38	38	38	14
42 RINS	21	38	30	30	38	38	55	38	38	38	38	38	38	38	38	38	38	38	30	30	30	30	30	30	30	30	30	15
21 MORBIDELLI	38	30	38	38	45	55	38	45	45	45	17	17	12	12	12	12	12	12	12	12	12	12	12	12	12	12	12	
38 SMITH	19	45	45	45	55	45	45	17	17	17	12	12	17	17	17	17	17	17	17	17	17	17	17	17	17	17	17	
44 P. ESPARGARO	30	55	55	55	17	17	17	12	12	12	10	10	10	10	10	10	10	10	10	10	10	10	10	10	10	10	10	
30 NAKAGAMI	45	17	17	17	12	12	12	10	10	10																		
19 BAUTISTA	55	10	10	12	10	10	10	5	53	53																		
12 LUTHI	17	12	12	10	53	53	53	53																				
45 REDDING	10	53	53	53																								
10 SIMEON	12																											
17 ABRAHAM																												

5 Pit stop

Moto2

RACE DISTANCE: 25 laps, 65.011 miles/104.625km · RACE WEATHER: Dry (air 21°C, humidity 46%, track 38°C)

Pos.	Rider	Nat.	No.	Entrant	Machine	Laps	Time & Speed
1	**Francesco Bagnaia**	ITA	42	SKY Racing Team VR46	Kalex	25	40m 40.162s 95.9mph/ 154.3km/h
2	**Alex Marquez**	SPA	73	EG 0,0 Marc VDS	Kalex	25	40m 42.871s
3	**Joan Mir**	SPA	36	EG 0,0 Marc VDS	Kalex	25	40m 45.027s
4	**Marcel Schrotter**	GER	23	Dynavolt Intact GP	Kalex	25	40m 47.203s
5	**Xavi Vierge**	SPA	97	Dynavolt Intact GP	Kalex	25	40m 49.973s
6	**Miguel Oliveira**	POR	44	Red Bull KTM Ajo	KTM	25	40m 50.105s
7	**Romano Fenati**	ITA	13	Marinelli Snipers Team	Kalex	25	40m 52.455s
8	**Fabio Quartararo**	FRA	20	MB Conveyors - Speed Up Racing	Speed Up	25	40m 54.747s
9	**Brad Binder**	RSA	41	Red Bull KTM Ajo	KTM	25	40m 55.591s
10	**Stefano Manzi**	ITA	62	Forward Racing Team	Suter	25	40m 57.390s
11	**Hector Barbera**	SPA	40	Pons HP40	Kalex	25	40m 58.971s
12	**Andrea Locatelli**	ITA	5	Italtrans Racing Team	Kalex	25	40m 59.703s
13	**Sam Lowes**	GBR	22	Swiss Innovative Investors	KTM	25	41m 01.274s
14	**Simone Corsi**	ITA	24	Tasca Racing Scuderia Moto2	Kalex	25	41m 03.672s
15	**Khairul Idham Pawi**	MAL	89	IDEMITSU Honda Team Asia	Kalex	25	41m 06.158s
16	Bo Bendsneyder	NED	64	Tech 3 Racing	Tech 3	25	41m 09.429s
17	Steven Odendaal	RSA	4	NTS RW Racing GP	NTS	25	41m 12.655s
18	Mattia Pasini	ITA	54	Italtrans Racing Team	Kalex	25	41m 24.168s
19	Joe Roberts	USA	16	NTS RW Racing GP	NTS	25	41m 25.771s
20	Jules Danilo	FRA	95	Nashi Argan SAG Team	Kalex	25	41m 26.002s
21	Danny Kent	GBR	52	MB Conveyors - Speed Up Racing	Speed Up	25	41m 26.214s
22	Niki Tuuli	FIN	66	SIC Racing Team	Kalex	25	41m 28.533s
23	Lukas Tulovic	GER	3	Kiefer Racing	KTM	25	41m 34.466s
24	Corentin Perolari	FRA	19	Promoto Sport	Transformers	25	41m 37.640s
25	Tetsuta Nagashima	JPN	45	IDEMITSU Honda Team Asia	Kalex	25	41m 47.874s
26	Xavi Cardelus	AND	18	Team Stylobike	Kalex	25	42m 01.918s
27	Cedric Tangre	FRA	80	Yohan Moto Sport	Tech 3	25	42m 16.704s
	Federico Fuligni	ITA	21	Tasca Racing Scuderia Moto2	Kalex	10	DNF
	Hector Garzo	SPA	14	Tech 3 Racing	Tech 3	10	DNF
	Lorenzo Baldassarri	ITA	7	Pons HP40	Kalex	8	DNF
	Iker Lecuona	SPA	27	Swiss Innovative Investors	KTM	6	DNF
	Jorge Navarro	SPA	9	Federal Oil Gresini Moto2	Kalex	5	DNF
	Eric Granado	BRA	51	Forward Racing Team	Suter	1	DNF
	Luca Marini	ITA	10	SKY Racing Team VR46	Kalex	1	DNF
	Isaac Vinales	SPA	32	SAG Team	Kalex	0	DNF

Fastest lap: Lorenzo Baldassarri, on lap 7, 1m 36.959s, 96.5mph/155.3km/h.

Lap record: Franco Morbidelli, 1m 36.836s, 96.6mph/155.5km/h (2017).

Event maximum speed: Hector Barbera, 158.3mph/254.7km/h (race).

Qualifying

Weather: Dry

Air Temp: 23° **Track Temp:** 45°

Humidity: 30%

1	Bagnaia	1m 36.188s
2	Vierge	1m 36.390s
3	Baldassarri	1m 36.583s
4	Mir	1m 36.659s
5	Schrotter	1m 36.671s
6	Marquez	1m 36.676s
7	Lowes	1m 36.784s
8	Binder	1m 36.920s
9	Corsi	1m 36.951s
10	Oliveira	1m 36.976s
11	Pasini	1m 37.099s
12	Fenati	1m 37.193s
13	Barbera	1m 37.193s
14	Quartararo	1m 37.243s
15	Navarro	1m 37.359s
16	Locatelli	1m 37.440s
17	Roberts	1m 37.444s
18	Pawi	1m 37.457s
19	Vinales	1m 37.460s
20	Lecuona	1m 37.485s
21	Bendsneyder	1m 37.565s
22	Nagashima	1m 37.673s
23	Manzi	1m 37.816s
24	Marini	1m 37.847s
25	Tulovic	1m 37.962s
26	Odendaal	1m 38.077s
27	Garzo	1m 38.191s
28	Danilo	1m 38.377s
29	Fuligni	1m 38.638s
30	Tuuli	1m 38.683s
31	Kent	1m 38.712s
32	Perolari	1m 38.769s
33	Cardelus	1m 38.802s
34	Granado	1m 38.927s
35	Tangre	1m 40.723s

Fastest race laps

1	Baldassarri	1m 36.959s
2	Bagnaia	1m 36.972s
3	Marquez	1m 37.004s
4	Mir	1m 37.155s
5	Vierge	1m 37.192s
6	Fenati	1m 37.309s
7	Schrotter	1m 37.331s
8	Oliveira	1m 37.357s
9	Manzi	1m 37.439s
10	Pasini	1m 37.488s
11	Quartararo	1m 37.512s
12	Barbera	1m 37.519s
13	Lowes	1m 37.520s
14	Nagashima	1m 37.534s
15	Binder	1m 37.544s
16	Corsi	1m 37.674s
17	Roberts	1m 37.766s
18	Locatelli	1m 37.818s
19	Pawi	1m 37.985s
20	Bendsneyder	1m 37.996s
21	Navarro	1m 38.037s
22	Odendaal	1m 38.162s
23	Kent	1m 38.514s
24	Tulovic	1m 38.530s
25	Danilo	1m 38.585s
26	Perolari	1m 38.643s
27	Tuuli	1m 38.799s
28	Lecuona	1m 38.940s
29	Garzo	1m 39.019s
30	Fuligni	1m 39.147s
31	Cardelus	1m 39.369s
32	Tangre	1m 40.611s

Championship Points

1	Bagnaia	98
2	Oliveira	73
3	Marquez	67
4	Baldassarri	64
5	Pasini	58
6	Vierge	52
7	Mir	48
8	Schrotter	37
9	Binder	37
10	Lecuona	23
11	Aegerter	16
12	Quartararo	15
13	Gardner	14
14	Navarro	14
15	Lowes	14
16	Corsi	12
17	Marini	10
18	Barbera	10
19	Fenati	9
20	Locatelli	8
21	Vinales	7
22	Manzi	6
23	Kent	4
24	Nagashima	3
25	Pawi	1

Constructor Points

1	Kalex	125
2	KTM	73
3	Speed Up	19
4	Tech 3	14
5	Suter	6

Moto3

RACE DISTANCE: 22 laps, 57.210 miles/92.070km · RACE WEATHER: Dry (air 19°C, humidity 53%, track 33°C)

Pos.	Rider	Nat.	No.	Entrant	Machine	Laps	Time & Speed
1	**Albert Arenas**	SPA	75	Angel Nieto Team Moto3	KTM	22	37m 40.056s 91.1mph/ 146.6km/h
2	**Andrea Migno**	ITA	16	Angel Nieto Team Moto3	KTM	22	37m 40.216s
3	**Marcos Ramirez**	SPA	42	Bester Capital Dubai	KTM	22	37m 40.765s
4	**Fabio Di Giannantonio**	ITA	21	Del Conca Gresini Moto3	Honda	22	37m 41.867s
5	**Niccolo Antonelli**	ITA	23	SIC58 Squadra Corse	Honda	22	37m 42.361s
6	**Jakub Kornfeil**	CZE	84	Redox PruestelGP	KTM	22	37m 45.543s
7	**Tony Arbolino**	ITA	14	Marinelli Snipers Team	Honda	22	37m 47.633s
8	**Aron Canet**	SPA	44	Estrella Galicia 0,0	Honda	22	37m 51.246s
9	**Tatsuki Suzuki**	JPN	24	SIC58 Squadra Corse	Honda	22	37m 51.573s
10	**Jaume Masia**	SPA	5	Bester Capital Dubai	KTM	22	37m 51.760s
11	**Darryn Binder**	RSA	40	Red Bull KTM Ajo	KTM	22	37m 52.067s
12	**John McPhee**	GBR	17	CIP - Green Power	KTM	22	37m 52.129s
13	**Makar Yurchenko**	KAZ	76	CIP - Green Power	KTM	22	37m 52.414s
14	**Dennis Foggia**	ITA	10	SKY Racing Team VR46	KTM	22	37m 52.537s
15	**Philipp Oettl**	GER	65	Sudmetal Schedl GP Racing	KTM	22	37m 52.802s
16	Ayumu Sasaki	JPN	71	Petronas Sprinta Racing	Honda	22	37m 52.864s
17	Kaito Toba	JPN	27	Honda Team Asia	Honda	22	37m 54.453s
18	Kazuki Masaki	JPN	22	RBA BOE Skull Rider	KTM	22	38m 08.071s
19	Alonso Lopez	SPA	72	Estrella Galicia 0,0	Honda	22	38m 16.535s
20	Nakarin Atiratphuvapat	THA	41	Honda Team Asia	Honda	22	38m 39.973s
21	Livio Loi	BEL	11	Reale Avintia Academy	KTM	22	38m 47.419s
	Marco Bezzecchi	ITA	12	Redox PruestelGP	KTM	21	DNF
	Jorge Martin	SPA	88	Del Conca Gresini Moto3	Honda	21	DNF
	Adam Norrodin	MAL	7	Petronas Sprinta Racing	Honda	21	DNF
	Enea Bastianini	ITA	33	Leopard Racing	Honda	20	DNF
	Lorenzo Dalla Porta	ITA	48	Leopard Racing	Honda	14	DNF
	Nicolo Bulega	ITA	8	SKY Racing Team VR46	KTM	9	DNF
	Gabriel Rodrigo	ARG	19	RBA BOE Skull Rider	KTM	3	DNF

Fastest lap: Jorge Martin, on lap 7, 1m 41.754s, 92.0mph/148.0km/h.

Lap record: Joan Mir, 1m 42.485s, 91.3mph/147.0km/h (2017).

Event maximum speed: Tony Arbolino, 134.0mph/215.6km/h (warm up).

Qualifying

Weather: Dry

Air Temp: 20° **Track Temp:** 37°

Humidity: 39%

1	Martin	1m 42.039s
2	Kornfeil	1m 42.162s
3	Bastianini	1m 42.163s
4	Ramirez	1m 42.189s
5	Arenas	1m 42.214s
6	Bezzecchi	1m 42.355s
7	Antonelli	1m 42.422s
8	Di Giannantonio	1m 42.447s
9	Migno	1m 42.509s
10	Canet	1m 42.512s
11	Dalla Porta	1m 42.520s
12	Oettl	1m 42.576s
13	Binder	1m 42.611s
14	Arbolino	1m 42.728s
15	Suzuki	1m 42.777s
16	Bulega	1m 42.813s
17	Masaki	1m 42.889s
18	Lopez	1m 42.982s
19	Yurchenko	1m 43.000s
20	Masia	1m 43.018s
21	Loi	1m 43.087s
22	Foggia	1m 43.099s
23	Rodrigo	1m 43.170s
24	Atiratphuvapat	1m 43.219s
25	McPhee	1m 43.290s
26	Sasaki	1m 43.380s
27	Toba	1m 43.419s
28	Norrodin	1m 43.450s

Fastest race laps

1	Martin	1m 41.754s
2	Bezzecchi	1m 41.860s
3	Bastianini	1m 41.957s
4	Di Giannantonio	1m 41.993s
5	Kornfeil	1m 42.011s
6	Ramirez	1m 42.026s
7	McPhee	1m 42.050s
8	Canet	1m 42.055s
9	Arbolino	1m 42.144s
10	Masia	1m 42.145s
11	Migno	1m 42.164s
12	Yurchenko	1m 42.174s
13	Antonelli	1m 42.183s
14	Arenas	1m 42.232s
15	Binder	1m 42.305s
16	Oettl	1m 42.335s
17	Masaki	1m 42.386s
18	Sasaki	1m 42.437s
19	Rodrigo	1m 42.466s
20	Suzuki	1m 42.485s
21	Dalla Porta	1m 42.488s
22	Foggia	1m 42.555s
23	Toba	1m 42.653s
24	Atiratphuvapat	1m 42.792s
25	Bulega	1m 42.964s
26	Loi	1m 43.087s
27	Norrodin	1m 43.169s
28	Lopez	1m 43.243s

Championship Points

1	Bezzecchi	63
2	Di Giannantonio	59
3	Canet	56
4	Martin	55
5	Migno	45
6	Ramirez	37
7	Antonelli	37
8	Oettl	36
9	Kornfeil	36
10	Bastianini	33
11	Rodrigo	28
12	Arenas	26
13	Dalla Porta	25
14	Suzuki	24
15	Lopez	23
16	Masia	21
17	Sasaki	17
18	Norrodin	16
19	Toba	16
20	Arbolino	15
21	Binder	8
22	Loi	7
23	McPhee	6
24	Yurchenko	5
25	Masaki	3
26	Foggia	2
27	Ogura	1

Constructor Points

1	KTM	102
2	Honda	96

Main: Swathes of Rossi yellow notwithstanding, Lorenzo was imperious in his return to victory.

Inset, below: Lorenzo jubilant, Dovizioso merely happy after Ducati's first one-two of the year – the first in Italy since taking the top five in the 125 class at Monza in 1958.
Photos: Gold & Goose

Inset, bottom: Pole position and a podium – with his national-flag helmet, Rossi celebrates a good home GP.
Photo: Movistar Yamaha

FIM WORLD CHAMPIONSHIP · ROUND 6

ITALIAN GRAND PRIX

MUGELLO CIRCUIT

F

WHEN Jorge Lorenzo announced to the media on Thursday that he would be leaving Ducati at the end of the season, he had a firm answer to those who thought they might be seeing the last of him. No, he was not thinking about retirement, but would be back for at least two more years. And "on a competitive bike".

That triggered a frenzy of twittering speculation, and a surprising conclusion. Lorenzo was obviously going back to Yamaha, to join the (still unconfirmed) satellite team due to replace Tech 3. This idea gained traction when Yamaha Racing boss Lin Jarvis suggested that factory-spec machinery might be made available to such a team.

Lorenzo had a second answer to Ducati, about the wisdom of failing to renew his contract, as he later confirmed would have been his preference. With nothing much more than reconfigured ergonomics – a jury-rigged piece of padding on the rear of the 'tank' to support him under braking – he was absolutely unbeatable. In the process, he proved that they had been wrong to let him go. At the same time, he took five points away from his supposedly senior team-mate, Dovizioso.

If Ducati had wanted to reconsider after that display, it was too late. Apparently, according to the rider, it had been between the previous round at Le Mans and Thursday's pre-race briefing, a matter of less than two weeks, when he'd put together the deal with Honda, which stunned the racing world when it was announced before the next race.

At Mugello, however, his destination remained unclear, and there was plenty else to occupy the mind. Much of it related to Ducati.

First off, a new top speed record, set by Dovi on Friday – a towering 221.45mph (356.4km/h).

Later the same day, Ducati set a new crash-speed record. The victim was wild-carding test rider Michele Pirro, who had lifted the front over a brow at top speed and landed with a major front-end shake. This spread the brake pads, and when he grabbed a handful, the lever went back to the bar. So he grabbed another handful, and locked the front at close

to top speed. The bike nose-dived violently and he was flung over the handlebars, high, far and fast. He landed very heavily, still on the asphalt.

The 31-year-old was instantly knocked out, and there were worried frowns in the pit lane, the session immediately red-flagged as he was treated trackside behind screens. But he had regained consciousness by the time he was taken away by ambulance, and had escaped any injury worse than a briefly dislocated shoulder. Marquez's crash in the same place in 2013, for a similar reason, had been measured at 337km/h. Pirro's was certainly faster than that.

Ducati made more headlines in the same place when Dovi suffered a smoky blow-up at top speed. This had been caused by over-revving as the back wheel hopped over the bump, in exactly the same manner as those that had afflicted the factory Yamahas here two years previously, Lorenzo in the morning, Rossi during the race. In theory, desmodromic valve gear should have made the Desmosedicis more capable of over-revving without damage, but everything has a limit. "We have put the rev-limiter down a bit," Ducati's Davide Tardozzi told media.

And still with Ducati, directly after the race, satellite-team rider Danilo Petrucci was told that he would be drafted into the factory team for 2019 to replace Lorenzo, leaving Miller to head the Pramac squad, although also on the latest GP19. Rather unexpectedly, of his own volition, Petrucci had only a one-year contract, having imposed his own performance clause for renewal.

There was more dream-come-true news from Suzuki, although only officially confirmed the following week, that Moto3 champion Mir was to be fast-tracked into the team after just one year in Moto2. In this way, he was following directly in the footsteps of Vinales, although by this stage of the season, Vinales had already taken the first of his four Moto2 race wins.

And Yamaha's future? Rumours were reinforced by the presence of Sepang International Circuit (SIC) CEO Dato Razlan Razali. He denied that SIC, already running a Moto2 team, was planning its own MotoGP squad, but not that its sponsor, Petronas (already also backing a Moto3 team), was interested. As well as the unresolved matter of the Marc VDS team, Jorge Martinez's Aspar team, currently running Ducatis under the 'Angel Nieto Team' name, was another candidate to take over from Tech 3.

There were a number of technical innovations. The most obvious change to Lorenzo's Ducati was a large moulded plastic extension to the rear of the 'tank' section (actually an airbox cover, the fuel being carried beneath the nose of the seat). This took his weight under hard braking, although it was not by itself the reason for his win, he would say, but only "the last piece" in making the best balanced Ducati ever. He also had a second new chassis, like the one seen at Le Mans.

Honda's carbon-fibre swing-arm reappeared for both riders, but only for qualifying and the race, numbers still being restricted. Both also had a slippery new rear seat unit. Suzuki had some chassis with carbon-fibre cladding, intended to fine-tune stiffness ratios. At Yamaha, where they were still searching for elusive traction, Vinales's bike settings had made it considerably shorter, to ensure more pitching and weight transfer: a move imitated at the next round by Rossi's crew. But Vinales's difficulties in the early laps with a full fuel tank persisted.

Brembo's annual list of bragging rights named the 'last of the late brakers' into the first corner, where speed goes from more than 350km/h to 90 and carbon discs reach temperatures of 700°C in a distance of 288m. The winner was Marquez, in spite of his own assertion (after Pirro's crash) that "since I crashed there in 2013, I always manage the risk". He beat Iannone, Rossi, Petrucci and fifth-placed Aleix Espargaro.

MOTOGP RACE – 23 laps

On a weekend of persistent sunshine, the capacity crowd got what they had come for, at least on Saturday, when Rossi took a 55th premier-class pole – his first in almost two years, and his first front row of the season.

Above: **Andrea Iannone leads Dovizioso, Rins, Crutchlow et al in the early laps.**
Photo: Team Ecstar Suzuki

Top left: **Plotting a course to victory. Lorenzo and crew chief Cristian Gabarrini lay their plans; Davide Tardozzi listens in.**
Photo: Monster Energy

Above far left: **"It's only a scratch." A battle-scarred Pirro was back at the track on Sunday after his record-speed crash.**

Above left: **A fierce-looking Crutchlow was sixth and top Honda, after misfortune for the factory pair.**

Left: **Petrucci was hoping for an all-Ducati podium before tyre wear took its toll.**
Photos: Gold & Goose

Below left: **Alex Rins had to be content with fifth place after a spirited battle with Rossi and Iannone.**
Photo: Team Ecstar Suzuki

Above: **He's back! Lorenzo takes the plaudits in the pit lane after his unexpected, but momentous win.**

Top right: **Miguel Oliveira leads Baldassarri, Mir and Bagnaia in the closely fought Moto2 race.**

Above right: **A year after his comeback win, Mattia Pasini took Moto2 pole, but crashed out early.**

Above far right: **Marcel Schrotter qualified a best-ever second, and led for just one corner before crashing out.**

Right: **Podium regulars Oliveira and KTM finally took their first victory of the year.**

Below right: **The tiniest bikes, a titanic battle. Martin leads Bezzecchi and Di Giannantonio. They finished in the same order.**

Photos: Gold & Goose

Vinales was on the far end of row one, Lorenzo in between; with Iannone heading row two from Petrucci and Marquez, at a track where five starts had given him only one win.

That record would not improve. After a typically aggressive start, he was up to second, but on lap five he suffered a front-end slide that for once he couldn't save – though he was still trying in the gravel trap.

He couldn't blame his sole use of the hard rear tyre, however. And he wasn't alone in choosing the asymmetric hard front, added at the riders' request following Mugello tests. Dovizioso, Rossi and Vinales had the same. Most of the rest, including Lorenzo, had opted for the medium.

It was about safety versus race-end drop-off, and as always was a difficult choice. Dovi said after the race, "I saw Valentino lose the front three times. I think we both made the wrong decision." Rossi didn't agree: "We knew it would be difficult, but at the end, those with the soft [medium] started to struggle on the right."

It made Lorenzo's surprise return to dominant form all the more impressive, as he barely lost speed in the final laps.

It was a trademark start-to-finish victory. Marquez did nose ahead into the first corner, but immediately ran wide. From there on, Lorenzo kept out of trouble as Rossi held on to second, while a number of crashes started when Pedrosa (qualified a lowly 20th) took down fellow Honda rider Nakagami on only the second corner. By the end of the lap, Abraham and Redding were also down and out; on the second, Luthi and Miller slipped off, ending a run of eight consecutive top tens for the Australian.

Also in the second corner on lap one, Marquez – desperate to regain momentum after his failed lunge – dived inside Petrucci for third, batting the independent Ducati rider wide, to finish the first lap eighth.

Things were more settled at the front, with Iannone fourth, ahead of Dovizioso, Rins was behind on the second Suzuki.

Lorenzo had led the previous two races, and most expected him to fade. He was steadfast, however, as Marquez outbraked Rossi into the first corner at the start of lap three; steadfast also when the Honda tucked the front two laps later; and he remained so on the following two laps as Dovizioso moved firmly up into second.

Instead, it was Rossi who appeared to be losing speed, and first Iannone and then, on lap 12, Petrucci came by, the latter also taking the Suzuki. Now there were three Ducatis up front: Lorenzo better than a second clear of Dovi, and Petrucci almost three adrift. These gaps would grow, and the triple podium would not see the flag.

Rins was gaining strength and also passed Rossi to hound Petrucci on lap 15; with Crutchlow now pressing at the back of the quintet.

Tyre wear would shuffle it. Petrucci said he'd had to push too hard to regain places lost on lap one, and from the 18th he began dropping to the back of the group.

Iannone had re-passed Rins, and now he and Rossi changed places several times. But on the penultimate lap, the older rider got ahead clearly and moved free. With Dovi slowing, he came within half a second of snitching second.

Iannone held off Rins; Crutchlow was still close.

Almost two seconds away, Petrucci only narrowly saved seventh. Vinales had finished lap one 11th, but once again recovered strongly, by the end his pace matching the leaders, and he brought a pressing Bautista with him. They'd surged past a lacklustre Zarco, who had been "fighting the bike in every corner".

Three seconds adrift of Zarco, Pol Espargaro was 11th, finally getting clear of a close trio, with top rookie Syahrin mere hundredths ahead of Rabat and Smith.

Morbidelli saved a point for a distant 15th. The remounted Marquez was 16th. Aleix Espargaro retired on the 21st lap with a rear tyre failure, after running in the points.

Rossi's second podium in a row put him in second place overall, and made him the first rider to score more than 5,000 points. But the big news was that Lorenzo was back: "A lot of people were saying my mentality was not right, and I just said I needed to be more comfortable and save more energy. Finally, when the team gave me a bike to feel comfortable, I could keep a constant pace. And today nobody could catch me."

MOTO2 RACE – 21 laps

Was this the best ever Moto2 race? Certainly it was for Oliveira, back to winning form from the fourth row of the grid, and victor in a race-long battle with the cream of the crop.

There was heartbreak, however, for pole-starter Pasini, He'd taken the lead on lap six, and had appeared comfortable and

set to repeat his win of 2017 – until he slipped off at the difficult first corner on lap 14.

He was the second to crash out of the lead. Marcel Schrotter had qualified a best ever second and had led into the first corner, only to slip off at the second.

Oliveira's blazing start was followed by a determined attack. He led for the first time on lap two, chased by Bagnaia, as well as Pasini, Alex Marquez and team-mate Mir, sandwiching fellow rookie Fenati.

Pasini would pick through; Fenati run straight at the first corner, with gear-shifting troubles. The rest would be joined by Baldassarri for a close and absorbing battle.

Oliveira had let Pasini go, divining that he was pushing too hard on a hot and tyre-punishing track.

When he fell, Oliveira had got back ahead of Bagnaia, as had Baldassarri, and the points leader dropped back slightly.

From lap 14, it was between Oli and Balda, the latter leading over the line for the first time on lap 16. Their battle raged to the end. Meanwhile, Mir had got ahead of Marquez, who'd been pushed wide at the first turn and lost touch. As the lead pair exchanged blows, both Mir and Bagnaia caught up again.

The last lap was a thriller. Baldassarri led on to it; Mir pushed Bagnaia to fourth at the first corner. Oliveira kept the pressure on, and it told – Baldassarri suffered a major slide at the top of the hill, losing drive and giving Oliveira his chance to get by. He won by 0.184 of a second.

Mir's third was a second podium in a row for the fast-rising star. He was barely a tenth adrift, with Bagnaia a similar distance behind. But Bagnaia had been suffering all weekend with unexpected arm-pump, and ominously it returned in the race. He said afterwards that he'd lost all feeling in one arm.

Marquez was alone in fifth; sixth was a fine result for Binder, who had qualified 19th, but finished lap one 12th. He had eventually escaped from Marini; close behind, Andrea Locatelli finally got the better of Vierge after a long battle.

Corsi had closed up again on this pair to round out the top ten, leaving Quartararo five seconds adrift.

With Aegerter back from injury in 12th and Lecuona a lone 13th, the welcome last points went to American Joe Roberts and South African Steven Odendaal, who took the first top-15 finishes for the new RW Racing NTS chassis.

Navarro, Lowes. Kent and Manzi crashed out, and late in the race Barbera knocked off Nagashima with such headlong violence that he was hit with a six-place grid penalty at the next race – but he wouldn't be there to take it.

MOTO3 RACE – 20 laps

After a string of poles and being knocked off in the previous two rounds, Jorge Martin claimed the cleverest and narrowest of wins.

It followed a 20-lap, three-bike fight that ended still all but three abreast. Martin managed a strong exit from the final corner that was just enough to keep him from being drafted over the line; Bezzecchi made the most of his KTM's straight-line speed to inch ahead of Martin's team-mate, Fabio Di Giannantonio. The three were covered by 0.049 of a second.

Martin had charged from the start to prevent the usual big group from forming. Only those two went with him, and they exchanged the lead constantly. Towards the end, Bezzecchi, struggling with a sliding front, was losing time everywhere, but getting it all back on the straight.

The usual Mugello muddle prevailed behind, until Bastianini managed to pick through from 14th on the grid. He took the KTMs of Rodrigo and 2017's winner Migno, plus Honda's Tony Arbolino, with him. Over the line, Rodrigo and Migno were ahead, Arbolini seventh.

The chase pack was still huge, from Dalla Porta in eighth to Bulega 21st covered by less than 1.5 seconds.

Antonelli and Pagliani completed the top ten; fancied runner Canet dropped to 11th with a last-lap slide. McPhee, Binder, Arenas and Ramirez wrapped up the points.

Bezzecchi's points lead over Martin shrank to three, with Di Giannantonio just another five behind.

GRAN PREMIO D'ITALIA OAKLEY

1–3 JUNE, 2018

AUTODROMO INTERNAZIONALE DEL MUGELLO

23 laps
Length: 5.245 km / 3.259 miles
Width: 14m

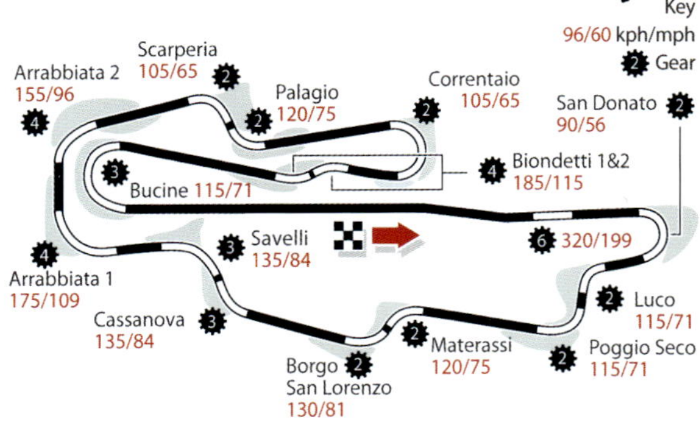

MotoGP

RACE DISTANCE: 23 laps, 74.959 miles/120.635km · RACE WEATHER: Dry (air 29°C, humidity 39%, track 51°C)

Pos.	Rider	Nat.	No.	Entrant	Machine	Tyres	Race tyre choice	Laps	Time & speed
1	**Jorge Lorenzo**	SPA	99	Ducati Team	Ducati Desmosedici	M	F: Medium/R: Soft	23	41m 43.230s 107.7mph/ 173.4km/h
2	**Andrea Dovizioso**	ITA	4	Ducati Team	Ducati Desmosedici	M	F: Hard*/R: Soft	23	41m 49.600s
3	**Valentino Rossi**	ITA	46	Movistar Yamaha MotoGP	Yamaha YZR-M1	M	F: Hard*/R: Medium	23	41m 49.859s
4	**Andrea Iannone**	ITA	29	Team SUZUKI ECSTAR	Suzuki GSX-RR	M	F: Medium/R: Soft	23	41m 51.115s
5	**Alex Rins**	SPA	42	Team SUZUKI ECSTAR	Suzuki GSX-RR	M	F: Medium/R: Soft	23	41m 51.137s
6	**Cal Crutchlow**	GBR	35	LCR Honda CASTROL	Honda RC213V	M	F: Medium/R: Medium	23	41m 52.350s
7	**Danilo Petrucci**	ITA	9	Alma Pramac Racing	Ducati Desmosedici	M	F: Medium/R: Soft	23	41m 54.128s
8	**Maverick Vinales**	SPA	25	Movistar Yamaha MotoGP	Yamaha YZR-M1	M	F: Hard*/R: Medium	23	41m 54.290s
9	**Alvaro Bautista**	SPA	19	Angel Nieto Team	Ducati Desmosedici	M	F: Medium/R: Soft	23	41m 54.384s
10	**Johann Zarco**	FRA	5	Monster Yamaha Tech 3	Yamaha YZR-M1	M	F: Medium/R: Medium	23	42m 00.874s
11	**Pol Espargaro**	SPA	44	Red Bull KTM Factory Racing	KTM RC16	M	F: Hard/R: Soft	23	42m 03.486s
12	**Hafizh Syahrin**	MAL	55	Monster Yamaha Tech 3	Yamaha YZR-M1	M	F: Medium/R: Soft	23	42m 05.665s
13	**Tito Rabat**	SPA	53	Reale Avintia Racing	Ducati Desmosedici	M	F: Medium/R: Soft	23	42m 05.694s
14	**Bradley Smith**	GBR	38	Red Bull KTM Factory Racing	KTM RC16	M	F: Medium/R: Soft	23	42m 05.725s
15	**Franco Morbidelli**	ITA	21	EG 0,0 Marc VDS	Honda RC213V	M	F: Medium/R: Soft	23	42m 09.874s
16	Marc Marquez	SPA	93	Repsol Honda Team	Honda RC213V	M	F: Hard*/R: Hard	23	42m 22.541s
17	Xavier Simeon	BEL	10	Reale Avintia Racing	Ducati Desmosedici	M	F: Medium/R: Soft	23	42m 44.441s
18	Takaaki Nakagami	JPN	30	LCR Honda IDEMITSU	Honda RC213V	M	F: Medium/R: Soft	18	42m 34.319s
	Aleix Espargaro	SPA	41	Aprilia Racing Team Gresini	Aprilia RS-GP	M	F: Medium/R: Soft	19	DNF-technical
	Jack Miller	AUS	43	Alma Pramac Racing	Ducati Desmosedici	M	F: Medium/R: Medium	1	DNF-crash
	Thomas Luthi	SWI	12	EG 0,0 Marc VDS	Honda RC213V	M	F: Medium/R: Soft	1	DNF-crash
	Dani Pedrosa	SPA	26	Repsol Honda Team	Honda RC213V	M	F: Hard/R: Medium	0	DNF-crash
	Karel Abraham	CZE	17	Angel Nieto Team	Ducati Desmosedici	M	F: Medium/R: Soft	0	DNF-crash
	Scott Redding	GBR	45	Aprilia Racing Team Gresini	Aprilia RS-GP	M	F: Medium/R: Soft	0	DNF-crash
	Michele Pirro	ITA	51	Ducati Team	Ducati Desmosedici	M	-	-	DNS-injured

*Asymmetric

Fastest lap: Danilo Petrucci, on lap 3, 1m 48.001s, 108.6mph/174.8km/h.
Lap record: Marc Marquez, 1m 47.639s, 109.0mph/175.4km/h (2013).
Event maximum speed: Andrea Dovizioso, 221.5mph/356.5km/h (race, all time MotoGP record).

Qualifying

Weather: Dry
Air Temp: 26° **Track Temp:** 47°
Humidity: 50%

1	Rossi	1m 46.208s
2	Lorenzo	1m 46.243s
3	Vinales	1m 46.304s
4	Iannone	1m 46.347s
5	Petrucci	1m 46.445s
6	Marquez	1m 46.454s
7	Dovizioso	1m 46.500s
8	Crutchlow	1m 46.813s
9	Zarco	1m 46.830s
10	Rins	1m 46.909s
11	Miller	1m 46.998s
12	Morbidelli	1m 47.002s
13	Rabat	1m 46.908s
14	Syahrin	1m 47.188s
15	P. Espargaro	1m 47.335s
16	Bautista	1m 47.708s
17	Smith	1m 47.818s
18	Nakagami	1m 47.868s
19	Luthi	1m 47.989s
20	Pedrosa	1m 48.065s
21	A. Espargaro	1m 48.286s
22	Abraham	1m 48.532s
23	Redding	1m 48.744s
24	Simeon	1m 48.794s

Fastest race laps

1	Petrucci	1m 48.001s
2	Dovizioso	1m 48.019s
3	Rins	1m 48.047s
4	Iannone	1m 48.073s
5	Marquez	1m 48.091s
6	Rossi	1m 48.096s
7	Lorenzo	1m 48.106s
8	Bautista	1m 48.255s
9	Crutchlow	1m 48.372s
10	Vinales	1m 48.467s
11	Zarco	1m 48.537s
12	A. Espargaro	1m 48.544s
13	Nakagami	1m 48.600s
14	P. Espargaro	1m 48.847s
15	Syahrin	1m 48.861s
16	Rabat	1m 48.865s
17	Smith	1m 48.886s
18	Morbidelli	1m 48.903s
19	Simeon	1m 50.151s

Grid order		1	2	3	4	5	6	7	8	9	10	11	12	13	14	15	16	17	18	19	20	21	22	23	
46	ROSSI	99	99	99	99	99	99	99	99	99	99	99	99	99	99	99	99	99	99	99	99	99	99	99	1
99	LORENZO	46	46	93	93	46	46	4	4	4	4	4	4	4	4	4	4	4	4	4	4	4	4	4	2
25	VINALES	93	93	46	46	29	4	46	29	29	29	29	9	9	9	9	9	9	46	46	46	46	46	46	3
29	IANNONE	29	29	29	29	4	29	29	46	46	46	46	29	46	46	42	42	46	29	29	29	29	29	29	4
9	PETRUCCI	4	4	4	4	42	42	9	9	9	9	9	46	42	42	46	46	29	9	42	42	42	42	42	5
93	MARQUEZ	42	42	42	42	9	9	42	42	42	42	42	42	29	29	29	29	42	42	9	9	35	35	35	6
4	DOVIZIOSO	35	9	9	9	35	35	35	35	35	35	35	35	35	35	35	35	35	35	35	35	9	9	9	7
35	CRUTCHLOW	9	35	35	35	5	5	5	5	5	25	25	25	25	25	25	25	25	25	25	25	25	25	25	8
5	ZARCO	43	5	5	5	25	25	25	25	25	19	19	19	19	19	19	19	19	19	19	19	19	19	19	9
42	RINS	5	25	25	25	19	19	19	19	19	5	5	5	5	5	5	5	5	5	5	5	5	5	5	10
43	MILLER	25	38	38	38	38	38	38	38	44	44	44	44	44	44	44	44	44	44	44	44	44	44	44	11
21	MORBIDELLI	38	44	44	19	44	44	44	44	38	38	41	41	41	41	41	41	41	41	41	38	53	53	55	12
53	RABAT	55	55	19	44	55	41	41	41	41	41	38	38	38	38	38	38	38	38	38	53	55	55	53	13
55	SYAHRIN	44	19	55	55	41	55	55	55	55	55	55	55	55	55	53	53	53	53	53	55	38	38	38	14
44	P. ESPARGARO	19	21	41	41	21	21	21	21	53	53	53	53	53	53	55	55	55	55	55	21	21	21	21	15
19	BAUTISTA	21	41	21	21	53	53	53	53	21	21	21	21	21	21	21	21	21	21	21	93	93	93	93	
38	SMITH	41	53	53	53	10	10	10	10	10	10	10	93	93	93	93	93	93	93	93	10	10	10	10	
30	NAKAGAMI	53	10	10	10	93	93	93	93	93	93	93	10	10	10	10	10	10	10	10					
12	LUTHI	10	30	30	30	30	30	30	30	30	30	30	30	30	30	30	30	30	30						
26	PEDROSA	12																							
41	A. ESPARGARO	30																							
17	ABRAHAM																								
45	REDDING																								
10	SIMEON																								

41 Pit stop 30 Lapped rider

Championship Points

1	Marquez	95
2	Rossi	72
3	Vinales	67
4	Dovizioso	66
5	Zarco	64
6	Petrucci	63
7	Iannone	60
8	Crutchlow	56
9	Miller	49
10	Lorenzo	41
11	Rins	33
12	Pedrosa	29
13	Rabat	27
14	P. Espargaro	23
15	Bautista	19
16	Syahrin	17
17	Morbidelli	17
18	A. Espargaro	13
19	Nakagami	10
20	Smith	7
21	Kallio	6
22	Redding	5
23	Abraham	1

Constructor Points

1	Honda	130
2	Yamaha	108
3	Ducati	107
4	Suzuki	74
5	KTM	24
6	Aprilia	18

Moto2

RACE DISTANCE: 21 laps, 68.441 miles/110.145km · RACE WEATHER: Dry (air 27°C, humidity 43%, track 43°C)

Pos.	Rider	Nat.	No.	Entrant	Machine	Laps	Time & Speed
1	**Miguel Oliveira**	POR	44	Red Bull KTM Ajo	KTM	21	39m 42.018s 103.4mph/ 166.4km/h
2	**Lorenzo Baldassarri**	ITA	7	Pons HP40	Kalex	21	39m 42.202s
3	**Joan Mir**	SPA	36	EG 0,0 Marc VDS	Kalex	21	39m 42.352s
4	**Francesco Bagnaia**	ITA	42	SKY Racing Team VR46	Kalex	21	39m 42.502s
5	**Alex Marquez**	SPA	73	EG 0,0 Marc VDS	Kalex	21	39m 45.555s
6	**Brad Binder**	RSA	41	Red Bull KTM Ajo	KTM	21	39m 48.003s
7	**Luca Marini**	ITA	10	SKY Racing Team VR46	Kalex	21	39m 51.926s
8	**Andrea Locatelli**	ITA	5	Italtrans Racing Team	Kalex	21	39m 53.237s
9	**Xavi Vierge**	SPA	97	Dynavolt Intact GP	Kalex	21	39m 54.389s
10	**Simone Corsi**	ITA	24	Tasca Racing Scuderia Moto2	Kalex	21	39m 54.693s
11	**Fabio Quartararo**	FRA	20	MB Conveyors - Speed Up Racing	Speed Up	21	39m 59.861s
12	**Dominique Aegerter**	SWI	77	Kiefer Racing	KTM	21	40m 02.371s
13	**Iker Lecuona**	SPA	27	Swiss Innovative Investors	KTM	21	40m 10.769s
14	**Joe Roberts**	USA	16	NTS RW Racing GP	NTS	21	40m 14.454s
15	**Steven Odendaal**	RSA	4	NTS RW Racing GP	NTS	21	40m 14.483s
16	Isaac Vinales	SPA	32	SAG Team	Kalex	21	40m 15.072s
17	Niki Tuuli	FIN	66	SIC Racing Team	Kalex	21	40m 15.523s
18	Khairul Idham Pawi	MAL	89	IDEMITSU Honda Team Asia	Kalex	21	40m 25.918s
19	Eric Granado	BRA	51	Forward Racing Team	Suter	21	40m 29.282s
20	Hector Garzo	SPA	14	Tech 3 Racing	Tech 3	21	40m 38.621s
21	Federico Fuligni	ITA	21	Tasca Racing Scuderia Moto2	Kalex	21	40m 55.627s
22	Xavi Cardelus	AND	18	Team Stylobike	Kalex	21	41m 09.945s
	Tetsuta Nagashima	JPN	45	IDEMITSU Honda Team Asia	Kalex	15	DNF
	Hector Barbera	SPA	40	Pons HP40	Kalex	15	DNF
	Mattia Pasini	ITA	54	Italtrans Racing Team	Kalex	13	DNF
	Jules Danilo	FRA	95	Nashi Argan SAG Team	Kalex	12	DNF
	Stefano Manzi	ITA	62	Forward Racing Team	Suter	10	DNF
	Danny Kent	GBR	52	MB Conveyors - Speed Up Racing	Speed Up	9	DNF
	Romano Fenati	ITA	13	Marinelli Snipers Team	Kalex	7	DNF
	Sam Lowes	GBR	22	Swiss Innovative Investors	KTM	6	DNF
	Jorge Navarro	SPA	9	Federal Oil Gresini Moto2	Kalex	4	DNF
	Bo Bendsneyder	NED	64	Tech 3 Racing	Tech 3	0	DNF
	Marcel Schrotter	GER	23	Dynavolt Intact GP	Kalex	0	DNF

Fastest lap: Miguel Oliveira, on lap 2, 1m 52.337s, 104.4mph/168.0km/h.
Lap record: Thomas Luthi, 1m 52.084s, 104.6mph/168.4km/h (2017).
Event maximum speed: Hector Barbera, 182.2mph/293.3km/h (qualifying).

Qualifying

Weather: Dry
Air Temp: 26° **Track Temp:** 49°
Humidity: 50%

1	Pasini	1m 51.575s
2	Schrotter	1m 51.605s
3	Marquez	1m 51.642s
4	Bagnaia	1m 51.921s
5	Corsi	1m 51.959s
6	Fenati	1m 51.973s
7	Marini	1m 51.979s
8	Baldassarri	1m 52.083s
9	Mir	1m 52.100s
10	Navarro	1m 52.112s
11	Oliveira	1m 52.145s
12	Vierge	1m 52.173s
13	Nagashima	1m 52.227s
14	Lowes	1m 52.244s
15	Kent	1m 52.245s
16	Quartararo	1m 52.318s
17	Locatelli	1m 52.387s
18	Pawi	1m 52.391s
19	Binder	1m 52.433s
20	Manzi	1m 52.618s
21	Barbera	1m 52.644s
22	Lecuona	1m 52.668s
23	Bendsneyder	1m 52.729s
24	Vinales	1m 52.840s
25	Odendaal	1m 52.842s
26	Aegerter	1m 52.879s
27	Tuuli	1m 53.390s
28	Roberts	1m 53.562s
29	Danilo	1m 53.606s
30	Granado	1m 54.038s
31	Fuligni	1m 54.389s
32	Garzo	1m 54.720s
33	Cardelus	1m 55.485s

Fastest race laps

1	Oliveira	1m 52.337s
2	Pasini	1m 52.371s
3	Bagnaia	1m 52.400s
4	Baldassarri	1m 52.450s
5	Mir	1m 52.482s
6	Fenati	1m 52.595s
7	Locatelli	1m 52.616s
8	Marquez	1m 52.653s
9	Navarro	1m 52.675s
10	Binder	1m 52.690s
11	Manzi	1m 52.739s
12	Vierge	1m 52.772s
13	Lowes	1m 52.859s
14	Marini	1m 52.950s
15	Quartararo	1m 52.988s
16	Corsi	1m 53.015s
17	Lecuona	1m 53.196s
18	Aegerter	1m 53.289s
19	Nagashima	1m 53.320s
20	Barbera	1m 53.431s
21	Odendaal	1m 53.562s
22	Kent	1m 53.622s
23	Vinales	1m 53.650s
24	Pawi	1m 53.681s
25	Roberts	1m 53.979s
26	Tuuli	1m 54.056s
27	Granado	1m 54.171s
28	Fuligni	1m 54.270s
29	Danilo	1m 54.292s
30	Garzo	1m 54.588s
31	Cardelus	1m 54.791s

Championship Points

1	Bagnaia	111
2	Oliveira	98
3	Baldassarri	84
4	Marquez	78
5	Mir	64
6	Vierge	59
7	Pasini	58
8	Binder	47
9	Schrotter	37
10	Lecuona	26
11	Aegerter	20
12	Quartararo	20
13	Marini	19
14	Corsi	18
15	Locatelli	16
16	Gardner	14
17	Navarro	14
18	Lowes	14
19	Barbera	10
20	Fenati	9
21	Vinales	7
22	Manzi	6
23	Kent	4
24	Nagashima	3
25	Roberts	2
26	Odendaal	1
27	Pawi	1

Constructor Points

1	Kalex	145
2	KTM	98
3	Speed Up	24
4	Tech 3	14
5	Suter	6
6	NTS	2

Moto3

RACE DISTANCE: 20 laps, 65.182 miles/104.900km · RACE WEATHER: Dry (air 27°C, humidity 45%, track 43°C)

Pos.	Rider	Nat.	No.	Entrant	Machine	Laps	Time & Speed
1	**Jorge Martin**	SPA	88	Del Conca Gresini Moto3	Honda	20	39m 20.810s 99.4mph/ 159.9km/h
2	**Marco Bezzecchi**	ITA	12	Redox PruestelGP	KTM	20	39m 20.829s
3	**Fabio Di Giannantonio**	ITA	21	Del Conca Gresini Moto3	Honda	20	39m 20.853s
4	**Gabriel Rodrigo**	ARG	19	RBA BOE Skull Rider	KTM	20	39m 31.758s
5	**Andrea Migno**	ITA	16	Angel Nieto Team Moto3	KTM	20	39m 31.893s
6	**Enea Bastianini**	ITA	33	Leopard Racing	Honda	20	39m 31.975s
7	**Tony Arbolino**	ITA	14	Marinelli Snipers Team	Honda	20	39m 32.004s
8	**Lorenzo Dalla Porta**	ITA	48	Leopard Racing	Honda	20	39m 35.377s
9	**Niccolo Antonelli**	ITA	23	SIC58 Squadra Corse	Honda	20	39m 35.486s
10	**Manuel Pagliani**	ITA	96	Leopard Junior Team	Honda	20	39m 35.492s
11	**Aron Canet**	SPA	44	Estrella Galicia 0,0	Honda	20	39m 35.503s
12	**John McPhee**	GBR	17	CIP - Green Power	KTM	20	39m 35.530s
13	**Darryn Binder**	RSA	40	Red Bull KTM Ajo	KTM	20	39m 35.543s
14	**Albert Arenas**	SPA	75	Angel Nieto Team Moto3	KTM	20	39m 35.580s
15	**Marcos Ramirez**	SPA	42	Bester Capital Dubai	KTM	20	39m 36.047s
16	Ayumu Sasaki	JPN	71	Petronas Sprinta Racing	Honda	20	39m 36.081s
17	Tatsuki Suzuki	JPN	24	SIC58 Squadra Corse	Honda	20	39m 36.178s
18	Alonso Lopez	SPA	72	Estrella Galicia 0,0	Honda	20	39m 36.441s
19	Philipp Oettl	GER	65	Sudmetal Schedl GP Racing	KTM	20	39m 36.763s
20	Kaito Toba	JPN	27	Honda Team Asia	Honda	20	39m 36.793s
21	Nicolo Bulega	ITA	8	SKY Racing Team VR46	KTM	20	39m 36.840s
22	Kazuki Masaki	JPN	22	RBA BOE Skull Rider	KTM	20	39m 43.302s
23	Jakub Kornfeil	CZE	84	Redox PruestelGP	KTM	20	39m 43.330s
24	Livio Loi	BEL	11	Reale Avintia Academy	KTM	20	40m 11.501s
25	Nakarin Atiratphuvapat	THA	41	Honda Team Asia	Honda	20	40m 43.855s
	Makar Yurchenko	KAZ	76	CIP - Green Power	KTM	18	DNF
	Jaume Masia	SPA	5	Bester Capital Dubai	KTM	16	DNF
	Dennis Foggia	ITA	10	SKY Racing Team VR46	KTM	6	DNF
	Stefano Nepa	ITA	81	NRT Junior Team	KTM	5	DNF
	Adam Norrodin	MAL	7	Petronas Sprinta Racing	Honda	2	DNF

Fastest lap: Fabio Di Giannantonio, on lap 2, 1m 56.628s, 100.5mph/161.8km/h.
Lap record: Aron Canet, 1m 57.071s, 100.2mph/161.2km/h (2017).
Event maximum speed: John McPhee, 153.0mph/246.3km/h (race).

Qualifying

Weather: Dry
Air Temp: 26° **Track Temp:** 47°
Humidity: 54%

1	Martin	1m 56.634s
2	Suzuki	1m 56.824s
3	Sasaki	1m 56.844s
4	Canet	1m 56.858s
5	Bezzecchi	1m 56.875s
6	Di Giannantonio	1m 56.905s
7	Antonelli	1m 56.937s
8	Norrodin	1m 56.993s
9	Ramirez	1m 57.087s
10	Toba	1m 57.266s
11	Masaki	1m 57.306s
12	Rodrigo	1m 57.358s
13	Masia	1m 57.366s
14	Bastianini	1m 57.463s
15	Migno	1m 57.513s
16	Bulega	1m 57.542s
17	Dalla Porta	1m 57.572s
18	Arbolino	1m 57.589s
19	McPhee	1m 57.606s
20	Oettl	1m 57.637s
21	Kornfeil	1m 57.678s
22	Arenas	1m 57.745s
23	Yurchenko	1m 57.779s
24	Pagliani	1m 57.863s
25	Binder	1m 58.181s
26	Lopez	1m 58.319s
27	Foggia	1m 58.458s
28	Atiratphuvapat	1m 58.578s
29	Nepa	1m 59.143s
30	Loi	1m 59.711s

Fastest race laps

1	Di Giannantonio	1m 56.628s
2	Bezzecchi	1m 56.695s
3	Masia	1m 56.950s
4	Antonelli	1m 56.982s
5	Arbolino	1m 57.069s
6	Rodrigo	1m 57.097s
7	Martin	1m 57.108s
8	Foggia	1m 57.154s
9	Dalla Porta	1m 57.193s
10	Bastianini	1m 57.214s
11	Canet	1m 57.243s
12	McPhee	1m 57.266s
13	Pagliani	1m 57.303s
14	Kornfeil	1m 57.304s
15	Binder	1m 57.309s
16	Oettl	1m 57.328s
17	Migno	1m 57.357s
18	Arenas	1m 57.388s
19	Toba	1m 57.400s
20	Sasaki	1m 57.417s
21	Suzuki	1m 57.446s
22	Norrodin	1m 57.459s
23	Bulega	1m 57.462s
24	Lopez	1m 57.467s
25	Ramirez	1m 57.713s
26	Masaki	1m 57.919s
27	Yurchenko	1m 57.935s
28	Loi	1m 58.360s
29	Nepa	1m 59.004s
30	Atiratphuvapat	1m 59.292s

Championship Points

1	Bezzecchi	83
2	Martin	80
3	Di Giannantonio	75
4	Canet	61
5	Migno	56
6	Antonelli	44
7	Bastianini	43
8	Rodrigo	41
9	Ramirez	38
10	Oettl	36
11	Kornfeil	36
12	Dalla Porta	33
13	Arenas	28
14	Suzuki	24
15	Arbolino	24
16	Lopez	23
17	Masia	21
18	Sasaki	17
19	Norrodin	16
20	Toba	16
21	Binder	11
22	McPhee	10
23	Loi	7
24	Pagliani	6
25	Yurchenko	5
26	Masaki	3
27	Foggia	2
28	Ogura	1

Constructor Points

1	KTM	122
2	Honda	121

FIM WORLD CHAMPIONSHIP · ROUND 7

CATALUNYA GRAND PRIX

BARCELONA-CATALUNYA CIRCUIT

LORENZO'S
Jorge Lorenzo
OFFICIAL FAN CLUB

Above: Lorenzo ran away again. Here on lap two, he's chased by Marquez, Dovizioso, Rossi, Iannone, Pedrosa, Petrucci and fast-starter Smith.

Top right: Moto2's Remy Gardner with father Wayne. A gutsy return earned him a point.

Above right: Plastic fantastic. A simple ergonomic modification made to Lorenzo's Ducati delivered rich rewards.

Right: Independent Ducati rider Alvaro Bautista earned a third top ten in four races.

Photos: Gold & Goose

Below right: Suzuki test rider Sylvain Guintoli was back as a wild-card – but not for long. The Frenchman was one of ten to crash out of a race of high attrition.

Photo: Team Ecstar Suzuki

Opening spread: Catalunya became Lorenzo's Land again, and his symbolic hammer was ready to wave to the fans.

Photo: Gold & Goose

THE talk was still all about Lorenzo, and he underlined it with not just his first pole position for Ducati, but also a second straight win, in imperious style, dominating a race of such attrition that there were not enough finishers to take all the points.

The confirmation of his move to Honda had come in the break after his first win in Italy and followed (as was proper) Honda's announcement of the split with Dani Pedrosa, ending a career-long commitment to the marque that included one 125 and two 250 titles, and 31 MotoGP wins. How had Lorenzo and Honda managed to keep it secret? "I didn't tell anybody," the rider said, disingenuously. He was equally calm when asked whether his smooth style could work with the point-and-squirt Honda. "I have the capacity," he said.

The weekend began with a packed assembly in Honda's hospitality, where Dani was expected to announce his retirement. Instead, with a mischievous grin, he noted that there were more present than had ever celebrated one of his race wins, then apologised for having nothing to tell them. He was considering his options.

One was with the expected Petronas Yamaha team, but this remained unconfirmed. Intriguing hints had to be enough. Yamaha Motor Racing's Lin Jarvis had previously suggested the possibility of at least one full factory bike for the team, and now said, "I've always been personally very curious to see how Dani Pedrosa would go on a Yamaha."

The uncertainty surrounding the troubled Marc VDS team also had the potential to affect Yamaha's situation, but at least threats of a court battle between owner Marc van der Straten and ex-team principal Michael Bartholemy were in abeyance. A team statement indicated that the pair had "reached a mutual agreement to end their association … due to differing strategic approaches." Van der Straten "did not hold against Bartholemy the allegations reported in the press, especially regarding any supposed embezzlement." In the coming weeks would come the news that the VDS MotoGP adventure would end in 2018, allowing the team to concentrate on Moto2.

Other teams had plenty of definite news. Suzuki confirmed their contract with Mir; Aprilia announced that they would pick up the thus dispossessed Iannone. Ducati confirmed that Danilo Petrucci would be taking Lorenzo's ride, although rather surprisingly the rider had requested only a one-year contract. Syahrin was signed to stay with Tech 3 alongside 2020 rookie Oliveira, with 2019's KTM. And Oliveira's current Ajo KTM Moto2 team announced that Moto3's Jorge Martin would take his place.

The circuit at Montmelo was also in a more definite state, not only fully resurfaced, but also largely restored to the original motorcycle-friendly layout. Although the tight left-hander at the end of the back straight remained, the penultimate right-hander – where two years before, Salom had crashed fatally – had been restored, the grandstand moved for extra run-off, and the F1 chicane between that and the final corner was off the MotoGP map. The reversion was welcomed, although Marquez noted that, after the F1 race a month before, "already there are some bumps in braking". He also had some doubts about the angled kerbing inside the corners, which reduced clearance for knees and elbows.

The kerbs had nothing to do with yet another of his sensational trademark saves – perhaps his best ever – at the fast final corner. He lost the front on full lean at more than 170km/h, but managed to get it back with his knee (in the process, the slider was pushed around to the back of his leg), only for the tyre to slide away again "when I was on the dirty part of the track". Nothing daunted, he recovered once more.

Test riders were on hand: Sylvain Guintoli for Suzuki and Mika Kallio again for KTM. Guintoli was exercising a modified chassis with carbon-fibre cladding to adjust stiffness, which Rins liked at once, and team-mate Iannone also, but only at the official Monday tests. Kallio, it was revealed, did not have the reverse-crank 2018 engine this time.

Yamaha had a modification, too, aimed at solving their difficulties in hot conditions. The rear hugger mudguard was slotted to pass more air over the rear tyre.

A delegation from Brazil was at the track, with the welcome announcement of a potential return to Rio in 2021, after an absence of 14 years. Dorna had signed "a preliminary agreement" with Rio Motosports, a company formed to promote racing there. The planned circuit in Rio would have to be designed, built and homologated, but hopes were

high. Brazil had a chequered history, with three races at the inland Goiania circuit between 1987 and 1989, a single controversial outing at scary Sao Paulo in 1992 (a riders' strike narrowly averted), and subsequent races between 1995 and 2004 at the now extinct Jacarepagua circuit outside the city.

A new balconied double-storey Clinica Mobile, now backed by European medical group Quirónsalud, made its debut, sized in keeping with the massive expansion of team hospitalities, but rather more useful to the riders, with more space and more equipment than previously. The Clinica had been founded by Dr Claudio Costa in 1977 and had grown in status ever since, with almost all riders owing it some sort of a debt, sometimes very large indeed.

Hector Barbera's return to Moto2 had come to an abrupt end after the trouble-prone rider was handed a one-year driving ban for failing a drink-drive test in Valencia the previous week. His contract with Sito Pons's HP40 team was terminated forthwith. His seat went to Augusto Fernandez (20) from Madrid, winner of the CEV Moto2 race at the Catalunya circuit one week before.

Also in Moto2, Remy Gardner was back after missing three races. Still on crutches after breaking both legs and his ankle in a motocross crash, he showed true grit and was rewarded by finishing in the points.

The weekend was run under a sombre shadow, following the death of 14-year-old Andrea Perez at the CEV meeting a week before; and the fresh tragedy was marked by a minute of silence before racing got under way. Perez had been backed by Avintia, and their MotoGP bikes for Rabat and Simeon ran in all-black livery.

MOTOGP RACE – 24 laps

On a second weekend rich in irony, Lorenzo was fast and consistent, while nearest rival and future team-mate Marc Marquez was quite the opposite, after falling in FP3 to miss going straight to Q2 for the second time ever. Straight after his knee-dragging FP4 save, in scarred leathers, he dominated Q1, then was knocked off pole by less than a tenth. Dovi was third, his first front-row start of the year.

Vinales led row two, less than half a second down, from Iannone and Petrucci; Rossi headed the third. Crutchlow's front-row bid had ended with a crash, leaving him tenth, but ahead of Pedrosa. Nakagami (12th) was through from Q1 for the first time.

Lorenzo chose soft tyres front and rear; Marquez was one of only two riders (the other Morbidelli) to choose the hard compound for both ends. The difference added a dimension to an otherwise uneventful duel in a race where the drama was all behind the pair.

Marquez led into the first corner, with Iannone shoving past Lorenzo into second and even leading for a couple of yards at the end of the back straight, before immediately running wide.

On the first run down the front straight, Lorenzo powered into the lead, while Dovizioso likewise surged past the Suzuki. Then Rossi dived underneath to put Iannone fifth on the way into the first right-left corner set.

The first three soon pulled clear, with Dovi a second ahead of Rossi by lap six. Three laps later, however, shaking his head in bafflement, as at Le Mans, he crashed out under brakes at the downhill entry to Turn Five, much like his equally uncharacteristic Le Mans crash.

By now, wild-cards Kallio and Guintoli, as well as Luthi, Simeon and Aleix Espargaro, had already crashed out, the grippy new surface treacherous when the grip ran out. Soon afterwards, Rins retired, from the back of the field.

The front three didn't change, and Marquez didn't give up pushing. But Lorenzo was in metronomic mood, turning one regular fast lap after another, and after lap ten, the gap started to grow – to almost 4.5 seconds at the end. By then, Marquez's times had dropped off, and the gap to Rossi had been halved to less than two seconds.

Pedrosa had started well from 11th on the grid, finishing lap one sixth and heading the pursuit as Iannone continued to drop back. Petrucci was pushing hard and was ahead once on lap eight, by which time Crutchlow had caught up and was clearly fastest of the trio. With seven laps left, the Briton found his way past the factory Honda, taking fourth, four seconds behind Rossi, though barely two-tenths clear of Pedrosa.

By now, Vinales had found his speed. His start had been disastrous and, as so often, his early pace uninspiring, but in the latter laps, he was as fast as the leaders. He repassed Zarco and left him behind, with Petrucci fading to the finish, taking eighth.

There had been a good battle behind, with Miller and Rabat shadowing the Yamahas, along with Syahrin, another strong run – until he crashed. By then, Miller had dropped back with fuel pump issues, which soon caused a second successive non-finish.

Meanwhile, Rabat had already departed in dramatic fashion. A plume of smoke in Syahrin's face at the start of the main straight was the prelude to gouts of flame at the end of it, the Spanish rider swerving off into the gravel and leaping off his burning Ducati. An exhaust leak, it transpired, had burned through an oil line, resulting in a fine conflagration.

Iannone had dropped right behind, and at the end gave way also to Bautista. Trailing in, Pol Espargaro was chased by Redding's Aprilia, while miles behind were Abraham and Morbidelli. The last-named had fallen, remounted and toured to the pits – only to be sent out again, with points guaranteed for every finisher, even though by then he was three laps adrift.

Above: Crutchlow hounds Pedrosa on the factory Honda. The Briton would prevail in the fight for fourth.

Above right: Lorenzo's second straight Ducati win came days after he'd signed for the opposition.
Photos: Gold & Goose

Above far right: Mutual admiration in *parc ferme*. It was Rossi's third podium in a row; Crutchlow's fourth time as top independent rider.
Photo: Monster Energy

Right: First-time winner Fabio Quartararo caught and outpaced Oliveira's KTM.

Far right: The Frenchman celebrates the reward for never giving up.

Below right: Four survivors. Moto3 winner Bastianini heads Rodrigo, Bezzecchi and McPhee. Bezzecchi would swap for second over the line.
Photos: Gold & Goose

Not among them were Nakagami and Smith. The Japanese rider had been in the process of taking 15th from the KTM man at the same corner that had claimed Dovizioso, but he lost the front and fell under the Briton's front wheel, ending the race for both.

It was an important race for the championship: Marquez making up for his Mugello no-score and stretching his lead; Dovizioso's title chances taking a hammer blow with a third no-score in four races; and the remarkable Rossi taking a third podium in a row. And Lorenzo jumping to seventh, fewer than 50 points off the leader.

MOTO2 RACE – 22 laps

French one-time bright hope Fabio Quartararo illustrated the strength of 'never give up'. First he qualified on pole, then he rode his Speed Up to not only his first GP win, but also his first podium since he had started in Moto3 in 2015.

He had been given a special 'under-age' entry into Moto3 as a reward for winning the previous two 'Junior World Championship' Spanish CEV titles. The hype had been overwhelming, and he had struggled to live up to it ever since. His best finish since moving to Moto2 in 2017 had been a single sixth place.

The win was convincing, outpacing Mugello winner Oliveira (KTM), who had blazed through from 17th on the grid. They consigned early leader Alex Marquez to third, his EG-VDS Kalex making it three different types of chassis on the grid for the first time since 2013.

Marquez had qualified second, with Schrotter alongside; Bagnaia headed row two from Binder and Pasini.

Marquez led Schrotter away, with Quartararo third. Oliveira made up nine places into the first corner and finished lap one fourth, ahead of Bagnaia.

Oliveira was still on the move, taking third from Quartararo on lap five, both now ahead of Schrotter. Next time around, trying to get back, Schrotter ran off at the first corner, rejoining in eighth, behind Binder, the troubled Bagnaia, Vierge and Pasini. It was the beginning of a strong fight back by the German.

Oliveira led on lap eight. A little further around, Quartararo also passed Marquez. When he passed Oliveira two laps later, it was for good, the gap stretching to more than a second on lap 15.

Marquez soon had his hands full fending off fiercely challenging team-mates Schrotter and Vierge, and they finished in that order.

Binder was sixth, while Bagnaia faded throughout, blaming a faulty rear tyre. With two laps to go, Baldassarri had got past, and with another lap, he might have taken Binder as well.

Only three seconds behind by the end, Sam Lowes stormed through ninth, having started from the back of the grid after suffering fuel pump problems on the sighting lap. His last victim was team-mate Iker Lecuona, who rounded out the top ten.

A brave ride allowed Gardner to take a point for 15th, in his first race since breaking both legs and an ankle before the start of the European season.

There were several crashes, starting on lap one when Bendsneyder, Tuuli and Manzi became tangled together. This was followed by Navarro; hot rookie Mir, for once nowhere near the front; Pasini, Fenati and Vinales.

Potentially, the worst came after the finish line.

Oliveira had slowed and was waving to the crowd when Simone Corsi, who had finished 12th, ran right up the back of him at speed. Miraculously, neither was badly hurt, and Corsi would start the next race from the back of the grid as punishment.

Bagnaia's title lead shrank to just one point from Oliveira: the battle was heating up.

MOTO3 RACE – 21 laps

Crashes and drama upset the formbook in Moto3. Bastianini took a first win of the year, while second-placed Bezzecchi extended his points advantage, after earlier favourite Martin crashed out of a commanding lead.

Martin had fallen twice in practice, but only narrowly missed a fifth straight pole, with Bastianini quickest. The Spaniard took off in the lead, shadowed by third front-row starter Suzuki, and the pair rapidly put a substantial gap on a big brawl behind. By lap eight, it was still more than two seconds, but beginning to close.

Martin got the message, but overreacted – and fell off.

Without his guide, Suzuki was soon swallowed up by a lively group, now 11 strong. Then more crashes began to cut it back.

Three fell together, after Le Mans winner Arenas tagged an on-form Nicolo Bulega and Canet. Arenas would be docked six grid positions at the next race as a consequence.

Shortly afterwards, Masia and Migno, who had both led at least once, collided and were out.

With Arbolino pitting, that left just five still battling to the end, and Bastianini was able to hold off Bezzecchi's last push. Rodrigo was inches behind in third, the Argentine rider's first podium, narrowly ahead of McPhee and Suzuki, the top five over the line inside less than a second.

Luckless Antonelli missed the race, having dislocated his shoulder in practice.

Bezzecchi's valuable score moved him to almost 20 points clear of new second-placer Di Giannantonio, who finished a distant ninth, with Martin now third after a third no-score, this time through his own error.

NetApp
Lenovo

Castrol
POWER1
rizoma
HONDA
MICHELIN
YAMAHA
EOS

44
20
HDR

Beta
HDR
KYT

LEOPARD
33
SEVENTY
BRESSER

GRAN PREMI MONSTER ENERGY DE CATALUNYA

15–17 JUNE, 2018

CIRCUIT DE CATALUNYA

24 laps
Length: 4.627km / 2.875 miles
Width: 12m

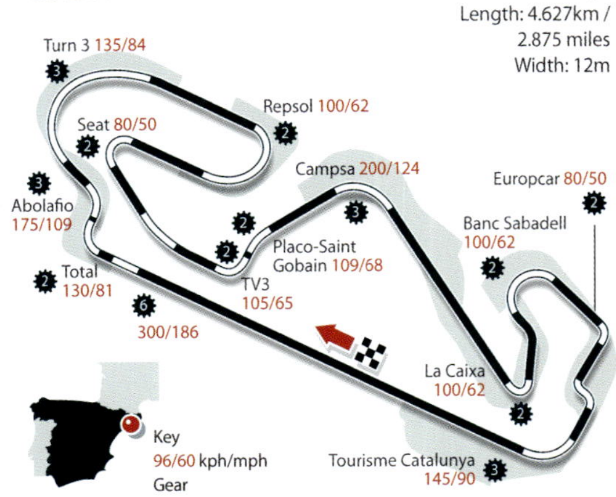

MotoGP

RACE DISTANCE: 24 laps, 69.002 miles/111.048km · RACE WEATHER: Dry (air 27°C, humidity 51%, track 45°C)

Pos.	Rider	Nat.	No.	Entrant	Machine	Tyres	Race tyre choice	Laps	Time & speed
1	**Jorge Lorenzo**	SPA	99	Ducati Team	Ducati Desmosedici	M	F: Soft/R: Soft	24	40m 13.566s 102.9mph/ 165.6km/h
2	**Marc Marquez**	SPA	93	Repsol Honda Team	Honda RC213V	M	F: Hard/R: Hard	24	40m 18.045s
3	**Valentino Rossi**	ITA	46	Movistar Yamaha MotoGP	Yamaha YZR-M1	M	F: Soft/R: Soft	24	40m 19.664s
4	**Cal Crutchlow**	GBR	35	LCR Honda CASTROL	Honda RC213V	M	F: Medium/R: Soft	24	40m 23.371s
5	**Dani Pedrosa**	SPA	26	Repsol Honda Team	Honda RC213V	M	F: Medium/R: Medium	24	40m 24.206s
6	**Maverick Vinales**	SPA	25	Movistar Yamaha MotoGP	Yamaha YZR-M1	M	F: Soft/R: Soft	24	40m 24.364s
7	**Johann Zarco**	FRA	5	Monster Yamaha Tech 3	Yamaha YZR-M1	M	F: Soft/R: Medium	24	40m 26.998s
8	**Danilo Petrucci**	ITA	9	Alma Pramac Racing	Ducati Desmosedici	M	F: Soft/R: Soft	24	40m 28.621s
9	**Alvaro Bautista**	SPA	19	Angel Nieto Team	Ducati Desmosedici	M	F: Soft/R: Soft	24	40m 35.623s
10	**Andrea Iannone**	ITA	29	Team SUZUKI ECSTAR	Suzuki GSX-RR	M	F: Soft/R: Soft	24	40m 37.707s
11	**Pol Espargaro**	SPA	44	Red Bull KTM Factory Racing	KTM RC16	M	F: Soft/R: Soft	24	40m 50.126s
12	**Scott Redding**	GBR	45	Aprilia Racing Team Gresini	Aprilia RS-GP	M	F: Hard/R: Soft	24	40m 51.795s
13	**Karel Abraham**	CZE	17	Angel Nieto Team	Ducati Desmosedici	M	F: Medium/R: Soft	24	41m 35.092s
14	**Franco Morbidelli**	ITA	21	EG 0,0 Marc VDS	Honda RC213V	M	F: Hard/R: Hard	21	41m 54.234s
	Hafizh Syahrin	MAL	55	Monster Yamaha Tech 3	Yamaha YZR-M1	M	F: Soft/R: Soft	20	DNF-crash
	Tito Rabat	SPA	53	Reale Avintia Racing	Ducati Desmosedici	M	F: Soft/R: Soft	18	DNF-technical
	Jack Miller	AUS	43	Alma Pramac Racing	Ducati Desmosedici	M	F: Soft/R: Soft	17	DNF-technical
	Bradley Smith	GBR	38	Red Bull KTM Factory Racing	KTM RC16	M	F: Medium/R: Soft	13	DNF-crash
	Takaaki Nakagami	JPN	30	LCR Honda IDEMITSU	Honda RC213V	M	F: Medium/R: Soft	13	DNF-crash
	Alex Rins	SPA	42	Team SUZUKI ECSTAR	Suzuki GSX-RR	M	F: Soft/R: Soft	11	DNF-technical
	Andrea Dovizioso	ITA	4	Ducati Team	Ducati Desmosedici	M	F: Soft/R: Soft	8	DNF-crash
	Xavier Simeon	BEL	10	Reale Avintia Racing	Ducati Desmosedici	M	F: Soft/R: Soft	7	DNF-crash
	Aleix Espargaro	SPA	41	Aprilia Racing Team Gresini	Aprilia RS-GP	M	F: Medium/R: Soft	4	DNF-crash
	Thomas Luthi	SWI	12	EG 0,0 Marc VDS	Honda RC213V	M	F: Medium/R: Soft	3	DNF-crash
	Sylvain Guintoli	FRA	50	Team SUZUKI ECSTAR	Suzuki GSX-RR	M	F: Soft/R: Soft	2	DNF-crash
	Mika Kallio	FIN	36	Red Bull KTM Factory Racing	KTM RC16	M	F: Medium/R: Soft	0	DNF-crash

Fastest lap: Jorge Lorenzo, on lap 9, 1m 40.021s, 103.5mph/166.5km/h.
Lap record: New layout.
Event maximum speed: Andrea Dovizioso, 216.7mph/348.8km/h (free practice).

Qualifying

Weather: Dry
Air Temp: 28° **Track Temp:** 48°
Humidity: 46%

1	Lorenzo	1m 38.680s
2	Marquez	1m 38.746s
3	Dovizioso	1m 38.923s
4	Vinales	1m 39.145s
5	Iannone	1m 39.148s
6	Petrucci	1m 39.178s
7	Rossi	1m 39.266s
8	Zarco	1m 39.331s
9	Rabat	1m 39.504s
10	Crutchlow	1m 39.556s
11	Pedrosa	1m 39.695s
12	Nakagami	1m 39.888s
13	Miller	1m 39.732s
14	Syahrin	1m 39.879s
15	Rins	1m 39.918s
16	A. Espargaro	1m 40.010s
17	Smith	1m 40.019s
18	Morbidelli	1m 40.058s
19	P. Espargaro	1m 40.178s
20	Redding	1m 40.300s
21	Abraham	1m 40.449s
22	Bautista	1m 40.524s
23	Kallio	1m 40.572s
24	Luthi	1m 40.590s
25	Guintoli	1m 40.834s
26	Simeon	1m 41.369s

Fastest race laps

1	Lorenzo	1m 40.021s
2	Marquez	1m 40.029s
3	Dovizioso	1m 40.209s
4	Crutchlow	1m 40.248s
5	Vinales	1m 40.299s
6	Rossi	1m 40.371s
7	Zarco	1m 40.380s
8	Syahrin	1m 40.512s
9	Petrucci	1m 40.528s
10	Pedrosa	1m 40.552s
11	Bautista	1m 40.581s
12	Rabat	1m 40.620s
13	Iannone	1m 40.621s
14	Miller	1m 40.667s
15	Morbidelli	1m 40.731s
16	Rins	1m 40.860s
17	A. Espargaro	1m 41.060s
18	Nakagami	1m 41.167s
19	Redding	1m 41.371s
20	Smith	1m 41.380s
21	P. Espargaro	1m 41.412s
22	Luthi	1m 42.104s
23	Simeon	1m 42.505s
24	Abraham	1m 42.595s
25	Guintoli	1m 43.339s

Grid order		1	2	3	4	5	6	7	8	9	10	11	12	13	14	15	16	17	18	19	20	21	22	23	24	·
99	LORENZO	93	99	99	99	99	99	99	99	99	99	99	99	99	99	99	99	99	99	99	99	99	99	99	99	1
93	MARQUEZ	99	93	93	93	93	93	93	93	93	93	93	93	93	93	93	93	93	93	93	93	93	93	93	93	2
4	DOVIZIOSO	29	4	4	4	4	4	4	4	46	46	46	46	46	46	46	46	46	46	46	46	46	46	46	46	3
25	VINALES	4	46	46	46	46	46	46	46	9	26	26	26	26	26	26	26	26	35	35	35	35	35	35	35	4
29	IANNONE	46	29	26	26	26	26	26	9	26	35	35	9	35	35	35	35	35	26	26	26	26	26	26	26	5
9	PETRUCCI	26	26	9	9	9	9	9	26	35	9	9	35	9	5	5	5	5	5	5	5	25	25	25	25	6
46	ROSSI	9	9	29	29	29	29	29	35	29	5	5	5	5	25	25	25	25	25	25	25	5	5	5	5	7
5	ZARCO	38	38	38	35	35	35	35	29	25	25	25	25	25	9	9	9	9	9	9	9	9	9	9	9	8
53	RABAT	35	35	35	25	25	25	25	25	5	29	43	43	43	43	43	53	53	53	55	55	29	29	19	19	9
35	CRUTCHLOW	25	25	25	5	5	5	5	5	43	43	29	53	53	53	53	43	43	55	29	29	19	19	29	29	10
26	PEDROSA	43	43	5	43	43	43	43	43	53	53	53	55	55	55	55	55	55	29	19	19	44	44	44	44	11
30	NAKAGAMI	5	5	43	53	53	53	53	53	55	55	55	29	29	29	29	29	29	19	21	44	45	45	45	45	12
43	MILLER	53	53	53	38	21	55	55	55	21	21	21	21	21	21	19	19	19	21	44	45	17	17	17	17	13
55	SYAHRIN	55	55	55	55	55	21	21	21	19	19	19	19	19	19	21	21	21	44	45	17	21				14
42	RINS	21	21	21	21	38	38	38	19	38	38	38	38	38	44	44	44	44	45	17	21					
38	SMITH	44	30	30	30	30	19	19	38	30	30	30	30	30	45	45	45	45	17							
21	MORBIDELLI	30	44	44	41	19	30	30	30	44	44	44	44	44	17	17	17	17								
44	P. ESPARGARO	42	42	41	42	44	44	44	44	45	45	45	45	45												
41	A. ESPARGARO	19	19	19	19	45	45	45	45	42	42	17	17	17												
45	REDDING	45	41	42	44	17	10	42	42	17	17	42														
17	ABRAHAM	41	45	45	45	10	42	10	17																	
19	BAUTISTA	12	12	12	17	42	17	17																		
36	KALLIO	17	17	17	10																					
12	LUTHI	10	10	10																						
50	GUINTOLI	50	50																							
10	SIMEON																									

42 Pit stop 21 Lapped rider

Championship Points

1	Marquez	115
2	Rossi	88
3	Vinales	77
4	Zarco	73
5	Petrucci	71
6	Crutchlow	69
7	Lorenzo	66
8	Dovizioso	66
9	Iannone	66
10	Miller	49
11	Pedrosa	40
12	Rins	33
13	P. Espargaro	28
14	Rabat	27
15	Bautista	26
16	Morbidelli	19
17	Syahrin	17
18	A. Espargaro	13
19	Nakagami	10
20	Redding	9
21	Smith	7
22	Kallio	6
23	Abraham	4

Constructor Points

1	Honda	150
2	Ducati	132
3	Yamaha	124
4	Suzuki	80
5	KTM	29
6	Aprilia	22

Moto2

RACE DISTANCE: 22 laps, 63.252 miles/101.794km · RACE WEATHER: Dry (air 27°C, humidity 50%, track 45°C)

Pos.	Rider	Nat.	No.	Entrant	Machine	Laps	Time & Speed
1	**Fabio Quartararo**	FRA	20	HDR - Speed Up Racing	Speed Up	22	38m 22.059s 98.9mph/ 159.1km/h
2	**Miguel Oliveira**	POR	44	Red Bull KTM Ajo	KTM	22	38m 24.551s
3	**Alex Marquez**	SPA	73	EG 0,0 Marc VDS	Kalex	22	38m 25.544s
4	**Marcel Schrotter**	GER	23	Dynavolt Intact GP	Kalex	22	38m 26.457s
5	**Xavi Vierge**	SPA	97	Dynavolt Intact GP	Kalex	22	38m 26.746s
6	**Brad Binder**	RSA	41	Red Bull KTM Ajo	KTM	22	38m 29.696s
7	**Lorenzo Baldassarri**	ITA	7	Pons HP40	Kalex	22	38m 29.783s
8	**Francesco Bagnaia**	ITA	42	SKY Racing Team VR46	Kalex	22	38m 32.670s
9	**Sam Lowes**	GBR	22	Swiss Innovative Investors	KTM	22	38m 35.968s
10	**Iker Lecuona**	SPA	27	Swiss Innovative Investors	KTM	22	38m 37.183s
11	**Andrea Locatelli**	ITA	5	Italtrans Racing Team	Kalex	22	38m 38.042s
12	**Simone Corsi**	ITA	24	Tasca Racing Scuderia Moto2	Kalex	22	38m 38.464s
13	**Tetsuta Nagashima**	JPN	45	IDEMITSU Honda Team Asia	Kalex	22	38m 41.054s
14	**Augusto Fernandez**	SPA	40	Pons HP40	Kalex	22	38m 42.300s
15	**Remy Gardner**	AUS	87	Tech 3 Racing	Tech 3	22	38m 42.468s
16	Edgar Pons	SPA	57	AGR Team	Kalex	22	38m 46.597s
17	Luca Marini	ITA	10	SKY Racing Team VR46	Kalex	22	38m 49.668s
18	Steven Odendaal	RSA	4	NTS RW Racing GP	NTS	22	38m 50.285s
19	Khairul Idham Pawi	MAL	89	IDEMITSU Honda Team Asia	Kalex	22	38m 50.699s
20	Dominique Aegerter	SWI	77	Kiefer Racing	KTM	22	38m 51.276s
21	Danny Kent	GBR	52	HDR - Speed Up Racing	Speed Up	22	38m 52.354s
22	Joe Roberts	USA	16	NTS RW Racing GP	NTS	22	38m 59.659s
23	Jules Danilo	FRA	95	Nashi Argan SAG Team	Kalex	22	39m 00.708s
24	Dimas Ekky Pratama	INA	30	Astra Honda Racing Team	Honda	22	39m 06.663s
25	Eric Granado	BRA	51	Forward Racing Team	Suter	22	39m 11.550s
	Isaac Vinales	SPA	32	SAG Team	Kalex	18	DNF
	Romano Fenati	ITA	13	Marinelli Snipers Team	Kalex	16	DNF
	Mattia Pasini	ITA	54	Italtrans Racing Team	Kalex	14	DNF
	Joan Mir	SPA	36	EG 0,0 Marc VDS	Kalex	12	DNF
	Federico Fuligni	ITA	21	Tasca Racing Scuderia Moto2	Kalex	12	DNF
	Jorge Navarro	SPA	9	Federal Oil Gresini Moto2	Kalex	7	DNF
	Bo Bendsneyder	NED	64	Tech 3 Racing	Tech 3	0	DNF
	Niki Tuuli	FIN	66	SIC Racing Team	Kalex	0	DNF
	Stefano Manzi	ITA	62	Forward Racing Team	Suter	0	DNF

Fastest lap: Fabio Quartararo, on lap 14, 1m 43.956s, 99.5mph/160.2km/h.

Lap record: New layout.

Event maximum speed: Marcel Schrotter, 178.7mph/287.6km/h (warm-up).

Qualifying

Weather: Dry
Air Temp: 28° **Track Temp:** 49°
Humidity: 42%

1	Quartararo	1m 43.474s
2	Marquez	1m 43.590s
3	Schrotter	1m 43.619s
4	Bagnaia	1m 43.821s
5	Binder	1m 43.867s
6	Pasini	1m 43.905s
7	Vierge	1m 44.136s
8	Mir	1m 44.170s
9	Lowes	1m 44.215s
10	Baldassarri	1m 44.227s
11	Corsi	1m 44.232s
12	Nagashima	1m 44.244s
13	Marini	1m 44.269s
14	Lecuona	1m 44.314s
15	Fenati	1m 44.383s
16	Locatelli	1m 44.419s
17	Oliveira	1m 44.429s
18	E. Pons	1m 44.512s
19	Navarro	1m 44.551s
20	Fernandez	1m 44.564s
21	Vinales	1m 44.725s
22	Pawi	1m 44.735s
23	Gardner	1m 44.760s
24	Aegerter	1m 44.780s
25	Odendaal	1m 44.972s
26	Bendsneyder	1m 45.089s
27	Kent	1m 45.155s
28	Roberts	1m 45.366s
29	Tuuli	1m 45.477s
30	Ekky Pratama	1m 45.532s
31	Manzi	1m 45.560s
32	Granado	1m 45.605s
33	Danilo	1m 45.902s
34	Fuligni	1m 46.544s

Fastest race laps

1	Quartararo	1m 43.956s
2	Schrotter	1m 44.119s
3	Vierge	1m 44.141s
4	Oliveira	1m 44.161s
5	Bagnaia	1m 44.285s
6	Pasini	1m 44.301s
7	Lowes	1m 44.308s
8	Baldassarri	1m 44.317s
9	Binder	1m 44.322s
10	Marquez	1m 44.356s
11	Mir	1m 44.394s
12	Lecuona	1m 44.434s
13	Locatelli	1m 44.476s
14	Fenati	1m 44.496s
15	Corsi	1m 44.525s
16	Nagashima	1m 44.538s
17	Navarro	1m 44.625s
18	Gardner	1m 44.663s
19	Fernandez	1m 44.708s
20	Vinales	1m 44.909s
21	E. Pons	1m 44.931s
22	Odendaal	1m 45.094s
23	Kent	1m 45.110s
24	Aegerter	1m 45.216s
25	Marini	1m 45.222s
26	Pawi	1m 45.243s
27	Ekky Pratama	1m 45.421s
28	Roberts	1m 45.586s
29	Danilo	1m 45.605s
30	Granado	1m 45.660s
31	Fuligni	1m 46.225s

Championship Points

1	Bagnaia	119
2	Oliveira	118
3	Marquez	94
4	Baldassarri	93
5	Vierge	70
6	Mir	64
7	Pasini	58
8	Binder	57
9	Schrotter	50
10	Quartararo	45
11	Lecuona	32
12	Corsi	22
13	Lowes	21
14	Locatelli	21
15	Aegerter	20
16	Marini	19
17	Gardner	15
18	Navarro	14
19	Barbera	10
20	Fenati	9
21	Vinales	7
22	Manzi	6
23	Nagashima	6
24	Kent	4
25	Roberts	2
26	Fernandez	2
27	Odendaal	1
28	Pawi	1

Constructor Points

1	Kalex	161
2	KTM	118
3	Speed Up	49
4	Tech 3	15
5	Suter	6
6	NTS	2

Moto3

RACE DISTANCE: 21 laps, 60.377 miles/97.167km · RACE WEATHER: Dry (air 27°C, humidity 61%, track 39°C)

Pos.	Rider	Nat.	No.	Entrant	Machine	Laps	Time & Speed
1	**Enea Bastianini**	ITA	33	Leopard Racing	Honda	21	38m 36.883s 93.8mph/ 150.9km/h
2	**Marco Bezzecchi**	ITA	12	Redox PruestelGP	KTM	21	38m 37.050s
3	**Gabriel Rodrigo**	ARG	19	RBA BOE Skull Rider	KTM	21	38m 37.053s
4	**John McPhee**	GBR	17	CIP - Green Power	KTM	21	38m 37.140s
5	**Tatsuki Suzuki**	JPN	24	SIC58 Squadra Corse	Honda	21	38m 37.522s
6	**Kaito Toba**	JPN	27	Honda Team Asia	Honda	21	38m 43.684s
7	**Fabio Di Giannantonio**	ITA	21	Del Conca Gresini Moto3	Honda	21	38m 43.755s
8	**Alonso Lopez**	SPA	72	Estrella Galicia 0,0	Honda	21	38m 43.483s
9	**Dennis Foggia**	ITA	10	SKY Racing Team VR46	KTM	21	38m 44.198s
10	**Raul Fernandez**	SPA	25	Angel Nieto Team	KTM	21	38m 44.390s
11	**Jakub Kornfeil**	CZE	84	Redox PruestelGP	KTM	21	38m 44.521s
12	**Makar Yurchenko**	KAZ	76	CIP - Green Power	KTM	21	38m 45.146s
13	**Adam Norrodin**	MAL	7	Petronas Sprinta Racing	Honda	21	33m 52.139s
14	**Nakarin Atiratphuvapat**	THA	41	Honda Team Asia	Honda	21	39m 03.504s
15	**Livio Loi**	BEL	11	Reale Avintia Academy 77	KTM	21	39m 05.442s
16	Philipp Oettl	GER	65	Sudmetal Schedl GP Racing	KTM	21	39m 09.863s
17	Lorenzo Dalla Porta	ITA	48	Leopard Racing	Honda	19	39m 11.677s
	Jaume Masia	SPA	5	Bester Capital Dubai	KTM	17	DNF
	Andrea Migno	ITA	16	Angel Nieto Team Moto3	KTM	17	DNF
	Aron Canet	SPA	44	Estrella Galicia 0,0	Honda	15	DNF
	Nicolo Bulega	ITA	8	SKY Racing Team VR46	KTM	15	DNF
	Albert Arenas	SPA	75	Angel Nieto Team Moto3	KTM	15	DNF
	Tony Arbolino	ITA	14	Marinelli Snipers Team	Honda	15	DNF
	Ayumu Sasaki	JPN	71	Petronas Sprinta Racing	Honda	15	DNF
	Marcos Ramirez	SPA	42	Bester Capital Dubai	KTM	14	DNF
	Jorge Martin	SPA	88	Del Conca Gresini Moto3	Honda	8	DNF
	Kazuki Masaki	JPN	22	RBA BOE Skull Rider	KTM	4	DNF
	Darryn Binder	RSA	40	Red Bull KTM Ajo	KTM	0	DNF

Fastest lap: Jaume Masia, on lap 4, 1m 49.005s, 94.9mph/152.8km/h.

Lap record: New layout.

Event maximum speed: Dennis Foggia, 151.4mph/243.6km/h (warm-up).

Qualifying:

Weather: Dry
Air Temp: 28° **Track Temp:** 45°
Humidity: 43%

1	Bastianini	1m 48.806s
2	Martin	1m 48.913s
3	Suzuki	1m 49.057s
4	Sasaki	1m 49.059s
5	Canet	1m 49.115s
6	Toba	1m 49.185s
7	McPhee	1m 49.191s
8	Rodrigo	1m 49.233s
9	Bezzecchi	1m 49.299s
10	Dalla Porta	1m 49.379s
11	Masaki	1m 49.398s
12	Bulega	1m 49.400s
13	Di Giannantonio	1m 49.414s
14	Kornfeil	1m 49.498s
15	Fernandez	1m 49.565s
16	Migno	1m 49.578s
17	Masia	1m 49.655s
18	Oettl	1m 49.691s
19	Arenas	1m 49.736s
20	Binder	1m 49.897s
21	Norrodin	1m 49.983s
22	Arbolino	1m 50.012s
23	Yurchenko	1m 50.022s
24	Lopez	1m 50.183s
25	Ramirez	1m 50.186s
26	Foggia	1m 50.197s
27	Loi	1m 50.247s
28	Perez	1m 50.469s
29	Atiratphuvapat	1m 51.306s

Fastest race laps

1	Masia	1m 49.005s
2	Bulega	1m 49.040s
3	McPhee	1m 49.119s
4	Kornfeil	1m 49.133s
5	Bezzecchi	1m 49.136s
6	Migno	1m 49.231s
7	Canet	1m 49.231s
8	Bastianini	1m 49.239s
9	Rodrigo	1m 49.303s
10	Sasaki	1m 49.328s
11	Arenas	1m 49.380s
12	Suzuki	1m 49.462s
13	Martin	1m 49.475s
14	Fernandez	1m 49.600s
15	Lopez	1m 49.600s
16	Di Giannantonio	1m 49.625s
17	Toba	1m 49.642s
18	Norrodin	1m 49.703s
19	Yurchenko	1m 49.752s
20	Foggia	1m 49.755s
21	Ramirez	1m 49.915s
22	Arbolino	1m 49.949s
23	Atiratphuvapat	1m 50.251s
24	Masaki	1m 50.260s
25	Oettl	1m 50.273s
26	Dalla Porta	1m 50.446s
27	Loi	1m 50.715s

Championship Points

1	Bezzecchi	103
2	Di Giannantonio	84
3	Martin	80
4	Bastianini	68
5	Canet	61
6	Rodrigo	57
7	Migno	56
8	Antonelli	44
9	Kornfeil	41
10	Ramirez	38
11	Oettl	36
12	Suzuki	35
13	Dalla Porta	33
14	Lopez	31
15	Arenas	28
16	Toba	26
17	Arbolino	24
18	McPhee	23
19	Masia	21
20	Norrodin	19
21	Sasaki	17
22	Binder	11
23	Foggia	9
24	Yurchenko	9
25	Loi	8
26	Fernandez	6
27	Pagliani	6
28	Masaki	3
29	Atiratphuvapat	2
30	Ogura	1

Constructor Points

1	Honda	146
2	KTM	142

Inset, above: Moto3 grows up. The MotoGP pack in the early stages: Lorenzo from Marquez, Dovizioso, Rins, Rossi (yellow helmet), Vinales, Crutchlow and Rins on the inside.

Inset, right: Phew, that was a tough one! Marquez was back on top.

Main: Rins stole second from Vinales into the final chicane.

Photos: Gold & Goose

FIM WORLD CHAMPIONSHIP · ROUND 8

DUTCH TT

ASSEN CIRCUIT

NOLAN
THE 42 BAKERY
SUZUKI
42
ECSTAR
Arai
movistar
25
ENEOS
YAMALUBE
MICHELIN

RIDERS, commentators and fans alike said the same thing about the Dutch TT. The MotoGP race was "like a Moto3 race". This was true, but only to a point. In fact, it was better. Moto3 only had five in the lead group, and two of them fell off. For most of the race, MotoGP had eight. And with the top 15 points scorers all within just over 16 seconds, it set a new grand prix record.

Perhaps the least unexpected thing was the name of the winner. Marc Marquez had appeared superior all weekend. But epic circumstances ensured that he had to work harder than perhaps ever in his career for the win.

Great tracks make great racing, but Assen had a bit of help in 2018 – from a significant headwind down the back straight. As Marquez explained, "It made the pace slower and easy to slipstream, and very hard to make a gap." But there were other factors, including a fund of talent riding bikes made more equal by ever more restrictive technical rules. For more than half of the 26-lap race, eight 270hp 1000c MotoGP bikes were locked in furious combat, and the group was hardly smaller at the end; it was only in the final three laps that Marquez was able to escape. He did so by two seconds for one of his best ever wins.

The European heat wave continued in the far north of the Netherlands, making for unfamiliar sunshine throughout the northernmost weekend of the long season. Also unfamiliar: a rumour that Assen was interested in hosting F1 in the future. This elicited an unhappy response from riders, fresh from whooping over braking bumps in Catalunya. Said Rossi, "I hope they don't come. F1 has a lot of tracks just for cars. Here at Assen, in history, it has been just for bikes." Lorenzo raised the point of modifications required to make the fast corners safe for the cars. There would need to be chicanes and barriers where "here there is green outside the track".

Assen's traditions may have been compromised somewhat by the still-resented cutting of track length in 2006, but it still had several fast corners, and still had sharp 'teeth' to punish errors.

The worst victim was in MotoGP. Franco Morbidelli suffered a heavy crash at the end of the back straight in FP3. The Moto2 champion, who at the previous race had moved clear of Syahrin as top rookie, lost the front in fourth gear and went tumbling end over end through the gravel, stopping only just short of the barrier. He broke the third metacarpal in his left hand and was out of this race, and, it would transpire, the next one as well.

Morbidelli's patron, Valentino Rossi, tested his luck at the same corner in FP4, but once again came out on the winning side. Not only did he slide harmlessly to a stop in the gravel, but so too did his factory Yamaha, rather than flipping to destruction. Alex Marquez also fell there, but escaped serious injury.

On Friday, Moto2 rider Nagashima was ruled out as well, after badly gashing a finger in a crash at the fast Ramshoek corner at the end of the lap; in the same class on Saturday, Finn Niki Tuuli injured his left hand in a high-side at the Strubben loop, bringing out the red flags at the end of qualifying. Another not to make the race was the first Kazakh rider in bike GP racing, Moto3 rookie Makar Yurchenko. The 19-year-old had scored points in three of the previous four races. The problem was money, promised sponsorship for the French CIP team having failed to materialise. His place alongside McPhee went to 16-year-old Italian Stefano Nepa.

The red flag for Tuuli brought problems also for previous race winner Quartararo, who was dropped three grid positions for not pulling directly into the pit lane.

There were other penalties, after a fresh bout of blatant dawdling in Moto3, this time somewhat pointlessly in FP2, rather than in qualifying, where there is little to be gained from a fast lap time. The increased penalties for being slow in three (not necessarily consecutive) sectors were 12 grid places for a first offence, back of the grid for a second. Adam Norrodin was slapped with the latter, Petronas team-mate Ayumu Sasaki the former, earning the opprobrium of team chief Johan Stigefelt. Jakub Kornfeil, Kaito Toba and rookie Dennis Foggia also suffered the lesser penalty.

There were several updates in the MotoGP class. More of Suzuki's new chassis was reinforced with carbon cladding, while Ducati had followed the trend, with patches bonded to the swing-arm pivot area. The reason, according to the factory team's Davide Tardozzi, was to improve cornering on worn tyres. Dovizioso liked his so much that he asked for a second chassis with the same treatment. This was impossible, but his team raised a laugh by using stick-on lookalike ca-fi on Saturday morning.

There was more carbon at Yamaha, where Vinales was still searching for a cure for his curious malady. He'd switched

Above: Sepang's Razlan Razali was at the track for meetings behind closed doors.

Top: Marquez holds off the Yamahas.
Photos: Gold & Goose

Top right: Downbeat Dani – Pedrosa netted only a single point for a desultory 15th.
Photo: HRC

Above right: Rossi fell in practice, but walked away. Protégé Morbidelli fell at the same place, and was out for two races.
Photo: Gold & Goose

Right: Iannone crossed the line ahead of Jack Miller, but the Australian took tenth when the Suzuki rider was penalised by two seconds for straying off-track.
Photo: www.suzuki-racing.com

to the carbon forks – which had become common to all teams – that he had rejected in tests in 2017. The team had also fitted a microswitch to his clutch, in an attempt to understand the reason for the poor start that had ruined his chances at the previous round in Catalunya.

Suzuki project leader Ken Kawauchi, in an interview with Dorna, revealed that plans for a satellite team had been shelved for the time being after they had run out of time. "Maybe in 2020 or 2021," he said. Talking of vague plans, Dani Pedrosa again had "no information" about his future, although Yamaha expectations were still in the air, with Sepang's Razlan Razali at the track for meetings behind closed doors.

There was news from Aragon, where competitive times were reported from first tests of 2019's 'all-change' Triumph-powered Moto2 bikes. Ex-racers Alex de Angelis, Ricky Cardus and Jonas Folger had been exercising (respectively) NTS, Kalex and KTM Moto2 chassis with the 675cc three-cylinder engines, which would not only bring more torque, but also more sophisticated electronics to the Cinderella class.

MOTOGP RACE – 26 laps

Marc Marquez took his 47th premier-class pole, but his first at Assen, crediting his looped front wings at what hitherto had been thought of as a Yamaha track. It came after the flag in a breathless Q2, 11 of the top 12 being just a thousandth over a half-second span. Iannone had been on top from Lorenzo when the flag fell, but they were down to ninth and tenth when the rest finished their lap.

Crutchlow had pushed into second, with Rossi alongside, his fourth straight front row. Dovi led row two from Rins (through from Q1) and Vinales. The 2017 pole-man, Zarco, was eighth, also through from Q1; Pedrosa was 18th.

Lorenzo surged off row four to seize the lap-one lead. Marquez took it back next time around, and by then Rossi and Dovi had also joined in. Then it was Rins up to third on lap nine; Vinales for once had started well, while Crutchlow – fourth on lap one – was still well in the mix. Zarco had caught up, though fast-starter Iannone had lost touch.

There would be five different leaders over the line, with Dovizioso heading laps 15–18, plus Rossi and Vinales one each. The action was breathtaking and non-stop; collisions were frequent.

One occurred on lap 12, when Rins dived inside Marquez

Above: The Espargaro brothers and Redding were within a couple of hundredths at the end.

Above right: Bagnaia celebrates an immaculate fourth Moto2 win.

Top far right: Quartararo on the Speed-Up cuts inside Schrotter's Kalex on his way through from a fourth-row start.

Above far right: Quartararo's second was his second straight podium.

Right: Hot pursuit. Jorge Martin starts his run to freedom in Moto3. Bastianini (33) and Canet (concealed) made the podium. McPhee (17) and Bezzecchi (12), both crashed out.

Below right: Backmarkers, maybe, but the battle for position was just as intense for Atiratphuvapat (41), Loi (11), wild-card Ogura (32), Masaki (22) and Sasaki (71).

Photos: Gold & Goose

at the Strubben loop to take second. They clashed; Marquez nearly fell. The Spaniard suffered another such moment later, with Vinales, the latter pushed off track at De Bult left-hander.

But the scariest and most miraculous collision had been on lap five. Lorenzo was leading, while Rossi had moved into second and was chasing him around to the fastest corners of the track, through the Meeuwenmeer right-hander to the flat-out Hoge Heide kink. Then Lorenzo lost the front at high speed, only saving it by a miracle. In the process, he slowed so suddenly that the Yamaha slammed into the back of the Ducati. Amazingly, there were no consequences.

The number of overtakes was uncountable. With just ten laps left, first to eighth was covered by 1.6 seconds, Dovizioso now heading Marquez and Vinales; Lorenzo was starting to drop back, his tyres shot.

With four laps left, Marquez – one of the very few to choose the soft rear tyre – made his move. "During practice, I was so comfortable, with a good rhythm, but I suspected it would be difficult to open a gap," he said. "So I decided to wait, but in that transition there was a big fight. I tried to manage the tyre, and in the last four laps, I gave it everything."

At the start of lap 23, he was 0.3 of a second from Dovizioso: "Then I could take my own lines. Before that, if you did, somebody would overtake. The most difficult thing was to defend and attack at the same time."

Next time around, he was a second ahead, and better than two at the flag,

Battle raged behind him to the end. By then, Rins had climbed back up, and last time around the Ramshoek, he dived underneath Vinales for second, making an all-Spanish podium. Vinales had suffered arm-pump, he said, "but I was able to have fun again. I have recovered a lot of confidence in the bike." That would prove a brief revival.

Rossi's podium hopes had been dashed at the start of the penultimate lap. He'd taken second off Dovizioso into the final chicane, where he'd done most of his overtaking, but Dovi was faster past the pits and took the inside into the first corner. Rossi was pushed wide and dropped to sixth, complaining bitterly, but in vain, afterwards. Last time into the chicane, he'd moved up again and passed Dovizioso, only to lose fourth on the run to the line. Second to fourth was inside seven-tenths – very Moto3.

Crutchlow was less than a second behind after running wide in the late stages, Lorenzo close. Both Ducati riders had chosen the hard rear tyre, and both complained of degradation. But overall, there seemed little difference in the performance of the Michelins on offer.

Zarco had lost touch and almost been caught over the line by Bautista, who had outpaced Miller. However, the Australian was promoted to tenth by a two-second penalty for Iannone for cutting the track.

Espargaro was 12th, a tenth ahead of his brother, Aleix, and Scott Redding; Pedrosa was right behind for the final point after a downbeat weekend. He was less than half a second clear of Rabat. Smith, Syahrin, Nakagami and Luthi trailed in.

Petrucci had crashed out of 12th on lap 18, bringing an undistinguished weekend to a conclusion.

MOTO2 RACE – 24 laps

The Moto2 field burst out of the pit lane *en masse* when it was re-opened after the late red flag in qualifying, but nobody could improve, and Bagnaia had already done enough early on to secure his second pole. Once again, times were very close, Schrotter barely seven-hundredths slower, and there were 22 within the first second.

Gaining strength after earlier injuries, Marini was third for his first front-row start. Marquez led row two, having survived a bruising fast crash at the end of the back straight. Vierge and Lowes were alongside. Oliveira was just over half a second off pole, but back on the sixth row.

The anticipated brawl didn't take place. Bagnaia made sure nobody got a sniff of him with another fault-free run to the flag. It was his fourth win of the season, and it increased his title lead ominously.

"It was hard to break away, but when I saw the gap go to 0.7, then one second, I could breathe a bit," the winner said. Rising wind had made the going difficult towards the finish.

He had led away from Schrotter and Marini, but the well-connected young Italian was soon shuffled backwards as first Mir and then also Marquez came through.

Marquez was ahead of Mir on lap six and past Schrotter one lap later, after the German had run wide. By then, however, Baldassarri had caught the group, after an impressive run through from 13th on the grid, setting fastest lap on the way. Before half-distance, he'd got by them all to second, albeit more than two seconds behind the leader.

He was Bagnaia's biggest threat, and with four laps left had closed to within just over 1.5 seconds. Then suddenly he slowed, with the most prosaic of problems. He had a puncture, his rear tyre as flat as the proverbial pancake.

Quartararo had sliced through from tenth on the grid, and by now had got ahead of Mir. He was pushing Schrotter and Marquez. After the next lap-and-a-half, he was through to second, Marquez half a second behind.

Schrotter held fourth from Mir, with Oliveira closing at the

end. He'd made another good start to finish the first lap 11th, but he'd had no answer when Quartararo had come upon him at around half-distance.

Four seconds away, Red Bull KTM team-mate Binder took seventh from Marini on the last lap; Lowes did the same for ninth to Andrea Locatelli, whose Italtrans Kalex team-mate, Mattia Pasini, had lost touch in 11th.

New boy Fernandez equalled his best previous finish in 12th, ahead of compatriot Navarro; but there was heart-break for home hero Bo Bendsneyder, who had started 23rd, but crossed the line 14th and in the points, only to be de-moted to 17th by a time penalty. That gave the final points to Aegerter and Corsi, with Lecuona missing out by a tenth.

Kent crashed out early, Vierge a bit later from the top ten, and at the end also Fenati from the points. Manzi preserved his impressive crash record with a fifth non-finish.

MOTO3 RACE – 22 laps

A dramatic last lap overturned the championship standings as pole-qualifier Jorge Martin returned with a fine fighting win, while erstwhile points-leader Marco Bezzecchi crashed out of the battle for second with less than half a lap to go.

It was the culmination of a race-long five-bike battle, with Martin leading away, but battered to and fro with the con-stant changing of places. Bezzecchi also led a number of laps, as did 2017 Assen winner Canet, while McPhee head-ed one lap after half-distance.

The only front-runner never to lead over the line was Cata-lunya winner Bastianini, but he was well in the fight as the finish drew near.

McPhee had dropped away, then caught up again, but crashed at the looping Strubben left-hander early on the pe-nultimate lap.

At the same time, Martin – who later said he had been battling with a soft-feeling front brake throughout – put his head down and opened a small, but significant gap.

Bezzecchi was at the back of the pursuit when he lost the rear at the first of the far pair of right-handers. That left Bastianini to mount a successful attack on Canet, only for the Spaniard to get him back by inches into the final chicane.

Masia headed a huge pursuit pack when it mattered, fourth to eleventh covered by just over two seconds. Kornfeil had come through from 23rd on the grid, but lost the place by a tenth on the final lap.

Dalla Porta, Binder, Rodrigo, Di Giannantonio and front-row starter Bulega completed the top ten. The last was pro-moted ahead of Ramirez after the Spaniard was one of five riders hit with time penalties for exceeding track limits.

TT ASSEN

26 laps
Length: 4.542km / 2.822 miles
Width: 10-14m

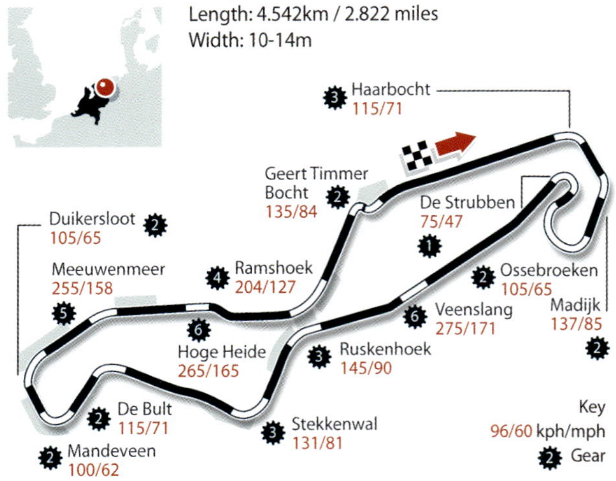

MotoGP

RACE DISTANCE: 26 laps, 73.379 miles/118.092km · RACE WEATHER: Dry (air 27°C, humidity 51%, track 45°C)

Pos.	Rider	Nat.	No.	Entrant	Machine	Tyres	Race tyre choice	Laps	Time & speed
1	**Marc Marquez**	SPA	93	Repsol Honda Team	Honda RC213V	M	F: Medium/R: Soft	26	41m 13.863s 106.8mph/ 171.8km/h
2	**Alex Rins**	SPA	42	Team SUZUKI ECSTAR	Suzuki GSX-RR	M	F: Medium/R: Hard	26	41m 16.132s
3	**Maverick Vinales**	SPA	25	Movistar Yamaha MotoGP	Yamaha YZR-M1	M	F: Medium/R: Soft	26	41m 16.171s
4	**Andrea Dovizioso**	ITA	4	Ducati Team	Ducati Desmosedici	M	F: Medium/R: Hard	26	41m 16.285s
5	**Valentino Rossi**	ITA	46	Movistar Yamaha MotoGP	Yamaha YZR-M1	M	F: Medium/R: Soft	26	41m 16.826s
6	**Cal Crutchlow**	GBR	35	LCR Honda CASTROL	Honda RC213V	M	F: Medium/R: Soft	26	41m 17.739s
7	**Jorge Lorenzo**	SPA	99	Ducati Team	Ducati Desmosedici	M	F: Soft/R: Hard	26	41m 18.325s
8	**Johann Zarco**	FRA	5	Monster Yamaha Tech 3	Yamaha YZR-M1	M	F: Medium/R: Hard	26	41m 20.864s
9	**Alvaro Bautista**	SPA	19	Angel Nieto Team	Ducati Desmosedici	M	F: Soft/R: Soft	26	41m 21.404s
10	**Jack Miller**	AUS	43	Alma Pramac Racing	Ducati Desmosedici	M	F: Medium/R: Hard	26	41m 26.919s
11	**Andrea Iannone**	ITA	29	Team SUZUKI ECSTAR	Suzuki GSX-RR	M	F: Medium/R: Hard	26	41m 28.118s
12	**Pol Espargaro**	SPA	44	Red Bull KTM Factory Racing	KTM RC16	M	F: Medium/R: Hard	26	41m 29.739s
13	**Aleix Espargaro**	SPA	41	Aprilia Racing Team Gresini	Aprilia RS-GP	M	F: Medium/R: Hard	26	41m 29.849s
14	**Scott Redding**	GBR	45	Aprilia Racing Team Gresini	Aprilia RS-GP	M	F: Medium/R: Soft	26	41m 29.882s
15	**Dani Pedrosa**	SPA	26	Repsol Honda Team	Honda RC213V	M	F: Medium/R: Soft	26	41m 29.906s
16	Tito Rabat	SPA	53	Reale Avintia Racing	Ducati Desmosedici	M	F: Medium/R: Soft	26	41m 30.279s
17	Bradley Smith	GBR	38	Red Bull KTM Factory Racing	KTM RC16	M	F: Medium/R: Soft	26	41m 42.936s
18	Hafizh Syahrin	MAL	55	Monster Yamaha Tech 3	Yamaha YZR-M1	M	F: Soft/R: Soft	26	41m 47.687s
19	Takaaki Nakagami	JPN	30	LCR Honda IDEMITSU	Honda RC213V	M	F: Medium/R: Hard	26	41m 47.900s
20	Thomas Luthi	SWI	12	EG 0,0 Marc VDS	Honda RC213V	M	F: Medium/R: Hard	26	42m 01.716s
	Danilo Petrucci	ITA	9	Alma Pramac Racing	Ducati Desmosedici	M	F: Medium/R: Hard	17	DNF-crash
	Xavier Simeon	BEL	10	Reale Avintia Racing	Ducati Desmosedici	M	F: Soft/R: Soft	17	DNF-technical
	Karel Abraham	CZE	17	Angel Nieto Team	Ducati Desmosedici	M	F: Medium/R: Hard	11	DNF-technical
	Franco Morbidelli	ITA	21	EG 0,0 Marc VDS	Honda RC213V	M	-	-	DNS-injured

Fastest lap: Maverick Vinales, on lap 6, 1m 34.113s, 107.9mph/173.7km/h.
Lap record: Marc Marquez, 1m 33.617s, 108.5mph/174.6km/h (2015).
Event maximum speed: Alvaro Bautista, 196.5mph/316.3km/h (free practice).

Qualifying

Weather: Dry
Air Temp: 24° **Track Temp:** 42°
Humidity: 30%

1	Marquez	1m 32.791s
2	Crutchlow	1m 32.832s
3	Rossi	1m 32.850s
4	Dovizioso	1m 32.870s
5	Rins	1m 32.933s
6	Vinales	1m 32.984s
7	A. Espargaro	1m 33.029s
8	Zarco	1m 33.072s
9	Iannone	1m 33.120s
10	Lorenzo	1m 33.167s
11	Petrucci	1m 33.292s
12	Bautista	1m 34.015s
13	Nakagami	1m 33.625s
14	Rabat	1m 33.666s
15	Syahrin	1m 33.666s
16	Miller	1m 33.672s
17	Redding	1m 33.995s
18	Pedrosa	1m 34.125s
19	Abraham	1m 34.145s
20	Smith	1m 34.149s
21	P. Espargaro	1m 34.268s
22	Luthi	1m 35.192s
23	Simeon	1m 35.646s

Fastest race laps

1	Vinales	1m 34.113s
2	Rossi	1m 34.201s
3	Marquez	1m 34.261s
4	Zarco	1m 34.292s
5	Dovizioso	1m 34.378s
6	Iannone	1m 34.439s
7	Rins	1m 34.463s
8	Lorenzo	1m 34.526s
9	Crutchlow	1m 34.555s
10	Pedrosa	1m 34.582s
11	Bautista	1m 34.674s
12	A. Espargaro	1m 34.774s
13	Petrucci	1m 34.791s
14	P. Espargaro	1m 34.867s
15	Rabat	1m 34.869s
16	Smith	1m 34.901s
17	Miller	1m 34.950s
18	Redding	1m 34.950s
19	Nakagami	1m 35.251s
20	Syahrin	1m 35.266s
21	Luthi	1m 35.752s
22	Abraham	1m 35.841s
23	Simeon	1m 36.570s

Championship Points

1	Marquez	140
2	Rossi	99
3	Vinales	93
4	Zarco	81
5	Dovizioso	79
6	Crutchlow	79
7	Lorenzo	75
8	Petrucci	71
9	Iannone	71
10	Miller	55
11	Rins	53
12	Pedrosa	41
13	Bautista	33
14	P. Espargaro	32
15	Rabat	27
16	Morbidelli	19
17	Syahrin	17
18	A. Espargaro	16
19	Redding	11
20	Nakagami	10
21	Smith	7
22	Kallio	6
23	Abraham	4

Constructor Points

1	Honda	175
2	Ducati	145
3	Yamaha	140
4	Suzuki	100
5	KTM	33
6	Aprilia	25

Grid order	1	2	3	4	5	6	7	8	9	10	11	12	13	14	15	16	17	18	19	20	21	22	23	24	25	26	
93 MARQUEZ	99	93	93	99	99	99	99	99	99	99	99	99	99	99	4	4	99	4	25	93	46	93	93	93	93	93	1
35 CRUTCHLOW	93	99	99	46	46	46	4	93	93	93	93	42	42	4	93	93	4	93	93	25	4	4	4	46	25	42	2
46 ROSSI	46	46	46	93	93	93	93	4	42	4	42	4	4	93	99	99	93	25	4	4	93	46	46	4	42	25	3
4 DOVIZIOSO	4	4	4	4	4	4	46	42	4	42	46	93	93	42	25	46	25	46	46	46	25	25	25	25	4	4	4
42 RINS	35	35	35	42	42	42	42	46	46	46	4	25	25	25	46	25	46	99	42	42	42	42	42	42	46	46	5
25 VINALES	42	42	42	35	35	35	25	25	25	25	25	5	46	46	42	42	42	42	99	99	35	35	35	35	35	35	6
41 A. ESPARGARO	29	29	29	29	25	25	35	35	35	5	5	46	5	5	35	35	35	35	35	35	99	99	99	99	99	99	7
5 ZARCO	25	25	25	25	5	5	5	5	5	35	35	35	35	35	5	5	5	5	5	5	5	5	5	5	5	5	8
29 IANNONE	41	41	5	5	29	29	29	29	29	29	29	29	29	19	19	19	19	19	19	19	19	19	19	19	19	19	9
99 LORENZO	5	5	43	43	43	43	19	19	19	19	19	19	19	29	29	29	29	29	29	29	29	29	29	29	29	29	10
9 PETRUCCI	9	9	9	9	19	19	43	43	43	43	43	43	43	43	43	43	43	43	43	43	43	43	43	43	43	43	11
19 BAUTISTA	43	43	19	19	9	9	41	41	41	41	41	9	9	9	9	9	9	53	53	53	53	53	44	41	44	44	12
30 NAKAGAMI	19	19	41	44	41	41	44	44	44	44	44	41	53	53	53	53	53	44	44	44	44	44	41	44	41	41	13
53 RABAT	44	44	44	41	44	44	45	45	9	9	9	53	44	44	44	44	44	41	41	41	41	45	45	45	45	45	14
55 SYAHRIN	30	30	30	30	45	45	9	9	45	53	53	44	41	41	41	41	41	45	45	45	45	41	53	53	26	26	15
43 MILLER	53	45	45	45	30	53	53	53	53	45	45	45	45	45	45	45	45	26	26	26	26	26	26	26	53	53	
45 REDDING	45	53	53	53	53	38	38	38	38	38	38	26	26	26	26	26	26	38	38	38	38	38	38	38	38	38	
26 PEDROSA	38	38	38	38	38	30	30	26	26	26	26	38	38	38	38	38	38	55	55	55	55	55	55	55	30	30	
17 ABRAHAM	26	26	26	26	26	26	26	30	55	55	55	55	55	55	55	55	55	30	30	30	30	30	30	30	55	55	
38 SMITH	55	55	55	55	55	55	55	55	30	30	30	30	30	30	30	30	30	12	12	12	12	12	12	12	12	12	
44 P. ESPARGARO	10	17	17	17	17	17	17	17	17	17	12	12	12	12	12	12	12										
12 LUTHI	17	10	10	10	10	10	10	10	12	12	17	10	10	10	10	10	10										
10 SIMEON	12	12	12	12	12	12	12	12	10	10	10																

17 Pit stop   10 Lapped rider

Moto2

RACE DISTANCE: 24 laps, 67.734 miles/109.008km · RACE WEATHER: Dry (air 23°C, humidity 33%, track 38°C)

Pos.	Rider	Nat.	No.	Entrant	Machine	Laps	Time & Speed
1	**Francesco Bagnaia**	ITA	42	SKY Racing Team VR46	Kalex	24	39m 30.436s 102.8mph/ 165.5km/h
2	**Fabio Quartararo**	FRA	20	Lightech - Speed Up Racing	Speed Up	24	39m 32.184s
3	**Alex Marquez**	SPA	73	EG 0,0 Marc VDS	Kalex	24	39m 32.615s
4	**Marcel Schrotter**	GER	23	Dynavolt Intact GP	Kalex	24	39m 34.530s
5	**Joan Mir**	SPA	36	EG 0,0 Marc VDS	Kalex	24	39m 34.778s
6	**Miguel Oliveira**	POR	44	Red Bull KTM Ajo	KTM	24	39m 35.666s
7	**Brad Binder**	RSA	41	Red Bull KTM Ajo	KTM	24	39m 40.004s
8	**Luca Marini**	ITA	10	SKY Racing Team VR46	Kalex	24	39m 40.396s
9	**Sam Lowes**	GBR	22	Swiss Innovative Investors	KTM	24	39m 44.569s
10	**Andrea Locatelli**	ITA	5	Italtrans Racing Team	Kalex	24	39m 44.768s
11	**Mattia Pasini**	ITA	54	Italtrans Racing Team	Kalex	24	39m 48.961s
12	**Augusto Fernandez**	SPA	40	Pons HP40	Kalex	24	39m 50.733s
13	**Jorge Navarro**	SPA	9	Federal Oil Gresini Moto2	Kalex	24	39m 51.303s
14	**Dominique Aegerter**	SWI	77	Kiefer Racing	KTM	24	39m 57.830s
15	**Simone Corsi**	ITA	24	Tasca Racing Scuderia Moto2	Kalex	24	39m 58.860s
16	Iker Lecuona	SPA	27	Swiss Innovative Investors	KTM	24	39m 58.941s
17	Bo Bendsneyder	NED	64	Tech 3 Racing	Tech 3	24	39m 59.110s
18	Remy Gardner	AUS	87	Tech 3 Racing	Tech 3	24	39m 59.324s
19	Khairul Idham Pawi	MAL	89	IDEMITSU Honda Team Asia	Kalex	24	39m 59.877s
20	Steven Odendaal	RSA	4	NTS RW Racing GP	NTS	24	40m 09.757s
21	Joe Roberts	USA	16	NTS RW Racing GP	NTS	24	40m 09.843s
22	Isaac Vinales	SPA	32	SAG Team	Kalex	24	40m 10.186s
23	Jules Danilo	FRA	95	Nashi Argan SAG Team	Kalex	24	40m 19.382s
24	Eric Granado	BRA	51	Forward Racing Team	Suter	24	40m 19.412s
25	Federico Fuligni	ITA	21	Tasca Racing Scuderia Moto2	Kalex	24	40m 58.315s
26	Lorenzo Baldassarri	ITA	7	Pons HP40	Kalex	23	39m 38.768s
	Romano Fenati	ITA	13	Marinelli Snipers Team	Kalex	20	DNF
	Xavi Vierge	SPA	97	Dynavolt Intact GP	Kalex	9	DNF
	Stefano Manzi	ITA	62	Forward Racing Team	Suter	6	DNF
	Danny Kent	GBR	52	Lightech - Speed Up Racing	Speed Up	0	DNF

Fastest lap: Lorenzo Baldassarri, on lap 8, 1m 38.030s, 103.6mph/166.7km/h.

Lap record: Tito Rabat, 1m 37.449s, 104.2mph/167.7km/h (2015).

Event maximum speed: Brad Binder, 160.9mph/258.9km/h (free practice).

Qualifying

Weather: Dry

Air Temp: 25° **Track Temp:** 42°

Humidity: 29%

1	Bagnaia	1m 37.608s
2	Schrotter	1m 37.681s
3	Marini	1m 37.689s
4	Marquez	1m 37.717s
5	Vierge	1m 37.768s
6	Lowes	1m 37.787s
7	Quartararo	1m 37.812s
8	Locatelli	1m 37.853s
9	Navarro	1m 37.856s
10	Mir	1m 37.895s
11	Pasini	1m 37.899s
12	Pawi	1m 37.940s
13	Baldassarri	1m 37.955s
14	Fenati	1m 38.061s
15	Vinales	1m 38.178s
16	Fernandez	1m 38.215s
17	Oliveira	1m 38.228s
18	Gardner	1m 38.245s
19	Lecuona	1m 38.305s
20	Corsi	1m 38.425s
21	Aegerter	1m 38.433s
22	Binder	1m 38.605s
23	Kent	1m 38.686s
24	Bendsneyder	1m 38.715s
25	Manzi	1m 38.986s
26	Odendaal	1m 39.121s
27	Tuuli	1m 39.301s
28	Granado	1m 39.337s
29	Roberts	1m 39.615s
30	Danilo	1m 39.663s
31	Cardelus	1m 41.117s
32	Fuligni	1m 41.388s
	Nagashima	No Time

Fastest race laps

1	Baldassarri	1m 38.030s
2	Bagnaia	1m 38.048s
3	Quartararo	1m 38.082s
4	Mir	1m 38.132s
5	Marquez	1m 38.143s
6	Vierge	1m 38.164s
7	Oliveira	1m 38.167s
8	Schrotter	1m 38.267s
9	Marini	1m 38.281s
10	Binder	1m 38.402s
11	Locatelli	1m 38.479s
12	Fenati	1m 38.484s
13	Pasini	1m 38.502s
14	Gardner	1m 38.543s
15	Navarro	1m 38.624s
16	Fernandez	1m 38.631s
17	Manzi	1m 38.656s
18	Lowes	1m 38.707s
19	Pawi	1m 38.779s
20	Lecuona	1m 38.995s
21	Corsi	1m 39.033s
22	Bendsneyder	1m 39.050s
23	Aegerter	1m 39.103s
24	Vinales	1m 39.462s
25	Roberts	1m 39.580s
26	Odendaal	1m 39.660s
27	Danilo	1m 39.816s
28	Granado	1m 39.828s
29	Fuligni	1m 40.963s

Championship Points

	Rider	Points
1	Bagnaia	144
2	Oliveira	128
3	Marquez	110
4	Baldassarri	93
5	Mir	75
6	Vierge	70
7	Binder	66
8	Quartararo	65
9	Pasini	63
10	Schrotter	63
11	Lecuona	32
12	Lowes	28
13	Marini	27
14	Locatelli	27
15	Corsi	23
16	Aegerter	22
17	Navarro	17
18	Gardner	15
19	Barbera	10
20	Fenati	9
21	Vinales	7
22	Manzi	6
23	Fernandez	6
24	Nagashima	6
25	Kent	4
26	Roberts	2
27	Odendaal	1
28	Pawi	1

Constructor Points

	Constructor	Points
1	Kalex	186
2	KTM	128
3	Speed Up	69
4	Tech 3	15
5	Suter	6
6	NTS	2

Moto3

RACE DISTANCE: 22 laps, 62.090 miles/99.924km · RACE WEATHER: Dry (air 23°C, humidity 36%, track 35°C)

Pos.	Rider	Nat.	No.	Entrant	Machine	Laps	Time & Speed
1	**Jorge Martin**	SPA	88	Del Conca Gresini Moto3	Honda	22	37m 56.485s 98.2mph/ 158.0km/h
2	**Aron Canet**	SPA	44	Estrella Galicia 0,0	Honda	22	37m 57.150s
3	**Enea Bastianini**	ITA	33	Leopard Racing	Honda	22	37m 57.203s
4	**Jaume Masia**	SPA	5	Bester Capital Dubai	KTM	22	38m 07.327s
5	**Jakub Kornfeil**	CZE	84	Redox PruestelGP	KTM	22	38m 07.438s
6	**Lorenzo Dalla Porta**	ITA	48	Leopard Racing	Honda	22	38m 07.806s
7	**Darryn Binder**	RSA	40	Red Bull KTM Ajo	KTM	22	38m 07.828s
8	**Gabriel Rodrigo**	ARG	19	RBA BOE Skull Rider	KTM	22	38m 08.222s
9	**Fabio Di Giannantonio**	ITA	21	Del Conca Gresini Moto3	Honda	22	38m 08.241s
10	**Marcos Ramirez**	SPA	42	Bester Capital Dubai	KTM	22	38m 08.251s
11	**Nicolo Bulega**	ITA	8	SKY Racing Team VR46	KTM	22	38m 08.262s
12	**Dennis Foggia**	ITA	10	SKY Racing Team VR46	KTM	22	38m 12.458s
13	**Tatsuki Suzuki**	JPN	24	SIC58 Squadra Corse	Honda	22	38m 19.768s
14	**Albert Arenas**	SPA	75	Angel Nieto Team Moto3	KTM	22	38m 20.252s
15	**Niccolo Antonelli**	ITA	23	SIC58 Squadra Corse	Honda	22	38m 20.312s
16	Kaito Toba	JPN	27	Honda Team Asia	Honda	22	38m 20.335s
17	Tony Arbolino	ITA	14	Marinelli Snipers Team	Honda	22	38m 20.525s
18	Philipp Oettl	GER	65	Sudmetal Schedl GP Racing	KTM	22	38m 22.287s
19	Ayumu Sasaki	JPN	71	Petronas Sprinta Racing	Honda	22	38m 23.582s
20	Kazuki Masaki	JPN	22	RBA BOE Skull Rider	KTM	22	38m 23.681s
21	Adam Norrodin	MAL	7	Petronas Sprinta Racing	Honda	22	38m 23.745s
22	Nakarin Atiratphuvapat	THA	41	Honda Team Asia	Honda	22	38m 23.888s
23	Ai Ogura	JPN	32	Asia Talent Team	Honda	22	38m 24.129s
24	Livio Loi	BEL	11	Reale Avintia Academy 77	KTM	22	38m 24.524s
25	Alonso Lopez	SPA	72	Estrella Galicia 0,0	Honda	22	38m 27.004s
26	Andrea Migno	ITA	16	Angel Nieto Team Moto3	KTM	22	38m 31.423s
27	Stefano Nepa	ITA	81	CIP - Green Power	KTM	22	38m 48.555s
28	Ryan van de Lagemaat	NED	18	Lamotec Lagemaat Racing	KTM	21	38m 12.927s
	Marco Bezzecchi	ITA	12	Redox PruestelGP	KTM	21	DNF
	John McPhee	GBR	17	CIP - Green Power	KTM	20	DNF

Fastest lap: Aron Canet, on lap 5, 1m 42.007s, 99.5mph/160.2km/h.

Lap record: Jorge Navarro, 1m 42.135s, 99.4mph/160.0km/h (2015).

Event maximum speed: Adam Norrodin, 138.6mph/223.0km/h (free practice).

Qualifying

Weather: Dry

Air Temp: 23° **Track Temp:** 40°

Humidity: 31%

1	Martin	1m 42.039s
2	Bastianini	1m 42.349s
3	Bulega	1m 42.445s
4	Canet	1m 42.562s
5	Dalla Porta	1m 42.594s
6	McPhee	1m 42.595s
7	Di Giannantonio	1m 42.749s
8	Bezzecchi	1m 42.764s
9	Ramirez	1m 42.811s
10	Rodrigo	1m 42.933s
11	Kornfeil	1m 43.030s
12	Norrodin	1m 43.067s
13	Arenas	1m 43.083s
14	Arbolino	1m 43.091s
15	Antonelli	1m 43.117s
16	Sasaki	1m 43.124s
17	Loi	1m 43.193s
18	Oettl	1m 43.212s
19	Foggia	1m 43.268s
20	Masia	1m 43.275s
21	Toba	1m 43.290s
22	Suzuki	1m 43.390s
23	Binder	1m 43.452s
24	Migno	1m 43.527s
25	Atiratphuvapat	1m 43.746s
26	Lopez	1m 43.894s
27	Ogura	1m 43.938s
28	Masaki	1m 44.271s
29	Nepa	1m 44.616s
30	Van de Lagemaat	1m 45.879s

Fastest race laps

1	Canet	1m 42.007s
2	McPhee	1m 42.217s
3	Bastianini	1m 42.337s
4	Bezzecchi	1m 42.351s
5	Martin	1m 42.561s
6	Kornfeil	1m 42.592s
7	Masia	1m 42.650s
8	Rodrigo	1m 42.865s
9	Ramirez	1m 42.916s
10	Suzuki	1m 42.921s
11	Bulega	1m 42.963s
12	Di Giannantonio	1m 42.967s
13	Dalla Porta	1m 43.008s
14	Foggia	1m 43.026s
15	Arenas	1m 43.041s
16	Binder	1m 43.055s
17	Toba	1m 43.070s
18	Oettl	1m 43.135s
19	Masaki	1m 43.177s
20	Sasaki	1m 43.287s
21	Arbolino	1m 43.300s
22	Ogura	1m 43.409s
23	Norrodin	1m 43.427s
24	Lopez	1m 43.445s
25	Atiratphuvapat	1m 43.506s
26	Antonelli	1m 43.745s
27	Migno	1m 43.748s
28	Loi	1m 43.749s
29	Nepa	1m 44.421s
30	Van de Lagemaat	1m 47.841s

Championship Points

	Rider	Points
1	Martin	105
2	Bezzecchi	103
3	Di Giannantonio	91
4	Bastianini	84
5	Canet	81
6	Rodrigo	65
7	Migno	56
8	Kornfeil	52
9	Antonelli	45
10	Ramirez	44
11	Dalla Porta	43
12	Suzuki	38
13	Oettl	36
14	Masia	34
15	Lopez	31
16	Arenas	30
17	Toba	26
18	Arbolino	24
19	McPhee	23
20	Binder	20
21	Norrodin	19
22	Sasaki	17
23	Foggia	13
24	Yurchenko	9
25	Loi	8
26	Fernandez	6
27	Pagliani	6
28	Bulega	5
29	Masaki	3
30	Atiratphuvapat	2
31	Ogura	1

Constructor Points

	Constructor	Points
1	Honda	171
2	KTM	155

FIM WORLD CHAMPIONSHIP · ROUND 9

GERMAN GRAND PRIX

SACHSENRING

Main: MotoGP bikes swing around the Omega curve, one of only three right-handers.
Photo: Gold & Goose

Inset: Unbeatable again. Marquez extended an unbroken pole-to-victory record dating back to 2010.
Photo: HRC

Above: Going, going... Pedrosa briefly succumbed to emotion as he announced his retirement.

Top: "Keep the flame alive, not the ashes." Banner responds to (ultimately hollow) threats that this was the last Sachsenring MotoGP.

Above right: Second was Rossi's best of the season so far.

Centre right: Luckily, Stefan Bradl had his leathers handy to take over when Morbidelli withdrew at lunchtime on Friday.

Centre far right: A top-ten finish for Bradley Smith on the KTM.

Below right: Bautista was on fire, beating both of the factory Ducatis to take fifth.

Photos: Gold & Goose

AFTER weeks of suspense and a half-hidden flirtation with Yamaha, Dani Pedrosa opened the weekend by announcing his retirement, after 18 years of GP racing. The former 125 and double 250 champion and triple MotoGP runner-up, who had won at least one GP every year since his first in the 125 class at Assen in 2002, held his emotions in check at the packed announcement, thanking Honda, his team and his fans for their support. He only faltered briefly, when asked to pick out a special moment. "There are many, but one was when I started racing in Jarama [in trials for the Movistar talent series]. I was very small, and I didn't imagine with so many riders that I would be picked. From that moment to here ... is amazing."

In trademark matter-of-fact style, he spoke about "a very hard decision", and that "despite having very good opportunities to keep racing, I didn't feel the same intensity, and I now have different priorities in my life."

The principal opportunity had been from the formative Petronas Yamaha team, alongside Franco Morbidelli. His refusal seemed to offer an opportunity for the displaced Bautista, but news broke that instead the seat would go to Moto2's Quartararo.

The next day, it was business as usual at the pocket-handkerchief track described by Cal Crutchlow as "horrible". But, the Briton continued, "It's fun to ride, and you often get good races here." The comments were in response to threats (not the first such) that this would be the last GP race at the little circuit outside the former Karl-Marx-Stadt. Riders accustomed to complaining about the ultra-tight layout and string of seven successive left-handers now discovered an affection for the characterful venue.

This was least surprising in Marc Marquez. As with his domination at the left-handed US circuits, the anticlockwise 'Ring played to strengths he had nurtured over years of left-hand dirt-track training. He had taken pole every year since 2010, in all three classes. Abandoning the track, he smiled, "would be bad for me". Just to prove it, he did the same again in 2018. He was kind enough to his rivals to say, "Every year, it gets more difficult." But his grip on the championship was tightening.

Where would the race go? With the Lausitzring sold to DEKRA for automotive testing, the alternatives were the Hockenheimring ("Too much an F1 circuit.") or the Nurburgring ("Okay, but the weather is bad," according to Rossi). It turned out to be a false alarm.

Safety remained an issue, with scant run-off compensated for by extensive air-fencing. Two prominent victims in MotoGP: Mika Kallio, back for another KTM wild-card; and Aprilia's Aleix Espargaro.

Kallio suffered serious knee injuries in a frightening crash early in FP2, having lost the rear under braking and run into the gravel trap outside the fast Turn Eight at barely reduced speed. He was thrown directly into the air-fence, and the bike followed him in. "I've broken ligaments before," he said, but it had never been as painful. He was out for the rest of the year.

Espargaro was also hit by his bike after a much slower crash in race-morning warm-up, having just set fastest time. He suffered such a big impact to his ribs that he was taken to hospital in Chemnitz for observation, out of the race.

That was a climax to a weekend that had gone bad on Saturday. During FP3, the Aprilia rider had come upon Simeon and Rins cruising in to the rather awkwardly placed pit lane. It spoiled a fast lap, and with typically fulsome gestures, he made his displeasure very clear. Only a few minutes later, however, he was cruising on the racing line on the entry to the same corner when Marquez came storming up behind, and had to back off. This time, Espargaro's waves were in apology; but when Race Direction examined the incident, they felt it was worthy of a six-place grid penalty, as his third such offence of the season. Rins and Simeon were also called before the stewards, but escaped punishment, and Espargaro was so incensed by this injustice that he cancelled his press debrief and stormed off in high dudgeon.

On a weekend when big brother Brad Binder was confirmed for another year with the official KTM Moto2 squad, his less fortunate younger brother, Darryn, missed the GP after breaking his collarbone in a training crash.

Others out of the race were carrying injuries from Assen. Moto2 rider Tuuli pulled out after the first day, in too much

pain after a partial finger amputation. Morbidelli also withdrew after FP1, for the same reason.

That left a vacant seat in MotoGP, and with HRC test rider Stefan Bradl on hand working for German TV, it was a short step from microphone to twist-grip, as the Marc VDS team passed him the ignition key. The former Moto2 champion was already down for a wild-card ride at the next round at Brno, so at worst this was a good chance to test. He was 21st in his first session, less than two-tenths down on Pedrosa, and would finish a creditable 16th. Sadly, his next outing would be less successful.

Oddly enough, there were no crashes all weekend at the track's finest – and most notorious – corner, the right-hand Turn 11, which follows a string of lefts and has claimed many victims. Michelin's Piero Taramasso said, "We have used a softer compound than last year;" while Rossi confirmed, "We now have the right tyres. You need one that is very, very soft on the right side. It was always very critical with Bridgestone and with Michelin for the last two years. They have taken a big forward step." And not only Michelin, because the Dunlop-shod Motos 2 and 3 enjoyed the same accident-free run.

Turn 11 leads spectacularly over a blind brow to the plunging 'Waterfall'. Now the corner had been officially named after the late Ralf Waldmann, who had died unexpectedly of a heart attack in March at the age of 51. Waldmann had finished second in the 250cc World Championship in 1996 and 1997, and had recently become a popular and humorous TV commentator in Germany.

Dorna's always impressive TV coverage took another little step, with a record 130 on-bike cameras, including new angles. And, in line with the other European races so far, bright sunshine for the three days ensured plenty of good light by which to film.

MOTOGP RACE – 30 laps

Marquez had run a two-stop strategy in a hectic Q2 to narrowly depose Petrucci from a first pole with a new track record. Petrucci had followed Lorenzo, who was third. He was better than a tenth ahead of Vinales, joined on row two by Dovizioso (from Q1) and Rossi. Crutchlow led the third, from Iannone and Bautista.

The race was close, at least until Marquez decided it was time to stop nursing his unusual choice of a soft rear tyre. By then, tyre wear had started some serious shuffling, and put some pre-race favourites out to grass – specifically both factory Ducatis.

Lorenzo made a great start to lead into the first tight corners, with Petrucci and Marquez following, and Rossi straight up to fourth, ahead of Vinales and Crutchlow.

Overtaking is difficult at this track and almost invariably takes place under braking into Turns One or 12, at the bottom of the 'Waterfall'. Marquez did it at the former to slip into second at the start of lap five; Crutchlow had made the same move on Vinales for fifth two laps earlier, the Yamaha rider directly ceding another place to Dovizioso.

Vinales would lose touch slightly, but the rest were still close – Rossi having taken third from Petrucci, also into the first corner – when Crutchlow crashed out on lap ten. He had lost the front in the final corner, and was puzzled and angry, having pushed harder in previous laps, and blamed a quirk that had troubled him before: that when in a big group, the front tyre is robbed of cooling air and can overheat.

By then, Bautista was closing, at this point fastest on the track, having got ahead of Pedrosa and then, on lap nine, also Vinales. As the half-distance point approached, he was pressing Dovizioso.

By this stage also, at the end of lap 12, Marquez had finally followed through on his long-standing threat to leader Lorenzo, moving cleanly inside into the last corner. Lorenzo was the only rider on the soft front, but he blamed the rear for grip problems. On lap 16, he ran wide at the last of the series of lefts, giving Rossi an easy way through into second.

Above: Third again… Vinales made it two Yamahas on the podium.

Top right: Crutchlow crashed out of a strong place on lap ten.

Above centre right: Luca Marini took his maiden Moto2 podium.

Above right: Second-placed Mir congratulates Binder on his first Moto2 victory.

Above far right: Moto2 coming-man Xavi Vierge (97) leads veteran Simone Corsi (24).

Right: Binder (41) leads Mir and Marini in Moto2.

Below right: Martin hustles his Honda ahead of Bezzecchi (12), Ramirez (42) and the rest for a fifth win of the year.

Below far right: John McPhee made a welcome podium return.

Photos: Gold & Goose

He was almost a second behind Marquez, and had taken back a couple of tenths when the Honda rider got the message and started to pull away, better than two seconds clear with six laps to go.

Second was not just Rossi's best result of the season so far, "but also my best race," he said. He added that half-brother Luca Marini's earlier maiden Moto2 podium "gave me extra power".

Lorenzo, in a fading third, succumbed to Petrucci on lap 26. By then, Vinales had picked up his pace again. He was back in front of Bautista, with Dovizioso dropping behind them. The Yamaha would easily dispose of Lorenzo (as did Bautista a couple of laps later). Then, with two laps to go, Vinales swept past Petrucci through the fast left-hand Turn Eight, taking a second podium in a row by just over half a second. The paradox of his early struggles and late-race speed was "crazy, but that's how it is."

Some five seconds behind, Pedrosa was back ahead of Zarco, to finish eighth. The latter had run into a slump that he struggled to explain, but that seemed to have started with his home GP blunder at Le Mans.

Smith had battled with the two of them earlier in the race, until he ran wide, but he regained ground for his first top-ten of the season.

Rookie Syahrin prevailed in a distant late-race battle with Iannone. The Suzuki rider had started from the middle of row three, but on only the third corner, he was pushed wide to finish lap one 18th. He'd gained places ever since, but too slowly to make much difference.

He was not the only Turn Three victim of a crash triggered when (according to Jack Miller) "Pol [Espargaro] came round the outside of everyone like an idiot and hit Rins." Both Espargaro and Rins went down and out; Miller was dropped to last. By the finish, he'd managed to get between Rabat and 15th-placed Redding.

Bradl was another four seconds away after an uneventful race, comfortably clear of temporary team-mate Luthi. Abraham and Simeon were a long way back; Nakagami was a third rider to crash out, on his fifth lap, after getting through to Q2 from Q1 the previous day. Hardly had he picked himself up than he was on his way back to Japan to resume testing for the forthcoming Suzuka 8 Hours race for Honda.

Marquez went into the short summer break with a handsome championship lead of 46 points – a nice round number for Rossi to contemplate.

MOTO2 RACE – 28 laps

Records tumbled also in Moto2 qualifying where, as usual, the best times came early, the Dunlops running on freshly laid Michelin rubber from MotoGP. There were 24 within a second of Pasini's second pole of the season. Marini was a career-best second, for a second successive front row, by two measly thousandths from team-mate Bagnaia – all three train together at the VR46 ranch outside Tavullia.

Lowes was the first non-Kalex, heading row two on his KTM, from Baldassarri and Vierge.

Again, Marquez was the victim of a heavy crash in FP3; he qualified seventh, but was badly battered. Oliveira was 15th to team-mate Binder's tenth; Quartararo 18th after an early tumble.

With track temperature peaking at a punishing 40 degrees, Dunlop decreed that the soft option would not be safe for race distance, so all riders were on identical rubber, with endurance of the hard even open to question.

Early drama upset the form book. Marini led away from Bagnaia; on lap two, Pasini had moved inside Bagnaia, but in the final corner he slid off, right under the title leader's front wheel.

Bagnaia swerved away for a giddy ride across the gravel. He would finish lap three down in 25th.

That was good news for Oliveira, in the top ten on lap one, although a bump with Vierge had dropped him two places by the end of it.

Up front, Mir had inherited second, ahead of Lowes and Marquez. Then, on lap three, Binder sliced past the pair for third. Two laps later, Mir consigned Marini to second; and the first three started moving clear.

The big change came on lap ten. Binder took Marini into the first corner, and Mir at the end of the lap, to gain a lead he would never lose.

They stayed close, every escape bid by Binder pegged back by Mir. But the KTM rider was able to sustain his narrow lead by seven-tenths over the line. At the same time, Marini

was gaining strength for his own final challenge, third by less than two-tenths. Binder was the first South African to win in an intermediate class since Jon Ekerold had won the 350 GP in Italy in 1981.

They'd been pursued until after half-distance by Schrotter, now ahead of Lowes. Then Oliveira got between them on lap 11. Eight laps later, the KTM was past the Kalex in fourth.

But by then, tyre grip was in short supply, and while Oliveira did close a gap of 1.6 seconds to less than a second, he was never close enough to attack. In his wake, Lowes reclaimed fifth from Schrotter on the final lap.

Marquez had been fading badly, towards the back of a big fight some ten seconds away, seventh to 13th covered by less than two seconds. With three laps to go, Vierge got to the front of this swarm. Inches behind, Corsi, Quartararo and Navarro completed the top ten. Then, in short order, Gardner, Bagnaia and Marquez, with the Italian taking 12th on the last lap. Aegerter was still close; Augusto Fernandez took the last point.

In addition to Pasini, Lorenzo Baldassarri, Danny Kent and Tetsuta Nagashima crashed out, the first two of them from strong positions.

MOTO3 RACE – 27 laps

Jorge Martin claimed a sixth pole of the season by the narrowest of margins, ahead of career-best Ramirez and Bastianini, with 21 within the first second. The order was shuffled by another rash of penalties, seven for riding "at an extreme slow speed" as they dawdled at the pit exit. Bulega, Antonelli, Fernandez, Atiratphuvapat, Perez, new boy Nepa and wild-card Luca Grunwald were all dropped three grid positions; rookie Foggia went to the back of the grid for a repeat of three slow track sectors.

The race was intense and complicated; Martin rose above it magnificently. He held a strong place at or near the front of a huge pack, then moved away over the last seven laps to win by 2.5 seconds, extending his narrow championship points lead. In his wake, second to seventh was covered by just over a second.

Former title leader Bezzecchi very narrowly held off long-time podium absentee McPhee; while three-tenths away, Ramirez was inches ahead of Canet, Kornfeil right behind, survivors of a swarming melee.

There were significant casualties. One was Di Giannantonio, who fell after tagging his team-mate into the first corner; Martin was lucky not to have fallen as well.

Another was Bastianini, fastest in morning warm-up, who took early front-running rookie Lopez with him. Gabriel Rodrigo also fell.

Oettl fought through to the front pack from 18th on lap one, but had dropped to eighth at the end. Raul Fernandez (replacement for the injured Darryn Binder on the Red Bull KTM) was an excellent ninth. Close behind, Sasaki held off team-mate Adam Norrodin to complete the top ten.

PRAMAC MOTORRAD GRAND PRIX DEUTSCHLAND

13–15 JULY, 2018

SACHSENRING GP CIRCUIT

30 laps
Length: 3.671 km / 3.259 miles
Width: 12m

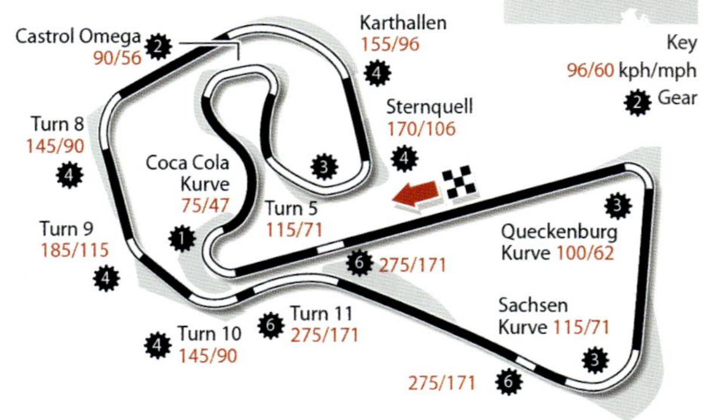

MotoGP

RACE DISTANCE: 30 laps, 68.432 miles/110.130km · RACE WEATHER: Dry (air 27°C, humidity 48%, track 48°C)

Pos.	Rider	Nat.	No.	Entrant	Machine	Tyres	Race tyre choice	Laps	Time & speed
1	**Marc Marquez**	SPA	93	Repsol Honda Team	Honda RC213V	M	F: Hard/R: Soft	30	41m 05.019s 99.9mph/ 160.8km/h
2	**Valentino Rossi**	ITA	46	Movistar Yamaha MotoGP	Yamaha YZR-M1	M	F: Medium/R: Medium	30	41m 07.215s
3	**Maverick Vinales**	SPA	25	Movistar Yamaha MotoGP	Yamaha YZR-M1	M	F: Medium/R: Soft	30	41m 07.795s
4	**Danilo Petrucci**	ITA	9	Alma Pramac Racing	Ducati Desmosedici	M	F: Medium/R: Medium	30	41m 08.395s
5	**Alvaro Bautista**	SPA	19	Angel Nieto Team	Ducati Desmosedici	M	F: Medium/R: Medium	30	41m 10.202s
6	**Jorge Lorenzo**	SPA	99	Ducati Team	Ducati Desmosedici	M	F: Soft/R: Medium	30	41m 10.799s
7	**Andrea Dovizioso**	ITA	4	Ducati Team	Ducati Desmosedici	M	F: Medium/R: Medium	30	41m 12.960s
8	**Dani Pedrosa**	SPA	26	Repsol Honda Team	Honda RC213V	M	F: Hard/R: Medium	30	41m 17.730s
9	**Johann Zarco**	FRA	5	Monster Yamaha Tech 3	Yamaha YZR-M1	M	F: Medium/R: Soft	30	41m 19.447s
10	**Bradley Smith**	GBR	38	Red Bull KTM Factory Racing	KTM RC16	M	F: Medium/R: Medium	30	41m 26.493s
11	**Hafizh Syahrin**	MAL	55	Monster Yamaha Tech 3	Yamaha YZR-M1	M	F: Medium/R: Soft	30	41m 30.828s
12	**Andrea Iannone**	ITA	29	Team SUZUKI ECSTAR	Suzuki GSX-RR	M	F: Medium/R: Medium	30	41m 30.982s
13	**Tito Rabat**	SPA	53	Reale Avintia Racing	Ducati Desmosedici	M	F: Medium/R: Medium	30	41m 34.059s
14	**Jack Miller**	AUS	43	Alma Pramac Racing	Ducati Desmosedici	M	F: Medium/R: Medium	30	41m 34.344s
15	**Scott Redding**	GBR	45	Aprilia Racing Team Gresini	Aprilia RS-GP	M	F: Hard/R: Medium	30	41m 39.142s
16	Stefan Bradl	GER	6	EG 0,0 Marc VDS	Honda RC213V	M	F: Medium/R: Medium	30	41m 43.226s
17	Thomas Luthi	SWI	12	EG 0,0 Marc VDS	Honda RC213V	M	F: Medium/R: Medium	30	41m 54.388s
18	Karel Abraham	CZE	17	Angel Nieto Team	Ducati Desmosedici	M	F: Medium/R: Medium	30	42m 06.041s
19	Xavier Simeon	BEL	10	Reale Avintia Racing	Ducati Desmosedici	M	F: Medium/R: Medium	30	42m 21.711s
	Cal Crutchlow	GBR	35	LCR Honda CASTROL	Honda RC213V	M	F: Hard/R: Soft	9	DNF-crash
	Takaaki Nakagami	JPN	30	LCR Honda IDEMITSU	Honda RC213V	M	F: Hard/R: Soft	4	DNF-crash
	Alex Rins	SPA	42	Team SUZUKI ECSTAR	Suzuki GSX-RR	M	F: Medium/R: Soft	0	DNF-crash
	Pol Espargaro	SPA	44	Red Bull KTM Factory Racing	KTM RC16	M	F: Medium/R: Medium	0	DNF-crash
	Aleix Espargaro	SPA	41	Aprilia Racing Team Gresini	Aprilia RS-GP	M	-	-	DNS-injured
	Mika Kallio	FIN	36	Red Bull KTM Factory Racing	KTM RC16	M	-	-	DNS-injured
	Franco Morbidelli	ITA	21	EG 0,0 Marc VDS	Honda RC213V	M	-	-	DNS-injured

Fastest lap: Marc Marquez, on lap 22, 1m 21.643s, 100.5mph/161.8km/h.
Lap record: Jonas Folger, 1m 21.442s, 100.8mph/162.2km/h (2017).
Event maximum speed: Andrea Dovizioso, 184.4mph/296.7km/h (qualifying).

Qualifying

Weather: Dry
Air Temp: 24° **Track Temp:** 46°
Humidity: 45%

1	Marquez	1m 20.270s
2	Petrucci	1m 20.295s
3	Lorenzo	1m 20.327s
4	Vinales	1m 20.441s
5	Dovizioso	1m 20.444s
6	Rossi	1m 20.532s
7	Crutchlow	1m 20.675s
8	Iannone	1m 20.682s
9	Bautista	1m 20.700s
10	Pedrosa	1m 20.831s
11	Rins	1m 20.847s
12	Nakagami	1m 20.938s
13	A. Espargaro	1m 20.972s
14	Zarco	1m 21.059s
15	Miller	1m 21.183s
16	P. Espargaro	1m 21.242s
17	Smith	1m 21.287s
18	Syahrin	1m 21.460s
19	Rabat	1m 21.546s
20	Redding	1m 21.749s
21	Bradl	1m 21.802s
22	Luthi	1m 22.012s
23	Abraham	1m 22.159s
24	Simeon	1m 22.709s

Fastest race laps

1	Marquez	1m 21.643s
2	Rossi	1m 21.776s
3	Bautista	1m 21.794s
4	Lorenzo	1m 21.806s
5	Vinales	1m 21.813s
6	Petrucci	1m 21.845s
7	Dovizioso	1m 21.861s
8	Crutchlow	1m 21.924s
9	Miller	1m 22.052s
10	Zarco	1m 22.185s
11	Smith	1m 22.240s
12	Pedrosa	1m 22.243s
13	Syahrin	1m 22.248s
14	Iannone	1m 22.271s
15	Nakagami	1m 22.343s
16	Redding	1m 22.498s
17	Rabat	1m 22.503s
18	Luthi	1m 22.651s
19	Bradl	1m 22.687s
20	Abraham	1m 23.010s
21	Simeon	1m 24.028s

Championship Points

1	Marquez	165
2	Rossi	119
3	Vinales	109
4	Dovizioso	88
5	Zarco	88
6	Lorenzo	85
7	Petrucci	84
8	Crutchlow	79
9	Iannone	75
10	Miller	57
11	Rins	53
12	Pedrosa	49
13	Bautista	44
14	P. Espargaro	32
15	Rabat	30
16	Syahrin	22
17	Morbidelli	19
18	A. Espargaro	16
19	Smith	13
20	Redding	12
21	Nakagami	10
22	Kallio	6
23	Abraham	4

Constructor Points

1	Honda	200
2	Yamaha	160
3	Ducati	158
4	Suzuki	104
5	KTM	39
6	Aprilia	26

Grid Order		1	2	3	4	5	6	7	8	9	10	11	12	13	14	15	16	17	18	19	20	21	22	23	24	25	26	27	28	29	30	
93	MARQUEZ	99	99	99	99	99	99	99	99	99	99	99	99	93	93	93	93	93	93	93	93	93	93	93	93	93	93	93	93	93	93	1
9	PETRUCCI	9	9	9	9	93	93	93	93	93	93	93	93	99	99	99	46	46	46	46	46	46	46	46	46	46	46	46	46	46	46	2
99	LORENZO	93	93	93	93	9	9	9	9	46	46	46	46	46	46	46	99	99	99	99	99	99	99	99	99	99	9	9	9	25	25	3
25	VINALES	46	46	46	46	46	46	46	46	9	9	9	9	9	9	9	9	9	9	9	9	9	9	9	9	9	25	25	25	9	9	4
4	DOVIZIOSO	25	25	35	35	35	35	35	35	35	4	4	4	4	4	4	4	4	4	4	4	19	19	19	19	25	99	99	19	19	19	5
46	ROSSI	35	35	25	4	4	4	4	4	4	19	19	19	19	19	19	19	19	19	19	19	4	4	25	25	19	19	19	99	99	99	6
35	CRUTCHLOW	4	4	4	25	25	25	25	25	19	25	25	25	25	25	25	25	25	25	25	25	25	25	4	4	4	4	4	4	4	4	7
29	IANNONE	26	26	26	26	19	19	19	19	25	5	5	5	5	5	5	5	5	5	5	5	5	5	5	26	26	26	26	26	26	26	8
19	BAUTISTA	19	19	19	19	26	26	26	26	26	26	26	26	26	26	26	26	26	26	26	26	26	26	26	5	5	5	5	5	5	5	9
26	PEDROSA	38	38	38	38	38	5	5	5	5	38	38	38	38	38	55	55	55	55	38	38	38	38	38	38	38	38	38	38	38	38	10
42	RINS	30	30	5	5	5	38	38	38	38	55	55	55	55	55	38	38	38	38	55	55	55	55	55	55	55	55	29	55	55	55	11
30	NAKAGAMI	5	5	30	30	55	55	55	55	55	53	53	53	53	53	53	53	53	53	53	53	53	29	29	29	29	29	55	29	29	29	12
5	ZARCO	45	45	55	55	45	45	45	53	53	45	45	45	45	45	45	45	45	45	45	45	29	53	53	53	53	53	53	53	53	53	13
43	MILLER	55	55	45	45	53	53	53	45	45	29	29	29	29	29	29	29	29	29	29	29	45	45	45	45	45	45	43	43	43	43	14
44	P. ESPARGARO	17	53	53	53	6	6	6	29	29	12	12	12	12	12	12	12	43	43	43	43	43	43	43	43	43	43	45	45	45	45	15
38	SMITH	53	17	6	6	29	29	29	6	6	6	6	6	6	6	6	43	12	12	12	12	6	6	6	6	6	6	6	6	6	6	
55	SYAHRIN	6	6	17	17	12	12	12	12	12	43	43	43	43	43	43	6	6	6	6	6	12	12	12	12	12	12	12	12	12	12	
53	RABAT	29	29	29	29	17	17	17	17	17	17	17	17	17	17	17	17	17	17	17	17	17	17	17	17	17	17	17	17	17	17	
45	REDDING	10	12	12	12	43	43	43	43	43	10	10	10	10	10	10	10	10	10	10	10	10	10	10	10	10	10	10	10	10	10	
6	BRADL	12	10	10	10	10	10	10	10	10																						
12	LUTHI	43	43	43	43																											
17	ABRAHAM																															
10	SIMEON																															

Moto2

RACE DISTANCE: 28 laps, 63.870 miles/102.788km · RACE WEATHER: Dry (air 24°C, humidity 60%, track 40°C)

Pos.	Rider	Nat.	No.	Entrant	Machine	Laps	Time & Speed
1	**Brad Binder**	RSA	41	Red Bull KTM Ajo	KTM	28	39m 46.306s 96.3mph/ 155.0km/h
2	**Joan Mir**	SPA	36	EG 0,0 Marc VDS	Kalex	28	39m 47.085s
3	**Luca Marini**	ITA	10	SKY Racing Team VR46	Kalex	28	39m 47.239s
4	**Miguel Oliveira**	POR	44	Red Bull KTM Ajo	KTM	28	39m 48.449s
5	**Sam Lowes**	GBR	22	Swiss Innovative Investors	KTM	28	39m 52.682s
6	**Marcel Schrotter**	GER	23	Dynavolt Intact GP	Kalex	28	39m 52.819s
7	**Xavi Vierge**	SPA	97	Dynavolt Intact GP	Kalex	28	40m 01.850s
8	**Simone Corsi**	ITA	24	Tasca Racing Scuderia Moto2	Kalex	28	40m 01.980s
9	**Fabio Quartararo**	FRA	20	MB Conveyors - Speed Up Racing	Speed Up	28	40m 02.310s
10	**Jorge Navarro**	SPA	9	Federal Oil Gresini Moto2	Kalex	28	40m 02.311s
11	**Remy Gardner**	AUS	87	Tech 3 Racing	Tech 3	28	40m 02.902s
12	**Francesco Bagnaia**	ITA	42	SKY Racing Team VR46	Kalex	28	40m 03.610s
13	**Alex Marquez**	SPA	73	EG 0,0 Marc VDS	Kalex	28	40m 03.764s
14	**Dominique Aegerter**	SWI	77	Kiefer Racing	KTM	28	40m 04.444s
15	**Augusto Fernandez**	SPA	40	Pons HP40	Kalex	28	40m 10.122s
16	Romano Fenati	ITA	13	Marinelli Snipers Team	Kalex	28	40m 10.917s
17	Khairul Idham Pawi	MAL	89	IDEMITSU Honda Team Asia	Kalex	28	40m 11.923s
18	Steven Odendaal	RSA	4	NTS RW Racing GP	NTS	28	40m 14.325s
19	Iker Lecuona	SPA	27	Swiss Innovative Investors	KTM	28	40m 14.479s
20	Bo Bendsneyder	NED	64	Tech 3 Racing	Tech 3	28	40m 22.704s
21	Eric Granado	BRA	51	Forward Racing Team	Suter	28	40m 26.505s
22	Joe Roberts	USA	16	NTS RW Racing GP	NTS	28	40m 27.815s
23	Federico Fuligni	ITA	21	Tasca Racing Scuderia Moto2	Kalex	28	40m 50.330s
24	Xavi Cardelus	AND	18	Team Stylobike	Kalex	27	41m 08.577s
25	Stefano Manzi	ITA	62	Forward Racing Team	Suter	21	41m 00.447s
	Isaac Vinales	SPA	32	SAG Team	Kalex	16	DNF
	Danny Kent	GBR	52	MB Conveyors - Speed Up Racing	Speed Up	7	DNF
	Tetsuta Nagashima	JPN	45	IDEMITSU Honda Team Asia	Kalex	4	DNF
	Lorenzo Baldassarri	ITA	7	Pons HP40	Kalex	2	DNF
	Mattia Pasini	ITA	54	Italtrans Racing Team	Kalex	1	DNF
	Andrea Locatelli	ITA	5	Italtrans Racing Team	Kalex	1	DNF
	Jules Danilo	FRA	95	Nashi Argan SAG Team	Kalex	-	DNS
	Niki Tuuli	FIN	66	SIC Racing Team	Kalex	-	DNS

Fastest lap: Joan Mir, on lap 3, 1m 24.634s, 97.0mph/156.1km/h.
Lap record: Miguel Oliveira, 1m 24.483s, 97.2mph/156.4km/h (2017).
Event maximum speed: Miguel Oliveira, 154.5mph/248.7km/h (free practice).

Qualifying

Weather: Dry
Air Temp: 24° **Track Temp:** 47°
Humidity: 41%

Pos.	Rider	Time
1	Pasini	1m 23.787s
2	Marini	1m 23.968s
3	Bagnaia	1m 23.970s
4	Lowes	1m 23.971s
5	Baldassarri	1m 24.021s
6	Vierge	1m 24.036s
7	Marquez	1m 24.079s
8	Mir	1m 24.092s
9	Schrotter	1m 24.102s
10	Binder	1m 24.178s
11	Fenati	1m 24.280s
12	Kent	1m 24.312s
13	Fernandez	1m 24.333s
14	Vinales	1m 24.341s
15	Oliveira	1m 24.360s
16	Navarro	1m 24.366s
17	Locatelli	1m 24.386s
18	Quartararo	1m 24.495s
19	Corsi	1m 24.546s
20	Gardner	1m 24.598s
21	Bendsneyder	1m 24.670s
22	Odendaal	1m 24.695s
23	Aegerter	1m 24.710s
24	Pawi	1m 24.737s
25	Lecuona	1m 24.801s
26	Nagashima	1m 24.834s
27	Manzi	1m 25.198s
28	Granado	1m 25.416s
29	Danilo	1m 25.441s
30	Roberts	1m 25.450s
31	Fuligni	1m 25.525s
32	Cardelus	1m 27.477s
	Tuuli	No Time

Fastest race laps

Pos.	Rider	Time
1	Mir	1m 24.634s
2	Binder	1m 24.718s
3	Oliveira	1m 24.881s
4	Schrotter	1m 24.889s
5	Lowes	1m 24.933s
6	Marini	1m 24.995s
7	Baldassarri	1m 25.112s
8	Bagnaia	1m 25.197s
9	Quartararo	1m 25.213s
10	Fenati	1m 25.266s
11	Vierge	1m 25.285s
12	Navarro	1m 25.296s
13	Kent	1m 25.310s
14	Marquez	1m 25.314s
15	Corsi	1m 25.374s
16	Fernandez	1m 25.387s
17	Gardner	1m 25.421s
18	Pawi	1m 25.479s
19	Aegerter	1m 25.485s
20	Lecuona	1m 25.614s
21	Odendaal	1m 25.682s
22	Bendsneyder	1m 25.745s
23	Granado	1m 25.991s
24	Vinales	1m 26.029s
25	Nagashima	1m 26.078s
26	Manzi	1m 26.136s
27	Roberts	1m 26.240s
28	Fuligni	1m 26.692s
29	Cardelus	1m 27.233s

Championship Points

Pos.	Rider	Points
1	Bagnaia	148
2	Oliveira	141
3	Marquez	113
4	Mir	95
5	Baldassarri	93
6	Binder	91
7	Vierge	79
8	Schrotter	73
9	Quartararo	72
10	Pasini	63
11	Marini	43
12	Lowes	39
13	Lecuona	32
14	Corsi	31
15	Locatelli	27
16	Aegerter	24
17	Navarro	23
18	Gardner	20
19	Barbera	10
20	Fenati	9
21	Vinales	7
22	Fernandez	7
23	Manzi	6
24	Nagashima	6
25	Kent	4
26	Roberts	2
27	Odendaal	1
28	Pawi	1

Constructor Points

Pos.	Constructor	Points
1	Kalex	206
2	KTM	153
3	Speed Up	76
4	Tech 3	20
5	Suter	6
6	NTS	2

Moto3

RACE DISTANCE: 27 laps, 61.588 miles/99.117km · RACE WEATHER: Dry (air 20°C, humidity 65%, track 35°C)

Pos.	Rider	Nat.	No.	Entrant	Machine	Laps	Time & Speed
1	**Jorge Martin**	SPA	88	Del Conca Gresini Moto3	Honda	27	39m 36.427s 93.3mph/ 150.1km/h
2	**Marco Bezzecchi**	ITA	12	Redox PruestelGP	KTM	27	39m 38.942s
3	**John McPhee**	GBR	17	CIP - Green Power	KTM	27	39m 38.998s
4	**Marcos Ramirez**	SPA	42	Bester Capital Dubai	KTM	27	39m 39.363s
5	**Aron Canet**	SPA	44	Estrella Galicia 0,0	Honda	27	39m 39.455s
6	**Jaume Masia**	SPA	5	Bester Capital Dubai	KTM	27	39m 39.768s
7	**Jakub Kornfeil**	CZE	84	Redox PruestelGP	KTM	27	39m 39.959s
8	**Philipp Oettl**	GER	65	Sudmetal Schedl GP Racing	KTM	27	39m 41.313s
9	**Raul Fernandez**	SPA	25	Red Bull KTM Ajo	KTM	27	39m 41.810s
10	**Ayumu Sasaki**	JPN	71	Petronas Sprinta Racing	Honda	27	39m 41.913s
11	**Adam Norrodin**	MAL	7	Petronas Sprinta Racing	Honda	27	39m 42.037s
12	**Andrea Migno**	ITA	16	Angel Nieto Team Moto3	KTM	27	39m 46.365s
13	**Lorenzo Dalla Porta**	ITA	48	Leopard Racing	Honda	27	39m 46.454s
14	**Nicolo Bulega**	ITA	8	SKY Racing Team VR46	KTM	27	39m 46.787s
15	**Kazuki Masaki**	JPN	22	RBA BOE Skull Rider	KTM	27	39m 46.894s
16	Niccolo Antonelli	ITA	23	SIC58 Squadra Corse	Honda	27	39m 47.941s
17	Tony Arbolino	ITA	14	Marinelli Snipers Team	Honda	27	39m 48.139s
18	Kaito Toba	JPN	27	Honda Team Asia	Honda	27	39m 56.466s
19	Dennis Foggia	ITA	10	SKY Racing Team VR46	KTM	27	40m 07.664s
20	Luca Grunwald	GER	43	Freudenberg Racing Team	KTM	27	40m 09.195s
21	Stefano Nepa	ITA	81	CIP - Green Power	KTM	27	40m 17.485s
	Gabriel Rodrigo	ARG	19	RBA BOE Skull Rider	KTM	24	DNF
	Ai Ogura	JPN	32	Asia Talent Team	Honda	24	DNF
	Enea Bastianini	ITA	33	Leopard Racing	Honda	22	DNF
	Alonso Lopez	SPA	72	Estrella Galicia 0,0	Honda	22	DNF
	Albert Arenas	SPA	75	Angel Nieto Team Moto3	KTM	20	DNF
	Vicente Perez	SPA	77	Reale Avintia Academy 77	KTM	18	DNF
	Nakarin Atiratphuvapat	THA	41	Honda Team Asia	Honda	16	DNF
	Fabio Di Giannantonio	ITA	21	Del Conca Gresini Moto3	Honda	15	DNF
	Tatsuki Suzuki	JPN	24	SIC58 Squadra Corse	Honda	5	DNF

Fastest lap: Aron Canet, on lap 11, 1m 27.136s, 94.2mph/151.6km/h.
Lap record: Brad Binder, 1m 26.877s, 94.5mph/152.1km/h (2014).
Event maximum speed: Tony Arbolino, 131.5mph/211.7km/h (warm-up).

Qualifying

Weather: Dry
Air Temp: 22° **Track Temp:** 44°
Humidity: 52%

Pos.	Rider	Time
1	Martin	1m 26.434s
2	Ramirez	1m 26.494s
3	Bastianini	1m 26.499s
4	Masia	1m 26.696s
5	Canet	1m 26.740s
6	Arbolino	1m 26.745s
7	Bezzecchi	1m 26.783s
8	McPhee	1m 26.792s
9	Sasaki	1m 26.827s
10	Di Giannantonio	1m 26.891s
11	Arenas	1m 26.969s
12	Rodrigo	1m 26.987s
13	Oettl	1m 27.016s
14	Fernandez	1m 27.017s
15	Antonelli	1m 27.161s
16	Dalla Porta	1m 27.199s
17	Norrodin	1m 27.237s
18	Ogura	1m 27.274s
19	Lopez	1m 27.287s
20	Kornfeil	1m 27.328s
21	Masaki	1m 27.339s
22	Suzuki	1m 27.489s
23	Bulega	1m 27.489s
24	Toba	1m 27.527s
25	Migno	1m 27.766s
26	Grunwald	1m 28.145s
27	Foggia	1m 28.305s
28	Perez	1m 28.427s
29	Atiratphuvapat	1m 28.647s
30	Nepa	1m 28.976s

Fastest race laps

Pos.	Rider	Time
1	Canet	1m 27.136s
2	Rodrigo	1m 27.158s
3	Ramirez	1m 27.231s
4	Arenas	1m 27.240s
5	Di Giannantonio	1m 27.271s
6	Kornfeil	1m 27.272s
7	Fernandez	1m 27.434s
8	Ogura	1m 27.464s
9	Martin	1m 27.465s
10	McPhee	1m 27.481s
11	Norrodin	1m 27.521s
12	Dalla Porta	1m 27.536s
13	Oettl	1m 27.549s
14	Bezzecchi	1m 27.556s
15	Bulega	1m 27.583s
16	Migno	1m 27.594s
17	Masia	1m 27.632s
18	Sasaki	1m 27.645s
19	Antonelli	1m 27.647s
20	Lopez	1m 27.652s
21	Arbolino	1m 27.674s
22	Bastianini	1m 27.725s
23	Toba	1m 27.805s
24	Masaki	1m 27.852s
25	Foggia	1m 27.918s
26	Suzuki	1m 28.078s
27	Nepa	1m 28.163s
28	Perez	1m 28.425s
29	Grunwald	1m 28.436s
30	Atiratphuvapat	1m 28.512s

Championship Points

Pos.	Rider	Points
1	Martin	130
2	Bezzecchi	123
3	Canet	92
4	Di Giannantonio	91
5	Bastianini	84
6	Rodrigo	65
7	Kornfeil	61
8	Migno	60
9	Ramirez	57
10	Dalla Porta	46
11	Antonelli	45
12	Oettl	44
13	Masia	44
14	McPhee	39
15	Suzuki	38
16	Lopez	31
17	Arenas	30
18	Toba	26
19	Norrodin	24
20	Arbolino	24
21	Sasaki	23
22	Binder	20
23	Fernandez	13
24	Foggia	13
25	Yurchenko	9
26	Loi	8
27	Bulega	7
28	Pagliani	6
29	Masaki	4
30	Atiratphuvapat	2
31	Ogura	1

Constructor Points

Pos.	Constructor	Points
1	Honda	196
2	KTM	175

FIM WORLD CHAMPIONSHIP · ROUND 10

CZECH REPUBLIC GRAND PRIX

BRNO CIRCUIT

Inset: Marquez congratulates Dovi on his long-awaited return to the top slot.

Main: Dovi's perfect exit from the last corner gave him clear air ahead of his team-mate.

Photos: Gold & Goose

Above: Just cruising. Rossi took a short-lived lead as Marquez, Dovizioso and Lorenzo saved their tyres for the end.

Right: Simmering tension between Vinales and crew chief Forcada.

Far right: Petrucci was back with the front-runners to take sixth.

Below right: Early bath – Vinales was out on lap one after a collision with Bradl. Smith was also eliminated.

Below far right: When a wing is not a wing. More creative aero bodywork from Ducati.

Photos: Gold & Goose

THE summer break had lasted just two weekends; the summer itself was still blazing, although a remote threat of rain led to riders practising bike swaps on Saturday. Sunday was sunny again, however, and though slightly cooler than in qualifying (28 degrees ambient, 41 degrees ground, compared with 32/50), there were still fears that tyre drop-off in the heat would affect the outcome of the race.

This did come to pass, but in an oblique way, thanks more to the fear than the fact. The top riders had all been running slowly and steadily to save their Michelins, with enough variety up front to sustain interest without overmuch excitement, even giving Rossi's relatively ill-favoured Yamaha a run in the lead. Then it came to a superlative last-lap climax, a gloves-off fight between the Ducatis and Marquez, with all three of them doing their fastest laps on the last.

It was the closest podium since the 2006 Portuguese GP, where Elias, Rossi and Roberts had been within 0.176 of a second – Brno's spread was 0.368; and the closest top ten in history. Begging an old question: why hurry a good race?

As usual at Brno, Dorna laid on the annual technical update conference, where each MotoGP factory sends a delegate to avoid revealing much. This is accomplished in a variety of ways, according to nationality. The Japanese companies are practised in the art of deliberate misunderstanding, the Italians in Machievellian verbal subterfuge. Austrian KTM required no such sophistry and bluntly refused to answer direct questions about their forthcoming reverse-crank engine. Later it emerged, however, that Bradley Smith was using this new engine (previously raced successfully by tester Kallio) at Brno, although mechanical issues obliged him to switch to the standard engine for the race.

Another matter on which delegates were more outspoken was aerodynamics, led by Ducati's Dall'Igna, who opened the conversation with the exasperated comment that enough had already been said about a science unfairly hobbled by the rules, asserting that Pirro's high-speed crash at Mugello "with proper aerodynamics doesn't happen". (Downforce would have prevented the head shake that spread the brake pads. But in truth, Pirro had been sent out without even the rudimentary wings now permitted.)

Ducati had introduced its own aero-body update at Brno, on day one for Petrucci's satellite bike, and the next day and henceforth on both factory Desmosedicis. Like those of the other manufacturers, this pushed the rules to the limits, comprising two boxes on each side – one high and one low. But for the side-plates, the upper ones especially were winglets in everything but name, but the same was true of the Yamaha and other aero-bodies. KTM's delegate, technical chief Sebastian Risse, had another blunt comment: "I think if we sitting here, if you had shown us photos of the bikes as they are now when the current rules were announced, we would have said … that they are not within the rules. The current interpretation is very wide."

The 2019 test schedule was announced, with one less outing after the winter break, but a three-day 'set-up' before the first Sepang tests at the start of February; while the limited private factory tests with active riders would end. The cut was meant to reduce costs, but the factories' response was to set up their own test teams, and at Brno Yamaha confirmed that they would be following suit with a new team based in Europe, Jonas Folger being pencilled in as a test rider. Honda already employed Stefan Bradl in Europe; Suzuki, Sylvain Guintoli; Ducati, Michele Pirro; and KTM, Mika Kallio. Until that point, Aprilia's team had concentrated on basic endurance testing, but team boss Romano Albesiano said they too planned to recruit a GP-level rider for the future, with Scott Redding a candidate, though this would change.

On the same topic, Pedrosa's name was linked with a possible test role at KTM, while it was confirmed that Casey Stoner's testing job with Ducati would also end. A few weeks later, the Australian poured cold water on Ducati's suggestion that this was because of surgery for a shoulder injury.

He told press that the real reason was because Ducati didn't seem to be taking any notice of his suggestions, and he was not prepared to risk running at racing speeds to be ignored.

Vinales's Yamaha difficulties were boiling over, with the rider telling the Spanish press that he was planning to replace current crew chief Ramon Forcada with former Moto3 ally Esteban Garcia for 2019. Forcada (a highly respected veteran who had taken Lorenzo to 44 wins and three titles) riposted that he thought the rider might have had the courtesy to tell him before the newspapers. Yamaha bosses then put a gagging order on the wayward rider to stem this overflow of ill will, but the rider's mime show at the end of FP3 was eloquent enough. He'd failed to make the top ten, obliging a Q1 outing with the slowcoaches for a fourth time in the season. Blaming the squad for not fitting the tyres he'd asked for, he stood up and slow-clapped them as he freewheeled into the pit.

Aleix Espargaro was back after his bruising pre-race elimination in Germany, still somewhat battered, and the race authorities were sufficiently sympathetic to cancel the six-place grid penalty he had been unable to serve there. Fate hadn't finished with the family, however, and younger brother Pol crashed so heavily in race-morning warm-up that he suffered worrying spinal damage, which put him out for the next three races.

The weekend opened with a major upset in Moto3. The first free practice was coming to an end, with points-leader Jorge Martin trying to regain top spot from Philipp Oettl, when the Spaniard slipped off, blaming a tyre that was too cool. The consequences were worse than the crash: he landed heavily on his left wrist. His worst fears were confirmed when he learned that he had fractured the top of the radius bone. With a points lead of only seven over KTM rival Bezzecchi, and the Austrian GP in just one week, it could hardly have come at a worse time.

MOTOGP RACE – 21 laps

Marquez, lining up for his 100th MotoGP start, had displaced Lorenzo for pole in Q2. But there was more to come from Dovizioso, who was making his 100th Ducati start. A smooth, unflustered final run gave him his first pole since 2016. Rossi was following and narrowly edged Marquez to third. That left Lorenzo to head row two from Crutchlow and Petrucci, who'd been left with just one bike after a blow-up at the end of FP4.

Zarco led the third from the Suzukis, Iannone from Rins, through from Q1. Vinales ditto, but he was only 12th, Morbidelli best of the rest.

The race started badly for Vinales, sent flying in a three-bike tangle triggered when HRC wild-card Stefan Bradl lost the front under braking, also skittling Smith's sole remaining KTM. Several others, including Jack Miller, were slowed.

Rossi had jumped into the lead from the middle of the front row, but before the first lap was half done, Dovi was in front, Marquez third; at the end of it, Lorenzo was fourth, ahead of Crutchlow, Petrucci and Zarco.

Dovi stayed ahead of some minor shuffling: Lorenzo to third, Petrucci past Crutchlow for a couple of laps only, and then on lap seven, Rossi through from second to steal inside Dovi on the right-hander before the stadium section.

It was a fine sight for his fans as he led for three laps, but he already knew that "I didn't have enough pace to fight with the Ducatis or Marquez."

That was in spite of the caution of his rivals, all saving their tyres. Dovi would say later, "Nobody could push at the beginning, and that's why we were a bit slow." It was unusual for Lorenzo, who generally preferred to gallop away and build up a lead, then take his tactics from there. Later it emerged that he had been strongly urged to change his approach by crew chief Gabarrini, and for once he'd actually taken somebody's advice. "This is new for me," he admitted.

Rossi was back to third on lap 11; two laps later, fifth, behind Crutchlow and Lorenzo, the Englishman ahead of the Ducati for a few laps until he succumbed to its superior acceleration, at the same time battling worsening off-throttle slides. "Usually, I have trouble with the front gaining too much heat when I'm with other riders, but this time it was different and the bike was floating mid-corner."

Lorenzo was second, ahead of Marquez, by the end of lap 18, and the front three began to pull clear over the final three laps.

The tension was rising, with Marquez probing at Lorenzo, the battle seeming to favour Dovi up front, but only slightly. Margins remained small.

On lap 20, they swapped twice, but Lorenzo was still a close second as they started the last – only for Marquez to nose ahead in Turn Three. Lorenzo took him back before the stadium section two bends later, but his game plan had been spoiled and his attack delayed.

It was a breathless final lap, with the Ducatis frequently if only briefly side by side. Lorenzo attacked again into the final left-right, but Dovi's lines were perfect and he could cut back for the narrowest of wins.

Marquez might have played a stronger role but for his own new tactics: "The Ducatis were really strong, in acceleration and braking more than top speed. Maybe before I would have tried to fight to win, but my main target this weekend was to increase my championship lead."

A little way back, Rossi got close enough to attack Crutchlow going into the crucial final left-right and managed to make the pass stick for a valuable fourth, by five-hundredths of a second.

Petrucci had never been close enough to attack, but had outpaced Zarco by better than two seconds for sixth. He was still less than 3.8 seconds away from the win.

A short way back, the Suzukis had battled all race long. Then, as their tyres dropped, Pedrosa was able to take advantage, passing both on the last lap. Alvaro Bautista went with him, having caught the group in the closing stages.

Miller had started well, but lost time in the lap-one tangle, finishing the lap 15th. He recovered strongly at first, passing Morbidelli and Syahrin, and for a spell also Bautista. But when his tyres dropped, he faded to 12th.

Morbidelli was safe in 13th, then Syahrin, and closing at the end, Aleix Espargaro for the last point.

Above: Kornfeil was ecstatic with his first home Moto3 podium after claiming pole.

Top: Marquez mixes it with the Ducatis.

Top right: Morbidelli was back from injury, and top rookie again.

Above centre right: Oliveira's win gave him the title lead.

Above right: Oliveira (44) and Marini (10) changed places six times on the last lap alone.

Far right: Moto3 1-2-3. Di Giannantonio heads Canet and Kornfeil for his first win.

Photos: Gold & Goose

Right: A measured Marquez settled for third and another haul of points.

Photo HRC

Luthi and Nakagami followed, then Abraham, Suzuki wild-card Guintoli and Simeon. Redding had crashed out early, while Rabat spluttered to a stop after a strong early run in the top ten.

MOTO2 RACE – 19 laps

Almost all the top-20 times, spanning only just over one second, were set on the second or third laps, Dunlops finding grip on MotoGP's freshly laid Michelin rubber. Thereafter, tyre drop on an increasingly slippery surface gave a foretaste of the race.

Marini narrowly claimed a first pole, third front row in succession; Marquez and Pasini were with him. Oliveira's fourth equalled his best qualifying of the year; he headed Schrotter and Bagnaia; Binder led the third row.

Close times presaged one of the best Moto2 races for years, fought to the final corner between Oliveira and Marini, the former victorious by just seven-hundredths. They had changed places six times on the last lap alone. By then, they'd only narrowly escaped a group that had been five-strong, leaving Bagnaia tooth and nail with latecomer Baldassarri, who had led three laps in the later stages. The top four were over the line within less than a second.

Marquez led away from Marini and Bagnaia; Oliveira finished the first lap fourth, ahead of Binder.

On lap two, Marini led; next time around, Bagnaia. It looked as though the team-mates might play tactics, Marini protecting the championship leader. All weekend, he'd been trumpeting their good relationship.

It didn't work like that. Oliveira was getting between them, Vierge closing, plus Pasini and Binder. Marquez dropped to seventh on lap five, but was back up to a close fourth three laps later – only to crash out on the final corner, his title hopes in tatters.

At this point, Marini was leading again, while Baldassarri had joined up and would cut through to the front on lap 13. He stayed there for three laps, but then with four laps left, he was sliding badly.

By then also, Vierge had lost touch with the front four.

They started the last lap with Oliveira in front of Marini, then Baldassarri heading Bagnaia close behind.

The front two swapped at almost every corner, and it looked as though Marini's final lunge through the last right-left combination had been enough. But Oliveira got a better drive for his second win of the year, giving him a two-point championship lead for the first time.

Vierge hung on to fifth from Binder, who had his hands full fighting off Schrotter and late arrivals Navarro and Lowes. A second behind, Pasini completed the top ten at the head of another close trio, with Quartararo next, then Fernandez, preserving his perfect points record since replacing Barbera four races before. Lecuona, Locatelli and Corsi rounded up the rest of the points, Nagashima and Aegerter narrowly missing out.

Mir had been the victim of a scary-looking three-bike crash on the first lap, when he and Remy Gardner touched, and both brought down the apologetic Australian's team-mate, Bendsneyder. Mir's bike bounced off the air-fence to land on Bendsneyder, but he escaped serious injury. Danny Kent and frequent faller Manzi also crashed out.

MOTO3 RACE – 18 laps

With Martin absent, his Del Conca Honda team-mate, Di Giannantonio, topped the time sheets, but mistimed his final run. Just too late for the flag. That let a quartet of KTMs ahead, with home rider Kornfeil taking a career-first pole by four-tenths after the flag. He'd followed, then drafted past former Brno winner McPhee, second fastest, barely two-hundredths quicker than Ramirez. Oettl led row two, with Canet on the far end.

Erstwhile title leader Bezzecchi was 14th, still coming to terms with a new KTM chassis that was meant to improve fast corners.

The race was a brawl, those fast corners keeping them close throughout – the top 15 points-scorers were over the line in 2.77 seconds, an all-time record; the top eight in 1.097. Tactics (and sharp elbows) were everything.

Di Giannantonio and Canet took control on the last lap, dashing Kornfeil's hopes of a win, though he became the first Czech national to stand on the podium at his home GP.

Bastianini just missed the top three by two-tenths, after a canny ride from 12th at half-distance. Rodrigo and Bezzecchi took the next two places, mired in the gang. Then came three more KTMs – Ramirez, Oettl and Arenas. Lorenzo Dalla Porta crossed the line tenth, ahead of Antonelli and impressive rookie Foggia.

McPhee had crashed out of the front group with nine laps left after a freak incident. A brush with Ramirez's bike had resulted in his front tyre being slashed by the bike-stand nubbin on the swing-arm, and he went flying.

Sixth was good enough for Bezzecchi to regain the championship lead by five points.

MONSTER ENERGY GRAND PRIX CESKE REPUBLIKY

AUTODROM BRNO

21 laps
Length: 5.403 km / 3.357 miles
Width: 15m

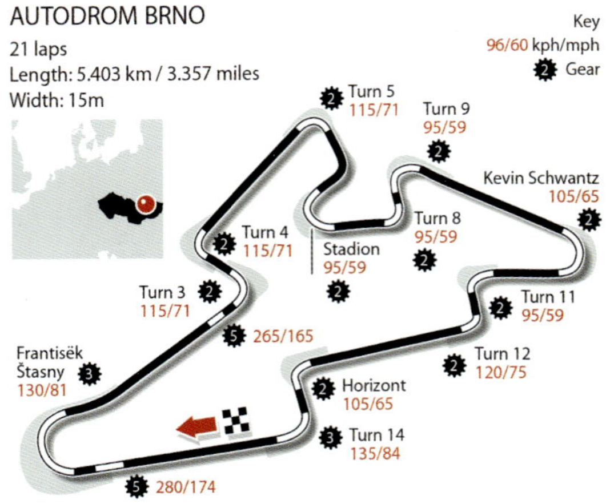

MotoGP

RACE DISTANCE: 21 laps, 70.503 miles/113.463km · RACE WEATHER: Dry (air 28°C, humidity 44%, track 41°C)

Pos.	Rider	Nat.	No.	Entrant	Machine	Tyres	Race tyre choice	Laps	Time & speed
1	**Andrea Dovizioso**	ITA	4	Ducati Team	Ducati Desmosedici	M	F: Hard/R: Hard	21	41m 07.728s 102.8mph/ 165.5km/h
2	**Jorge Lorenzo**	SPA	99	Ducati Team	Ducati Desmosedici	M	F: Hard/R: Hard	21	41m 07.906s
3	**Marc Marquez**	SPA	93	Repsol Honda Team	Honda RC213V	M	F: Hard/R: Hard	21	41m 08.096s
4	**Valentino Rossi**	ITA	46	Movistar Yamaha MotoGP	Yamaha YZR-M1	M	F: Medium/R: Hard	21	41m 10.630s
5	**Cal Crutchlow**	GBR	35	LCR Honda CASTROL	Honda RC213V	M	F: Hard/R: Hard	21	41m 10.686s
6	**Danilo Petrucci**	ITA	9	Alma Pramac Racing	Ducati Desmosedici	M	F: Hard/R: Hard	21	41m 11.496s
7	**Johann Zarco**	FRA	5	Monster Yamaha Tech 3	Yamaha YZR-M1	M	F: Medium/R: Soft	21	41m 13.887s
8	**Dani Pedrosa**	SPA	26	Repsol Honda Team	Honda RC213V	M	F: Hard/R: Hard	21	41m 15.207s
9	**Alvaro Bautista**	SPA	19	Angel Nieto Team	Ducati Desmosedici	M	F: Medium/R: Soft	21	41m 15.303s
10	**Andrea Iannone**	ITA	29	Team SUZUKI ECSTAR	Suzuki GSX-RR	M	F: Hard/R: Hard	21	41m 16.054s
11	**Alex Rins**	SPA	42	Team SUZUKI ECSTAR	Suzuki GSX-RR	M	F: Medium/R: Hard	21	41m 16.381s
12	**Jack Miller**	AUS	43	Alma Pramac Racing	Ducati Desmosedici	M	F: Hard/R: Hard	21	41m 24.277s
13	**Franco Morbidelli**	ITA	21	EG 0,0 Marc VDS	Honda RC213V	M	F: Hard/R: Hard	21	41m 27.331s
14	**Hafizh Syahrin**	MAL	55	Monster Yamaha Tech 3	Yamaha YZR-M1	M	F: Hard/R: Hard	21	41m 29.109s
15	**Aleix Espargaro**	SPA	41	Aprilia Racing Team Gresini	Aprilia RS-GP	M	F: Hard/R: Hard	21	41m 30.887s
16	Thomas Luthi	SWI	12	EG 0,0 Marc VDS	Honda RC213V	M	F: Hard/R: Hard	21	41m 35.401s
17	Takaaki Nakagami	JPN	30	LCR Honda IDEMITSU	Honda RC213V	M	F: Hard/R: Hard	21	41m 36.039s
18	Karel Abraham	CZE	17	Angel Nieto Team	Ducati Desmosedici	M	F: Hard/R: Hard	21	41m 48.900s
19	Sylvain Guintoli	FRA	50	Team SUZUKI ECSTAR	Suzuki GSX-RR	M	F: Medium/R: Hard	21	41m 50.139s
20	Xavier Simeon	BEL	10	Reale Avintia Racing	Ducati Desmosedici	M	F: Hard/R: Hard	21	41m 58.669s
	Tito Rabat	SPA	53	Reale Avintia Racing	Ducati Desmosedici	M	F: Medium/R: Hard	8	DNF-technical
	Scott Redding	GBR	45	Aprilia Racing Team Gresini	Aprilia RS-GP	M	F: Hard/R: Hard	5	DNF-crash
	Bradley Smith	GBR	38	Red Bull KTM Factory Racing	KTM RC16	M	F: Medium/R: Soft	1	DNF-crash
	Maverick Vinales	SPA	25	Movistar Yamaha MotoGP	Yamaha YZR-M1	M	F: Medium/R: Soft	0	DNF-crash
	Stefan Bradl	GER	6	HRC Honda Team	Honda RC213V	M	F: Hard/R: Hard	0	DNF-crash
	Pol Espargaro	SPA	44	Red Bull KTM Factory Racing	KTM RC16	M	-	-	DNS-injured

Fastest lap: Jorge Lorenzo, on lap 21, 1m 56.640s, 103.6mph/166.7km/h.
Lap record: Dani Pedrosa, 1m 56.027s, 104.1mph/167.6km/h (2014).
Event maximum speed: Andrea Dovizioso, 195.5mph/314.7km/h (qualifying).

Qualifying

Weather: Dry
Air Temp: 32° **Track Temp:** 50°
Humidity: 33%

1	Dovizioso	1m 54.689s
2	Rossi	1m 54.956s
3	Marquez	1m 54.961s
4	Lorenzo	1m 55.038s
5	Crutchlow	1m 55.055s
6	Petrucci	1m 55.203s
7	Zarco	1m 55.221s
8	Iannone	1m 55.270s
9	Rins	1m 55.431s
10	Pedrosa	1m 55.474s
11	Rabat	1m 55.686s
12	Vinales	1m 55.823s
13	Morbidelli	1m 56.029s
14	Bautista	1m 56.031s
15	Smith	1m 56.218s
16	Syahrin	1m 56.285s
17	Miller	1m 56.316s
18	Bradl	1m 56.330s
19	P. Espargaro	1m 56.353s
20	Nakagami	1m 56.512s
21	Guintoli	1m 57.037s
22	Luthi	1m 57.208s
23	Abraham	1m 57.217s
24	A. Espargaro	1m 57.250s
25	Redding	1m 57.438s
26	Simeon	1m 58.048s

Fastest race laps

1	Lorenzo	1m 56.640s
2	Marquez	1m 56.729s
3	Dovizioso	1m 56.742s
4	Bautista	1m 56.772s
5	Rabat	1m 56.947s
6	Petrucci	1m 56.975s
7	Rossi	1m 56.992s
8	Crutchlow	1m 57.003s
9	Rins	1m 57.101s
10	Zarco	1m 57.156s
11	Pedrosa	1m 57.173s
12	Iannone	1m 57.264s
13	Syahrin	1m 57.608s
14	Morbidelli	1m 57.627s
15	Miller	1m 57.632s
16	A. Espargaro	1m 57.658s
17	Luthi	1m 57.978s
18	Redding	1m 58.055s
19	Nakagami	1m 58.108s
20	Abraham	1m 58.438s
21	Guintoli	1m 58.528s
22	Simeon	1m 58.769s

Championship Points

1	Marquez	181
2	Rossi	132
3	Dovizioso	113
4	Vinales	109
5	Lorenzo	105
6	Zarco	97
7	Petrucci	94
8	Crutchlow	90
9	Iannone	81
10	Miller	61
11	Rins	58
12	Pedrosa	57
13	Bautista	51
14	P. Espargaro	32
15	Rabat	30
16	Syahrin	24
17	Morbidelli	22
18	A. Espargaro	17
19	Smith	13
20	Redding	12
21	Nakagami	10
22	Kallio	6
23	Abraham	4

Constructor Points

1	Honda	216
2	Ducati	183
3	Yamaha	173
4	Suzuki	110
5	KTM	39
6	Aprilia	27

Grid order		1	2	3	4	5	6	7	8	9	10	11	12	13	14	15	16	17	18	19	20	21	
4	DOVIZIOSO	4	4	4	4	4	4	4	46	46	46	4	4	4	4	4	4	4	4	4	4	4	1
46	ROSSI	46	46	46	46	46	46	46	4	4	4	93	93	93	93	93	93	93	99	99	99	99	2
93	MARQUEZ	93	99	99	99	93	93	93	99	93	93	46	35	35	35	35	99	99	93	93	93	93	3
99	LORENZO	99	93	93	93	99	99	99	93	99	35	35	46	99	99	99	35	35	35	35	35	46	4
35	CRUTCHLOW	35	35	9	9	9	9	35	35	35	99	99	99	46	46	46	46	46	46	46	46	35	5
9	PETRUCCI	9	9	5	35	35	35	9	9	9	9	9	9	9	9	9	9	9	9	9	9	9	6
5	ZARCO	5	5	35	5	5	5	5	5	5	5	5	5	5	5	5	5	5	5	5	5	5	7
29	IANNONE	42	42	42	42	42	42	29	29	29	29	29	42	42	42	29	29	29	29	26	26	26	8
42	RINS	29	29	29	29	29	29	42	42	42	42	42	29	29	29	42	42	42	42	29	29	19	9
26	PEDROSA	26	26	26	26	26	26	26	26	26	26	26	26	26	26	26	26	26	26	19	19	29	10
53	RABAT	53	53	53	53	53	53	53	53	19	19	19	19	19	19	19	19	19	19	42	42	42	11
25	VINALES	19	19	19	19	19	43	43	43	43	43	43	43	43	43	43	43	43	43	43	43	43	12
21	MORBIDELLI	55	55	55	43	43	19	19	19	55	21	21	21	21	21	21	21	21	21	21	21	21	13
19	BAUTISTA	21	43	43	55	55	55	55	55	21	55	55	55	55	55	55	55	55	55	55	55	55	14
38	SMITH	43	21	21	21	21	21	21	21	41	41	41	41	41	41	41	41	41	41	41	41	41	15
55	SYAHRIN	50	50	45	45	45	41	41	41	12	12	12	12	12	12	12	12	12	12	12	12	12	
43	MILLER	12	45	50	41	41	12	12	12	30	30	30	30	30	30	30	30	30	30	30	30	30	
6	BRADL	45	12	41	50	12	30	30	30	17	17	17	17	17	17	17	17	17	17	17	17	17	
30	NAKAGAMI	41	41	12	12	50	50	17	17	50	50	50	50	50	50	10	50	50	50	50	50	50	
50	GUINTOLI	30	30	30	30	30	17	50	50	10	10	10	10	10	10	50	10	10	10	10	10	10	
12	LUTHI	10	10	17	17	17	10	10	10														
17	ABRAHAM	17	17	10	10	10																	
41	A. ESPARGARO	38																					
45	REDDING																						
10	SIMEON																						

38 Pit stop/Lapped rider

Moto2

RACE DISTANCE: 19 laps, 63.788 miles/102.657km · RACE WEATHER: Dry (air 28°C, humidity 44%, track 39°C)

Pos.	Rider	Nat.	No.	Entrant	Machine	Laps	Time & Speed
1	**Miguel Oliveira**	POR	44	Red Bull KTM Ajo	KTM	19	39m 22.324s 97.2mph/ 156.4km/h
2	**Luca Marini**	ITA	10	SKY Racing Team VR46	Kalex	19	39m 22.394s
3	**Francesco Bagnaia**	ITA	42	SKY Racing Team VR46	Kalex	19	39m 22.849s
4	**Lorenzo Baldassarri**	ITA	7	Pons HP40	Kalex	19	39m 23.069s
5	**Xavi Vierge**	SPA	97	Dynavolt Intact GP	Kalex	19	39m 25.686s
6	**Brad Binder**	RSA	41	Red Bull KTM Ajo	KTM	19	39m 25.967s
7	**Marcel Schrotter**	GER	23	Dynavolt Intact GP	Kalex	19	39m 26.018s
8	**Jorge Navarro**	SPA	9	Federal Oil Gresini Moto2	Kalex	19	39m 26.052s
9	**Sam Lowes**	GBR	22	Swiss Innovative Investors	KTM	19	39m 26.362s
10	**Mattia Pasini**	ITA	54	Italtrans Racing Team	Kalex	19	39m 27.354s
11	**Fabio Quartararo**	FRA	20	Boost - Speed Up Racing	Speed Up	19	39m 27.477s
12	**Augusto Fernandez**	SPA	40	Pons HP40	Kalex	19	39m 28.163s
13	**Iker Lecuona**	SPA	27	Swiss Innovative Investors	KTM	19	39m 29.181s
14	**Andrea Locatelli**	ITA	5	Italtrans Racing Team	Kalex	19	39m 31.797s
15	**Simone Corsi**	ITA	24	Tasca Racing Scuderia Moto2	Kalex	19	39m 32.378s
16	Tetsuta Nagashima	JPN	45	IDEMITSU Honda Team Asia	Kalex	19	39m 32.950s
17	Dominique Aegerter	SWI	77	Kiefer Racing	KTM	19	39m 32.982s
18	Joe Roberts	USA	16	NTS RW Racing GP	NTS	19	39m 40.460s
19	Steven Odendaal	RSA	4	NTS RW Racing GP	NTS	19	39m 41.364s
20	Khairul Idham Pawi	MAL	89	IDEMITSU Honda Team Asia	Kalex	19	39m 43.658s
21	Niki Tuuli	FIN	66	Petronas Sprinta Racing	Kalex	19	39m 50.402s
22	Jules Danilo	FRA	95	Nashi Argan SAG Team	Kalex	19	39m 56.894s
23	Eric Granado	BRA	51	Forward Racing Team	Suter	19	40m 07.493s
24	Sheridan Morais	POR	12	Willi Race Racing Team	Kalex	19	40m 31.177s
	Danny Kent	GBR	52	Boost - Speed Up Racing	Speed Up	11	DNF
	Alex Marquez	SPA	73	EG 0,0 Marc VDS	Kalex	8	DNF
	Romano Fenati	ITA	13	Marinelli Snipers Team	Kalex	7	DNF
	Stefano Manzi	ITA	62	Forward Racing Team	Suter	5	DNF
	Xavi Cardelus	AND	18	Team Stylobike	Kalex	2	DNF
	Alejandro Medina	SPA	55	SAG Team	Kalex	1	DNF
	Joan Mir	SPA	36	EG 0,0 Marc VDS	Kalex	0	DNF
	Bo Bendsneyder	NED	64	Tech 3 Racing	Tech 3	0	DNF
	Remy Gardner	AUS	87	Tech 3 Racing	Tech 3	0	DNF

Fastest lap: Xavi Vierge, on lap 4, 2m 3.103s, 98.2mph/158.0km/h.

Lap record: Tito Rabat, 2m 2.383s, 98.7mph/158.9km/h (2014).

Event maximum speed: Iker Lecuona, 160.7mph/258.7km/h (qualifying).

Qualifying

Weather: Dry

Air Temp: 33° **Track Temp:** 53°

Humidity: 30%

1	Marini	2m 02.244s
2	Marquez	2m 02.359s
3	Pasini	2m 02.417s
4	Oliveira	2m 02.446s
5	Schrotter	2m 02.449s
6	Bagnaia	2m 02.451s
7	Binder	2m 02.493s
8	Vierge	2m 02.505s
9	Aegerter	2m 02.520s
10	Baldassarri	2m 02.649s
11	Navarro	2m 02.653s
12	Mir	2m 02.748s
13	Lecuona	2m 02.749s
14	Quartararo	2m 02.760s
15	Locatelli	2m 02.824s
16	Corsi	2m 02.905s
17	Fenati	2m 03.106s
18	Bendsneyder	2m 03.235s
19	Gardner	2m 03.273s
20	Pawi	2m 03.301s
21	Fernandez	2m 03.363s
22	Lowes	2m 03.385s
23	Roberts	2m 03.540s
24	Kent	2m 03.548s
25	Nagashima	2m 03.569s
26	Odendaal	2m 03.594s
27	Manzi	2m 03.613s
28	Tuuli	2m 03.873s
29	Morais	2m 04.126s
30	Danilo	2m 04.281s
31	Cardelus	2m 04.659s
32	Medina	2m 04.869s
	Granado	No Time

Fastest race laps

1	Vierge	2m 03.103s
2	Oliveira	2m 03.224s
3	Pasini	2m 03.271s
4	Bagnaia	2m 03.341s
5	Marini	2m 03.356s
6	Navarro	2m 03.389s
7	Binder	2m 03.426s
8	Baldassarri	2m 03.432s
9	Schrotter	2m 03.519s
10	Marquez	2m 03.548s
11	Corsi	2m 03.571s
12	Fenati	2m 03.623s
13	Lowes	2m 03.711s
14	Quartararo	2m 03.745s
15	Lecuona	2m 03.800s
16	Fernandez	2m 03.870s
17	Nagashima	2m 03.983s
18	Locatelli	2m 03.985s
19	Aegerter	2m 04.000s
20	Kent	2m 04.104s
21	Manzi	2m 04.171s
22	Roberts	2m 04.270s
23	Odendaal	2m 04.282s
24	Pawi	2m 04.309s
25	Tuuli	2m 04.459s
26	Cardelus	2m 05.080s
27	Danilo	2m 05.256s
28	Granado	2m 05.310s
29	Morais	2m 06.570s

Championship Points

1	Oliveira	166
2	Bagnaia	164
3	Marquez	113
4	Baldassarri	106
5	Binder	101
6	Mir	95
7	Vierge	90
8	Schrotter	82
9	Quartararo	77
10	Pasini	69
11	Marini	63
12	Lowes	46
13	Lecuona	35
14	Corsi	32
15	Navarro	31
16	Locatelli	29
17	Aegerter	24
18	Gardner	20
19	Fernandez	11
20	Barbera	10
21	Fenati	9
22	Vinales	7
23	Manzi	6
24	Nagashima	6
25	Kent	4
26	Roberts	2
27	Odendaal	1
28	Pawi	1

Constructor Points

1	Kalex	226
2	KTM	178
3	Speed Up	81
4	Tech 3	20
5	Suter	6
6	NTS	2

Moto3

RACE DISTANCE: 18 laps, 60.431 miles/97.254km · RACE WEATHER: Dry (air 30°C, humidity 46%, track 42°C)

Pos.	Rider	Nat.	No.	Entrant	Machine	Laps	Time & Speed
1	**Fabio Di Giannantonio**	ITA	21	Del Conca Gresini Moto3	Honda	18	39m 09.124s 92.6mph/ 149.0km/h
2	**Aron Canet**	SPA	44	Estrella Galicia 0,0	Honda	18	39m 09.236s
3	**Jakub Kornfeil**	CZE	84	Redox PruestelGP	KTM	18	39m 09.463s
4	**Enea Bastianini**	ITA	33	Leopard Racing	Honda	18	39m 09.684s
5	**Gabriel Rodrigo**	ARG	19	RBA BOE Skull Rider	KTM	18	39m 09.895s
6	**Marco Bezzecchi**	ITA	12	Redox PruestelGP	KTM	18	39m 10.020s
7	**Marcos Ramirez**	SPA	42	Bester Capital Dubai	KTM	18	39m 10.154s
8	**Philipp Oettl**	GER	65	Sudmetal Schedl GP Racing	KTM	18	39m 10.221s
9	**Albert Arenas**	SPA	75	Angel Nieto Team Moto3	KTM	18	39m 11.158s
10	**Lorenzo Dalla Porta**	ITA	48	Leopard Racing	Honda	18	39m 11.180s
11	**Niccolo Antonelli**	ITA	23	SIC58 Squadra Corse	Honda	18	39m 11.217s
12	**Dennis Foggia**	ITA	10	SKY Racing Team VR46	KTM	18	39m 11.483s
13	**Kazuki Masaki**	JPN	22	RBA BOE Skull Rider	KTM	18	39m 11.641s
14	**Tatsuki Suzuki**	JPN	24	SIC58 Squadra Corse	Honda	18	39m 11.740s
15	**Tony Arbolino**	ITA	14	Marinelli Snipers Team	Honda	18	39m 11.894s
16	Nakarin Atiratphuvapat	THA	41	Honda Team Asia	Honda	18	39m 12.798s
17	Jaume Masia	SPA	5	Bester Capital Dubai	KTM	18	39m 13.742s
18	Alonso Lopez	SPA	72	Estrella Galicia 0,0	Honda	18	39m 13.994s
19	Nicolo Bulega	ITA	8	SKY Racing Team VR46	KTM	18	39m 14.066s
20	Andrea Migno	ITA	16	Angel Nieto Team Moto3	KTM	18	39m 14.078s
21	Vicente Perez	SPA	77	Reale Avintia Academy 77	KTM	18	39m 22.047s
22	Ayumu Sasaki	JPN	71	Petronas Sprinta Racing	Honda	18	39m 22.066s
23	Darryn Binder	RSA	40	Red Bull KTM Ajo	KTM	18	39m 22.080s
24	Filip Salac	CZE	15	Cuna de Campeones Czech Talent	KTM	18	39m 50.635s
	Adam Norrodin	MAL	7	Petronas Sprinta Racing	Honda	17	DNF
	Stefano Nepa	ITA	81	CIP - Green Power	KTM	14	DNF
	John McPhee	GBR	17	CIP - Green Power	KTM	9	DNF
	Kaito Toba	JPN	27	Honda Team Asia	Honda	2	DNF

Fastest lap: Aron Canet, on lap 2, 2m 8.480s, 94.0mph/151.3km/h.

Lap record: Romano Fenati, 2m 8.064s, 94.3mph/151.8km/h (2014).

Event maximum speed: Gabriel Rodrigo, 139.9mph/225.1km/h (free practice).

Qualifying

Weather: Dry

Air Temp: 31° **Track Temp:** 46°

Humidity: 32%

1	Kornfeil	2m 07.981s
2	McPhee	2m 08.400s
3	Ramirez	2m 08.426s
4	Oettl	2m 08.445s
5	Di Giannantonio	2m 08.473s
6	Canet	2m 08.556s
7	Rodrigo	2m 08.778s
8	Atiratphuvapat	2m 08.885s
9	Antonelli	2m 09.004s
10	Bastianini	2m 09.078s
11	Masia	2m 09.144s
12	Masaki	2m 09.159s
13	Foggia	2m 09.162s
14	Bezzecchi	2m 09.205s
15	Arenas	2m 09.333s
16	Arbolino	2m 09.494s
17	Dalla Porta	2m 09.524s
18	Bulega	2m 09.591s
19	Binder	2m 09.709s
20	Toba	2m 09.807s
21	Norrodin	2m 10.146s
22	Migno	2m 10.274s
23	Nepa	2m 10.408s
24	Perez	2m 10.439s
25	Lopez	2m 11.049s
26	Salac	2m 11.119s
	Suzuki	No Time
	Sasaki	No Time

Fastest race laps

1	Canet	2m 08.480s
2	Masia	2m 08.599s
3	Di Giannantonio	2m 08.645s
4	McPhee	2m 08.661s
5	Bezzecchi	2m 08.711s
6	Antonelli	2m 08.724s
7	Foggia	2m 08.731s
8	Lopez	2m 08.794s
9	Arenas	2m 08.806s
10	Oettl	2m 08.829s
11	Rodrigo	2m 08.844s
12	Kornfeil	2m 08.868s
13	Bulega	2m 08.929s
14	Dalla Porta	2m 08.944s
15	Arbolino	2m 09.008s
16	Bastianini	2m 09.058s
17	Toba	2m 09.109s
18	Ramirez	2m 09.112s
19	Norrodin	2m 09.196s
20	Atiratphuvapat	2m 09.215s
21	Suzuki	2m 09.243s
22	Perez	2m 09.341s
23	Sasaki	2m 09.381s
24	Migno	2m 09.427s
25	Masaki	2m 09.561s
26	Binder	2m 09.709s
27	Salac	2m 09.946s
28	Nepa	2m 10.953s

Championship Points

1	Bezzecchi	133
2	Martin	130
3	Di Giannantonio	116
4	Canet	112
5	Bastianini	97
6	Kornfeil	77
7	Rodrigo	76
8	Ramirez	66
9	Migno	60
10	Oettl	52
11	Dalla Porta	52
12	Antonelli	50
13	Masia	44
14	Suzuki	40
15	McPhee	39
16	Arenas	37
17	Lopez	31
18	Toba	26
19	Arbolino	25
20	Norrodin	24
21	Sasaki	23
22	Binder	20
23	Foggia	17
24	Fernandez	13
25	Yurchenko	9
26	Loi	8
27	Bulega	7
28	Masaki	7
29	Pagliani	6
30	Atiratphuvapat	2
31	Ogura	1

Constructor Points

1	Honda	221
2	KTM	191

FIM WORLD CHAMPIONSHIP · ROUND 11

AUSTRIAN GRAND PRIX

RED BULL RING

SHOEI
REPSOL
93
HRC
FLEX-BOX
DUCATI

Above: Fast in the wet, angry in the dry, Aprilia's Scott Redding showed his talents.

Top right: Caught in the storm – Vinales is sheltered by rider coach Wilco Zeelenberg.

Above right: Rossi qualified a lowly 14th, but ground his way to sixth.
Photos: Gold & Goose

Right: Where do we go from here? Crew chief Silvano Galbusera scratches his head while they fiddle with Rossi's Yamaha.
Photo: Monster Energy

Opening spread: Triumverate. Only Marquez could challenge the Ducatis at the wide-open Red Bull Ring.
Photo: Gold & Goose

THREE days after climbing off their bikes at post-Brno tests, the MotoGP riders were back on them again in Austria. In one way, however, the situation had changed. It rained. After a dry stretch that had begun directly after round two in Argentina, it was a first chance to brush up on their wet-weather skills.

One notable result was the sudden appearance of Scott Redding at the top of the FP2 time sheet, although ultimately he was second, to Marquez, by half a second. He shone again the next morning, third behind another Briton favoured by the conditions, Smith. Sunday's race, however, was a familiar story for the youngest ever GP winner on the ill-starred Aprilia. He was 20th, almost 60 seconds behind winner Lorenzo, and more than 20 behind his team-mate, Aleix Espargaro.

It was difficult not to feel sympathy, given his position – no ride for 2019, and no fun in 2018. He considered that the rain had proved his talent, and that Aprilia's bike and a lack of team support compared to Espargaro was undermining it. He employed some pretty fruity language in condemning them. Less than a week later, having been censured and hit financially, he recanted – but by then, it was too late to save any hopes he may have had of a testing role with the Italian firm.

Redding's apology hardly made a ripple compared with the same thing at Yamaha. Already well into their longest winless spell in 19 years (Regis Laconi's Valencia win in 1999 had been the first in 18 races; Germany 2018 their 20th loss), the factory team's qualifying positions were the worst of the year. Their response was almost unprecedented, a public apology. Joined by a solemn-faced Yamaha Motor Racing MD Lin Jarvis, factory project leader Kouji Tsuya said, "We are struggling with acceleration performance and power delivery. We couldn't address the power delivery more precisely, and we have to apologise to our riders ... but now we are working as hard as ever to find the solution." Marketing and communications manager William Favero added, "We hope it's the very bottom of our crisis." Next day, the race results were again the worst of the season so far.

As well as forthcoming tests at Misano and Aragon before and after the next race, behind the scenes they had borrowed electronics expert Michele Gadda from their own Superbike team; but they would have to wait still longer for the much awaited change in fortunes.

If nothing else, the apology was a very Yamaha thing to do; the sole precedent had occurred at Phillip Island in 2001, after Max Biaggi had complained of "structural faults" that had caused him many crashes in his unsuccessful battle against Rossi on the Honda. Masahiko Nakajima, project leader for the YZR500 two-stroke, had stopped short of apologising, but admitted that they "may have been mistaken" in certain areas of chassis setting development. "It's very tough to beat Rossi and the Honda combination, and the riders are forced to push harder than ever before. It seems our bike does not accept this entry speed for the corners. Recently, we focused on stability under braking – biased the set-up direction toward that. The result is that the cornering performance or chassis balance may be a little unstable because of that."

Rossi reacted to the latest apology by reminding Yamaha of the improvement they had made to their sub-standard first M1 in 2004, when he had joined them from Honda, winning the title at his first attempt on a significantly upgraded bike with the new cross-plane-crankshaft engine. For 2005, they had built what he regarded as the best M1 ever. Yamaha had "put in different organisation, more money and more people. Now we have to try the same," he said. Poor acceleration was the key, blamed on wheelspin caused by aggressive throttle response, which was especially problematic at Austria's Red Bull Ring, where slow corners precede fast straights. "The rest of the bike is good," he said.

Not that good, according to news from the post-Brno tests, where all the other factories announced progress. Vinales, still bruised from his race crash, had missed the session, but of all the riders, only Rossi had no progress to report.

KTM experienced a downbeat time at their and their sponsor's home race, with Smith the sole rider. He managed his best qualifying position of the year, 13th, and finished in the points again. But the new engine configuration was absent once more, after its brief practice outing at Brno, and would remain in abeyance for the next race as well.

Pol Espargaro's injury complications kept him at home: as well as a fractured collarbone, spinal inflammation had had very painful consequences. Compatriot Jorge Martin was ignoring his own pain, a week after breaking his left forearm. Strapped and full of the Clinica's finest blockers, the Moto3 title hopeful put in a remarkable weekend, fighting for pole position and the race win.

The rain revived memories of a crash-strewn Moto2 FP2 at this circuit in 2017, when almost all of 14 falls had been blamed on dirt and rubber in the hard braking zones. MotoGP riders had threatened a strike if race-day turned out to be wet, while safety adviser Loris Capirossi – who had tested in the wet before the event and suffered the same problem – had been panned for not taking action when there had still been time to clean the track. In 2018, a thorough sandblasting had quite solved the problem; a couple of identikit Moto2 crashes at Turn One were down to rider error. In one, Lecuona had been shadowing Oliveira, missed his braking point and skittled them both, luckily without serious consequences. In the other, NTS rider Steven Odendaal did the same thing to Vierge, and the Spaniard suffered horrible fractures to his right hand and wrist.

Vierge was a top name on the Moto2 transfer list, switching from his Dynavolt Intact team to replace Mir at the Marc VDS squad. That left a spot for Luthi, whose foray into MotoGP had brought no joy. Two more names piqued the interest: Moto3 race winners Bezzecchi and Oettl were bound for the Tech 3 Moto2 team, which in 2019 would switch from its home-built chassis to a KTM for the new Triumph engine.

MOTOGP RACE – 28 laps

Dry qualifying came to a tense climax, the top three inside two-tenths, Marquez claiming his fourth pole of the year by two-thousandths. In spite of dubbing the circuit "Ducati-land", he had led every session, wet or dry.

The Ducatis were alongside, Dovizioso second, then Lorenzo: the trio had swapped pole between them throughout.

Petrucci, less than two-tenths down, led row two from Crutchlow and Zarco on the independent Yamaha; the factory riders were back in 11th (Vinales) and 14th (Rossi). It was Valentino's worst since Phillip Island in 2016, where he'd qualified 15th, but finished second.

The front running in the race involved the same trio as in Brno. The issue was doubt until the final yards of the short and deceptively simple lap, fastest of the year by some 3km/h over Phillip Island. Dovi set a new lap record on the sixth, but he would miss the final battle.

That was between Lorenzo and Marquez, and after an increasingly frantic exchange of the lead, it went to the Ducati rider by just 0.130 of a second. It was Ducati's second in a row, and third in succession at the track. Ducati-land indeed.

For a second race, Lorenzo had abandoned runaway tactics to save tyres and energy, and described it as one of his best wins. "When you beat Marc, it is always special … when you have to fight with a monster like him to the last lap."

Unusually, the top three were all employing different tyres: Lorenzo soft front/soft rear, Marquez medium/hard and Dovizioso medium/medium – a choice that played him foul as their grip faded. The variety, at least in part, was because of a shortage of time to explore options, with only two dry free practices.

Dovi led away, but the trio tangled at Turn Three's hard braking zone, and Lorenzo led the first lap. It was Marquez's favourite passing spot, and on lap two he used it to take a

Above: Marquez and Lorenzo approach the showdown. Dovi has been consigned to a spectator's role.
Photo: Repsol Honda

Right: Moto3 winner Bezzecchi leads hero Martin (88), Arenas, Masia (5) and Dalla Porta.

Below: right: With a smile like that, who needs emojis? Bezzecchi and crew celebrate his victory.
Photos: Gold & Goose

lead he would hold until lap 18; with Dovi third, peering over Lorenzo's shoulder, but never able to get by. After lap 12, the gap had stretched to almost a full second, and the race took on a familiar feel. Then things started to change.

One- or two-tenths at a time, the Ducatis began closing, their power telling on the dragstrip straights.

At the start of lap 19, Lorenzo pounced into the first corner. At the same time, Dovi was caught out – almost hitting Marquez's back wheel and running wide. He would never get back into an attacking position.

Marquez fought straight back. And so did Lorenzo. They would be only inches apart for the rest of the race, with the Honda in front again three or four more times, almost always at Turn Three, but never for very long. They were shaping up for the final battle.

They started the last lap with Marquez a couple of hundredths ahead over the line, but Lorenzo retook the lead into the first corner. There's a fast kink next, then Turn Three. Lorenzo ran in wide, giving Marquez room. He took the bait. But Lorenzo was able to open the throttle sooner and get back ahead, and to hold off the furiously pressing Honda to the line.

Dovi was less than two seconds behind, and watched as Marquez's final attempt to line up Lorenzo through the last two corners went wrong as both wheels slid under braking.

Crutchlow was alone, another eight seconds away, after successfully fending off a persistent Petrucci, until the Italian had to back off his mapping to avoid running out of fuel. He'd fallen back to lead Rossi and Pedrosa. The latter pair had passed a fading Rins with three laps to go, leaving him three seconds behind in eighth. Sixth was a fine effort from Rossi, who had finished the first lap 11th and gained places all race long. All the same, he lost more ground to podium regular Marquez in the championship, second place now under threat from both Ducati riders.

Zarco was ninth, having regained two places on the last lap from Bautista, through from a slow start, and Rabat, fast away, but fading.

The increasingly dispirited Vinales was a couple of seconds behind in 12th, never having been on the pace, but ahead of Iannone, who had been in the group chasing the leaders until he ran off at Turn Three. Smith and Nakagami took the last of the points, Syahrin having missed out by less than half a second.

Espargaro had faded badly to 17th after a strong start well up in the top ten; likewise 18th-placed Miller, who blamed overheating tyres. Morbidelli, Redding, Abraham and Luthi trailed in; Simeon crashed out.

MOTO2 RACE – 25 laps

Two of the front-row qualifiers – pole-sitter Bagnaia and Quartararo – didn't finish the session. Bagnaia out of fuel, Quartararo out of sparks. Between them, Oliveira claimed his first front row of the season.

As usual, times were very close – 18 within the first second. Navarro led row two from Marquez and Pasini; Schrotter the third from Binder and Baldassarri.

Oliveira led away, while Bagnaia, chasing him into Turn One, had his back wheel tagged by Quartararo. That pushed him wide, but while his assailant dropped away to finish the first lap 22nd, Bagnaia merely ceded second to Navarro.

It took him four more laps to get past the Spaniard, with Oliveira now clear by a second. Tenth by tenth, he chipped away, and by half-distance he had caught up. Irresistible force meets immovable object.

Bagnaia did nose ahead a handful of times in the later laps, but Oliveira always responded immediately, to lead every time over the line. He appeared to have things under control. As it transpired, it was the other way round. The Kalex seemed to have more front grip for braking and turning; the KTM had better drive. The third and twistiest section favoured Bagnaia.

Last lap, last corner, and Bagnaia moved ahead again, then ran a wide entry line. Oliveira dived inside, and in a replay of 2017's Dovizioso-Marquez battle at the same corner, he briefly took the lead again. But Bagnaia's exit line was better, and he won by half a second.

Thus Bagnaia regained the title lead after "a very nice race", while Oliveira's sportsmanship was conspicuous: with

Above: Crutchlow fends off Petrucci in their battle for fourth.

Left: Alex Marquez crashed again as his hard year became harder.

Above right: Bagnaia snatches victory from Oliveira at the final corner.

Photos: Gold & Goose

a smile, he said, "It sucks a bit to lose like this, but it was a great battle."

The fight for third was hardly less fierce.

Marquez had taken it off Navarro on lap ten, and they were joined by Pasini, Marini and Binder. Navarro had lost touch by a couple of seconds at the end, so when Binder was instructed to lose one place for exceeding track limits (one of several riders so punished), he had to slow down by that much to get behind the Spaniard.

The other three fought to the end. Marquez prevailed early on the final lap, but Marini got back inside him, precisely as the Spaniard ran out of grip and slid off for a second successive race crash. Thus a third successive podium finish for Marini.

Pasini was a couple of tenths adrift; Navarro held off Binder for fifth.

Schrotter had closed at the finish after dealing with a fading Mir. Quartararo came through from 20th on lap one to head the next group, with Lecuona completing the top ten. Fenati was on his back wheel, and Kent not far adrift for only his second points of the year. Locatelli, Manzi and Nagashima took the rest of them.

Team-mates Baldassarri and Fernandez had crashed with Corsi in the early stages, with Gardner also put off the track. He got going again, only to fall later around the lap. Baldassarri, who had caused it all, remounted to finish last. Sam Lowes was another to crash out.

MOTO3 RACE – 23 laps

Drying as it came to a close, qualifying ended in a pole shootout. Good timing gave Bezzecchi his first by 0.078 of a second. But the returned Martin was the hero of the hour, one of five or six riders to hold provisional pole in the final flurry, and ending up second. Bezzecchi slowed at the end of the session to symbolically tip his cap to his rival.

Arenas was third; Canet headed row two from Arbolino and Rodrigo. Brno winner Di Giannantonio was 16th, two seconds off. McPhee, unqualified after two crashes, would start from the back of the grid.

Bezzecchi took a flawless win, but like his pole, it was overshadowed by Martin's determination and courage. He fought up front throughout, and even led briefly with three laps to go,

He was consigned to fourth in a hectic last lap, when the front four were joined at the last by Bastianini and Dalla Porta, who had come through a big pursuit battle. Bastianini zipped through to take second from Martin, then Spanish teenager Masia also moved ahead. But as they ran into the final corner, Martin attacked again as the KTM rider ran wide, to secure a classic podium finish.

In tears afterwards, he said, "It was a really hard weekend for me. To be here is unbelievable."

Arenas, with the leaders throughout, was fourth, less than a second adrift; mere hundredths behind him came Dalla Porta, followed by the disappointed Masia.

McPhee had also come through from the back, up to eighth, but had dropped to 12th in the last-lap shuffle.

EYETIME MOTORRAD GRAND PRIX VON ÖSTERREICH

10-12 AUGUST, 2018

RED BULL RING, SPIELBERG

Circuit: 4.318km / 2.683 miles

28 laps

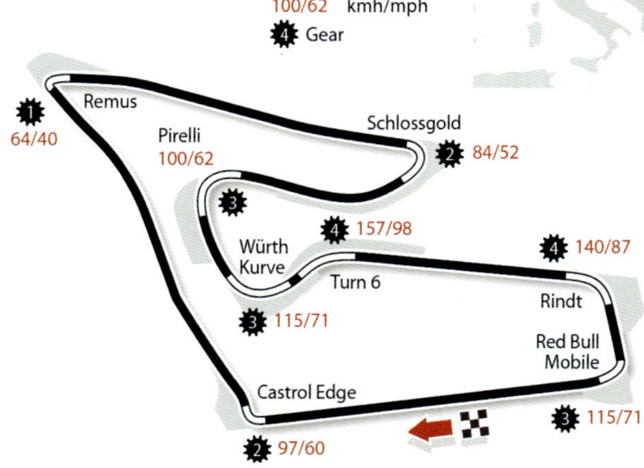

MotoGP

RACE DISTANCE: 28 laps, 75.126 miles/120.904km · RACE WEATHER: Dry (air 27°C, humidity 41%, track 43°C)

Pos.	Rider	Nat.	No.	Entrant	Machine	Tyres	Race tyre choice	Laps	Time & speed
1	**Jorge Lorenzo**	SPA	99	Ducati Team	Ducati Desmosedici	M	F: Soft/R: Soft	28	39m 40.688s 113.6mph/ 182.8km/h
2	**Marc Marquez**	SPA	93	Repsol Honda Team	Honda RC213V	M	F: Medium/R: Hard	28	39m 40.818s
3	**Andrea Dovizioso**	ITA	4	Ducati Team	Ducati Desmosedici	M	F: Medium/R: Medium	28	39m 42.344s
4	**Cal Crutchlow**	GBR	35	LCR Honda CASTROL	Honda RC213V	M	F: Hard/R: Medium	28	39m 50.122s
5	**Danilo Petrucci**	ITA	9	Alma Pramac Racing	Ducati Desmosedici	M	F: Medium/R: Medium	28	39m 53.857s
6	**Valentino Rossi**	ITA	46	Movistar Yamaha MotoGP	Yamaha YZR-M1	M	F: Medium/R: Medium	28	39m 54.714s
7	**Dani Pedrosa**	SPA	26	Repsol Honda Team	Honda RC213V	M	F: Medium/R: Medium	28	39m 54.844s
8	**Alex Rins**	SPA	42	Team SUZUKI ECSTAR	Suzuki GSX-RR	M	F: Hard/R: Medium	28	39m 57.332s
9	**Johann Zarco**	FRA	5	Monster Yamaha Tech 3	Yamaha YZR-M1	M	F: Medium/R: Soft	28	40m 01.448s
10	**Alvaro Bautista**	SPA	19	Angel Nieto Team	Ducati Desmosedici	M	F: Soft/R: Soft	28	40m 01.532s
11	**Tito Rabat**	SPA	53	Reale Avintia Racing	Ducati Desmosedici	M	F: Soft/R: Soft	28	40m 01.802s
12	**Maverick Vinales**	SPA	25	Movistar Yamaha MotoGP	Yamaha YZR-M1	M	F: Medium/R: Soft	28	40m 03.627s
13	**Andrea Iannone**	ITA	29	Team SUZUKI ECSTAR	Suzuki GSX-RR	M	F: Medium/R: Medium	28	40m 07.211s
14	**Bradley Smith**	GBR	38	Red Bull KTM Factory Racing	KTM RC16	M	F: Medium/R: Soft	28	40m 09.856s
15	**Takaaki Nakagami**	JPN	30	LCR Honda IDEMITSU	Honda RC213V	M	F: Medium/R: Medium	28	40m 10.760s
16	Hafizh Syahrin	MAL	55	Monster Yamaha Tech 3	Yamaha YZR-M1	M	F: Medium/R: Soft	28	40m 11.031s
17	Aleix Espargaro	SPA	41	Aprilia Racing Team Gresini	Aprilia RS-GP	M	F: Medium/R: Medium	28	40m 12.463s
18	Jack Miller	AUS	43	Alma Pramac Racing	Ducati Desmosedici	M	F: Medium/R: Soft	28	40m 15.063s
19	Franco Morbidelli	ITA	21	EG 0,0 Marc VDS	Honda RC213V	M	F: Medium/R: Soft	28	40m 20.859s
20	Scott Redding	GBR	45	Aprilia Racing Team Gresini	Aprilia RS-GP	M	F: Hard/R: Medium	28	40m 33.708s
21	Karel Abraham	CZE	17	Angel Nieto Team	Ducati Desmosedici	M	F: Soft/R: Soft	28	40m 33.949s
22	Thomas Luthi	SWI	12	EG 0,0 Marc VDS	Honda RC213V	M	F: Medium/R: Medium	28	40m 35.043s
	Xavier Simeon	BEL	10	Reale Avintia Racing	Ducati Desmosedici	M	F: Soft/R: Soft	10	DNF-crash

Fastest lap: Andrea Dovizioso, on lap 8, 1m 24.277s, 114.6mph/184.4km/h.

Lap record: Johann Zarco, 1m 24.312s, 114.5mph/184.3km/h (2017).

Event maximum speed: Andrea Dovizioso, 196.2mph/315.8km/h (warm-up).

Qualifying

Weather: Dry

Air Temp: 22° **Track Temp:** 31°

Humidity: 65%

1	Marquez	1m 23.241s
2	Dovizioso	1m 23.243s
3	Lorenzo	1m 23.376s
4	Petrucci	1m 23.503s
5	Crutchlow	1m 23.812s
6	Zarco	1m 23.887s
7	Rabat	1m 23.922s
8	Iannone	1m 24.091s
9	Pedrosa	1m 24.124s
10	Rins	1m 24.227s
11	Vinales	1m 24.284s
12	Bautista	1m 24.342s
13	Smith	1m 24.245s
14	Rossi	1m 24.309s
15	A. Espargaro	1m 24.762s
16	Morbidelli	1m 24.767s
17	Miller	1m 24.805s
18	Syahrin	1m 24.834s
19	Simeon	1m 24.868s
20	Redding	1m 25.067s
21	Nakagami	1m 25.178s
22	Luthi	1m 25.310s
23	Abraham	1m 25.339s

Fastest race laps

1	Dovizioso	1m 24.277s
2	Marquez	1m 24.292s
3	Lorenzo	1m 24.327s
4	Iannone	1m 24.722s
5	Crutchlow	1m 24.753s
6	Petrucci	1m 24.825s
7	Pedrosa	1m 24.827s
8	Rins	1m 24.861s
9	Rossi	1m 24.965s
10	Bautista	1m 24.978s
11	Rabat	1m 25.005s
12	Vinales	1m 25.024s
13	A. Espargaro	1m 25.127s
14	Zarco	1m 25.128s
15	Miller	1m 25.130s
16	Smith	1m 25.333s
17	Syahrin	1m 25.392s
18	Nakagami	1m 25.453s
19	Morbidelli	1m 25.529s
20	Redding	1m 25.746s
21	Simeon	1m 25.875s
22	Abraham	1m 26.053s
23	Luthi	1m 26.305s

Championship Points

1	Marquez	201
2	Rossi	142
3	Lorenzo	130
4	Dovizioso	129
5	Vinales	113
6	Petrucci	105
7	Zarco	104
8	Crutchlow	103
9	Iannone	84
10	Rins	66
11	Pedrosa	66
12	Miller	61
13	Bautista	57
14	Rabat	35
15	P. Espargaro	32
16	Syahrin	24
17	Morbidelli	22
18	A. Espargaro	17
19	Smith	15
20	Redding	12
21	Nakagami	11
22	Kallio	6
23	Abraham	4

Constructor Points

1	Honda	236
2	Ducati	208
3	Yamaha	183
4	Suzuki	118
5	KTM	41
6	Aprilia	27

Grid order	1	2	3	4	5	6	7	8	9	10	11	12	13	14	15	16	17	18	19	20	21	22	23	24	25	26	27	28	·
93 MARQUEZ	99	93	93	93	93	93	93	93	93	93	93	93	93	93	93	93	93	93	99	99	99	99	99	99	99	99	93	99	1
4 DOVIZIOSO	93	99	99	99	99	99	99	99	99	99	99	99	99	99	99	99	99	99	93	93	93	93	93	93	93	93	99	93	2
99 LORENZO	4	4	4	4	4	4	4	4	4	4	4	4	4	4	4	4	4	4	4	4	4	4	4	4	4	4	4	4	3
9 PETRUCCI	35	35	35	35	35	35	35	35	35	35	35	35	35	35	35	35	35	35	35	35	35	35	35	35	35	35	35	35	4
35 CRUTCHLOW	42	42	9	9	9	9	9	9	9	9	9	9	9	9	9	9	9	9	9	9	9	9	9	9	9	9	9	9	5
5 ZARCO	9	9	42	42	42	42	42	42	42	42	42	42	42	42	42	42	42	42	42	42	42	42	42	46	46	46	46	46	6
53 RABAT	53	53	53	53	53	53	53	53	53	53	53	53	53	53	53	53	53	53	46	46	46	46	46	42	42	26	26	26	7
29 IANNONE	29	5	41	41	41	41	41	41	46	46	46	46	46	46	46	46	46	46	53	53	26	26	26	26	26	42	42	42	8
26 PEDROSA	5	41	5	5	5	46	46	46	41	41	41	41	26	26	26	26	26	26	26	26	53	53	53	53	53	53	53	5	9
42 RINS	38	29	46	46	46	5	5	5	5	26	26	26	41	41	41	41	5	5	5	5	5	5	5	5	5	19	19	19	10
25 VINALES	46	46	29	29	29	29	29	26	26	5	5	5	5	5	5	5	41	41	41	41	19	19	19	19	19	5	5	53	11
19 BAUTISTA	41	38	43	43	26	26	26	29	43	43	43	43	43	43	19	19	19	19	19	19	25	25	25	25	25	25	25	25	12
38 SMITH	43	43	38	26	43	43	43	43	19	19	19	19	19	19	25	25	25	25	25	25	29	29	29	29	29	29	29	29	13
46 ROSSI	26	26	26	38	19	19	19	19	38	38	38	38	38	25	29	29	29	29	29	29	41	41	41	41	41	38	38	38	14
41 A. ESPARGARO	25	19	19	19	38	38	38	38	25	25	25	25	25	38	38	38	38	38	38	38	38	38	38	38	38	41	30	30	15
43 MILLER	19	25	25	25	25	25	25	25	30	30	29	29	29	29	30	30	30	30	30	30	30	30	30	30	30	30	41	55	
55 SYAHRIN	30	30	30	30	30	30	30	30	29	29	30	30	30	30	43	43	43	43	43	43	43	55	55	55	55	55	55	41	
10 SIMEON	10	10	10	21	21	21	21	21	21	21	21	21	55	55	55	55	55	55	55	55	55	43	43	43	43	43	43	43	
21 MORBIDELLI	45	45	21	10	10	10	55	55	55	55	55	55	21	21	21	21	21	21	21	21	21	21	21	21	21	21	21	21	
45 REDDING	21	21	45	55	55	55	10	10	10	10	45	17	17	17	17	45	45	45	45	45	45	45	45	17	17	17	17	45	
30 NAKAGAMI	55	55	55	45	45	45	45	45	45	45	17	45	45	45	45	17	17	17	17	17	17	17	17	45	45	45	45	17	
12 LUTHI	17	17	17	17	17	17	17	17	17	17	12	12	12	12	12	12	12	12	12	12	12	12	12	12	12	12	12	12	
17 ABRAHAM	12	12	12	12	12	12	12	12	12	12																			

Moto2

RACE DISTANCE: 25 laps, 67.077 miles/107.950km · RACE WEATHER: Dry (air 27°C, humidity 43%, track 41°C)

Pos.	Rider	Nat.	No.	Entrant	Machine	Laps	Time & Speed
1	**Francesco Bagnaia**	ITA	42	SKY Racing Team VR46	Kalex	25	37m 45.914s 106.6mph/ 171.5km/h
2	**Miguel Oliveira**	POR	44	Red Bull KTM Ajo	KTM	25	37m 46.178s
3	**Luca Marini**	ITA	10	SKY Racing Team VR46	Kalex	25	37m 51.867s
4	**Mattia Pasini**	ITA	54	Italtrans Racing Team	Kalex	25	37m 52.028s
5	**Jorge Navarro**	SPA	9	Federal Oil Gresini Moto2	Kalex	25	37m 54.468s
6	**Brad Binder**	RSA	41	Red Bull KTM Ajo	KTM	25	37m 54.858s
7	**Marcel Schrotter**	GER	23	Dynavolt Intact GP	Kalex	25	37m 55.040s
8	**Joan Mir**	SPA	36	EG 0,0 Marc VDS	Kalex	25	37m 58.318s
9	**Fabio Quartararo**	FRA	20	(+)Ego - Speed Up Racing	Speed Up	25	38m 02.164s
10	**Iker Lecuona**	SPA	27	Swiss Innovative Investors	KTM	25	38m 02.632s
11	**Romano Fenati**	ITA	13	Marinelli Snipers Team	Kalex	25	38m 02.743s
12	**Danny Kent**	GBR	52	(+)Ego - Speed Up Racing	Speed Up	25	38m 03.630s
13	**Andrea Locatelli**	ITA	5	Italtrans Racing Team	Kalex	25	38m 09.114s
14	**Stefano Manzi**	ITA	62	Forward Racing Team	Suter	25	38m 13.858s
15	**Tetsuta Nagashima**	JPN	45	IDEMITSU Honda Team Asia	Kalex	25	38m 13.908s
16	Khairul Idham Pawi	MAL	89	IDEMITSU Honda Team Asia	Kalex	25	38m 14.407s
17	Dominique Aegerter	SWI	77	Kiefer Racing	KTM	25	38m 14.957s
18	Steven Odendaal	RSA	4	NTS RW Racing GP	NTS	25	38m 24.090s
19	Joe Roberts	USA	16	NTS RW Racing GP	NTS	25	38m 26.458s
20	Jules Danilo	FRA	95	Nashi Argan SAG Team	Kalex	25	38m 27.569s
21	Niki Tuuli	FIN	66	Petronas Sprinta Racing	Kalex	25	38m 27.641s
22	Bo Bendsneyder	NED	64	Tech 3 Racing	Tech 3	25	38m 28.680s
23	Isaac Vinales	SPA	32	Forward Racing Team	Suter	25	38m 29.725s
24	Alejandro Medina	SPA	55	SAG Team	Kalex	25	38m 31.286s
25	Xavi Cardelus	AND	18	Team Stylobike	Kalex	25	38m 37.099s
26	Lorenzo Baldassarri	ITA	7	Pons HP40	Kalex	25	38m 59.815s
	Alex Marquez	SPA	73	EG 0,0 Marc VDS	Kalex	24	DNF
	Sam Lowes	GBR	22	Swiss Innovative Investors	KTM	17	DNF
	Federico Fuligni	ITA	21	Tasca Racing Scuderia Moto2	Kalex	17	DNF
	Simone Corsi	ITA	24	Tasca Racing Scuderia Moto2	Kalex	3	DNF
	Remy Gardner	AUS	87	Tech 3 Racing	Tech 3	3	DNF
	Augusto Fernandez	SPA	40	Pons HP40	Kalex	3	DNF

Fastest lap: Brad Binder, on lap 11, 1m 30.157s, 107.1mph/172.4km/h.

Lap record: Johann Zarco, 1m 29.497s, 107.9mph/173.6km/h (2016)

Event maximum speed: Miguel Oliveira, 159.4mph/256.6km/h (warm-up).

Qualifying

Weather: Dry
Air Temp: 23° **Track Temp:** 36°
Humidity: 60%

1	Bagnaia	1m 29.409s
2	Oliveira	1m 29.719s
3	Quartararo	1m 29.930s
4	Navarro	1m 29.971s
5	Marquez	1m 30.058s
6	Pasini	1m 30.069s
7	Schrotter	1m 30.095s
8	Binder	1m 30.125s
9	Baldassarri	1m 30.135s
10	Marini	1m 30.194s
11	Gardner	1m 30.195s
12	Lecuona	1m 30.197s
13	Fernandez	1m 30.215s
14	Locatelli	1m 30.270s
15	Fenati	1m 30.286s
16	Lowes	1m 30.336s
17	Kent	1m 30.401s
18	Corsi	1m 30.409s
19	Aegerter	1m 30.452s
20	Mir	1m 30.486s
21	Nagashima	1m 30.555s
22	Pawi	1m 30.555s
23	Manzi	1m 30.654s
24	Roberts	1m 30.794s
25	Odendaal	1m 30.959s
26	Danilo	1m 31.093s
27	Bendsneyder	1m 31.132s
28	Vierge	1m 31.377s
29	Tuuli	1m 31.404s
30	Vinales	1m 31.468s
31	Medina	1m 31.790s
32	Cardelus	1m 32.012s
33	Fuligni	1m 33.725s

Fastest race laps

1	Binder	1m 30.157s
2	Marini	1m 30.165s
3	Bagnaia	1m 30.185s
4	Oliveira	1m 30.234s
5	Pasini	1m 30.266s
6	Marquez	1m 30.268s
7	Schrotter	1m 30.356s
8	Navarro	1m 30.417s
9	Fenati	1m 30.427s
10	Lecuona	1m 30.538s
11	Mir	1m 30.556s
12	Quartararo	1m 30.589s
13	Lowes	1m 30.634s
14	Kent	1m 30.717s
15	Locatelli	1m 30.816s
16	Nagashima	1m 30.821s
17	Pawi	1m 30.833s
18	Manzi	1m 30.861s
19	Baldassarri	1m 30.969s
20	Aegerter	1m 30.985s
21	Roberts	1m 31.105s
22	Corsi	1m 31.124s
23	Fernandez	1m 31.173s
24	Odendaal	1m 31.236s
25	Vinales	1m 31.473s
26	Danilo	1m 31.482s
27	Tuuli	1m 31.498s
28	Bendsneyder	1m 31.530s
29	Cardelus	1m 31.621s
30	Gardner	1m 31.692s
31	Medina	1m 31.721s
32	Fuligni	1m 33.367s

Championship Points

1	Bagnaia	189
2	Oliveira	186
3	Marquez	113
4	Binder	111
5	Baldassarri	106
6	Mir	103
7	Schrotter	91
8	Vierge	90
9	Quartararo	84
10	Pasini	82
11	Marini	79
12	Lowes	46
13	Navarro	42
14	Lecuona	41
15	Locatelli	32
16	Corsi	32
17	Aegerter	24
18	Gardner	20
19	Fenati	14
20	Fernandez	11
21	Barbera	10
22	Manzi	8
23	Kent	8
24	Vinales	7
25	Nagashima	7
26	Roberts	2
27	Pawi	1
28	Odendaal	1

Constructor Points

1	Kalex	251
2	KTM	198
3	Speed Up	88
4	Tech 3	20
5	Suter	8
6	NTS	2

Moto3

RACE DISTANCE: 23 laps, 61.711 miles/99.314km · RACE WEATHER: Dry (air 25°C, humidity 50%, track 37°C)

Pos.	Rider	Nat.	No.	Entrant	Machine	Laps	Time & Speed
1	**Marco Bezzecchi**	ITA	12	Redox PruestelGP	KTM	23	37m 13.198s 99.4mph/ 160.0km/h
2	**Enea Bastianini**	ITA	33	Leopard Racing	Honda	23	37m 13.671s
3	**Jorge Martin**	SPA	88	Del Conca Gresini Moto3	Honda	23	37m 13.742s
4	**Albert Arenas**	SPA	75	Angel Nieto Team Moto3	KTM	23	37m 14.571s
5	**Lorenzo Dalla Porta**	ITA	48	Leopard Racing	Honda	23	37m 14.619s
6	**Jaume Masia**	SPA	5	Bester Capital Dubai	KTM	23	37m 14.717s
7	**Ayumu Sasaki**	JPN	71	Petronas Sprinta Racing	Honda	23	37m 21.783s
8	**Gabriel Rodrigo**	ARG	19	RBA BOE Skull Rider	KTM	23	37m 21.856s
9	**Tony Arbolino**	ITA	14	Marinelli Snipers Team	Honda	23	37m 21.889s
10	**Aron Canet**	SPA	44	Estrella Galicia 0,0	Honda	23	37m 22.007s
11	**Fabio Di Giannantonio**	ITA	21	Del Conca Gresini Moto3	Honda	23	37m 22.022s
12	**John McPhee**	GBR	17	CIP - Green Power	KTM	23	37m 22.142s
13	**Jakub Kornfeil**	CZE	84	Redox PruestelGP	KTM	23	37m 22.869s
14	**Philipp Oettl**	GER	65	Sudmetal Schedl GP Racing	KTM	23	37m 27.883s
15	**Marcos Ramirez**	SPA	42	Bester Capital Dubai	KTM	23	37m 27.895s
16	Kaito Toba	JPN	27	Honda Team Asia	Honda	23	37m 32.575s
17	Adam Norrodin	MAL	7	Petronas Sprinta Racing	Honda	23	37m 32.617s
18	Tatsuki Suzuki	JPN	24	SIC58 Squadra Corse	Honda	23	37m 32.702s
19	Darryn Binder	RSA	40	Red Bull KTM Ajo	KTM	23	37m 32.748s
20	Ai Ogura	JPN	32	Asia Talent Team	Honda	23	37m 32.800s
21	Kazuki Masaki	JPN	22	RBA BOE Skull Rider	KTM	23	37m 32.904s
22	Niccolo Antonelli	ITA	23	SIC58 Squadra Corse	Honda	23	37m 33.179s
23	Nicolo Bulega	ITA	8	SKY Racing Team VR46	KTM	23	37m 36.617s
24	Alonso Lopez	SPA	72	Estrella Galicia 0,0	Honda	23	37m 37.254s
25	Vicente Perez	SPA	77	Reale Avintia Academy 77	KTM	23	37m 40.832s
26	Dennis Foggia	ITA	10	SKY Racing Team VR46	KTM	23	37m 40.945s
27	Stefano Nepa	ITA	81	CIP - Green Power	KTM	23	37m 49.136s
28	Nakarin Atiratphuvapat	THA	41	Honda Team Asia	Honda	23	38m 00.066s
29	Maximilian Kofler	AUT	73	Motosport Kofler	KTM	23	38m 00.487s
	Andrea Migno	ITA	16	Angel Nieto Team Moto3	KTM	11	DNF

Fastest lap: Lorenzo Dalla Porta, on lap 20, 1m 36.307s, 100.2mph/161.4km/h.

Lap record: Jaume Masia, 1m 36.436s, 100.1mph/161.1km/h (2017).

Event maximum speed: Marco Bezzecchi, 136.6mph/219.8km/h (warm-up).

Qualifying

Weather: Wet-dry
Air Temp: 20° **Track Temp:** 26°
Humidity: 85%

1	Bezzecchi	1m 38.617s
2	Martin	1m 38.695s
3	Arenas	1m 39.255s
4	Canet	1m 39.500s
5	Arbolino	1m 39.548s
6	Rodrigo	1m 39.876s
7	Ramirez	1m 39.901s
8	Oettl	1m 40.022s
9	Bastianini	1m 40.125s
10	Norrodin	1m 40.295s
11	Dalla Porta	1m 40.406s
12	Masia	1m 40.420s
13	Kornfeil	1m 40.494s
14	Antonelli	1m 40.496s
15	Foggia	1m 40.608s
16	Di Giannantonio	1m 40.712s
17	Suzuki	1m 40.759s
18	Sasaki	1m 40.848s
19	Migno	1m 40.944s
20	Lopez	1m 40.996s
21	Nepa	1m 41.127s
22	Bulega	1m 41.779s
23	Kofler	1m 42.171s
24	Atiratphuvapat	1m 42.362s
25	Masaki	1m 42.501s
26	Ogura	1m 43.361s
27	Binder	1m 43.945s
28	Toba	1m 43.993s
29	Perez	1m 45.474s
30	McPhee	1m 46.150s

Fastest race laps

1	Dalla Porta	1m 36.307s
2	Bastianini	1m 36.322s
3	Masia	1m 36.512s
4	Martin	1m 36.535s
5	Di Giannantonio	1m 36.541s
6	Arenas	1m 36.573s
7	Bezzecchi	1m 36.610s
8	McPhee	1m 36.616s
9	Sasaki	1m 36.693s
10	Arbolino	1m 36.733s
11	Rodrigo	1m 36.741s
12	Canet	1m 36.760s
13	Kornfeil	1m 36.837s
14	Oettl	1m 36.843s
15	Toba	1m 36.904s
16	Ramirez	1m 36.917s
17	Ogura	1m 36.942s
18	Masaki	1m 36.945s
19	Bulega	1m 37.130s
20	Norrodin	1m 37.154s
21	Binder	1m 37.218s
22	Suzuki	1m 37.271s
23	Antonelli	1m 37.303s
24	Lopez	1m 37.427s
25	Perez	1m 37.516s
26	Foggia	1m 37.603s
27	Kofler	1m 37.615s
28	Nepa	1m 37.820s
29	Migno	1m 37.935s
30	Atiratphuvapat	1m 38.141s

Championship Points

1	Bezzecchi	158
2	Martin	146
3	Di Giannantonio	121
4	Canet	118
5	Bastianini	117
6	Rodrigo	84
7	Kornfeil	80
8	Ramirez	67
9	Dalla Porta	63
10	Migno	60
11	Oettl	54
12	Masia	54
13	Arenas	50
14	Antonelli	50
15	McPhee	43
16	Suzuki	40
17	Arbolino	32
18	Sasaki	32
19	Lopez	31
20	Toba	26
21	Norrodin	24
22	Binder	20
23	Foggia	17
24	Fernandez	13
25	Yurchenko	9
26	Loi	8
27	Bulega	7
28	Masaki	7
29	Pagliani	6
30	Atiratphuvapat	2
31	Ogura	1

Constructor Points

1	Honda	241
2	KTM	216

FIM WORLD CHAMPIONSHIP · ROUND 12

BRITISH GRAND PRIX

SILVERSTONE CIRCUIT

Above: Multi-champion Phil Read (*right*) joins photographers snapping pole-sitter Lorenzo before the race that never was.
Photo: Monster Energy

Above right: Dorna Safety Officer Franco Uncini faced criticism for homologating the circuit without being aware of problems in the rain.

Right: "This hurts me more than it hurts you." Embattled Silverstone CEO Stuart Pringle faces the media.
Photos: Gold & Goose

THE 2018 British GP at Silverstone made history. It was the first GP of the modern era in which no racing took place, thanks to sheets of standing water on the fully resurfaced circuit.

The water came from rain, a frequent phenomenon at Silverstone. Somehow, however, the new surface couldn't cope with it. It smacked of incompetence on an impressive scale; for that a premier event at a classic circuit had to be cancelled simply because of the British weather left a deep scar on the reputation of British motor sport, and threatened the future of the British GP.

The decision came from the riders, arrived at in a scrappy impromptu meeting late in the afternoon, but it was endorsed by Dorna Safety Officer Franco Uncini, Safety Advisor Loris Capirossi and Race Director Mike Webb. It sent some 55,000 spectators home disappointed, after spending a day exposed to the windy, cold and damp conditions. They'd seen no track action after morning warm-up and a couple of tentative sighting laps, save for some exaggerated aquaplaning and drifting by the safety car, and sundry road-sweeping attempts to clear the flooding.

"We were forced to cancel today's event due to track conditions," said Webb. "Primarily, it was water on the surface – in some places, it was not safe because of the way the water didn't run off.

"We have a number of years' experience of racing in bad weather on the old surface. This year is the first time we have encountered such surface water, so it must be blamed on the new surface."

He continued, "The track people made enormous efforts." But the water could not be cleared, and nor was the long-term prospect much better. "We want to have a British GP and we have to expect rain ... and the surface must be able to handle it."

Safety concerns were foremost after a very local cloudburst in Saturday's FP4 had caused a multiple pile-up and left Tito Rabat badly injured. Overnight earthworks and drainage slots cut in the track were aimed at alleviating the problem, while the schedule was changed to run MotoGP first at 11:30, in the hope of avoiding the rain that was forecast for later in the day.

But the rain, which was not heavy, but was persistent, came early.

There followed a black comedy of delays and deferments. The smaller classes remained in abeyance, while MotoGP's start was rescheduled for 2pm, pending an inspection half an hour earlier. Then it was to be at 3pm. Track still flooded. A new inspection was scheduled for 4pm, aiming at a 4:50 start. At that time, given the long hours of daylight, it was put about that racing would be possible until 7:30pm, thanks to an expected so-called weather window. This did duly arrive, but by then, it was too late.

The riders arranged an ad-hoc Safety Commission meeting at around 3:30, although at least one – Dovizioso – was not aware of it. Most team managers were also present, and five minutes before the planned 4pm inspection, the races were cancelled.

Crucially, the next day was a bank holiday; and with dry weather forecast, Dorna at least were keen on repeating the 2009 Qatar arrangement of running the race on the Monday. Doubtless most of the crowd would have agreed, but the kibosh came not only from Silverstone, but also some teams,

notably Yamaha, who had a test scheduled at Aragon on Wednesday, which they regarded as more important.

Recriminations and repercussions continued long afterwards. While Silverstone did refund racegoers the price of their Sunday tickets and promised to address the problem, and Dorna planned to introduce compulsory Monday reruns should the circumstances arise again, rumblings from within were that without a complete fresh resurfacing, the track would not be homologated.

At the time of writing, the chances of a full resurface seemed negligible, and the survival of the race was under serious threat. After all, Silverstone and owner-operators the British Racing Drivers Club were infamous for pleading poverty, not least in driving down Dorna's race fee when they rescued the GP from the ephemeral Circuit of Wales. And they had already paid for a full resurface at the start of 2018.

The results of this work were incomprehensibly bad. F1 drivers had complained about the bumps at the earlier car GP, and riders found the same thing as practice began on a fine sunny Friday. "It's a disaster," said Marquez, while Miller joked, "I asked Ohlins for motocross suspension." It was, he continued, "bumpy in strange places. I don't think it's because of the cars. It's more like a road laid on soft soil that has settled a bit." Pedrosa told how rear-wheel bouncing was fooling the electronics into cutting power to reduce wheelspin, but that if the electronics were turned down, the bike went sideways in the corners. Dovizioso said ruefully, "You have to fight on every exit. It's bad for everybody when you have to fight the bumps at the best track in Europe."

Rossi had an insouciant view. "The secret to riding a bumpy track," he said, "is to don't care."

When the rain came on Friday, as water puddled in the hollows, discomfort and difficulty were supplanted by serious danger. Shockingly, the new surface was unable to cope. The key incident came at the end of FP4, when a severe local downpour at the end of the Hangar Straight left standing water so deep that riders said it looked like a mirror. Even on wet tyres, they simply aquaplaned out of control.

Stowe Corner is approached at more than 320km/h and taken at around 120. Crutchlow, one of the first to arrive, had managed to get through, running wide after the front lifted off in sixth gear. Marquez also made it. Seeing confusion ahead, "luckily I closed the gas halfway down the straight. I was very slow, but it was still amazing aquaplaning." Six other riders were not so lucky.

The first to run straight had been Rins, who jumped off before hitting the air-fence. He was followed by Aleix Espargaro, Petrucci and Lorenzo, who avoided falling. Then Tito Rabat went down, and was getting to his feet when Morbidelli's VDS Honda came barrelling across the gravel and knocked him flying. He didn't get up again, having suffered serious leg injuries – femur and both lower bones badly broken, and major blood loss causing further complications. Luckily, Silverstone was better served by its medical arrangements than its resurfacing contractor. He underwent surgery in Coventry directly, but was out for the rest of the season.

On Saturday evening, all believed that it was only freak rain that had made the new surface unrideable; that in 'normal' rain it would be usable. The next day proved that view very wrong.

The full resurface had been carried out in February by British company Aggregate Industries, whose website boasts of "unsurpassed technical knowledge", and which had surfaced Silverstone in the past. Aggregate Industries has an impressive portfolio, including surfacing major British motorways, the Mersey and Channel Tunnels, and foundation work on The Shard, London's tallest structure.

Given this reputation, it was very difficult to understand how Silverstone's surface could have such major shortcomings. Silverstone manager Stuart Higgs promised a full independent investigation; at the time of writing, no findings had been released. He declined to condemn the contractor, nor say if he expected to seek compensation. "I know that Aggregate Industries are proud of their product, and they did this job for Brownie points rather than purely commercial reasons. It would be unfair to round on them now, without full data, but we need to get to the bottom of this."

Certainly, there were mixed feelings among teams and riders, with Jack Miller pretty much a lone voice at the riders' meeting in wanting to race. It was possible, he believed, "to ride to the conditions". That meant taking a less than ideal line past the puddles, but it could be done. "It feels worse than a crash – doing all the work and not racing," he said. "I think they give too much power to the riders. Yes, it was dangerous, but we are paid to do this job, and if you feel out of your comfort zone, then slow down."

Redding and Loris Baz (on the KTM in place of the still-absent Pol Espargaro) wanted to race as well, but did not attend the meeting.

Yamaha also might have regretted not voting for a Monday race instead of what turned out to be a rather ineffectual Aragon test, since for once, both riders were looking strong. Particularly Vinales, who was fastest on Friday and Sunday mornings, and third on combined free practice times.

However, cancellation was a relief for Moto2's erstwhile title leader Oliveira, way down in 23rd – the eighth row of the grid, while Bagnaia was on pole, with Remy Gardner alongside for his first front-row start. A release also for Jorge

THE cancellation of all classes on race-day was unprecedented in the modern era. The last time a complete meeting had been abandoned had been at Austria's Salzburgring in 1980. The reason? Thick snow in the Alpine foothills before practice even began.

In Qatar in 2009, the 125 race had been hit by rain and red-flagged after four laps, with half-points awarded; the subsequent 250 race also affected. Then a heavy rainstorm had hit just as the late-night main MotoGP race was about to begin. The race was postponed to the next day.

The previous year, the first race at Indianapolis had been hit by Hurricane Ike. Both the 125 and the MotoGP race had been shortened, the latter red-flagged as debris blew across the track; the subsequent 250 race was abandoned.

Above: Zarco's Yamaha and Smith's KTM are wheeled back from the grid.

Above right: NASA astronaut and MotoGP fan Drew Feustel was live at the pre-race press conference.

Above far right: Crews cut slots in the asphalt and dug drains, working overnight in a vain attempt to make the track fit for purpose.

Top right: The only entertainment for most of the day was drifting by the BMW safety car.

Photos: Gold & Goose

Martin, still hurting, although on Moto3 pole, with Bezzecchi only 11th.

Friday had been dry, and Saturday mixed, allowing practice and qualifying to go ahead.

Two Ducati riders had a narrow escape on Friday afternoon. Lorenzo, on an out-lap, swung into a left-hand corner, still warming his tyres, while Petrucci was approaching at very high speed from behind. Hard on the brakes, one foot down and smoking, Petrucci missed Lorenzo's back wheel by centimetres. "He is one of those riders who thinks there isn't anybody else on the track with him," said Petrucci.

There might as well not have been, when next day Lorenzo rose above dauntingly difficult mixed conditions in qualifying to take his second pole of the year. Team-mate Dovizioso was alongside, while Zarco completed the front row; slip-sliding Marquez was in the middle of row two, between independents Crutchlow and Petrucci.

Only Miller gambled on slicks on the half-dry track, hoping to repeat his classic Argentine pole. He had already done enough to place ninth, on row three, alongside Iannone and Smith, through from Q1.

The factory Yamahas had been strong in the dry, but ended up 11th and 12th, behind second Q1 escapee Rins. Rossi's problem was mainly timing – just too late out of the pits to complete a long lap for one last run at the end of the session. Morbidelli was best of the rest.

In Moto2 – the track now dry – the top 15 were within one second of pole-man Bagnaia, who had only displaced Gardner from a career-first pole at the finish. Marquez was alongside, while Schrotter headed row two and Sam Lowes was on row three.

Rain hit towards the end of the lunchtime Moto3 qualifying, leaving Di Giannantonio celebrating a second pole – until the sun reappeared, the track dried and he was pushed to fifth, with Martin, Masia and Dalla Porta on the front row.

In the end, none of this would make any difference.

The race-day disaster pushed other news to the background, but there had been plenty of it, starting with the usual Day of Champions for the renamed Two Wheels for Life charity (formerly Riders for Health), which realised more than £290,000 to support motorcycles providing health care in rural Africa.

Later that evening, the pre-race press conference was upstaged by NASA astronaut and MotoGP fan Drew Feustel, whose snaps from space of circuits are a social-media hit. 'Interviewed' by Marquez, Rossi, Dovi, Lorenzo, Crutchlow and Bautista, he adopted a sideways posture at times as he answered their wide-eyed questions.

Bautista was present because he had his own announcement: unable to find a MotoGP ride, he was off to World Superbikes instead, where he would replace Marco Melandri alongside Chaz Davies in the factory Ducati squad, on the new V4 Panigale.

That preceded the forthcoming confirmation of the paddock's worst kept secret. A raft of Malaysian dignitaries, including the minister for youth and sport, the chairman of the Sepang circuit (SIC) and top Petronas management, officially announced the new Petronas Yamaha MotoGP team, which would take over from the KTM-bound Tech 3 squad, extending the circuit and sponsor's joint involvement across all three classes. MotoGP riders were confirmed as Franco Morbidelli and Fabio Quartararo; Moto2's Malaysian Khairul Idham Pawi would switch from Honda Team Asia; and in Moto3, John McPhee would replace Adam Norrodin alongside Ayumu Sasaki. Current junior-class team manager Johan Stigefelt would be team director, while current Yamaha teamsters Wilco Zeelenberg and Ramon Forcada would join the new MotoGP squad, Zeelenberg as team manager, and Forcada as crew chief to Morbidelli, who would get a factory-spec M1.

The other major contract announcement came from Cal Crutchlow, whose tenure with the LCR team had been extended by another year to include 2020, still contracted directly to HRC.

FIM WORLD CHAMPIONSHIP ROUND 12

MotoGP · TISSOT OFFICIAL TIMEKEEPER

GOPRO BRITISH GRAND PRIX

24–26 AUGUST, 2018

MotoGP Race cancelled due to track conditions

Rider	Nat.	No.	Entrant	Machine	Tyres
Andrea Dovizioso	ITA	4	Ducati Team	Ducati Desmosedici	M
Johann Zarco	FRA	5	Monster Yamaha Tech 3	Yamaha YZR-M1	M
Danilo Petrucci	ITA	9	Alma Pramac Racing	Ducati Desmosedici	M
Xavier Simeon	BEL	10	Reale Avintia Racing	Ducati Desmosedici	M
Thomas Luthi	SWI	12	EG 0,0 Marc VDS	Honda RC213V	M
Karel Abraham	CZE	17	Angel Nieto Team	Ducati Desmosedici	M
Alvaro Bautista	SPA	19	Angel Nieto Team	Ducati Desmosedici	M
Franco Morbidelli	ITA	21	EG 0,0 Marc VDS	Honda RC213V	M
Maverick Vinales	SPA	25	Movistar Yamaha MotoGP	Yamaha YZR-M1	M
Dani Pedrosa	SPA	26	Repsol Honda Team	Honda RC213V	M
Andrea Iannone	ITA	29	Team SUZUKI ECSTAR	Suzuki GSX-RR	M
Takaaki Nakagami	JPN	30	LCR Honda IDEMITSU	Honda RC213V	M
Cal Crutchlow	GBR	35	LCR Honda CASTROL	Honda RC213V	M
Bradley Smith	GBR	38	Red Bull KTM Factory Racing	KTM RC16	M
Aleix Espargaro	SPA	41	Aprilia Racing Team Gresini	Aprilia RS-GP	M
Alex Rins	SPA	42	Team SUZUKI ECSTAR	Suzuki GSX-RR	M
Jack Miller	AUS	43	Alma Pramac Racing	Ducati Desmosedici	M
Loris Baz	SPA	76	Red Bull KTM Factory Racing	KTM RC16	M
Scott Redding	GBR	45	Aprilia Racing Team Gresini	Aprilia RS-GP	M
Valentino Rossi	ITA	46	Movistar Yamaha MotoGP	Yamaha YZR-M1	M
Tito Rabat	SPA	53	Reale Avintia Racing	Ducati Desmosedici	M
Hafizh Syahrin	MAL	55	Monster Yamaha Tech 3	Yamaha YZR-M1	M
Marc Marquez	SPA	93	Repsol Honda Team	Honda RC213V	M
Jorge Lorenzo	SPA	99	Ducati Team	Ducati Desmosedici	M

Qualifying

Weather: Wet

Air Temp: 16° **Track Temp:** 24°

Humidity: 59%

1	Lorenzo	2m 10.155s
2	Dovizioso	2m 10.314s
3	Zarco	2m 10.439s
4	Crutchlow	2m 10.615s
5	Marquez	2m 11.083s
6	Petrucci	2m 11.317s
7	Iannone	2m 11.495s
8	Smith	2m 11.514s
9	Miller	2m 12.173s
10	Rins	2m 12.504s
11	Vinales	2m 12.514s
12	Rossi	2m 13.504s
13	Morbidelli	2m 13.945s
14	Redding	2m 14.171s
15	Luthi	2m 14.198s
16	Pedrosa	2m 14.866s
17	A. Espargaro	2m 15.141s
18	Baz	2m 15.299s
19	Nakagami	2m 15.377s
20	Abraham	2m 15.721s
21	Bautista	2m 16.106s
22	Simeon	2m 16.451s
23	Syahrin	2m 16.483s
	Rabat	No Time

SILVERSTONE GRAND PRIX CIRCUIT

Length: 5.900km / 3.666 miles

Width: 17m

Key: 96/60 kph/mph; Gear

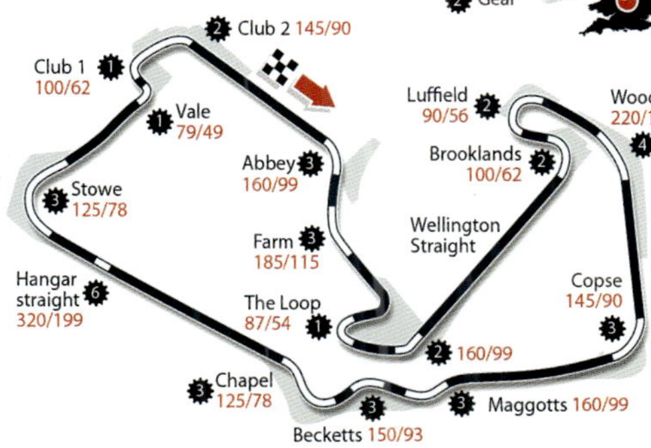

Championship Points

Pos	Rider	Points
1	Marquez	201
2	Rossi	142
3	Lorenzo	130
4	Dovizioso	129
5	Vinales	113
6	Petrucci	105
7	Zarco	104
8	Crutchlow	103
9	Iannone	84
10	Rins	66
11	Pedrosa	66
12	Miller	61
13	Bautista	57
14	Rabat	35
15	P. Espargaro	32
16	Syahrin	24
17	Morbidelli	22
18	A. Espargaro	17
19	Smith	15
20	Redding	12
21	Nakagami	11
22	Kallio	6
23	Abraham	4

Constructor Points

Pos	Constructor	Points
1	Honda	236
2	Ducati	208
3	Yamaha	183
4	Suzuki	118
5	KTM	41
6	Aprilia	27

Moto2 Race cancelled due to track conditions.

Rider	Nat.	No.	Entrant	Machine
Steven Odendaal	RSA	4	NTS RW Racing GP	NTS
Andrea Locatelli	ITA	5	Italtrans Racing Team	Kalex
Lorenzo Baldassarri	ITA	7	Pons HP40	Kalex
Jorge Navarro	SPA	9	Federal Oil Gresini Moto2	Kalex
Luca Marini	ITA	10	SKY Racing Team VR46	Kalex
Romano Fenati	ITA	13	Marinelli Snipers Team	Kalex
Joe Roberts	USA	16	NTS RW Racing GP	NTS
Xavi Cardelus	AND	18	Team Stylobike	Kalex
Fabio Quartararo	FRA	20	MB Conveyors - Speed Up Racing	Speed Up
Federico Fuligni	ITA	21	Tasca Racing Scuderia Moto2	Kalex
Sam Lowes	GBR	22	Swiss Innovative Investors	KTM
Marcel Schrotter	GER	23	Dynavolt Intact GP	Kalex
Simone Corsi	ITA	24	Tasca Racing Scuderia Moto2	Kalex
Iker Lecuona	SPA	27	Swiss Innovative Investors	KTM
Isaac Vinales	SPA	32	SAG Team	Kalex
Joan Mir	SPA	36	EG 0,0 Marc VDS	Kalex
Augusto Fernandez	SPA	40	Pons HP40	Kalex
Brad Binder	RSA	41	Red Bull KTM Ajo	KTM
Francesco Bagnaia	ITA	42	SKY Racing Team VR46	Kalex
Miguel Oliveira	POR	44	Red Bull KTM Ajo	KTM
Tetsuta Nagashima	JPN	45	IDEMITSU Honda Team Asia	Kalex
Eric Granado	BRA	51	Forward Racing Team	Suter
Danny Kent	GBR	52	MB Conveyors - Speed Up Racing	Speed Up
Mattia Pasini	ITA	54	Italtrans Racing Team	Kalex
Alejandro Medina	SPA	55	SAG Team	Kalex
Stefano Manzi	ITA	62	Forward Racing Team	Suter
Bo Bendsneyder	NED	64	Tech 3 Racing	Tech 3
Josh Owens	GBR	65	Tickhill Labour and Plant	Kalex
Niki Tuuli	FIN	66	SIC Racing Team	Kalex
Alex Marquez	SPA	73	EG 0,0 Marc VDS	Kalex
Dominique Aegerter	SWI	77	Kiefer Racing	KTM
Remy Gardner	AUS	87	Tech 3 Racing	Tech 3
Khairul Idham Pawi	MAL	89	IDEMITSU Honda Team Asia	Kalex
Jules Danilo	FRA	95	Nashi Argan SAG Team	Kalex
Xavi Vierge	SPA	97	Dynavolt Intact GP	Kalex

Qualifying

Weather: Dry

Air Temp: 24° **Track Temp:** 47°

Humidity: 41%

1	Bagnaia	2m 08.153s
2	Gardner	2m 08.347s
3	Marquez	2m 08.411s
4	Schrotter	2m 08.442s
5	Marini	2m 08.643s
6	Quartararo	2m 08.756s
7	Pasini	2m 08.772s
8	Lecuona	2m 08.774s
9	Lowes	2m 08.785s
10	Fenati	2m 08.908s
11	Vierge	2m 08.921s
12	Baldassarri	2m 08.976s
13	Locatelli	2m 09.007s
14	Mir	2m 09.041s
15	Fernandez	2m 09.129s
16	Binder	2m 09.252s
17	Aegerter	2m 09.301s
18	Bendsneyder	2m 09.323s
19	Tuuli	2m 09.578s
20	Roberts	2m 09.582s
21	Nagashima	2m 09.706s
22	Navarro	2m 09.838s
23	Oliveira	2m 09.968s
24	Manzi	2m 09.994s
25	Odendaal	2m 10.112s
26	Kent	2m 10.285s
27	Pawi	2m 10.888s
28	Owens	2m 11.033s
29	Danilo	2m 11.522s
30	Fuligni	2m 12.355s
31	Medina	2m 12.847s
32	Corsi	2m 13.871s
33	Cardelus	2m 14.055s

Moto3 Race cancelled due to track conditions.

Rider	Nat.	No.	Entrant	Machine
Jaume Masia	SPA	5	Bester Capital Dubai	KTM
Adam Norrodin	MAL	7	Petronas Sprinta Racing	Honda
Nicolo Bulega	ITA	8	SKY Racing Team VR46	KTM
Dennis Foggia	ITA	10	SKY Racing Team VR46	KTM
Marco Bezzecchi	ITA	12	Redox PruestelGP	KTM
Tony Arbolino	ITA	14	Marinelli Snipers Team	Honda
Andrea Migno	ITA	16	Angel Nieto Team Moto3	KTM
John McPhee	GBR	17	CIP - Green Power	KTM
Gabriel Rodrigo	ARG	19	RBA BOE Skull Rider	KTM
Jake Archer	GBR	20	City Lifting RS Racing	KTM
Fabio Di Giannantonio	ITA	21	Del Conca Gresini Moto3	Honda
Kazuki Masaki	JPN	22	RBA BOE Skull Rider	KTM
Niccolo Antonelli	ITA	23	SIC58 Squadra Corse	Honda
Tatsuki Suzuki	JPN	24	SIC58 Squadra Corse	Honda
Raul Fernandez	SPA	25	Red Bull KTM Ajo	KTM
Kaito Toba	JPN	27	Honda Team Asia	Honda
Enea Bastianini	ITA	33	Leopard Racing	Honda
Nakarin Atiratphuvapat	THA	41	Honda Team Asia	Honda
Marcos Ramirez	SPA	42	Bester Capital Dubai	KTM
Aron Canet	SPA	44	Estrella Galicia 0,0	Honda
Lorenzo Dalla Porta	ITA	48	Leopard Racing	Honda
Philipp Oettl	GER	65	Sudmetal Schedl GP Racing	KTM
Tom Booth-Amos	GBR	69	Leopard Racing	Honda
Ayumu Sasaki	JPN	71	Petronas Sprinta Racing	Honda
Alonso Lopez	SPA	72	Estrella Galicia 0,0	Honda
Albert Arenas	SPA	75	Angel Nieto Team Moto3	KTM
Vicente Perez	SPA	77	Reale Avintia Academy 77	KTM
Stefano Nepa	ITA	81	CIP - Green Power	KTM
Jakub Kornfeil	CZE	84	Redox PruestelGP	KTM
Jorge Martin	SPA	88	Del Conca Gresini Moto3	Honda

Qualifying

Weather: Dry

Air Temp: 24° **Track Temp:** 47°

Humidity: 41%

1	Martin	2m 13.292s
2	Masia	2m 13.293s
3	Dalla Porta	2m 13.313s
4	Arenas	2m 13.443s
5	Di Giannantonio	2m 13.574s
6	Suzuki	2m 13.819s
7	Rodrigo	2m 13.839s
8	Bastianini	2m 13.885s
9	Bulega	2m 13.899s
10	Ramirez	2m 13.940s
11	Bezzecchi	2m 13.962s
12	Antonelli	2m 14.009s
13	Canet	2m 14.035s
14	Oettl	2m 14.052s
15	Norrodin	2m 14.060s
16	Masaki	2m 14.140s
17	Kornfeil	2m 14.183s
18	Arbolino	2m 14.284s
19	McPhee	2m 14.311s
20	Sasaki	2m 14.370s
21	Foggia	2m 14.603s
22	Lopez	2m 14.946s
23	Perez	2m 15.022s
24	Atiratphuvapat	2m 15.058s
25	Migno	2m 15.134s
26	Toba	2m 15.171s
27	Binder	2m 15.424s
28	Booth-Amos	2m 15.969s
29	Nepa	2m 16.098s
30	Archer	2m 17.227s

FIM WORLD CHAMPIONSHIP · ROUND 13

SAN MARINO GRAND PRIX

MISANO WORLD CIRCUIT MARCO SIMONCELLI

Delight for Dovi and Ducati after victory on home turf.
Photos: Gold & Goose

Above: Disqualified and vilified. Romano Fenati ended his race – and probably his career – in disgrace.

Above centre: Electrifying – the five-round 2019 MotoE World Cup was formally announced.

Top: Arms firmly folded, Rossi dismissed Marquez's proffered handshake.

Top right: Lorenzo took a second successive pole.

Photos: Gold & Goose

POLES apart, there were two different displays of Italian temperament at Misano, each of them in the full glare of the television cameras, and each in its way more or less scandalous.

Perhaps 'scandalous' is too strong a word for Valentino Rossi's icy public refusal to shake hands with Marc Marquez, although given the status of the participants, it was still important enough, and sufficiently arrogant and ill-tempered to remind everybody that motorcycle racing is (in the immortal words of Max Biaggi) not chamber music.

Romano Fenati performed a different kind of handshake, which provoked scandal across the full spectrum of world opinion, from tut-tutting disapproval in major newspapers to hysterical death threats on social media. And which cost a talented rider his career.

In all conscience, his behaviour was ridiculous, even for a hothead who had been in trouble several times before, including for kicking out at Niklas Ajo and then hitting his kill switch in morning warm-up in the Argentine in 2015; then getting the boot from Rossi's SKY Moto3 team for losing his temper once too often in the pit.

In the Moto2 race, Fenati and multiple crasher Stefano Manzi were embroiled in a big gang disputing 11th. Fenati had worked his way through to near the front of it by lap 16, but Manzi fought back in his usual headstrong manner, taking both of them on to the run-off area and to the back of the group.

Fenati was so cross that when he managed to catch his assailant a couple of laps later, he pulled alongside on the pit straight, leaned across and squeezed his front brake lever.

It was outrageous – both hugely amusing and viciously dangerous. Manzi wobbled, but didn't crash, although very soon afterwards he did, for a 22nd time in 2018. Fenati pitted and rejoined, only to be black-flagged. And that was just the start of it. Within hours, he had been suspended for two races by Race Direction; within a day, sacked by his prospective 2019 Italtrans team (for whom Manzi had ridden in 2018) and also his current Marinelli Snipers team. The Italian federation suspended his racing licence, and soon after that, the FIM extended his two-race ban to six.

By then, there was an international furore, with people who knew little about racing and probably had never heard of him baying for his blood. Fenati himself apologised, and announced that he would quit racing forthwith. A sad end for a rider who was always both promising and exciting.

The Rossi-Marquez incident in the pre-event press conference was much calmer. During the break, a Marquez interview revealed that he'd be happy to "make peace" with Rossi. Well then, came a question, would you shake hands? Marquez gave his best PR-friendly smile and reached across. Rossi kept his arms folded, saying, "It sounds to me a bit strange, because in reality we don't have any problems between me and Marc. So I don't know why we have to 'make peace'. For me, it's okay." He briefly glanced at his rival; and the next day, he told Italian media that personal relationships were unimportant. "It is not written anywhere that we must go out to dinner." Some deplored that Rossi had not taken the opportunity to cool the poisonous atmosphere that meant Marquez faced boos on the podium, but this showed a misunderstanding of the nature of their rivalry. In terms of racing, each drew strength from it. Rossi in particular also made money, with boosted sales of merchandising tat.

(There was somebody else with whom Rossi did not shake hands, for he was not included in an unusual pre-event promotion at the Vatican City, where the Pope granted an audience to Marquez, Pedrosa, Miller, Dorna's Carmelo Ezpeleta and others, and affably discussed the spiritual importance of sport. His Holiness's reaction to not being granted an audience with Rossi was not recorded.)

Marquez failed to perform one of his miracle saves in Q2, but accomplished another astonishing feat. On his feet before he had stopped sliding and on a scooter directly after-

Top: Tipping point. For once, Marquez didn't save the crash.

Above: The Repsol Honda cartwheels through the gravel.

Left: Up and at 'em! Marquez sees at a glance that his bike is unfit to continue.

Below left: The world champion races back to the pits for his spare.
Photos: Gold & Goose

wards, he sprinted through his pit to get back out on his second bike just 135 seconds after falling. Only then did he discover that he had a piece of grit in his eye, which spoiled his final attempt for pole.

The Reale Avintia team blamed short notice and a lack of suitable candidates for their choice of a grand prix novice, Christophe Ponsson, to replace the injured Rabat, though it became clear when he was banned from the next round that the Frenchman had actually paid for the seat for four races. For now, riders were adamant that a GP weekend was not the right time or place for anybody to make first acquaintance with a MotoGP bike. Ponsson used Xavier Simeon's bits-and-pieces Ducati, the Belgian being promoted to Rabat's GP17, and generally managed to keep out of the way, although almost lapped twice.

Simeon, meanwhile, was also on sufferance, accused of underperforming and having had his two-year contract cut in half. His seat for 2019 would go instead to Karel Abraham, another rider who could bring finance.

Pol Espargaro was back on his KTM, though he pulled out of the race too weak to continue. He and team-mate Smith were riding the 2019 prototype with the backward-spin crankshaft (and a newly be-winged fairing) for its first full race since tester Kallio had taken it to tenth at Jerez. KTM are notoriously close with information, so it was a touch awkward when news broke at Misano that Smith, having close acquaintance with their future plans, would be joining Aprilia's upgraded factory test team for 2019, with a few wild-card rides thrown in.

The provisional 2019 calendar was released, identical to 2018's, with the British GP at Silverstone included, at least for the present. At the same time, the five venues for the new MotoE championship were also confirmed – Jerez, Le Mans, Sachsenring, Red Bull Ring and Misano.

Brembo published another late-braking sheet, not from the daunting first of three reducing-speed right-handers at the end of the main straight, but from the Quercia corner earlier on the lap, where speeds are cut from around 295km/h to less than 80 over 222m. After conceding to Marquez at Mugello, Dovizioso was back on top, then Marquez, Rossi, Crutchlow and Lorenzo.

MOTOGP RACE – 27 laps

Lorenzo claimed his third pole of the year with a new all-out record. Marquez's opportunity to better it had been lost in his dramatic fall. Miller was alongside the factory Duke, his first dry-weather front row, and a somewhat revived Vinales was third, crediting chassis and electronic improvements after the Aragon test. His hopes would prove ill-founded.

Dovi was displaced to lead row two, from Marquez and Crutchlow; Rossi headed the third. Morbidelli had got through from Q1, but – short of tyres – had tumbled without setting a time to remain 12th. Ponsson comfortably made the 107-per cent qualifying cut, but was last.

Sunday was hot and dry after evening rain on the previous days, with a crowd not far short of 100,000. Local idol Rossi was wearing a special 'Back to Misano' helmet (he had missed the previous year, injured), but was not able to reward his legion of fans.

Lorenzo took off in the lead, with Dovizioso second, ahead of Miller, by the end of lap one. The Australian would surrender third to Marquez next time around, then lose the front at the slowest corner, bamboozled by a full fuel load.

From there, the front three were on their own.

Dovi was surprised that Lorenzo didn't push harder in the early laps. "I passed him [on lap six] because I didn't want the heat from his bike." He set a new record three laps later, but expected to have to fight at the end. Instead, he had an advantage of a second by lap 11, better than two seconds six laps later.

Marquez overtook Lorenzo on lap 14, but admitted later that, with their acceleration advantage and strong braking,

Above: Promoted. Crutchlow was back on the podium after Lorenzo's Ducati demise.

Centre, from top: Rins leads Vinales and Pedrosa in the fight for fourth; Lorenzo is helped back on board his Ducati; a first Moto3 win for Italy's Dalla Porta.

Top far right: Moto2 winner Pecco Bagnaia seized control from the off – from Schrotter, Binder, Pasini (54) and the rest. Prominent in the pursuit pack, Marini (10), Quartararo (purple cowling) and behind him, runner-up Oliveira.

Above far right: Grand prix novice Christophe Ponsson was a controversial replacement for Rabat.

Below right: Close finish. Moto3 winner Dalla Porta was this far ahead of Martin and Di Giannantonio.

Photos: Gold & Goose

"it was because he made a mistake. I was only able to follow the Ducatis." Six laps later, after several close encounters between the two, that's what he was doing again. But he remained poised, and when Lorenzo pushed on lap 24 to cut Dovi's lead to less than two seconds for an end-of-race charge, Marquez went with him.

Thus he had a grandstand seat when the Ducati bounced under braking at Quercia corner, ran a little wide on the entry, then tucked the front and slid away for a rare Lorenzo race crash. He'd wanted to use the soft front tyre, but had been dissuaded, and now he had paid the price.

Vinales had been leading the pursuit when Miller fell, but soon succumbed to a charging Rins, who – with nothing to lose – had switched to the soft rear and pushed through from the fourth row. He had Crutchlow in his wake, and on lap nine, "he looked over his shoulder in a corner and gave me his place. I don't know why."

Crutchlow now had the benefit of clear air ahead and no risk of his front tyre overheating because of bikes in front, though "I'd rather have been in the front battle and managed it." He had a lonely ride to an eventual third, his first podium since victory in round two in Argentina.

Rins had continued to lose ground, but while Vinales had closed right up, he wasn't able to do anything more. After five laps, Pedrosa, up from 11th on the grid, had displaced Rossi and was pressing the other Yamaha. He too wouldn't get past, but was comfortably clear of Rossi by the finish.

Nor was there anything more than pressure from second Suzuki rider Iannone, who was within a second before dropping away in the last couple of laps.

Alvaro Bautista had a strong run through from 14th on lap one to tenth on lap nine, having passed Zarco and fast-starting Morbidelli on the way; but he would get no further, though promoted to ninth by Lorenzo's fall.

Zarco was next, and then Petrucci, in an undistinguished home race.

Morbidelli hung on to 12th, the best of what had become a big gang after 13th-placed Nakagami had gained speed in the latter stages, dropping off long-term companion Aleix Espargaro, who had wild-card Michele Pirro as close company over the line for the last point. Smith had lost touch with this group, but had got narrowly back in front of the remounted Lorenzo for 16th. Miller, also remounted, was 17th; then Syahrin, Abraham, Redding, Luthi and Ponsson followed along, the last almost two laps adrift.

Wild-card Stefan Bradl had been with the gang disputing the last points, but crashed out on lap 17. Returned injury victim Pol Espargaro retired, likewise Xavier Simeon, after falling and remounting.

Dovizioso took over second from Rossi in the championship table, but Marquez extended his lead still further.

MOTO2 RACE – 25 laps

Bagnaia's fifth pole of the year was also a new track record, but with the top 20 within a second, "I'll try to make a break early. I think it will be a tough race because the front tyre goes down a lot after ten or twelve laps."

Schrotter was second, Pasini third; Oliveira was ninth. Fenati qualified 22nd, just over a second down, and two places ahead of his nemesis, Manzi.

Bagnaia's strategy worked perfectly, and he led from first to last, adding another five points to his overall lead over second-placed Oliveira. Schrotter almost cost the Portuguese those points, closing at the end and making a last-lap lunge, only to run wide, nearly taking Oliveira with him.

Bagnaia's first-lap lead had been seven-tenths, with Pasini third, and about to pounce on Schrotter. A lap later, he had stretched it to better than a second.

Pasini closed briefly, but Bagnaia got the message, and just before half-distance, the gap was better than two seconds. "It was one of the longest races of my life, and maybe the best," Bagnaia said later.

Binder had finished lap one fourth from his second-row start. Team-mate Oliveira had started even more strongly from the third row, however, and was ahead of him next time around, and directly past Schrotter as well.

Now he had to hunt down the flying Pasini, and it took him until lap 17 before he could to mount a successful attack. At this point, he was more than three seconds adrift of Bagnaia and he had to settle for second. Once again, bad qualifying had cost him, "but we minimised the damage, and we're on the podium again."

Schrotter had followed him past Pasini, and a couple of laps later, Mir did the same, in an impressive run through from tenth on the grid. But his podium chances would be thwarted by a penalty for exceeding track limits, and he was obliged to drop back behind Pasini with three laps to go.

That left Schrotter for his risky last-lap lunge. He was still delighted with a long awaited first podium after 151 starts.

Behind Pasini and Mir, Baldassarri had come through from 11th on lap one to take sixth, at the end comfortably clear of Quartararo and Binder, with fading tyre grip.

Jorge Navarro had a strong ride to an erstwhile fifth, but

also was penalised and dropped to an eventual ninth. Vierge overcame the pain from his practice injury in Austria; Corsi was 11th, having escaped from the next group, led by Gardner's Tech 3 from Aegerter and Locatelli. SAG Kalex substitute rider Jesko Raffin took the last point, having started from the back of the grid following problems on the warm-up lap.

Marini's hopes of a fourth consecutive podium were dashed when he stopped in plumes of smoke on lap ten, a dislodged rear brake link rubbing on the tyre.

Luckless Alex Marquez had a third consecutive zero score after he was taken down on the first lap by apologetic fellow Spaniard Augusto Fernandez. That dropped him from third overall to sixth.

MOTO3 RACE – 23 laps

The championship took another twist in a crash-hit Moto3 race, and Martin was the beneficiary, a whisker-close second after twice narrowly escaping involvement in other riders' indiscretions.

Martin was 0.058 of a second behind first-time winner Lorenzo Dalla Porta; his team-mate Di Giannantonio a similar distance behind in third for an all-Honda podium. KTM-mounted Rodrigo had just lost touch.

They were the survivors of a five-bike crash on only the second lap, Martin having avoided involvement by microseconds. He had just overtaken charging teenager Jaume Masia when the Spaniard's KTM slid sideways and tipped him off under the wheels of the front pack. He took down Honda riders Bastianini, Canet and Sasaki, as well as Bulega (KTM). Sasaki suffered a fractured left arm; later, Canet was also diagnosed with a fractured shoulder.

That split the field, leaving five away up front, with erstwhile points leader Bezzecchi doing most of the leading.

Martin's second big fright came two laps from the end, when Bezzecchi high-sided right in front of him. He hit his rival's stricken bike, but stayed on board.

Kornfeil also narrowly survived the first crash to head the next group, from Arenas, Foggia and Darryn Binder, the South African's first top ten of the year. Migno and Antonelli had closed by the end.

The usual shuffling was complicated by 'drop one position' penalties for exceeding track limits: for Binder, Suzuki, Perez, Arenas, Foggia, Atiratphuvapat, Ramirez and Nepa, the last-named twice. McPhee crashed out.

Martin extended his championship lead over Bezzecchi to eight points; Di Giannantonio closed to 21 off second overall.

GP OCTO DI SAN MARINO E DELLA RIVIERA DI RIMINI

7-9 SEPTEMBER, 2018

MISANO WORLD CIRCUIT

27 laps
Length: 4.226 km / 2.626 miles
Width: 14m

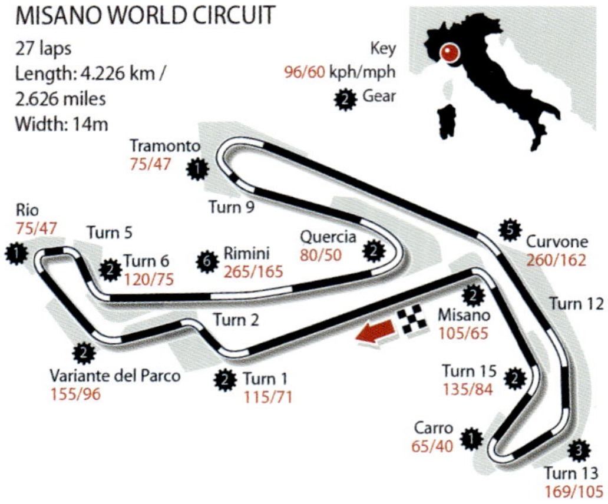

MotoGP

RACE DISTANCE: 27 laps, 70.900 miles/114.102km · RACE WEATHER: Dry (air 27°C, humidity 57%, track 41°C)

Pos.	Rider	Nat.	No.	Entrant	Machine	Tyres	Race tyre choice	Laps	Time & speed
1	**Andrea Dovizioso**	ITA	4	Ducati Team	Ducati Desmosedici	M	F: Medium/R: Medium	27	42m 05.426s 101.0mph/ 162.6km/h
2	**Marc Marquez**	SPA	93	Repsol Honda Team	Honda RC213V	M	F: Hard/R: Medium	27	42m 08.248s
3	**Cal Crutchlow**	GBR	35	LCR Honda CASTROL	Honda RC213V	M	F: Hard/R: Medium	27	42m 12.695s
4	**Alex Rins**	SPA	42	Team SUZUKI ECSTAR	Suzuki GSX-RR	M	F: Medium/R: Soft	27	42m 20.113s
5	**Maverick Vinales**	SPA	25	Movistar Yamaha MotoGP	Yamaha YZR-M1	M	F: Medium/R: Soft	27	42m 21.442s
6	**Dani Pedrosa**	SPA	26	Repsol Honda Team	Honda RC213V	M	F: Hard/R: Medium	27	42m 22.834s
7	**Valentino Rossi**	ITA	46	Movistar Yamaha MotoGP	Yamaha YZR-M1	M	F: Medium/R: Medium	27	42m 24.512s
8	**Andrea Iannone**	ITA	29	Team SUZUKI ECSTAR	Suzuki GSX-RR	M	F: Medium/R: Soft	27	42m 27.230s
9	**Alvaro Bautista**	SPA	19	Angel Nieto Team	Ducati Desmosedici	M	F: Soft/R: Soft	27	42m 29.345s
10	**Johann Zarco**	FRA	5	Monster Yamaha Tech 3	Yamaha YZR-M1	M	F: Soft/R: Soft	27	42m 32.985s
11	**Danilo Petrucci**	ITA	9	Alma Pramac Racing	Ducati Desmosedici	M	F: Medium/R: Medium	27	42m 36.124s
12	**Franco Morbidelli**	ITA	21	EG 0,0 Marc VDS	Honda RC213V	M	F: Hard/R: Medium	27	42m 38.367s
13	**Takaaki Nakagami**	JPN	30	LCR Honda IDEMITSU	Honda RC213V	M	F: Hard/R: Medium	27	42m 38.887s
14	**Aleix Espargaro**	SPA	41	Aprilia Racing Team Gresini	Aprilia RS-GP	M	F: Medium/R: Soft	27	42m 41.112s
15	**Michele Pirro**	ITA	51	Ducati Team	Ducati Desmosedici	M	F: Soft/R: Medium	27	42m 41.238s
16	Bradley Smith	GBR	38	Red Bull KTM Factory Racing	KTM RC16	M	F: Medium/R: Soft	27	42m 51.926s
17	Jorge Lorenzo	SPA	99	Ducati Team	Ducati Desmosedici	M	F: Medium/R: Medium	27	42m 52.040s
18	Jack Miller	AUS	43	Alma Pramac Racing	Ducati Desmosedici	M	F: Medium/R: Medium	27	42m 56.019s
19	Hafizh Syahrin	MAL	55	Monster Yamaha Tech 3	Yamaha YZR-M1	M	F: Medium/R: Soft	27	43m 00.594s
20	Karel Abraham	CZE	17	Angel Nieto Team	Ducati Desmosedici	M	F: Medium/R: Soft	27	43m 07.681s
21	Scott Redding	GBR	45	Aprilia Racing Team Gresini	Aprilia RS-GP	M	F: Medium/R: Soft	27	43m 14.901s
22	Thomas Luthi	SWI	12	EG 0,0 Marc VDS	Honda RC213V	M	F: Medium/R: Soft	27	43m 18.034s
23	Christophe Ponsson	FRA	23	Reale Avintia Racing	Ducati Desmosedici	M	F: Soft/R: Soft	26	43m 02.996s
	Stefan Bradl	GER	6	HRC Honda Team	Honda RC213V	M	F: Hard/R: Hard	17	DNF-crash
	Pol Espargaro	SPA	44	Red Bull KTM Factory Racing	KTM RC16	M	F: Medium/R: Soft	17	DNF-injured
	Xavier Simeon	BEL	10	Reale Avintia Racing	Ducati Desmosedici	M	F: Medium/R: Soft	2	DNF-crash

Fastest lap: Andrea Dovizioso, on lap 9, 1m 32.678s, 102.0mph/164.1km/h.
Lap record: Dani Pedrosa, 1m 32.979s, 101.7mph/163.6km/h (2016).
Event maximum speed: Andrea Dovizioso, 184.3mph/296.6km/h (warm-up).

Qualifying

Weather: Dry
Air Temp: 25° **Track Temp:** 39°
Humidity: 74%

1	Lorenzo	1m 31.629s
2	Miller	1m 31.916s
3	Vinales	1m 31.950s
4	Dovizioso	1m 32.003s
5	Marquez	1m 32.016s
6	Crutchlow	1m 32.025s
7	Rossi	1m 32.028s
8	Petrucci	1m 32.136s
9	Zarco	1m 32.250s
10	Rins	1m 32.338s
11	Pedrosa	1m 32.369s
12	Morbidelli	No Time
13	Iannone	1m 32.566s
14	Pirro	1m 32.624s
15	Bautista	1m 32.792s
16	A. Espargaro	1m 33.084s
17	Smith	1m 33.085s
18	Bradl	1m 33.361s
19	Nakagami	1m 33.437s
20	P. Espargaro	1m 33.502s
21	Redding	1m 33.572s
22	Simeon	1m 33.705s
23	Luthi	1m 33.755s
24	Abraham	1m 33.812s
25	Syahrin	1m 34.080s
26	Ponsson	1m 37.180s

Fastest race laps

1	Dovizioso	1m 32.678s
2	Lorenzo	1m 32.849s
3	Marquez	1m 32.891s
4	Crutchlow	1m 33.185s
5	Rins	1m 33.410s
6	Vinales	1m 33.488s
7	Iannone	1m 33.589s
8	Pedrosa	1m 33.608s
9	Morbidelli	1m 33.620s
10	Rossi	1m 33.631s
11	Petrucci	1m 33.666s
12	Bautista	1m 33.716s
13	Miller	1m 33.808s
14	Zarco	1m 33.953s
15	A. Espargaro	1m 33.968s
16	Pirro	1m 34.030s
17	Bradl	1m 34.098s
18	Nakagami	1m 34.292s
19	Smith	1m 34.304s
20	Syahrin	1m 34.393s
21	Redding	1m 34.459s
22	Abraham	1m 34.860s
23	P. Espargaro	1m 34.974s
24	Luthi	1m 35.413s
25	Simeon	1m 36.547s
26	Ponsson	1m 37.375s

Championship Points

1	Marquez	221
2	Dovizioso	154
3	Rossi	151
4	Lorenzo	130
5	Vinales	124
6	Crutchlow	119
7	Zarco	110
8	Petrucci	110
9	Iannone	92
10	Rins	79
11	Pedrosa	76
12	Bautista	64
13	Miller	61
14	Rabat	35
15	P. Espargaro	32
16	Morbidelli	26
17	Syahrin	24
18	A. Espargaro	19
19	Smith	15
20	Nakagami	14
21	Redding	12
22	Kallio	6
23	Abraham	4
24	Pirro	1

Constructor Points

1	Honda	256
2	Ducati	233
3	Yamaha	194
4	Suzuki	131
5	KTM	41
6	Aprilia	29

Grid order	1	2	3	4	5	6	7	8	9	10	11	12	13	14	15	16	17	18	19	20	21	22	23	24	25	26	27	
99 LORENZO	99	99	99	99	99	4	4	4	4	4	4	4	4	4	4	4	4	4	4	4	4	4	4	4	4	4	4	1
43 MILLER	4	4	4	4	4	99	99	99	99	99	99	99	99	93	93	93	93	93	99	99	99	99	99	99	99	93	93	2
25 VINALES	43	93	93	93	93	93	93	93	93	93	93	93	93	99	99	99	99	99	93	93	93	93	93	93	93	35	35	3
4 DOVIZIOSO	93	43	25	42	42	42	42	42	35	35	35	35	35	35	35	35	35	35	35	35	35	35	35	35	35	42	42	4
93 MARQUEZ	25	25	42	25	35	35	35	35	42	42	42	42	42	42	42	42	42	42	42	42	42	42	42	42	42	25	25	5
35 CRUTCHLOW	42	42	35	35	25	25	25	25	25	25	25	25	25	25	25	25	25	25	25	25	25	25	25	25	25	26	26	6
46 ROSSI	35	35	46	46	26	26	26	26	26	26	26	26	26	26	26	26	26	26	26	26	26	26	26	26	26	46	46	7
9 PETRUCCI	46	46	26	26	46	46	46	46	46	46	46	46	46	46	46	46	46	46	46	46	46	46	46	46	46	29	29	8
5 ZARCO	5	26	21	21	21	29	29	29	29	29	29	29	29	29	29	29	29	29	29	29	29	29	29	29	29	19	19	9
42 RINS	26	21	29	29	29	21	21	21	19	19	19	19	19	19	19	19	19	19	19	19	19	19	19	19	19	5	5	10
26 PEDROSA	9	9	9	9	9	9	19	19	21	21	21	5	5	5	5	5	5	5	5	5	5	5	5	5	5	9	9	11
21 MORBIDELLI	21	29	5	5	5	5	5	5	5	5	5	21	21	21	21	21	21	9	9	9	9	9	9	9	9	21	21	12
29 IANNONE	29	5	19	19	19	19	9	9	9	9	9	9	9	9	9	9	9	21	21	21	21	21	21	21	21	30	30	13
51 PIRRO	19	19	41	41	41	41	41	41	41	30	30	30	30	30	30	30	30	30	30	30	30	30	30	30	30	41	41	14
19 BAUTISTA	30	41	30	30	30	30	30	30	30	41	41	41	41	41	41	41	41	41	41	41	41	41	41	41	41	51	51	15
41 A. ESPARGARO	41	30	38	38	38	38	38	38	38	38	38	38	38	51	51	51	51	51	51	51	51	51	51	51	51	99	38	
38 SMITH	6	38	6	6	6	6	6	6	6	6	51	51	51	6	6	6	6	38	38	38	38	38	38	38	38	38	99	
6 BRADL	38	6	44	51	51	51	51	51	51	51	6	6	6	38	38	38	38	55	55	55	55	55	55	55	43	43	43	
30 NAKAGAMI	44	44	51	44	44	44	44	44	44	44	55	55	55	55	55	55	55	17	17	17	43	43	43	43	55	55	55	
44 P. ESPARGARO	51	45	45	45	55	55	55	55	55	55	44	44	44	44	44	44	44	43	43	43	17	17	17	17	17	17	17	
45 REDDING	45	51	17	55	45	17	17	17	17	17	17	17	17	17	17	17	17	12	12	12	12	12	12	45	45	45	45	
10 SIMEON	12	17	55	17	17	12	12	12	12	12	12	12	12	12	43	43	43	45	45	45	45	45	45	12	12	12	12	
12 LUTHI	17	12	12	12	12	45	45	45	45	43	43	43	43	43	12	12	12	23	23	23	23	23	23	23	23	23		
17 ABRAHAM	10	55	23	23	43	43	43	43	43	45	45	45	45	45	45	45	45											
55 SYAHRIN	55	10	43	43	23	23	23	23	23	23	23	23	23	23	23	23	23											
23 PONSSON	23	23																										

10 Pit stop 23 Lapped rider

Moto2

RACE DISTANCE: 25 laps, 65.648 miles/105.650km · RACE WEATHER: Dry (air 26°C, humidity 64%, track 39°C)

Pos.	Rider	Nat.	No.	Entrant	Machine	Laps	Time & Speed
1	**Francesco Bagnaia**	ITA	42	SKY Racing Team VR46	Kalex	25	41m 02.106s 95.9mph/ 154.4km/h
2	**Miguel Oliveira**	POR	44	Red Bull KTM Ajo	KTM	25	41m 05.214s
3	**Marcel Schrotter**	GER	23	Dynavolt Intact GP	Kalex	25	41m 06.200s
4	**Mattia Pasini**	ITA	54	Italtrans Racing Team	Kalex	25	41m 08.426s
5	**Joan Mir**	SPA	36	EG 0,0 Marc VDS	Kalex	25	41m 08.834s
6	**Lorenzo Baldassarri**	ITA	7	Pons HP40	Kalex	25	41m 11.576s
7	**Fabio Quartararo**	FRA	20	+ Ego Speed Up Racing	Speed Up	25	41m 14.174s
8	**Brad Binder**	RSA	41	Red Bull KTM Ajo	KTM	25	41m 14.240s
9	**Jorge Navarro**	SPA	9	Federal Oil Gresini Moto2	Kalex	25	41m 19.531s
10	**Xavi Vierge**	SPA	97	Dynavolt Intact GP	Kalex	25	41m 24.092s
11	**Simone Corsi**	ITA	24	Tasca Racing Scuderia Moto2	Kalex	25	41m 26.807s
12	**Remy Gardner**	AUS	87	Tech 3 Racing	Tech 3	25	41m 27.688s
13	**Dominique Aegerter**	SWI	77	Kiefer Racing	KTM	25	41m 27.866s
14	**Andrea Locatelli**	ITA	5	Italtrans Racing Team	Kalex	25	41m 28.824s
15	**Jesko Raffin**	SWI	2	Temporary Lavorint SAG Team	Kalex	25	41m 33.274s
16	Joe Roberts	USA	16	NTS RW Racing GP	NTS	25	41m 40.813s
17	Steven Odendaal	RSA	4	NTS RW Racing GP	NTS	25	41m 41.538s
18	Alex Marquez	SPA	73	EG 0,0 Marc VDS	Kalex	25	41m 41.657s
19	Iker Lecuona	SPA	27	Swiss Innovative Investors	KTM	25	41m 42.542s
20	Bo Bendsneyder	NED	64	Tech 3 Racing	Tech 3	25	41m 43.920s
21	Niki Tuuli	FIN	66	Petronas Sprinta Racing	Kalex	25	41m 50.149s
22	Khairul Idham Pawi	MAL	89	IDEMITSU Honda Team Asia	Kalex	25	41m 55.496s
23	Jules Danilo	FRA	95	Nashi Argan SAG Team	Kalex	25	42m 07.711s
24	Federico Fuligni	ITA	21	Tasca Racing Scuderia Moto2	Kalex	25	42m 18.708s
25	Xavi Cardelus	AND	18	Team Stylobike	Kalex	25	42m 33.356s
	Augusto Fernandez	SPA	40	Pons HP40	Kalex	21	DNF
	Stefano Manzi	ITA	62	Forward Racing Team	Suter	18	DNF
	Tetsuta Nagashima	JPN	45	IDEMITSU Honda Team Asia	Kalex	15	DNF
	Sheridan Morais	POR	12	Willi Race Racing Team	Kalex	13	DNF
	Sam Lowes	GBR	22	Swiss Innovative Investors	KTM	11	DNF
	Luca Marini	ITA	10	SKY Racing Team VR46	Kalex	9	DNF
	Danny Kent	GBR	52	+ Ego Speed Up Racing	Speed Up	1	DNF
	Romano Fenati	ITA	13	Marinelli Snipers Team	Kalex	-	DSQ

Fastest lap: Mattia Pasini, on lap 3, 1m 37.860s, 96.6mph/155.4km/h.

Lap record: Jonas Folger, 1m 37.422s, 97.0mph/156.1km/h (2015).

Event maximum speed: Miguel Oliveira, 159.4mph/256.6km/h (warm-up).

Qualifying

Weather: Dry

Air Temp: 25° **Track Temp:** 39°

Humidity: 71%

1	Bagnaia	1m 37.121s
2	Schrotter	1m 37.331s
3	Pasini	1m 37.416s
4	Quartararo	1m 37.540s
5	Binder	1m 37.621s
6	Navarro	1m 37.632s
7	Marini	1m 37.645s
8	Marquez	1m 37.661s
9	Oliveira	1m 37.678s
10	Mir	1m 37.714s
11	Vierge	1m 37.774s
12	Fernandez	1m 37.826s
13	Baldassarri	1m 37.834s
14	Aegerter	1m 37.954s
15	Lowes	1m 37.970s
16	Nagashima	1m 37.974s
17	Raffin	1m 37.982s
18	Lecuona	1m 38.010s
19	Gardner	1m 38.050s
20	Locatelli	1m 38.053s
21	Corsi	1m 38.156s
22	Fenati	1m 38.160s
23	Bendsneyder	1m 38.317s
24	Manzi	1m 38.505s
25	Odendaal	1m 38.671s
26	Roberts	1m 38.732s
27	Pawi	1m 38.766s
28	Tuuli	1m 39.128s
29	Danilo	1m 39.496s
30	Fuligni	1m 39.626s
31	Kent	1m 39.685s
32	Vinales	1m 40.591s
33	Morais	1m 40.600s
34	Cardelus	1m 40.647s

Fastest race laps

1	Pasini	1m 37.860s
2	Bagnaia	1m 37.931s
3	Oliveira	1m 38.026s
4	Navarro	1m 38.047s
5	Schrotter	1m 38.075s
6	Mir	1m 38.168s
7	Baldassarri	1m 38.201s
8	Fernandez	1m 38.203s
9	Marquez	1m 38.216s
10	Vierge	1m 38.236s
11	Quartararo	1m 38.385s
12	Fenati	1m 38.400s
13	Binder	1m 38.401s
14	Manzi	1m 38.451s
15	Nagashima	1m 38.472s
16	Gardner	1m 38.540s
17	Lowes	1m 38.579s
18	Marini	1m 38.580s
19	Lecuona	1m 38.596s
20	Locatelli	1m 38.644s
21	Corsi	1m 38.699s
22	Raffin	1m 38.700s
23	Aegerter	1m 38.741s
24	Roberts	1m 39.128s
25	Odendaal	1m 39.220s
26	Bendsneyder	1m 39.322s
27	Tuuli	1m 39.563s
28	Pawi	1m 39.615s
29	Danilo	1m 39.804s
30	Fuligni	1m 39.898s
31	Cardelus	1m 40.758s
32	Morais	1m 41.145s

Championship Points

1	Bagnaia	214
2	Oliveira	206
3	Binder	119
4	Baldassarri	116
5	Mir	114
6	Marquez	113
7	Schrotter	107
8	Vierge	96
9	Pasini	95
10	Quartararo	93
11	Marini	79
12	Navarro	49
13	Lowes	46
14	Lecuona	41
15	Corsi	37
16	Locatelli	34
17	Aegerter	27
18	Gardner	24
19	Fenati	14
20	Fernandez	11
21	Barbera	10
22	Manzi	8
23	Kent	8
24	Vinales	7
25	Nagashima	7
26	Roberts	2
27	Pawi	1
28	Odendaal	1
29	Raffin	1

Constructor Points

1	Kalex	276
2	KTM	218
3	Speed Up	97
4	Tech 3	24
5	Suter	8
6	NTS	2

Moto3

RACE DISTANCE: 23 laps, 60.396 miles/97.198km · RACE WEATHER: Dry (air 27°C, humidity 63%, track 37°C)

Pos.	Rider	Nat.	No.	Entrant	Machine	Laps	Time & Speed
1	**Lorenzo Dalla Porta**	ITA	48	Leopard Racing	Honda	23	39m 38.684s 91.4mph/ 147.1km/h
2	**Jorge Martin**	SPA	88	Del Conca Gresini Moto3	Honda	23	39m 38.742s
3	**Fabio Di Giannantonio**	ITA	21	Del Conca Gresini Moto3	Honda	23	39m 38.806s
4	**Gabriel Rodrigo**	ARG	19	RBA BOE Skull Rider	KTM	23	39m 39.506s
5	**Jakub Kornfeil**	CZE	84	Redox PruestelGP	KTM	23	39m 45.237s
6	**Albert Arenas**	SPA	75	Angel Nieto Team Moto3	KTM	23	39m 45.543s
7	**Dennis Foggia**	ITA	10	SKY Racing Team VR46	KTM	23	39m 45.999s
8	**Darryn Binder**	RSA	40	Red Bull KTM Ajo	KTM	23	39m 46.064s
9	**Andrea Migno**	ITA	16	Angel Nieto Team Moto3	KTM	23	39m 47.292s
10	**Niccolo Antonelli**	ITA	23	SIC58 Squadra Corse	Honda	23	39m 47.537s
11	**Tony Arbolino**	ITA	14	Marinelli Snipers Team	Honda	23	39m 49.092s
12	**Adam Norrodin**	MAL	7	Petronas Sprinta Racing	Honda	23	39m 49.467s
13	**Kaito Toba**	JPN	27	Honda Team Asia	Honda	23	40m 06.501s
14	**Vicente Perez**	SPA	77	Reale Avintia Academy 77	KTM	23	40m 06.581s
15	**Kazuki Masaki**	JPN	22	RBA BOE Skull Rider	KTM	23	40m 06.746s
16	Marcos Ramirez	SPA	42	Bester Capital Dubai	KTM	23	40m 25.839s
17	Stefano Nepa	ITA	81	CIP - Green Power	KTM	23	40m 13.069s
18	Nakarin Atiratphuvapat	THA	41	Honda Team Asia	Honda	23	40m 26.194s
19	Yari Montella	ITA	55	SIC58 Squadra Corse	Honda	23	40m 26.261s
20	Kevin Zannoni	ITA	3	TM Racing Factory 3570 MTA	TM RACING	22	39m 40.425s
	Marco Bezzecchi	ITA	12	Redox PruestelGP	KTM	21	DNF
	Tatsuki Suzuki	JPN	24	SIC58 Squadra Corse	Honda	19	DNF
	John McPhee	GBR	17	CIP - Green Power	KTM	11	DNF
	Jaume Masia	SPA	5	Bester Capital Dubai	KTM	1	DNF
	Aron Canet	SPA	44	Estrella Galicia 0,0	Honda	1	DNF
	Ayumu Sasaki	JPN	71	Petronas Sprinta Racing	Honda	1	DNF
	Enea Bastianini	ITA	33	Leopard Racing	Honda	1	DNF
	Nicolo Bulega	ITA	8	SKY Racing Team VR46	KTM	1	DNF
	Alonso Lopez	SPA	72	Estrella Galicia 0,0	Honda	1	DNF

Fastest lap: Gabriel Rodrigo, on lap 5, 1m 42.381s, 92.3mph/148.5km/h.

Lap record: Andrea Locatelli, 1m 42.627s, 92.1mph/148.2km/h (2016).

Event maximum speed: John McPhee, 129.9mph/209.1km/h (race).

Qualifying

Weather: Dry

Air Temp: 24° **Track Temp:** 38°

Humidity: 76%

1	Martin	1m 41.823s
2	Rodrigo	1m 42.134s
3	Canet	1m 42.270s
4	Di Giannantonio	1m 42.271s
5	Bastianini	1m 42.294s
6	Bezzecchi	1m 42.318s
7	Bulega	1m 42.355s
8	Dalla Porta	1m 42.442s
9	Kornfeil	1m 42.474s
10	Sasaki	1m 42.578s
11	Masia	1m 42.662s
12	Arbolino	1m 42.681s
13	Arenas	1m 42.694s
14	Norrodin	1m 42.790s
15	Antonelli	1m 42.860s
16	Suzuki	1m 43.071s
17	Toba	1m 43.227s
18	Zannoni	1m 43.282s
19	Migno	1m 43.328s
20	Foggia	1m 43.370s
21	Ramirez	1m 43.409s
22	Masaki	1m 43.410s
23	Binder	1m 43.632s
24	Oettl	1m 43.640s
25	McPhee	1m 43.830s
26	Atiratphuvapat	1m 43.962s
27	Perez	1m 44.163s
28	Montella	1m 44.233s
29	Nepa	1m 44.239s
30	Lopez	1m 44.556s

Fastest race laps

1	Rodrigo	1m 42.381s
2	Martin	1m 42.418s
3	Dalla Porta	1m 42.424s
4	Bezzecchi	1m 42.503s
5	Di Giannantonio	1m 42.557s
6	Ramirez	1m 42.607s
7	McPhee	1m 42.688s
8	Kornfeil	1m 42.748s
9	Foggia	1m 42.814s
10	Arbolino	1m 42.822s
11	Arenas	1m 42.902s
12	Migno	1m 42.907s
13	Antonelli	1m 42.921s
14	Norrodin	1m 42.960s
15	Suzuki	1m 42.968s
16	Binder	1m 42.976s
17	Masaki	1m 43.075s
18	Nepa	1m 43.492s
19	Perez	1m 43.699s
20	Toba	1m 43.755s
21	Atiratphuvapat	1m 43.777s
22	Montella	1m 43.954s
23	Zannoni	1m 44.100s

Championship Points

1	Martin	166
2	Bezzecchi	158
3	Di Giannantonio	137
4	Canet	118
5	Bastianini	117
6	Rodrigo	97
7	Kornfeil	91
8	Dalla Porta	88
9	Migno	67
10	Ramirez	67
11	Arenas	60
12	Antonelli	56
13	Oettl	54
14	Masia	54
15	McPhee	43
16	Suzuki	40
17	Arbolino	37
18	Sasaki	32
19	Lopez	31
20	Toba	29
21	Norrodin	28
22	Binder	28
23	Foggia	26
24	Fernandez	13
25	Yurchenko	9
26	Loi	8
27	Masaki	8
28	Bulega	7
29	Pagliani	6
30	Atiratphuvapat	2
31	Perez	2
32	Ogura	1

Constructor Points

1	Honda	266
2	KTM	229

FIM WORLD CHAMPIONSHIP · ROUND 14

ARAGON GRAND PRIX

ARAGON CIRCUIT

Inset, above: The Maniac puts his head in order.

Inset, above left: A clenched fist greets Marquez's first win since the summer break.

Inset, left: All puffed up – his airbag couldn't prevent luckless Lorenzo's painful foot injuries.
Photos: Gold & Goose

Inset, top: Iannone and Rins took third and fourth for Suzuki, which was enough for them to lose their concession-team status.
Photo: www.suzuki-racing.com

Main: Marquez, invincible again.
Photo: Gold & Goose

Above: Pole-starter Lorenzo loops out as his race goes haywire.

Top right: An outstanding effort by Aleix Espargaro gave Aprilia a best ever sixth.

Above right: Jordi Torres happily switched to MotoGP from WorldSBK as a more acceptable replacement for Reale Avintia's Rabat.

Photos: Gold & Goose

Right: Dovizioso led much of the race, but had to shadow Marquez at the end.

Photo: Repsol Honda

WHEN things go right, they keep going right. And vice versa. In the third of four outings at home in Spain, Marc Marquez and Jorge Lorenzo bore that out.

Marquez had just become the latest Spanish rider to have a corner that bore his name. When that happened to Lorenzo, at Jerez's final hairpin in 2013, he came off second best in a barging match with newcomer Marquez at that very spot. Naturally, he was very critical of the young rider's tactics.

It went the other way at Aragon, though Lorenzo didn't get as far as Turn Ten, the newly christened left-hander. In another barging match with the same rider, first time through the first corner, again he came off worse, but this time was precipitated into a vicious high-side and a heavy landing, which left him with costly and painful foot injuries: a dislocated toe and compound fracture of one metatarsal.

Once again, he muttered dark imprecations, blaming over-aggressive Marquez for pushing him wide on to the dirty part of the track, where he felt he had no option but to open the throttle early to avoid losing the advantage of his third straight pole.

And Marquez? He quite avoided the curse of the corner name and won his sixth victory, his first in four consecutive outings. When the luck is going your way…

This rule applied also to the increasingly beleaguered Yamaha troops, whose 23rd race without a win set an unwelcome new record for the factory, the worst run since they had joined the premier class in 1973. Again, Rossi was the better of the factory riders, but down in eighth, where in 2017 he had come back from injury to the podium.

For Vinales, a lonely tenth, things started to go sour on Saturday, when he was hit with a three-place grid penalty, dropping him to 14th. Along with Morbidelli, he was sanctioned for blocking Bradley Smith's KTM in Q1; Morbidelli by a more costly six grid places, for Vinales at least had tried to get out of the way.

Such penalties generally occurred in Moto3, and it was a busy weekend for sanctioning officials in that class. Thirteen penalties for dawdling in practice and qualifying may not have been a record, but it was the first time that the most severe of 2018's heavier punishment was unleashed, with rookie Dennis Foggia starting from the pit lane for a third offence. Migno, Antonelli, Rodrigo and Kornfeil were sent to the back of the grid (second offence), with mere 12-place penalties for erstwhile front-row qualifier Bastianini and second-row man Bezzecchi, who complained bitterly of unfairness after the race, insisting, "I was the only rider in qualifying who rode by himself." Also thus punished: wild-card Alcoba, Arbolino, Bulega, Dalla Porta, Fernandez and Masaki.

The baulking of Bradley was ill-timed, because he was on a run that might have put him through to Q2 for a second time in the season. Whether it would have lasted to the end of the session remained moot. Once again, he was the sole KTM rider after returnee Pol Espargaro had crashed again on Saturday morning, rebreaking the collarbone that he had fractured in his ruinous Brno tumble. He had chosen natural healing then; this time, he went straight back home for quick-fix surgery.

This was costly for KTM, still without main tester/back-up rider Kallio (a renewal of whose testing contract had just been confirmed). Reluctant to reveal detailed future plans to Aprilia-bound Smith, race boss Pit Beirer bemoaned "a terrible situation. We have so many things on our agenda, and we have been waiting six weeks for him [Pol] to return." This race and a following test had been important for finalising

the 2019 bike. "Now it looks like we will have to do it blind."

Rabat was sending out optimistic messages of an imminent return; his Avintia Reale team, meanwhile, had responded to criticism of their novice Misano substitute, replacing Ponsson with Superbike rider Jordi Torres. He was also a MotoGP beginner, and again riders looked askance, but at least he had GP experience, including a Moto2 win and two further podiums in 2013, and he rode impressively. An aggrieved Ponsson issued a statement that revealed he had paid to ride the Ducati for four races, and while he admitted his lack of experience, he said he'd intended for Misano to be a test, then to show his paces in subsequent events. In any case, all were subject to *force majeure*, as the GP Commission now responded to rider complaints: henceforth, substitute riders would be subject to the same selection committee as full-timers.

Aprilia joined the trend towards carbon-fibre swing-arms, with chief Romano Albesiano describing the main advantage as weight reduction, with development in stiffness ratios to follow. The Ducati and Honda factory riders were using them regularly; Crutchlow was still awaiting his, and frequently bemoaning the fact.

With Iannone's third podium added to Rins's two, Suzuki would now lose their concession-team status from the start of the next season, with engine allocation down from nine to seven, no more free testing by factory riders and no free engine development. This, boss Davide Brivio would say, was entirely positive: "It was our target ... to compete on equal terms with the other factories." And in any case, with a 19-race schedule, there hadn't been time to make much use of the right to test.

There was a formal launch of 2019's Triumph Moto2 engines, lined up on the grid in their packing cases, lacking only chassis and wheels (and riders). Encouraging reports had already filtered out from earlier tests; now Dorna reporter and former 500cc GP winner Simon Crafar had given the new bikes a ringing endorsement after his own Silverstone test. With one fewer cylinders and 165cc more than the Honda engines, the Triumphs yielded valuable increased torque and improved throttle response.

Double Superbike champion and former 500-class rider Troy Corser was at the track and revealed that he was in the market for a ride in 2019's new MotoE series. With Randy de Puniet and possibly also Bradley Smith on the list, another confirmed addition came in the following week: the Aspar team would be fielding former 125 champion Nico Terol.

MOTOGP RACE – 23 laps

The usual top three had dominated in qualifying: the Ducatis being rampant, Marquez's brinkmanship keeping him within hundredths of Lorenzo and Dovizioso. Said Dovi, "The life of the tyre we will understand during the race, but the speed is there."

Less than two-tenths down, Crutchlow headed row two, attempts to improve thwarted, as at Misano, by a late tumble, his second of the day. Iannone was alongside, then Pedrosa, his best showing since Jerez at the start of the European season.

Petrucci and Bautista headed Rins on row three. Vinales had got through from Q1, but his three-place penalty put him 14th, one down on Zarco; Rossi was 17th, his worst since he had been injured at Assen in 2006, and promoted there after Morbidelli was dropped to 19th.

The last race of the European season was as sunny as the first, and Marquez had to argue with Michelin and his team before they approved of his late gamble, changing to a soft rear tyre on the grid. A fall in warm-up had precipitated the risk. "It was a risk, because I'd never used it in the afternoon sessions, but I thought it would be the only way I could fight the Ducatis," he said.

Only Lorenzo chose the soft front, most of the rest going for the hardest of three options. For the rear, both Suzuki

Above: Nakagami (30) would eventually pass Bradley Smith for 12th, but Zarco (5) couldn't keep up.

Top right: Brad Binder took a clear second win of the year.

Top far right: With team-mate Oliveira nowhere to be seen, Binder was free to stamp his authority on Moto2.

Above right: Baldassarri has passed Schrotter on his way to joining the leaders.

Right: Martin sprints away. With his main rivals penalised, his plan for an early escape worked perfectly.

Below right: Starting from the sixth row, Bezzecchi stormed to the front of the pursuit pack for second, chased by Bastianini (33), Ramirez (42) and Di Giannantonio (21).

Photos: Gold & Goose

riders were also among six risking the soft; all the rest were on the hard.

With Lorenzo having looped out early, the front four were on their own throughout: Dovi straight into the lead, Marquez in hot pursuit, Iannone leading Rins.

The Suzukis swapped on lap three, then Pedrosa got ahead of Iannone briefly, only to be passed straight back. Iannone had been nursing his tyres.

The first half of the race looked like a dogged pursuit, and then on lap 12, Dovizioso pulled clear by three-quarters of a second. Was the chase over? It was not. The Ducati was strong under brakes and on the straight, but the Honda could close again through the long corners, especially Marquez's favourite left-handers, including his new namesake. Next time around, he was right on his tail, and used his better exit from Turns 10 and 11 to push ahead through Turn 12.

The game was afoot, and Iannone switched back to third as Dovi retook the lead two laps further on.

Rins remained a close spectator as it became a three-way fight for the lead, Iannone taking advantage as the other two traded blows. At one point on lap 18, they were side by side at the entrance to the straight, and while the Ducati's surging power put Dovi back in front, Marquez continued to push ahead now and again. "I could see he was sliding more, and I didn't want the race to go to the last corner as we did a few times last year," he said.

On lap 21, the two leaders changed places three times, and with two to go, Marquez gained enough daylight to remain invulnerable.

Dovi had to be content with second, albeit by only six-tenths. He found a positive side: "We did a huge step compared with last year. I couldn't really fight with Marc, but the podium confirms our improvement." In 2017, he'd finished seventh, although Lorenzo had been second.

Iannone was a similar distance behind and spoke of how the Suzuki's "fantastic chassis means we can gain a lot in fast corners, especially in the entry. But the Honda and Ducati are a lot faster on the straight. That is our weakness."

With Rins finally a second adrift, it was fairly processional behind him. Especially after Bautista crashed out on lap two and soon afterwards also Crutchlow, both of them from seventh position.

Pedrosa enjoyed a better than usual run because of the heat, but later bemoaned that he had not also switched to the soft rear. He had his hands full fending off a surprise pursuer, Aleix Espargaro, who did have the soft. Eventually he lost touch by some four seconds, but sixth still equalled Aprilia's best ever result.

Rossi had closed to within just over a second of a lone seventh-placed Petrucci by the end, salvaging some self-respect after starting on the sixth row. "I wasn't particularly fast, but I was consistent," he said.

His last victim had been Miller, nursing the bike home with a bad vibration, but still comfortably clear of the baffling Vinales, who finished lap one 19th, only picking up speed in the latter half of the race.

Morbidelli had been his final prey. He'd got to the front of a group from Nakagami, erstwhile leader Smith and, dropping away, Zarco.

Abraham took a lone last point, a couple of seconds clear of Redding, who got by the fading Luthi with two laps to go.

MOTO2 RACE – 21 laps

Binder took a first Moto2 pole at the track where in 2016 he had secured his Moto3 title, displacing Schrotter at the end by less than a tenth. Three-hundredths down, Navarro took his first front row, with an identical time to Marquez, but having set it earlier.

Bagnaia was alongside Marquez, then Pasini, with Quartararo and Baldassarri heading row three from Corsi. The top 19 were within a second of pole, Oliveira mired among them, at the far end of the sixth row.

Binder led away, but Marquez – anxious to put three consecutive zero scores behind him – flew off row two and took over as Binder ran wide into the fast final corner on lap two.

A couple of laps later, Bagnaia recovered from an average start to pass Schrotter and soon made it three up front.

As they passed half-distance, Marquez manfully resisted the growing pressure. Binder twice outbraked him into the first corner, only to be passed straight back. But the deed was finally done at Turn 12 on lap 15, and from then on,

Binder quickly gained a cushion that stretched to 1.5 seconds at the finish.

By half-distance, Baldassarri had left Schrotter and closed on the front trio. Then Bagnaia clipped Binder's back wheel at the last corner on lap 13, narrowly saving the crash and letting Baldassarri ahead.

The trio fought over second to the end. Bagnaia displaced Marquez with three laps to go; then Baldassarri finally battled past on lap 20 to deny him a home podium. Second to fourth were over the line in less than a second.

Binder was fresh from fruitful Valencia tests. Team-mate Oliveira also had a strong ride, but starting from 18th on the grid meant he could get no higher than a close seventh, behind Schrotter and Mir.

A couple of seconds behind, veteran Pasini managed to hold off Quartararo and Navarro to complete the top ten. Marini was less than a second behind, with Corsi out of touch by the finish.

Another four seconds away, Augusto Fernandez eventually outpaced Lecuona and Nagashima. Locatelli was less than two-tenths behind the Japanese, but out of the points after having to lose one place for exceeding track limits.

Manzi, Kent and Vierge crashed out; Sam Lowes was 20th after running off and rejoining. Kent's tumble, the tenth in a dire season for the former Moto3 champion, was the last straw for his Speed Up team. He had scored points only twice, and neither rider nor pit crew had gelled. It would be the Briton's last GP for the foreseeable future.

Bagnaia pronounced his second "important for the championship", as he extended his lead over Oliveira to 19 points. Binder took over third, ahead of Baldassarri and Marquez.

MOTO3 RACE – 19 laps

Martin waited until the very end to obliterate the record as well as the opposition for pole number nine. His 1m 57.066s was almost seven-tenths inside the previous best lap, and better than half a second clear of Masia, after a final flurry ended with Bastianini mere hundredths down. Arbolino and Foggia likewise nosed ahead of Bezzecchi on row two. Antonelli was seventh, but was dropped 12 grid places for dawdling.

The dominant Spaniard went on to make his first win since breaking his arm at Brno look easy. He kept stretching away while the rest scrapped. By the end, he was able to cruise and still win by almost six seconds.

He had a little help. Bezzecchi and Bastianini were among 13 shoved back down the grid, so gaining a crucial early lead was relatively untroubled.

Bezzecchi also had a fine fighting day. Starting from 18th, he'd joined the big chase group disputing second by half-distance. By the end, the gang had shrunk to six, with Bastianini seizing the last podium spot, inches behind Bezzecchi. Second to seventh was covered by just half a second, with Di Giannantonio fourth, then Ramirez, Suzuki and Arenas, two Hondas and two KTMs.

Norrodin and Masia, beaten up from a crash in warm-up, had lost the group by the end, with McPhee on their heels in tenth.

Canet started from the front row, but fell back rapidly and retired, in too much pain to continue. A scan discovered fractures in his shoulder blade from the Misano crash.

Rodrigo crashed out of the lead group; Antonelli also fell after working through to the top ten.

GRAN PREMIO MOVISTAR DE ARAGÓN

21–23 SEPTEMBER, 2018

MOTORLAND ARAGÓN

23 laps
Length: 5.077 km / 3.154 miles
Width: 15m

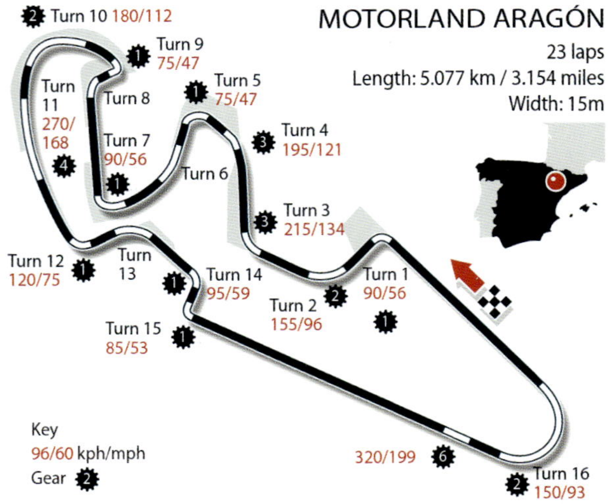

MotoGP

RACE DISTANCE: 23 laps, 72.558 miles/116.771km · RACE WEATHER: Dry (air 30°C, humidity 36%, track 45°C)

Pos.	Rider	Nat.	No.	Entrant	Machine	Tyres	Race tyre choice	Laps	Time & speed
1	**Marc Marquez**	SPA	93	Repsol Honda Team	Honda RC213V	M	F: Hard/R: Soft	23	41m 55.949s 103.8mph/ 167.0km/h
2	**Andrea Dovizioso**	ITA	4	Ducati Team	Ducati Desmosedici	M	F: Hard/R: Hard	23	41m 56.597s
3	**Andrea Iannone**	ITA	29	Team SUZUKI ECSTAR	Suzuki GSX-RR	M	F: Hard/R: Soft	23	41m 57.208s
4	**Alex Rins**	SPA	42	Team SUZUKI ECSTAR	Suzuki GSX-RR	M	F: Hard/R: Soft	23	41m 58.587s
5	**Dani Pedrosa**	SPA	26	Repsol Honda Team	Honda RC213V	M	F: Hard/R: Hard	23	42m 01.223s
6	**Aleix Espargaro**	SPA	41	Aprilia Racing Team Gresini	Aprilia RS-GP	M	F: Medium/R: Soft	23	42m 05.345s
7	**Danilo Petrucci**	ITA	9	Alma Pramac Racing	Ducati Desmosedici	M	F: Hard/R: Hard	23	42m 10.234s
8	**Valentino Rossi**	ITA	46	Movistar Yamaha MotoGP	Yamaha YZR-M1	M	F: Medium/R: Hard	23	42m 11.148s
9	**Jack Miller**	AUS	43	Alma Pramac Racing	Ducati Desmosedici	M	F: Hard/R: Hard	23	42m 12.324s
10	**Maverick Vinales**	SPA	25	Movistar Yamaha MotoGP	Yamaha YZR-M1	M	F: Hard/R: Hard	23	42m 18.406s
11	**Franco Morbidelli**	ITA	21	EG 0,0 Marc VDS	Honda RC213V	M	F: Hard/R: Hard	23	42m 22.974s
12	**Takaaki Nakagami**	JPN	30	LCR Honda IDEMITSU	Honda RC213V	M	F: Hard/R: Hard	23	42m 23.906s
13	**Bradley Smith**	GBR	38	Red Bull KTM Factory Racing	KTM RC16	M	F: Hard/R: Hard	23	42m 24.770s
14	**Johann Zarco**	FRA	5	Monster Yamaha Tech 3	Yamaha YZR-M1	M	F: Medium/R: Soft	23	42m 28.294s
15	**Karel Abraham**	CZE	17	Angel Nieto Team	Ducati Desmosedici	M	F: Hard/R: Hard	23	42m 33.588s
16	Scott Redding	GBR	45	Aprilia Racing Team Gresini	Aprilia RS-GP	M	F: Hard/R: Soft	23	42m 35.534s
17	Thomas Luthi	SWI	12	EG 0,0 Marc VDS	Honda RC213V	M	F: Hard/R: Hard	23	42m 36.712s
18	Hafizh Syahrin	MAL	55	Monster Yamaha Tech 3	Yamaha YZR-M1	M	F: Medium/R: Soft	23	42m 52.245s
19	Xavier Simeon	BEL	10	Reale Avintia Racing	Ducati Desmosedici	M	F: Medium/R: Hard	23	42m 54.930s
20	Jordi Torres	SPA	81	Reale Avintia Racing	Ducati Desmosedici	M	F: Medium/R: Hard	23	42m 55.462s
	Cal Crutchlow	GBR	35	LCR Honda CASTROL	Honda RC213V	M	F: Hard/R: Hard	4	DNF-crash
	Alvaro Bautista	SPA	19	Angel Nieto Team	Ducati Desmosedici	M	F: Medium/R: Soft	1	DNF-crash
	Jorge Lorenzo	SPA	99	Ducati Team	Ducati Desmosedici	M	F: Soft/R: Hard	0	DNF-crash
	Pol Espargaro	SPA	44	Red Bull KTM Factory Racing	KTM RC16	M	-	-	DNS-Injured

Fastest lap: Andrea Dovizioso, on lap 12, 1m 48.385s, 104.8mph/168.6km/h.
Lap record: Jorge Lorenzo, 1m 48.120s, 105.0mph/169.0km/h (2015).
Event maximum speed: Dani Pedrosa, 213.8mph/344.1km/h (qualifying).

Qualifying

Weather: Dry
Air Temp: 28° **Track Temp:** 46°
Humidity: 40%

1	Lorenzo	1m 46.881s
2	Dovizioso	1m 46.895s
3	Marquez	1m 46.960s
4	Crutchlow	1m 47.146s
5	Iannone	1m 47.169s
6	Pedrosa	1m 47.224s
7	Petrucci	1m 47.351s
8	Bautista	1m 47.678s
9	Rins	1m 47.737s
10	Miller	1m 47.792s
11	Vinales	1m 47.810s
12	Nakagami	1m 48.284s
13	Morbidelli	1m 48.009s
14	Zarco	1m 48.052s
15	A. Espargaro	1m 48.181s
16	Smith	1m 48.216s
17	Abraham	1m 48.398s
18	Rossi	1m 48.627s
19	Syahrin	1m 48.975s
20	Luthi	1m 48.988s
21	Redding	1m 49.303s
22	Simeon	1m 49.699s
23	Torres	1m 50.336s
	P. Espargaro	No Time

Fastest race laps

1	Dovizioso	1m 48.385s
2	Marquez	1m 48.478s
3	Iannone	1m 48.775s
4	Petrucci	1m 48.870s
5	Pedrosa	1m 48.904s
6	Rins	1m 49.014s
7	A. Espargaro	1m 49.083s
8	Crutchlow	1m 49.090s
9	Miller	1m 49.137s
10	Rossi	1m 49.256s
11	Morbidelli	1m 49.287s
12	Vinales	1m 49.361s
13	Syahrin	1m 49.443s
14	Zarco	1m 49.479s
15	Nakagami	1m 49.499s
16	Smith	1m 49.612s
17	Redding	1m 49.916s
18	Abraham	1m 49.927s
19	Luthi	1m 50.203s
20	Simeon	1m 50.864s
21	Torres	1m 51.163s

Championship Points

1	Marquez	246
2	Dovizioso	174
3	Rossi	159
4	Lorenzo	130
5	Vinales	130
6	Crutchlow	119
7	Petrucci	119
8	Zarco	112
9	Iannone	108
10	Rins	92
11	Pedrosa	87
12	Miller	68
13	Bautista	64
14	Rabat	35
15	P. Espargaro	32
16	Morbidelli	31
17	A. Espargaro	29
18	Syahrin	24
19	Smith	18
20	Nakagami	18
21	Redding	12
22	Kallio	6
23	Abraham	5
24	Pirro	1

Constructor Points

1	Honda	281
2	Ducati	253
3	Yamaha	202
4	Suzuki	147
5	KTM	44
6	Aprilia	39

Grid order		1	2	3	4	5	6	7	8	9	10	11	12	13	14	15	16	17	18	19	20	21	22	23	
99	LORENZO	4	4	4	4	4	4	4	4	4	4	4	4	4	93	93	4	4	4	4	4	93	93	93	1
4	DOVIZIOSO	93	93	93	93	93	93	93	93	93	93	93	93	93	4	4	93	93	93	93	93	4	4	4	2
93	MARQUEZ	29	29	42	42	42	42	42	42	42	42	42	42	42	29	29	29	29	29	29	29	29	29	29	3
35	CRUTCHLOW	42	42	29	29	29	29	29	29	29	29	29	29	29	42	42	42	42	42	42	42	42	42	42	4
29	IANNONE	26	26	26	26	26	26	26	26	26	26	26	26	26	26	26	26	26	26	26	26	26	26	26	5
26	PEDROSA	41	41	41	41	41	41	41	41	41	41	41	41	41	41	41	41	41	41	41	41	41	41	41	6
9	PETRUCCI	19	35	35	35	9	9	9	9	9	9	9	9	9	9	9	9	9	9	9	9	9	9	9	7
19	BAUTISTA	35	9	9	9	43	43	43	43	43	43	43	43	43	43	43	43	43	43	43	43	43	46	46	8
42	RINS	5	43	43	43	46	46	46	46	46	46	46	46	46	46	46	46	46	46	46	46	46	43	43	9
43	MILLER	9	5	5	5	5	5	5	5	5	5	38	38	38	25	25	25	25	25	25	25	25	25	25	10
30	NAKAGAMI	43	46	46	46	30	38	38	38	38	38	30	30	25	38	38	21	21	21	21	21	21	21	21	11
5	ZARCO	30	30	30	30	55	30	30	30	30	30	5	25	30	21	21	38	38	38	38	38	30	30	30	12
41	A. ESPARGARO	46	55	55	55	38	55	55	21	21	21	21	21	21	30	30	30	30	30	30	30	38	38	38	13
25	VINALES	55	38	38	38	21	21	21	25	25	25	25	5	5	5	5	5	5	5	5	5	5	5	5	14
38	SMITH	38	45	21	21	25	25	25	55	55	55	55	55	17	17	17	17	17	17	17	17	17	17	17	15
17	ABRAHAM	12	12	45	45	17	17	12	17	17	17	17	17	12	12	12	12	12	12	12	12	12	45	45	
46	ROSSI	45	21	25	25	12	12	17	12	12	12	12	12	55	45	45	45	45	45	45	45	45	12	12	
55	SYAHRIN	21	25	12	17	45	45	45	45	45	45	45	45	45	55	55	55	55	55	55	55	55	55	55	
21	MORBIDELLI	25	17	17	12	10	10	10	10	10	10	10	10	10	10	10	10	10	10	10	10	10	10	10	
12	LUTHI	17	10	10	10	81	81	81	81	81	81	81	81	81	81	81	81	81	81	81	81	81	81	81	
45	REDDING	10	81	81	81																				
10	SIMEON	81																							
81	TORRES																								

Moto2

RACE DISTANCE: 21 laps, 66.249 miles/106.617km · RACE WEATHER: Dry (air 28°C, humidity 38%, track 41°C)

Pos.	Rider	Nat.	No.	Entrant	Machine	Laps	Time & Speed
1	**Brad Binder**	RSA	41	Red Bull KTM Ajo	KTM	21	39m 59.247s 99.4mph/ 159.9km/h
2	**Francesco Bagnaia**	ITA	42	SKY Racing Team VR46	Kalex	21	40m 00.773s
3	**Lorenzo Baldassarri**	ITA	7	Pons HP40	Kalex	21	40m 01.302s
4	**Alex Marquez**	SPA	73	EG 0,0 Marc VDS	Kalex	21	40m 01.643s
5	**Marcel Schrotter**	GER	23	Dynavolt Intact GP	Kalex	21	40m 05.097s
6	**Joan Mir**	SPA	36	EG 0,0 Marc VDS	Kalex	21	40m 05.452s
7	**Miguel Oliveira**	POR	44	Red Bull KTM Ajo	KTM	21	40m 05.988s
8	**Mattia Pasini**	ITA	54	Italtrans Racing Team	Kalex	21	40m 08.897s
9	**Fabio Quartararo**	FRA	20	MB Conveyors - Speed Up	Speed Up	21	40m 08.993s
10	**Jorge Navarro**	SPA	9	Federal Oil Gresini Moto2	Kalex	21	40m 09.095s
11	**Luca Marini**	ITA	10	SKY Racing Team VR46	Kalex	21	40m 10.815s
12	**Simone Corsi**	ITA	24	Tasca Racing Scuderia Moto2	Kalex	21	40m 13.033s
13	**Augusto Fernandez**	SPA	40	Pons HP40	Kalex	21	40m 17.103s
14	**Iker Lecuona**	SPA	27	Swiss Innovative Investors	KTM	21	40m 18.479s
15	**Tetsuta Nagashima**	JPN	45	IDEMITSU Honda Team Asia	Kalex	21	40m 20.505s
16	Andrea Locatelli	ITA	5	Italtrans Racing Team	Kalex	21	40m 20.640s
17	Edgar Pons	SPA	57	AGR Team	Kalex	21	40m 25.800s
18	Steven Odendaal	RSA	4	NTS RW Racing GP	NTS	21	40m 26.994s
19	Remy Gardner	AUS	87	Tech 3 Racing	Tech 3	21	40m 27.586s
20	Sam Lowes	GBR	22	Swiss Innovative Investors	KTM	21	40m 31.073s
21	Dominique Aegerter	SWI	77	Kiefer Racing	KTM	21	40m 31.461s
22	Niki Tuuli	FIN	66	Petronas Sprinta Racing	Kalex	21	40m 34.208s
23	Jesko Raffin	SWI	2	SAG Team	Kalex	21	40m 35.816s
24	Joe Roberts	USA	16	NTS RW Racing GP	NTS	21	40m 36.390s
25	Bo Bendsneyder	NED	64	Tech 3 Racing	Tech 3	21	40m 41.469s
26	Jules Danilo	FRA	95	Nashi Argan SAG Team	Kalex	21	40m 52.804s
27	Khairul Idham Pawi	MAL	89	IDEMITSU Honda Team Asia	Kalex	18	40m 52.922s
28	Xavi Cardelus	AND	18	Marinelli Snipers Team	Kalex	15	41m 14.246s
	Xavi Vierge	SPA	97	Dynavolt Intact GP	Kalex	14	DNF
	Federico Fuligni	ITA	21	Tasca Racing Scuderia Moto2	Kalex	14	DNF
	Danny Kent	GBR	52	MB Conveyors - Speed Up	Speed Up	3	DNF
	Sheridan Morais	POR	12	Willi Race Racing Team	Kalex	3	DNF
	Stefano Manzi	ITA	62	Forward Racing Team	Suter	1	DNF

Fastest lap: Alex Marquez, on lap 2, 1m 53.479s, 100.0mph/161.0km/h.

Lap record: Alex Rins, 1m 52.767s, 100.7mph/162.1km/h (2015).

Event maximum speed: Andrea Locatelli, 173.8mph/279.7km/h (race).

Qualifying

Weather: Dry

Air Temp: 29° **Track Temp:** 46°

Humidity: 37%

1	Binder	1m 53.149s
2	Schrotter	1m 53.223s
3	Navarro	1m 53.257s
4	Marquez	1m 53.257s
5	Bagnaia	1m 53.275s
6	Pasini	1m 53.317s
7	Quartararo	1m 53.466s
8	Baldassarri	1m 53.480s
9	Corsi	1m 53.605s
10	Marini	1m 53.629s
11	Fernandez	1m 53.671s
12	Vierge	1m 53.676s
13	Lecuona	1m 53.681s
14	Nagashima	1m 53.688s
15	Mir	1m 53.747s
16	Locatelli	1m 53.913s
17	E. Pons	1m 53.976s
18	Oliveira	1m 54.011s
19	Lowes	1m 54.043s
20	Gardner	1m 54.202s
21	Odendaal	1m 54.269s
22	Manzi	1m 54.293s
23	Pawi	1m 54.385s
24	Kent	1m 54.524s
25	Raffin	1m 54.685s
26	Bendsneyder	1m 54.720s
27	Roberts	1m 54.763s
28	Tuuli	1m 54.979s
29	Vinales	1m 55.009s
30	Aegerter	1m 55.112s
31	Danilo	1m 55.340s
32	Fuligni	1m 55.740s
33	Morais	1m 55.832s
34	Cardelus	1m 55.864s

Fastest race laps

1	Marquez	1m 53.479s
2	Baldassarri	1m 53.639s
3	Bagnaia	1m 53.659s
4	Mir	1m 53.742s
5	Binder	1m 53.748s
6	Oliveira	1m 53.752s
7	Schrotter	1m 53.767s
8	Pasini	1m 53.863s
9	Lecuona	1m 53.937s
10	Fernandez	1m 54.002s
11	Vierge	1m 54.015s
12	Corsi	1m 54.035s
13	Quartararo	1m 54.072s
14	Navarro	1m 54.124s
15	Marini	1m 54.209s
16	Lowes	1m 54.324s
17	E. Pons	1m 54.383s
18	Nagashima	1m 54.400s
19	Locatelli	1m 54.491s
20	Gardner	1m 54.777s
21	Odendaal	1m 54.812s
22	Bendsneyder	1m 55.092s
23	Aegerter	1m 55.107s
24	Tuuli	1m 55.161s
25	Kent	1m 55.219s
26	Raffin	1m 55.288s
27	Roberts	1m 55.391s
28	Pawi	1m 55.620s
29	Danilo	1m 55.739s
30	Fuligni	1m 56.430s
31	Cardelus	1m 56.682s
32	Morais	1m 57.493s

Championship Points

1	Bagnaia	234
2	Oliveira	215
3	Binder	144
4	Baldassarri	132
5	Marquez	126
6	Mir	124
7	Schrotter	118
8	Pasini	103
9	Quartararo	100
10	Vierge	96
11	Marini	84
12	Navarro	55
13	Lowes	46
14	Lecuona	43
15	Corsi	41
16	Locatelli	34
17	Aegerter	27
18	Gardner	24
19	Fenati	14
20	Fernandez	14
21	Barbera	10
22	Manzi	8
23	Kent	8
24	Nagashima	8
25	Vinales	7
26	Roberts	2
27	Pawi	1
28	Odendaal	1
29	Raffin	1

Constructor Points

1	Kalex	296
2	KTM	243
3	Speed Up	104
4	Tech 3	24
5	Suter	8
6	NTS	2

Moto3

RACE DISTANCE: 19 laps, 59.939 miles/96.463km · RACE WEATHER: Dry (air 26°C, humidity 44%, track 35°C)

Pos.	Rider	Nat.	No.	Entrant	Machine	Laps	Time & Speed
1	**Jorge Martin**	SPA	88	Del Conca Gresini Moto3	Honda	19	37m 49.030s 95.1mph/ 153.0km/h
2	**Marco Bezzecchi**	ITA	12	Redox PruestelGP	KTM	19	37m 55.014s
3	**Enea Bastianini**	ITA	33	Leopard Racing	Honda	19	37m 55.075s
4	**Fabio Di Giannantonio**	ITA	21	Del Conca Gresini Moto3	Honda	19	37m 55.125s
5	**Marcos Ramirez**	SPA	42	Bester Capital Dubai	KTM	19	37m 55.191s
6	**Tatsuki Suzuki**	JPN	24	SIC58 Squadra Corse	Honda	19	37m 55.299s
7	**Albert Arenas**	SPA	75	Angel Nieto Team Moto3	KTM	19	37m 55.570s
8	**Adam Norrodin**	MAL	7	Petronas Sprinta Racing	Honda	19	37m 59.322s
9	**Jaume Masia**	SPA	5	Bester Capital Dubai	KTM	19	37m 59.359s
10	**John McPhee**	GBR	17	CIP - Green Power	KTM	19	37m 59.567s
11	**Jakub Kornfeil**	CZE	84	Redox PruestelGP	KTM	19	37m 59.709s
12	**Andrea Migno**	ITA	16	Angel Nieto Team Moto3	KTM	19	38m 00.953s
13	**Lorenzo Dalla Porta**	ITA	48	Leopard Racing	Honda	19	38m 01.002s
14	**Nicolo Bulega**	ITA	8	SKY Racing Team VR46	KTM	19	38m 01.043s
15	**Vicente Perez**	SPA	77	Reale Avintia Academy 77	KTM	19	38m 01.037s
16	Tony Arbolino	ITA	14	Marinelli Snipers Team	Honda	19	38m 01.514s
17	Raul Fernandez	SPA	25	Angel Nieto Team	KTM	19	38m 01.686s
18	Darryn Binder	RSA	40	Red Bull KTM Ajo	KTM	19	38m 03.672s
19	Philipp Oettl	GER	65	Sudmetal Schedl GP Racing	KTM	19	38m 06.120s
20	Alonso Lopez	SPA	72	Estrella Galicia 0,0	Honda	19	38m 23.997s
21	Kazuki Masaki	JPN	22	RBA BOE Skull Rider	KTM	19	38m 24.030s
22	Stefano Nepa	ITA	81	CIP - Green Power	KTM	19	38m 24.052s
23	Jeremy Alcoba	SPA	52	Junior Team Estrella Galicia 0,0	Honda	19	38m 24.230s
24	Nakarin Atiratphuvapat	THA	41	Honda Team Asia	Honda	19	38m 43.937s
25	Dennis Foggia	ITA	10	SKY Racing Team VR46	KTM	19	38m 32.896s
26	Kaito Toba	JPN	27	Honda Team Asia	Honda	19	38m 44.012s
	Gabriel Rodrigo	ARG	19	RBA BOE Skull Rider	KTM	17	DNF
	Niccolo Antonelli	ITA	23	SIC58 Squadra Corse	Honda	16	DNF
	Aron Canet	SPA	44	Estrella Galicia 0,0	Honda	11	DNF

Fastest lap: Jaume Masia, on lap 6, 1m 58.540s, 95.8mph/154.1km/h.

Lap record: Fabio Di Giannantonio, 1m 58.347s, 95.9mph/154.4km/h (2017).

Event maximum speed: Tony Arbolino, 148.8mph/239.4km/h (race).

Qualifying

Weather: Dry

Air Temp: 27° **Track Temp:** 42°

Humidity: 45%

1	Martin	1m 57.066s
2	Masia	1m 57.603s
3	Bastianini	1m 57.659s
4	Arbolino	1m 57.774s
5	Foggia	1m 57.791s
6	Bezzecchi	1m 57.855s
7	Antonelli	1m 57.879s
8	Rodrigo	1m 57.937s
9	Canet	1m 57.953s
10	Di Giannantonio	1m 58.149s
11	Norrodin	1m 58.388s
12	Ramirez	1m 58.389s
13	Kornfeil	1m 58.391s
14	Bulega	1m 58.449s
15	Arenas	1m 58.451s
16	Dalla Porta	1m 58.602s
17	Suzuki	1m 58.691s
18	Oettl	1m 58.715s
19	Fernandez	1m 58.718s
20	Masaki	1m 58.789s
21	Migno	1m 58.802s
22	Alcoba	1m 58.822s
23	McPhee	1m 58.836s
24	Perez	1m 58.925s
25	Lopez	1m 59.011s
26	Binder	1m 59.052s
27	Nepa	1m 59.601s
28	Toba	1m 59.998s
29	Atiratphuvapat	2m 01.054s

Fastest race laps

1	Masia	1m 58.540s
2	Bastianini	1m 58.643s
3	Norrodin	1m 58.728s
4	Bezzecchi	1m 58.734s
5	Ramirez	1m 58.745s
6	Arenas	1m 58.767s
7	Martin	1m 58.865s
8	Rodrigo	1m 58.891s
9	Oettl	1m 58.929s
10	Suzuki	1m 58.933s
11	Di Giannantonio	1m 58.941s
12	Migno	1m 58.963s
13	Kornfeil	1m 58.981s
14	Bulega	1m 59.002s
15	Masaki	1m 59.026s
16	McPhee	1m 59.047s
17	Antonelli	1m 59.053s
18	Fernandez	1m 59.143s
19	Perez	1m 59.174s
20	Binder	1m 59.193s
21	Dalla Porta	1m 59.210s
22	Canet	1m 59.244s
23	Arbolino	1m 59.252s
24	Alcoba	1m 59.362s
25	Lopez	1m 59.594s
26	Nepa	2m 00.025s
27	Foggia	2m 00.093s
28	Atiratphuvapat	2m 00.383s
29	Toba	2m 00.724s

Championship Points

1	Martin	191
2	Bezzecchi	178
3	Di Giannantonio	150
4	Bastianini	133
5	Canet	118
6	Rodrigo	97
7	Kornfeil	96
8	Dalla Porta	91
9	Ramirez	78
10	Migno	71
11	Arenas	69
12	Masia	61
13	Antonelli	56
14	Oettl	54
15	Suzuki	50
16	McPhee	49
17	Arbolino	37
18	Norrodin	36
19	Sasaki	32
20	Lopez	31
21	Toba	29
22	Binder	28
23	Foggia	26
24	Fernandez	13
25	Bulega	9
26	Yurchenko	9
27	Loi	8
28	Masaki	8
29	Pagliani	6
30	Perez	3
31	Atiratphuvapat	2
32	Ogura	1

Constructor Points

1	Honda	291
2	KTM	249

FIM WORLD CHAMPIONSHIP · ROUND 15

THAI GRAND PRIX

CHANG INTERNATIONAL CIRCUIT

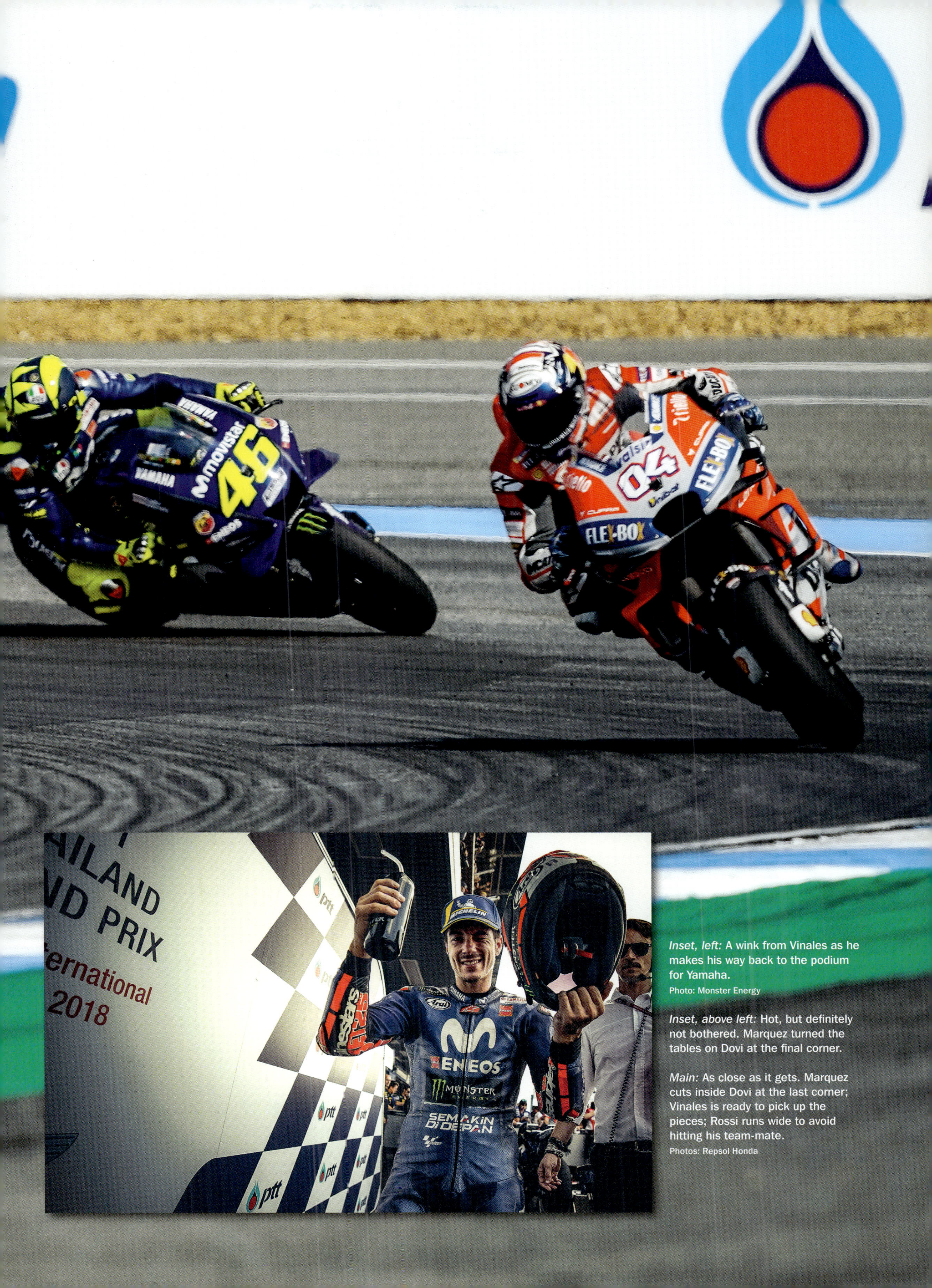

Inset, left: A wink from Vinales as he makes his way back to the podium for Yamaha.
Photo: Monster Energy

Inset, above left: Hot, but definitely not bothered. Marquez turned the tables on Dovi at the final corner.

Main: As close as it gets. Marquez cuts inside Dovi at the last corner; Vinales is ready to pick up the pieces; Rossi runs wide to avoid hitting his team-mate.
Photos: Repsol Honda

Above: Close formation. The Yamahas of Vinales and Rossi.

Top right: Crutchlow cools off with the help of an ice bag and the ubiquitous fan.

Top far right: Rossi found the new-compound Michelins to his liking.
Photos: Monster Energy

Above right: Marshals remove Lorenzo's battered Ducati from the gravel trap.

Right: Lorenzo arrived on crutches after his Aragon crash.
Photos: Gold & Goose

Far right: Rins and Pedrosa battled for sixth.
Photo: www.suzuki-racing.com

Right: Zarco rediscovered his form and brought his Tech 3 Yamaha home in fifth.
Photo: Gold & Goose

THOSE who might wish to believe in divine intervention (or even interest) in motorcycle racing would have found affirmation at Buriram. The inaugural Thai Grand Prix was particularly blessed.

Just one indication was the sustained dry weather – in the last month of the monsoon season, when those who had tested at the track earlier in the year had been told to expect rain at least once every day.

There were many other favourable omens as a 100,000-strong crowd gathered in gaudy, steamy heat to be rewarded with a truly splendid day of racing. The Chang circuit had not been expected to find much favour – a simplistic layout with long straights preceded by slow corners, and then an artificial-looking twisty section at the end. The opposite turned out to be the case.

Most particularly blessed were the Yamaha troops, fresh from their latest humiliation at Aragon. In Thailand, however, it was completely different: fully competitive in practice, and even more so in the race. Both factory riders were still in the hunt for the lead right to the end. The only problem was that nobody could really understand why. Vinales spoke of a setting change to the balance that "we should have done months ago", but the biggest change to the bike had been new aero bodywork with novel staggered biplane 'not-wings'. This appeared only on Friday afternoon, and only on Rossi's bike. So nobody could know if they would take the huge improvement with them to the remaining races.

There was one significant change for all teams, which might have explained why Yamaha's hot-weather wheelspin problems had melted away in the furnace-like conditions. After major tyre-life problems due to heat build-up at the tests, Michelin had made special hard-construction tyres for this race, to which they added a unique special brew of compounds. Further, the usual allocation of three different rear tyres was expanded to four, with two different mediums.

There were miracles also for Marquez, although by now these were a regular event. A spill in FP3 meant that he had to go through Q1 for the second time in the season and the fourth in his career. Of course, he made it to Q2, where he became the first such graduate to take pole. He was not the first Q1 rider to win a GP, however: both Miller and Crutchlow had done so. But his thrilling and narrow victory did bring his career total to 68, putting him fifth overall, behind Agostini (122), Rossi (115), Nieto (90) and Hailwood (76), and on level pegging with Lorenzo.

Ah, Lorenzo – once again Yang to Marquez's Yin; once more the spectre at the feast. For a second time in the season, he had the great misfortune to suffer a mechanical malfunction. The first had been mid-race brake failure in Qatar, where he had been obliged to abandon ship. The reason was never explained. The Chang failure was equally mysterious, but was 100 times more cruel.

The soon-to-be-ex-Ducati star was already hurt, on crutches around the paddock, but able – he said later – to ride in a reasonably effective manner. He was working up to speed on Friday afternoon when, approaching the first-gear Turn Three hairpin at the end of the longest straight, he was scrubbing off speed when suddenly his bike slewed violently sideways and sent him arcing through the air to another very heavy landing. He immediately reached for his injured right foot, starting to take the boot off before they stretchered him away, but later it would transpire that the injury that ruled him out was a small, but painful fracture in his left radius bone, at the wrist.

But what had happened? On-board footage revealed that after Jorge had been down through the gears, the revs suddenly dropped – not instantly, as with a complete seize, but rapidly enough to break rear traction. Had it been the rider's error? Had his injured right foot robbed him of sensitivity on the pedal? Or, if he had been using the thumb brake, had he misjudged it? Much to his relief, Ducati confirmed that it had been "a technical problem". But they declined to give details, merely saying that they were confident it would not happen again. That left the field wide open for speculation, ranging from a mechanic's error that had caused the transmission or a wheel bearing to bind; through the brakes failing to release; to a glitch in the engine braking software, which gives a little throttle opening that combines with the slipper clutch to limit reverse torque.

Torres was back in place of Rabat, and it was confirmed

that he would be on strength for the remaining three flyaways as well. The former Moto2 winner had sacrificed the remainder of his contract with the MV Superbike team to fill the role, because of a race clash – the Australian GP with the Qatar Superbike round – and made the most of the chance to showcase his talents. Again riding Simeon's hybrid Ducati while his temporary team-mate exercised Rabat's GP17, he qualified two-tenths slower than the Belgian and was two seconds behind him in the race, although both were out of the points.

Di Giannantonio and his Gresini team had settled their differences, and the Italian was off to Moto2 as he wanted, joining Speed Up. A second victory showed his appreciation. The same Moto2 team had recruited Edgar Pons in place of the dropped Danny Kent.

Moto3 leader Jorge Martin suffered an extraordinary fresh misfortune, after he was rubbed up the wrong way in a routine Clinica Mobile massage to his previously injured left wrist. A nerve was trapped, leaving his hand numb and making it difficult to operate the clutch. He borrowed a solution pioneered many years before by Japanese star Nobbie Ueda – a spring-loaded prosthesis inside the glove to help his movement.

The race came a week after former Moto3 rider Ana Carrasco had become the first woman to win a motorcycle world championship. The top riders paid tribute to her success, but demurred when asked if she might have a future in MotoGP. "It is a big step from 300 to MotoGP," said Rossi, "for a man or a woman."

MOTOGP RACE – 26 laps

Nothing could stop Marquez's 50th MotoGP pole, though he'd been quicker in Q1. Rossi was second, his fourth front row of the year, Dovi alongside.

Times were close, Q2's top 12 inside nine-tenths. Vinales had moved through at the finish to lead row two, ahead of Crutchlow and Iannone. Pedrosa, who had set the pace at pre-season tests, was seventh, from Zarco and Petrucci; erstwhile leader Miller led row four from Rins (from Q1) and Bautista; Morbidelli was best of the rest.

Michelin had briefed all the riders beforehand, strongly recommending, though not demanding, use of the hard rear. Piero Taramasso explained that while the soft and medium would last the race, lap times would drop off radically in the closing stages. All but one followed that advice, the exception being Aprilia's Espargaro. Front tyre choice was a little more mixed, with six riders choosing the medium, but the fastest taking the hard.

Marquez led away, Rossi and Dovi in hot pursuit. The track layout and the fact that they were all saving tyres kept them close. On lap five, Rossi outbraked Marquez into the Turn Three hairpin, one of the few overtaking spots, to lead for the next five laps. Also on lap five, Dovizioso found another possible passing place, taking second into the final corner.

Most of the action to come would be at these two key locations, and most of it was contained in the last five laps. Five times, Marquez took the lead, and each time Dovi would take it straight back.

Above: Dovi and Marquez enjoyed a spectacular duel.

Top right: Again, Bradley Smith was KTM's lone rider following Pol Espargaro's withdrawal.

Above right: Jorge Martin used a spring-loaded prosthesis inside his glove to help operate the clutch.

Right: The SKY VR46 Kalexes of Bagnaia and Marini prevailed over the KTMs of Binder and Oliveira in a furious four-way Moto2 battle.

Far right: 1-2 joy for Marini and Bagnaia.

Below right: Fabio Di Giannantonio on his way to victory, ahead of Dalla Porta and Foggia (10), while Bastianini is skittled by Bezzecchi. A compromised Kornfeil (84) dropped to tenth.

Below far right: Foggia leads Bezzecchi on his way to a maiden podium.
Photos: Gold & Goose

On the final lap, Marquez saved his overtake to Turn Five and stayed ahead. Until the final corner. There, Dovi moved up inside to outbrake the Honda and claim the apex. But he was a touch overambitious and ran wide on the exit. Marquez flicked back underneath and crossed the line just over a tenth ahead.

Three times in 2017, the climax had been the other way round. "This time, it was the opposite," said an exultant Marquez, whose seventh win of the year extended his points lead. "I was Dovi and he was Marquez."

Dovi at least had enjoyed the battle, praising Marquez for the fact that they could fight so closely so often without any rough riding (a dig at complaining team-mate Lorenzo), and he was pleased at fresh proof that the improved Ducati was able to preserve its tyres even in hot conditions. "It's an even bigger step than Aragon," he said, adding, "Because I'd been in front all the time, I didn't understand Marc's weak points and I was too far behind to outbrake him in the last corner."

Their battle had been absorbing, but did not overshadow the astonishing revival of the Yamahas. Vinales, strong again in the later stages, hadn't been able to overtake, but had been poised to profit from any error, just over a tenth adrift at the finish. Rossi, who had ceded third to his team-mate on lap 20, would have been as close, after pulling right up again in the final lap, but had to swerve wide to avoid hitting Vinales's back wheel in the last corner. Said an unusually happy Vinales, "I am very curious to see at the next race if our improvements are just this track and this tyre. I have no expectations, but I am looking forward to it."

The remaining top ten positions were keenly fought.

Crutchlow had started strongly, tailing the front three until after half-distance, Vinales behind him, apart from a brief early skirmish with Zarco. On lap 18, the Spaniard finally got past. Crutchlow had run out of grip and would continue to lose places.

By then, Pedrosa had passed Rins, and the pair had got ahead of Zarco and then also Crutchlow. Pedrosa would not last another lap, however, losing the front and sliding out at Turn Five on lap 19.

Also speeding up, Zarco was promptly ahead of Crutchlow and closed on Rins for fifth, getting past him on the final lap.

Bautista was on the move as well. Dropped to 15th on the first lap after clashing with Morbidelli, he'd been firmly gaining places ever since and was just two-tenths behind seventh-placed Crutchlow over the line.

Behind him, Miller – blaming disappearing grip – had finally given way to team-mate Petrucci. They'd been fighting with Iannone, but he'd also slowed radically at the end for the same reason, almost five seconds down in 11th.

Syahrin was a strong 12th, top rookie, with his rival for that title, Morbidelli, 14th, Espargaro's Aprilia between them. Smith finally won a long and close fight with Redding for the final point. The rest were well behind, Nakagami a distant last after falling early, pitting, then rejoining.

MOTO2 RACE – 24 laps

A hard-fought Moto2 qualifying put 19 riders inside just over half a second, positions decided by hundredths. Less than three-hundredths for pole, Baldassarri's second of the season. That came early, but was enough, in a session during which, unusually, most riders kept getting quicker.

Marini fell narrowly short; then in the dying seconds, Alex Marquez slid between to the middle of the front row. This foiled Friday leader Pasini, who slipped off on his own attempt, but headed row two from the title rivals, Oliveira a tantalising two-thousandths quicker than Bagnaia. Aragon winner Binder headed row three from Quartararo and Fernandez; fancied runners Schrotter and Mir were right behind.

A compelling race became fascinating at the finish – and deeply depressing for the Red Bull KTM teamsters, as Bagnaia's seventh win of the year was backed up when SKY VR46 Kalex team-mate Marini pushed past into a valuable second place on the final lap.

Oliveira had disputed the lead in the early stages, but suffering brake problems had been obliged to settle for second as Bagnaia took firm control at half-distance. Then it became third, costing him another four points.

Team-mate Binder had dutifully shadowed him throughout, with each having at least a spell in the lead in the early stages, but he had succumbed to the late-charging Marini on the 22nd lap.

It had taken time for Bagnaia to apply his stranglehold. He'd leapt straight into the lead from the second row, but at

the end of lap three, Oliveira took over, while Binder and Baldassarri squabbled over third. The latter took it, lost it again when he missed a gear and ran wide, then crashed trying to regain lost ground.

By that stage, Marini had shuffled Marquez back to sixth. Then the Spaniard also slipped off after regaining the position, his fourth crash in five races.

Now Quartararo caught up and engaged with Marini, ahead of him for three laps. That gave the three up front a gap of a second. Then Marini took over again from the Frenchman, but it wasn't until the last five laps that he started to gain speed even as the KTMs were losing it, giving Bagnaia the chance he needed to escape.

On lap 16, Marini had been almost 1.5 seconds adrift of Binder. Six laps later, not only had he caught up, but also he went sailing past. When they started the last lap, he was looming over Oliveira's shoulder and could see that the KTM rider was comparatively short of grip. All it took was for Oliveira to run wide at Turn Three, and Marini was firmly ahead.

Quartararo was a lone fifth, Pasini likewise in sixth, having dropped off Lecuona and an on-form Tetsuta Nagashima. Andrea Locatelli had lost touch in ninth; veteran Corsi completed the top ten, after passing and outpacing Vierge and fast-starting Gardner, who had gained eight places in a blazing first lap.

American Joe Roberts had closed to within less than a second at the finish for his second points of the season. Bendsneyder and Tuuli took the final points, the first for each of them.

Among several crashers were Marcel Schrotter and Joan Mir, on the first lap.

MOTO3 RACE – 22 laps

Qualifying times were close also in Moto3, but only from second to 24th, within a second. Bezzecchi was all but half a second clear for his second pole. Masia was best of the rest from first-timer Masaki, for an all-KTM front row. Binder was sixth, a career best; Martin on row five, 13th fastest.

The long straights kept the 30-strong field packed close, five or six abreast into the corners. With so many close finishes in this class (this was the fifth top three of 2018 in less than half a second), it was not atypical. But it was still one of the best, as fine tactics (or perhaps chance) brought a second win for Di Giannantonio, inches clear of Dalla Porta, with a classic first podium for rookie Dennis Foggia, up from 25th on the grid.

But there was a major casualty of the close running, when Enea Bastianini made a big lunge for third place at the last corner, cutting under Bezzecchi, only to slip off and take both of them down. Zero points was a heavy blow to the erstwhile points leader's chances, with Di Giannantonio's win bringing him within three points.

The tangle promoted Martin to fourth and a valuable 26-point title lead.

The lead group had been 20 strong for most of the way – and there were other casualties. At last finding form, Binder had been an early leader, but he was knocked off by a headstrong Arenas; front-running Sic 58 Honda team-mates Antonelli and Suzuki collided and fell; while rookie Masaki had been running with the leaders, only to fall after a clash with Martin.

PTT THAILAND GRAND PRIX

5-7 OCTOBER, 2018

CHANG INTERNATIONAL CIRCUIT

26 laps
Length: 4.554 km / 2.829 miles
Width: 12m

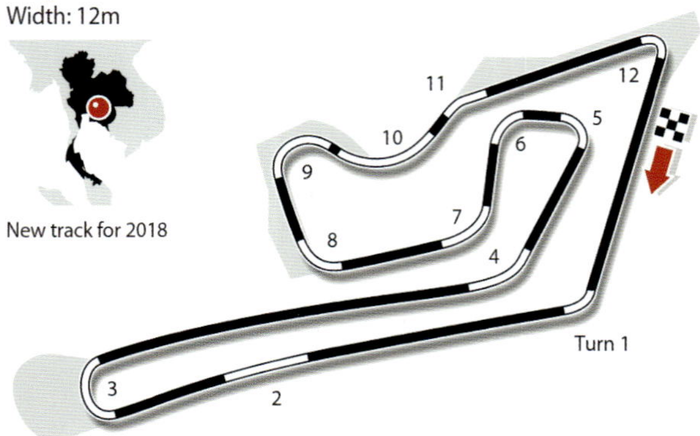

MotoGP

RACE DISTANCE: 26 laps, 73.573 miles/118.404km · RACE WEATHER: Dry (air 32°C, humidity 46%, track 49°C)

Pos.	Rider	Nat.	No.	Entrant	Machine	Tyres	Race tyre choice	Laps	Time & speed
1	**Marc Marquez**	SPA	93	Repsol Honda Team	Honda RC213V	M	F: Hard/R: Hard	26	39m 55.722s 110.5mph/ 177.9km/h
2	**Andrea Dovizioso**	ITA	4	Ducati Team	Ducati Desmosedici	M	F: Hard/R: Hard	26	39m 55.837s
3	**Maverick Vinales**	SPA	25	Movistar Yamaha MotoGP	Yamaha YZR-M1	M	F: Hard/R: Hard	26	39m 55.992s
4	**Valentino Rossi**	ITA	46	Movistar Yamaha MotoGP	Yamaha YZR-M1	M	F: Hard/R: Hard	26	39m 57.286s
5	**Johann Zarco**	FRA	5	Monster Yamaha Tech 3	Yamaha YZR-M1	M	F: Medium/R: Hard	26	39m 58.469s
6	**Alex Rins**	SPA	42	Team SUZUKI ECSTAR	Suzuki GSX-RR	M	F: Hard/R: Hard	26	39m 58.745s
7	**Cal Crutchlow**	GBR	35	LCR Honda CASTROL	Honda RC213V	M	F: Hard/R: Hard	26	40m 02.242s
8	**Alvaro Bautista**	SPA	19	Angel Nieto Team	Ducati Desmosedici	M	F: Medium/R: Hard	26	40m 02.413s
9	**Danilo Petrucci**	ITA	9	Alma Pramac Racing	Ducati Desmosedici	M	F: Hard/R: Hard	26	40m 05.666s
10	**Jack Miller**	AUS	43	Alma Pramac Racing	Ducati Desmosedici	M	F: Medium/R: Hard	26	40m 06.799s
11	**Andrea Iannone**	ITA	29	Team SUZUKI ECSTAR	Suzuki GSX-RR	M	F: Medium/R: Hard	26	40m 11.210s
12	**Hafizh Syahrin**	MAL	55	Monster Yamaha Tech 3	Yamaha YZR-M1	M	F: Hard/R: Hard	26	40m 13.413s
13	**Aleix Espargaro**	SPA	41	Aprilia Racing Team Gresini	Aprilia RS-GP	M	F: Hard/R: Soft	26	40m 17.135s
14	**Franco Morbidelli**	ITA	21	EG 0,0 Marc VDS	Honda RC213V	M	F: Hard/R: Hard	26	40m 18.524s
15	**Bradley Smith**	GBR	38	Red Bull KTM Factory Racing	KTM RC16	M	F: Hard/R: Hard	26	40m 19.350s
16	Scott Redding	GBR	45	Aprilia Racing Team Gresini	Aprilia RS-GP	M	F: Hard/R: Hard	26	40m 19.526s
17	Karel Abraham	CZE	17	Angel Nieto Team	Ducati Desmosedici	M	F: Hard/R: Hard	26	40m 28.229s
18	Xavier Simeon	BEL	10	Reale Avintia Racing	Ducati Desmosedici	M	F: Medium/R: Hard	26	40m 32.938s
19	Jordi Torres	SPA	81	Reale Avintia Racing	Ducati Desmosedici	M	F: Medium/R: Hard	26	40m 34.926s
20	Thomas Luthi	SWI	12	EG 0,0 Marc VDS	Honda RC213V	M	F: Hard/R: Hard	26	40m 35.143s
21	Pol Espargaro	SPA	44	Red Bull KTM Factory Racing	KTM RC16	M	F: Hard/R: Hard	26	40m 49.110s
22	Takaaki Nakagami	JPN	30	LCR Honda IDEMITSU	Honda RC213V	M	F: Hard/R: Hard	24	40m 21.117s
	Dani Pedrosa	SPA	26	Repsol Honda Team	Honda RC213V	M	F: Hard/R: Hard	18	DNF-crash
	Jorge Lorenzo	SPA	99	Ducati Team	Ducati Desmosedici	M	-	-	DNS-injured

Fastest lap: Marc Marquez, on lap 16, 1m 31.471s, 111.3mph/179.2km/h.
Lap record: New circuit.
Event maximum speed: Andrea Dovizioso, 205.3mph/330.4km/h (free practice).

Qualifying

Weather: Dry
Air Temp: 31° **Track Temp:** 50°
Humidity: 54%

1	Marquez	1m 30.088s
2	Rossi	1m 30.099s
3	Dovizioso	1m 30.227s
4	Vinales	1m 30.328s
5	Crutchlow	1m 30.356s
6	Iannone	1m 30.419s
7	Pedrosa	1m 30.458s
8	Zarco	1m 30.471s
9	Petrucci	1m 30.599s
10	Miller	1m 30.660s
11	Rins	1m 30.738s
12	Bautista	1m 30.976s
13	Morbidelli	1m 30.923s
14	Nakagami	1m 30.995s
15	Smith	1m 31.207s
16	A. Espargaro	1m 31.243s
17	Abraham	1m 31.374s
18	Syahrin	1m 31.389s
19	P. Espargaro	1m 31.399s
20	Simeon	1m 31.686s
21	Torres	1m 31.819s
22	Luthi	1m 31.830s
23	Redding	1m 31.835s

Fastest race laps

1	Marquez	1m 31.471s
2	Dovizioso	1m 31.492s
3	Rossi	1m 31.500s
4	Pedrosa	1m 31.533s
5	Vinales	1m 31.602s
6	Crutchlow	1m 31.664s
7	Bautista	1m 31.670s
8	Rins	1m 31.686s
9	Zarco	1m 31.704s
10	Miller	1m 31.708s
11	Iannone	1m 31.745s
12	Petrucci	1m 31.754s
13	A. Espargaro	1m 31.987s
14	Syahrin	1m 32.121s
15	Morbidelli	1m 32.146s
16	Nakagami	1m 32.170s
17	Smith	1m 32.370s
18	Redding	1m 32.387s
19	Abraham	1m 32.482s
20	Luthi	1m 32.542s
21	P. Espargaro	1m 32.618s
22	Simeon	1m 32.717s
23	Torres	1m 32.831s

Championship Points

1	Marquez	271
2	Dovizioso	194
3	Rossi	172
4	Vinales	146
5	Lorenzo	130
6	Crutchlow	128
7	Petrucci	126
8	Zarco	123
9	Iannone	113
10	Rins	102
11	Pedrosa	87
12	Miller	74
13	Bautista	72
14	Rabat	35
15	Morbidelli	33
16	A. Espargaro	32
17	P. Espargaro	32
18	Syahrin	28
19	Smith	19
20	Nakagami	18
21	Redding	12
22	Kallio	6
23	Abraham	5
24	Pirro	1
27	Guintoli	1

Constructor Points

1	Honda	306
2	Ducati	273
3	Yamaha	218
4	Suzuki	157
5	KTM	45
6	Aprilia	42

Grid order	1	2	3	4	5	6	7	8	9	10	11	12	13	14	15	16	17	18	19	20	21	22	23	24	25	26	
93 MARQUEZ	93	93	93	93	46	46	46	46	46	46	4	4	4	4	4	4	4	4	4	4	4	4	4	4	4	93	1
46 ROSSI	46	46	46	46	4	4	4	4	4	4	93	93	93	93	93	93	93	93	93	93	93	93	93	93	93	4	2
4 DOVIZIOSO	4	4	4	4	93	93	93	93	93	93	46	46	46	46	46	46	46	46	46	25	25	25	25	25	25	25	3
25 VINALES	35	35	35	35	35	35	35	35	35	35	35	35	35	35	35	35	35	25	25	46	46	46	46	46	46	46	4
35 CRUTCHLOW	25	5	25	25	25	25	25	25	25	25	25	25	25	25	25	25	25	26	42	42	42	42	42	42	42	5	5
29 IANNONE	5	25	5	5	5	5	5	5	5	5	5	5	42	42	42	26	26	42	5	5	5	5	5	5	5	42	6
26 PEDROSA	43	43	43	43	43	43	43	43	42	42	42	42	26	26	26	42	42	35	35	35	35	35	35	35	35	35	7
5 ZARCO	29	29	29	42	42	42	42	42	26	26	26	26	5	5	5	5	5	5	9	29	29	19	19	19	19	19	8
9 PETRUCCI	42	9	42	26	26	26	26	26	43	43	43	43	43	43	43	43	43	43	29	19	19	43	43	43	9	9	9
43 MILLER	9	42	9	9	9	9	9	9	9	9	9	9	9	9	9	9	9	9	19	43	43	9	9	9	43	43	10
42 RINS	26	26	26	29	29	29	29	29	29	29	29	29	29	29	29	29	29	29	43	9	9	29	29	29	29	29	11
19 BAUTISTA	38	41	41	41	41	41	41	19	19	19	19	19	19	19	19	19	19	19	55	55	55	55	55	55	55	55	12
21 MORBIDELLI	41	38	38	38	38	38	19	41	41	41	41	55	55	55	55	55	55	55	41	41	41	41	41	41	41	41	13
30 NAKAGAMI	21	21	21	19	19	19	38	38	38	55	55	41	41	41	41	41	41	41	21	21	21	21	21	21	21	21	14
38 SMITH	19	19	19	21	21	21	21	55	55	38	38	38	21	21	21	21	21	21	45	38	38	38	38	38	38	38	15
41 A. ESPARGARO	45	45	45	45	45	45	55	21	45	45	45	21	38	38	38	38	45	45	38	45	45	45	45	45	45	45	
17 ABRAHAM	17	17	55	55	55	55	45	45	21	21	21	45	45	45	45	45	38	38	44	17	17	17	17	17	17	17	
55 SYAHRIN	30	55	44	44	44	44	44	44	44	44	44	44	44	44	44	44	44	44	17	44	44	10	10	10	10	10	
44 P. ESPARGARO	55	30	17	17	17	17	17	17	17	17	17	17	17	17	17	17	17	17	10	10	10	81	81	81	81	81	
10 SIMEON	44	44	10	10	10	10	10	10	10	10	10	10	10	10	10	10	10	10	81	81	81	44	12	12	12	12	
81 TORRES	10	10	81	81	81	81	81	81	81	81	81	81	81	81	81	81	81	81	12	12	12	12	44	44	44	44	
12 LUTHI	81	81	12	12	12	12	12	12	12	12	12	12	12	12	12	12	12	12	30	30	30	30	30	30			
45 REDDING	12	12	30	30	30	30	30	30	30	30	30	30	30	30	30	30	30	30									

30 Pit stop 30 Lapped rider

Moto2

RACE DISTANCE: 24 laps, 67.913 miles/109.296km · RACE WEATHER: Dry (air 33°C, humidity 45%, track 56°C)

Pos.	Rider	Nat.	No.	Entrant	Machine	Laps	Time & Speed
1	**Francesco Bagnaia**	ITA	42	SKY Racing Team VR46	Kalex	24	39m 00.009s 104.5mph/ 168.1km/h
2	**Luca Marini**	ITA	10	SKY Racing Team VR46	Kalex	24	39m 01.521s
3	**Miguel Oliveira**	POR	44	Red Bull KTM Ajo	KTM	24	39m 01.660s
4	**Brad Binder**	RSA	41	Red Bull KTM Ajo	KTM	24	39m 01.817s
5	**Fabio Quartararo**	FRA	20	MB Conveyors - Speed Up	Speed Up	24	39m 06.269s
6	**Mattia Pasini**	ITA	54	Italtrans Racing Team	Kalex	24	39m 11.793s
7	**Iker Lecuona**	SPA	27	Swiss Innovative Investors	KTM	24	39m 15.299s
8	**Tetsuta Nagashima**	JPN	45	IDEMITSU Honda Team Asia	Kalex	24	39m 16.912s
9	**Andrea Locatelli**	ITA	5	Italtrans Racing Team	Kalex	24	39m 18.617s
10	**Simone Corsi**	ITA	24	Tasca Racing Scuderia Moto2	Kalex	24	39m 21.190s
11	**Xavi Vierge**	SPA	97	Dynavolt Intact GP	Kalex	24	39m 22.030s
12	**Remy Gardner**	AUS	87	Tech 3 Racing	Tech 3	24	39m 23.966s
13	**Joe Roberts**	USA	16	NTS RW Racing GP	NTS	24	39m 24.677s
14	**Bo Bendsneyder**	NED	64	Tech 3 Racing	Tech 3	24	39m 26.311s
15	**Niki Tuuli**	FIN	66	Petronas Sprinta Racing	Kalex	24	39m 26.826s
16	Dominique Aegerter	SWI	77	Kiefer Racing	KTM	24	39m 30.767s
17	Jorge Navarro	SPA	9	Federal Oil Gresini Moto2	Kalex	24	39m 34.791s
18	Thitipong Warokorn	THA	99	SAG Team	Kalex	24	39m 38.324s
19	Edgar Pons	SPA	57	MB Conveyors - Speed Up	Speed Up	24	39m 40.303s
20	Jules Danilo	FRA	95	Nashi Argan SAG Team	Kalex	24	39m 40.854s
21	Khairul Idham Pawi	MAL	89	IDEMITSU Honda Team Asia	Kalex	24	39m 41.358s
22	Xavi Cardelus	AND	18	Marinelli Snipers Team	Kalex	24	39m 43.917s
23	Steven Odendaal	RSA	4	NTS RW Racing GP	NTS	24	39m 57.266s
24	Isaac Vinales	SPA	32	Forward Racing Team	Suter	24	39m 59.216s
25	Federico Fuligni	ITA	21	Tasca Racing Scuderia Moto2	Kalex	24	39m 59.392s
	Sam Lowes	GBR	22	Swiss Innovative Investors	KTM	23	DNF
	Lorenzo Baldassarri	ITA	7	Pons HP40	Kalex	10	DNF
	Alex Marquez	SPA	73	EG 0,0 Marc VDS	Kalex	6	DNF
	Stefano Manzi	ITA	62	Forward Racing Team	Suter	1	DNF
	Augusto Fernandez	SPA	40	Pons HP40	Kalex	0	DNF
	Marcel Schrotter	GER	23	Dynavolt Intact GP	Kalex	0	DNF
	Joan Mir	SPA	36	EG 0,0 Marc VDS	Kalex	0	DNF

Fastest lap: Francesco Bagnaia, on lap 12, 1m 36.924s, 105.1mph/169.1km/h.

Lap record: New circuit.

Event maximum speed: Miguel Oliveira, 170.6mph/274.5km/h (free practice).

Qualifying

Weather: Dry

Air Temp: 31° **Track Temp:** 46°

Humidity: 54%

1	Baldassarri	1m 36.374s
2	Marquez	1m 36.400s
3	Marini	1m 36.408s
4	Pasini	1m 36.527s
5	Oliveira	1m 36.529s
6	Bagnaia	1m 36.531s
7	Binder	1m 36.545s
8	Quartararo	1m 36.589s
9	Fernandez	1m 36.661s
10	Schrotter	1m 36.689s
11	Mir	1m 36.744s
12	Lecuona	1m 36.797s
13	Corsi	1m 36.865s
14	Aegerter	1m 36.867s
15	Lowes	1m 36.877s
16	Locatelli	1m 36.878s
17	Navarro	1m 36.894s
18	Nagashima	1m 36.898s
19	Gardner	1m 36.933s
20	Vierge	1m 37.069s
21	Odendaal	1m 37.287s
22	Roberts	1m 37.432s
23	Bendsneyder	1m 37.474s
24	Pawi	1m 37.537s
25	E. Pons	1m 37.588s
26	Warokorn	1m 37.673s
27	Manzi	1m 37.686s
28	Tuuli	1m 37.722s
29	Cardelus	1m 37.997s
30	Danilo	1m 38.260s
31	Vinales	1m 38.622s
32	Fuligni	1m 38.772s

Fastest race laps

1	Bagnaia	1m 36.924s
2	Binder	1m 36.943s
3	Marini	1m 37.084s
4	Oliveira	1m 37.100s
5	Quartararo	1m 37.254s
6	Nagashima	1m 37.275s
7	Marquez	1m 37.302s
8	Lecuona	1m 37.308s
9	Navarro	1m 37.318s
10	Baldassarri	1m 37.323s
11	Pasini	1m 37.496s
12	Locatelli	1m 37.652s
13	Lowes	1m 37.684s
14	Bendsneyder	1m 37.696s
15	Vierge	1m 37.714s
16	Gardner	1m 37.797s
17	Tuuli	1m 37.824s
18	Corsi	1m 37.851s
19	Roberts	1m 37.907s
20	Aegerter	1m 38.042s
21	E. Pons	1m 38.086s
22	Odendaal	1m 38.138s
23	Warokorn	1m 38.332s
24	Danilo	1m 38.454s
25	Pawi	1m 38.467s
26	Cardelus	1m 38.649s
27	Vinales	1m 39.117s
28	Fuligni	1m 39.249s

Championship Points

1	Bagnaia	259
2	Oliveira	231
3	Binder	157
4	Baldassarri	132
5	Marquez	126
6	Mir	124
7	Schrotter	118
8	Pasini	113
9	Quartararo	111
10	Marini	104
11	Vierge	101
12	Navarro	55
13	Lecuona	52
14	Corsi	47
15	Lowes	46
16	Locatelli	41
17	Gardner	28
18	Aegerter	27
19	Nagashima	16
20	Fenati	14
21	Fernandez	14
22	Barbera	10
23	Manzi	8
24	Kent	8
25	Vinales	7
26	Roberts	5
27	Bendsneyder	2
28	Pawi	1
29	Odendaal	1
30	Tuuli	1
31	Raffin	1

Constructor Points

1	Kalex	321
2	KTM	259
3	Speed Up	115
4	Tech 3	28
5	Suter	8
6	NTS	5

Moto3

RACE DISTANCE: 22 laps, 62.254 miles/100.188km · RACE WEATHER: Dry (air 31°C, humidity 52%, track 52°C)

Pos.	Rider	Nat.	No.	Entrant	Machine	Laps	Time & Speed
1	**Fabio Di Giannantonio**	ITA	21	Del Conca Gresini Moto3	Honda	22	38m 10.789s 97.8mph/ 157.4km/h
2	**Lorenzo Dalla Porta**	ITA	48	Leopard Racing	Honda	22	38m 10.924s
3	**Dennis Foggia**	ITA	10	SKY Racing Team VR46	KTM	22	38m 11.255s
4	**Jorge Martin**	SPA	88	Del Conca Gresini Moto3	Honda	22	38m 11.769s
5	**Gabriel Rodrigo**	ARG	19	RBA BOE Skull Rider	KTM	22	38m 11.873s
6	**Vicente Perez**	SPA	77	Reale Avintia Academy 77	KTM	22	38m 12.021s
7	**Nicolo Bulega**	ITA	8	SKY Racing Team VR46	KTM	22	38m 12.101s
8	**Marcos Ramirez**	SPA	42	Bester Capital Dubai	KTM	22	38m 12.229s
9	**Somkiat Chantra**	THA	35	AP Honda Racing Thailand	Honda	22	38m 12.432s
10	**Jakub Kornfeil**	CZE	84	Redox PruestelGP	KTM	22	38m 12.507s
11	**Andrea Migno**	ITA	16	Angel Nieto Team Moto3	KTM	22	38m 14.175s
12	**Kaito Toba**	JPN	27	Honda Team Asia	Honda	22	38m 14.402s
13	**Philipp Oettl**	GER	65	Sudmetal Schedl GP Racing	KTM	22	38m 14.919s
14	**Tony Arbolino**	ITA	14	Marinelli Snipers Team	Honda	22	38m 15.108s
15	**Adam Norrodin**	MAL	7	Petronas Sprinta Racing	Honda	22	38m 15.446s
16	Apiwath Wongthananon	THA	9	VR46 Master Camp Team	KTM	22	38m 15.591s
17	Jaume Masia	SPA	5	Bester Capital Dubai	KTM	22	38m 15.673s
18	Jeremy Alcoba	SPA	52	Estrella Galicia 0,0	Honda	22	38m 34.704s
19	Stefano Nepa	ITA	81	CIP - Green Power	KTM	22	38m 34.753s
20	Kazuki Masaki	JPN	22	RBA BOE Skull Rider	KTM	22	39m 10.179s
	Marco Bezzecchi	ITA	12	Redox PruestelGP	KTM	22	DNF
	Enea Bastianini	ITA	33	Leopard Racing	Honda	21	DNF
	John McPhee	GBR	17	CIP - Green Power	KTM	20	DNF
	Nakarin Atiratphuvapat	THA	41	Honda Team Asia	Honda	19	DNF
	Ayumu Sasaki	JPN	71	Petronas Sprinta Racing	Honda	13	DNF
	Albert Arenas	SPA	75	Angel Nieto Team Moto3	KTM	6	DNF
	Niccolo Antonelli	ITA	23	SIC58 Squadra Corse	Honda	4	DNF
	Tatsuki Suzuki	JPN	24	SIC58 Squadra Corse	Honda	4	DNF
	Darryn Binder	RSA	40	Red Bull KTM Ajo	KTM	3	DNF
	Alonso Lopez	SPA	72	Estrella Galicia 0,0	Honda	3	DNF

Fastest lap: Dennis Foggia, on lap 3, 1m 42.963s, 98.9mph/159.2km/h.

Lap record: New circuit.

Event maximum speed: Vicente Perez, 144.8mph/233.1km/h (warm-up).

Qualifying

Weather: Dry

Air Temp: 32° **Track Temp:** 56°

Humidity: 52%

1	Bezzecchi	1m 42.235s
2	Masia	1m 42.697s
3	Masaki	1m 42.716s
4	Arbolino	1m 42.720s
5	Antonelli	1m 42.776s
6	Binder	1m 42.799s
7	Bulega	1m 42.815s
8	Bastianini	1m 42.818s
9	Di Giannantonio	1m 42.831s
10	Dalla Porta	1m 42.835s
11	Sasaki	1m 42.942s
12	Perez	1m 42.961s
13	Martin	1m 43.042s
14	Suzuki	1m 43.058s
15	Wongthananon	1m 43.071s
16	Ramirez	1m 43.114s
17	Arenas	1m 43.131s
18	Oettl	1m 43.133s
19	McPhee	1m 43.179s
20	Atiratphuvapat	1m 43.365s
21	Norrodin	1m 43.399s
22	Kornfeil	1m 43.424s
23	Chantra	1m 43.437s
24	Rodrigo	1m 43.445s
25	Foggia	1m 43.723s
26	Toba	1m 43.738s
27	Nepa	1m 43.929s
28	Migno	1m 43.964s
29	Alcoba	1m 43.972s
30	Lopez	1m 44.767s

Fastest race laps

1	Foggia	1m 42.963s
2	Migno	1m 43.006s
3	Sasaki	1m 43.019s
4	Rodrigo	1m 43.030s
5	Arenas	1m 43.039s
6	Kornfeil	1m 43.055s
7	Dalla Porta	1m 43.062s
8	Bastianini	1m 43.088s
9	Suzuki	1m 43.099s
10	Ramirez	1m 43.143s
11	Binder	1m 43.165s
12	Oettl	1m 43.184s
13	Masia	1m 43.204s
14	Atiratphuvapat	1m 43.253s
15	Chantra	1m 43.283s
16	Bulega	1m 43.294s
17	McPhee	1m 43.300s
18	Di Giannantonio	1m 43.353s
19	Bezzecchi	1m 43.395s
20	Martin	1m 43.420s
21	Antonelli	1m 43.442s
22	Perez	1m 43.448s
23	Arbolino	1m 43.475s
24	Wongthananon	1m 43.616s
25	Toba	1m 43.633s
26	Norrodin	1m 43.669s
27	Alcoba	1m 43.672s
28	Masaki	1m 43.688s
29	Lopez	1m 43.732s
30	Nepa	1m 43.901s

Championship Points

1	Martin	204
2	Bezzecchi	178
3	Di Giannantonio	175
4	Bastianini	133
5	Canet	118
6	Dalla Porta	111
7	Rodrigo	108
8	Kornfeil	102
9	Ramirez	86
10	Migno	76
11	Arenas	69
12	Masia	61
13	Oettl	57
14	Antonelli	56
15	Suzuki	50
16	McPhee	49
17	Foggia	42
18	Arbolino	39
19	Norrodin	37
20	Toba	33
21	Sasaki	32
22	Lopez	31
23	Binder	28
24	Bulega	18
25	Perez	13
26	Fernandez	13
27	Yurchenko	9
28	Loi	8
29	Masaki	8
30	Chantra	7
31	Pagliani	6
32	Atiratphuvapat	2
33	Ogura	1

Constructor Points

1	Honda	316
2	KTM	265

MARC
MARQUEZ
PRO RACE
CHALLENGE
LEVEL
7
WORLD
CHAMPION
2018
REPSOL HONDA

FIM WORLD CHAMPIONSHIP · ROUND 16

JAPANESE GRAND PRIX

TWIN RING MOTEGI

Above: The crucial overtake – Marquez slips inside Dovi's Duke in their battle for the lead.

Top right: Rookie Hafizh Syahrin took tenth on the Monster Yamaha.

Centre, clockwise from top left: Quartararo's celebration was short-lived; attention-seeking Redding sported blue braids; home boy Nakagami poses with some young fans; Lorenzo tried, but had to give up.

Below right: Veteran Katsuyuki Nakasuga wild-carded for Yamaha and preserved a perfect points record.

Opening spread: Game Boy. Marquez's inner circle orchestrated an elaborate victory celebration.

Photos: Gold & Goose

ONLY Dovizioso could stop Marc Marquez from making more history in Japan, and the best he could hope for was to delay the inevitable. This looked achievable. At this track in 2017, he'd accomplished his third last-corner defeat of the Repsol Honda. Ducati had five wins here, and the GP18 had added better cornering to its class-leading braking and acceleration. Stop-and-go Motegi and the Desmosedici seemed made for one another.

It all came to an abrupt end on the penultimate lap, though, when Dovi fell at the far hairpin. It was a small mistake on the Italian's part. But it was illustrative of how, all season, Marquez had come up smiling in all circumstances.

Thus his seventh world championship, fifth MotoGP title in six years, third in a row, and third secured in front of top Honda management, this time Honda Motor President Takehiro Hachigo. "I think the big boss will be happy," he said.

This was after an extraordinary moment, when he'd stopped trackside to cue up his elaborate and forgivably cheesy 'Level Seven' celebration (climbing six steps up a specially-made podium, then miming winning to the next level in a retro video game). Former Moto2 rival Scott Redding pulled alongside to give him a hug – which dislocated his left shoulder. Later he explained that this was a fairly frequent occurrence during training, and his brother Alex was on hand to pop it straight back. He would face surgery to repair it over the winter. One little sign of mortality.

For the rest, the records speak for themselves. Here are some: he was the youngest to win seven championships, taking over from Mike Hailwood. He had deposed Rossi as the youngest to win five premier-class crowns; he was one of just eight riders to have taken seven or more titles, with Agostini (15), Nieto (13), Rossi, Hailwood and Carlo Ubbiali (nine), John Surtees and Phil Read (seven). Only Rossi and Agostini had more premier-class titles, and now he equalled Mick Doohan. And he was the only rider to have won at least five GPs per season in all classes, over nine years, two more than Hailwood.

Would 2019's new team-mate change the dynamic? Lorenzo was in no position to do so as a rival in 2018. Ducati's Motegi prospects had tempted an early return after his heavy Thai crash, but when he upped his training regime, the pain had returned to his left arm with a vengeance. A scan in a Mito hospital on Thursday, from a different angle, revealed that the originally diagnosed hairline fracture was more serious. He elected to try anyway, but didn't even complete one timed lap in FP1 before pulling in, face etched with pain. Subsequently, back in Spain, famed GP medic Dr Xavier Mir discovered ligament damage.

Speculation about the following weekend's replacement produced the intriguing prospect of six-times Phillip Island winner Casey Stoner. It was a figment, however. More realistically, how about Jack Miller for his home GP? That didn't fly either. Miller's Pramac team had a championship position to protect; team-mate Petrucci one in the independent team riders' championship. The seat would go to Alvaro Bautista.

Both Suzuki and Yamaha fielded wild-cards. For the former, Sylvain Guintoli again, fresh from two days of testing at Motegi. He had been essaying chassis and engine ideas for 2019's bike, or at least a version of it for Valencia tests. With 2019's engine design frozen, it was important to get it right.

Yamaha also had important development work to do, but nothing new for Katsuyuki Nakasuga to test on behalf of its beleaguered factory riders. The 37-year-old veteran multiple national champion was merely being rewarded for many years of loyalty. This was his 12th GP, and he would preserve an enviable record of taking points every time, the highlight being an extraordinary second in a weather-affected Valencia race in 2012, substituting for the injured Ben Spies.

Neither the unexpected strengths that had surfaced at Chang, nor the weaknesses at the Red Bull Ring were in great evidence in a somewhat average weekend for Yamaha. Given the similar nature of Motegi to the latter track, this did indicate some progress.

A controversial post-race decision stripped Moto2 winner Quartararo of victory, after his rear tyre pressure was found to be fractionally under the 1.4-bar minimum. Speed Up team owner Luca Boscoscuro was not in Japan, and the team missed the 30-minute protest window. But he was consider-

ing an appeal to the Court of Arbitration for Sport, since the transgression of 0.04-bar was less than the maker's specified tolerance for the measuring equipment, and in any case, pressure could have been lost through a tyre fault during the race.

There were two victims of bizarre accidents. The first, back in Italy, was Nicolo Bulega. The Moto3 rider had fallen through a glass table while playing with his dog, suffering bad ligament damage to one hand. His substitute, 17-year-old fellow Rossi protégé Celestino Vietti, made the points at his first attempt.

The other was in Moto2, on the last lap of the race. The alternator on the Honda CBR600 engine in Bo Bensneyder's Tech 3 disintegrated with such violence that shrapnel hitting his left leg caused a compound fracture of the tibia, described as being like a shotgun wound.

In other news, Takaaki Nakagami's Idemitsu-backed contract with LCR was renewed, unsurprisingly. The rider was unable to celebrate with a strong result – after a first-lap collision, he struggled back into the lower points and ended the weekend apologising to his fans.

It was announced that the man deposed as 'youngest ever' by Marquez, 1983 and 1985 champion Freddie Spencer, had been appointed to take over from Race Director Mike Webb as chairman of the stewards panel, which decides on punishment for riders, with effect from 2019. News was also released that Avintia rider Xavier Simeon, after a disappointing MotoGP debut, was to ride for the same team's 2019 MotoE effort, alongside displaced ex-Moto2 rider Eric Granado.

MOTOGP RACE – 24 laps

Marquez's 43rd premier-class win, the 69th in his career, came at the end of what had become a typical MotoGP race in the latter part of the season. In the absence of Lorenzo, he and Dovizioso were joined up front by Crutchlow, all playing a wait-for-it game of tyre preservation.

Light rain on Friday afternoon was the only interruption, and just two-tenths covered the front row, led by Dovizioso from Zarco and another Ducati, Miller's private bike. A late flurry in times had consigned Marquez to sixth, less than three-tenths down on pole, and confined to one bike for Q2, after a tumble late in the preceding FP4. Crutchlow was top Honda, heading row two, with Iannone between him and Marquez. The factory Yamahas spanned Rins on row three, Vinales the better of them.

Bautista led row four, he and Nakagami through from Q1, the latter having prevented Smith's Q2 bid by less than a tenth. Petrucci was mired in Q1 after a morning crash left him on his spare bike.

Dovi led away; Marquez took a flyer to get straight into second. "I knew the first lap would be one of the most important," he said later.

From there, he dogged the Ducati's wheel tracks. He did pass once, briefly, on lap 14, only to run off on to the dirt out of the far hairpin, letting Dovi straight back. A little earlier, Crutchlow – frustrated by the slow pace – had got in front of Marquez for two laps and had been looking for a way into the lead. Afterwards, he regretted that he hadn't pushed past "and left Dovi and Marc to sort it out for second". But when Marquez nipped ahead once more, he dutifully followed along.

It was down to Dovizioso's tactics, lap times see-sawing so much that by half-distance, the pursuers had closed up, much to Crutchlow's dismay. At this point, Iannone was heading the group, from Rins and Rossi, but he would soon crash out.

Marquez's pass on Dovi, however, signalled a change. "Now he started to push harder," said Marquez later. "But I was able to go with him, in a good way."

Rather than risk losing another last-corner skirmish, Marquez dived past on the 21st, at Turn Nine, approaching the

far hairpin and the swoop downhill. This time, he stayed narrowly ahead, but surely it would go to another last-lap battle.

Not so. On the penultimate lap, poised to counterattack as they ran into Turn Ten, Dovi was a little wide, and a little fast. The Ducati's front wheel tucked, he was down, Marquez was alone. "I was faster in some places, but I prepared the corner too early. I asked too much of the front tyre," the Italian said.

For Marquez, "When I saw the pit board 'DOVI OUT' at the start of the last lap, my first reaction was to be pleased, because I knew I had won the championship. But now I am disappointed, because Andrea rode a great race and he deserves to be on the podium with us."

Crutchlow had his hands full with Rins at the end, but the Suzuki rider wasn't strong enough to attack, having used up his tyres fighting with Iannone and Rossi.

The hoped-for Yamaha revival remained on hold, although Rossi had bucked the odds with fourth, after being out-accelerated by the Suzukis. "This is our potential," he said. "Suzuki did a big step because they worked in the right way. Not like us."

He managed to stay half a second clear of Bautista, storming through from 11th on the first lap, and past Zarco on the last.

Vinales was left glum again, five seconds away in seventh, saying, "Every area was an issue". He'd taken the place off Pedrosa with five laps left. Petrucci was a lone ninth.

Syahrin won a lively scrap for tenth, a second ahead of rival rookie Morbidelli, who had passed Smith. The KTM rider managed to stay a couple of tenths ahead of team-mate Pol Espargaro.

Nakasuga got points again, clear of Nakagami by the end. Simeon and Torres were less than two seconds down, ahead of a remounted Dovi.

Miller had started well, but slipped off out of seventh on lap nine, let down by his slightly eccentric choice of a soft rather than medium rear Michelin. Aleix Espargaro, battered from a morning warm-up spill, was an early retirement.

With Marquez invulnerable, Dovizioso's no-score put him under threat from Rossi in the championship fight, nine points adrift.

MOTO2 RACE – 22 laps

Fabio Quartararo took his Speed Up chassis to a copybook second Moto2 win at Motegi, having resisted constant pressure from championship leader Bagnaia, who had led the first two laps. But with Oliveira off the podium in fourth, second was another valuable boost to Bagnaia's title hopes. Baldassarri, celebrating his 100th start, was a lone third.

Then the copybook was blotted. Quartararo's bike had failed the technical inspection – the rear tyre pressure was fractionally lower than the regulation 1.4 bar minimum. He was disqualified, stripped of the win.

That promoted everybody else by one position, giving Bagnaia an eighth win and extending his advantage over Oliveira from an erstwhile 35 points to 37. Even though the Portuguese was now effectively a podium finisher, it left him another two points worse off.

The leading pair had taken off from the start, Quartararo in front off the line from the middle of the front row, only to run a little wide, ceding the lead to pole-starter Bagnaia. Third front-row man Iker Lecuona was slow away, and losing places in the jostle.

Instead, it was Baldassarri up to third from the middle of row two, chased by Vierge, Marquez and hard-charging Oliveira, who had qualified ninth.

The next change came on lap three at the bottom of the downhill straight, where Quartararo cleanly outbraked Bagnaia. From there to the end, the front three positions didn't change – although Bagnaia did make a few attempts in the closing laps. He was still less than half a second behind over the line; by then, Baldassarri was more than five seconds away, with a similar margin of safety behind him.

There was some shuffling in the big chase group, though it was mainly through small errors in the heat of battle, for the pressure was intense.

Vierge led the group until lap 14, then ran wide into the crucial Turn 11. That finally let Oliveira through, and he stayed ahead of the rest to the end.

Marquez had crashed heavily on a wet white line on the first day of practice, and was battered and in pain; he had dropped back to ninth by lap eight. By the end, he had

Above: The top eight in Moto3 were covered by less than two seconds.

Right: With Martin gone, Moto3 winner Bezzecchi heads Binder, Dalla Porta, McPhee, Foggia and Arbolino.

Top: Seven-Up. Record-breaker Marquez celebrates with his crew.

Photos: Gold & Goose

Left: Saving tyres, entertaining the crowd. Dovi leads Marquez, Crutchlow lurks with intent.
Photo: Gold & Goose

Below left: A good move. Rins took third, and presented his helmet to company president Toshihiro Suzuki.
Photo: www.suzuki-racing.com

Below: The luckless Quartararo leads Bagnaia and Baldassarri.
Photo: Gold & Goose

picked up speed to reverse his fortunes, regaining one place after another, finally battling back ahead of second Red Bull KTM rider Binder for an eventual fourth. Second Pons HP40 rider Augusto Fernandez was close behind the pair.

Vierge was now a little back, holding off Lecuona, with Marini still close. Marcel Schrotter was never in touch with the gang, but was promoted to tenth.

The next trio also gained one place, with Mir, Nagashima and Aegerter all close. Mattia Pasini was some three seconds adrift; and Remy Gardner, having fended off Locatelli, was moved up into the points.

Sam Lowes was 17th, American Joe Roberts 18th, having held off NTS team-mate Odendaal and new European champion Jesko Raffin. The latter was riding the SAG Kalex in place of Alejandro Medini.

Corsi crashed out in the early stages, followed by Fuligni and Navarro; Bendsneyder did not complete the last lap.

MOTO3 RACE – 20 laps

What comes around goes around. Two weeks before, Bezzecchi had been brought down on the last corner for zero points. In Japan, it was Martin's turn again, while Bezzecchi snatched his third win on the final run to the line, and closed the points gap to just one.

Martin fell at tricky Turn 11, put off line while fighting to regain positions in a ten-strong lead pack. A couple of laps earlier, he'd banged Bezzecchi at the same place and dropped to the back of the gang.

Team-mate Di Giannantonio had fallen earlier at the next corner, spoiling his title challenge.

Top Honda was Dalla Porta, his third podium in four races. He claimed second by 0.001 of a second in a photo finish with podium first-timer Darren Binder, bouncing back after a dire season on the Red Bull KTM following a front-end settings breakthrough. He'd led the last lap, but a missed gear out of the last corner dropped him to third.

The top three were covered by 0.042 of a second, the top seven still inside half a second, but the Hondas' usual edge was somewhat blunted at a track where the KTMs' acceleration tipped the balance.

MOTUL GRAND PRIX OF JAPAN

19–21 OCTOBER, 2018

TWIN RING MOTEGI

24 laps
Length: 4.801 km / 2.983 miles
Width: 15m

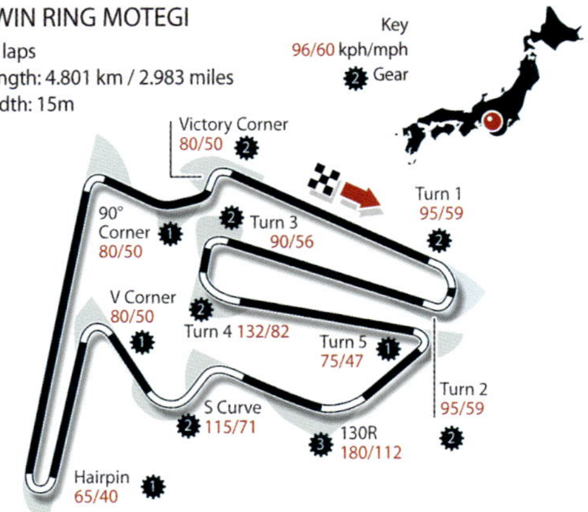

MotoGP

RACE DISTANCE: 24 laps, 71.597 miles/115.224km · RACE WEATHER: Dry (air 23°C, humidity 34%, track 35°C)

Pos.	Rider	Nat.	No.	Entrant	Machine	Tyres	Race tyre choice	Laps	Time & speed
1	**Marc Marquez**	SPA	93	Repsol Honda Team	Honda RC213V	M	F: Medium/R: Medium	24	42m 36.438s 100.8mph/ 162.2km/h
2	**Cal Crutchlow**	GBR	35	LCR Honda CASTROL	Honda RC213V	M	F: Medium/R: Medium	24	42m 38.011s
3	**Alex Rins**	SPA	42	Team SUZUKI ECSTAR	Suzuki GSX-RR	M	F: Medium/R: Medium	24	42m 38.158s
4	**Valentino Rossi**	ITA	46	Movistar Yamaha MotoGP	Yamaha YZR-M1	M	F: Medium/R: Medium	24	42m 42.851s
5	**Alvaro Bautista**	SPA	19	Angel Nieto Team	Ducati Desmosedici	M	F: Soft/R: Soft	24	42m 43.357s
6	**Johann Zarco**	FRA	5	Monster Yamaha Tech 3	Yamaha YZR-M1	M	F: Soft/R: Medium	24	42m 44.462s
7	**Maverick Vinales**	SPA	25	Movistar Yamaha MotoGP	Yamaha YZR-M1	M	F: Soft/R: Medium	24	42m 49.768s
8	**Dani Pedrosa**	SPA	26	Repsol Honda Team	Honda RC213V	M	F: Medium/R: Medium	24	42m 52.020s
9	**Danilo Petrucci**	ITA	9	Alma Pramac Racing	Ducati Desmosedici	M	F: Soft/R: Medium	24	42m 57.022s
10	**Hafizh Syahrin**	MAL	55	Monster Yamaha Tech 3	Yamaha YZR-M1	M	F: Medium/R: Medium	24	43m 01.423s
11	**Franco Morbidelli**	ITA	21	EG 0,0 Marc VDS	Honda RC213V	M	F: Medium/R: Medium	24	43m 02.369s
12	**Bradley Smith**	GBR	38	Red Bull KTM Factory Racing	KTM RC16	M	F: Medium/R: Medium	24	43m 03.313s
13	**Pol Espargaro**	SPA	44	Red Bull KTM Factory Racing	KTM RC16	M	F: Medium/R: Soft	24	43m 03.507s
14	**Katsuyuki Nakasuga**	JPN	89	Yamalube Yamaha Factory Racing	Yamaha YZR-M1	M	F: Medium/R: Medium	24	43m 08.988s
15	**Takaaki Nakagami**	JPN	30	LCR Honda IDEMITSU	Honda RC213V	M	F: Medium/R: Soft	24	43m 14.156s
16	Xavier Simeon	BEL	10	Reale Avintia Racing	Ducati Desmosedici	M	F: Soft/R: Medium	24	43m 16.021s
17	Jordi Torres	SPA	81	Reale Avintia Racing	Ducati Desmosedici	M	F: Soft/R: Medium	24	43m 16.277s
18	Andrea Dovizioso	ITA	4	Ducati Team	Ducati Desmosedici	M	F: Soft/R: Medium	24	43m 19.136s
19	Scott Redding	GBR	45	Aprilia Racing Team Gresini	Aprilia RS-GP	M	F: Soft/R: Soft	24	43m 26.381s
20	Thomas Luthi	SWI	12	EG 0,0 Marc VDS	Honda RC213V	M	F: Medium/R: Medium	24	43m 29.145s
21	Sylvain Guintoli	FRA	50	Team SUZUKI ECSTAR	Suzuki GSX-RR	M	F: Medium/R: Medium	24	43m 38.286s
	Andrea Iannone	ITA	29	Team SUZUKI ECSTAR	Suzuki GSX-RR	M	F: Medium/R: Medium	14	DNF-crash
	Karel Abraham	CZE	17	Angel Nieto Team	Ducati Desmosedici	M	F: Medium/R: Soft	12	DNF-crash
	Jack Miller	AUS	43	Alma Pramac Racing	Ducati Desmosedici	M	F: Soft/R: Soft	10	DNF-crash
	Aleix Espargaro	SPA	41	Aprilia Racing Team Gresini	Aprilia RS-GP	M	F: Medium/R: Soft	6	DNF-technical
	Jorge Lorenzo	SPA	99	Ducati Team	Ducati Desmosedici	M	-	-	DNS-injured

Fastest lap: Marc Marquez, on lap 19, 1m 45.646s, 101.6mph/163.5km/h.
Lap record: Jorge Lorenzo, 1m 45.350s, 101.9mph/164.0km/h (2014).
Event maximum speed: Maverick Vinales, 193.8mph/311.9km/h (race).

Qualifying

Weather: Dry
Air Temp: 20° **Track Temp:** 29°
Humidity: 60%

1	Dovizioso	1m 44.590s
2	Zarco	1m 44.658s
3	Miller	1m 44.727s
4	Crutchlow	1m 44.820s
5	Iannone	1m 44.832s
6	Marquez	1m 44.889s
7	Vinales	1m 45.140s
8	Rins	1m 45.225s
9	Rossi	1m 45.265s
10	Bautista	1m 45.396s
11	Pedrosa	1m 45.519s
12	Nakagami	1m 46.168s
13	Smith	1m 45.722s
14	P. Espargaro	1m 45.742s
15	Petrucci	1m 45.759s
16	Syahrin	1m 45.765s
17	Morbidelli	1m 45.969s
18	Abraham	1m 46.072s
19	A. Espargaro	1m 46.183s
20	Nakasuga	1m 46.441s
21	Redding	1m 46.571s
22	Simeon	1m 46.573s
23	Luthi	1m 46.817s
24	Guintoli	1m 47.106s
25	Torres	1m 47.147s

Fastest race laps

1	Marquez	1m 45.646s
2	Dovizioso	1m 45.696s
3	Iannone	1m 45.812s
4	Crutchlow	1m 45.858s
5	Rins	1m 45.961s
6	Bautista	1m 45.987s
7	Zarco	1m 46.005s
8	Rossi	1m 46.024s
9	Miller	1m 46.167s
10	Vinales	1m 46.175s
11	Pedrosa	1m 46.365s
12	Syahrin	1m 46.481s
13	Petrucci	1m 46.573s
14	Smith	1m 46.799s
15	Morbidelli	1m 46.834s
16	Nakasuga	1m 46.883s
17	P. Espargaro	1m 46.895s
18	Abraham	1m 47.041s
19	Nakagami	1m 47.068s
20	Simeon	1m 47.182s
21	Redding	1m 47.275s
22	Torres	1m 47.281s
23	A. Espargaro	1m 47.547s
24	Luthi	1m 47.631s
25	Guintoli	1m 48.115s

Championship Points

1	Marquez	296
2	Dovizioso	194
3	Rossi	185
4	Vinales	155
5	Crutchlow	148
6	Zarco	133
7	Petrucci	133
8	Lorenzo	130
9	Rins	118
10	Iannone	113
11	Pedrosa	95
12	Bautista	83
13	Miller	74
14	Morbidelli	38
15	Rabat	35
16	P. Espargaro	35
17	Syahrin	34
18	A. Espargaro	32
19	Smith	23
20	Nakagami	19
21	Redding	12
22	Kallio	6
23	Abraham	5
24	Nakasuga	2
25	Pirro	1

Constructor Points

1	Honda	331
2	Ducati	284
3	Yamaha	231
4	Suzuki	173
5	KTM	49
6	Aprilia	42

	Grid order	1	2	3	4	5	6	7	8	9	10	11	12	13	14	15	16	17	18	19	20	21	22	23	24	
4	DOVIZIOSO	4	4	4	4	4	4	4	4	4	4	4	4	4	4	4	4	4	4	4	4	93	93	93	93	1
5	ZARCO	93	93	93	93	35	35	93	93	93	93	93	93	93	93	93	93	93	93	93	93	4	4	35	35	2
43	MILLER	43	43	35	35	93	93	35	35	35	35	35	35	35	35	35	35	35	35	35	35	35	35	42	42	3
35	CRUTCHLOW	35	35	43	43	46	46	46	46	46	29	29	29	29	29	42	42	42	42	42	42	42	42	46	46	4
29	IANNONE	46	46	46	46	43	43	29	29	29	46	42	42	42	42	46	46	46	46	46	46	46	46	19	19	5
93	MARQUEZ	42	42	42	42	42	42	42	42	42	42	46	46	46	46	5	5	5	5	5	5	5	19	5	5	6
25	VINALES	5	5	5	29	29	29	43	43	43	43	5	5	5	5	19	19	19	19	19	19	19	5	25	25	7
42	RINS	26	26	29	5	5	5	5	5	5	5	26	26	19	19	26	26	26	26	26	25	25	25	26	26	8
46	ROSSI	29	29	26	26	26	26	26	26	26	26	19	19	26	26	25	25	25	25	25	26	26	26	9	9	9
19	BAUTISTA	25	25	25	25	25	25	19	19	19	19	25	25	25	25	9	9	9	9	9	9	9	9	55	55	10
26	PEDROSA	19	19	19	19	19	19	25	25	25	25	9	9	9	9	38	38	38	38	55	55	55	55	38	21	11
30	NAKAGAMI	44	9	9	9	9	9	9	9	9	9	38	38	38	38	55	55	55	55	38	38	38	38	21	38	12
38	SMITH	9	44	44	44	38	38	38	38	38	38	21	55	55	55	21	21	21	21	21	21	21	21	44	44	13
44	P. ESPARGARO	38	38	38	38	44	44	44	44	21	21	55	21	21	21	44	44	44	44	44	44	44	44	89	89	14
9	PETRUCCI	45	45	45	45	21	21	21	21	44	55	44	44	44	44	89	89	89	89	89	89	89	89	30	30	15
55	SYAHRIN	21	21	21	21	55	55	55	55	55	44	89	89	89	89	30	30	30	30	30	30	30	30	4	10	
21	MORBIDELLI	41	41	55	55	45	45	45	45	17	17	30	30	30	30	45	10	10	10	10	10	10	10	10	81	
17	ABRAHAM	55	55	17	17	17	17	17	89	89	89	45	45	45	45	10	81	81	81	81	81	81	81	81	4	
41	A. ESPARGARO	17	17	89	89	89	89	89	17	45	30	10	10	10	10	81	45	45	45	45	45	45	45	45	45	
89	NAKASUGA	89	89	30	30	30	30	30	30	30	45	81	81	81	81	12	12	12	12	12	12	12	12	12	12	
45	REDDING	81	30	81	81	10	10	10	10	10	10	50	12	12	12	50	50	50	50	50	50	50	50	50	50	
10	SIMEON	30	81	10	10	81	81	81	81	81	81	12	50	50	50											
12	LUTHI	10	10	41	41	41	41	50	50	50	50	17	17													
50	GUINTOLI	12	50	50	50	50	50	12	12	12	12															
81	TORRES	50	12	12	12	12	12																			

41 Pit stop

Moto2

RACE DISTANCE: 22 laps, 65.630 miles/105.622km · **RACE WEATHER:** Dry (air 23°C, humidity 32%, track 35°C)

Pos.	Rider	Nat.	No.	Entrant	Machine	Laps	Time & Speed
1	**Francesco Bagnaia**	ITA	42	SKY Racing Team VR46	Kalex	22	41m 04.294s 95.8mph/ 154.2km/h
2	**Lorenzo Baldassarri**	ITA	7	Pons HP40	Kalex	22	41m 10.521s
3	**Miguel Oliveira**	POR	44	Red Bull KTM Ajo	KTM	22	41m 15.847s
4	**Alex Marquez**	SPA	73	EG 0,0 Marc VDS	Kalex	22	41m 16.377s
5	**Brad Binder**	RSA	41	Red Bull KTM Ajo	KTM	22	41m 16.642s
6	**Augusto Fernandez**	SPA	40	Pons HP40	Kalex	22	41m 16.995s
7	**Xavi Vierge**	SPA	97	Dynavolt Intact GP	Kalex	22	41m 17.946s
8	**Iker Lecuona**	SPA	27	Swiss Innovative Investors	KTM	22	41m 18.105s
9	**Luca Marini**	ITA	10	SKY Racing Team VR46	Kalex	22	41m 19.898s
10	**Marcel Schrotter**	GER	23	Dynavolt Intact GP	Kalex	22	41m 21.850s
11	**Joan Mir**	SPA	36	EG 0,0 Marc VDS	Kalex	22	41m 23.515s
12	**Tetsuta Nagashima**	JPN	45	IDEMITSU Honda Team Asia	Kalex	22	41m 24.105s
13	**Dominique Aegerter**	SWI	77	Kiefer Racing	KTM	22	41m 24.572s
14	**Mattia Pasini**	ITA	54	Italtrans Racing Team	Kalex	22	41m 27.385s
15	**Remy Gardner**	AUS	87	Tech 3 Racing	Tech 3	22	41m 28.762s
16	Andrea Locatelli	ITA	5	Italtrans Racing Team	Kalex	22	41m 28.916s
17	Sam Lowes	GBR	22	Swiss Innovative Investors	KTM	22	41m 30.582s
18	Joe Roberts	USA	16	NTS RW Racing GP	NTS	22	41m 38.181s
19	Steven Odendaal	RSA	4	NTS RW Racing GP	NTS	22	41m 38.368s
20	Jesko Raffin	SWI	2	SAG Team	Kalex	22	41m 38.597s
21	Niki Tuuli	FIN	66	Petronas Sprinta Racing	Kalex	22	41m 41.752s
22	Khairul Idham Pawi	MAL	89	IDEMITSU Honda Team Asia	Kalex	22	41m 42.215s
23	Edgar Pons	SPA	57	MB Conveyors - Speed Up	Speed Up	22	41m 46.864s
24	Stefano Manzi	ITA	62	Forward Racing Team	Suter	22	41m 50.961s
25	Jules Danilo	FRA	95	Nashi Argan SAG Team	Kalex	22	42m 00.794s
26	Isaac Vinales	SPA	32	Forward Racing Team	Suter	22	42m 03.953s
27	Xavi Cardelus	AND	18	Marinelli Snipers Team	Kalex	22	42m 11.359s
	Bo Bendsneyder	NED	64	Tech 3 Racing	Tech 3	21	DNF
	Jorge Navarro	SPA	9	Federal Oil Gresini Moto2	Kalex	13	DNF
	Federico Fuligni	ITA	21	Tasca Racing Scuderia Moto2	Kalex	9	DNF
	Simone Corsi	ITA	24	Tasca Racing Scuderia Moto2	Kalex	3	DNF
	Fabio Quartararo	FRA	20	MB Conveyors - Speed Up	Speed Up	-	DSQ

Fastest lap: Francesco Bagnaia, on lap 11, 1m 51.367s, 96.4mph/155.1km/h.
Lap record: Franco Morbidelli, 1m 50.788s, 96.9mph/156.0km/h (2016).
Event maximum speed: Brad Binder, 160.8mph/258.8km/h (qualifying).

Qualifying

Weather: Dry
Air Temp: 19° **Track Temp:** 26°
Humidity: 65%

Pos.	Rider	Time
1	Bagnaia	1m 50.759s
2	Quartararo	1m 50.924s
3	Lecuona	1m 50.990s
4	Schrotter	1m 51.043s
5	Baldassarri	1m 51.092s
6	Marquez	1m 51.250s
7	Vierge	1m 51.313s
8	Nagashima	1m 51.327s
9	Oliveira	1m 51.331s
10	Binder	1m 51.340s
11	Marini	1m 51.343s
12	Fernandez	1m 51.359s
13	Gardner	1m 51.505s
14	Mir	1m 51.555s
15	Navarro	1m 51.638s
16	Corsi	1m 51.666s
17	Aegerter	1m 51.769s
18	Roberts	1m 51.797s
19	Lowes	1m 51.808s
20	Locatelli	1m 51.822s
21	Pasini	1m 51.862s
22	E. Pons	1m 51.899s
23	Pawi	1m 52.258s
24	Raffin	1m 52.378s
25	Odendaal	1m 52.505s
26	Bendsneyder	1m 52.549s
27	Manzi	1m 52.625s
28	Tuuli	1m 52.775s
29	Vinales	1m 53.222s
30	Danilo	1m 53.755s
31	Cardelus	1m 53.870s
32	Fuligni	1m 54.199s

Fastest race laps

Pos.	Rider	Time
1	Bagnaia	1m 51.367s
2	Quartararo	1m 51.381s
3	Oliveira	1m 51.682s
4	Baldassarri	1m 51.684s
5	Fernandez	1m 51.692s
6	Binder	1m 51.701s
7	Marini	1m 51.815s
8	Mir	1m 51.847s
9	Lecuona	1m 51.882s
10	Marquez	1m 51.913s
11	Vierge	1m 51.930s
12	Schrotter	1m 52.039s
13	Navarro	1m 52.040s
14	Nagashima	1m 52.064s
15	Lowes	1m 52.073s
16	Pasini	1m 52.120s
17	Aegerter	1m 52.128s
18	Corsi	1m 52.230s
19	Gardner	1m 52.358s
20	Locatelli	1m 52.364s
21	Odendaal	1m 52.459s
22	Roberts	1m 52.663s
23	Manzi	1m 52.769s
24	E. Pons	1m 52.810s
25	Raffin	1m 52.846s
26	Tuuli	1m 52.929s
27	Pawi	1m 52.941s
28	Bendsneyder	1m 53.197s
29	Danilo	1m 53.598s
30	Vinales	1m 53.638s
31	Cardelus	1m 53.702s
32	Fuligni	1m 54.109s

Championship Points

Pos.	Rider	Points
1	Bagnaia	284
2	Oliveira	247
3	Binder	168
4	Baldassarri	152
5	Marquez	139
6	Mir	129
7	Schrotter	124
8	Pasini	115
9	Quartararo	111
10	Marini	111
11	Vierge	110
12	Lecuona	60
13	Navarro	55
14	Corsi	47
15	Lowes	46
16	Locatelli	41
17	Aegerter	30
18	Gardner	29
19	Fernandez	24
20	Nagashima	20
21	Fenati	14
22	Barbera	10
23	Manzi	8
24	Kent	8
25	Vinales	7
26	Roberts	5
27	Bendsneyder	2
28	Pawi	1
29	Odendaal	1
30	Tuuli	1
31	Raffin	1

Constructor Points

Pos.	Constructor	Points
1	Kalex	346
2	KTM	275
3	Speed Up	115
4	Tech 3	29
5	Suter	8
6	NTS	5

Moto3

RACE DISTANCE: 20 laps, 59.664 miles/96.020km · **RACE WEATHER:** Dry (air 21°C, humidity 34%, track 33°C)

Pos.	Rider	Nat.	No.	Entrant	Machine	Laps	Time & Speed
1	**Marco Bezzecchi**	ITA	12	Redox PruestelGP	KTM	20	39m 35.653s 90.4mph/ 145.5km/h
2	**Lorenzo Dalla Porta**	ITA	48	Leopard Racing	Honda	20	39m 35.694s
3	**Darryn Binder**	RSA	40	Red Bull KTM Ajo	KTM	20	39m 35.695s
4	**Dennis Foggia**	ITA	10	SKY Racing Team VR46	KTM	20	39m 35.865s
5	**John McPhee**	GBR	17	CIP - Green Power	KTM	20	39m 35.904s
6	**Tony Arbolino**	ITA	14	Marinelli Snipers Team	Honda	20	39m 36.003s
7	**Enea Bastianini**	ITA	33	Leopard Racing	Honda	20	39m 36.057s
8	**Gabriel Rodrigo**	ARG	19	RBA BOE Skull Rider	KTM	20	39m 37.214s
9	**Ayumu Sasaki**	JPN	71	Petronas Sprinta Racing	Honda	20	39m 38.790s
10	**Jakub Kornfeil**	CZE	84	Redox PruestelGP	KTM	20	39m 43.618s
11	**Jaume Masia**	SPA	5	Bester Capital Dubai	KTM	20	39m 44.017s
12	**Marcos Ramirez**	SPA	42	Bester Capital Dubai	KTM	20	39m 44.088s
13	**Andrea Migno**	ITA	16	Angel Nieto Team Moto3	KTM	20	39m 44.214s
14	**Celestino Vietti**	ITA	31	SKY Racing Team VR46	KTM	20	39m 44.694s
15	**Tatsuki Suzuki**	JPN	24	SIC58 Squadra Corse	Honda	20	39m 44.890s
16	Philipp Oettl	GER	65	Sudmetal Schedl GP Racing	KTM	20	39m 45.551s
17	Kaito Toba	JPN	27	Honda Team Asia	Honda	20	39m 46.550s
18	Alonso Lopez	SPA	72	Estrella Galicia 0,0	Honda	20	39m 51.344s
19	Adam Norrodin	MAL	7	Petronas Sprinta Racing	Honda	20	39m 51.357s
20	Stefano Nepa	ITA	81	CIP - Green Power	KTM	20	39m 59.838s
21	Nakarin Atiratphuvapat	THA	41	Honda Team Asia	Honda	20	40m 00.234s
22	Kazuki Masaki	JPN	22	RBA BOE Skull Rider	KTM	20	40m 17.581s
23	Shizuka Okazaki	JPN	13	Kohara Racing Team	Honda	20	41m 23.989s
24	Yuto Fukushima	JPN	36	Team Plus One	Honda	19	39m 40.420s
	Jorge Martin	SPA	88	Del Conca Gresini Moto3	Honda	14	DNF
	Albert Arenas	SPA	75	Angel Nieto Team Moto3	KTM	10	DNF
	Fabio Di Giannantonio	ITA	21	Del Conca Gresini Moto3	Honda	5	DNF
	Niccolo Antonelli	ITA	23	SIC58 Squadra Corse	Honda	1	DNF
	Vicente Perez	SPA	77	Reale Avintia Academy 77	KTM	1	DNF
	Aron Canet	SPA	44	Estrella Galicia 0,0	Honda	0	DNF

Fastest lap: Darryn Binder, on lap 2, 1m 57.361s, 91.5mph/147.2km/h.
Lap record: Alex Marquez, 1m 57.112s, 91.7mph/147.5km/h (2014).
Event maximum speed: Vicente Perez, 137.6mph/221.4km/h (qualifying).

Qualifying

Weather: Dry
Air Temp: 22° **Track Temp:** 33°
Humidity: 48%

Pos.	Rider	Time
1	Rodrigo	1m 56.894s
2	McPhee	1m 56.969s
3	Bezzecchi	1m 57.014s
4	Martin	1m 57.118s
5	Binder	1m 57.120s
6	Bastianini	1m 57.194s
7	Foggia	1m 57.202s
8	Masaki	1m 57.260s
9	Arenas	1m 57.410s
10	Dalla Porta	1m 57.453s
11	Ramirez	1m 57.476s
12	Arbolino	1m 57.507s
13	Sasaki	1m 57.610s
14	Perez	1m 57.627s
15	Di Giannantonio	1m 57.636s
16	Kornfeil	1m 57.692s
17	Antonelli	1m 57.755s
18	Migno	1m 57.862s
19	Canet	1m 57.910s
20	Lopez	1m 58.002s
21	Masia	1m 58.020s
22	Oettl	1m 58.034s
23	Norrodin	1m 58.107s
24	Vietti	1m 58.236s
25	Nepa	1m 58.315s
26	Suzuki	1m 58.411s
27	Atiratphuvapat	1m 58.659s
28	Toba	1m 58.659s
29	Okazaki	2m 03.453s
30	Fukushima	2m 03.584s

Fastest race laps

Pos.	Rider	Time
1	Binder	1m 57.361s
2	Arenas	1m 57.458s
3	McPhee	1m 57.515s
4	Dalla Porta	1m 57.564s
5	Bastianini	1m 57.565s
6	Masaki	1m 57.586s
7	Foggia	1m 57.587s
8	Martin	1m 57.599s
9	Bezzecchi	1m 57.704s
10	Di Giannantonio	1m 57.730s
11	Arbolino	1m 57.735s
12	Rodrigo	1m 57.826s
13	Sasaki	1m 57.889s
14	Norrodin	1m 58.123s
15	Oettl	1m 58.155s
16	Vietti	1m 58.252s
17	Suzuki	1m 58.257s
18	Ramirez	1m 58.286s
19	Kornfeil	1m 58.296s
20	Masia	1m 58.321s
21	Toba	1m 58.340s
22	Migno	1m 58.364s
23	Lopez	1m 58.434s
24	Atiratphuvapat	1m 58.722s
25	Nepa	1m 58.746s
26	Fukushima	2m 03.237s
27	Okazaki	2m 03.276s

Championship Points

Pos.	Rider	Points
1	Martin	204
2	Bezzecchi	203
3	Di Giannantonio	175
4	Bastianini	142
5	Dalla Porta	131
6	Canet	118
7	Rodrigo	116
8	Kornfeil	108
9	Ramirez	90
10	Migno	79
11	Arenas	69
12	Masia	66
13	McPhee	60
14	Oettl	57
15	Antonelli	56
16	Foggia	55
17	Suzuki	51
18	Arbolino	49
19	Binder	44
20	Sasaki	39
21	Norrodin	37
22	Toba	33
23	Lopez	31
24	Bulega	18
25	Perez	13
26	Fernandez	13
27	Yurchenko	9
28	Loi	8
29	Masaki	8
30	Chantra	7
31	Pagliani	6
32	Atiratphuvapat	2
33	Vietti	2
34	Ogura	1

Constructor Points

Pos.	Constructor	Points
1	Honda	336
2	KTM	290

FIM WORLD CHAMPIONSHIP · ROUND 17

AUSTRALIAN GRAND PRIX

PHILLIP ISLAND CIRCUIT

Inset, left: Friends at last – crew chief Ramon Forcada and rider Maverick Vinales united in victory.

Inset, far left: Brad Binder took a third Moto2 win.

Inset, centre left: Albert Arenas won by inches in Moto3.

Main: Out on his own. Vinales ended Yamaha's longest win drought.
Photos: Gold & Goose

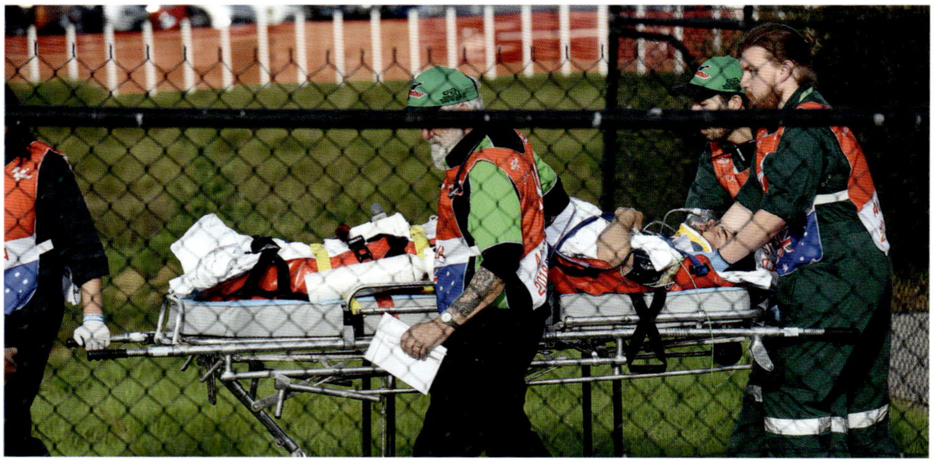

Above: Game over for Cal Crutchlow, whose run of form ended painfully.
Photo: Gold & Goose

Above right: Honda's five-timers formed an elite mutual admiration group. Marquez wore Doohan-replica gloves and boots.
Photo: Repsol Honda

Top: Franco Morbidelli and Aleix Espargaro battle over eighth place. Debris from the Zarco-Marquez crash had damaged a plate in the Spaniard's hand.
Photo: Monster Energy

Top right: Hit and miss in practice. Bautista was a hit in the race on Lorenzo's factory Ducati.

Above far right: Still standing. Johann Zarco was lucky to escape unhurt from a very fast crash.

Right: Seat smashed, tyre slashed – Marquez checks the damage on his hobbled Honda.
Photos: Gold & Goose

GP RACING held its breath on Sunday at Phillip Island, for as long as it took Johann Zarco to slide to a stop and get to his feet. The odds suggested that he might not be able to do so. He had crashed spectacularly after slamming into Marquez's back wheel at fully 280km/h, a whisker short of 174mph. His bike reared up over the back of the Honda, the rider flew high, then slammed down. His great good fortune was to be on grass, so he slid right over the pit exit road and on to more greensward without too much injurious flipping. A few metres to the right and he would have been in the gravel trap, and in great peril.

Miraculously, the Frenchman was unhurt. Meanwhile, Marquez toured to the pits with terminal tyre and bodywork damage, while Iannone – who had missed Zarco's reverse-ground-looping Yamaha by inches – had recovered his poise.

Racing had got away with it. Attention could turn back to yet another superb contest at one of the world's finest tracks – a feast of rhythm and speed, where Vinales was able to turn his and Yamaha's fortunes around and finally break the company's longest ever winless spell. His own first win for (as he pointed out) almost 18 months. That it was in the absence of Marquez, and that his closest, though distant, challenger was Iannone on the Suzuki, did not detract from the hard reality.

But the spectacular crash underlined a number of facts – primarily that fast corners are prone to hosting very scary accidents, where nobody is really to blame. The effects of slipstreaming on the flat-out downhill approach to Turn One, aka Doohan Corner, are just one factor that make braking distances hard to judge. There are also Phillip Island's notorious crosswinds and general lack of warmth, which have frequently taken riders and tyres respectively out of their safe performance zones. There were the usual rider calls, quietly ignored, to move the date of the GP from the cold and squall-prone early southern spring to a more amenable late summer date.

Doohan Corner is not the only very fast turn at the track, but generally it is the scariest. There were other crashes there over the three days, and the victims included Pedrosa and Syahrin, and Moto2 riders Lecuona and Odendaal. All escaped injury.

And Cal Crutchlow, on Friday afternoon, whose blind luck was facing the other way. His helter-skelter through the gravel broke his right ankle above and below the joint, with three separate fractures requiring two bouts of surgery in Melbourne in the coming the week. His season was over, a strong run of form abruptly terminated, and his position as top independent-team rider in the championship undermined, opening the way for a late-season stand-off between Petrucci and (ironically) Zarco.

The tricky conditions, with high winds and moments of generally light rain on both practice days (happily not repeated on Sunday), caused a number of other crashes. Remy Gardner opened his home-race weekend with a big high-side at the last corner; other tumblers included Moto2's Navarro and Lowes (both twice on Friday), plus Binder, Corsi, Pawi and Bryan Staring (in place of Bendsneyder), and in Moto3, Bezzecchi (also twice) and spectacularly Di Giannantonio. More crashes on Saturday eliminated Moto2's Manzi (wrist) and Moto3's Masaki (hand).

Bautista was on Lorenzo's GP18, and until the race, his performance was a little worrying, as he struggled to adapt from his GP17. He fell on Friday afternoon, managed to make Q2 from Q1, but promptly crashed again. He crashed once more in morning warm-up. By then, Ducati must have been regretting the unavoidable absence of tester and regular substitute Michele Pirro, engaged in vitally important tests of the 2019 bike at Valencia. Come the race, Bautista

didn't just vindicate himself, but even looked as though he might beat full-timer Dovizioso, before finishing a year's best fourth. This was potentially valuable to Ducati's position in the constructors' and teams' championships. It also begged the question, again, why had he been unable to secure a 2019 MotoGP ride? That, at least partly, had been due to an unusually early round of contract signings – Iannone another victim who had lost his seat before he'd had a real chance to prove himself.

The weekend got off to a slow start, thanks to an oil spill on the very first lap of the very first free practice. It came from Stefano Nepa's CIP Green Power KTM and stretched from Turn Two (Southern Loop) to Turn Eight (Hayshed); pretty much half the lap. Only one rider fell, Bezzecchi, and the red flags came out promptly. It took the best part of two-and-a-half hours and vigorous broomwork to render the track usable. Nepa was suspended from FP2 for irresponsible riding "by not determining the state of your motorcycle prior to restarting after a machine problem". FP sessions were cut for the smaller classes, Moto3 losing 15 minutes and Moto2 ten, and the lunch break was abandoned. Only MotoGP ran full length, finishing at 17:05 rather than the scheduled 16:50.

At Misano, Aleix Espargaro had tested a 2017 Aprilia and found it better in several respects, but his request to switch back had been put on hold. Now the factory had sent a sort of 'lab bike', one race later than had been hoped. This combined elements of the 2017 chassis with 2018 and even 2019 parts and ideas. The rider liked it, but his race was marred when he was struck on the hand by flying debris from the Marquez-Zarco clash.

News came at the race of Pedrosa's surprising, though not altogether unexpected, abandonment of HRC to test for KTM; and that KTM had signed Rookies Cup champion Can Oncu for their Red Bull Ajo Moto3 team. And, very promptly, that Bradl would step in for Crutchlow the following weekend at Sepang.

And former double 250/350 champion (that's four titles) Kork Ballington was appointed the 28th MotoGP Legend. Rhodesian born, the South African was now resident in Australia. "For starters, I'm honoured, because Randy [Mamola] flew all the way from California to see me," he joked, adding, "I'm amongst friends, this is my fraternity. To be put alongside the 27 other fantastic riders is an honour and a privilege."

MOTOGP RACE - 27 laps

Isolated, but scary spots of rain exactly as the pit lane opened meant that QP2 favoured the brave. Like Miller, hoping to repeat his Argentine pole, on slicks on a damp track. But the rain never quite arrived, and a fifth consecutive Phillip Island pole went to Marquez, from the Yamahas of Vinales and Zarco.

Iannone (who had topped free practice) led row two and was widely tipped as a victory contender. Rins and Miller were alongside; behind them, Rossi headed Petrucci and Dovizioso, with Syahrin back from his fast morning crash an impressive tenth.

Marquez – wearing Doohan replica boots and gloves in tribute to his fellow five-times Honda champion – started well, but Vinales and Zarco were swamped, finishing lap one ninth and eighth respectively. Instead it was Petrucci who surged off row three to seize a short-lived lead into Turn One. On Turn Two, he ran off, dropping to last place before beginning an impressive fight back: "It was the best start of my career, but in the second corner the [slipper] clutch didn't release and locked the back wheel."

Miller was fast and determined, and led lap one, but he was shuffled to fourth next time around, with Marquez, Dovizioso and Iannone ahead of him; and then Zarco on the following lap, after the two had traded blows in a generally furious battle.

Above: Free at last. Suzuki's Iannone eventually escaped the Ducatis for second.
Photo: www.suzuki-racing.com

Top right: Binder heads Mir, Marini and Aegerter mid-race. Victory came just 0.036 clear of Mir.
Photo: Gold & Goose

Above right: Jorge Martin was lucky to avoid this tangle between Arbolino and Foggia two laps from the finish.
Photo: John Morris – Mpix Photography

Centre right: Winners and losers. A sensational first podium for Sky VR46 youngster Celestino Vietti (*left*); broken dreams for the deflated Marco Bezzecchi, eliminated for a second time in three races.
Photos: Monster Energy

Right: Whose line is it anyway? Albert Arenas (75) emerged victorious from a torrid Moto3 race.
Photo: Gold & Goose

At the end of lap five, the Ducatis of Dovi and Miller surged past Marquez; and Zarco, aggressively past Iannone, almost got ahead as well. Marquez moved across to take his line for Turn One; Zarco, later on the brakes, couldn't prevent his front wheel from touching the Honda's rear, triggering mayhem, if only momentarily.

Vinales, meanwhile, had been quietly gaining places, now ahead of Bautista. On lap seven, he dodged past Rossi, Miller and Iannone in turn; next time around, Dovizioso as well to take a lead he would hold to the finish. He set fastest lap on the tenth, now 1.3 seconds clear. That would stretch to better than four seconds ten laps later.

Rossi held second for a while, but it was all very close. Then Iannone made a big mistake when braking for Turn Four, dropping behind the factory Ducatis, with Bautista for a while ahead of Dovi.

Both would soon pass Rossi; and on lap 17, Iannone did so as well. By then, Rins was ahead of Miller and pulling the pair back into touch.

Iannone had the pace, but once again was continually frustrated by the hard-braking, fast-accelerating Ducatis. On lap 20, he was back between them, Dovi now in front again – only to repeat his Turn Four mistake. But on the 23rd, he slipped past Bautista, then accomplished a spectacular pass on Dovi around the Hayshed corner. Now he was up to second, and he took a full second out of Vinales's lead next time around. Was there a sting in the tail?

Vinales was worried, he admitted, as his tyre performance had dropped badly. But Iannone had lost too much through earlier errors, and it was too little too late. He was left to fend off a furious last-lap assault by Dovizioso.

In their wake, Bautista claimed a safe fourth; Rins passed Rossi for fifth on the final lap, while Miller crossed the line a close seventh.

Pedrosa had qualified a dismal 18th in the cold, but had managed to move up into the points until he became one of the many victims of the Turn Four hairpin before half-distance. This meant that Morbidelli, in eighth, was the top Honda. He'd got back ahead of Aleix Espargaro on the final lap, with Smith right behind to complete the top ten. All had benefited when Syahrin crashed out of a strong eighth with nine laps to go.

Karel Abraham was a season-best 11th, proving a point in a one-race outing on Bautista's Desmosedici GP17. Petrucci had all but caught him at the end after his race-long recovery. Just over a second behind, Redding took 13th from Nakagami on the last lap, with a lone Xavier Simeon claiming his career-first point, riding Rabat's GP17.

Australian Mike Jones, on Abraham's vacant bike, rode to a steady 18th, well behind Luthi and Torres; Pol Espargaro (Red Bull KTM) retired, blaming a bad call on the Michelin rear tyre lottery.

Vinales greeted his win with some caution: "We have a great chassis, but we need to improve engine and electronics to make a challenge next season." But it moved him to within an intriguing 15 points of Rossi, who in turn had fallen the same number behind second-placed Dovizioso.

MOTO2 RACE – 25 laps

Pasini had an anxious wait after falling late in a dry and gusty qualifying, but he was safe for a third pole of the year, ahead of Schrotter and a fearsomely close batch of times, 16 inside one second. Vierge completed row one; Aegerter and Quartararo straddled Binder on row two.

The title rivals, facing a possible decider, were nowhere to be seen: Bagnaia 16th, 2017's winner Oliveira 20th, on rows six and seven. Neither would play much part in a race so close that it reminded Binder of his days in Moto3. As he had done there, he won.

He'd led from laps three to 11, but the leading group was still eight strong at half-distance. Unable to escape, he decided to wait for the finale.

Most of the leading after that was done by Vierge, with

Baldassarri having a stab and team-mate Augusto Fernandez threatening to make it a Pons team 1-2.

But Baldassarri ran out of road at the Turn Ten hairpin, and with two laps to go, Binder reassumed control. It remained close. A slide on the last fast corners gave 2017 Moto3 champion Mir his chance for a last-ditch slipstream attack, but he fell short by a minuscule 0.036 of a second.

Vierge had led away from Pasini, who took over at the second corner only to slide off at the fourth.

When Binder moved ahead on lap three, Lecuona was up to third, past Aegerter and challenging Vierge. But on lap seven, a clash of lines into the Hayshed put Lecuona on the grass and down, and dropped Vierge behind Aegerter, Baldassarri and Marini.

All were close, with Marquez falling victim to team-mate Mir. Gardner and Fernandez were in the group; there was clear air behind to the next gang, led now by Oliveira.

Gardner would only last until lap 13. He was sixth, then Mir pushed past and slowed in front of him, and he crashed trying to avoid him.

Just before half-distance, Binder let Vierge through; then Baldassarri made his bid on laps 20–22. His fall decided Binder that it was time to take to the front again, this time for good.

With Mir a close second, Vierge held off Fernandez for third, less than a second behind; Marini recovered from a late slip to save fifth from Aegerter, with Marquez closing again at the finish.

Oliveira and Bagnaia were nowhere near. Oliveira was 11th, Bagnaia a fairly close, but definitely despondent 12th.

Ahead of them, new European champion Jesko Raffin had broken free for eighth. Schrotter had stormed through to ninth, narrowly ahead of Quartararo. He'd stalled on the dummy grid and had to start from the back, losing his front-row slot.

Navarro and Locatelli joined the crash list.

Bagnaia still had a 36-point advantage with 50 left; Binder's third win put him 41 points clear of Baldassarri, not quite yet invulnerable for third overall.

MOTO3 RACE – 23 laps

Jorge Martin claimed pole number 19, tenth of the year, with Bezzecchi in 15th. Front-row first-timer Binder was alongside, then Sasaki; with Kornfeil, Rodrigo and Oettl on an all-KTM second row.

The race was thrilling – the top 14 over the line in less than a second. It might have been 15, had Oettl not been batted wide on the first corner. It was slipstreaming and elbows, art and aggression, and wildly changing fortunes throughout.

For example, Martin led over the line on lap 17, but as they piled into Turn One, he was eighth. The Hondas generally gained time through the corners, but the KTMs took it back on the run down the straight. And frequent leader Binder ended up 12th.

Eventually, Arenas took his second win of the year by inches. Almost alongside, from 17th on the grid, was Di Giannantonio. And a sensational third went to replacement rider Celestino Vietti, in only his second GP.

Martin was fifth, behind Suzuki after a difficult race, his dash showing the message "Drop One Place" throughout. But he scored important points, for Bezzecchi had a nightmare, ending the afternoon in floods of tears. He had been one of a number of leaders only to fall victim to a mistake by another, Rodrigo. It was the second time in three races that Bezzecchi had been taken down by others' errors. It was worth little to him that Rodrigo was blamed and dropped six grid places in punishment.

With the pack running into the fast corners six or eight abreast, collisions were inevitable. Arbolino and Foggia fell together at Turn Four; Dalla Porta alone out of second. Jaume Massa was taken out at the very fast Turn Three (Stoner Corner) by team-mate Marcos Ramirez, breaking his ankle.

MICHELIN AUSTRALIAN MOTORCYCLE GRAND PRIX

26–28 OCTOBER, 2018

PHILLIP ISLAND

27 laps
Length: 4.448 km / 2.764 miles
Width: 13m

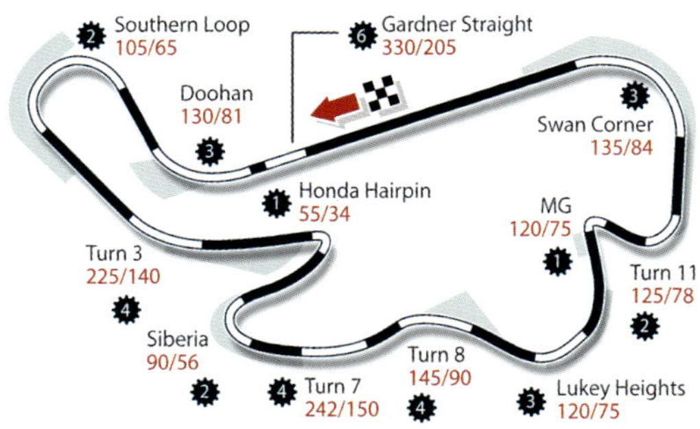

MotoGP

RACE DISTANCE: 27 laps, 74.624 miles/120.096km · RACE WEATHER: Dry (air 13°C, humidity 55%, track 32°C)

Pos.	Rider	Nat.	No.	Entrant	Machine	Tyres	Race tyre choice	Laps	Time & speed
1	**Maverick Vinales**	SPA	25	Movistar Yamaha MotoGP	Yamaha YZR-M1	M	F: Soft/R: Hard	27	40m 51.081s 109.5mph/ 176.3km/h
2	**Andrea Iannone**	ITA	29	Team SUZUKI ECSTAR	Suzuki GSX-RR	M	F: Medium/R: Hard	27	40m 52.624s
3	**Andrea Dovizioso**	ITA	4	Ducati Team	Ducati Desmosedici	M	F: Medium/R: Hard	27	40m 52.913s
4	**Alvaro Bautista**	SPA	19	Ducati Team	Ducati Desmosedici	M	F: Soft/R: Hard	27	40m 55.153s
5	**Alex Rins**	SPA	42	Team SUZUKI ECSTAR	Suzuki GSX-RR	M	F: Medium/R: Hard	27	40m 56.098s
6	**Valentino Rossi**	ITA	46	Movistar Yamaha MotoGP	Yamaha YZR-M1	M	F: Medium/R: Hard	27	40m 56.213s
7	**Jack Miller**	AUS	43	Alma Pramac Racing	Ducati Desmosedici	M	F: Medium/R: Hard	27	40m 57.837s
8	**Franco Morbidelli**	ITA	21	EG 0,0 Marc VDS	Honda RC213V	M	F: Medium/R: Hard	27	41m 12.886s
9	**Aleix Espargaro**	SPA	41	Aprilia Racing Team Gresini	Aprilia RS-GP	M	F: Medium/R: Soft	27	41m 13.985s
10	**Bradley Smith**	GBR	38	Red Bull KTM Factory Racing	KTM RC16	M	F: Soft/R: Hard	27	41m 14.021s
11	**Karel Abraham**	CZE	17	Angel Nieto Team	Ducati Desmosedici	M	F: Soft/R: Hard	27	41m 25.467s
12	**Danilo Petrucci**	ITA	9	Alma Pramac Racing	Ducati Desmosedici	M	F: Soft/R: Hard	27	41m 26.106s
13	**Scott Redding**	GBR	45	Aprilia Racing Team Gresini	Aprilia RS-GP	M	F: Soft/R: Soft	27	41m 27.429s
14	**Takaaki Nakagami**	JPN	30	LCR Honda IDEMITSU	Honda RC213V	M	F: Medium/R: Soft	27	41m 27.470s
15	**Xavier Simeon**	BEL	10	Reale Avintia Racing	Ducati Desmosedici	M	F: Soft/R: Hard	27	41m 35.295s
16	Thomas Luthi	SWI	12	EG 0,0 Marc VDS	Honda RC213V	M	F: Medium/R: Hard	27	41m 39.307s
17	Jordi Torres	SPA	81	Reale Avintia Racing	Ducati Desmosedici	M	F: Soft/R: Hard	27	41m 56.046s
18	Mike Jones	AUS	7	Angel Nieto Team	Ducati Desmosedici	M	F: Soft/R: Soft	27	42m 10.898s
	Pol Espargaro	SPA	44	Red Bull KTM Factory Racing	KTM RC16	M	F: Soft/R: Soft	22	DNF-technical
	Hafizh Syahrin	MAL	55	Monster Yamaha Tech 3	Yamaha YZR-M1	M	F: Medium/R: Hard	18	DNF-crash
	Dani Pedrosa	SPA	26	Repsol Honda Team	Honda RC213V	M	F: Medium/R: Soft	11	DNF-crash
	Marc Marquez	SPA	93	Repsol Honda Team	Honda RC213V	M	F: Medium/R: Hard	5	DNF-crash
	Johann Zarco	FRA	5	Monster Yamaha Tech 3	Yamaha YZR-M1	M	F: Soft/R: Soft	5	DNF-crash
	Cal Crutchlow	GBR	35	LCR Honda CASTROL	Honda RC213V	M	-	-	DNS-injured

Fastest lap: Maverick Vinales, on lap 10, 1m 29.632s, 111.0mph/178.6km/h.
Lap record: Marc Marquez, 1m 28.108s, 112.9mph/181.7km/h (2013).
Event maximum speed: Danilo Petrucci, 212.4mph/341.8km/h (race).

Qualifying

Weather: Dry
Air Temp: 15° **Humidity:** 77%
Track Temp: 25°

1	Marquez	1m 29.199s
2	Vinales	1m 29.509s
3	Zarco	1m 29.705s
4	Iannone	1m 29.712s
5	Rins	1m 30.026s
6	Miller	1m 30.140s
7	Rossi	1m 30.270s
8	Petrucci	1m 30.328s
9	Dovizioso	1m 30.519s
10	Syahrin	1m 30.593s
11	P. Espargaro	1m 30.640s
12	Bautista	1m 32.367s
13	Abraham	1m 30.174s
14	Nakagami	1m 30.452s
15	Morbidelli	1m 30.518s
16	Smith	1m 30.646s
17	Simeon	1m 30.679s
18	Pedrosa	1m 30.770s
19	A. Espargaro	1m 30.911s
20	Luthi	1m 30.958s
21	Torres	1m 31.141s
22	Redding	1m 31.309s
23	Jones	1m 32.639s

Fastest race laps

1	Vinales	1m 29.632s
2	Iannone	1m 29.699s
3	Bautista	1m 29.714s
4	Dovizioso	1m 29.778s
5	Rossi	1m 29.879s
6	Rins	1m 30.040s
7	Miller	1m 30.044s
8	Syahrin	1m 30.233s
9	A. Espargaro	1m 30.272s
10	Smith	1m 30.364s
11	Zarco	1m 30.400s
12	Marquez	1m 30.413s
13	Abraham	1m 30.440s
14	P. Espargaro	1m 30.523s
15	Morbidelli	1m 30.524s
16	Petrucci	1m 30.616s
17	Nakagami	1m 31.030s
18	Pedrosa	1m 31.259s
19	Redding	1m 31.261s
20	Simeon	1m 31.422s
21	Luthi	1m 31.425s
22	Torres	1m 31.904s
23	Jones	1m 32.486s

Championship Points

1	Marquez	296
2	Dovizioso	210
3	Rossi	195
4	Vinales	180
5	Crutchlow	148
6	Petrucci	137
7	Zarco	133
8	Iannone	133
9	Lorenzo	130
10	Rins	129
11	Bautista	96
12	Pedrosa	95
13	Miller	83
14	Morbidelli	46
15	A. Espargaro	39
16	Rabat	35
17	P. Espargaro	35
18	Syahrin	34
19	Smith	29
20	Nakagami	21
21	Redding	15
22	Abraham	10
23	Kallio	6
24	Nakasuga	2
25	Simeon	1
26	Pirro	1

Constructor Points

1	Honda	339
2	Ducati	300
3	Yamaha	256
4	Suzuki	193
5	KTM	55
6	Aprilia	49

Grid order	1	2	3	4	5	6	7	8	9	10	11	12	13	14	15	16	17	18	19	20	21	22	23	24	25	26	27	
93 MARQUEZ	43	93	93	93	4	4	4	25	25	25	25	25	25	25	25	25	25	25	25	25	25	25	25	25	25	25	25	1
25 VINALES	93	4	4	4	43	43	25	46	46	46	46	29	46	46	19	19	19	4	4	4	4	4	29	29	29	29	29	2
5 ZARCO	29	29	29	43	93	46	43	4	29	29	29	46	19	19	46	4	4	19	29	46	19	19	4	4	4	4	4	3
29 IANNONE	42	43	5	29	5	29	29	29	4	4	4	19	4	4	4	46	29	29	19	19	29	29	19	19	19	19	19	4
42 RINS	4	46	43	5	29	25	46	43	19	19	19	4	29	29	29	29	46	46	46	29	46	46	42	42	46	46	42	5
43 MILLER	46	5	46	46	46	19	42	42	43	43	43	43	43	43	42	42	42	42	42	42	42	42	46	46	42	42	46	6
46 ROSSI	44	42	42	42	19	42	19	19	42	42	42	42	42	42	43	43	43	43	43	43	43	43	43	43	43	43	43	7
9 PETRUCCI	5	44	44	25	25	55	55	55	55	55	55	55	55	55	55	55	55	55	38	38	38	38	38	38	41	41	21	8
4 DOVIZIOSO	25	25	25	44	42	38	38	38	38	38	38	38	38	38	38	38	38	38	41	41	41	41	41	41	38	21	41	9
55 SYAHRIN	38	55	55	19	55	17	44	44	44	44	21	44	44	41	41	41	41	41	21	21	21	21	21	21	21	38	38	10
44 P. ESPARGARO	30	19	19	55	38	44	21	21	21	21	44	21	41	21	21	21	21	21	44	44	44	44	17	17	17	17	17	11
19 BAUTISTA	21	38	38	38	44	21	41	41	41	41	41	41	21	44	44	44	44	44	17	17	17	17	30	30	9	9	9	12
17 ABRAHAM	55	21	17	17	17	41	17	17	17	17	17	17	17	17	17	17	17	17	30	30	30	30	45	45	30	30	45	13
30 NAKAGAMI	19	17	41	41	41	10	10	45	10	26	26	10	10	10	10	30	30	30	45	45	45	45	9	9	45	45	30	14
21 MORBIDELLI	41	41	21	21	21	45	45	10	26	10	10	45	45	45	30	10	10	45	10	10	10	9	10	10	10	10	10	15
38 SMITH	26	26	26	26	10	26	26	26	45	45	45	30	30	30	45	45	45	10	9	9	9	10	12	12	12	12	12	
10 SIMEON	17	10	10	10	26	12	12	12	12	30	30	12	12	12	12	12	9	9	12	12	12	12	81	81	81	81	81	
26 PEDROSA	10	12	12	12	45	30	30	30	30	12	12	9	9	9	9	9	12	12	81	81	81	81	7	7	7	7	7	
41 A. ESPARGARO	12	45	45	45	12	81	81	81	81	81	81	81	81	81	81	81	81	81	7	7	7	7						
12 LUTHI	81	30	30	30	30	7	7	7	9	9	9	7	7	7	7	7	7	7										
81 TORRES	45	81	81	81	81	9	9	9	7	7	7																	
45 REDDING	7	7	7	7	7																							
7 JONES	9	9	9	9	9																							

93 Pit stop

Moto2

RACE DISTANCE: 25 laps, 69.096 miles/111.200km · RACE WEATHER: Dry (air 13°C, humidity 541%, track 35°C)

Pos.	Rider	Nat.	No.	Entrant	Machine	Laps	Time & Speed
1	**Brad Binder**	RSA	41	Red Bull KTM Ajo	KTM	25	39m 23.427s 105.2mph/ 169.3km/h
2	**Joan Mir**	SPA	36	EG 0,0 Marc VDS	Kalex	25	39m 23.463s
3	**Xavi Vierge**	SPA	97	Dynavolt Intact GP	Kalex	25	39m 24.376s
4	**Augusto Fernandez**	SPA	40	Pons HP40	Kalex	25	39m 24.384s
5	**Luca Marini**	ITA	10	SKY Racing Team VR46	Kalex	25	39m 25.194s
6	**Dominique Aegerter**	SWI	77	Kiefer Racing	KTM	25	39m 25.909s
7	**Alex Marquez**	SPA	73	EG 0,0 Marc VDS	Kalex	25	39m 27.186s
8	**Jesko Raffin**	SWI	2	SAG Team	Kalex	25	39m 28.277s
9	**Marcel Schrotter**	GER	23	Dynavolt Intact GP	Kalex	25	39m 29.677s
10	**Fabio Quartararo**	FRA	20	MB Conveyors - Speed Up	Speed Up	25	39m 30.880s
11	**Miguel Oliveira**	POR	44	Red Bull KTM Ajo	KTM	25	39m 32.102s
12	**Francesco Bagnaia**	ITA	42	SKY Racing Team VR46	Kalex	25	39m 33.152s
13	**Tetsuta Nagashima**	JPN	45	IDEMITSU Honda Team Asia	Kalex	25	39m 33.214s
14	**Sam Lowes**	GBR	22	Swiss Innovative Investors	KTM	25	39m 34.636s
15	**Edgar Pons**	SPA	57	MB Conveyors - Speed Up	Speed Up	25	39m 37.503s
16	Khairul Idham Pawi	MAL	89	IDEMITSU Honda Team Asia	Kalex	25	39m 38.777s
17	Steven Odendaal	RSA	4	NTS RW Racing GP	NTS	25	39m 38.823s
18	Joe Roberts	USA	16	NTS RW Racing GP	NTS	25	39m 46.657s
19	Simone Corsi	ITA	24	Tasca Racing Scuderia Moto2	Kalex	25	39m 57.163s
20	Andrea Locatelli	ITA	5	Italtrans Racing Team	Kalex	25	40m 05.751s
21	Bryan Staring	AUS	67	Tech 3 Racing	Tech 3	25	40m 15.724s
22	Lorenzo Baldassarri	ITA	7	Pons HP40	Kalex	25	40m 27.315s
	Xavi Cardelus	AND	18	Marinelli Snipers Team	Kalex	14	DNF
	Remy Gardner	AUS	87	Tech 3 Racing	Tech 3	13	DNF
	Jorge Navarro	SPA	9	Federal Oil Gresini Moto2	Kalex	8	DNF
	Iker Lecuona	SPA	27	Swiss Innovative Investors	KTM	6	DNF
	Federico Fuligni	ITA	21	Tasca Racing Scuderia Moto2	Kalex	6	DNF
	Jules Danilo	FRA	95	Nashi Argan SAG Team	Kalex	4	DNF
	Isaac Vinales	SPA	32	Forward Racing Team	Suter	4	DNF
	Mattia Pasini	ITA	54	Italtrans Racing Team	Kalex	1	DNF

Fastest lap: Augusto Fernandez, on lap 11, 1m 33.715s, 106.1mph/170.8km/h.
Lap record: Franco Morbidelli, 1m 50.788s, 96.9mph/156.0km/h (2016).
Event maximum speed: Brad Binder, 178.0mph/286.5km/h (qualifying).

Qualifying

Weather: Dry
Air: 16° **Track:** 26°
Humidity: 76%

1	Pasini	1m 33.368s
2	Schrotter	1m 33.624s
3	Vierge	1m 33.721s
4	Aegerter	1m 33.841s
5	Binder	1m 33.929s
6	Quartararo	1m 33.951s
7	Marini	1m 33.963s
8	Lecuona	1m 33.988s
9	Marquez	1m 34.007s
10	Raffin	1m 34.039s
11	Baldassarri	1m 34.050s
12	Navarro	1m 34.086s
13	Fernandez	1m 34.094s
14	Mir	1m 34.149s
15	Gardner	1m 34.181s
16	Bagnaia	1m 34.367s
17	Manzi	1m 34.413s
18	Locatelli	1m 34.491s
19	Lowes	1m 34.540s
20	Oliveira	1m 34.556s
21	Nagashima	1m 34.784s
22	E. Pons	1m 34.844s
23	Pawi	1m 34.850s
24	Roberts	1m 34.851s
25	Corsi	1m 34.934s
26	Odendaal	1m 34.958s
27	Staring	1m 35.760s
28	Danilo	1m 35.978s
29	Fuligni	1m 35.986s
30	Vinales	1m 36.173s
31	Cardelus	1m 37.065s

Fastest race laps

1	Fernandez	1m 33.715s
2	Baldassarri	1m 33.718s
3	Mir	1m 33.719s
4	Vierge	1m 33.804s
5	Binder	1m 33.822s
6	Gardner	1m 33.852s
7	Schrotter	1m 33.857s
8	Marquez	1m 33.877s
9	Marini	1m 33.909s
10	Aegerter	1m 33.934s
11	Nagashima	1m 33.938s
12	Quartararo	1m 33.974s
13	Raffin	1m 34.001s
14	Lecuona	1m 34.022s
15	Locatelli	1m 34.047s
16	E. Pons	1m 34.080s
17	Lowes	1m 34.103s
18	Oliveira	1m 34.115s
19	Bagnaia	1m 34.216s
20	Odendaal	1m 34.262s
21	Navarro	1m 34.297s
22	Pawi	1m 34.388s
23	Corsi	1m 34.407s
24	Roberts	1m 34.645s
25	Danilo	1m 34.981s
26	Fuligni	1m 35.351s
27	Staring	1m 35.964s
28	Vinales	1m 36.009s
29	Cardelus	1m 36.010s

Championship Points

1	Bagnaia	288
2	Oliveira	252
3	Binder	193
4	Baldassarri	152
5	Mir	149
6	Marquez	148
7	Schrotter	131
8	Vierge	126
9	Marini	122
10	Quartararo	117
11	Pasini	115
12	Lecuona	60
13	Navarro	55
14	Lowes	48
15	Corsi	47
16	Locatelli	41
17	Aegerter	40
18	Fernandez	37
19	Gardner	29
20	Nagashima	23
21	Fenati	14
22	Barbera	10
23	Raffin	9
24	Manzi	8
25	Kent	8
26	Vinales	7
27	Roberts	5
28	Bendsneyder	2
29	Pawi	1
30	E. Pons	1
31	Odendaal	1
32	Tuuli	1

Constructor Points

1	Kalex	366
2	KTM	300
3	Speed Up	121
4	Tech 3	29
5	Suter	8
6	NTS	5

Moto3

RACE DISTANCE: 23 laps, 63.569 miles/102.304km · RACE WEATHER: Dry (air 14°C, humidity 54%, track 31°C)

Pos.	Rider	Nat.	No.	Entrant	Machine	Laps	Time & Speed
1	**Albert Arenas**	SPA	75	Angel Nieto Team Moto3	KTM	23	37m 48.073s 100.8mph/ 162.3km/h
2	**Fabio Di Giannantonio**	ITA	21	Del Conca Gresini Moto3	Honda	23	37m 48.125s
3	**Celestino Vietti**	ITA	31	SKY Racing Team VR46	KTM	23	37m 48.132s
4	**Tatsuki Suzuki**	JPN	24	SIC58 Squadra Corse	Honda	23	37m 48.154s
5	**Jorge Martin**	SPA	88	Del Conca Gresini Moto3	Honda	23	37m 48.172s
6	**Aron Canet**	SPA	44	Estrella Galicia 0,0	Honda	23	37m 48.227s
7	**Adam Norrodin**	MAL	7	Petronas Sprinta Racing	Honda	23	37m 48.261s
8	**Enea Bastianini**	ITA	33	Leopard Racing	Honda	23	37m 48.308s
9	**Jakub Kornfeil**	CZE	84	Redox PruestelGP	KTM	23	37m 48.401s
10	**Ayumu Sasaki**	JPN	71	Petronas Sprinta Racing	Honda	23	37m 48.479s
11	**Alonso Lopez**	SPA	72	Estrella Galicia 0,0	Honda	23	37m 48.648s
12	**Darryn Binder**	RSA	40	Red Bull KTM Ajo	KTM	23	37m 48.962s
13	**Andrea Migno**	ITA	16	Angel Nieto Team Moto3	KTM	23	37m 49.060s
14	**John McPhee**	GBR	17	CIP - Green Power	KTM	23	37m 49.062s
15	**Philipp Oettl**	GER	65	Sudmetal Schedl GP Racing	KTM	23	37m 50.221s
16	Yari Montella	ITA	55	SIC58 Squadra Corse	Honda	23	38m 22.773s
17	Stefano Nepa	ITA	81	CIP - Green Power	KTM	23	38m 23.042s
18	Nakarin Atiratphuvapat	THA	41	Honda Team Asia	Honda	23	38m 27.440s
19	Kaito Toba	JPN	27	Honda Team Asia	Honda	23	38m 36.127s
20	Vicente Perez	SPA	77	Reale Avintia Academy 77	KTM	23	38m 37.043s
	Tony Arbolino	ITA	14	Marinelli Snipers Team	Honda	21	DNF
	Dennis Foggia	ITA	10	SKY Racing Team VR46	KTM	21	DNF
	Marcos Ramirez	SPA	42	Bester Capital Dubai	KTM	13	DNF
	Jaume Masia	SPA	5	Bester Capital Dubai	KTM	13	DNF
	Lorenzo Dalla Porta	ITA	48	Leopard Racing	Honda	12	DNF
	Marco Bezzecchi	ITA	12	Redox PruestelGP	KTM	10	DNF
	Gabriel Rodrigo	ARG	19	RBA BOE Skull Rider	KTM	10	DNF

Fastest lap: Lorenzo Dalla Porta, on lap 4, 1m 36.826s, 102.8mph/165.3km/h.
Lap record: Jack Miller, 1m 36.302s, 103.3mph/166.2km/h (2014).
Event maximum speed: Jaume Masia, 151.6mph/244.0km/h (race).

Qualifying:

Weather: Dry
Air: 15° **Track:** 24°
Humidity: 77%

1	Martin	1m 36.591s
2	Binder	1m 36.848s
3	Sasaki	1m 37.117s
4	Kornfeil	1m 37.357s
5	Rodrigo	1m 37.465s
6	Oettl	1m 37.540s
7	Arbolino	1m 37.579s
8	Ramirez	1m 37.711s
9	Foggia	1m 37.757s
10	Canet	1m 37.844s
11	Arenas	1m 37.892s
12	Toba	1m 37.896s
13	Norrodin	1m 37.943s
14	Bastianini	1m 37.995s
15	Bezzecchi	1m 38.011s
16	Lopez	1m 38.017s
17	Di Giannantonio	1m 38.021s
18	McPhee	1m 38.034s
19	Masia	1m 38.414s
20	Dalla Porta	1m 38.590s
21	Perez	1m 38.828s
22	Vietti	1m 38.853s
23	Montella	1m 38.905s
24	Suzuki	1m 38.934s
25	Nepa	1m 39.027s
26	Atiratphuvapat	1m 39.228s
27	Migno	1m 39.516s

Fastest race laps

1	Dalla Porta	1m 36.826s
2	Bezzecchi	1m 36.919s
3	Canet	1m 36.933s
4	Masia	1m 36.951s
5	McPhee	1m 36.957s
6	Oettl	1m 37.148s
7	Suzuki	1m 37.150s
8	Ramirez	1m 37.173s
9	Martin	1m 37.180s
10	Perez	1m 37.196s
11	Lopez	1m 37.199s
12	Vietti	1m 37.210s
13	Foggia	1m 37.216s
14	Arbolino	1m 37.217s
15	Rodrigo	1m 37.232s
16	Bastianini	1m 37.266s
17	Arenas	1m 37.350s
18	Di Giannantonio	1m 37.365s
19	Montella	1m 37.367s
20	Kornfeil	1m 37.379s
21	Norrodin	1m 37.409s
22	Migno	1m 37.440s
23	Binder	1m 37.443s
24	Sasaki	1m 37.449s
25	Atiratphuvapat	1m 38.147s
26	Nepa	1m 38.179s
27	Toba	1m 39.629s

Championship Points

1	Martin	215
2	Bezzecchi	203
3	Di Giannantonio	195
4	Bastianini	150
5	Dalla Porta	131
6	Canet	128
7	Rodrigo	116
8	Kornfeil	115
9	Arenas	94
10	Ramirez	90
11	Migno	82
12	Masia	66
13	Suzuki	64
14	McPhee	62
15	Oettl	58
16	Antonelli	56
17	Foggia	55
18	Arbolino	49
19	Binder	48
20	Norrodin	46
21	Sasaki	45
22	Lopez	36
23	Toba	33
24	Vietti	18
25	Bulega	18
26	Perez	13
27	Fernandez	13
28	Yurchenko	9
29	Loi	8
30	Masaki	8
31	Chantra	7
32	Pagliani	6
33	Atiratphuvapat	2
34	Ogura	1

Constructor Points

1	Honda	356
2	KTM	315

ADVANCE
SHOEI
REPSOL
93
HRC
HRC

FIM WORLD CHAMPIONSHIP · ROUND 18

MALAYSIAN GRAND PRIX

SEPANG INTERNATIONAL CIRCUIT

Inset, top: Pure joy after the tensions. Martin and team owner Fausto Gresini celebrate the Moto3 title win.

Inset, left: Black, gold and victorious. Pecco Bagnaia took the Moto2 crown with a race to spare.

Main: After Rossi's crash, Marquez was in total control and claimed win number nine.

Photos: Gold & Goose

Above: Heartbreak for Rossi, and his legion of fans. He had led from the start.

Top right: Keeping it in the family. Rossi hugs half-brother Marini after his maiden win.

Photos: Monster Energy

Above centre right: Vinales reveals his "ugly" hairstyle, a week after his close shave.

Above right: Lorenzo rode on day one, but pulled out on Saturday morning still in considerable pain.

Photos: Gold & Goose

Right: Rins, heading Dovizioso, pulled through the field for second, repeating his Assen result.

Photo: Monster Energy

IN a paddock peopled by overheated and jaded world travellers, rumours needed to develop a momentum of their own. This was a big one. Rossi, went the buzz, was planning to retire early. If Yamaha proved unable to build a world-beater for 2019, he would not bother to see out 2020, the second year of his renewed contract.

The response, if such it was, was classic Rossi, classic racer. He threatened to win the race. For the first 16 of its 20 laps.

What happened next did nothing to dispel the doubts about his future, for the pattern of the race had changed. Marquez, having started from a very unusual third row, had risen to second, but then didn't seem to have anything left in the wilting heat. But now he started to close again, by tenths, but remorselessly. And under the growing pressure, Rossi crashed.

It really did look like the turning of some sort of a tide. Then again, Rossi had bounced back from worse in the past. And if there were times, in the debilitating hot and humid run-up to the race, when he had looked every one of his nearly 40 years – why shouldn't he? He's Rossi. And that says a lot.

In the middle class, on the same day, came the clarification of Rossi's overall position in the world of racing – nothing less than the one-man saviour of Italian GP honour. The Godfather. For while his half-brother, Luca Marini, claimed a first Moto2 win, yet another family landmark, his protégé (one of many) secured a classic world championship. No matter that Pecco Bagnaia's Kalex had refused to start, after he'd stopped for a complete livery change on the slow-down lap. The VR46 triumph was already complete.

The monsoon that had stayed away in Thailand had a final sting at Sepang, with several heavy falls and then a proper biblical downpour on Saturday. Apart from threatening to cancel qualifying, this had two major effects.

The first was an unprecedented race-eve rejig of Sunday's timing. With more rain forecast for precisely 3pm, the scheduled start time of the main race, all three races were advanced by two hours, with warm-up starting an hour early and the Idemitsu Asia Talent Cup shifted from the morning to the potentially rainy afternoon (in fact, it didn't rain, but nobody had predicted that).

The second was to put Avintia Reale substitute Jordi Torres out of the race, and awaken memories of a similar incident in 2011, which had threatened to end Marc Marquez's career before it had really begun. As then, heavy rain struck out of the blue, at the end of MotoGP's FP4. Torres was one of several riders who arrived at speed on slicks before warning flags had been shown. Vinales and Abraham also fell, but Torres was the only one hurt, suffering hand fractures that required surgery back in Spain.

In 2011, Marquez had been just three points adrift of Stefan Bradl in his first attempt at the Moto2 title. He suffered a complex concussion that left him with double vision. Not only was he out for the rest of the season, but also his participation the following year and thereafter was in serious doubt until damage to the nerves was repaired by microsurgery.

The Sepang circuit had been sanctioned and fined. In 2018, any such judgement remained in abeyance, while the track was again presented with the GP Commission's award for the best grand prix of 2017.

After their Phillip Island encounter, both Zarco and Marquez appeared unaffected. Marquez was fastest in dry free practice, then took pole in the delayed wet Q2; Zarco alongside him second fastest. Then came the surprise news that Marquez would be dropped six grid places for having inadvertently baulked Iannone during qualifying. Zarco was promoted to pole; Marquez (he would say after taking his ninth race win of the year) had gained extra motivation from having to start from the third row. Zarco's inherited pole made up for a 1,000-euro fine on Friday, imposed after he'd been caught using a scooter for track inspection on Thursday. Only cyclists or pedestrians were allowed, following an injurious scooter crash at this track in 2017.

Lorenzo took part in the first day of practice, but withdrew on Saturday morning, handing his bike to Pirro, who was there on standby. Keyhole surgery in Spain had repaired his tendon damage, but he'd only taken the cast off the day before practice, and after he'd placed last in both Friday's sessions, Saturday morning was painful enough to convince him to call it a day. Hostile team-mate Dovizioso questioned whether he'd had any intention of riding, though it was hard to understand why.

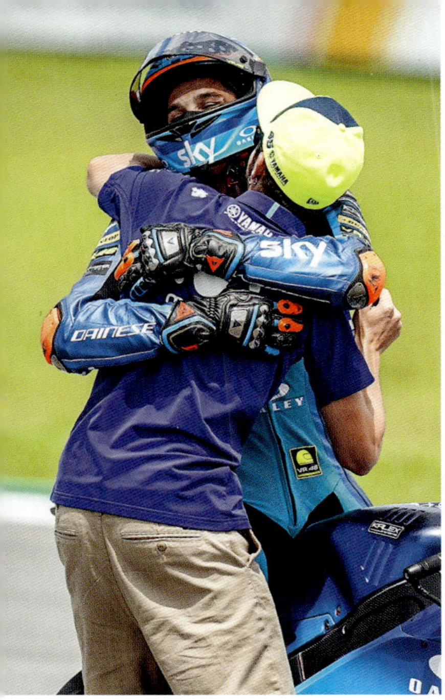

Vinales arrived as a reluctant slaphead, having had a post-race scalp shave after his Australian win. After setting fastest time in FP1, he explained, he'd told his crew that he felt he could win the race. The bet was concluded: if he did win, he would forfeit his hair. "I feel so ugly like this," he smiled, after removing his cap at the pre-race press conference.

The weekend started with drama at the Suzuki pit. On Thursday afternoon, as usual, the bikes were on the apron for an exploratory warm-up when Rins's machine burst into flames. It wasn't as bad as it had looked, said team boss Davide Brivio the next day, after the bike had been completely rebuilt overnight. The cause had been a fuel leak.

News came of a six-place grid penalty for Rodrigo, for "irresponsible riding" after he had knocked Bezzecchi off the weekend before in Australia. But his own injuries from that crash, mainly flesh wounds to his leg, had ruled him out of the race anyway. The penalty, the statement confirmed, would be dropped if he was unable to serve it during the current season.

With the hot conditions helping Pedrosa to equal his year's best fifth, it was a valuable race for Honda and the Repsol team. Marquez's win secured the constructors' title, Honda's 25th; while the combined riders' score gave the team a 39-point advantage over Movistar Yamaha in the run-up to the final race.

MOTOGP RACE – 27 laps

With Zarco now on pole and Rossi alongside, Iannone moved up to his first front-row since round three in Texas. Dovizioso, winner in the wet for the previous two years, but a faller late in Q2, led row two from Miller and Petrucci.

Marquez had Rins alongside and Bautista, from Q1 and back on his own GP17. Espargaro had also made it through, for the fourth time in the year, but ended up 12th. The previous week's winner, Vinales, was fast in the dry, but 11th in wet Q2. Redding was a best-of-the-year 13th, again enjoying the wet.

The race was dry and humidity 55 per cent, against 100 per cent in qualifying. But the track was 32 degrees, and temperature a punishing 34.

Rossi made a superb start, heading Zarco and Miller through the first twists, with Marquez having forced his way to fourth by the end of the lap.

On the second, he was firmly past Miller, and over the next couple of laps, the leading trio would have a little gap. Dovi was now fourth, with Pedrosa pressing Miller, the only rider to risk the medium over the soft rear, and starting to pay the price.

Next time around, Zarco made a slip that let Marquez through to second, but the champion didn't get away. He explained that he'd overheated his tyres somewhat and been forced "to be cool. Now Valentino was really pushing, and we were really on the limit. I was just riding by instinct."

An instinct that, on lap 13, told him it was time to get going. At the start of that lap, he was more than 1.2 seconds adrift. At the end of it, less than a second.

Little by little, he got closer, taking around a tenth every lap. By then, Zarco was also suffering and losing touch.

The crucial moment came at the beginning of lap 17, as Rossi peeled over to take the first slow right-hander. Almost in slow motion, the front tucked and the rear let go, and he was down. "I don't understand what happened," he said later. "I was feeling comfortable. I made a mistake, because I crashed."

Said Marquez, "It was a pity. I was looking forward to the last lap."

So too everybody watching. Marquez was able to settle his pace; Zarco felt safe in second.

There were chasers behind, but Iannone was not one of them. He'd been on Marquez's back wheel as they came to the final hairpin for the first time. Marquez lost the front and slowed suddenly as he recovered with his usual knee-and-elbow style. Iannone flinched, and that was enough to put him down and out.

It was left to Rins, at this point eighth, to demonstrate again the growing strength of the Suzuki. He set fastest lap on the fifth; next time around, he was cleanly past Miller; and the next also Dovizioso, and pressing Pedrosa, who had taken fourth shortly before. Just after half-distance, Rins swept past. His next target was Zarco, at this point more than three seconds away.

Zarco was worried: "I could see Alex was catching me at half a second a lap, but I was struggling a lot for grip." On the last lap, Rins was close enough to attack, and fast enough to get by easily. It was his fourth podium of the year, and his second time in second place. Zarco was barely half a second behind.

The other big mover was Vinales, who had finished the first lap tenth and picked up places throughout. His last victim was Pedrosa for fourth, with seven laps left. Dovizioso's top Ducati had been left trailing.

Bautista was also making progress, and with five laps to go, he took seventh ahead of Miller.

Above: Zarco tries to stay ahead of the advancing Rins; Vinales tries to catch up.

Top right: Syahrin rewarded the packed grandstands with tenth. Here he leads Bradley Smith.

Above right: The title decider – Oliveira got past Bagnaia, but it wasn't enough to save his chances.

Photos: Gold & Goose

Centre right: Marini's first win crowned his growing strength in the latter half of the year.

Photo: Monster Energy

Centre far right: Martin starts his successful bid for freedom, ahead of Arbolino and Dalla Porta.

Photo: Gold & Goose

Right: Bagnaia's title celebrations included a change of livery for bike and rider – but then his machine wouldn't start to complete his victory lap.

Photo: Monster Energy

Far right: Canet slips off, handing a short-lived lead to Bezzecchi in the Moto3 race.

Photo: Gold & Goose

Ninth was hotly disputed, with the capacity crowd cheering Syahrin, the first Malaysian in the premier class, as he hounded Petrucci. He got ahead for a spell, but was four seconds behind at the end.

Aleix Espargaro had been tailing brother Pol's KTM until the latter pitted to retire. Less than two seconds down, Morbidelli pulled clear of a battling trio, leaving Crutchlow's replacement, Bradl, to 13th; and Smith to fall behind Nakagami for the last point. Luthi was a frustrated 16th yet again, missing points by two seconds.

Simeon was next, then a crestfallen remounted Rossi, ahead of Redding. Abraham was an early trackside retirement; Pirro another victim of the last hairpin.

Sixth was good enough to secure second overall for Dovi, with third-placed Rossi no-scoring and team-mate Vinales just two points adrift. Zarco was five points ahead of Petrucci for top independent rider.

MOTO2 RACE – 18 laps

Remy Gardner was the first to smash Moto2's 2015 record (set by Luthi), but by the end he'd been consigned to fourth, with Alex Marquez on pole, almost half a second clear of Marini and Quartararo. Pasini was fifth, then Bagnaia – Oliveira six-hundredths and one place down.

In the punishing conditions, the race was somewhat austere, but a triumph for the VR46 troops, with Marini taking his first GP win, and Bagnaia his first title. Oliveira was able to salvage some pride by finishing second.

Quartararo took a flying start from the front row, but he and Marquez had a big touch running into the first corner. They were swamped as they recovered, finishing lap one seventh and ninth respectively.

That gave Marini the opening he needed, and he seized a lead he would hold to the end. Oliveira was right behind him, losing second place to Bagnaia on lap two, but taking it back five laps later.

Gardner chased the front men for four laps, losing fourth to Pasini on lap four. Then Marquez, fighting his way back though the crowd, passed him before the final hairpin. This pushed the Tech 3 wide and off the grippy line. Trying to fight back, he slipped off instead.

Marquez would never catch the leading quartet, out on their own. Oliveira did close to within a few tenths of the leader, but Marini withstood the pressure; Pasini also got close to Bagnaia, but didn't challenge.

Marini looked fresher than doubtless he felt in the heat. "It was really, really hard, but when you are leading, it is a bit easier," he said.

Team-mate Bagnaia was close to speechless with emotion, paying tribute to Marini and all his team: "This season is together. Together we win, together we lose. And together we are world champion."

Oliveira was gracious, warmly congratulating Bagnaia: "Pecco has been really strong. I am proud of my riding, proud of my season; we have been really constant. Our package wasn't enough to beat Pecco, but it was a championship full of emotion."

The action was behind them, with Marquez dropping back towards the end as Quartararo was recovering positions. The hard-riding Frenchman was getting the best of a long battle with Pons HP40 Kalex team-mates Baldassari and Fernandez, the latter eventually stretchered off after a fall. Finally Quartararo took fifth on the last lap from Baldassari, with Marquez sixth.

A couple of seconds behind, second Red Bull KTM rider Binder held off Schrotter; behind them, Mir won a long fight for tenth from second Dynavolt rider Xavi Vierge.

By the finish, the next group had closed up, with Locatelli getting ahead of Navarro at two-thirds distance. Aegerter had been with them to the end. Sam Lowes, again disadvantaged by poor qualifying, came through from 22nd to outpace Corsi for the final point.

The top three in the championship were settled: Bagnaia, Oliveira, Binder; fourth still disputed between Baldassarri (162), Marquez (157), Mir (155) and Marini (147).

MOTO3 RACE – 17 laps

Martin's 11th pole of the season was 0.032 of a second clear of Bezzecchi. Arbolino was third, all three inside the track record.

Martin rode a perfect trademark runaway victory, while Bezzecchi was caught in the usual brawling pursuit.

The pair had been up and down in the pack. Bezzecchi led more often than Martin, at one point tenth.

His first runaway failed. Then with five laps to go, he took the lead from Bezzecchi once again and pulled steadily away to a clear 3.5-second win.

In his wake, Bezzecchi had his hands full on the multi-line corners of the widest track on the calendar. He started the last lap in second place; by the end of it, he was fifth, and left to rue his five often innocent non-finishes.

Dalla Porta, strong at season's end, was second; team-mate Bastianini a photo-finish third ahead of Arenas, after pushing steadily through from 18th on lap two. His 24th class podium was a new record.

Di Giannantonio was sixth, frequent early leader Binder a tenth behind; the Hondas of Arbolino, Suzuki and Antonelli rounded out the top ten. The final points went to Ramirez, Toba, Perez, Atiratphuvapat and Masaki; Migno and the returned Yurchenko narrowly missed out.

Canet had grabbed the lead on lap ten, but fell directly; McPhee, Lopez and Foggia crashed together from the front pack; stunning novice Vietti also. Local hero Norrodin started from the pit lane (dawdling in practice) and worked his way into the top ten, but crashed.

Martin was unassailable, Bezzecchi and Di Giannantonio close on 214 and 205 respectively. The podium lock-out finalised the hat trick for Honda, taking the title for constructors, and Gresini that for teams.

SHELL MALAYSIA MOTORCYCLE GRAND PRIX

2-4 NOVEMBER, 2018

SEPANG INTERNATIONAL CIRCUIT

20 laps
Length: 5.543 km / 3.444 miles
Width: 25m

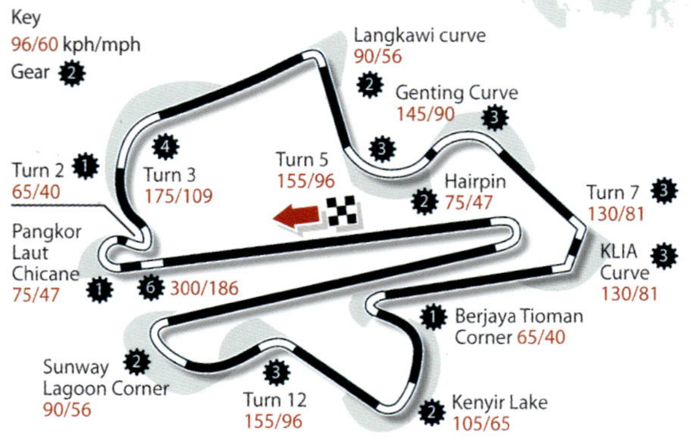

MotoGP

RACE DISTANCE: 20 laps, 68.885 miles/110.860km · RACE WEATHER: Dry (air 34°C, humidity 55%, track 53°C)

Pos.	Rider	Nat.	No.	Entrant	Machine	Tyres	Race tyre choice	Laps	Time & speed
1	**Marc Marquez**	SPA	93	Repsol Honda Team	Honda RC213V	M	F: Medium/R: Soft	20	40m 32.372s 101.9mph/ 164.0km/h
2	**Alex Rins**	SPA	42	Team SUZUKI ECSTAR	Suzuki GSX-RR	M	F: Medium/R: Soft	20	40m 34.270s
3	**Johann Zarco**	FRA	5	Monster Yamaha Tech 3	Yamaha YZR-M1	M	F: Medium/R: Soft	20	40m 34.846s
4	**Maverick Vinales**	SPA	25	Movistar Yamaha MotoGP	Yamaha YZR-M1	M	F: Medium/R: Soft	20	40m 37.039s
5	**Dani Pedrosa**	SPA	26	Repsol Honda Team	Honda RC213V	M	F: Medium/R: Soft	20	40m 38.562s
6	**Andrea Dovizioso**	ITA	4	Ducati Team	Ducati Desmosedici	M	F: Medium/R: Soft	20	40m 43.620s
7	**Alvaro Bautista**	SPA	19	Angel Nieto Team	Ducati Desmosedici	M	F: Medium/R: Soft	20	40m 47.983s
8	**Jack Miller**	AUS	43	Alma Pramac Racing	Ducati Desmosedici	M	F: Medium/R: Medium	20	40m 51.381s
9	**Danilo Petrucci**	ITA	9	Alma Pramac Racing	Ducati Desmosedici	M	F: Medium/R: Soft	20	40m 55.293s
10	**Hafizh Syahrin**	MAL	55	Monster Yamaha Tech 3	Yamaha YZR-M1	M	F: Medium/R: Soft	20	40m 59.291s
11	**Aleix Espargaro**	SPA	41	Aprilia Racing Team Gresini	Aprilia RS-GP	M	F: Medium/R: Soft	20	41m 01.875s
12	**Franco Morbidelli**	ITA	21	EG 0,0 Marc VDS	Honda RC213V	M	F: Hard/R: Soft	20	41m 03.305s
13	**Stefan Bradl**	GER	6	LCR Honda CASTROL	Honda RC213V	M	F: Medium/R: Soft	20	41m 07.694s
14	**Takaaki Nakagami**	JPN	30	LCR Honda IDEMITSU	Honda RC213V	M	F: Medium/R: Soft	20	41m 10.284s
15	**Bradley Smith**	GBR	38	Red Bull KTM Factory Racing	KTM RC16	M	F: Medium/R: Soft	20	41m 12.047s
16	Thomas Luthi	SWI	12	EG 0,0 Marc VDS	Honda RC213V	M	F: Medium/R: Soft	20	41m 14.192s
17	Xavier Simeon	BEL	10	Reale Avintia Racing	Ducati Desmosedici	M	F: Medium/R: Soft	20	41m 16.350s
18	Valentino Rossi	ITA	46	Movistar Yamaha MotoGP	Yamaha YZR-M1	M	F: Medium/R: Soft	20	41m 30.660s
19	Scott Redding	GBR	45	Aprilia Racing Team Gresini	Aprilia RS-GP	M	F: Hard/R: Soft	20	41m 32.563s
	Pol Espargaro	SPA	44	Red Bull KTM Factory Racing	KTM RC16	M	F: Medium/R: Soft	16	DNF-technical
	Michele Pirro	ITA	51	Ducati Team	Ducati Desmosedici	M	F: Medium/R: Soft	5	DNF-crash
	Karel Abraham	CZE	17	Angel Nieto Team	Ducati Desmosedici	M	F: Medium/R: Soft	3	DNF-technical
	Andrea Iannone	ITA	29	Team SUZUKI ECSTAR	Suzuki GSX-RR	M	F: Medium/R: Soft	0	DNF-crash
	Jordi Torres	SPA	81	Reale Avintia Racing	Ducati Desmosedici	M	-	-	DNS-injured
	Jorge Lorenzo	SPA	99	Ducati Team	Ducati Desmosedici	M	-	-	DNS-injured

Fastest lap: Alex Rins, on lap 5, 2m 0.762s, 102.7mph/165.2km/h.
Lap record: Jorge Lorenzo, 2m 0.606s, 102.8mph/165.4km/h (2015).
Event maximum speed: Danilo Petrucci, 204.2mph/328.6km/h (free practice).

Qualifying

Weather: Wet
Air Temp: 25° **Track Temp:** 28°
Humidity: 100%

1	Marquez	2m 12.161s
2	Zarco	2m 12.709s
3	Rossi	2m 13.009s
4	Iannone	2m 13.097s
5	Dovizioso	2m 13.183s
6	Miller	2m 13.274s
7	Petrucci	2m 13.413s
8	Rins	2m 13.463s
9	Bautista	2m 14.185s
10	Pedrosa	2m 14.443s
11	Vinales	2m 14.856s
12	A. Espargaro	2m 15.340s
13	Redding	2m 13.786s
14	Pirro	2m 13.823s
15	Simeon	2m 13.971s
16	P. Espargaro	2m 14.132s
17	Smith	2m 14.332s
18	Luthi	2m 14.843s
19	Morbidelli	2m 14.994s
20	Bradl	2m 15.364s
21	Abraham	2m 15.679s
22	Nakagami	2m 16.558s
23	Syahrin	2m 16.825s

Fastest race laps

1	Rins	2m 00.762s
2	Zarco	2m 00.780s
3	Marquez	2m 00.808s
4	Rossi	2m 00.912s
5	Dovizioso	2m 00.930s
6	Vinales	2m 00.964s
7	Pedrosa	2m 00.987s
8	Miller	2m 01.274s
9	Petrucci	2m 01.686s
10	Bautista	2m 01.737s
11	Syahrin	2m 01.894s
12	Pirro	2m 01.907s
13	A. Espargaro	2m 02.039s
14	Morbidelli	2m 02.067s
15	P. Espargaro	2m 02.108s
16	Nakagami	2m 02.243s
17	Luthi	2m 02.619s
18	Bradl	2m 02.641s
19	Smith	2m 02.854s
20	Simeon	2m 02.931s
21	Abraham	2m 02.953s
22	Redding	2m 03.147s

Championship Points

1	Marquez	321
2	Dovizioso	220
3	Rossi	195
4	Vinales	193
5	Rins	149
6	Zarco	149
7	Crutchlow	148
8	Petrucci	144
9	Iannone	133
10	Lorenzo	130
11	Pedrosa	106
12	Bautista	105
13	Miller	91
14	Morbidelli	50
15	A. Espargaro	44
16	Syahrin	40
17	Rabat	35
18	P. Espargaro	35
19	Smith	30
20	Nakagami	23
21	Redding	15
22	Abraham	10
23	Kallio	6
24	Bradl	3
25	Nakasuga	2
26	Simeon	1
27	Pirro	1

Constructor Points

1	Honda	364
2	Ducati	310
3	Yamaha	272
4	Suzuki	213
5	KTM	56
6	Aprilia	54

Grid order		1	2	3	4	5	6	7	8	9	10	11	12	13	14	15	16	17	18	19	20	
5	ZARCO	46	46	46	46	46	46	46	46	46	46	46	46	46	46	46	46	93	93	93	93	1
46	ROSSI	5	5	5	5	93	93	93	93	93	93	93	93	93	93	93	93	5	5	5	42	2
29	IANNONE	43	93	93	93	5	5	5	5	5	5	5	5	5	5	5	5	42	42	42	5	3
4	DOVIZIOSO	93	43	43	4	4	26	26	26	26	26	26	42	42	42	42	42	25	25	25	25	4
43	MILLER	4	4	4	43	43	4	42	42	42	42	42	26	26	25	25	25	26	26	26	26	5
9	PETRUCCI	26	26	26	26	26	42	4	4	4	4	25	25	25	26	26	26	4	4	4	4	6
93	MARQUEZ	9	42	42	42	42	43	43	43	25	25	4	4	4	4	4	4	19	19	19	19	7
42	RINS	42	9	9	9	25	25	25	25	43	43	43	43	43	43	43	19	43	43	43	43	8
19	BAUTISTA	19	19	25	25	9	9	9	9	19	19	19	19	19	19	19	43	9	9	9	9	9
26	PEDROSA	25	25	19	19	19	19	19	19	9	9	9	9	9	9	9	9	55	55	55	55	10
25	VINALES	55	55	55	55	55	55	55	55	55	55	55	55	55	55	55	55	41	41	41	41	11
41	A. ESPARGARO	44	44	44	44	44	44	44	44	44	44	44	44	44	44	44	41	21	21	21	21	12
45	REDDING	38	51	51	51	51	41	41	41	41	41	41	41	41	41	41	44	6	6	6	6	13
51	PIRRO	51	38	38	41	41	38	38	38	38	21	21	21	21	21	21	21	30	30	30	30	14
10	SIMEON	6	6	41	38	38	6	6	21	21	38	6	6	6	6	6	6	38	38	38	38	15
44	P. ESPARGARO	12	41	6	6	6	21	21	6	6	6	38	38	38	38	38	30	12	12	12	12	
38	SMITH	41	21	21	21	21	12	12	12	12	12	12	12	12	30	30	38	10	10	10	10	
12	LUTHI	45	12	12	12	12	30	30	30	30	30	30	30	30	12	12	12	46	46	46	46	
21	MORBIDELLI	21	45	17	30	30	45	45	45	10	10	10	10	10	10	10	10	45	45	45	45	
6	BRADL	17	17	45	45	45	10	10	10	45	45	45	45	45	45	45	45					
17	ABRAHAM	30	30	30	10	10																
30	NAKAGAMI	10	10	10																		
55	SYAHRIN																					

Moto2

RACE DISTANCE: 18 laps, 61.997 miles/99.774km · RACE WEATHER: Dry (air 32°C, humidity 61%, track 48°C)

Pos.	Rider	Nat.	No.	Entrant	Machine	Laps	Time & Speed
1	**Luca Marini**	ITA	10	SKY Racing Team VR46	Kalex	18	38m 25.689s 96.7mph/ 155.7km/h
2	**Miguel Oliveira**	POR	44	Red Bull KTM Ajo	KTM	18	38m 26.883s
3	**Francesco Bagnaia**	ITA	42	SKY Racing Team VR46	Kalex	18	38m 28.709s
4	**Mattia Pasini**	ITA	54	Italtrans Racing Team	Kalex	18	38m 30.186s
5	**Fabio Quartararo**	FRA	20	MB Conveyors - Speed Up	Speed Up	18	38m 30.939s
6	**Lorenzo Baldassarri**	ITA	7	Pons HP40	Kalex	18	38m 30.994s
7	**Alex Marquez**	SPA	73	EG 0,0 Marc VDS	Kalex	18	38m 33.379s
8	**Brad Binder**	RSA	41	Red Bull KTM Ajo	KTM	18	38m 34.632s
9	**Marcel Schrotter**	GER	23	Dynavolt Intact GP	Kalex	18	38m 35.376s
10	**Joan Mir**	SPA	36	EG 0,0 Marc VDS	Kalex	18	38m 44.236s
11	**Xavi Vierge**	SPA	97	Dynavolt Intact GP	Kalex	18	38m 44.505s
12	**Andrea Locatelli**	ITA	5	Italtrans Racing Team	Kalex	18	38m 45.428s
13	**Jorge Navarro**	SPA	9	Federal Oil Gresini Moto2	Kalex	18	38m 46.866s
14	**Dominique Aegerter**	SWI	77	Kiefer Racing	KTM	18	38m 47.649s
15	**Sam Lowes**	GBR	22	Swiss Innovative Investors	KTM	18	38m 52.564s
16	Simone Corsi	ITA	24	Tasca Racing Scuderia Moto2	Kalex	18	38m 54.204s
17	Khairul Idham Pawi	MAL	89	IDEMITSU Honda Team Asia	Kalex	18	38m 54.491s
18	Joe Roberts	USA	16	NTS RW Racing GP	NTS	18	38m 55.480s
19	Jesko Raffin	SWI	2	SAG Team	Kalex	18	38m 56.246s
20	Edgar Pons	SPA	57	MB Conveyors - Speed Up	Speed Up	18	38m 56.758s
21	Steven Odendaal	RSA	4	NTS RW Racing GP	NTS	18	39m 04.119s
22	Jules Danilo	FRA	95	Nashi Argan SAG Team	Kalex	18	39m 08.619s
23	Dimas Ekky Pratama	INA	30	Tech 3 Racing	Tech 3	18	39m 23.196s
24	Isaac Vinales	SPA	32	Forward Racing Team	Suter	18	39m 23.599s
25	Federico Fuligni	ITA	21	Tasca Racing Scuderia Moto2	Kalex	18	39m 29.426s
26	Rafid Topan Sucipto	INA	50	Forward Racing Team	Suter	18	40m 29.755s
	Augusto Fernandez	SPA	40	Pons HP40	Kalex	8	DNF
	Niki Tuuli	FIN	66	Petronas Sprinta Racing	Kalex	7	DNF
	Tetsuta Nagashima	JPN	45	IDEMITSU Honda Team Asia	Kalex	7	DNF
	Remy Gardner	AUS	87	Tech 3 Racing	Tech 3	5	DNF
	Xavi Cardelus	AND	18	Marinelli Snipers Team	Kalex	5	DNF
	Iker Lecuona	SPA	27	Swiss Innovative Investors	KTM	2	DNF

Fastest lap: Luca Marini, on lap 2, 2m 7.423s, 97.3mph/156.6km/h.
Lap record: Miguel Oliveira, 2m 6.952s, 97.6mph/157.1km/h (2017).
Event maximum speed: Tetsuta Nagashima, 168.1mph/270.6km/h (qualifying).

Qualifying

Weather: Dry
Air Temp: 32° **Track Temp:** 42°
Humidity: 62%

	Rider	Time
1	Marquez	2m 05.629s
2	Marini	2m 06.117s
3	Quartararo	2m 06.295s
4	Gardner	2m 06.347s
5	Pasini	2m 06.439s
6	Bagnaia	2m 06.549s
7	Oliveira	2m 06.617s
8	Vierge	2m 06.687s
9	Binder	2m 06.741s
10	Schrotter	2m 06.742s
11	Fernandez	2m 06.878s
12	Navarro	2m 06.901s
13	Baldassarri	2m 06.964s
14	Lecuona	2m 07.041s
15	Locatelli	2m 07.086s
16	Nagashima	2m 07.220s
17	Aegerter	2m 07.243s
18	Mir	2m 07.251s
19	E. Pons	2m 07.251s
20	Raffin	2m 07.365s
21	Lowes	2m 07.379s
22	Corsi	2m 07.494s
23	Roberts	2m 07.516s
24	Odendaal	2m 07.566s
25	Pawi	2m 07.683s
26	Tuuli	2m 08.425s
27	Danilo	2m 08.500s
28	Ekky Pratama	2m 08.769s
29	Cardelus	2m 08.989s
30	Vinales	2m 09.524s
31	Fuligni	2m 09.942s
32	Sucipto	2m 10.553s

Fastest race laps

	Rider	Time
1	Marini	2m 07.423s
2	Marquez	2m 07.434s
3	Bagnaia	2m 07.442s
4	Oliveira	2m 07.451s
5	Pasini	2m 07.498s
6	Quartararo	2m 07.539s
7	Binder	2m 07.572s
8	Baldassarri	2m 07.575s
9	Nagashima	2m 07.643s
10	Gardner	2m 07.721s
11	Fernandez	2m 07.760s
12	Schrotter	2m 07.827s
13	Aegerter	2m 07.901s
14	Mir	2m 08.028s
15	Navarro	2m 08.195s
16	Vierge	2m 08.247s
17	E. Pons	2m 08.301s
18	Locatelli	2m 08.311s
19	Odendaal	2m 08.431s
20	Pawi	2m 08.605s
21	Corsi	2m 08.680s
22	Lowes	2m 08.721s
23	Roberts	2m 08.754s
24	Raffin	2m 08.839s
25	Tuuli	2m 09.037s
26	Danilo	2m 09.193s
27	Ekky Pratama	2m 09.654s
28	Cardelus	2m 09.921s
29	Fuligni	2m 10.108s
30	Vinales	2m 10.144s
31	Sucipto	2m 12.510s

Championship Points

	Rider	Points
1	Bagnaia	304
2	Oliveira	272
3	Binder	201
4	Baldassarri	162
5	Marquez	157
6	Mir	155
7	Marini	147
8	Schrotter	138
9	Vierge	131
10	Quartararo	128
11	Pasini	128
12	Lecuona	60
13	Navarro	58
14	Lowes	49
15	Corsi	47
16	Locatelli	45
17	Aegerter	42
18	Fernandez	37
19	Gardner	29
20	Nagashima	23
21	Fenati	14
22	Barbera	10
23	Raffin	9
24	Manzi	8
25	Kent	8
26	Vinales	7
27	Roberts	5
28	Bendsneyder	2
29	Pawi	1
30	E. Pons	1
31	Odendaal	1
32	Tuuli	1

Constructor Points

	Constructor	Points
1	Kalex	391
2	KTM	320
3	Speed Up	132
4	Tech 3	29
5	Suter	8
6	NTS	5

Moto3

RACE DISTANCE: 17 laps, 58.552 miles/94.231km · RACE WEATHER: Dry (air 31°C, humidity 65%, track 41°C)

Pos.	Rider	Nat.	No.	Entrant	Machine	Laps	Time & Speed
1	**Jorge Martin**	SPA	88	Del Conca Gresini Moto3	Honda	17	38m 34.799s 91.0mph/ 146.5km/h
2	**Lorenzo Dalla Porta**	ITA	48	Leopard Racing	Honda	17	38m 38.355s
3	**Enea Bastianini**	ITA	33	Leopard Racing	Honda	17	38m 38.556s
4	**Albert Arenas**	SPA	75	Angel Nieto Team Moto3	KTM	17	38m 38.594s
5	**Marco Bezzecchi**	ITA	12	Redox PruestelGP	KTM	17	38m 38.894s
6	**Fabio Di Giannantonio**	ITA	21	Del Conca Gresini Moto3	Honda	17	38m 38.905s
7	**Darryn Binder**	RSA	40	Red Bull KTM Ajo	KTM	17	38m 39.031s
8	**Tony Arbolino**	ITA	14	Marinelli Snipers Team	Honda	17	38m 39.503s
9	**Tatsuki Suzuki**	JPN	24	SIC58 Squadra Corse	Honda	17	38m 39.506s
10	**Niccolo Antonelli**	ITA	23	SIC58 Squadra Corse	Honda	17	38m 39.514s
11	**Marcos Ramirez**	SPA	42	Bester Capital Dubai	KTM	17	38m 39.526s
12	**Kaito Toba**	JPN	27	Honda Team Asia	Honda	17	38m 39.900s
13	**Vicente Perez**	SPA	77	Reale Avintia Academy 77	KTM	17	38m 41.191s
14	**Nakarin Atiratphuvapat**	THA	41	Honda Team Asia	Honda	17	38m 41.862s
15	**Kazuki Masaki**	JPN	22	RBA BOE Skull Rider	KTM	17	38m 42.152s
16	Andrea Migno	ITA	16	Angel Nieto Team Moto3	KTM	17	38m 42.277s
17	Makar Yurchenko	KAZ	76	Marinelli Snipers Team	Honda	17	38m 42.425s
18	Ayumu Sasaki	JPN	71	Petronas Sprinta Racing	Honda	17	38m 48.642s
19	Philipp Oettl	GER	65	Sudmetal Schedl GP Racing	KTM	17	38m 54.791s
20	Jakub Kornfeil	CZE	84	Redox PruestelGP	KTM	17	39m 01.477s
21	Stefano Nepa	ITA	81	CIP - Green Power	KTM	17	39m 08.983s
22	Apiwath Wongthananon	THA	9	VR46 Master Camp Team	KTM	17	39m 09.267s
23	Adam Norrodin	MAL	7	Petronas Sprinta Racing	Honda	17	40m 12.186s
	Aron Canet	SPA	44	Estrella Galicia 0,0	Honda	10	DNF
	Alonso Lopez	SPA	72	Estrella Galicia 0,0	Honda	6	DNF
	John McPhee	GBR	17	CIP - Green Power	KTM	6	DNF
	Dennis Foggia	ITA	10	SKY Racing Team VR46	KTM	6	DNF
	Celestino Vietti	ITA	31	SKY Racing Team VR46	KTM	2	DNF

Fastest lap: Jorge Martin, on lap 14, 2m 13.931s, 92.5mph/148.9km/h.
Lap record: Adam Norrodin, 2m 12.775s, 93.3mph/150.2km/h (2017).
Event maximum speed: Niccolo Antonelli, 144.3mph/232.2km/h (race).

Qualifying

Weather: Dry
Air Temp: 25° **Track Temp:** 42°
Humidity: 100%

	Rider	Time
1	Martin	2m 11.731s
2	Bezzecchi	2m 11.763s
3	Arbolino	2m 12.065s
4	McPhee	2m 12.081s
5	Arenas	2m 12.211s
6	Bastianini	2m 12.222s
7	Suzuki	2m 12.543s
8	Masaki	2m 12.627s
9	Sasaki	2m 12.637s
10	Antonelli	2m 12.679s
11	Binder	2m 12.748s
12	Vietti	2m 12.763s
13	Di Giannantonio	2m 12.797s
14	Dalla Porta	2m 12.812s
15	Canet	2m 12.873s
16	Foggia	2m 12.940s
17	Lopez	2m 12.975s
18	Norrodin	2m 13.089s
19	Ramirez	2m 13.113s
20	Toba	2m 13.160s
21	Perez	2m 13.181s
22	Kornfeil	2m 13.644s
23	Migno	2m 13.679s
24	Atiratphuvapat	2m 13.718s
25	Oettl	2m 13.955s
26	Wongthananon	2m 14.502s
27	Nepa	2m 14.692s
28	Yurchenko	2m 14.868s

Fastest race laps

	Rider	Time
1	Martin	2m 13.931s
2	Arbolino	2m 14.346s
3	Antonelli	2m 14.405s
4	Dalla Porta	2m 14.485s
5	Di Giannantonio	2m 14.538s
6	Suzuki	2m 14.569s
7	Bezzecchi	2m 14.571s
8	Bastianini	2m 14.585s
9	Norrodin	2m 14.653s
10	Toba	2m 14.656s
11	Binder	2m 14.780s
12	Arenas	2m 14.797s
13	Perez	2m 14.807s
14	Canet	2m 14.882s
15	Kornfeil	2m 14.975s
16	Masaki	2m 14.994s
17	Migno	2m 14.995s
18	Atiratphuvapat	2m 15.003s
19	Ramirez	2m 15.011s
20	Yurchenko	2m 15.068s
21	Sasaki	2m 15.527s
22	Oettl	2m 15.619s
23	McPhee	2m 15.623s
24	Lopez	2m 15.797s
25	Foggia	2m 15.866s
26	Wongthananon	2m 16.151s
27	Vietti	2m 16.513s
28	Nepa	2m 16.612s

Championship Points

	Rider	Points
1	Martin	240
2	Bezzecchi	214
3	Di Giannantonio	205
4	Bastianini	166
5	Dalla Porta	151
6	Canet	128
7	Rodrigo	116
8	Kornfeil	115
9	Arenas	107
10	Ramirez	95
11	Migno	82
12	Suzuki	71
13	Masia	66
14	McPhee	62
15	Antonelli	62
16	Oettl	58
17	Binder	57
18	Arbolino	57
19	Foggia	55
20	Norrodin	46
21	Sasaki	45
22	Toba	37
23	Lopez	36
24	Vietti	18
25	Bulega	18
26	Perez	16
27	Fernandez	13
28	Yurchenko	9
29	Masaki	9
30	Loi	8
31	Chantra	7
32	Pagliani	6
33	Atiratphuvapat	4
34	Ogura	1

Constructor Points

	Constructor	Points
1	Honda	381
2	KTM	328

Inset, above: A KTM double for Oliveira in Moto2 and novice Oncu in Moto3.

Inset, above right: Sixth was a career best for Takaaki Nakagami, and as top independent teamster he was in *parc fermé*.

Inset, top: Rins (Suzuki), Dovizioso (Ducati) and Espargaro (KTM) on the first podium – the first time with no Honda or Yamaha since 2007.

Main: Steady now. Red Bull Rookies champion Can Oncu heads towards a sensational debut victory.
Photos: Gold & Goose

FIM WORLD CHAMPIONSHIP · ROUND 19

VALENCIA GRAND PRIX

CIRCUIT RICARDO TORMO

AFTER a summer of record heat and sunshine, Valencia could hardly have been different from every other European race – except the British GP at Silverstone. The management at the British circuit might even have allowed themselves a pinched smile when track flooding brought out the red flags on three separate occasions: twice on Friday and once during the main race, occasioning the first restart of the year.

Any such comparison, however, was not valid. For one thing, the rain in Spain was torrential – that on the Sunday at Silverstone merely sustained; for another, the floods quickly drained away. The longest delay, on race-day, was 40 minutes.

Conditions led to a record number of crashes over the weekend – 155, 15 more than at Misano in 2017, with some riders falling several times. It was a tribute to both modern equipment like air-bag leathers and the track's secondary safety that only two riders were hurt badly enough to miss the race – a concussed Xavier Simeon and Moto2 Bendsneyder replacement Hector Garzo.

Fifty-seven of these were on race-day, which left severely depleted fields, particularly in MotoGP, where one faller, Jack Miller, was angered that the red flags had not come out a few laps previously. He'd long gone by then, but was watching in dismay and gesturing angrily from the pit lane as the bikes' revs rose and fell with the aquaplaning down the straight. It was as though officials were trying to get the race to two-thirds distance to avoid a restart, he said, adding, "Maverick fell almost in a straight line."

Vinales was one of the last to fall in the first attempt, when conditions were no respecter of status. By then, Marquez had already departed, at Turn Nine. Other crashes were spread out; in practice, most had been at Turns 12 or Four, the first right-hander for some time.

Altogether there had been 11 fallers, with three of them able to restart. In Smith's case, this was not because he'd been able to remount, but because he'd fallen on lap 14, coincidental with the red flag, and the restart grid was made up in the finishing order of lap 13, per regulations. There would be more fallers in the second leg, among them Rossi, out of the podium positions for the second race in a row, after a fine ride up from 16th on the original grid.

Remarkable conditions gave rise to remarkable feats. One such was in qualifying, when Marquez fell (Turn Four again) on his first flying lap and trudged off in obvious agony, clutching at his left shoulder, which had been dislocated again. Less than seven minutes later, he was back on the bike and making a serious attempt at pole.

Another was by Pol Espargaro, who had also fallen and remounted in the first leg (the other to have done so was Michele Pirro), after showing great courage and skill in the conditions to battle over third with Marquez. He demonstrated similar qualities in the restart, earning his and a jubilant KTM's first podium.

And yet another was in Moto3, where Red Bull Rookies Cup winner Can Oncu was taking advantage of the recent rule change to make an under-age debut on the Ajo team KTM. He had already impressed in qualifying, leading at one point and ending up fourth. His race was even more impressive. He inherited the lead at half-distance after pole-starter Tony Arbolino fell – and hung on to the bitter end. In the process, at 15 years and 115 days, he became the youngest ever winner, displacing Scott Redding by 55 days; the first GP winner from Turkey; and the first rider to win his first race since Noboru Ueda back in 1991. A historic display.

Then there was the make-up of the podium – the first since Misano in 2007 with not a single Yamaha or Honda.

Also somewhat historic, the retirement of Dani Pedrosa, marked by his induction into the Hall of Fame. This was a good-natured ceremony attended by several Spanish world champions past and present, an antidote to some mean-spirited observers who pointed out that he had never won a premier-class title. His accolades were well deserved, for more than just the simple reason that he had ridden the fastest bikes in the world with the physical attributes of a pre-teenage boy. His record of at least one win per year for 16 years is unequalled.

Rumours were rife, with official confirmation that Stoner's

Above: **Dovi was in calm control in the restarted MotoGP race.**

Top left: **Marquez was just one of many to crash out of the first race.**

Above far left: **Miller made his own contribution to a record number of 155 crashes. This was his fifth.**

Above left: **From 16th to a sniff of the podium, but Rossi fell again. He took solace in being so competitive.**

Above right: **FIM president Vito Ippolito and Dorna boss Carmelo Ezpeleta welcomed Dani Pedrosa as the latest MotoGP Legend.**

Above far right: **Vinales came from Q1 to take his first pole, but ended up as another victim.**

Right: **Last waltz for Pedrosa. The little Spaniard took fifth at the track where he had claimed seven of his 54 grand prix wins.**

Photos: Gold & Goose

three-year role with Ducati was over, that the Australian would be crossing the divide once again to take the same testing and ambassadorial role with Honda, for whom he had won his second world title in 2011. They were given impetus by Repsol team boss Alberto Puig who, while denying any actuality, did agree that it was obviously an interesting prospect. Stoner had been a Honda champion and had tested for HRC before rejoining Ducati, he said. In addition, Puig had been instrumental in launching his GP career. "We have a long personal relationship," he said. Marquez, however, was very lukewarm. His information from within Honda, he said, was that Stoner had not always been available to test, which was one of the first requirements. "We already have a good test rider that is Stefan Bradl. I would like to keep him."

More surprising news came with the release of provisional entry lists for 2019, with the return of racing bad-boy Romano Fenati. Less than three months earlier, he'd been widely vilified, both inside and outside racing, had his licence suspended for two races and then for the rest of the year, been sacked by his Marinelli team and by MV Agusta from his Moto2 ride for 2019, and said he was going to quit racing. Now, all was forgiven, or at least held in abeyance, and the same team was ready to give him another chance – well deserved, if talent is the criterion. But there was an element of start again, for he was going back to Moto3.

The entry list confirmed that the Forward Racing/MV Agusta ride had gone to the previously displaced Domi Aegerter, with the second seat given to Stefano Manzi, Fenati's victim. Pasini had been hoping to take the job, but the veteran's name was not on the list.

MOTOGP RACE – 14 laps (restarted)

Vinales equalled Marquez's new record from Buriram: through from Q1 to take pole, his first in over a year. Rins was alongside, then Dovizioso, with Petrucci leading row two. But Marquez, fifth, was hero of the afternoon, after coming back from dislocating his shoulder. Pol Espargaro was sixth, with five different makes in the top six; brother Aleix's Aprilia was eighth.

Pedrosa was ninth, Rossi mired in Q1 and placed 16th behind Morbidelli.

Heavy rain started simultaneously with the main race, although more than 97,000 drenched fans at least would see two races, after the deluge redoubled shortly before half-distance, bringing out red flags.

By then, the field had been radically cut. Vinales and Marquez were just two of eight riders unable to restart, along with team-mates Petrucci and Miller, Iannone, Aleix Espargaro, plus team-mates Morbidelli and Luthi.

The first running was gruelling. Rins took a flyer and forged away, his first time leading and fully four seconds clear of Dovizioso by lap five.

By then, the tentative Vinales had dropped back to seventh, Rossi about to pass him. And the carnage had begun. Aleix Espargaro was first out on lap two; two laps later, Miller, his fifth fall of the weekend, while climbing from tenth on lap one. Then Pirro, who rejoined, and Luthi.

After six laps, Marquez seemed finally to have shaken off Pol Espargaro and was close to Dovi; Rossi a couple of seconds adrift of the KTM. Then Espargaro fell, scrambling straight back on, and then Marquez as well, clutching again at his left shoulder.

Iannone fell on lap nine. Morbidelli inherited his fifth place, then fell himself three laps later.

Up front, Rins's pace was dropping as the conditions worsened. Dovi and Rossi closed right up. Vinales had recovered momentum and was on Rossi's tail – until he too went looping over the high side at the track's fastest corner on lap 13.

As they started the 14th, Rins ran wide and dropped to third, while at the end of it Rossi challenged Dovizioso for the lead at the final corner. But down the straight, Dovi raised his hand. At Friday's Safety Commission meeting, he explained,

Above: **Survival of the wettest. Pol Espargaro was lucky he could re-mount after crashing in the first race. He revelled in the wet to take his and KTM's first MotoGP podium.**

Top right: **Ducati tester Pirro heads Nakagami on his way to a career-best fourth.**

Above right: **Moto2's Iker Lecuona wheelies in celebration of taking his first podium.**

Right: **John McPhee heads for third. Behind him, Di Giannantonio (21) would give way to Martin (88), who was second, while Arenas (75) was one of many to crash out.**

Photos: Gold & Goose

Race Direction had asked the riders "for some feedback" if the expected bad weather came.

Track position to determine the new grid was taken back to lap 13, when Rins was still leading, with Dovi and Rossi on the front row; then Pedrosa, Zarco and Nakagami. The remounted Espargaro was eighth.

It started raining again as they lined up 40 minutes later, but not as heavily.

Rins led away again; Dovizioso took over on lap two and, when Rossi moved into second place five laps later, was almost two seconds clear and pulling away. With new soft tyres and a minor bike change to improve braking, he was in control. "I could push as hard as I wanted. Harder than my competitors."

Rossi was dropping back when, on lap ten, he had a second successive race crash, losing the rear at Turn 12. He remounted, but way back in 13th. With Vinales gone, at least third overall was safe. Later he bemoaned that he'd had only used tyres available, but at least he had been competitive in the last two races: "I'll take that into the winter."

Rins was a comfortable second, underlining strong end-of-season form. "Now we test a new bike, with more power," he said, reaching across to tap Dovizioso playfully and adding, "Watch out next year."

The attention was on Espargaro, the only other rider with new tyres front and rear. Fourth from the start, he'd been to and fro with Pedrosa, but "My confidence was high because we were fast in wet practice," the jubilant younger rider said, after his first podium. By half-distance, he'd broken free, leaving Pedrosa to tussle with Pirro, a fight he would eventually lose.

Pirro's fourth was also his best result; likewise Nakagami's sixth. He'd been alone until the last laps, and fended off Zarco and the bullish Smith by half a second. Bautista had been with them, but fell at half-distance.

Bradl narrowly got the better of Syahrin in the last two laps; some way back, Redding repassed Lorenzo's Ducati on the last lap, his best of probably his last GP year.

Rossi was almost 20 seconds away, then Abraham and a distant Jordi Torres taking last place and last point, on a day when even finishing was a real accomplishment.

Pedrosa's valedictory fifth was enough to secure the teams' championship for Repsol Honda – another triple-crown for the manufacturer. Rins drew comfortably clear of Zarco for fifth, the Frenchman already independent-team rider winner ahead of Crutchlow; while in spite of non-scoring, Morbidelli was Rookie of the Year.

MOTO2 RACE – 25 laps

Marini had struggled in wet practice, but in dry qualifying he took a narrow second pole; the top three covered by under two-tenths, and 21 riders in the first second. Team-mates Vierge and Schrotter were alongside; Bagnaia led row two from Baldassarri and Sam Lowes, enjoying a welcome return to form.

The last race of the Honda-powered Moto2 had a dramatic start on the wet and treacherous track.

Vierge led away from Bagnaia, but into only the second corner, Marini lost the front as he touched the brakes, tagging his team-mate's back wheel. A little way back, quite independently, Mir did the same thing to Baldassarri.

Bagnaia survived, but finished the first lap way down in 21st, his chances gone. The other three were out, giving Alex Marquez a golden chance to secure fourth overall. Several other riders had been forced wide.

There were only 20 finishers: not among them Binder, who had a rare crash after having dropped to sixth by lap four, blaming tyre problems. Lowes and Navarro were also on the crash list.

MOTO3 RACE – 23 laps

They had to change the rules to let Can Oncu into the GPs under the minimum age of 16. Just in time for him to win his first race by beating not just new champion Martin by four seconds, but also conditions that caused 16 crashes. These included (from a big lead) second-time pole qualifier Tony Arbolino, and race winners Dalla Porta, Canet, Arenas and (twice) Bezzecchi.

Arbolino's pole came on a drying track, the brave having fitted slicks. Atiratphuvapat was second, his first front row; while McPhee slipped into third at the end, pushing Oncu down to lead the second row.

Arbolino had been in control, with a lead of almost three seconds when he fell on the 12th lap. At this stage, Oncu had already seen Bezzecchi fall in front of him on lap four, and was 6.5 seconds ahead of team-mates Di Giannantonio and Martin.

He continued alone, his Ajo team and elder twin brother, Deniz, biting their nails on the pit wall. On the last lap, he slipped and was out of the seat. But he recovered for a classic win. "It's an incredible feeling – my first time. I don't know what's going on," he said.

It was a race of survival, with champion Martin finally getting clear of the pursuing trio, where McPhee came back to overtake Di Giannantonio, who was happy with fourth. With Bezzecchi out of the points, it was good enough for second overall, a 1-2 championship result for the Del Conca Gresini Honda team.

Bezzecchi finally finished in 20th place and last, a lap down, after having pitted for running repairs following his second crash.

Bastianini finished strongly for fifth, leading Rookie of the Year Masia by seven seconds at the end.

The EG-VDS Kalex rider made the most of it, hunting down Oliveira, who had taken over from Pasini on lap two. On lap six, Marquez took the lead, looking set for his first win in a difficult season, almost two seconds clear at half-distance. But Oliveira kept the pressure on, and the gap was back to just over 1.5 seconds as they started lap 15. At the end of it, Marquez crashed.

But while Oliveira swept on to a clear third win and Iker Lecuona was safe for second, by that time, there had been so many crashes and the field was so spread that Marquez was able to remount and finish third.

"It was not about being fast. It was about being constant," said Oliveira, who would move to MotoGP for 2019. Lecuona said, "I knew when I saw it was raining this morning, it was perfect for me." And Marquez was smiling. "It's good to still finish third when you've had a crash," he said.

Vierge had been struggling for grip and crashed out of third on lap 12, and there were so many others – 15 in all – including American Joe Roberts (NTS), who had been dropped to 19th by the lap-one tangle. Revelling in the wet, he was back up into the top ten when he tumbled.

Pasini was fourth pretty much throughout. He'd almost gained third as Marquez remounted just in front of him, but had lost touch again by the end.

A lively quartet had closed up in the latter laps. Remy Gardner had worked through to the front of it, a second down on the veteran for a career-best fifth, now a couple of seconds clear of Quartararo. The Frenchman had started from the back after stalling on the form-up grid. Schrotter and Augusto Fernandez were still close, Locatelli and Corsi not far behind to close out the top ten.

Aegerter was a lone 11th, then Nagashima, with Odendaal finally moving clear of Bagnaia.

GP MOTUL DE LA COMUNITAT VALENCIANA

16-18 NOVEMBER, 2018

CIRCUITO DE LA COMUNITAT VALENCIANA

Restarted race at 14 laps
Length: 4.005 km / 2.488 miles
Width: 12m

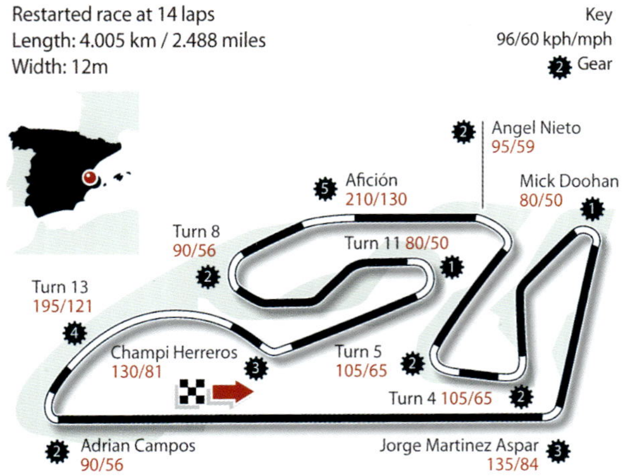

MotoGP

RACE DISTANCE (Part 2): 14 laps, 38.840 miles/56.070km · RACE WEATHER: Wet (air 13°C, humidity 98%, track 13°C)

Pos.	Rider	Nat.	No.	Entrant	Machine	Tyres	Race tyre choice	Laps	Time & speed
1	**Andrea Dovizioso**	ITA	4	Ducati Team	Ducati Desmosedici	M	F: Soft Wet/R: Soft Wet	14	24m 03.408s 86.9mph/ 139.8km/h
2	**Alex Rins**	SPA	42	Team SUZUKI ECSTAR	Suzuki GSX-RR	M	F: Med. Wet/R: Soft Wet	14	24m 06.158s
3	**Pol Espargaro**	SPA	44	Red Bull KTM Factory Racing	KTM RC16	M	F: Soft Wet/R: Soft Wet	14	24m 10.814s
4	**Michele Pirro**	ITA	51	Ducati Team	Ducati Desmosedici	M	F: Soft Wet/R: Soft Wet	14	24m 12.055s
5	**Dani Pedrosa**	SPA	26	Repsol Honda Team	Honda RC213V	M	F: Soft Wet/R: Soft Wet	14	24m 16.759s
6	**Takaaki Nakagami**	JPN	30	LCR Honda IDEMITSU	Honda RC213V	M	F: Soft Wet/R: Soft Wet	14	24m 35.696s
7	**Johann Zarco**	FRA	5	Monster Yamaha Tech 3	Yamaha YZR-M1	M	F: Soft Wet/R: Soft Wet	14	24m 36.214s
8	**Bradley Smith**	GBR	38	Red Bull KTM Factory Racing	KTM RC16	M	F: Soft Wet/R: Soft Wet	14	24m 36.519s
9	**Stefan Bradl**	GER	6	LCR Honda CASTROL	Honda RC213V	M	F: Soft Wet/R: Soft Wet	14	24m 39.784s
10	**Hafizh Syahrin**	MAL	55	Monster Yamaha Tech 3	Yamaha YZR-M1	M	F: Soft Wet/R: Soft Wet	14	24m 40.606s
11	**Scott Redding**	GBR	45	Aprilia Racing Team Gresini	Aprilia RS-GP	M	F: Soft Wet/R: Soft Wet	14	24m 47.734s
12	**Jorge Lorenzo**	SPA	99	Ducati Team	Ducati Desmosedici	M	F: Soft Wet/R: Soft Wet	14	24m 49.554s
13	**Valentino Rossi**	ITA	46	Movistar Yamaha MotoGP	Yamaha YZR-M1	M	F: Soft Wet/R: Soft Wet	14	24m 56.217s
14	**Karel Abraham**	CZE	17	Angel Nieto Team	Ducati Desmosedici	M	F: Soft Wet/R: Soft Wet	14	25m 14.036s
15	**Jordi Torres**	SPA	81	Reale Avintia Racing	Ducati Desmosedici	M	F: Soft Wet/R: Soft Wet	14	25m 20.147s
	Alvaro Bautista	SPA	19	Angel Nieto Team	Ducati Desmosedici	M	-	7	DNF-crash
	Maverick Vinales	SPA	25	Movistar Yamaha MotoGP	Yamaha YZR-M1	M	-	-	DNS Part 2
	Danilo Petrucci	ITA	9	Alma Pramac Racing	Ducati Desmosedici	M	-	-	DNS Part 2
	Marc Marquez	SPA	93	Repsol Honda Team	Honda RC213V	M	-	-	DNS Part 2
	Andrea Iannone	ITA	29	Team SUZUKI ECSTAR	Suzuki GSX-RR	M	-	-	DNS Part 2
	Aleix Espargaro	SPA	41	Aprilia Racing Team Gresini	Aprilia RS-GP	M	-	-	DNS Part 2
	Jack Miller	AUS	43	Alma Pramac Racing	Ducati Desmosedici	M	-	-	DNS Part 2
	Franco Morbidelli	ITA	21	EG 0,0 Marc VDS	Honda RC213V	M	-	-	DNS Part 2
	Thomas Luthi	SWI	12	EG 0,0 Marc VDS	Honda RC213V	M	-	-	DNS Part 2

Fastest lap: Andrea Dovizioso, on lap 6, 1m 41.863s, 87.9mph/141.5km/h.
Lap record: Jorge Lorenzo, 1m 31.171s, 98.2mph/158.1km/h (2016).
Event maximum speed: Stefan Bradl, 198.2mph/319.0km/h (qualifying).

Qualifying

Weather: Dry
Air Temp: 18° **Track Temp:** 20°
Humidity: 79%

1	Vinales	1m 31.312s
2	Rins	1m 31.380s
3	Dovizioso	1m 31.392s
4	Petrucci	1m 31.414s
5	Marquez	1m 31.442s
6	P. Espargaro	1m 31.577s
7	Iannone	1m 31.629s
8	A. Espargaro	1m 31.630s
9	Pedrosa	1m 32.140s
10	Miller	1m 32.145s
11	Zarco	1m 32.179s
12	Pirro	1m 32.310s
13	Lorenzo	1m 31.900s
14	Nakagami	1m 31.928s
15	Morbidelli	1m 32.385s
16	Rossi	1m 32.452s
17	Luthi	1m 32.545s
18	Abraham	1m 32.547s
19	Bautista	1m 32.568s
20	Bradl	1m 32.708s
21	Syahrin	1m 32.749s
22	Smith	1m 33.011s
23	Torres	1m 34.427s
24	Redding	1m 35.171s

Fastest race laps

1	Dovizioso	1m 41.863s
2	Rossi	1m 41.864s
3	Pirro	1m 42.081s
4	Rins	1m 42.233s
5	P. Espargaro	1m 42.501s
6	Pedrosa	1m 42.901s
7	Bautista	1m 43.889s
8	Smith	1m 43.997s
9	Zarco	1m 44.042s
10	Nakagami	1m 44.223s
11	Syahrin	1m 44.238s
12	Redding	1m 44.269s
13	Bradl	1m 44.409s
14	Lorenzo	1m 44.742s
15	Abraham	1m 45.778s
16	Torres	1m 46.948s

Championship Points

1	Marquez	321
2	Dovizioso	245
3	Rossi	198
4	Vinales	193
5	Rins	169
6	Zarco	158
7	Crutchlow	148
8	Petrucci	144
9	Lorenzo	134
10	Iannone	133
11	Pedrosa	117
12	Bautista	105
13	Miller	91
14	P. Espargaro	51
15	Morbidelli	50
16	Syahrin	46
17	A. Espargaro	44
18	Smith	38
19	Rabat	35
20	Nakagami	33
21	Redding	20
22	Pirro	14
23	Abraham	12
24	Bradl	10
25	Kallio	6
26	Nakasuga	2
27	Simeon	1
28	Torres	1

Constructor Points

1	Honda	375
2	Ducati	335
3	Yamaha	281
4	Suzuki	233
5	KTM	72
6	Aprilia	59

	Grid order	1	2	3	4	5	6	7	8	9	10	11	12	13	14	
42	RINS	42	4	4	4	4	4	4	4	4	4	4	4	4	4	1
4	DOVIZIOSO	4	42	42	42	42	42	46	46	46	42	42	42	42	42	2
46	ROSSI	46	46	46	46	46	46	42	42	42	44	44	44	44	44	3
26	PEDROSA	44	44	44	44	44	44	44	44	44	51	51	51	51	51	4
5	ZARCO	26	26	26	26	26	26	51	51	51	26	26	26	26	26	5
30	NAKAGAMI	30	30	30	51	51	51	26	26	26	30	30	30	30	30	6
19	BAUTISTA	19	51	51	30	30	30	30	30	30	5	5	5	5	5	7
44	P. ESPARGARO	51	19	19	19	5	5	5	5	5	38	38	38	38	38	8
45	REDDING	5	5	5	5	38	38	38	38	38	55	55	55	6	6	9
55	SYAHRIN	38	38	38	38	19	19	19	55	55	6	6	6	55	55	10
99	LORENZO	55	45	45	45	45	45	45	6	6	45	45	45	45	45	11
6	BRADL	99	55	55	55	55	6	55	45	45	99	99	99	99	99	12
51	PIRRO	45	6	6	6	6	55	6	99	99	46	46	46	46	46	13
17	ABRAHAM	6	99	99	99	99	99	99	17	17	17	17	17	17	17	14
81	TORRES	17	17	17	17	17	17	17	81	81	81	81	81	81	81	15
38	SMITH	81	81	81	81	81	81	81								

Moto2

RACE DISTANCE: 25 laps, 66.215 miles/100.125km · RACE WEATHER: Wet (air 14°C, humidity 98%, track 14°C)

Pos.	Rider	Nat.	No.	Entrant	Machine	Laps	Time & Speed
1	**Miguel Oliveira**	POR	44	Red Bull KTM Ajo	KTM	25	45m 07.639s 82.7mph/ 133.1km/h
2	**Iker Lecuona**	SPA	27	Swiss Innovative Investors	KTM	25	45m 20.840s
3	**Alex Marquez**	SPA	73	EG 0,0 Marc VDS	Kalex	25	45m 29.814s
4	**Mattia Pasini**	ITA	54	Italtrans Racing Team	Kalex	25	45m 36.531s
5	**Remy Gardner**	AUS	87	Tech 3 Racing	Tech 3	25	45m 37.745s
6	**Fabio Quartararo**	FRA	20	HDR Heidrun - Speed Up	Speed Up	25	45m 39.765s
7	**Marcel Schrotter**	GER	23	Dynavolt Intact GP	Kalex	25	45m 40.725s
8	**Augusto Fernandez**	SPA	40	Pons HP40	Kalex	25	45m 41.589s
9	**Andrea Locatelli**	ITA	5	Italtrans Racing Team	Kalex	25	45m 43.346s
10	**Simone Corsi**	ITA	24	Tasca Racing Scuderia Moto2	Kalex	25	45m 44.658s
11	**Dominique Aegerter**	SWI	77	Kiefer Racing	KTM	25	45m 51.483s
12	**Tetsuta Nagashima**	JPN	45	IDEMITSU Honda Team Asia	Kalex	25	45m 53.510s
13	**Steven Odendaal**	RSA	4	NTS RW Racing GP	NTS	25	45m 56.752s
14	**Francesco Bagnaia**	ITA	42	SKY Racing Team VR46	Kalex	25	46m 00.927s
15	**Jesko Raffin**	SWI	2	SAG Team	Kalex	25	46m 16.351s
16	Isaac Vinales	SPA	32	Forward Racing Team	Suter	25	46m 33.305s
17	Xavi Cardelus	AND	18	Marinelli Snipers Team	Kalex	25	46m 39.805s
18	Jules Danilo	FRA	95	Nashi Argan SAG Team	Kalex	25	46m 55.141s
19	Federico Fuligni	ITA	21	Tasca Racing Scuderia Moto2	Kalex	24	45m 26.874s
20	Lukas Tulovic	GER	23	Forward Racing Team	Suter	24	47m 03.737s
	Niki Tuuli	FIN	66	Petronas Sprinta Racing	Kalex	19	DNF
	Xavi Vierge	SPA	97	Dynavolt Intact GP	Kalex	13	DNF
	Joe Roberts	USA	16	NTS RW Racing GP	NTS	8	DNF
	Tommaso Marcon	ITA	70	HDR Heidrun - Speed Up	Speed Up	7	DNF
	Jorge Navarro	SPA	9	Federal Oil Gresini Moto2	Kalex	5	DNF
	Brad Binder	RSA	41	Red Bull KTM Ajo	KTM	3	DNF
	Sam Lowes	GBR	22	Swiss Innovative Investors	KTM	3	DNF
	Khairul Idham Pawi	MAL	89	IDEMITSU Honda Team Asia	Kalex	2	DNF
	Luca Marini	ITA	10	SKY Racing Team VR46	Kalex	0	DNF
	Lorenzo Baldassarri	ITA	7	Pons HP40	Kalex	0	DNF
	Joan Mir	SPA	36	EG 0,0 Marc VDS	Kalex	0	DNF

Fastest lap: Alex Marquez, on lap 13, 1m 47.089s, 83.6mph/134.6km/h.
Lap record: Thomas Luthi, 1m 35.312s, 94.0mph/151.2km/h (2014).
Event maximum speed: Mattia Pasini, 162.5mph/261.5km/h (qualifying).

Qualifying

Weather: Dry
Air Temp: 17° **Track Temp:** 18°
Humidity: 79%

1	Marini	1m 35.777s
2	Vierge	1m 35.804s
3	Schrotter	1m 35.945s
4	Bagnaia	1m 36.173s
5	Baldassarri	1m 36.270s
6	Lowes	1m 36.335s
7	Mir	1m 36.336s
8	Fernandez	1m 36.380s
9	Quartararo	1m 36.396s
10	Oliveira	1m 36.429s
11	Binder	1m 36.464s
12	Raffin	1m 36.499s
13	Corsi	1m 36.515s
14	Pasini	1m 36.532s
15	Pawi	1m 36.572s
16	Marquez	1m 36.580s
17	Gardner	1m 36.595s
18	Locatelli	1m 36.638s
19	Roberts	1m 36.656s
20	Nagashima	1m 36.667s
21	Lecuona	1m 36.671s
22	Odendaal	1m 36.819s
23	Navarro	1m 36.909s
24	Aegerter	1m 36.976s
25	Garzo	1m 37.444s
26	Tuuli	1m 37.457s
27	Marcon	1m 37.483s
28	Fuligni	1m 38.351s
29	Vinales	1m 38.406s
30	Cardelus	1m 38.718s
31	Danilo	1m 39.275s
32	Tulovic	1m 39.600s

Fastest race laps

1	Marquez	1m 47.089s
2	Oliveira	1m 47.136s
3	Lecuona	1m 47.510s
4	Vierge	1m 47.713s
5	Tuuli	1m 48.121s
6	Quartararo	1m 48.209s
7	Schrotter	1m 48.237s
8	Gardner	1m 48.263s
9	Fernandez	1m 48.336s
10	Pasini	1m 48.432s
11	Locatelli	1m 48.468s
12	Corsi	1m 48.476s
13	Nagashima	1m 48.602s
14	Roberts	1m 48.734s
15	Bagnaia	1m 48.983s
16	Aegerter	1m 49.087s
17	Odendaal	1m 49.125s
18	Raffin	1m 49.414s
19	Binder	1m 49.575s
20	Vinales	1m 49.650s
21	Cardelus	1m 49.725s
22	Danilo	1m 49.760s
23	Navarro	1m 49.891s
24	Lowes	1m 49.926s
25	Tulovic	1m 50.174s
26	Pawi	1m 50.737s
27	Fuligni	1m 51.482s
28	Marcon	1m 53.129s

Championship Points

1	Bagnaia	306
2	Oliveira	297
3	Binder	201
4	Marquez	173
5	Baldassarri	162
6	Mir	155
7	Marini	147
8	Schrotter	147
9	Pasini	141
10	Quartararo	138
11	Vierge	131
12	Lecuona	80
13	Navarro	58
14	Corsi	53
15	Locatelli	52
16	Lowes	49
17	Aegerter	47
18	Fernandez	45
19	Gardner	40
20	Nagashima	27
21	Fenati	14
22	Raffin	10
23	Barbera	10
24	Manzi	8
25	Kent	8
26	Vinales	7
27	Roberts	5
28	Odendaal	4
29	Bendsneyder	2
30	Pawi	1
31	E. Pons	1
32	Tuuli	1

Constructor Points

1	Kalex	407
2	KTM	345
3	Speed Up	142
4	Tech 3	40
5	Suter	8
6	NTS	8

Moto3

RACE DISTANCE: 23 laps, 57.238 miles/92.115km · RACE WEATHER: Wet (air 14°C, humidity 98%, track 14°C)

Pos.	Rider	Nat.	No.	Entrant	Machine	Laps	Time & Speed
1	**Can Oncu**	TUR	61	Red Bull KTM Ajo	KTM	23	43m 06.370s 79.7mph/ 128.2km/h
2	**Jorge Martin**	SPA	88	Del Conca Gresini Moto3	Honda	23	43m 10.441s
3	**John McPhee**	GBR	17	CIP - Green Power	KTM	23	43m 12.500s
4	**Fabio Di Giannantonio**	ITA	21	Del Conca Gresini Moto3	Honda	23	43m 19.267s
5	**Enea Bastianini**	ITA	33	Leopard Racing	Honda	23	43m 21.105s
6	**Jaume Masia**	SPA	5	Bester Capital Dubai	KTM	23	43m 28.354s
7	**Niccolo Antonelli**	ITA	23	SIC58 Squadra Corse	Honda	23	43m 33.011s
8	**Nakarin Atiratphuvapat**	THA	41	Honda Team Asia	Honda	23	43m 37.128s
9	**Marcos Ramirez**	SPA	42	Bester Capital Dubai	KTM	23	43m 39.781s
10	**Celestino Vietti**	ITA	31	SKY Racing Team VR46	KTM	23	43m 45.378s
11	**Ayumu Sasaki**	JPN	71	Petronas Sprinta Racing	Honda	23	43m 48.702s
12	**Stefano Nepa**	ITA	81	CIP - Green Power	KTM	23	43m 55.301s
13	**Raul Fernandez**	SPA	25	Angel Nieto Team	KTM	23	44m 00.804s
14	**Andrea Migno**	ITA	16	Angel Nieto Team Moto3	KTM	23	44m 00.955s
15	**Jakub Kornfeil**	CZE	84	Redox PruestelGP	KTM	23	44m 02.794s
16	Kazuki Masaki	JPN	22	RBA BOE Skull Rider	KTM	23	44m 03.592s
17	Gabriel Rodrigo	ARG	19	RBA BOE Skull Rider	KTM	23	44m 06.911s
18	Lorenzo Dalla Porta	ITA	48	Leopard Racing	Honda	23	44m 41.463s
19	Darryn Binder	RSA	40	Red Bull KTM Ajo	KTM	23	43m 32.841s
20	Marco Bezzecchi	ITA	12	Redox PruestelGP	KTM	23	44m 00.405s
	Vicente Perez	SPA	77	Reale Avintia Academy 77	KTM	22	DNF
	Philipp Oettl	GER	65	Sudmetal Schedl GP Racing	KTM	22	DNF
	Tony Arbolino	ITA	14	Marinelli Snipers Team	Honda	21	DNF
	Izam Ikmal	MAL	26	Petronas Sprinta Racing	Honda	15	DNF
	Albert Arenas	SPA	75	Angel Nieto Team Moto3	KTM	11	DNF
	Kaito Toba	JPN	27	Honda Team Asia	Honda	7	DNF
	Dennis Foggia	ITA	10	SKY Racing Team VR46	KTM	6	DNF
	Aron Canet	SPA	44	Estrella Galicia 0,0	Honda	4	DNF
	Alonso Lopez	SPA	72	Estrella Galicia 0,0	Honda	1	DNF
	Tatsuki Suzuki	JPN	24	SIC58 Squadra Corse	Honda	0	DNF

Fastest lap: Tony Arbolino, on lap 8, 1m 51.172s, 80.5mph/129.6km/h.
Lap record: Marcos Ramirez, 1m 39.109s, 90.3mph/145.4km/h (2017).
Event maximum speed: Dennis Foggia, 137.1mph/220.6km/h (qualifying).

Qualifying

Weather: Wet
Air Temp: 16° **Track Temp:** 18°
Humidity: 89%

1	Arbolino	1m 46.773s
2	Atiratphuvapat	1m 47.017s
3	McPhee	1m 47.116s
4	Oncu	1m 47.336s
5	Canet	1m 47.431s
6	Bezzecchi	1m 47.776s
7	Ramirez	1m 47.783s
8	Kornfeil	1m 47.796s
9	Arenas	1m 47.826s
10	Fernandez	1m 47.880s
11	Lopez	1m 47.896s
12	Perez	1m 48.069s
13	Martin	1m 48.124s
14	Bastianini	1m 48.216s
15	Di Giannantonio	1m 48.357s
16	Masia	1m 48.435s
17	Foggia	1m 48.543s
18	Suzuki	1m 48.614s
19	Binder	1m 48.772s
20	Dalla Porta	1m 48.894s
21	Toba	1m 49.027s
22	Masaki	1m 49.469s
23	Rodrigo	1m 49.696s
24	Vietti	1m 49.802s
25	Sasaki	1m 49.980s
26	Antonelli	1m 50.011s
27	Oettl	1m 50.145s
28	Migno	1m 51.870s
29	Nepa	1m 52.119s
30	Ikmal	1m 53.093s

Fastest race laps

1	Arbolino	1m 51.172s
2	Oncu	1m 51.373s
3	Di Giannantonio	1m 51.477s
4	Bezzecchi	1m 51.533s
5	Martin	1m 51.541s
6	McPhee	1m 51.666s
7	Bastianini	1m 51.771s
8	Masia	1m 51.911s
9	Atiratphuvapat	1m 51.957s
10	Antonelli	1m 51.965s
11	Arenas	1m 52.014s
12	Fernandez	1m 52.255s
13	Kornfeil	1m 52.514s
14	Ramirez	1m 52.713s
15	Sasaki	1m 52.765s
16	Migno	1m 52.834s
17	Vietti	1m 52.876s
18	Perez	1m 52.905s
19	Dalla Porta	1m 53.012s
20	Rodrigo	1m 53.086s
21	Masaki	1m 53.337s
22	Nepa	1m 53.345s
23	Binder	1m 54.378s
24	Toba	1m 54.507s
25	Oettl	1m 55.053s
26	Ikmal	1m 55.652s

Championship Points

1	Martin	260
2	Di Giannantonio	218
3	Bezzecchi	214
4	Bastianini	177
5	Dalla Porta	151
6	Canet	128
7	Rodrigo	116
8	Kornfeil	116
9	Arenas	107
10	Ramirez	102
11	Migno	84
12	McPhee	78
13	Masia	76
14	Suzuki	71
15	Antonelli	71
16	Oettl	58
17	Binder	57
18	Arbolino	57
19	Foggia	55
20	Sasaki	50
21	Norrodin	46
22	Toba	37
23	Lopez	36
24	Oncu	25
25	Vietti	24
26	Bulega	18
27	Perez	16
28	Fernandez	16
29	Atiratphuvapat	12
30	Yurchenko	9
31	Masaki	9
32	Loi	8
33	Chantra	7
34	Pagliani	6
35	Nepa	4
36	Ogura	1

Constructor Points

1	Honda	401
2	KTM	353

sky
OAKLEY
DAINESE
42
REPSOL
HONDA
One HEART
Red Bull
TEAM
DEL CONCA
Gresini Moto3
88
SAGTUBI
DEL CONCA
Kaprìol

REPSOL
93
26

WORLD CHAMPIONSHIP POINTS 2018

Compiled by PETER McLAREN

MotoGP – Riders

Position	Rider	Nationality	Machine	Qatar	Argentina	United States	Spain	France	Italy	Catalunya	Netherlands	Germany	Czech Republic	Austria	Great Britain	San Marino	Aragon	Thailand	Japan	Australia	Malaysia	Valencia	Points total
1	**Marc Marquez**	SPA	Honda	20	0	25	25	25	0	20	25	25	16	20	–	20	25	25	25	–	25	–	**321**
2	**Andrea Dovizioso**	ITA	Ducati	25	10	11	–	–	20	–	13	9	25	16	–	25	20	20	0	16	10	25	**245**
3	**Valentino Rossi**	ITA	Yamaha	16	0	13	11	16	16	16	11	20	13	10	–	9	8	13	13	10	0	3	**198**
4	**Maverick Vinales**	SPA	Yamaha	10	11	20	9	9	8	10	16	16	–	4	–	11	6	16	9	25	13	–	**193**
5	**Alex Rins**	SPA	Suzuki	–	16	–	–	6	11	–	20	–	5	8	–	13	13	10	16	11	20	20	**169**
6	**Johann Zarco**	FRA	Yamaha	8	20	10	20	–	6	9	8	7	9	7	–	6	2	11	10	–	16	9	**158**
7	**Cal Crutchlow**	GBR	Honda	13	25	0	–	8	10	13	10	–	11	13	–	16	–	9	20	–	–	–	**148**
8	**Danilo Petrucci**	ITA	Ducati	11	6	4	13	20	9	8	–	13	10	11	–	5	9	7	7	4	7	–	**144**
9	**Jorge Lorenzo**	SPA	Ducati	–	1	5	–	10	25	25	9	10	20	25	–	0	–	–	–	–	–	4	**134**
10	**Andrea Iannone**	ITA	Suzuki	7	8	16	16	–	13	6	5	4	6	3	–	8	16	5	–	20	–	–	**133**
11	**Dani Pedrosa**	SPA	Honda	9	–	9	–	11	–	11	1	8	8	9	–	10	11	–	8	–	11	11	**117**
12	**Alvaro Bautista**	SPA	Ducati	3	0	1	8	–	7	7	7	11	7	6	–	7	–	8	11	13	9	–	**105**
13	**Jack Miller**	AUS	Ducati	6	13	7	10	13	–	–	6	2	4	0	–	0	7	6	–	9	8	–	**91**
14	**Pol Espargaro**	SPA	KTM	–	5	3	5	5	5	5	4	–	–	–	–	–	–	0	3	–	–	16	**51**
15	**Franco Morbidelli**	ITA	Honda	4	2	0	7	3	1	2	–	–	3	0	–	4	5	2	5	8	4	–	**50**
16	**Hafizh Syahrin**	MAL	Yamaha	2	7	–	0	4	4	–	0	5	2	0	–	0	0	4	6	–	6	6	**46**
17	**Aleix Espargaro**	SPA	Aprilia	0	–	6	–	7	–	–	3	–	1	0	–	2	10	3	–	7	5	–	**44**
18	**Bradley Smith**	GBR	KTM	0	–	0	3	2	2	–	0	6	–	2	–	0	3	1	4	6	1	8	**38**
19	**Tito Rabat**	SPA	Ducati	5	9	8	2	–	3	–	0	3	–	5	–	–	–	–	–	–	–	–	**35**
20	**Takaaki Nakagami**	JPN	Honda	0	3	2	4	1	0	–	0	–	0	1	–	3	4	0	1	2	2	10	**33**
21	**Scott Redding**	GBR	Aprilia	0	4	0	1	–	–	4	2	1	–	0	–	0	0	0	0	3	0	5	**20**
22	**Michele Pirro**	ITA	Ducati	–	–	–	–	–	–	–	–	–	–	–	–	1	–	–	–	–	–	13	**14**
23	**Karel Abraham**	CZE	Ducati	1	0	–	0	0	–	3	–	0	0	0	–	0	1	0	–	5	–	2	**12**
24	**Stefan Bradl**	GER	Honda	–	–	–	–	–	–	–	–	0	–	–	–	–	–	–	–	–	3	7	**10**
25	**Mika Kallio**	FIN	KTM	–	–	–	6	–	–	–	–	–	–	–	–	–	–	–	–	–	–	–	**6**
26	**Katsuyuki Nakasuga**	JPN	Yamaha	–	–	–	–	–	–	–	–	–	–	–	–	–	–	–	2	–	–	–	**2**
27	**Xavier Simeon**	BEL	Ducati	0	0	0	0	0	0	–	–	0	0	–	–	–	0	0	0	1	0	–	**1**
28	**Jordi Torres**	SPA	Ducati	–	–	–	–	–	–	–	–	–	–	–	–	–	0	0	0	0	–	1	**1**
	Thomas Luthi	SWI	Honda	0	0	0	–	0	–	–	0	0	0	0	–	0	0	0	0	0	0	–	**0**
	Mike Jones	AUS	Ducati	–	–	–	–	–	–	–	–	–	–	–	–	–	–	–	–	0	–	–	**0**
	Sylvain Guintoli	FRA	Suzuki	–	–	–	–	–	–	–	–	–	0	–	–	–	–	–	0	–	–	–	**0**
	Christophe Ponsson	FRA	Ducati	–	–	–	–	–	–	–	–	–	–	–	–	0	–	–	–	–	–	–	**0**

MotoGP - Teams

Position	Team	Qatar	Argentina	United States	Spain	France	Italy	Catalunya	Netherlands	Germany	Czech Republic	Austria	Great Britain	San Marino	Aragon	Thailand	Japan	Australia	Malaysia	Valencia	Points total
1	**Repsol Honda Team**	29	–	34	25	36	–	31	26	33	24	29	–	30	36	25	33	–	36	11	**438**
2	**Ducati Team**	25	11	16	–	10	45	25	22	19	45	41	–	25	20	20	–	29	10	29	**392**
3	**Movistar Yamaha MotoGP**	26	11	33	20	25	24	26	27	36	13	14	–	20	14	29	22	35	13	3	**391**
4	**Team SUZUKI ECSTAR**	7	24	16	16	6	24	6	25	4	11	11	–	21	29	15	16	31	20	20	**302**
5	**Alma Pramac Racing**	17	19	11	23	33	9	8	6	15	14	11	–	5	16	13	7	13	15	–	**235**
6	**Monster Yamaha Tech 3**	10	27	10	20	4	10	9	8	12	11	7	–	6	2	15	16	–	22	15	**204**
7	**LCR Honda**	13	28	2	4	9	10	13	10	–	11	14	–	19	4	9	21	2	5	17	**191**
8	**Angel Nieto Team**	4	–	1	8	–	7	10	7	11	7	6	–	7	1	8	11	5	9	2	**104**
9	**Red Bull KTM Factory Racing**	–	5	3	8	7	7	5	4	6	–	2	–	–	3	1	7	6	1	24	**89**
10	**Aprilia Racing Team Gresini**	–	4	6	1	7	–	4	5	1	1	–	–	2	10	3	–	10	5	5	**64**
11	**EG 0,0 Marc VDS**	4	2	–	7	3	1	2	–	–	3	–	–	4	5	2	5	8	4	–	**50**
12	**Reale Avintia Racing**	5	9	8	2	–	3	–	–	3	–	5	–	–	–	–	–	1	–	1	**37**

Moto2

Position	Rider	Nationality	Machine	Qatar	Argentina	United States	Spain	France	Italy	Catalunya	Netherlands	Germany	Czech Republic	Austria	Great Britain	San Marino	Aragon	Thailand	Japan	Australia	Malaysia	Valencia	Points total
1	**Francesco Bagnaia**	ITA	Kalex	25	7	25	16	25	13	8	25	4	16	25	–	25	20	25	25	4	16	2	**306**
2	**Miguel Oliveira**	POR	KTM	11	16	16	20	10	25	20	10	13	25	20	–	20	9	16	16	5	20	25	**297**
3	**Brad Binder**	RSA	KTM	10	–	10	10	7	10	10	9	25	10	10	–	8	25	13	11	25	8	–	**201**
4	**Alex Marquez**	SPA	Kalex	16	11	20	–	20	11	16	16	3	–	–	–	0	13	–	13	9	9	16	**173**
5	**Lorenzo Baldassarri**	ITA	Kalex	20	13	6	25	–	20	9	0	–	13	0	–	10	16	–	20	0	10	–	**162**
6	**Joan Mir**	SPA	Kalex	5	9	13	5	16	16	–	11	20	–	8	–	11	10	–	5	20	6	–	**155**
7	**Luca Marini**	ITA	Kalex	7	0	3	–	–	9	0	8	16	20	16	–	–	5	20	7	11	25	–	**147**
8	**Marcel Schrotter**	GER	Kalex	9	6	–	9	13	–	13	13	10	9	9	–	16	11	–	6	7	7	9	**147**
9	**Mattia Pasini**	ITA	Kalex	13	25	9	11	0	–	–	5	–	6	13	–	13	8	10	2	–	13	13	**141**
10	**Fabio Quartararo**	FRA	Speed Up	0	0	1	6	8	5	25	20	7	5	7	–	9	7	11	–	6	11	10	**138**
11	**Xavi Vierge**	SPA	Kalex	8	20	–	13	11	7	11	–	9	11	–	–	6	–	5	9	16	5	–	**131**
12	**Iker Lecuona**	SPA	KTM	–	5	11	7	–	3	6	0	0	3	6	–	0	2	9	8	–	–	20	**80**
13	**Jorge Navarro**	SPA	Kalex	6	–	8	0	–	–	–	3	6	8	11	–	7	6	0	–	–	3	–	**58**
14	**Simone Corsi**	ITA	Kalex	2	0	4	4	2	6	4	1	8	1	–	–	5	4	6	–	0	0	6	**53**
15	**Andrea Locatelli**	ITA	Kalex	0	1	2	1	4	8	5	6	–	2	3	–	2	0	7	0	0	4	7	**52**
16	**Sam Lowes**	GBR	KTM	–	3	0	8	3	–	7	7	11	7	–	–	–	0	–	0	2	1	–	**49**
17	**Dominique Aegerter**	SWI	KTM	1	8	7	–	–	4	0	2	2	0	0	–	3	0	0	3	10	2	5	**47**
18	**Augusto Fernandez**	SPA	Kalex	–	–	–	–	–	–	2	4	1	4	–	–	–	3	–	10	13	–	8	**45**
19	**Remy Gardner**	AUS	Tech 3	4	10	0	–	–	–	1	0	5	–	–	–	4	0	4	1	–	–	11	**40**
20	**Tetsuta Nagashima**	JPN	Kalex	0	0	0	3	0	–	3	–	–	0	1	–	–	1	8	4	3	–	4	**27**
21	**Romano Fenati**	ITA	Kalex	0	0	0	–	9	–	–	–	0	–	5	–	–	–	–	–	–	–	–	**14**
22	**Jesko Raffin**	SWI	Kalex	–	–	–	–	–	–	–	–	–	–	–	–	1	0	–	0	8	0	1	**10**
23	**Hector Barbera**	SPA	Kalex	3	0	0	2	5	–	–	–	–	–	–	–	–	–	–	–	–	–	–	**10**
24	**Stefano Manzi**	ITA	Suter	0	0	–	–	6	–	–	–	0	–	2	–	–	–	–	0	–	–	–	**8**
25	**Danny Kent**	GBR	Speed Up	0	4	–	–	0	–	0	–	–	–	4	–	–	–	–	–	–	–	–	**8**
26	**Isaac Vinales**	SPA	Suter	0	2	5	0	–	0	–	0	–	–	0	–	–	–	0	0	–	0	0	**7**
27	**Joe Roberts**	USA	NTS	0	0	0	–	0	2	0	0	0	0	0	–	0	0	3	0	0	0	–	**5**
28	**Steven Odendaal**	RSA	NTS	0	0	0	–	0	1	0	0	0	0	0	–	0	0	0	0	0	0	3	**4**
29	**Bo Bendsneyder**	NED	Tech 3	0	0	0	0	0	–	–	0	0	–	0	–	0	0	2	–	–	–	–	**2**
30	**Khairul Idham Pawi**	MAL	Kalex	0	0	0	0	1	0	0	0	0	0	0	–	0	0	0	0	0	0	–	**1**
31	**Edgar Pons**	SPA	Kalex/Speed Up	–	–	–	–	–	–	0	–	–	–	–	–	–	0	0	0	1	0	–	**1**
32	**Niki Tuuli**	FIN	Kalex	–	–	–	–	0	0	–	–	–	0	0	–	0	0	1	0	–	–	–	**1**
	Xavi Cardelus	AND	Kalex	–	–	–	0	0	0	–	–	0	–	0	–	0	0	0	0	–	–	0	**0**
	Jules Danilo	FRA	Kalex	0	–	0	0	0	–	0	0	–	0	0	–	0	0	0	0	–	0	0	**0**
	Thitipong Warokorn	THA	Kalex	–	–	–	–	–	–	–	–	–	–	–	–	–	–	0	–	–	–	–	**0**
	Federico Fuligni	ITA	Kalex	0	0	0	0	–	0	–	0	0	–	–	–	0	–	0	–	–	0	0	**0**
	Eric Granado	BRA	Suter	0	0	0	–	–	0	0	0	0	0	–	–	–	–	–	–	–	–	–	**0**
	Lukas Tulovic	GER	Suter	–	–	–	0	0	–	–	–	–	–	–	–	–	–	–	–	–	–	0	**0**
	Hector Garzo	SPA	Tech 3	–	–	–	0	–	0	–	–	–	–	–	–	–	–	–	–	–	–	–	**0**
	Bryan Staring	AUS	Tech 3	–	–	–	–	–	–	–	–	–	–	–	–	–	–	–	–	0	–	–	**0**
	Dimas Ekky Pratama	INA	Honda/Tech 3	–	–	–	–	–	–	0	–	–	–	–	–	–	–	–	–	–	0	–	**0**
	Alejandro Medina	SPA	Kalex	–	–	–	–	–	–	–	–	–	0	–	–	–	–	–	–	–	–	–	**0**
	Sheridan Morais	POR	Kalex	–	–	–	–	0	–	–	–	–	–	–	–	–	–	–	–	–	–	–	**0**
	Corentin Perolari	FRA	Transformiers	0	0	0	–	–	–	–	–	–	–	–	–	–	–	–	–	–	–	–	**0**
	Zulfahmi Khairuddin	MAL	Kalex	0	0	0	–	–	–	–	–	–	–	–	–	–	–	–	–	–	–	–	**0**
	Rafid Topan Sucipto	INA	Suter	–	–	–	–	–	–	–	–	–	–	–	–	–	–	–	–	–	0	–	**0**
	Cedric Tangre	FRA	Tech 3	–	–	–	–	0	–	–	–	–	–	–	–	–	–	–	–	–	–	–	**0**

Photos: Gold & Goose

Moto3

Position	Rider	Nationality	Machine	Qatar	Argentina	United States	Spain	France	Italy	Catalunya	Netherlands	Germany	Czech Republic	Austria	Great Britain	San Marino	Aragon	Thailand	Japan	Australia	Malaysia	Valencia	Points total
1	**Jorge Martin**	SPA	Honda	25	5	25	–	–	25	–	25	25	–	16	–	20	25	13	–	11	25	20	**260**
2	**Fabio Di Giannantonio**	ITA	Honda	10	16	11	9	13	16	9	7	–	25	5	–	16	13	25	–	20	10	13	**218**
3	**Marco Bezzecchi**	ITA	KTM	2	25	16	20	–	20	20	–	20	10	25	–	–	20	–	25	–	11	0	**214**
4	**Enea Bastianini**	ITA	Honda	–	13	20	–	–	10	25	16	–	13	20	–	–	16	–	9	8	16	11	**177**
5	**Lorenzo Dalla Porta**	ITA	Honda	16	9	0	–	–	8	0	10	3	6	11	–	25	3	20	20	–	20	0	**151**
6	**Aron Canet**	SPA	Honda	20	20	8	–	8	5	–	20	11	20	6	–	–	–	–	–	10	–	–	**128**
7	**Gabriel Rodrigo**	ARG	KTM	11	7	4	6	–	13	16	8	–	11	8	–	13	–	11	8	–	–	0	**116**
8	**Jakub Kornfeil**	CZE	KTM	7	2	9	8	10	0	5	11	9	16	3	–	11	5	6	6	7	0	1	**116**
9	**Albert Arenas**	SPA	KTM	–	–	1	–	25	2	–	2	–	7	13	–	10	9	–	–	25	13	–	**107**
10	**Marcos Ramirez**	SPA	KTM	1	4	–	16	16	1	–	6	13	9	1	–	0	11	8	4	–	5	7	**102**
11	**Andrea Migno**	ITA	KTM	6	3	13	3	20	11	–	0	4	0	–	–	7	4	5	3	3	0	2	**84**
12	**John Mcphee**	GBR	KTM	–	0	2	–	4	4	13	–	16	–	4	–	–	6	–	11	2	–	16	**78**
13	**Jaume Masia**	SPA	KTM	4	–	0	11	6	–	–	13	10	0	10	–	–	7	0	5	–	–	10	**76**
14	**Tatsuki Suzuki**	JPN	Honda	–	0	7	10	7	0	11	3	–	2	0	–	–	10	–	1	13	7	–	**71**
15	**Niccolo Antonelli**	ITA	Honda	13	8	0	5	11	7	–	1	0	5	0	–	6	–	–	–	–	6	9	**71**
16	**Philipp Oettl**	GER	KTM	–	0	10	25	1	0	0	0	8	8	2	–	–	0	3	0	1	0	–	**58**
17	**Darryn Binder**	RSA	KTM	–	0	3	–	5	3	–	9	–	0	0	–	8	0	–	16	4	9	0	**57**
18	**Tony Arbolino**	ITA	Honda	0	6	0	–	9	9	–	0	0	1	7	–	5	0	2	10	–	8	–	**57**
19	**Dennis Foggia**	ITA	KTM	0	–	0	–	2	–	7	4	0	4	0	–	9	0	16	13	–	–	–	**55**
20	**Ayumu Sasaki**	JPN	Honda	8	0	5	4	0	0	–	0	6	0	9	–	–	–	–	7	6	0	5	**50**
21	**Adam Norrodin**	MAL	Honda	5	11	–	0	–	–	3	0	5	–	0	–	4	8	1	0	9	0	–	**46**
22	**Kaito Toba**	JPN	Honda	9	0	–	7	0	0	10	0	0	–	0	–	3	0	4	0	0	4	–	**37**
23	**Alonso Lopez**	SPA	Honda	–	10	0	13	0	0	8	0	–	0	0	–	–	0	–	0	5	–	–	**36**
24	**Can Oncu**	TUR	KTM	–	–	–	–	–	–	–	–	–	–	–	–	–	–	–	–	–	–	25	**25**
25	**Celestino Vietti**	ITA	KTM	–	–	–	–	–	–	–	–	–	–	–	–	–	–	–	2	16	–	6	**24**
26	**Nicolo Bulega**	ITA	KTM	–	–	–	0	–	0	–	5	2	0	0	–	–	2	9	–	–	–	–	**18**
27	**Vicente Perez**	SPA	KTM	–	–	–	–	–	–	–	–	–	0	0	–	2	1	10	–	0	3	–	**16**
28	**Raul Fernandez**	SPA	KTM	–	–	–	–	–	–	6	–	7	–	–	–	–	0	–	–	–	–	3	**16**
29	**Nakarin Atiratphuvapat**	THA	Honda	0	0	0	0	0	0	2	0	–	0	0	–	0	0	–	0	0	2	8	**12**
30	**Makar Yurchenko**	KAZ	KTM/Honda	0	0	0	2	3	–	4	–	–	–	–	–	–	–	–	–	–	0	–	**9**
31	**Kazuki Masaki**	JPN	KTM	3	0	0	0	0	0	–	0	1	3	0	–	1	0	0	0	–	1	0	**9**
32	**Livio Loi**	BEL	KTM	–	1	6	0	0	0	1	0	–	–	–	–	–	–	–	–	–	–	–	**8**
33	**Somkiat Chantra**	THA	Honda	–	–	–	–	–	–	–	–	–	–	–	–	–	–	7	–	–	–	–	**7**
34	**Manuel Pagliani**	ITA	Honda	–	–	–	–	–	6	–	–	–	–	–	–	–	–	–	–	–	–	–	**6**
35	**Stefano Nepa**	ITA	KTM	–	–	–	–	–	–	–	0	0	–	0	–	0	0	0	0	0	0	4	**4**
36	**Ai Ogura**	JPN	Honda	–	–	–	1	–	–	–	0	–	–	0	–	–	–	–	–	–	–	–	**1**
	Yari Montella	ITA	Honda	–	–	–	–	–	–	–	–	–	–	–	–	0	–	–	–	0	–	–	**0**
	Apiwath Wongthananon	THA	KTM	–	–	–	–	–	–	–	–	–	–	–	–	–	–	0	–	–	0	–	**0**
	Jeremy Alcoba	SPA	Honda	–	–	–	–	–	–	–	–	–	–	–	–	–	0	0	–	–	–	–	**0**
	Kevin Zannoni	ITA	TM Racing	–	–	–	–	–	–	–	–	–	–	–	–	0	–	–	–	–	–	–	**0**
	Luca Grunwald	GER	KTM	–	–	–	–	–	–	–	–	0	–	–	–	–	–	–	–	–	–	–	**0**
	Shizuka Okazaki	JPN	Honda	–	–	–	–	–	–	–	–	–	–	–	–	–	–	–	0	–	–	–	**0**
	Izam Ikmal	MAL	Honda	–	–	–	–	–	–	–	–	–	–	–	–	–	–	–	–	–	–	0	**0**
	Yuto Fukushima	JPN	Honda	–	–	–	–	–	–	–	–	–	0	–	–	–	–	–	–	–	–	–	**0**

TWIN TRIUMPH

RED BULL ROOKIES CUP REVIEW by PETER CLIFFORD

Above: The Oncu twins, Can (61) and Deniz (53), battle for supremacy at the Sachsenring.

Top right: Champion Can Oncu took five victories, and won the right for an under-age GP wild-card at Valencia. He made history with victory at his first attempt.

Above right: Filip Salac (12) and Xavier Artigas (24) head the brawl at the Red Bull Ring.

Right: Fifth-placed Carlos Tatay took a victory in Jerez.

Far right: Year-two rookie Ryusei Yamanaka, here on the Sachsenring podium, claimed a first win during the season.

Below right: Deniz Oncu celebrates his race-one victory in Germany. He was second overall.

Photos: Red Bull/Gold & Goose

BY the time we heard Deniz Oncu singing along to the Turkish national anthem, after winning the final race of the 2018 Red Bull MotoGP Rookies Cup in Aragon, at least we should have been able to hum along with him. It was the eighth time that the catchy number had been played during the year.

Oncu's 15-year-old twin brother, Can, stood on the top step for five of those renditions, and seized the Cup itself by backing up those victories with a record-breaking run of ten podium finishes that left no one else with much of a chance. Three wins for Deniz put him second in the points table and made their family virtually Rookies Cup royalty.

Their reign had been far from easy, however. Every weekend, they had come under attack from the world's fastest teens, all with ideas of following ex-Rookies like Brad Binder, Joan Mir and Jorge Martin to grand prix glory.

There were four other winners, and all had got the better of the Oncu twins in fair fights. Can only managed the double at Assen, something that he'd achieved 12 months earlier in his first Cup season. He'd won four of the first seven races in 2017 and appeared to be on his way to the title, only for his campaign to come unravelled. He ended the season third. But in 2018, it was a very different Can Oncu, who had the measure of both himself and the opposition.

That opposition was pretty clear from race one at Jerez, when Can was still only 14. He had to work very hard for victory, defeating first-timer Carlos Tatay, the 14-year-old Spaniard, with two immaculate final laps. It had been an eight-man battle for the lead, and only over the last four of the 16 laps did Tatay and Oncu get away. Sixteen-year-old Czech Filip Salac closed them down, though, and chased them home, with Deniz Oncu a close fourth.

Tatay turned the tables on Can and won race two with a perfect outbraking move at the final turn. Can, and brother Deniz and Salac (third and fourth) all thought that there was another lap to go and didn't see the chequered flag. However this happened, Can Oncu and Tatay, who turned 15 the next day, left tied on points, with Deniz Oncu and third-year Rookie Salac sharing third.

Tatay was out of his comfort zone at Mugello, but was still a fine fourth after another fantastic race. Just 1.5 seconds separated the top 13 at the end of 16 incredible laps, Japanese 15-year-old Yuki Kunii winning from Can Oncu and 15-year-old Spaniard Adrian Carrasco. The smooth and stylish win propelled Kuni into possible Cup contention. Unfortunately, he broke his hand in a Spanish CEV event and missed the next four Cup races.

While Kuni was recovering, Can Oncu was dominating in the Netherlands, matching his 2017 double and extending his lead to 24 points. Brother Deniz led a five-man battle in hot pursuit, but just lost a podium place coming out of the last chicane when he was passed by Xavi Artigas and Ryusei Yamanaka.

It was a first podium for Spaniard Artigas (15) and a first of the year for Japanese fellow year-two Rookie Yamanaka (16). Both were worth watching. Yamanaka needed to find more consistency, while Artigas was steadily and impressively building skills and experience, and making precious few mistakes.

It was still Can Oncu doing the winning, though, and he emerged in front after an incredible opening few laps of race two at Assen, stretching his points advantage to an impressive 49 after five of 12 races.

The chasing pack of KTM RC 250 Rs provided plenty of entertainment. Salac made a strong run to second, having finished fourth on Saturday, holding off Artigas.

Can's domination in the Netherlands made it look as though he could put together more doubles, but when the Rookies lined up in Germany, it was brother Deniz who produced a perfect performance to win race one at the Sachsenring, beating Can by 4.455 seconds after 19 laps. Can had to battle just to make the podium, chased over the line by Yamanaka, Salac, Carrasco and Steward Garcia, the 18-year-old Colombian, all covered by half a second.

Can said that he had had a small problem with the bike in the Saturday race. It was fixed for Sunday, however, and there was no stopping him; he led his brother home by less than two-tenths.

Three seconds back, the battle for third was even closer as Salac snatched the final podium place by the same rim

width by which he had lost it on Saturday, after a similarly brilliant battle with Carrasco, Artigas and Yamanaka.

Suddenly just five races were left as the teens gathered at the Red Bull Ring. The Turkish twins had turned 15 on 26th July, and while Can had a 52-point advantage over Deniz, there were still 125 on offer from the remaining races. Salac was a further 13 adrift. But there was no sense of inevitability about the continued domination by the Turks. Both knew how quickly things could come unravelled. Can had only picked up two points from race one at the Red Bull Ring the previous year, after a second-corner collision. He had missed out on points completely in half of the last six races of 2017 and seen his big lead collapse.

As if to emphasise unpredictability, the weather jumped in, inflicting dry, soaking and drying sessions of practice and qualifying that left Yamanaka, Artigas and 16-year-old Brazilian Meikon Kawakami lining up on the front row, with Can Oncu eighth and Deniz 14th.

Yamanaka converted his first pole into his first win, with a perfect final thrust on the last lap, outbraking everyone into the second tight right-hander up the hill and holding on to the flag. He'd fought a huge lead pack throughout the 17 laps, crossing the line just ahead of Artigas and Can Oncu. Deniz had rapidly charged through from 14th to the front, but Can had gone backwards from eighth and had had a big struggle to get that rostrum.

In race two, Artigas put together the perfect final 4.318km to claim his first Cup victory. Again, there had been a huge group swapping places at each corner, and while the Spaniard had featured at the front, as he had done on Saturday, it was only the perfect last tour that had clinched it ahead of Can Oncu and Salac.

Just 1.3 seconds covered the top nine at the finish, but Artigas had been learning all year, and again from his second place on Saturday: "I saw that Yamanaka led the last lap and it just wasn't possible to pass him. So I knew I had to try the same thing. I got ahead and pushed hard. It worked."

So no win for Can, but a third and a second were strong steps to the title and opened up the possibility of resolving the Cup on the Adriatic coast, where Misano would give us a single race. Deniz had picked up two fourth places in Austria, dropping points to his brother as well as to Artigas and Salac, who were chasing him for second, now just ten and 12 points respectively behind.

Seeing him munching pizza and looking forward to the weekend, you might have recalled that Can Oncu had scored zero in Misano in 2017, and again in race two at Aragon. But a year on, this was a much more level-headed racer, who seemed to have banished errors from his portfolio. There was little apparent caution, though, and he and Deniz were quickest in qualifying, and it was no surprise that they were chased around by half of the remaining KTMs, all looking for a tow towards a quick lap. Yamanaka got closest on time and completed the front row, ahead of Kawakami.

Once again, the brothers did the leading, with Can in front when it counted. They had to fight all the way with seven other Rookies, and while Deniz did most of the front running, a minor error at the end left him a furious eighth. Salac took a super-close second, ahead of Carrasco. Just 1.3 seconds covered the top eight.

That gave Can Oncu the Cup, and put Salac equal on points with Deniz for second; Artigas was just seven behind.

Two races remained, and no one was betting much against Can Oncu wrapping up the season with at least another two podium finishes to keep his perfect score. Strangely, he didn't feature in the Motorland Aragon action at all: tenth in qualifying, tenth in race one and eighth in race two. The bike hadn't felt right and neither had he. Winning the Cup hadn't looked that hard for him, but at 15 (at any age), such things take a toll, and for that weekend at least Can Oncu was spent.

There was no problem for brother Deniz, however, who picked up the Turkish flag and ran with it to a superb double. He had been energised by what he considered to be unfair tactics in qualifying, accusing other riders of trailing him for a quick time, particularly Artigas, who had taken pole, 0.455 of a second quicker than Deniz. His other rival for second overall, Salac, completed the front row.

Perhaps the smaller of the Oncu twins needed to feed on a bit of perceived injustice. He certainly made it work for him, and while both races featured big battles, he triumphed on both occasions: by 0.548 of a second over Artigas on Saturday, and half that ahead of Tatay on Sunday.

Salac had been brought down on Saturday, so Artigas took third in the Cup chase. It was great to see Tatay end the year with second after his third of the day before, completing his season with a podium double, the way he had started in Jerez. The mid-season had not been quite as stellar, but he had put together a very intelligent first year and marked himself as a favourite for 2019, finishing fifth in the points.

The four ahead of him would all move on to Moto3 Grand Prix and Junior World championships, keeping the stream of potential world champions flowing.

SUPERBIKE WORLD CHAMPIONSHIP REVIEW OF 2018

By GORDON RITCHIE

Photo: Gold & Goose

OVERARCHING OVER-PERFORMANCE

By GORDON RITCHIE

Above: **Jonathan Rea scored 17 wins and amassed a staggering 545 points to finish 189 clear of Ducati's Chaz Davies (7), his closest challenger.**

Right, from top: **Wins were thin on the ground for Rea's rivals. As well as Davies, those who made the top step were Alex Lowes (22, Pata Yamaha), Marco Melandri (33, Aruba.IT Ducati), Tom Sykes (66, Kawasaki Racing Team) and Michael van der Mark (60, Pata Yamaha).**

Photos: Gold & Goose

IT'S hard to look at the fourth straight WorldSBK success for Jonathan Rea, Kawasaki and the Provec Racing Team and not acknowledge that they have simply smashed this whole thing out of the park. As with Mick Doohan's all-conquering five-year run in GPs, the best rider, machine and team were completely dominant.

KRT, of course, was elevated by greater resources than its closest rivals. For those without sneer-goggles refracting their vision, it's not hard to see that the combination of Rea's speed, accuracy and confidence, his team's set-up ability and the supporting manufacturer's appropriate response to each rule change was always going to prevail.

Even now, KHI's rivals are missing some key elements for the overall championship challenge.

It can be boring if one man wins nearly all the time, but there were several brilliant contests to watch in 2018. Without Rea in the field, it would have been a different story for the championship fight. The same was true elsewhere: MotoGP without Marquez, who won with races to spare; or BSB without Haslam, who would have done the same without the Shootout gimmick. Were these series panned and trolled on social media in the same way as WorldSBK?

The 2018 championship featured just 59 points from second to fifth. The fight would have gone all the way without JR in the paddock. The class, the concept was far from broken.

Six riders won at least one race in 2018, despite Rea's transcendence, and two of those were first-timers. But the fact that none of them won more than two races showed what was missing. This lack of consistency and repeatability of performance seemed to have been forgotten by some who said that things needed to change to compete with Rea and his package.

In all, nine riders stood on the podium in 2018. Yamaha delivered breakthrough wins for both their riders, and a privateer Ducati often beat the official bikes. WorldSBK might have been predictable in Rea's case, but everything else was a game of "Who's round is it?"

Why? WorldSBK technical and balancing rules, and access to the same material as the top men had never been more even and open.

It must be unspeakably frustrating to be nearly there in terms of overall performance, to have a race-winning pedigree going back several seasons, yet still the best of them finished 189 points behind Rea. Even after his shaky start under the new rev-limit rules.

As a salve to their wounded pride, they should note that they were racing against the statistical new Superbike GOAT.

Still there were calls for changes. Everybody needs to see tight races and unpredictability. Especially the fans.

After four years of watching their best legions breaking on the walls of the green fortress, some elements of the Superbike paddock were in open (though off-the-record) rebellion. Clashes of interest, unfair technical resources, tyre trickery and too many new-model homologations – the rumours and conspiracy theories grew each weekend.

We had not quite reached the stage when voodoo was suspected. But 2018 will be remembered as the season when Rea and Kawasaki put the psychological hoodoo on even their most level-headed and talented rivals.

Ducati and Yamaha looked pretty much like factory efforts – or what passes for them in WorldSBK. Decrying Kawasaki for spending a bit more than them seemed incredibly hypocritical, given WorldSBK's history.

And demanding the end of new Kawasaki homologations seemed odd. The bike they brought in 2018 won by such a huge margin. Would it suddenly be more catchable in 2019 if no new homologations were allowed?

Racing is essentially unpredictable, but in all probability Rea will be catchable in 2019 only if the new V4 Ducati and new BMW exceed expectations from the very start. Or Yamaha makes another jump to be competitive at every track.

For 2019, we will get new bikes, top rider shuffles and a change of weekend format.

Again.

If those elements combine to make for a greater number of close and unpredictable races, then WorldSBK should regain something of the profile and prestige it once enjoyed.

NEW RULES EXPLAINED

IN a continuing attempt to achieve closer racing, Dorna introduced new 'balancing' regulations and revised older ones for 2018. Once again, each rider was allowed seven engines for the season.

Rev Limits

New for 2018, the initial rev limit was the dynamometer-measured rev limit of third and fourth gears (averaged) plus three per cent, or 1,100rpm above the measured peak horsepower rpm – whichever was lower.

A complicated algorithm was applied every three rounds to determine if any increases or decreases were required, manufacturer by manufacturer, with a possible 250rpm adjustment each time.

Honda, BMW and MV Agusta were allowed one step up after round six at Donington.

Start-of-Season Rev Limits

Aprilia	14,700
BMW	14,700
Ducati	12,400
Honda	14,300
Kawasaki	14,100
MV Agusta	14,700
Suzuki	14,700
Yamaha	14,700

Concession Parts

To further balance performance of homologated motorcycles, concession points were scored for each podium place – 3-2-1 for the top three.

After the first three rounds, any manufacturer that was nine points or more behind the leading manufacturer was allowed to adopt a specific range of new 'concession parts' thereafter. These included camshafts and other valve-train elements.

After early-season success by the Panigale R, everyone except Ducati was allowed to adopt concession parts. Not all manufacturers took up the offer, for logistical, financial and time-constraint reasons.

Approved Parts

To keep costs under control and make 'factory' parts available to all at a controlled cost, the readily available cost-capped parts of recent seasons (brakes and suspension units, for example) were expanded to manufacturer-supplied items. These included swing-arms, triple clamps and other individual performance components. They were called 'approved parts'.

CHAMPION PROFILE: JONATHAN REA

THE BEST EVER

By GORDON RITCHIE

Photos: Gold & Goose

JONATHAN REA and KRT had dominated the FIM Superbike World Championship since he had joined in 2015, but in 2018, racing was made a bit more difficult for him. The goal had been a more exciting show – Rea winning everything could often be dull, for all but those directly involved.

Despite even more levelling of the tech rules, none of Rea's rivals was truly competitive over race distance in 2018, not for more than a race or two. JR and his team alone were able to adapt to the reality of a rev deficit, even after some tough early races.

Rea prefers a heavier-inertia engine; he likes a chassis set-up that rolls into and around corners; and he would always opt for a mechanical partner he can guide and glide across the dance floor, rather than break-dancing over kerbstones. He likes to fight the other riders, not the bike.

In 2018, Rea eventually had a bike and set-up that suited him just fine, even if he had lost any vestige of the straight-line advantage he might have once enjoyed. In all other aspects, the spec was peachy for his preferred way of riding.

Rea makes record breaking look easy, especially as he never appears to be going fast, such is his body language and demeanour. He is a cool customer when on track, operating at the height of his hard-won self-confidence.

He is a good qualifier, but seldom fastest. His Superpole-win tally lags massively behind his race-win tally. The 16:71 ratio is extreme, even allowing for the fact that riders only get one chance at pole for every two races.

All-time top riders, in MotoGP, Superbike or any other high-level racing discipline, are often like this. It is all very well being fast for one lap, but a rider needs to be fastest for 20-odd laps. In the wet, in the dry, at tracks they might not like, at every single opportunity, they have to find a way to make the game winnable.

Rea and Co did that at almost every race in 2018. And it was just as well that there was some disturbance to his race-winning ways at the beginning of the year, otherwise he would have taken the title even earlier than five races before the end.

His season was not flawless, just nearly so, and peerlessly record breaking. A coming together with Tom Sykes in Brno resulted in a no-score. Arguments raged for a long time about where the blame lay, but this seemed to be his only costly mistake.

A tyre issue in Australia and then chassis problems in Thailand held him back. This was mainly because his heavily rev-limited machine meant that KHI and his track crew had to push the chassis set-up to make up for a reduction in top speed and overtaking power.

Rea believed that 2018 had probably been his best season, and it is hard to imagine a better one. Refusing to let the technical hobbling of the big Ninja pre-season get to them, KHI worked to make their bike a torque monster, and Rea used its new nature to the full. It seems obvious now that the organisers' action had the opposite of the desired effect. Sykes and the rest were the ones who suffered most, not Rea.

Now with a Fogarty-equalling four world titles, Rea's golden years have arrived consecutively. All agreed that four in row made him statistically the best ever, especially given that he had taken Foggy's all-time race-winning record during the season, too.

But could Rea really be the WorldSBK absolute greatest already?

In addition to the impressive statistics, he has to be an extremely strong candidate for the biggest GOAT in the diamond-standard herd. Especially after being able to keep on keeping on at the very top for four amazing years.

Rea's opponents have to add consistency to their occasional winning race pace to break through his force-field of self-confidence and dent his unshakeable trust in his package. If not, Jonathan Andrew Rea will most probably be the subject of this page of MOTOCOURSE next season, too.

Motocard.com
Motorcycle Gear Store
elf
Kawasaki
Racing Team
MONSTER

SUPERBIKE WORLD CHAMPIONSHIP

2018 TEAMS & RIDERS

By GORDON RITCHIE

APRILIA

Milwaukee Aprilia

Eugene Laverty (32) had 13 WorldSBK race-winning trophies in his cabinet, but could not quite add another in 2018. He did score podiums, however, as he and his bike caught up significantly after all the rule changes and chassis allowances. He also had to recover from a nasty pelvic fracture suffered in Thailand.

Aprilia's homeboy, **Lorenzo Savadori** (25), played a big part in the British-run team in 2018, and was often the Aprilia rider to take the most most points in any particular race. **Davide Giugliano** (28) rode as a stand-in for Laverty at two rounds.

Dream Team Company Aprilia

Mathieu Lussiana (30) rode as a wild-card for Dream Team Company at his native Magny-Cours, but no-scored twice.

BMW

Althea Gulf Racing BMW

Loris Baz (25) returned to his paddock of global origin after his experiences in the MotoGP middle ground, and showed some flashes of his undoubted talent. Genesio Bevilacqua's small, but experienced team dealt with the chassis side, BMW with the engines and electronics, under their customer support plan.

Althea was the only team to use the S1000RR in 2018, but their lone gunman was not counted as an independent rider, although in reality he was more of a privateer than some others who were.

DUCATI

Aruba.it Racing - Ducati World Superbike Team

At one early stage for both **Chaz Davies** (31) and **Marco Melandri** (36), 2018 looked like being their year, as the off-season rev-limit changes seemed to affect them less than many of the four-cylinder riders. However, as the season moved on, under the control of former racer Serafino Foti, it became obvious that without more tech freedom, their official challenge would be for the odd win at best.

A somewhat muted last hurrah for the legendary Ducati V-twins.

Aruba.it Racing Junior Team Ducati

Racing only in the European rounds, **Michael Ruben Rinaldi** (22) was occasionally potent, more often middling. However, the 2017 STK1000 champion was still at the base of his learning curve in WorldSBK competition.

Barni Racing Ducati

An undulating season in some ways, but only a fool would consider anything other than awarding hyper-high marks to **Javier 'Xavi' Fores** (33) and his privateer Italian team. They won the independent teams' award with time to spare, on a bike that was so close to the official ones – partly through regulation and partly because Barni Racing was sometimes equal to, and sometimes better than, the official effort.

HONDA

Red Bull Honda World Superbike Team

It would have been almost impossible to repeat the horrid 2017 season experienced by the official Honda Europe effort, even with a major change of electronics early in the season and a whole new riding line-up. At times, **Leon Camier** (32) was on course for a podium, but it never quite came, and after suffering injuries, he could not ride to the peaks everyone expected.

Rookie **Jake Gagne** (25) was a compromise pick, but he applied himself well and was a popular addition to the paddock. There were too many challenges for him to overcome, however – he needed more stability to progress further.

BSB regular **Jason O'Halloran** (30) rode as a replacement for Camier at Imola, but was also injured.

New team manager Kervin Bos had his hands full all year.

Triple M Honda World Superbike Team

A truly welcome sight in 2018, an all-new and entirely rookie WorldSBK team even got to develop Honda's Magneti Marelli electronics from the very start.

Team owner Matthias Moser's squad was an official satellite team. But it was too much of an ask in year one, and **Patrick 'PJ' Jacobsen** (22) moved out with two rounds to go.

Florian Marino (25) scored points in Argentina, but suffered a broken leg in race two, and they did not compete in Qatar.

Penrite Honda

Phillip Island wild-cards, Penrite launched soon-to-be again ASBK Champion **Troy Herfoss** (31) into big Superbike school, qualifying 18th.

KAWASAKI

Kawasaki Racing Team

Jonathan Rea (31) and **Tom Sykes** (33) were the only active WorldSBK riders to have won the championship, and the official KRT/Provec Racing squad had both of them on their books again.

Rea, manufacturer and team were all conquering for the fourth year in succession. Sykes's highly individual riding style and personal domestic issues took a toll on his results, but he still won a race at Rea's favourite track, Assen.

The best overall package and set-up of all.

Kawasaki Puccetti Racing

In the second season, Manuel Puccetti's team adopted the unquestioned, but sometimes unfathomable talents of Turkish rider **Toprak Razgatlioglu**. At Donington, he took his first podium, ahead of occasional wild-card team member **Leon Haslam** (35). Toprak repeated his podium prowess in Argentina.

Team Pedercini Racing Kawasaki

Lucio Pedercini's perennial paddock ambition caused him to sign ex-MotoGP Colombian **Yonny Hernandez** (30), but it did not work out well for either party. He finished no higher than 11th in any race.

A bizarre pre-Magny-Cours split, about hotels apparently, led to **Jeremy Guarnoni** (24) being a late draftee for the French round and STK1000 rider **Gabriele Ruiu** (18) joining the class. He became the youngest points scorer ever.

BSB regular **Luke Mossey** (26) also got on board at Donington.

Team GoEleven Kawasaki

Once again, **Roman Ramos** (27) rode for Dennis Sacchetti, but the altered state for the Ninja in 2018 made it very difficult.

Orelac Racing VerdNatura Kawasaki

Leandro 'Tati' Mercado got to take Orelac into the WorldSBK league, and also got to race at home in Argentina. Although just another Kawasaki toiler at times, he was especially impressive at Assen.

SPB Racing Kawasaki

The Russian wild-cards arrived at Motorland and Assen with former triple WorldSSP podium man **Vladimir Leonov** (31) at the controls. It started well, but no points came.

Team WD40 Kawasaki

Mason Law (22) arrived for a wild-card ride at home in Donington. He left with experience, but no points.

MV AGUSTA

MV Agusta Reparto Corse

Jordi Torres (31) seemed a great choice for MV, and he gave it his all, taking a best of fifth at Imola. A chance to ride in MotoGP finally lured him away, however, and STK1000 top-runner **Maximilian Scheib** (23) took over, scoring points. In possibly their last year, MV found that elusive first podium always just too far away.

SUZUKI

Buildbase Suzuki

Wild-carding at Donington, BSB race winner **Bradley Ray** (23) scored points in each race.

OMG Racing Suzuki

Former WorldSSP podium rider **Gino Rea** (29) took his BSB bike into WorldSBK at Donington, but left with no points.

YAMAHA

Pata Yamaha Official WorldSBK Team

Alex Lowes (28) was in his third official Yamaha season, **Michael van der Mark** (26) his second. Once again, a split personality and personnel group, with Paul Denning's Crescent Racing doing the race operations from the UK, and the development and manufacturer side operated from Italy, all controlled by Andrea Dosoli.

Important breakthrough race victories came at Donington for van der Mark, and Brno for Lowes.

Niccolo Canepa (30) created a Yamaha Motor Europe sideshow to the main Pata element at Donington and Misano.

Guandalini Racing Yamaha

Very much privateers, the team had an unwanted revolving-door rider policy. Early-season regular **Ondrej Jezek** (29) left after his native Brno round, to be replaced by **Karel Hanika** (22) at Laguna only. **Alessandro Andreozzi** (27) took over the ride in Misano, and **Jakub 'Kuba' Smrz** (35) rode from then on.

Yamaha Racing Team Australia

Daniel Falzon (24) and **Wayne Maxwell** (36) joined the wild-card ranks at PI, but had little good fortune.

Attack Performance Two Wheel Legal Racing Yamaha

Josh Herrin (28) rode at home in America, just missing out on a point in race two.

onathan Rea

Chaz Davies

Michael van der Mark

om Sykes

Marco Melandri

Alex Lowes

Xavi Fores

Eugene Laverty

Toprak Razgatlioglu

Lorenzo Savadori

Loris Baz

eon Camier

Jordi Torres

Leandro Mercado

Michael Ruben Rinaldi

Roman Ramos

Jake Gagne

Yonny Hernandez

PJ Jacobsen

Leon Haslam

Maximilian Scheib

Niccolo Canepa

Florian Marino

SUPERBIKE WORLD CHAMPIONSHIP

THE SUPERBIKES OF 2018

By GORDON RITCHIE

BMW S1000RR

APRILIA RSV-4 RF

DUCATI PANIGALE R

APRILIA RSV-4 RF

UNIQUE in WorldSBK racing, Aprilia's V4 ran a 78 x 52.3mm bore and stroke in an ageing design. Its permissible revs were cut hardest of all, but eventually that left the machine with an engine that put out more usable torque than in 2017, which proved to be a benefit in many ways. The camshaft design was less radical than in the previous season, which helped.

With several adjustable chassis parameters and engine positions, the Aprilia had been locked down quite significantly in recent years. Freedom of movement came again in 2018, and thus – eventually – the team made a breakthrough mid-season that allowed Laverty to score podiums. He chose to have the engine higher in the chassis than Savadori, to aid weight transfer. Putting the correct forces into the back tyre allowed it to work properly over race distance for the first time in 18 months.

This was aided by centralising the end-of-race fuel load. In 2017, the mass had changed from being forward and high to rearward and lower. That was the key for corner entry and exit in 2018.

A new design of rear linkage and pull-rod shock also helped tyre life, with a minor redesign from Portimao onwards. Front forks were Ohlins, the longer-than-usual 770 model.

Laverty liked a more rigid chassis, Savadori more flexibility, which even extended to removing the centre engine mounting bolts. The former also opted for slightly softer damping for the rear shock.

Max revs remained unchanged at 14,700rpm throughout the year, but Aprilia did qualify for concession parts. Aprilia's in-house APX2 ECU control box and engine management system were still used.

BMW S1000RR

IN some ways still the state of the art for in-line four performance, the 80 x 49.7mm engine architecture of the BMW, and finger-style camshaft followers, kept the S1000RR spinning relatively fast. But the upper rev limit for the bike at the start of 2018 was 14,700rpm, just like most other fours.

BMW's customer support programme provided the engines and electronics again, while the Althea side of the team looked after chassis parts.

Front and rear suspension came from Ohlins, with 42mm-diameter RVP25 front forks and a custom-made RSP rear shock. As with all the Ohlins units in WorldSBK, compression damping was done in one leg, rebound in the other.

Brakes were Brembo, with 336 x 6.5mm front rotors. All Brembo brakes feature T-type connection between the rotors and hubs. Aluminium wheels were from OZ, and a Termignoni exhaust, with a very short and squat silencer section, was the final part of the combustion process.

The team claimed more than 230CV at 13,500rpm (less than maximum rev potential). BMW was allowed an extra potential 250rpm after mid-season balancing calculations. All up, it was claimed to be a kilo over the mandatory 168kg lower limit.

DUCATI PANIGALE R

THE last big twin to run in a category once dominated by them, the Panigale series carried Ducati's world championship hopes perhaps for one year too many.

The monocoque chassis section under the tank, both airbox and steering-head, is distinctive enough. The most obvious visual clue that this bike is not like the others is a triangular external rising-rate link on the left side, which pushes on an almost horizontal rear shock absorber from Ohlins.

Other than the headstock/airbox section, the rest of the chassis was vestigial, holding the subframe, engine and suspension mounts in place, with the engine the main element. Ducati spent the winter trying to maximise chassis performance after the rev drop, and they introduced different braking and power exit strategies to help. They worked with Brembo to maximise airflow to the calipers to keep them cool under extreme use.

A new swing-arm increased grip at maximum lean, and both riders employed the same version. They also used all the new tolerances on bodywork to make their bike more aerodynamic. Melandri's infamous wobble, caused by rider ergonomics and how they worked with the aerodynamic package for a short rider, was cured at a Brno test, but only after a lot of simulation and experimentation.

At the start of the season, Ducati's maximum revs were 12,400rpm, causing the loss of perhaps close to 10bhp compared to 2017. It was also a little more difficult for the V-twin to cut its power cleanly as the limit approached.

Engineers tried to find more torque, but that was tough work with their massively oversquare 112 x 60.8mm bore and stroke. Inside the engine, they worked on reducing friction, and used different cams and less radical cam profiles.

The 2018 exhaust had a different layout, and each could be open or closed independently of the other. But they were either fully open or closed; there was no gradual transition.

Again, the exit bores of the tiny Akrapovic exhausts were of different diameters, to balance exhaust waves against each other, as the exhausts were of differing lengths. Alternate intake trumpets, varying in length and shape, were tried until an optimum set was finally adopted. Overall development stopped mid-season as Ducati started to concentrate on the all-new V4. They had concession parts and a new engine spec ready to go, but were the only ones who could not use them by regulation.

HONDA CBR1000RR SP2

THE always-evolutionary Honda Fireblade development continued in 2018, with a major change occurring when the Red Bull Honda official team adopted the Magneti Marelli ECU system a few rounds in. A completely redesigned wiring harness was introduced, as was a new suite of sensors. The

HONDA CBR1000RR SP2

MV AGUSTA F4 RR

KAWASAKI NINJA ZX-10RR

YAMAHA YZF-R1

Photos: courtesy WorldSBK/Gold & Goose

team took the opportunity to include two junction boxes to allow quicker changes of bodywork and crash damage repair, plus the replacement of any faulty sensors without the need to dismantle too much of the bike. Effectively, that broke the electrics down into front, middle and rear sections.

The Akrapovic exhaust went through continuous development, with a third spec arriving at Portimao.

Brake temperatures became even more critical in 2018, partly because of the greater demands on the chassis, and partly because of the greater levels of grip from the latest generation of Pirelli tyres. The Nissin calipers, with Yutaka discs, were the same as tried at the end of 2017. Ten Kate used Marchesini wheels with a new internal coating to prevent tyre creep.

With a wide spread of top power, Honda did not lose as much at the start of the season, with their revs pegged at a lower-than-most 14,300rpm (of the fours, only Kawasaki started with fewer), but the engine lost its over-rev facility. Ten Kate got this back to an extent after they were allowed an extra 250rpm, by regulation, mid-season.

The biggest change in the engine occurred after qualification for concession parts, ready in time for the final two rounds.

The team claimed that the biggest improvement was in the 'rideability' of the ECU software, and they had a stand-alone private test in which to prove it before final race use. Their software co-operation with Cosworth survived the change to Magneti Marelli's ECU.

Ten Kate employed carbon F1-style chassis bracing technology, with carbon sheets melted on to the alloy chassis in key areas to provide bracing around the swing-arm and still allow flex in other planes. There were three different overall chassis stiffness types. Carbon stiffening cuts thermal distortion and the sheer size of panels when compared with welded plates and internal bracing.

The swing-arm was the same as in 2017, and 2018 was the first year that Honda hit the 168kg weight limit exactly, thanks to a complete re-evaluation of every nut, bolt and bracket.

KAWASAKI NINJA ZX-10RR

ANOTHER new homologation, to help with internal friction, the 2018 Kawasaki played its part in Rea's record, but other riders could not take as much advantage.

The 'new' bike had to take on the sudden loss of 1,100rpm from the top, as the Kawasaki's engine rev limit at the start of the season was the lowest of the four-cylinders at 14,100rpm. This would remain all year. Kawasaki lost possibly 7bhp compared to 2017.

Bizarrely, Kawasaki was one of the manufacturers allowed to use concession parts after the first balancing calculation was made.

The main problem Kawasaki had to overcome emerged in Thailand: a drop-off in the reliability of some highly stressed braking and chassis components. They introduced some brake ducts (built into the mudguard) and switched to some other readily available Brembo parts compared to their planned set-up. Sykes opted for thicker discs than most others, as he was always the last of the late brakers.

Kawasaki used Magneti Marelli electronics and handed out ECU boxes with engine maps already loaded to their many customer teams, as well as KRT.

There were some evolutions to the Showa suspension, which again were available to all by regulation.

MV AGUSTA F4 RR

THE now-venerable 79 x 50.9mm MV engine, with its radial-valve head, produced even more power in 2018, thanks to hard work from the team. The rev ceiling of 14,700rpm, by regulation at the start of the year, was allowed to rise to nearly 15,000rpm in mid-season.

The performance was well up, with the MV regularly inside the top five or six through the speed trap, not the last five or six as in 2017.

The gas flow change in the intake side was one factor in their improvement. Reducing valve spring forces and other power-sapping friction allowed the team to achieve nearly double the 300–400rpm expected winter gain.

Due to budget constraints, and with each rider allowed only seven engines per season, the team could not use all of those top-spec engines.

The small electronics team was reorganised, which led to improvements in mapping and throttle control.

The chassis was also changed, with a 'family' of swing-arms and links that gave the team more options. There had been one set of rear links in 2017, but there were three in 2018. The way the rear swing-arm, link and suspension unit worked was rationalised, with revised stiffness, and two options available. The fuel tank was also a more rational design.

MV ran older-style Ohlins TTX25 forks and TTX36 shock, presumably for budget reasons.

Yamaha YZF-R1

WITH its 79 x 50.9mm bore and stroke, and a crossplane crankshaft design, the R1 was almost like a demented V-twin. It featured many detail changes and was the second or perhaps third most desirable bike.

One obvious change was to van der Mark's 'puller' handlebar-mounted rear brake, which gave him greater control than the 'pusher' design used by most others.

The team fitted 328mm Brembo rotors and the same spec of brakes as in 2017. Yamaha also employed the longer 770 Ohlins forks, with revised internal set-up, the same as for the final few races in 2017.

The focus of chassis development was to increase stability and grip in slow-speed corners, with a development in both swing-arm design and stiffness ratios, plus rear linkage upgrades that were homologated.

The engine itself had more everywhere than the 2017 bike, so rider complaints of being outgunned were much reduced. A new Akrapovic exhaust, with a much bigger link pipe and layout below the bodywork, was a big help for the overall power range. No new concession parts were used, as they were not considered a requirement mid-season.

The biggest operational change involved increased direct support from Yamaha Japan at the track, which went beyond only the updated Magneti Marelli software package.

SUPERBIKE WORLD CHAMPIONSHIP

PHILLIP ISLAND

ROUND 1 · AUSTRALIA

Above: Melandri just pips Rea in race two, despite suffering dramatic wobbles at high speed.

Right: Pirelli's Giorgio Barbier oversaw a mandatory tyre change for race two.

Centre right: Kawasaki's Ichiro Yoda and Pere Riba in deep discussion after a tough opener.
Photos: Gold & Goose

Below right: Chaz Davies practises the race-two tyre-change drill.
Photo: John Morris/MPix

Facing page, from top:
Melandri heads Rea in race one, around one of the circuit's many left-handers; Laverty crashed in race two, remounted for 15th; tyre picture (*left*) tells a thousand words; wild-card rider Falzon (*right*) was disqualified from race two for missing the pit-lane entry window.
Photos: Gold & Goose

Centre right: Classic Phillip Island backdrop as top independent rider Fores briefly leads Sykes and Rea.

Far right: Melandri scored a sensational opening double for Ducati.
Photos: Gold & Goose

THE curtain raiser to the 2018 MOTUL FIM Superbike World Championship was played out on an old stage at Phillip Island, with a largely similar cast of seasoned performers as the previous year.

Of all the top teams, the greatest pre-season intrigue surrounded Red Bull Honda, still using their Cosworth electronics after a temporary dispensation, with a new rider pairing of Leon Camier and Jake Gagne.

At the official pre-season tests at Phillip Island, in February, Marco Melandri had placed above Tom Sykes, Jonathan Rea – and then Camier. The top seven in testing included machines from five different manufacturers – so no Rea dominance on the race weekend then? No, really not, as the more stringent rev limits applied to him and all the other Kawasaki riders made a difference, especially on the long main straight.

Sykes won his 43rd career Superpole in windy conditions that caused many riders to run off track at a key time. His new total equalled that of previous Superpole win record holder Troy Corser.

Lorenzo Savadori was a Superpole casualty early on, suffering a broken collarbone that ruled him out. Camier and Jordi Torres also fell in Superpole 2.

On this evidence, it had become a weird weekend even by Saturday lunchtime, and it became positively dystopian for some of the big names on Saturday afternoon.

Tyres were the undoing of some top riders in race one, as the old Phillip Island problem of long left-handers wrought havoc among some of WorldSBK's best talents.

The design philosophy inherent in the Pirelli control tyres deliberately avoided exotic materials, so everyone from track-day amateurs to world champions were offered the same standard choices. This became mission-critical in Australia, even for development versions. New rules would soon come into force to ensure that teams ran the recommended minimum pressures in 2018, too.

Rea lost all chance of recovering from sixth in Superpole when his tyre overheated, and he lost drive and confidence. Others had similar issues. Sunday's race even had the unwanted novelty of a mandatory tyre change mid-race.

Sykes led the first race for the most part, while Rea and Melandri were in the podium places for most of it. But as Melandri moved forward to catch a fading Sykes (despite an alarming and incurable top-speed wobble), Rea's race was falling apart along with his rear rubber. He dropped to fifth, four seconds behind Xavi Fores.

The podium places were taken by Melandri – his first WorldSBK race win at Phillip Island – then Sykes and Chaz Davies.

The pace had been all out from lap one, unusual for PI, and that may have been why race two was so different. Sunday's mandatory pit stop was enthralling and also contributed to a photo finish at the end of the 22 laps.

Melandri's double came only after early leader Eugene Laverty had crashed out, and Camier had also shown early pace. The Italian had to recover from the middle of the pack for a last-lap scrap with Rea, after everyone had taken new tyres. Melandri prevailed by just 0.025 of a second; right behind the pair, top independent rider Fores added third to his race-one fourth, having led for two laps as he and his team grew in stature again. Sykes was fourth this time. The podium trio were covered by just 0.304 of a second, the top seven by just over three.

Davies, third in race one, crashed out of the lead in the second 'half' of race two.

Another cast-iron PI classic season-opener, if a highly unusual one.

SUPERBIKE WORLD CHAMPIONSHIP

BURIRAM

ROUND 2 · THAILAND

Above: Back in the victory business. Rea takes the honours by 1.550 seconds in race one.

Right: Fores was a happy second in race one.

Top right: The Pata Yamaha pairing of Lowes and van der Mark celebrate their noteworthy race-two podiums.

Above right: Prodigal son Baz (76), new boy Gagne (45) and perennial privateer Ramos (40) engage in a race-two battle.

Below right: The heat is on for Savadori on the steamy grid.

Centre right: Camier leads Fores in race one, his Honda showing more than mere potential.

Far right: One-time Chang struggler Davies took the win ahead of van der Mark in race two.

Photos: Gold & Goose

THE heat and humidity that shrouded all 4.554km of the Chang International Circuit in Thailand were omnipresent discomforts for the WorldSBK riders and teams. Mandatory engine rev limits in 2018 were a new curve ball for Kawasaki in particular to overcome.

In Thailand, KRT's difficult start to the season ended, and then immediately returned, mainly because the riders were having to ask a lot more of their chassis settings and vital components than in previous years. None of those things prevented Jonathan Rea from taking his first victory in race one on Saturday. Earlier, he had taken pole position from his team-mate.

Tom Sykes had passed Rea twice early on and made a race of it for a while, with the entire top flight comprising a super-steamy freight train behind.

As Rea reasserted himself, Leon Camier and his rejuvenated Honda (albeit at this point with 2017 Cosworth electronics) came howling through a gap left by the two battling Kawasakis. Then, as Rea escaped, the early-season privateer whirlwind of Xavi Fores moved up to second, a position he would keep until the end. Another strong demonstration of a positive new privateer era.

Rea won the opening race, but Chang was no longer the Kawasaki benefit gig it had been. Ducati, thanks to the rule changes and two riders on basically the same factory bikes, showed that this peak was climbable, with Fores second and Chaz Davies 2.118 seconds back. The latter, often a struggler in the Thai heat, pushed through to third from a lowly ninth on the grid.

In the birthplace of Red Bull, Honda's Camier showed he still had all the speed required, as the top four finished within three seconds. He had qualified third in Superpole.

Alex Lowes, a past podium finisher at this circuit, placed fifth, just ahead of a slowing Sykes, who was facing issues at a circuit with lots of hard braking. The British duo were over seven seconds down on the lead, while Michael van der Mark was a second behind them, and PI double winner Melandri eighth, again on an unstable bike set-up.

Opinions about the reverse grid, where the top three from race one become the third row for race two, vary wildly, but at this round, it appeared to play a part in ensuring that Rea would not double up. That and his bike's sporadic technical glitches, which resulted in him being only fourth at the flag, while other top riders benefited.

Davies was excellent value for his eventual win, and he became the third different victor in four races after he passed early pace-setters van der Mark and Alex Lowes. The Yamaha duo took their first podiums of the season well clear of the chasing Rea and Fores.

Two seconds back on the privateer Ducati, Camier was sixth. Melandri, so brilliant in Australia, was 17 seconds behind the winner this time around, and mystified as to why his Ducati had behaved so oddly at full speed.

Sykes dropped off the pace early on and finished as a retiree. Again, he endured brake issues, at a very hot circuit where riders spend 26 seconds out of 94 braking hard. Along with chassis settings that were pushed closer to the edge than ever, problems were emerging.

New championship leader Rea, despite his own tech problems, was happy that the rules apparently were compressing the capabilities of the top machines. He understood that close racing makes for a more compelling spectacle, and more personal satisfaction for the winner.

Eugene Laverty suffered a pelvic fracture after a crash and then scary collision with the MV of Jordi Torres, who was too close to avoid the fallen Aprilia runner. Fortunately, Laverty would make a strong recovery.

SUPERBIKE WORLD CHAMPIONSHIP

ARAGON

ROUND 3 · SPAIN

Above: Racing in word and deed at Motorland. Van der Mark leads Melandri, Fores, Lowes and Rea.

Left: Roman Ramos scored good home-town points in both races.

Right: Lowes just missed out on another podium for Yamaha.

Below: Heads you win. Melandri and mechanic greet the Italian's rare Superpole success.

Photos: Gold & Goose

Above left and above: Leon Camier crashed in race one, Torres hit him and Savadori also fell, bringing out the red flag.

Above centre: Sunday's win was satisfying for Davies, but would be his last of the season.

Top: After his collision and dnf in race one, Torres was eighth in race two.

Right: Davies leads Rea, both showing how much more was being asked of the brakes in 2018.

Left: After his ride through the mid-field, Davies finally saw off Fores for second in race one.

Photos: Gold & Goose

MOTORLAND offered a complete contrast to the previous Thai venue: less asphalted football stadium, more tarmac safari park. Saturday's race was preceded by Superpole One and Two, and pole position was a rare success for Marco Melandri. It was only the third pre-race 'win' of his WorldSBK career.

Jonathan Rea was victorious in race one, but it was no dominant lap count-down like some of his other wins. It was tense and tricky.

The first race was red-flagged early on, after Leon Camier, Jordi Torres and Lorenzo Savadori crashed together. Camier would miss several rounds through injury as a consequence. You felt for him – and for Torres, once again blamelessly involved in a collision with another prostrate rider.

At the restart, over 17 laps in cool conditions, Rea had to work hard to keep Alex Lowes behind him, giving best to the Yamaha rider for a time on lap three.

Xavi Fores took the opportunity to lead from laps nine to 11, until Rea went back to the prow. He stretched out an eventual advantage of 1.450 seconds at the flag, but the gap could have been closer had three Ducati riders – Chaz Davies, Fores and Melandri – not been held back by their individual sort-outs.

Welshman Davies had come through from an 11th-place start, but on the wrong option rear tyre for the conditions, while Melandri had endured back brake issues. Davies got his factory Ducati up to Fores's privateer bike and had a great last-lap desmo dogfight with the Spanish rider, bringing the locals to their feet. The works rider got the best of it for second, but Motorland made it three podiums in five races for top Independent rider Fores.

Race two would be much less happy, however, as he fell while leading on lap eight.

In the second Spanish thriller, over 18 laps, race-one fifth-place rider Michael van der Mark led for a lap, until Melandri and Fores passed him almost as one, and then Rea a little later.

Seventh on lap one, Davies was up to third on lap nine, after Fores had grabbed too much front brake going into the fast left-hand corner at the end of the straight.

Taking the lead at that point, Rea did not get away from the battling Ducatis this time, the leading bunch keeping close company. Rea was out front until Davies made a move with five laps to go, slipping inside at Turn One and powering on to take an eventual advantage of 1.184 seconds over Rea.

Melandri, wildly wobbling and weaving down the straights, was unable to keep pace as the laps counted down. Davies took over second place in the title fight, which perhaps was going to swing towards Kawasaki. And everyone else, as it happened, as the much vaunted concession parts rules were triggered to allow everyone in the championship – except Ducati – to introduce concession parts to improve their engine performance.

If, as some said, the concession parts initiative had been conceived to allow other manufacturers to close the gap that Kawasaki would normally have opened up at this early stage, then the plan had clearly backfired. Ducati, in fact, dominated the early-season podiums, and they were not allowed to use any concession parts as a result.

But by that early stage, with Rea starting to win despite the rev limit drop, maybe it was Ducati who needed more regulatory assistance.

Behind the Motorland race-two podium trio, Lowes got the better of a last-lap fight with team-mate van der Mark; with Tom Sykes as unhappy in sixth in the second race as he had been in the first.

SUPERBIKE WORLD CHAMPIONSHIP

ASSEN

ROUND 4 · NETHERLANDS

Top: Racing connoisseurs. Dutch fans enjoy the majesty of Assen as Rea leads at his favourite circuit.

Right: Sykes became the season's fourth race winner in race two.

Facing page, from top: Mercado (36) leads Baz (76) and Razgatlioglu (54); Rea stands tall from the saddle after winning Saturday's race from local favourite van der Mark; Lowes (*left*) took his first Superpole, while Fores (*right*) was top privateer again in both races.

Centre right: Davies scored a podium, but never seriously challenged.

Far right: Dutchman van der Mark teased and pleased his local fans with a pair of podiums.

Photos: Gold & Goose

A FIRST double race win of the season for Jonathan Rea was on the cards long before the transporters and trailers made the quick-turnaround trip from northern Spain to the very north of the Netherlands. The triple champion's Assen record was immense: he had won 11 races there in all, the last seven in succession, including the six since he had joined Kawasaki.

What the local crowd really wanted to see, however, were two wins for local hero Michael van der Mark. After FP3, they got his name at the top of the Friday times. What they got after Superpole was the other Pata Yamaha rider, Alex Lowes, on pole – a first and career milestone for the British rider.

Sunny conditions were welcomed by a healthy crowd on Saturday afternoon, and it would be even warmer on Sunday.

Off the line in race one, Xavi Fores and Rea led the charge into the first corner, with the latter out front soon after.

On the seventh lap, the gradually advancing van der Mark took his opportunity to pass Rea as seven riders formed a breakaway slipstreaming group. Two laps later, Rea took back the place at the final chicane.

With van der Mark tailing Rea, the rapidly advancing Chaz Davies put in a pass to take second. While the two riders fought for the position, Rea was able to make sure of the win, his eighth in succession at the venerable Dutch racetrack.

Just behind, van der Mark took a popular second, with Davies third and Tom Sykes in the podium riders' wake. Rea was 0.981 of a second ahead at the flag, the next three within less than half a second of each other.

Fores placed fifth after his early showing in the lead, but Marco Melandri was 14 seconds down, in sixth. A strong ride by Loris Baz on the Gulf Althea BMW resulted in seventh.

Fourth made Sykes the new pole-man for race two under WorldSBK's reverse-grid rule. He made use of it to lead into the first corner, but had to make a confident outbraking move to repass Fores, who had outdragged him to a stronger inside line. Davies had been run out wide at Turn One and had a lot of work to do from then on.

Sykes, no fan of the latest tech restrictions and heavy engine inertia, wound back the clock as he drove his front and rear tyres deep into the cambered and non-cambered asphalt of the modern Assen. It was like the glory days of 2013, building his advantage out front and easily taking the biggest winning margin of the season to that point.

After 21 laps, he was 5.445 seconds ahead of team-mate Rea, who had had to fight for too long with other riders. A Sykes win was a stunning result, given Rea's recent Assen imperium.

Rea's rhythm had been disrupted when he offered a gap to home-town charger van der Mark, and any last hope he had of running down Sykes took a terminal knock. But he was safely clear of van der Mark at the end, with Fores top independent again in fourth place, and Davies recovering for fifth.

Melandri's form continued its lull, and he came home seventh, over a second a lap slower than the winner.

Sykes became the fourth different race winner in 2018, and although Rea's 30-point championship lead was sure to grow again, it proved that those behind him could still wrestle at least some races from him.

With Leon Camier out, the Netherlands-based Red Bull Honda team only had rookie US rider Jake Gagne available, but after a fast practice high-side, he too was unable to race.

SUPERBIKE WORLD CHAMPIONSHIP

IMOLA

ROUND 5 · ITALY

Above: Rea and Sykes lead all three Ducatis and the field at the start of race one.

Right: Leon Haslam put in an appearance on the Elf-liveried Puccetti Racing Team Kawasaki.

Centre right: Jason O'Halloran subbed for Camier on the Red Bull Honda, but suffered an injury in race one.

Below right: Fores, sporting a one-off Italian helmet design at his team's home round, rides ahead of Sykes – for a time at least.

Facing page, from top: MV's loner Torres leads Lowes, Rinaldi and Razgatlioglu through the tight final chicane; Rea celebrates his first double of the year in enthusiastic fashion; Rea leads Davies through one of Imola's many chicanes.

Centre right: Razgatlioglu on the grid with his compatriot and mentor, Kenan Sofuoglu.

Far right: Savadori leads Haslam, Lowes and Razgatlioglu in race one.

Photos: Gold & Goose

NOTHING beats Imola in the sunshine, even though its 1970s design and city-centre location have obvious drawbacks in terms of primary safety in some areas. As a rider challenge, the parkland circuit has few equals, but in 2018 one rider had the place to himself, more or less.

Jonathan Rea's Imola rampage began with him taking pole, then going on to run clear of all his rivals at the end of 19 laps on Saturday, conquering the peak of the Variante Alto and the trough of the Rivazza double rights; indeed all points along the 4.936km ribbon of risk and reward.

Both KRT riders got away cleanly from their 1-2 grid places on Saturday, with Marco Melandri and Xavi Fores staying closest to them at the beginning. Chaz Davies, former conqueror at Imola, with double wins in 2016 and 2017, was down the order, despite his front-row start. Fifth, then fourth, then making a mistake into the start-line Variante Basso and having to take to the escape road to eighth on lap three.

After a determined slog back to the top four, he finished over eight seconds down on Rea. A great ride, in its own way, but more valuable points needlessly lost.

Tom Sykes, behind Rea by 3.755 seconds at the flag, was similarly clear of Melandri. Fores slotted into fifth, with Michael van der Mark chipping in with a sixth, still nearly 20 seconds adrift of Rea. Maddening inconsistency inside the Yamaha camp.

Rookie Michael Ruben Rinaldi was riding at home and had been fourth early on, but finished seventh. Another local man, Lorenzo Savadori, was eighth.

Ninth, in his first ride of the year for the Kawasaki Puccetti Racing squad (in his father Ron's old ELF GP colours) was regular BSB rider Leon Haslam.

Up to this point in the season, Rea had enjoyed greater success in the Saturday races, but his first double win of the year took him into rarefied company. It was his 59th, equalling Carl Fogarty's previous record. History made, and at a suitably classic Italian circuit.

His winning advantage of over four seconds on Sunday did not tell the whole story, however, as he had had to start from ninth – again under the reverse-grid rules – and fight. Being the fastest man yet again, he sliced past top-class riders one by one, and on lap four got behind second-race pole-man, and early contender for the lead, Davies.

Some great overtaking action between the two top riders in WorldSBK was the precursor to Rea's final attack, with seven laps left.

Davies did not go quietly, but by the finish ran out second, nearly five seconds back. Sykes placed third and was almost ten big clicks of the second hand behind Rea, the man set to become the most successful Superbike racer of all time.

Fores took fourth; Jordi Torres and the local MV Agusta contrived a fifth, a good performance to get and stay ahead of Alex Lowes in sixth. Rinaldi, so potent early on that he had led the first two laps, was seventh.

An ambitious overtake by van der Mark on Melandri on lap nine resulted in them both going down at the Rivazzas.

A potential top-ten again for Haslam was wiped out when he ran on to the gravel and then restarted to finish 16th.

Out front, the celebrations for matching Fogarty's win total were heartfelt, with Rea riding into the novel *parc fermé* podium display with his electronics engineer, Davide Gentile, on the pillion, just before the Prosecco spray became airborne.

Rea's first double of the year clearly proved that he could overcome the disadvantage of the reverse-grid rules. Maximum Imola points meant that he would take a whopping lead of 47 into his home round.

SUPERBIKE WORLD CHAMPIONSHIP

DONINGTON PARK

ROUND 6 · GREAT BRITAIN

AFTER many seasons of KRT rider Tom Sykes taking double wins at Donington, he and Jonathan Rea had shared a victory apiece in 2017. In 2018, WorldSBK returned to the British track where the whole venture had begun in 1988, but this time there was no British race winner.

Michael van der Mark scored not only his first WorldSBK race win, but also his second at the old parkland circuit. Moreover, his victories were the first for any Dutch rider in the series.

The result for the green guard was that the celebrations for Rea securing an all-time record 60th race win had to be put on ice – for now. But there was another record for Kawasaki to celebrate. In costume, no less.

Having equalled Troy Corser's previous all-time best of 43 Superpoles at Phillip Island, Sykes went ahead by one at Donington. He duly appeared as his new alter ego, 'Superpoleman', in cape and spandex, at the Superpole celebration stage.

Then he faced a tough race one a short time later.

It was a great opener, on a weekend when any British fan should have been happy to come along. Although not that many did, again.

BMW rider Loris Baz was one of the front-row trio in race one. In the race, however, it was Rea, Sykes and van der Mark, inseparable for most of the 23 circuits of the 4.023km track.

Uncharacteristic problems in downshifting experienced by Rea let first Sykes and then van der Mark into the lead. Rea repassed Sykes, but was a little behind van der Mark by that time and could not get back ahead. After a few nervous final laps and one or two tiny errors that gave his pursuers hope for a while, van der Mark signed his name in the winners' register for the first time.

Rea was second, Sykes third, only 2.193 seconds from the win.

At home, Alex Lowes found some pace and pushed up to fourth, ahead of Aprilia riders Lorenzo Savadori and Eugene Laverty. Leon Haslam was back, in ninth, behind Loris Baz and an out-of-sorts Chaz Davies.

Race two, with van der Mark ninth off the grid, was simply mind-blowing. Early leader Savadori was caught and passed by Lowes, and then van der Mark in relatively quick succession. Desperate for his own first WorldSBK win, especially at home, Lowes drove the pace until lap 17, when Rea went inside to lead. A record 60th win, surely?

But it was van der Mark who asserted his authority for a second time, going ahead on lap 18 and squeezing every granule of concentration to keep Rea behind him. A damp start to the weekend might have helped the Dutchman and Yamaha, as Kawasaki simply did not get enough track time to do their usual peerless job of making a 'full-race-distance' bike for Rea.

The surprises kept coming, as an inspired Kawasaki Puccetti Racing rider Toprak Razgatlioglu attacked right at the end, and to great effect. He had been tenth on lap one, but was up to fourth on lap 16 of 23.

First, the flying young Turk passed Lowes, then dispatched Rea on the final lap with a pass up the inside at Schwantz corner. Van der Mark was too far away to catch, however, and the Dutchman won by a clear 2.328 seconds. Razgatlioglu was only just ahead of the astounded Rea.

On form again, Lowes was a shadow behind the points leader in what had become an exciting and truly unpredictable fight for the podium.

Davies was fifth on this occasion, Sykes sixth. So in the championship, Rea was still pulling away like a bullet train, despite his disappointment at not breaking the win record at home.

Above: A record-breaking 44th career pole position for Tom 'Superpoleman' Sykes.

Top: A sensational ride by Razgatlioglu delivered second in race two.

Above left: Michael van der Mark leads Rea and Razgatlioglu during a race meeting when he came of age.
Photos: Gold & Goose

Left: British wild-cards in full dress rehearsal. Leon Haslam, Gino Rea (no relation), Luke Mossey and Bradley Ray.

Above right: Arms aloft, van der Mark takes his second win of the weekend.
Photos: Clive Challinor Motorsport Photography

Above far left: Leon Camier (2) was back in action and back in the points after his Motorland injury.

Far left: Razgatlioglu is congratulated by van der Mark after both reached new career highs.

Left: Lowes leads Rea in their battle for the final podium place in race two. Rea would take it.

Right: Double top. Celebration time for the official Pata Yamaha team after taking both race wins.
Photos: Gold & Goose

SUPERBIKE WORLD CHAMPIONSHIP

BRNO

ROUND 7 · CZECH REPUBLIC

Above: Alex Lowes leads van der Mark to a memorable Yamaha 1-2 in race two.

Top right: Brno old-stager Melandri was back on the podium pace in race one, taking second place behind a simply faster Rea.

Above right: Camier tails Fores during a bizarre race two.

Right: Sykes heads up Lowes, van der Mark, Davies and Laverty in race one.

Far right: Rea and the KRT crew celebrate his record-breaking 60th WorldSBK win.

Below right: A pensive record-breaker-in-waiting before the start of race one.

Centre right: Laverty leads team-mate Savadori in race two.

Far right: No number-one plate in sight as van der Mark, winner Lowes and Davies fill the race-two podium.

Photos: Gold & Goose

IT had been six long years since WorldSBK had last raced among the forests of Brno. Every gap in the wooded hills that embrace the fabulous 5.403km circuit is crammed with racing history, ancient and modern, so returning to the long chicanes and challenging undulations for the first time since 2012 was a treat for veteran and rookie riders alike.

After another check of the 2018 balancing-rule criteria by the powers that be, BMW, Honda and MV Agusta were given another potential 250rpm to play with from this race onwards.

Tom Sykes kicked off the combat on Saturday with another Superpole win, and a new Superbike circuit record of 1 minute 57.687 seconds. The real racing was delayed well beyond the original 13:00 starting time, however, after accidents suffered by Michael Ruben Rinaldi and Jordi Torres brought out the red flag. Then the attempted restart was delayed yet again, making for a final 16-lap race, not 18.

Jonathan Rea quickly passed Sykes to score a legendary 60th win – one more than even Carl Fogarty could manage. In doing so, Rea moved another step closer to becoming the undisputed World Superbike GOAT.

His win had seemed inevitable once the Kawasaki had hit the front, his pace being reliably better than anybody else's. He was, as he said, able to ride to his pit board and ease his way into the history books.

Behind for second were Marco Melandri and Ducati. He was still a full 5.3 seconds from Rea in race one, but on a more stable bike after some testing.

Sykes was third in the first race, before a long run of zero top-three finishes in succession. Michael van der Mark and Alex Lowes closed out the top five, with Eugene Laverty and Lorenzo Savadori both ahead of Chaz Davies, who complained about a lack of edge grip. Eighth was not the way to take the championship fight to Rea.

Fight was the operative word in race two on Sunday. For once, Rea did not make every effort to pass every rider as soon as humanly possible, from his usual third-row grid slot. He knew he would have enough pace to get to the front. Add in the fact that Brno's long chicanes allow repassing of almost every potential overtake, and Rea's moderate early tactic seemed sound.

Later, he would rue that decision, as he became involved in some mid-pack action and finally a collision with team-mate Sykes. Each rider blamed the other, but their corner-exit contact had sent Rea off and out of the race for the first time in 2018. The personal acrimony was long lasting, and made all the more bitter when later Sykes also fell, in a strange low-sider crash.

Oblivious to the internecine Kawasaki interactions behind, van der Mark had the early lead, which was soon taken by Lowes.

Then Melandri, back to his best, was up front, before a broken brake lever caused him to run wide and eventually lose enough ground to finish 15th.

Lowes had the concentration and set-up to continue his sudden advantage all the way to lap 18, cleaving out his own important bit of history with his first win. Van der Mark placed second, by just over two seconds for a Yamaha 1-2, with third place for Davies a real result after Rea had no-scored.

Laverty gave a glimpse of things to come with fourth place for Aprilia, while team-mate Savadori was fifth and rookie Rinaldi sixth. Leon Camier, who had returned to action at Donington, scored in each Brno race as well, while early-season potential winner Xavi Fores continued to struggle compared to his usual high standards.

Brno had promised a lot, and despite weather-inspired confusion on Friday, it delivered a lot as well: Rea's historic win, Lowes's very first, and a serious internal fall-out at KRT.

SUPERBIKE WORLD CHAMPIONSHIP

LAGUNA SECA

ROUND 8 · UNITED STATES

Left: Eugene Laverty leads Melandri, Fores, van der Mark and the rest at the start of race two. Note Rea (1) looking for an inside-line advantage already

Below far left: Laverty and his crew celebrate their Sunday podium, a first for SMR in WorldSBK.

Below left. Rea leads Davies on the drop down the famous Corkscrew.

Below: Fores heads Torres in their race-two scrap over sixth place.

Bottom far left: Davies makes a successful and very definite pass on Laverty.

Bottom: Very welcome Yamaha wild-card Josh Herrin leads Gagne and Baz.

Below right: American WorldSBK rookie Jacobsen leading Mercado, one-off Guandalini rider Karel Hanika and Baz.

Photos: Gold & Goose

FOR the 16th time, Laguna Seca hosted a WorldSBK round, and for the 16th time, it blew everybody's mind on lap one of practice to suddenly flick it left and then right, hurtling down the infamous Corkscrew section like a mini-skydiving course. Be it a corner, a chicane or an asphalt sculpture, it is unique, but only one of California's many attractions for race fans.

In 2018, America would be the place where Jonathan Rea and one half of the KRT garage really started motoring to satisfy their greed for race wins, and nothing less. Maybe it was because of all the new rules that they thought punished them for delivering consistent success, but Rea set about the US races with a vigour that netted him maximum points.

He was challenged, of course, but only for fleeting moments, even by Chaz Davies, who was the best of his rivals. Pole position even went to the Welshman, and a new lap record, on lap two of race one. But there was nothing to be done about Rea on race-days one and two. Davies would take two second places, but still Rea stretched his lead.

Davies had sparred with Rea in the early laps, while Tom Sykes had run third. Then a minor glitch under braking forced Davies to run wide entering the Corkscrew on lap seven. He went over the apex rumble strips, and Rea was through.

The fight behind Rea in race one never developed. Davies finished three seconds down; Alex Lowes well adrift, but still a podium participant, 12 seconds from Rea.

Eugene Laverty was potent again after his long recovery from the pelvic injury sustained in Thailand, taking fourth place for the second race in succession. Marco Melandri scored fifth, 16 seconds from Rea; Xavi Fores was sixth and top independent rider, ahead of Sykes, whose early podium challenge was first negated by Lowes, then Laverty, Melandri and finally Fores. Seventh was not in the 2013 champion's plan, but it would be even worse in race two. Struggling in the heat with his tyres, like Michael van der Mark, in the opener Sykes rode as hard as he could, but finished 25 gaping seconds from his team-mate.

Toprak Razgatlioglu was a first-time rider at Laguna and suffered a gigantic crash out of tenth down the Corkscrew after his back tyre unloaded. He would miss Sunday's race with an injured foot.

Five of the riders never made it to the finish of race one, on asphalt that reached 50°C.

Race two was a demonstration of confidence in both set-up and overtaking by Rea, which occasionally makes him unplayable by the other riders. He made up eight places to the lead after eight laps, taking all his chances as soon as they presented themselves and running away cleanly for his eighth win of the year.

Just over five seconds behind, Davies limited the damage by taking second place, again.

American rider and 2018 championship rookie Jake Gagne put this Red Bull Honda ninth, his best finish.

Soaking up the pressure to get back on the podium, Laverty was a clear third, aided by the warring Pata Yamaha factions of Lowes and van der Mark, jousting just behind him at the flag.

Fores was sixth, Jodi Torres seventh and Sykes eighth.

It was a tough Sunday for Melandri. After running near the front, despite his tenth-place grid start, he crashed out for no points, and that was probably the moment his fate was sealed with his Ducati employers.

Rea's latest victory meant that he had won half of all the races so far. He had three races' worth of points advantage leaving America, and the championship at least half in his pocket already.

SUPERBIKE WORLD CHAMPIONSHIP

MISANO

ROUND 9 · ITALY

Above: Xavi Fores leads van der Mark, Melandri, Sykes et al at the start of race two.

Right: Rea pays tribute to the memory of his compatriot, William Dunlop.

Centre right: Wild-card Niccolo Canepa delivered two points-scoring races for Yamaha.

Below right: Rea leads Davies, Laverty, Fores and Savadori at the very beginning of the weekend's race action.

Photos: Gold & Goose

Above: Rea leads van der Mark and Davies in race two. It would be this close all the way to the flag.

Left: Despite taking pole, Sykes failed to secure a podium in either race, scoring only two fifth places.

Below left: Former champion Troy Corser and MV rider Torres compare sun hats on the toasty grid.

Below: Chaz Davies took second in race one, but a miss was as good as another mile.

Bottom: Lorenzo Savadori bettered race one's eighth place with seventh in race two.

Below right: Melandri matched team-mate Davies in gaining a race-two podium.

Photos: Gold & Goose

THE last round before the monumental summer break was held at the ever-popular Misano World Circuit Marco Simoncelli. The sea is close to the track, and usually in the thoughts of many in the WorldSBK paddock and among the fans, especially in early July. They needed to look forward to a cool dip in the Adriatic after experiencing the near 30°C temperatures in which they watched and raced in 2018.

Superpole, and a new track best of 1 minute 33.640 seconds, went to a certain Mr Tom Sykes. He would be joined on the race-one front row by his soon-to-be-ex-team-mate Jonathan Rea and the revved-up Eugene Laverty.

In the opening race, Chaz Davies was up from seventh to fourth early on, after Rea had taken a quick advantage over Sykes. Loris Baz was an early faller on his BMW. He restarted it, but then was forced to retire to the pits.

Laverty was next to pile past Sykes into Turn One; then Davies at the Quercia left-hander. Sykes slipped back to fifth at the end, as Michael van der Mark made a pass for fourth.

Rea would eventually win by 2.791 seconds, but not from long-time second-place runner Laverty. The Irish rider had run wide into the last turn on the circuit, right out over the green paint no less, and the following Davies had pounced, making it stick to the end.

Brno race winner Alex Lowes suffered two falls in race one, and his bike could not recover from the second.

The opener was almost processional at times, but also much more closely contested than the spaced-out top-five classification would suggest. From Rea back to Sykes, 6.713 seconds covered the top five.

Rea was making winning a habit now. Each weekend, he increased his points lead enough to ensure that he would be champion long before the end of the year.

Laverty's second podium in succession proved that the Aprilia really was a weapon still, in the right hands at least, but only after the team had made a set-up breakthrough at an earlier Brno test.

There was drama in the second 21-lap race when early leader Xavi Fores, riding his Barni Racing Ducati in a patriotic team-inspired *tricolore* paint job, was forced out by a tech issue after only two laps.

Van der Mark led for a while, with Sykes and then Marco Melandri for close company. Melandri went inside Sykes, and then Rea also won a very short green-on-green tussle for track position. Melandri was next in Rea's sights and was dispatched with confidence and firmness.

Van der Mark hung on for as long as he could, but inevitably Rea slid through to lead. As the top three crossed the line, they were separated by only 0.595 of a second, completing a thrilling race that required true commitment and guts on some of the fastest sections of the circuit.

Having finished fourth, after being block-passed by Rea as the points leader made his way through from row three, Davies fell further behind in the championship fight. Any hopes that Rea's rivals had of planting doubts in his mind, doubts that he might linger over during the following nine weekends with no championship racing, melted in the heat of his intense ninth and tenth wins of the year.

The fight for second in the championship was bubbling away nicely, but once again the headlines were about Rea and his latest double win. He was 92 points ahead at this stage.

Some of the WorldSBK riders, including Rea, Lowes, van der Mark and PJ Jacobsen, headed for the Suzuka 8 Hours after Misano, but they all longed to get back to action at Portimao. And they would do so on two occasions, because the popular Algarve circuit would host an all-out official WorldSBK test before the next competitive round there.

SUPERBIKE WORLD CHAMPIONSHIP

PORTIMAO

ROUND 10 · PORTUGAL

Above: All downhill from here, lads. Melandri takes a short-lived lead from Rea and Laverty at the start of race one.

Left: Another step forward – a Superpole win for Eugene Laverty, SMR and Aprilia.

Below left: Kisses and lensless comedy specs from double podium man Melandri.

Right: The leading riders flow around the hairpin, with the VIP hospitality tower as their backdrop.

Above right: A battered Davies did well to claim two fourth places. The pain of missing two podiums was probably worse than the broken collarbone.

Top right: Michael van der Mark went Davies hunting with two well-timed podiums.

Top far right: Rea revelled where others toiled, at another one of his many best tracks.

Photos: Gold & Goose

PORTIMAO has been a talking point ever since its appearance on the Superbike scene over a decade ago. The best conceived and executed 'stadium' circuit imaginable, its actual track layout was also a bit of a handful even then for 1000cc machines, with all those blind entries, huge elevation changes and overstressed anti-wheelie algorithms. MotoGP, we must imagine, will not go there until wing technology exceeds aircraft standards and riders get pilots' licences.

That's why many of the old BSB riders like it, because it is a bit like some of the gnarliest British circuits, albeit with more run-off.

Portimao's intensity was tamed most effectively pre-race by Eugene Laverty, no less, who recorded his own first Superpole win since 2013, and Aprilia's since 2015. It had been a long nine-weekend summer break, but that had done Aprilia no harm at all on their first days back at school.

The rebooted No. 50 RSV-4 was unmissable in its race-one starting slot, and just for good measure, Lorenzo Savadori's example was right behind, in fourth place.

It would all go wrong for both of them in that first race, however. An out-braking manoeuvre by Xavi Fores on lap one took out Laverty, while Savadori crashed trying to match the increasing pace of eventual second-place rider Marco Melandri.

So who won?

At this stage of Jonathan Rea's peerless season, that question was becoming superfluous. He took the first race victory by a slowing 1.575 seconds from Melandri, and by 4.215 seconds from third-placed Michael van der Mark. Career win 65 for Rea brought out special start/finish-line signals from 'Team 65', as he laid another finger on the base of the championship trophy.

In race two, of course, he added yet another, from van der Mark this time and Melandri in third.

Behind the podium perps in each race, the recently injured Chaz Davies had turned up in Portimao with a fresh injury. A training accident had mashed his right collarbone. Again.

Thus, he had had two summer breaks and consequently was 14th in qualifying. Conducting Ducati manoeuvres under the long green shadow of the 'Rea Era' in WorldSBK, on a V-twin that was becoming just too long in the tooth, Davies was discovering that challenging the GOAT was growing increasingly difficult.

His recovery from row five to fourth in race one was one of his best rides. He followed it up with another in race two, leading for 11 laps, defending his ground, but inevitably being swallowed up by first Rea, then van der Mark and finally his own team-mate, Melandri.

Tom Sykes, fifth in race one, was also fifth in race two, missing just a bit of tyre and set-up performance in each race. He was less than five seconds from Rea second time around, but in race one, it had been almost 13 seconds.

Relatively hot weather was a feature of the entire Portimao race weekend, and it played its full part in tyre and set-up choice.

Having qualified eighth in Superpole, Loris Baz took his BMW to sixth in race one, a season best.

Back in the mix in race two, Laverty started from tenth place and finished seventh, behind Savadori. Michael Ruben Rinaldi rejoined the party on a third Aruba.it Ducati, finishing ninth and eighth.

Fresh back from another successful Suzuka 8 Hours race, Alex Lowes could show none of team-mate van der Mark's podium confidence, going tenth and then eleventh.

A resurgent Aprilia... Yamaha with a perennially podium-ready bike... A new V4 and MotoGP Ducati jockey coming... Many people were already excited about the prospects for 2019. For now, however, Rea was still making all the front running, especially at what he had always said was one of his favourite tracks, where he had made his WorldSBK debut in 2008.

SUPERBIKE WORLD CHAMPIONSHIP

MAGNY-COURS

ROUND 11 · FRANCE

Above: Camier and Baz duelled in both races, official bike versus customer-support machine.

Left: Savadori shone brightly on the Aprilia, claiming fourth- and sixth-place finishes.

Above left: Golden boy Rea disputes the leading position with van der Mark in race two.

Top: A rejuvenated and motivated Fores sped to a podium in race one.

Above right: The new champ's team celebrates his title, with three human 'Rea replicas' eventually joining in.

Far left: Sykes turned Superpole into stopwatch hyperbole, then led Fores and Savadori on his way to second place in race one.

Below left: The newly-crowned GOAT points out his unprecedented four consecutive WorldSBK titles.

Photos: Gold & Goose

JONATHAN REA is not the kind of rider who needs a second invitation to a race-winning party. He had another kind of invitation this time around, too: his first chance to win the 2018 championship. If he had a sufficiently good showing in France – and Chaz Davies and Michael van der Mark sufficiently poor outings – it would be all over. Even on Saturday.

Just as in 2017, Rea got the biggest job done in race one, completing the championship journal five chapters early as Davies finished fifth and van der Mark seventh.

Rea would launch his autobiography a few days after his historic fourth championship, but he had already written a personal fairy-tale in taking an unprecedented fourth successive title. Carl Fogarty also had four gold FIM medals, but the years stamped on his were not an unbroken sequence. And Rea already had many more wins.

The weekend began with both KRT riders, Rea and Tom Sykes, raising their personal bests and pushing each other on. Generally, Rea was ahead, and come Superpole, he pitched in with a new track best, well into the 1m 35s region. At first, the crowd was shocked, and then a little later, awed.

Sykes, with the doors of Superpole's last-chance saloon still swinging in Rea's slipstream, aced his team-mate's wonder-time with a 1m 35.696s. Astounding pace, real rivalry; Sykes was back from summer injury almost 100 per cent fit, and with a slightly clearer head than of late.

Indeed, he would push Rea hardest and longest in the first warm and sunny Magny-Cours race, finishing second, but by just over three seconds. He led for a lap and tried to hang on, but Rea was destined to greedily consume another win.

After some difficult periods following his great early season, Xavi Fores clambered back on to the podium by riding fast and free on his Ducati. Tellingly, he was well ahead of the toiling Davies, who had front-row qualifier Lorenzo Savadori just under a second ahead of him. The Welshman's fifth place was not enough to halt the Rea juggernaut before Sunday's race.

Marco Melandri was sixth, and with van der Mark seventh, the battle for second overall was hotting up nicely.

While Rea had settled the championship, he had another race win on his mind on Sunday, and he duly converted his now perennial third-row starting position into another victory, but only after some decent scrapping with Davies and van der Mark. They finished in that order behind Rea, in a race that was a second slower than Saturday's.

Sykes was a disappointed fourth, having changed tyre options in an effort to close the gap to Rea after being so close on Saturday. Nearly five seconds down, he was part of another relatively close top five. Melandri was only 6.5 seconds back, on one of his odd okay-ish weekends.

Savadori hung in there with a sixth, while Alex Lowes recovered from a race-one crash and restart (to 18th and last) to finish seventh.

After all the Portimao promise, Eugene Laverty was 13th in Superpole, then ninth and 11th in the races. Fourth and sixth places produced team-mate Savadori's best overall weekend results, however.

With Leon Camier still not fully fit, Honda struggled all weekend again. He finished 11th and ninth, having battled with the customer-support BMW of Loris Baz.

With the hum of forklifts and clatter of flight cases being loaded for the journey to Argentina creating a discordant symphony to celebrate Rea's latest and greatest championship win, the fight was now for second. For the rest of the best, anyway.

Meanwhile, the statistically greatest Superbike rider of all time would take another record with him on the series' first ever South American adventure. Rea had secured his 131st WorldSBK podium, from the 240 races to that point, overtaking Troy Corser's seemingly unbeatable record by one.

SUPERBIKE WORLD CHAMPIONSHIP

VILLICUM

ROUND 12 · ARGENTINA

YOU can't keep a good man down, they say. Or even in sight at times, in the case of Jonathan Rea at the all-new and almost perfectly formed Circuito San Juan Villicum.

The week's anticipation in the perennial game of "Who can beat Rea?" revolved around the unknowns in Argentina. There was no previous data for the KRT and KHI techies to get their avaricious teeth into, which should have levelled the playing field, right?

Not really, but that did not prevent the new circuit from providing plenty of race drama and excitement for over 80,000 weekend fans who witnessed the first ever visit of WorldSBK to South America.

There were snags. Garage roofs leaked after a Saturday-night deluge, and there was the small matter of the track surface breaking up here and there. That was so bad that a long narrow section of Turn Nine was resurfaced on Friday evening.

The track would worsen, but remain usable, even if the hot second race was slower than the first. But otherwise, Villicum was surprisingly magnificent.

Rea's record breaking possibilities on this particular weekend were centred on his ability to match, or beat, the previous best consecutive wins record in a season, which sat at nine, and his latest duo took the running green flush into double digits. Ten in a row: from Laguna in June through Misano, Portimao, Magny-Cours and Villicum.

He was astoundingly confident out of the blocks on day one, seconds faster than the rest in the first full lap of the dirty and slippery track, which had building dust and sand clinging stubbornly to the surface, brought in by the infamous Zonda wind.

The tarmac had no bumps and had been laid out in a very interesting way for a modern track, with lots of run-off. But something in the cure of the tarmac mix, the temperature when the surface had been laid or a film of dust had prevented the last few centimetres from sticking as it should, causing it to break up in some places. This was not deemed severe enough to affect the races, but it was one of the very few negatives of a truly excellent addition to the WorldSBK portfolio.

Marco Melandri had taken Superpole, and by an impressive margin. But Rea just disappeared up front after passing him in race one.

He had to work harder and risk a bit more in race two, from his usual third-row starting place. Passing was tricky, with the track still so dirty and slippery off line. Chaz Davies learned that the hard way when trying to get by Tom Sykes. He fell and was lucky not to hurt his broken and abused right collarbone too badly.

With Rea beating Melandri by 9.163 seconds, Toprak Razgatlioglu repeated his Donington podium prowess to take third, having just won a last-corner exit sprint with Xavi Fores to become top independent rider.

Eugene Laverty took a happy Aprilia fifth, Sykes an unhappy sixth. It was not a Yamaha track: Alex Lowes was seventh and Michael van der Mark eighth.

It was a Kawasaki track, though, and a Kawasaki season, as the greatly rev-limited 2018 Ninja was still enough for Rea, Sykes and Razgatlioglu to contribute sufficient points to take the constructors' award with three races to spare.

After many early passes, and despite Rea being up all night with a tummy bug, he won the second race at Villicum by just over three seconds – from a Ducati again, but it was privateer Fores this time. The latter scored his fifth podium and with it the independent riders' championship.

Melandri was third, 4.6 seconds back; Davies a salvage-yard fourth, and Sykes fifth, having been down in ninth on lap one.

Above: Podium capable again, Razgatlioglu leads Fores and local star Mercado in race one.

Top: Razgatlioglu and his crew played their part in Kawasaki's manufacturers' championship win, and had the T-shirts to prove it.

Top left: Racing gets under way at the impressive Circuito San Juan Villicum as pole-man Marco Melandri leads Rea, Sykes and a very small overall entry into a new chapter of WorldSBK history.

Left: With the mountains as a stunning backdrop in almost all directions, Fores leads Laverty and the rest of the pack in race two.

Far left: Over 80,000 fans made it to Villicum across the weekend – semi-flooded access roads on Sunday morning notwithstanding.

Below far left: Fores celebrates his second place in race two. He was 2018's top independent rider by some distance.

Right: Not quite complete, but endlessly convivial in nature, the noisy new paddock hosted many happy Argentineans.

Photos: Gold & Goose

SUPERBIKE WORLD CHAMPIONSHIP

LOSAIL

ROUND 13 · QATAR

Above: A desert storm brought a halt to proceedings.

Above right: Baz to sixth, best of the year for the BMW.

Right: The KRT crew bid Tom Sykes a fond farewell.

Photos: Gold & Goose

Left: Dorna WorldSBK executive director Daniel Carrera watches the weather.

Far left: Jonathan Rea took a comfortable win in race one, but cancellation of race two denied him the chance of a record-breaking 18 wins in one year.

Below left: Podium companions Alex Lowes and Rea.

Below: Submerged. The chequered flag was not needed.

Bottom centre: Melandri made a top-five farewell to Ducati.

Bottom right: Laverty and Lowes fight over third.

Photos: Gold & Goose

THE otherworldly nature of the entire Losail race weekend, from setting to schedule, has always singled it out as special. The fact that it is the final page of the yearbook just adds to the slightly disorientating, but always compelling, Qatar narrative for riders and teams to deal with.

Unfortunately, we only had one race, and the championship came to an end a whole day earlier than planned. And with race days on Friday and Saturday, rather than the more usual Saturday and Sunday, it was already going to be an early finish to a weekend's work.

Friday's lone race was close for the top two spots, but not thrilling.

Tom Sykes had set a new record of 1m 56.124s in Superpole earlier in the evening to extend his tally to 48 all in, signing off from his KRT career in some style. He was not able to beat 2018 champion Jonathan Rea into the first corner of the floodlit race, however. Once in front, Rea moved ahead a safe distance and stayed there. While Sykes was clearly rejuvenated, despite leaving his long-term employers after this round, he could not finish any closer than 1.424 seconds behind his team-mate.

Rea's 17th win of the year equalled Doug Polen's 1991 record, which would have set him up for stand-alone status with 18 on Saturday, had the race taken place.

Behind the KRT 1-2, the resurgent Alex Lowes got the better of Eugene Laverty, the top four covered by 4.723 seconds.

It was a tough farewell weekend for the last of the class-defining factory Ducati V-twins. Marco Melandri was fifth, but for Chaz Davies it was an unlucky ending, and a horribly surreal one for privateer Xavi Fores. It transpired that the 'Last Lap' board had been put out one lap early. The lucky ones, counting the laps from their own pit boards or the timing tower, didn't notice, but Davies did and slowed up – losing a place to his potential rival for overall second, Michael van der Mark. He was eighth. Fores, in fifth as the actual last lap approached, really slowed up and was passed by many as he cruised around, finishing 13th.

Loris Baz equalled his year's best with sixth place for BMW; Jake Gagne crafted the same personal-best story, in ninth.

Filled with mixed end-of-season emotions, the middle order joined the top riders in looking forward to dancing in the moonlight again in race two. They would be disappointed, and the weather was to blame.

Normally an open-air oven, Losail became first a wind tunnel, then a sandblasting cubicle, then a demented car wash as rain fell with a ferocity and duration that challenged reality. It left flooding and storm damage all over Qatar.

Rea had arrived in the teeth of the gale, wondering why he had bothered to show up at all, given the devastation. But after lots of hard work and several delays, there was some track action: warm-up sessions and the WorldSSP championship-deciding race.

But with trapped water in the gravel beds seeping back on to the track at Turn 15, and rivulets in the Superbikes' key braking zone into the first corner, Race Direction took the advice of the riders – and the evidence of their own eyes – and called it, sensibly and firmly.

So Rea 'only' had race one to add to his record collection on this weekend, and did not break his own season points best, but he did take his consecutive winning spree to 11. He had been unbeaten since June. Except by Mother Nature in Qatar.

Davies was runner-up in the championship, van der Mark overall third and Sykes fourth.

2018 WORLD SUPERBIKE CHAMPIONSHIP RESULTS

Compiled by Peter McLaren

Round 1 PHILLIP ISLAND, Australia · 24–25 February, 2018 · 2.762-mile/4.445km circuit · WEATHER: Race 1 · Dry · Track 31°C · Air 20°C; Race 2 · Dry · Track 29°C · Air 20°C

Race 1: 22 laps, 60.764 miles/97.790km

Time of race: 33m 40.354s · **Average speed:** 108.273mph/174.249km/h

Pos.	Rider	Nat.	No.	Entrant	Machine	Tyres	Time & Gap	Laps
1	**Marco Melandri**	ITA	33	Aruba.it Racing - Ducati	Ducati Panigale R	P		22
2	**Tom Sykes**	GBR	66	Kawasaki Racing Team WorldSBK	Kawasaki ZX-10RR	P	1.180s	22
3	**Chaz Davies**	GBR	7	Aruba.it Racing - Ducati	Ducati Panigale R	P	9.265s	22
4	**Xavi Fores**	ESP	12	Barni Racing Team	Ducati Panigale R	P	9.821s	22
5	**Jonathan Rea**	GBR	1	Kawasaki Racing Team WorldSBK	Kawasaki ZX-10RR	P	13.896s	22
6	**Alex Lowes**	GBR	22	Pata Yamaha Official WorldSBK Team	Yamaha YZF R1	P	17.028s	22
7	**Leon Camier**	GBR	2	Red Bull Honda World Superbike Team	Honda CBR1000RR	P	21.514s	22
8	**Eugene Laverty**	IRL	50	Milwaukee Aprilia	Aprilia RSV4 RF	P	23.662s	22
9	**Michael van der Mark**	NED	60	Pata Yamaha Official WorldSBK Team	Yamaha YZF R1	P	27.430s	22
10	**Leandro Mercado**	ARG	36	Orelac Racing VerdNatura	Kawasaki ZX-10RR	P	27.446s	22
11	**Loris Baz**	FRA	76	GULF ALTHEA BMW Racing Team	BMW S 1000 RR	P	27.748s	22
12	**Jake Gagne**	USA	45	Red Bull Honda World Superbike Team	Honda CBR1000RR	P	28.466s	22
13	**Toprak Razgatlioglu**	TUR	54	Kawasaki Puccetti Racing	Kawasaki ZX-10RR	P	30.000s	22
14	**Roman Ramos**	ESP	40	Team GoEleven Kawasaki	Kawasaki ZX-10RR	P	53.619s	22
15	**Ondrej Jezek**	CZE	37	Guandalini Racing	Yamaha YZF R1	P	1m 02.682s	22
16	PJ Jacobsen	USA	99	TripleM Honda World Superbike Team	Honda CBR1000RR	P	1m 09.775s	22
	Jordi Torres	ESP	81	MV Agusta Reparto Corse	MV Agusta 1000 F4	P	DNF	19
	Troy Herfoss	AUS	17	Penrite Honda	Honda CBR1000RR	P	DNF	19
	Yonny Hernandez	COL	68	Team Pedercini Racing	Kawasaki ZX-10RR	P	DNF	13
	Daniel Falzon	AUS	25	Yamaha Racing Team	Yamaha YZF R1	P	DNF	9
	Wayne Maxwell	AUS	47	Yamaha Racing Team	Yamaha YZF R1	P	DNF	1

Fastest race lap: T.Sykes on lap 2, 1m 30.971s, 109.30mph/175.90km/h.

Race 2: 22 laps, 60.764 miles/97.790km

Time of race: 34m 42.633s · **Average speed:** 105.035mph/169.038km/h

Pos.	Rider	Time & Gap	Laps
1	**Marco Melandri**		22
2	**Jonathan Rea**	0.021s	22
3	**Xavi Fores**	0.304s	22
4	**Tom Sykes**	1.488s	22
5	**Alex Lowes**	2.474s	22
6	**Leon Camier**	2.745s	22
7	**Michael van der Mark**	3.098s	22
8	**Jordi Torres**	14.301s	22
9	**Loris Baz**	14.361s	22
10	**Toprak Razgatlioglu**	19.785s	22
11	**Roman Ramos**	25.237s	22
12	**Leandro Mercado**	40.504s	22
13	**Jake Gagne**	58.923s	22
14	**PJ Jacobsen**	1m 00.084s	22
15	**Eugene Laverty**	2 Laps	20
	Chaz Davies	DNF	11
	Ondrej Jezek	DNF	0
	Daniel Falzon	DSQ	12

Fastest race lap: M.Melandri on lap 15, 1m 30.848s, 109.45mph/176.14km/h.

Lap record: C. Davies, 1m 30.949s, 109.324mph/175.940km/h (2014).

Superpole		
1	Sykes	1m 30.099s
2	Laverty	1m 30.339s
3	Melandri	1m 30.660s
4	Lowes	1m 30.767s
5	Davies	1m 31.009s
6	Rea	1m 31.056s
7	Fores	1m 31.080s
8	Van der Mark	1m 31.240s
9	Razgatlioglu	1m 31.581s
10	Savadori	No Time
11	Camier	No Time
12	Torres	No Time
13	Gagne	1m 31.957s
14	Baz	1m 32.016s
15	Ramos	1m 32.161s
16	Maxwell	1m 32.193s
17	Mercado	1m 32.386s
18	Hernandez	1m 32.554s
19	Herfoss	1m 32.640s
20	Jezek	1m 33.088s
21	Falzon	1m 33.126s
22	Jacobsen	1m 33.875s

Points

1, Melandri 50; 2, Sykes 33; 3, Rea 31; 4, Fores 29; 5, Lowes 21; 6, Camier 19; 7, Davies 16; 8, Van der Mark 16; 9, Baz 12; 10, Mercado 10; 11, Laverty 9; 12, Razgatlioglu 9; 13, Torres 8; 14, Ramos 7; 15, Gagne 7; 16, Jacobsen 2; 17, Jezek 1.

WORLD SUPERBIKE CHAMPIONSHIP · 2018

MOTUL

Round 2 · BURIRAM, Thailand · 24–25 March, 2018 · 2.830-mile/4.554km circuit · WEATHER: Race 1 · Dry · Track 42°C · Air 32°C; Race 2 · Dry · Track 41°C · Air 33°C

Race 1: 20 laps, 56.594 miles/91.080km

Time of race: 31m 24.203s · **Average speed:** 108.130mph/174.019km/h

Pos.	Rider	Nat.	No.	Entrant	Machine	Tyres	Time & Gap	Laps
1	**Jonathan Rea**	GBR	1	Kawasaki Racing Team WorldSBK	Kawasaki ZX-10RR	P		20
2	**Xavi Fores**	ESP	12	Barni Racing Team	Ducati Panigale R	P	1.550s	20
3	**Chaz Davies**	GBR	7	Aruba.it Racing - Ducati	Ducati Panigale R	P	2.118s	20
4	**Leon Camier**	GBR	2	Red Bull Honda World Superbike Team	Honda CBR1000RR	P	2.981s	20
5	**Alex Lowes**	GBR	22	Pata Yamaha Official WorldSBK Team	Yamaha YZF R1	P	7.258s	20
6	**Tom Sykes**	GBR	66	Kawasaki Racing Team WorldSBK	Kawasaki ZX-10RR	P	7.501s	20
7	**Michael van der Mark**	NED	60	Pata Yamaha Official WorldSBK Team	Yamaha YZF R1	P	8.500s	20
8	**Marco Melandri**	ITA	33	Aruba.it Racing - Ducati	Ducati Panigale R	P	10.184s	20
9	**Eugene Laverty**	IRL	50	Milwaukee Aprilia	Aprilia RSV4 RF	P	11.072s	20
10	**Jordi Torres**	ESP	81	MV Agusta Reparto Corse	MV Agusta 1000 F4	P	11.178s	20
11	**Loris Baz**	FRA	76	GULF ALTHEA BMW Racing Team	BMW S 1000 RR	P	24.062s	20
12	**Lorenzo Savadori**	ITA	32	Milwaukee Aprilia	Aprilia RSV4 RF	P	24.632s	20
13	**Leandro Mercado**	ARG	36	Orelac Racing VerdNatura	Kawasaki ZX-10RR	P	26.114s	20
14	**Roman Ramos**	ESP	40	Team GoEleven Kawasaki	Kawasaki ZX-10RR	P	26.142s	20
15	**Toprak Razgatlioglu**	TUR	54	Kawasaki Puccetti Racing	Kawasaki ZX-10RR	P	26.320s	20
16	Yonny Hernandez	COL	68	Team Pedercini Racing	Kawasaki ZX-10RR	P	30.665s	20
17	PJ Jacobsen	USA	99	TripleM Honda World Superbike Team	Honda CBR1000RR	P	32.625s	20
18	Jake Gagne	USA	45	Red Bull Honda World Superbike Team	Honda CBR1000RR	P	38.752s	20
	Ondrej Jezek	CZE	37	Guandalini Racing	Yamaha YZF R1	P	DNF	16

Fastest race lap: J.Rea on lap 11, 1m 33.714s, 108.70mph/174.94km/h.

Race 2: 20 laps, 56.594 miles/91.080km

Time of race: 31m 23.406s · **Average speed:** 108.176mph/174.093km/h

Pos.	Rider	Time & Gap	Laps
1	**Chaz Davies**		20
2	**Michael van der Mark**	2.185s	20
3	**Alex Lowes**	3.884s	20
4	**Jonathan Rea**	6.554s	20
5	**Xavi Fores**	8.973s	20
6	**Leon Camier**	10.647s	20
7	**Marco Melandri**	17.523s	20
8	**Toprak Razgatlioglu**	21.618s	20
9	**Lorenzo Savadori**	25.345s	20
10	**PJ Jacobsen**	27.076s	20
11	**Yonny Hernandez**	28.668s	20
12	**Loris Baz**	29.004s	20
13	**Roman Ramos**	30.434s	20
14	**Jake Gagne**	30.527s	20
	Leandro Mercado	DNF	18
	Tom Sykes	DNF	7
	Eugene Laverty	DNF	4
	Jordi Torres	DNF	4
	Ondrej Jezek	DSQ	5

Superpole		
1	Rea	1m 32.814s
2	Sykes	1m 32.817s
3	Camier	1m 32.922s
4	Torres	1m 32.972s
5	Fores	1m 33.022s
6	Lowes	1m 33.036s
7	Melandri	1m 33.103s
8	Laverty	1m 33.119s
9	Davies	1m 33.148s
10	Van der Mark	1m 33.373s
11	Savadori	1m 33.450s
12	Razgatlioglu	1m 34.570s
13	Mercado	1m 34.271s
14	Gagne	1m 34.404s
15	Baz	1m 34.477s
16	Ramos	1m 34.729s
17	Jacobsen	1m 34.782s
18	Hernandez	1m 34.783s
19	Jezek	1m 35.925s

Fastest race lap: C.Davies on lap 11, 1m 33.627s, 108.80mph/175.10km/h.

Lap record: J.Rea, 1m 33.436s, 109.03mph/175.46km/h (2017).

Points

1, Rea 69; 2, Melandri 67; 3, Fores 60; 4, Davies 57; 5, Lowes 48; 6, Van der Mark 45; 7, Sykes 43; 8, Camier 42; 9, Baz 21; 10, Razgatlioglu 18; 11, Laverty 16; 12, Torres 14; 13, Mercado 13; 14, Ramos 12; 15, Savadori 11; 16, Gagne 9; 17, Jacobsen 8; 18, Hernandez 5; 19, Jezek 1.

Round 3 · ARAGON, Spain · 14–15 April, 2018 · 3.155-mile/5.077km circuit · WEATHER: Race 1 · Dry · Track 18°C · Air 11°C; Race 2 · Dry · Track 31°C · Air 19°C

Race 1: 17 laps, 53.630 miles/86.309km

Time of race: 31m 38.578s · **Average speed:** 101.691mph/163.655km/h

Pos.	Rider	Nat.	No.	Entrant	Machine	Tyres	Time & Gap	Laps
1	**Jonathan Rea**	GBR	1	Kawasaki Racing Team WorldSBK	Kawasaki ZX-10RR	P		17
2	**Chaz Davies**	GBR	7	Aruba.it Racing - Ducati	Ducati Panigale R	P	1.450s	17
3	**Xavi Fores**	ESP	12	Barni Racing Team	Ducati Panigale R	P	1.473s	17
4	**Marco Melandri**	ITA	33	Aruba.it Racing - Ducati	Ducati Panigale R	P	6.108s	17
5	**Michael van der Mark**	NED	60	Pata Yamaha Official WorldSBK Team	Yamaha YZF R1	P	8.932s	17
6	**Tom Sykes**	GBR	66	Kawasaki Racing Team WorldSBK	Kawasaki ZX-10RR	P	9.450s	17
7	**Alex Lowes**	GBR	22	Pata Yamaha Official WorldSBK Team	Yamaha YZF R1	P	9.985s	17
8	**Michael Ruben Rinaldi**	ITA	21	Aruba.it Racing - Junior Team	Ducati Panigale R	P	19.303s	17
9	**Toprak Razgatlioglu**	TUR	54	Kawasaki Puccetti Racing	Kawasaki ZX-10RR	P	26.081s	17
10	**Roman Ramos**	ESP	40	Team GoEleven Kawasaki	Kawasaki ZX-10RR	P	26.325s	17
11	**Loris Baz**	FRA	76	GULF ALTHEA BMW Racing Team	BMW S 1000 RR	P	26.571s	17
12	**Jake Gagne**	USA	45	Red Bull Honda World Superbike Team	Honda CBR1000RR	P	26.858s	17
13	**Davide Giugliano**	ITA	34	Milwaukee Aprilia	Aprilia RSV4 RF	P	27.219s	17
14	**Yonny Hernandez**	COL	68	Team Pedercini Racing	Kawasaki ZX-10RR	P	28.340s	17
15	**Lorenzo Savadori**	ITA	32	Milwaukee Aprilia	Aprilia RSV4 RF	P	28.400s	17
16	PJ Jacobsen	USA	99	TripleM Honda World Superbike Team	Honda CBR1000RR	P	30.799s	17
17	Ondrej Jezek	CZE	37	Guandalini Racing	Yamaha YZF R1	P	58.926s	17
	Leandro Mercado	ARG	36	Orelac Racing VerdNatura	Kawasaki ZX-10RR	P	DNF	11
	Jordi Torres	ESP	81	MV Agusta Reparto Corse	MV Agusta 1000 F4	P	DNF	0
	Leon Camier	GBR	2	Red Bull Honda World Superbike Team	Honda CBR1000RR	P	DNS	0
	Vladimir Leonov	RUS	5	SPB Racing Team	Kawasaki ZX-10RR	P	DNS	0

Fastest race lap: M.Melandri on lap 2, 1m 50.663s, 102.63mph/165.16km/h.

Race 2: 18 laps, 56.785 miles/91.386km

Time of race: 33m 29.519s · **Average speed:** 101.728mph/163.716km/h

Pos.	Rider	Time & Gap	Laps
1	**Chaz Davies**		18
2	**Jonathan Rea**	1.184s	18
3	**Marco Melandri**	4.584s	18
4	**Alex Lowes**	10.251s	18
5	**Michael van der Mark**	10.687s	18
6	**Tom Sykes**	13.729s	18
7	**Michael Ruben Rinaldi**	14.819s	18
8	**Jordi Torres**	15.215s	18
9	**Toprak Razgatlioglu**	19.812s	18
10	**Lorenzo Savadori**	20.272s	18
11	**Roman Ramos**	25.604s	18
12	**Jake Gagne**	25.745s	18
13	**Leandro Mercado**	27.973s	18
14	**PJ Jacobsen**	28.469s	18
15	**Loris Baz**	32.094s	18
16	Yonny Hernandez	32.113s	18
17	Ondrej Jezek	56.590s	18
18	Vladimir Leonov	1m 23.992s	18
19	Davide Giugliano	1 Lap	17
	Xavi Fores	DNF	7
	Leon Camier	DNS	0

Superpole		
1	Melandri	1m 49.543s
2	Rea	1m 49.574s
3	Sykes	1m 49.644s
4	Fores	1m 49.667s
5	Lowes	1m 49.853s
6	Van der Mark	1m 49.863s
7	Torres	1m 50.055s
8	Rinaldi	1m 50.197s
9	Camier	1m 50.607s
10	Savadori	1m 50.809s
11	Davies	1m 51.065s
12	Leonov	1m 53.033s
13	Gagne	1m 51.609s
14	Giugliano	1m 51.632s
15	Mercado	1m 51.718s
16	Razgatlioglu	1m 51.777s
17	Jacobsen	1m 51.832s
18	Ramos	1m 51.845s
19	Baz	1m 51.867s
20	Hernandez	1m 51.961s
21	Jezek	1m 53.349s

Fastest race lap: M.Melandri on lap 16, 1m 51.048s, 102.27mph/164.59km/h.

Lap record: C. Davies, 1m 50.421s, 102.85mph/165.52km/h (2016)..

Points

1, Rea 114; 2, Davies 102; 3, Melandri 96; 4, Fores 76; 5, Lowes 70; 6, Van der Mark 67; 7, Sykes 63; 8, Camier 42; 9, Razgatlioglu 32; 10, Baz 27; 11, Ramos 23; 12, Torres 22; 13, Savadori 18; 14, Rinaldi 17; 15, Gagne 17; 16, Laverty 16; 17, Mercado 16; 18, Jacobsen 10; 19, Hernandez 7; 20, Giugliano 3; 21, Jezek 1.

WORLD SUPERBIKE CHAMPIONSHIP · 2018

MOTUL

Round 4 — ASSEN, Netherlands · 21–22 April, 2018 · 2.822-mile/4.542km circuit · WEATHER: Race 1 · Dry · Track 30°C · Air 18°C; Race 2 · Dry · Track 30°C · Air 23°C

Race 1: 21 laps, 59.268 miles/95.382km
Time of race: 33m 40.360s · **Average speed:** 105.606mph/169.957km/h

Pos.	Rider	Nat.	No.	Entrant	Machine	Tyres	Time & Gap	Laps
1	**Jonathan Rea**	GBR	1	Kawasaki Racing Team WorldSBK	Kawasaki ZX-10RR	P		21
2	**Michael van der Mark**	NED	60	Pata Yamaha Official WorldSBK Team	Yamaha YZF R1	P	0.981s	21
3	**Chaz Davies**	GBR	7	Aruba.it Racing - Ducati	Ducati Panigale R	P	1.282s	21
4	**Tom Sykes**	GBR	66	Kawasaki Racing Team WorldSBK	Kawasaki ZX-10RR	P	1.413s	21
5	**Xavi Fores**	ESP	12	Barni Racing Team	Ducati Panigale R	P	8.625s	21
6	**Marco Melandri**	ITA	33	Aruba.it Racing - Ducati	Ducati Panigale R	P	14.903s	21
7	**Loris Baz**	FRA	76	GULF ALTHEA BMW Racing Team	BMW S 1000 RR	P	17.301s	21
8	**Leandro Mercado**	ARG	36	Orelac Racing VerdNatura	Kawasaki ZX-10RR	P	21.482s	21
9	**Jordi Torres**	ESP	81	MV Agusta Reparto Corse	MV Agusta 1000 F4	P	21.938s	21
10	**Toprak Razgatlioglu**	TUR	54	Kawasaki Puccetti Racing	Kawasaki ZX-10RR	P	24.939s	21
11	**Roman Ramos**	ESP	40	Team GoEleven Kawasaki	Kawasaki ZX-10RR	P	27.049s	21
12	**Alex Lowes**	GBR	22	Pata Yamaha Official WorldSBK Team	Yamaha YZF R1	P	33.226s	21
13	**Davide Giugliano**	ITA	34	Milwaukee Aprilia	Aprilia RSV4 RF	P	35.630s	21
14	**PJ Jacobsen**	USA	99	TripleM Honda World Superbike Team	Honda CBR1000RR	P	38.480s	21
15	**Lorenzo Savadori**	ITA	32	Milwaukee Aprilia	Aprilia RSV4 RF	P	38.604s	21
16	Yonny Hernandez	COL	68	Team Pedercini Racing	Kawasaki ZX-10RR	P	44.690s	21
17	Ondrej Jezek	CZE	37	Guandalini Racing	Yamaha YZF R1	P	51.135s	21
	Michael Ruben Rinaldi	ITA	21	Aruba.it Racing - Junior Team	Ducati Panigale R	P	DNF	5

Fastest race lap: M. van der Mark on lap 2, 1m 35.248s, 160.67mph/171.67km/h.

Race 2: 21 laps, 59.268 miles/95.382km
Time of race: 33m 36.444s · **Average speed:** 105.811mph/170.287km/h

Pos.	Rider	Time & Gap	Laps
1	**Tom Sykes**		21
2	**Jonathan Rea**	5.445s	21
3	**Van der Mark**	7.507s	21
4	**Xavi Fores**	11.316s	21
5	**Chaz Davies**	18.953s	21
6	**Jordi Torres**	22.414s	21
7	**Marco Melandri**	22.515s	21
8	**Loris Baz**	23.997s	21
9	**Toprak Razgatlioglu**	24.245s	21
10	**Lorenzo Savadori**	24.653s	21
11	**Davide Giugliano**	41.807s	21
12	**Michael Ruben Rinaldi**	41.846s	21
13	**PJ Jacobsen**	47.516s	21
14	**Alex Lowes**	53.355s	21
15	**Ondrej Jezek**	54.065s	21
16	Yonny Hernandez	57.758s	21
	Leandro Mercado	DNF	5
	Roman Ramos	DNF	5

Superpole		
1	Lowes	1m 34.066s
2	Rea	1m 34.112s
3	Fores	1m 34.387s
4	Savadori	1m 34.739s
5	Melandri	1m 34.838s
6	Sykes	1m 34.840s
7	Van der Mark	1m 34.873s
8	Davies	1m 34.986s
9	Torres	1m 35.099s
10	Baz	1m 35.541s
11	Razgatlioglu	1m 35.858s
12	Rinaldi	1m 35.875s
13	Mercado	1m 35.854s
14	Ramos	1m 35.982s
15	Jacobsen	1m 36.199s
16	Giugliano	1m 36.417s
17	Hernandez	1m 36.478s
18	Jezek	1m 36.734s
19	Gagne	No Time

Fastest race lap: T.Sykes on lap 3, 1m 35.218s, 106.70mph/171.72km/h.
Lap record: J.Rea, 1m 34.880s, 107.09mph/172.34km/h (2017).

Points

1, Rea 159; 2, Davies 129; 3, Melandri 115; 4, Van Der Mark 103; 5, Sykes 101; 6, Fores 100; 7, Lowes 76; 8, Razgatlioglu 45; 9, Baz 44; 10, Camier 42; 11, Torres 39; 12, Ramos 28; 13, Savadori 25; 14, Mercado 24; 15, Rinaldi 21; 16, Gagne 17; 17, Laverty 16; 18, Jacobsen 15; 19, Giugliano 11; 20, Hernandez 7; 21, Jezek 2.

Round 5 — IMOLA, Italy · 12–13 May, 2018 · 3.067-mile/4.936km circuit · WEATHER: Race 1 · Dry · Track 40°C · Air 27°C; Race 2 · Dry · Track 43°C · Air 25°C

Race 1: 19 laps, 58.275 miles/93.784km
Time of race: 33m 58.989s · **Average speed:** 102.889mph/165.583km/h

Pos.	Rider	Nat.	No.	Entrant	Machine	Tyres	Time & Gap	Laps
1	**Jonathan Rea**	GBR	1	Kawasaki Racing Team WorldSBK	Kawasaki ZX-10RR	P		19
2	**Tom Sykes**	GBR	66	Kawasaki Racing Team WorldSBK	Kawasaki ZX-10RR	P	3.755s	19
3	**Marco Melandri**	ITA	33	Aruba.it Racing - Ducati	Ducati Panigale R	P	6.906s	19
4	**Chaz Davies**	GBR	7	Aruba.it Racing - Ducati	Ducati Panigale R	P	8.191s	19
5	**Xavi Fores**	ESP	12	Barni Racing Team	Ducati Panigale R	P	15.550s	19
6	**Michael van der Mark**	NED	60	Pata Yamaha Official WorldSBK Team	Yamaha YZF R1	P	19.339s	19
7	**Michael Ruben Rinaldi**	ITA	21	Aruba.it Racing - Junior Team	Ducati Panigale R	P	22.522s	19
8	**Lorenzo Savadori**	ITA	32	Milwaukee Aprilia	Aprilia RSV4 RF	P	25.772s	19
9	**Leon Haslam**	GBR	91	Kawasaki Puccetti Racing	Kawasaki ZX-10RR	P	30.269s	19
10	**Alex Lowes**	GBR	22	Pata Yamaha Official WorldSBK Team	Yamaha YZF R1	P	30.377s	19
11	**Toprak Razgatlioglu**	TUR	54	Kawasaki Puccetti Racing	Kawasaki ZX-10RR	P	30.660s	19
12	**Eugene Laverty**	IRL	50	Milwaukee Aprilia	Aprilia RSV4 RF	P	34.188s	19
13	**Loris Baz**	FRA	76	GULF ALTHEA BMW Racing Team	BMW S 1000 RR	P	36.494s	19
14	**Jordi Torres**	ESP	81	MV Agusta Reparto Corse	MV Agusta 1000 F4	P	36.671s	19
15	**Leandro Mercado**	ARG	36	Orelac Racing VerdNatura	Kawasaki ZX-10RR	P	38.041s	19
16	Jake Gagne	USA	45	Red Bull Honda World Superbike Team	Honda CBR1000RR	P	41.312s	19
17	Yonny Hernandez	COL	68	Team Pedercini Racing	Kawasaki ZX-10RR	P	55.007s	19
18	Ondrej Jezek	CZE	37	Guandalini Racing	Yamaha YZF R1	P	1m 07.522s	19
	Roman Ramos	ESP	40	Team GoEleven Kawasaki	Kawasaki ZX-10RR	P	DNF	15
	Vladimir Leonov	RUS	5	SPB Racing Team	Kawasaki ZX-10RR	P	DNF	2
	Jason O'Halloran	AUS	20	Red Bull Honda World Superbike Team	Honda CBR1000RR	P	DNF	1
	PJ Jacobsen	USA	99	TripleM Honda World Superbike Team	Honda CBR1000RR	P	DNF	0

Fastest race lap: J.Rea on lap 2, 1m 46.850s, 103.33mph/166.30km/h.

Race 2: 19 laps, 58.275 miles/93.784km
Time of race: 34m 3.420s · **Average speed:** 102.665mph/165.224km/h

Pos.	Rider	Time & Gap	Laps
1	**Jonathan Rea**		19
2	**Chaz Davies**	4.019s	19
3	**Tom Sykes**	9.530s	19
4	**Xavi Fores**	14.159s	19
5	**Jordi Torres**	15.479s	19
6	**Alex Lowes**	16.162s	19
7	**Michael Ruben Rinaldi**	17.197s	19
8	**Toprak Razgatlioglu**	17.554s	19
9	**Eugene Laverty**	22.331s	19
10	**Leandro Mercado**	30.176s	19
11	**Loris Baz**	30.267s	19
12	**Roman Ramos**	40.061s	19
13	**Yonny Hernandez**	51.973s	19
14	**PJ Jacobsen**	55.268s	19
15	**Ondrej Jezek**	1m 09.455s	19
16	Leon Haslam	1m 43.833s	19
	Marco Melandri	DNF	8
	Michael van der Mark	DNF	8
	Vladimir Leonov	DNF	6
	Lorenzo Savadori	DNF	4
	Jake Gagne	DNF	4
	Jason O'Halloran	DNS	0

Superpole		
1	Rea	1m 45.797s
2	Sykes	1m 46.109s
3	Davies	1m 46.162s
4	Melandri	1m 46.227s
5	Fores	1m 46.689s
6	Laverty	1m 46.692s
7	Torres	1m 46.820s
8	Rinaldi	1m 46.853s
9	Savadori	1m 46.921s
10	Lowes	1m 47.115s
11	Haslam	1m 47.547s
12	Van der Mark	1m 47.710s
13	Baz	1m 47.776s
14	Razgatlioglu	1m 48.020s
15	Ramos	1m 48.086s
16	Mercado	1m 48.138s
17	Jacobsen	1m 48.313s
18	O'Halloran	1m 48.411s
19	Gagne	1m 48.518s
20	Jezek	1m 48.606s
21	Hernandez	1m 48.958s
22	Leonov	1m 50.062s

Fastest race lap: J.Rea on lap 15, 1m 46.898s, 103.29mph/166.23km/h.
Lap record: C.Davies, 1m 46.393s, 103.78mph/167.02km/h (2017).

Points

1, Rea 209; 2, Davies 162; 3, Sykes 137; 4, Melandri 131; 5, Fores 124; 6, Van der Mark 113; 7, Lowes 92; 8, Razgatlioglu 58; 9, Torres 52; 10, Baz 52; 11, Camier 42; 12, Rinaldi 39; 13, Savadori 33; 14, Ramos 32; 15, Mercado 31; 16, Laverty 27; 17, Jacobsen 17; 18, Gagne 17; 19, Giugliano 11; 20, Hernandez 11; 21, Haslam 7; 22, Jezek 2.

WORLD SUPERBIKE CHAMPIONSHIP · 2018

MOTUL

Round 6 DONINGTON PARK, Great Britain · 26–27 May 2018 · 2.500-mile/4.023km circuit · WEATHER: Race 1 · Dry · Track 30°C · Air 18°C; Race 2 · Dry · Track 33°C · Air 23°C

Race 1: 23 laps, 57.495 miles/92.529km

Time of race: 33m 56.530s · **Average speed:** 101.635mph/163.565km/h

Pos.	Rider	Nat.	No.	Entrant	Machine	Tyres	Time & Gap	Laps
1	**Michael van der Mark**	NED	60	Pata Yamaha Official WorldSBK Team	Yamaha YZF R1	P		23
2	**Jonathan Rea**	GBR	1	Kawasaki Racing Team WorldSBK	Kawasaki ZX-10RR	P	1.136s	23
3	**Tom Sykes**	GBR	66	Kawasaki Racing Team WorldSBK	Kawasaki ZX-10RR	P	2.193s	23
4	**Alex Lowes**	GBR	22	Pata Yamaha Official WorldSBK Team	Yamaha YZF R1	P	6.642s	23
5	**Lorenzo Savadori**	ITA	32	Milwaukee Aprilia	Aprilia RSV4 RF	P	7.331s	23
6	**Eugene Laverty**	IRL	50	Milwaukee Aprilia	Aprilia RSV4 RF	P	13.374s	23
7	**Loris Baz**	FRA	76	GULF ALTHEA BMW Racing Team	BMW S 1000 RR	P	15.992s	23
8	**Chaz Davies**	GBR	7	Aruba.it Racing - Ducati	Ducati Panigale R	P	18.532s	23
9	**Leon Haslam**	GBR	91	Kawasaki Puccetti Racing	Kawasaki ZX-10RR	P	20.478s	23
10	**Leon Camier**	GBR	2	Red Bull Honda World Superbike Team	Honda CBR1000RR	P	20.634s	23
11	**Jordi Torres**	ESP	81	MV Agusta Reparto Corse	MV Agusta 1000 F4	P	22.503s	23
12	**Michael Ruben Rinaldi**	ITA	21	Aruba.it Racing - Junior Team	Ducati Panigale R	P	33.250s	23
13	**Leandro Mercado**	ARG	36	Orelac Racing VerdNatura	Kawasaki ZX-10RR	P	33.771s	23
14	**Bradley Ray**	GBR	28	Buildbase Suzuki	Suzuki GSX-R1000	P	36.715s	23
15	**PJ Jacobsen**	USA	99	TripleM Honda World Superbike Team	Honda CBR1000RR	P	38.850s	23
16	Jake Gagne	USA	45	Red Bull Honda World Superbike Team	Honda CBR1000RR	P	42.536s	23
17	Luke Mossey	GBR	41	Team Pedercini Racing	Kawasaki ZX-10RR	P	42.682s	23
18	Ondrej Jezek	CZE	37	Guandalini Racing	Yamaha YZF R1	P	47.849s	23
19	Roman Ramos	ESP	40	Team GoEleven Kawasaki	Kawasaki ZX-10RR	P	50.256s	23
20	Niccolo Canepa	ITA	94	Yamaha Motor Europe	Yamaha YZF R1	P	52.188s	23
21	Toprak Razgatlioglu	TUR	54	Kawasaki Puccetti Racing	Kawasaki ZX-10RR	P	55.588s	23
22	Marco Melandri	ITA	33	Aruba.it Racing - Ducati	Ducati Panigale R	P	1m 19.859s	23
23	Jonathan Rea	GBR	44	OMG Racing UK	Suzuki GSX-R1000	P	1m 36.779s	23
	Xavi Fores	ESP	12	Barni Racing Team	Ducati Panigale R	P	DNF	10
	Mason Law	GBR	55	Team WD40	Kawasaki ZX-10RR	P	DNF	0

Fastest race lap: J.Rea on lap 18, 1m 27.974s, 102.30mph/164.63km/h.

Race 2: 23 laps, 57.495 miles/92.529km

Time of race: 34m 2.406s · **Average speed:** 101.342mph/163.094km/h

Pos.	Rider	Time & Gap	Laps
1	**Michael van der Mark**		23
2	**Toprak Razgatlioglu**	2.328s	23
3	**Jonathan Rea**	2.614s	23
4	**Alex Lowes**	2.894s	23
5	**Chaz Davies**	4.797s	23
6	**Tom Sykes**	8.224s	23
7	**Lorenzo Savadori**	9.169s	23
8	**Leon Camier**	18.488s	23
9	**Jordi Torres**	19.964s	23
10	**Loris Baz**	20.207s	23
11	**Marco Melandri**	23.803s	23
12	**Leandro Mercado**	28.845s	23
13	**Jake Gagne**	29.741s	23
14	**Luke Mossey**	31.156s	23
15	**Bradley Ray**	33.321s	23
16	PJ Jacobsen	34.175s	23
17	Ondrej Jezek	47.350s	23
18	Niccolo Canepa	47.701s	23
19	Jonathan Rea	57.365s	23
	Mason Law	DNF	16
	Eugene Laverty	DNF	15
	Roman Ramos	DNF	14
	Xavi Fores	DNF	13
	Leon Haslam	DNF	8
	Michael Ruben Rinaldi	DNF	0

Superpole		
1	Sykes	1m 26.663s
2	Rea	1m 26.956s
3	Baz	1m 27.348s
4	Savadori	1m 27.355s
5	Lowes	1m 27.422s
6	Van der Mark	1m 27.472s
7	Laverty	1m 27.508s
8	Razgatlioglu	1m 27.631s
9	Davies	1m 27.749s
10	Ray	1m 27.946s
11	Haslam	1m 27.967s
12	Melandri	1m 28.130s
13	Camier	1m 28.108s
14	Torres	1m 28.230s
15	Rinaldi	1m 28.376s
16	Mossey	1m 28.885s
17	Jezek	1m 28.958s
18	Mercado	1m 28.969s
19	Jacobsen	1m 29.119s
20	Ramos	1m 29.172s
21	Gagne	1m 29.173s
22	Fores	1m 29.315s
23	Rea	1m 29.376s
24	Canepa	1m 29.530s
25	Law	No Time

Fastest race lap: J.Rea on lap 9, 1m 27.983s, 102.28mph/164.61km/h.

Lap record: J.Rea, 1m 27.605s, 102.73mph/165.32km/h (2016).

Points

1, Rea 245; 2, Davies 181; 3, Van der Mark 163; 4, Sykes 163; 5, Melandri 136; 6, Fores 124; 7, Lowes 118; 8, Razgatlioglu 78; 9, Baz 67; 10, Torres 64; 11, Camier 56; 12, Savadori 53; 13, Rinaldi 43; 14, Mercado 38; 15, Laverty 37; 16, Ramos 32; 17, Gagne 20; 18, Jacobsen 18; 19, Haslam 14; 20, Giugliano 11; 21, Hernandez 11; 22, Ray 3; 23, Mossey 2; 24, Jezek 2.

Round 7 BRNO, Czech Republic · 9–10 June, 2018 · 3.360-mile/5.403km circuit · WEATHER: Race 1 · Dry · Track 35°C · Air 24°C; Race 2 · Dry · Track 43°C · Air 27°C

Race 1: 16 laps, 53.716 miles/86.448km

Time of race: 32m 8.759s · **Average speed:** 100.261mph/161.354km/h

Pos.	Rider	Nat.	No.	Entrant	Machine	Tyres	Time & Gap	Laps
1	**Jonathan Rea**	GBR	1	Kawasaki Racing Team WorldSBK	Kawasaki ZX-10RR	P		16
2	**Marco Melandri**	ITA	33	Aruba.it Racing - Ducati	Ducati Panigale R	P	5.381s	16
3	**Tom Sykes**	GBR	66	Kawasaki Racing Team WorldSBK	Kawasaki ZX-10RR	P	7.336s	16
4	**Michael van der Mark**	NED	60	Pata Yamaha Official WorldSBK Team	Yamaha YZF R1	P	11.893s	16
5	**Alex Lowes**	GBR	22	Pata Yamaha Official WorldSBK Team	Yamaha YZF R1	P	13.145s	16
6	**Eugene Laverty**	IRL	50	Milwaukee Aprilia	Aprilia RSV4 RF	P	14.210s	16
7	**Lorenzo Savadori**	ITA	32	Milwaukee Aprilia	Aprilia RSV4 RF	P	17.051s	16
8	**Chaz Davies**	GBR	7	Aruba.it Racing - Ducati	Ducati Panigale R	P	17.743s	16
9	**Leon Camier**	GBR	2	Red Bull Honda World Superbike Team	Honda CBR1000RR	P	18.104s	16
10	**Toprak Razgatlioglu**	TUR	54	Kawasaki Puccetti Racing	Kawasaki ZX-10RR	P	21.783s	16
11	**Yonny Hernandez**	COL	68	Team Pedercini Racing	Kawasaki ZX-10RR	P	30.614s	16
12	**Leandro Mercado**	ARG	36	Orelac Racing VerdNatura	Kawasaki ZX-10RR	P	31.111s	16
13	**Roman Ramos**	ESP	40	Team GoEleven Kawasaki	Kawasaki ZX-10RR	P	31.188s	16
14	**Xavi Fores**	ESP	12	Barni Racing Team	Ducati Panigale R	P	31.864s	16
15	**Michael Ruben Rinaldi**	ITA	21	Aruba.it Racing - Junior Team	Ducati Panigale R	P	33.079s	16
16	PJ Jacobsen	USA	99	TripleM Honda World Superbike Team	Honda CBR1000RR	P	33.685s	16
17	Ondrej Jezek	CZE	37	Guandalini Racing	Yamaha YZF R1	P	53.662s	16
18	Loris Baz	FRA	76	GULF ALTHEA BMW Racing Team	BMW S 1000 RR	P	1m 44.844s	16
	Jordi Torres	ESP	81	MV Agusta Reparto Corse	MV Agusta 1000 F4	P	DNF	6
	Jake Gagne	USA	45	Red Bull Honda World Superbike Team	Honda CBR1000RR	P	DNF	4

Fastest race lap: J.Rea on lap 2, 1m 59.535s, 101.11mph/162.72km/h.

Race 2: 18 laps, 60.431 miles/97.254km

Time of race: 36m 23.516s · **Average speed:** 99.633mph/160.344km/h

Pos.	Rider	Time & Gap	Laps
1	**Alex Lowes**		18
2	**Michael van der Mark**	2.167s	18
3	**Chaz Davies**	7.649s	18
4	**Eugene Laverty**	9.422s	18
5	**Lorenzo Savadori**	9.716s	18
6	**Michael Ruben Rinaldi**	12.967s	18
7	**Leon Camier**	17.341s	18
8	**Xavi Fores**	20.293s	18
9	**Toprak Razgatlioglu**	23.613s	18
10	**Roman Ramos**	24.670s	18
11	**Loris Baz**	25.106s	18
12	**Jake Gagne**	25.212s	18
13	**PJ Jacobsen**	28.172s	18
14	**Yonny Hernandez**	31.659s	18
15	**Marco Melandri**	32.407s	18
16	Tom Sykes	36.305s	18
17	Leandro Mercado	39.367s	18
18	Ondrej Jezek	44.976s	18
	Jordi Torres	DNF	5
	Jonathan Rea	DNF	2

Superpole		
1	Sykes	1m 57.687s
2	Rea	1m 57.885s
3	Melandri	1m 57.899s
4	Lowes	1m 58.172s
5	Laverty	1m 58.187s
6	Van der Mark	1m 58.223s
7	Savadori	1m 58.300s
8	Baz	1m 58.389s
9	Davies	1m 59.011s
10	Camier	1m 59.041s
11	Rinaldi	1m 59.346s
12	Hernandez	1m 59.508s
13	Fores	1m 59.854s
14	Ramos	1m 59.989s
15	Razgatlioglu	2m 00.107s
16	Mercado	2m 00.391s
17	Jacobsen	2m 00.437s
18	Torres	2m 00.672s
19	Gagne	2m 00.845s
20	Jezek	2m 02.766s

Fastest race lap: M.Melandri on lap 3, 2m 0.176s, 100.57mph/161.85km/h.

Lap record: C.Crutchlow, 1m 59.291s, 101.31mph/163.05km/h (2010).

Points

1, Rea 270; 2, Davies 205; 3, Van der Mark 196; 4, Sykes 179; 5, Melandri 157 6, Lowes 154; 7, Fores 134; 8, Razgatlioglu 91; 9, Savadori 73; 10, Camier 72; 11, Baz 72; 12, Torres 64; 13, Laverty 60; 14, Rinaldi 54; 15, Mercado 42; 16, Ramos 41; 17, Gagne 24; 18, Jacobsen 21; 19, Hernandez 18; 20, Haslam 14; 21, Giugliano 11; 22, Ray 3; 23, Mossey 2; 24, Jezek 2.

WORLD SUPERBIKE CHAMPIONSHIP · 2018

MOTUL

Round 8 LAGUNA SECA, USA · 23–24 June, 2018 · 2.240-mile/3.610km circuit · WEATHER: Race 1 · Dry · Track 48°C · Air 28°C; Race 2 · Dry · Track 41°C · Air 20°C

Race 1: 25 laps, 56.079 miles/90.250km
Time of race: 35m 15.071s · **Average speed:** 95.450mph/153.612km/h

Pos.	Rider	Nat.	No.	Entrant	Machine	Tyres	Time & Gap	Laps
1	**Jonathan Rea**	GBR	1	Kawasaki Racing Team WorldSBK	Kawasaki ZX-10RR	P		25
2	**Chaz Davies**	GBR	7	Aruba.it Racing - Ducati	Ducati Panigale R	P	2.978s	25
3	**Alex Lowes**	GBR	22	Pata Yamaha Official WorldSBK Team	Yamaha YZF R1	P	12.212s	25
4	**Eugene Laverty**	IRL	50	Milwaukee Aprilia	Aprilia RSV4 RF	P	14.309s	25
5	**Marco Melandri**	ITA	33	Aruba.it Racing - Ducati	Ducati Panigale R	P	16.712s	25
6	**Xavi Fores**	ESP	12	Barni Racing Team	Ducati Panigale R	P	18.929s	25
7	**Tom Sykes**	GBR	66	Kawasaki Racing Team WorldSBK	Kawasaki ZX-10RR	P	25.638s	25
8	**Michael van der Mark**	NED	60	Pata Yamaha Official WorldSBK Team	Yamaha YZF R1	P	26.211s	25
9	**Jordi Torres**	ESP	81	MV Agusta Reparto Corse	MV Agusta 1000 F4	P	31.579s	25
10	**Jake Gagne**	USA	45	Red Bull Honda World Superbike Team	Honda CBR1000RR	P	38.084s	25
11	**Yonny Hernandez**	COL	68	Team Pedercini Racing	Kawasaki ZX-10RR	P	44.971s	25
12	**Roman Ramos**	ESP	40	Team GoEleven Kawasaki	Kawasaki ZX-10RR	P	45.412s	25
13	**Karel Hanika**	CZE	98	Guandalini Racing	Yamaha YZF R1	P	50.768s	25
14	**Lorenzo Savadori**	ITA	32	Milwaukee Aprilia	Aprilia RSV4 RF	P	1m 06.063s	25
15	**Loris Baz**	FRA	76	GULF ALTHEA BMW Racing Team	BMW S 1000 RR	P	1 Lap	24
	Toprak Razgatlioglu	TUR	54	Kawasaki Puccetti Racing	Kawasaki ZX-10RR	P	DNF	19
	Josh Herrin	USA	57	Attack 2Wheel Legal Yamaha	Yamaha YZF R1	P	DNF	18
	Leon Camier	GBR	2	Red Bull Honda World Superbike Team	Honda CBR1000RR	P	DNF	17
	PJ Jacobsen	USA	99	TripleM Honda World Superbike Team	Honda CBR1000RR	P	DNF	10
	Leandro Mercado	ARG	36	Orelac Racing VerdNatura	Kawasaki ZX-10RR	P	DNF	10

Fastest race lap: C.Davies on lap 2, 1m 23.041s, 97.24mph/156.50km/h.

Race 2: 25 laps, 56.079 miles/90.250km
Time of race: 35m 9.683s · **Average speed:** 95.694mph/154.004km/h

Pos.	Rider	Time & Gap	Laps
1	**Jonathan Rea**		25
2	**Chaz Davies**	5.099s	25
3	**Eugene Laverty**	6.711s	25
4	**Alex Lowes**	8.011s	25
5	**Michael van der Mark**	9.746s	25
6	**Xavi Fores**	14.791s	25
7	**Jordi Torres**	16.711s	25
8	**Tom Sykes**	17.284s	25
9	**Jake Gagne**	35.421s	25
10	**Loris Baz**	39.802s	25
11	**Leandro Mercado**	42.946s	25
12	**Roman Ramos**	43.437s	25
13	**Leon Camier**	44.563s	25
14	**Karel Hanika**	47.257s	25
15	**Yonny Hernandez**	53.415s	25
16	Josh Herrin	58.107s	25
	PJ Jacobsen	DNF	16
	Lorenzo Savadori	DNF	6
	Marco Melandri	DNF	3
	Toprak Razgatlioglu	DNS	0

Superpole		
1	Davies	1m 22.282s
2	Sykes	1m 22.297s
3	Rea	1m 22.359s
4	Laverty	1m 22.636s
5	Lowes	1m 22.729s
6	Savadori	1m 22.919s
7	Camier	1m 23.088s
8	Fores	1m 23.244s
9	Van der Mark	1m 23.253s
10	Melandri	1m 23.302s
11	Torres	1m 23.321s
12	Baz	No Time
13	Razgatlioglu	1m 23.776s
14	Mercado	1m 24.105s
15	Herrin	1m 24.182s
16	Gagne	1m 24.291s
17	Hernandez	1m 24.382s
18	Hanika	1m 24.746s
19	Jacobsen	1m 24.802s
20	Ramos	1m 24.836s

Fastest race lap: J.Rea on lap 5, 1m 23.480s, 96.74mph/155.68km/h.
Lap record: J.Rea, 1m 23.275s, 96.97mph/156.06km/h (2017).

Points

1, Rea 320; 2, Davies 245; 3, Van der Mark 215; 4, Sykes 196; 5, Lowes 183; 6, Melandri 168; 7, Fores 154; 8, Razgatlioglu 91; 9, Laverty 89; 10, Torres 80; 11, Baz 79; 12, Camier 75; 13, Savadori 75; 14, Rinaldi 54; 15, Ramos 49; 16, Mercado 47; 17, Gagne 37; 18, Hernandez 24; 19, Jacobsen 21; 20, Haslam 14; 21, Giugliano 11; 22, Hanika 5; 23, Ray 3; 24, Mossey 2; 25, Jezek 2.

Round 9 MISANO, Italy · 7–8 July, 2018 · 2.626-mile/4.226km circuit · WEATHER: Race 1 · Dry · Track 46°C · Air 28°C; Race 2 · Dry · Track 45°C · Air 29°C

Race 1: 21 laps, 55.144mi/88.746km
Time of race: 33m 31.846s · **Average speed:** 98.675mph/158.802km/h

Pos.	Rider	Nat.	No.	Entrant	Machine	Tyres	Time & Gap	Laps
1	**Jonathan Rea**	GBR	1	Kawasaki Racing Team WorldSBK	Kawasaki ZX-10RR	P		21
2	**Chaz Davies**	GBR	7	Aruba.it Racing - Ducati	Ducati Panigale R	P	2.791s	21
3	**Eugene Laverty**	IRL	50	Milwaukee Aprilia	Aprilia RSV4 RF	P	3.700s	21
4	**Michael van der Mark**	NED	60	Pata Yamaha Official WorldSBK Team	Yamaha YZF R1	P	4.921s	21
5	**Tom Sykes**	GBR	66	Kawasaki Racing Team WorldSBK	Kawasaki ZX-10RR	P	6.713s	21
6	**Xavi Fores**	ESP	12	Barni Racing Team	Ducati Panigale R	P	11.065s	21
7	**Marco Melandri**	ITA	33	Aruba.it Racing - Ducati	Ducati Panigale R	P	12.375s	21
8	**Lorenzo Savadori**	ITA	32	Milwaukee Aprilia	Aprilia RSV4 RF	P	12.995s	21
9	**Leon Camier**	GBR	2	Red Bull Honda World Superbike Team	Honda CBR1000RR	P	13.840s	21
10	**Leandro Mercado**	ARG	36	Orelac Racing VerdNatura	Kawasaki ZX-10RR	P	32.317s	21
11	**Toprak Razgatlioglu**	TUR	54	Kawasaki Puccetti Racing	Kawasaki ZX-10RR	P	36.316s	21
12	**Niccolo Canepa**	ITA	94	Yamaha Motor Europe	Yamaha YZF R1	P	37.665s	21
13	**Roman Ramos**	ESP	40	Team GoEleven Kawasaki	Kawasaki ZX-10RR	P	39.466s	21
14	**Jake Gagne**	USA	45	Red Bull Honda World Superbike Team	Honda CBR1000RR	P	39.896s	21
15	**Alessandro Andreozzi**	ITA	24	Guandalini Racing	Yamaha YZF R1	P	48.461s	21
16	PJ Jacobsen	USA	99	TripleM Honda World Superbike Team	Honda CBR1000RR	P	54.364s	21
17	Michael Ruben Rinaldi	ITA	21	Aruba.it Racing - Junior Team	Ducati Panigale R	P	3 Laps	18
18	Jordi Torres	ESP	81	MV Agusta Reparto Corse	MV Agusta 1000 F4	P	4 Laps	17
	Alex Lowes	GBR	22	Pata Yamaha Official WorldSBK Team	Yamaha YZF R1	P	DNF	9
	Yonny Hernandez	COL	68	Team Pedercini Racing	Kawasaki ZX-10RR	P	DNF	3
	Loris Baz	FRA	76	GULF ALTHEA BMW Racing Team	BMW S 1000 RR	P	DNF	1

Fastest race lap: J.Rea on lap 2, 1m 34.948s, 99.56mph/160.23km/h.

Race 2: 21 laps, 55.144mi/88.746km
Time of race: 33m 34.637s · **Average speed:** 98.538mph/158.582km/h

Pos.	Rider	Time & Gap	Laps
1	**Jonathan Rea**		21
2	**Michael van der Mark**	0.334s	21
3	**Marco Melandri**	0.595s	21
4	**Chaz Davies**	2.382s	21
5	**Tom Sykes**	4.535s	21
6	**Alex Lowes**	6.559s	21
7	**Lorenzo Savadori**	7.193s	21
8	**Eugene Laverty**	9.972s	21
9	**Loris Baz**	13.874s	21
10	**Leon Camier**	14.047s	21
11	**Michael Ruben Rinaldi**	26.003s	21
12	**Toprak Razgatlioglu**	28.886s	21
13	**Niccolo Canepa**	33.758s	21
14	**Jake Gagne**	34.751s	21
15	**Roman Ramos**	36.892s	21
16	Yonny Hernandez	36.983s	21
17	Leandro Mercado	56.465s	21
	PJ Jacobsen	DNF	19
	Alessandro Andreozzi	DNF	15
	Xavi Fores	DNF	2
	Jordi Torres	DNF	2

Superpole		
1	Sykes	1m 33.640s
2	Rea	1m 33.673s
3	Laverty	1m 34.281s
4	Fores	1m 34.363s
5	Savadori	1m 34.400s
6	Baz	1m 34.527s
7	Davies	1m 34.532s
8	Melandri	1m 34.533s
9	Torres	1m 34.569s
10	Camier	1m 34.597s
11	Van der Mark	1m 34.605s
12	Lowes	1m 35.239s
13	Mercado	1m 35.473s
14	Razgatlioglu	1m 35.869s
15	Hernandez	1m 35.918s
16	Canepa	1m 36.064s
17	Jacobsen	1m 36.233s
18	Ramos	1m 36.348s
19	Gagne	1m 36.599s
20	Rinaldi	1m 36.644s
21	Andreozzi	1m 37.297s

Fastest race lap: J.Rea on lap 10, 1m 34.944s, 99.57mph/160.24km/h.
Lap record: J.Rea, 1m 34.720s, 99.80mph/160.62km/h (2015).

Points

1, Rea 370; 2, Davies 278; 3, Van der Mark 248; 4, Sykes 218; 5, Melandri 193; 6, Lowes 193; 7, Fores 164; 8, Laverty 113; 9, Razgatlioglu 100; 10, Savadori 92; 11, Camier 88; 12, Baz 86; 13, Torres 80; 14, Rinaldi 59; 15, Mercado 53; 16, Ramos 53; 17, Gagne 41; 18, Hernandez 24; 19, Jacobsen 21; 20, Haslam 14; 21, Giugliano 11; 22, Canepa 7; 23, Hanika 5; 24, Ray 3; 25, Mossey 2; 26, Jezek 2; 27, Andreozzi 1.

WORLD SUPERBIKE CHAMPIONSHIP · 2018

MOTUL

Round 10 **PORTIMAO, Portugal** · 15–16 September, 2018 · 2.853-mile/4.592km circuit · WEATHER: Race 1 · Dry · Track 39°C · Air 29°C; Race 2 · Dry · Track 41°C · Air 29°C

Race 1: 20 laps, 57.067 miles/91.840km
Time of race: 34m 22.331s · **Average speed:** 99.616mph/160.316km/h

Pos.	Rider	Nat.	No.	Entrant	Machine	Tyres	Time & Gap	Laps
1	**Jonathan Rea**	GBR	1	Kawasaki Racing Team WorldSBK	Kawasaki ZX-10RR	P		20
2	**Marco Melandri**	ITA	33	Aruba.it Racing - Ducati	Ducati Panigale R	P	1.575s	20
3	**Michael van der Mark**	NED	60	Pata Yamaha Official WorldSBK Team	Yamaha YZF R1	P	4.215s	20
4	**Chaz Davies**	GBR	7	Aruba.it Racing - Ducati	Ducati Panigale R	P	10.760s	20
5	**Tom Sykes**	GBR	66	Kawasaki Racing Team WorldSBK	Kawasaki ZX-10RR	P	12.911s	20
6	**Loris Baz**	FRA	76	GULF ALTHEA BMW Racing Team	BMW S 1000 RR	P	19.685s	20
7	**Jordi Torres**	ESP	81	MV Agusta Reparto Corse	MV Agusta 1000 F4	P	21.974s	20
8	**Toprak Razgatlioglu**	TUR	54	Kawasaki Puccetti Racing	Kawasaki ZX-10RR	P	24.855s	20
9	**Michael Ruben Rinaldi**	ITA	21	Aruba.it Racing - Junior Team	Ducati Panigale R	P	30.302s	20
10	**Alex Lowes**	GBR	22	Pata Yamaha Official WorldSBK Team	Yamaha YZF R1	P	32.408s	20
11	**Leandro Mercado**	ARG	36	Orelac Racing VerdNatura	Kawasaki ZX-10RR	P	32.875s	20
12	**Yonny Hernandez**	COL	68	Team Pedercini Racing	Kawasaki ZX-10RR	P	39.178s	20
13	**Jake Gagne**	USA	45	Red Bull Honda World Superbike Team	Honda CBR1000RR	P	44.028s	20
14	**Roman Ramos**	ESP	40	Team GoEleven Kawasaki	Kawasaki ZX-10RR	P	56.896s	20
	PJ Jacobsen	USA	99	TripleM Honda World Superbike Team	Honda CBR1000RR	P	DNF	16
	Lorenzo Savadori	ITA	32	Milwaukee Aprilia	Aprilia RSV4 RF	P	DNF	11
	Jakub Smrz	CZE	96	Guandalini Racing	Yamaha YZF R1	P	DNF	11
	Leon Camier	GBR	2	Red Bull Honda World Superbike Team	Honda CBR1000RR	P	DNF	10
	Eugene Laverty	IRL	50	Milwaukee Aprilia	Aprilia RSV4 RF	P	DNF	0
	Xavi Fores	ESP	12	Barni Racing Team	Ducati Panigale R	P	DNF	0

Fastest race lap: J.Rea on lap 3, 1m 42.304s, 100.41mph/161.59km/h.

Race 2: : 20 laps, 57.067 miles/91.840km
Time of race: 34m 25.661s · **Average speed:** 99.455mph/160.057km/h

Pos.	Rider	Time & Gap	Laps
1	**Jonathan Rea**		20
2	**Michael van der Mark**	1.189s	20
3	**Marco Melandri**	2.813s	20
4	**Chaz Davies**	4.594s	20
5	**Tom Sykes**	4.834s	20
6	**Lorenzo Savadori**	11.417s	20
7	**Eugene Laverty**	11.732s	20
8	**Michael Ruben Rinaldi**	12.507s	20
9	**Loris Baz**	12.741s	20
10	**Xavi Fores**	18.973s	20
11	**Alex Lowes**	20.244s	20
12	**Jake Gagne**	20.943s	20
13	**Jordi Torres**	23.395s	20
14	**Leon Camier**	31.216s	20
15	**Leandro Mercado**	32.183s	20
16	Yonny Hernandez	33.076s	20
17	PJ Jacobsen	45.173s	20
	Jakub Smrz	DNF	13
	Toprak Razgatlioglu	DNF	12
	Roman Ramos	DNF	9

Superpole		
1	Laverty	1m 40.705s
2	Rea	1m 40.765s
3	Melandri	1m 40.856s
4	Savadori	1m 40.901s
5	Van der Mark	1m 40.926s
6	Sykes	1m 41.103s
7	Fores	1m 41.202s
8	Baz	1m 41.213s
9	Torres	1m 41.422s
10	Razgatlioglu	1m 41.960s
11	Rinaldi	1m 42.047s
12	Lowes	1m 42.709s
13	Camier	1m 42.019s
14	Davies	1m 42.045s
15	Gagne	1m 42.653s
16	Mercado	1m 42.812s
17	Hernandez	1m 42.844s
18	Jacobsen	1m 43.018s
19	Ramos	1m 43.586s
20	Smrz	1m 43.984s

Fastest race lap: M.Melandri on lap 2, 1m 42.385s, 100.33mph/161.46km/h.
Lap record: T. Sykes, 1m 42.475s, 100.24mph/161.32km/h (2013).

Points

1, Rea 420; 2, Davies 304; 3, Van der Mark 284; 4, Sykes 240; 5, Melandri 229; 6, Lowes 204; 7, Fores 170; 8, Laverty 122; 9, Razgatlioglu 108; 10, Baz 103; 11, Savadori 102; 12, Torres 92; 13, Camier 90; 14, Rinaldi 74; 15, Mercado 59; 16, Ramos 55; 17, Gagne 48; 18, Hernandez 28; 19, Jacobsen 21; 20, Haslam 14; 21, Giugliano 11; 22, Canepa 7; 23, Hanika 5; 24, Ray 3; 25, Mossey 2; 26, Jezek 2; 27, Andreozzi 1.

Round 11 **MAGNY-COURS, France** · 29–30 September, 2018 · 2.741-mile/4.411km circuit · WEATHER: Race 1 · Dry · Track 28°C · Air 18°C; Race 2 · Dry · Track 30°C · Air 20°C

Race 1: 21 laps, 57.558 miles/92.631km
Time of race: 34m 15.613s · **Average speed:** 100.802mph/162.225km/h

Pos.	Rider	Nat.	No.	Entrant	Machine	Tyres	Time & Gap	Laps
1	**Jonathan Rea**	GBR	1	Kawasaki Racing Team WorldSBK	Kawasaki ZX-10RR	P		21
2	**Tom Sykes**	GBR	66	Kawasaki Racing Team WorldSBK	Kawasaki ZX-10RR	P	3.091s	21
3	**Xavi Fores**	ESP	12	Barni Racing Team	Ducati Panigale R	P	8.558s	21
4	**Lorenzo Savadori**	ITA	32	Milwaukee Aprilia	Aprilia RSV4 RF	P	9.193s	21
5	**Chaz Davies**	GBR	7	Aruba.it Racing - Ducati	Ducati Panigale R	P	10.074s	21
6	**Marco Melandri**	ITA	33	Aruba.it Racing - Ducati	Ducati Panigale R	P	12.509s	21
7	**Michael van der Mark**	NED	60	Pata Yamaha Official WorldSBK Team	Yamaha YZF R1	P	14.733s	21
8	**Toprak Razgatlioglu**	TUR	54	Kawasaki Puccetti Racing	Kawasaki ZX-10RR	P	22.878s	21
9	**Eugene Laverty**	IRL	50	Milwaukee Aprilia	Aprilia RSV4 RF	P	23.028s	21
10	**Loris Baz**	FRA	76	GULF ALTHEA BMW Racing Team	BMW S 1000 RR	P	23.109s	21
11	**Leon Camier**	GBR	2	Red Bull Honda World Superbike Team	Honda CBR1000RR	P	24.709s	21
12	**Jordi Torres**	ESP	81	MV Agusta Reparto Corse	MV Agusta 1000 F4	P	32.766s	21
13	**Jake Gagne**	USA	45	Red Bull Honda World Superbike Team	Honda CBR1000RR	P	33.456s	21
14	**Leandro Mercado**	ARG	36	Orelac Racing VerdNatura	Kawasaki ZX-10RR	P	37.808s	21
15	**Roman Ramos**	ESP	40	Team GoEleven Kawasaki	Kawasaki ZX-10RR	P	46.558s	21
16	PJ Jacobsen	USA	99	TripleM Honda World Superbike Team	Honda CBR1000RR	P	49.525s	21
17	Jeremy Guarnoni	FRA	11	Team Pedercini Racing	Kawasaki ZX-10RR	P	57.484s	21
18	Alex Lowes	GBR	22	Pata Yamaha Official WorldSBK Team	Yamaha YZF R1	P	1m 12.942s	21
	Michael Ruben Rinaldi	ITA	21	Aruba.it Racing - Junior Team	Ducati Panigale R	P	DNF	2
	Matthieu Lussiana	FRA	121	Dreamteamcompany	Aprilia RSV4 RF	P	DNF	1
	Jakub Smrz	CZE	96	Guandalini Racing	Yamaha YZF R1	P	DNF	0

Fastest race lap: J. Rea on lap 8, 1m 37.152s, 101.56mph/163.45km/h.

Race 2: 21 laps, 57.558 miles/92.631km
Time of race: 34m 16.364s · **Average speed:** 100.765mph/162.166km/h

Pos.	Rider	Time & Gap	Laps
1	**Jonathan Rea**		21
2	**Chaz Davies**	1.804s	21
3	**Michael van der Mark**	3.552s	21
4	**Tom Sykes**	4.879s	21
5	**Marco Melandri**	6.505s	21
6	**Lorenzo Savadori**	11.477s	21
7	**Alex Lowes**	15.077s	21
8	**Xavi Fores**	17.339s	21
9	**Leon Camier**	17.655s	21
10	**Loris Baz**	22.725s	21
11	**Eugene Laverty**	23.257s	21
12	**Toprak Razgatlioglu**	23.637s	21
13	**Michael Ruben Rinaldi**	26.756s	21
14	**Jordi Torres**	28.178s	21
15	**Leandro Mercado**	29.292s	21
16	Jake Gagne	38.534s	21
17	PJ Jacobsen	42.776s	21
18	Roman Ramos	46.765s	21
19	Jeremy Guarnoni	51.689s	21
	Jakub Smrz	DNF	17
	Matthieu Lussiana	DNF	2

Superpole		
1	Sykes	1m 35.696s
2	Rea	1m 35.843s
3	Savadori	1m 36.564s
4	Fores	1m 36.613s
5	Lowes	1m 36.765s
6	Davies	1m 36.954s
7	Rinaldi	1m 36.999s
8	Baz	1m 37.055s
9	Razgatlioglu	1m 37.103s
10	Van der Mark	1m 37.239s
11	Camier	1m 37.398s
12	Melandri	1m 37.595s
13	Laverty	1m 37.617s
14	Gagne	1m 37.747s
15	Torres	1m 38.129s
16	Mercado	1m 38.176s
17	Jacobsen	1m 38.878s
18	Ramos	1m 39.188s
19	Guarnoni	1m 39.490s
20	Smrz	1m 39.713s
21	Lussiana	No Time

Fastest race lap: C. Davies on lap 2, 1m 37.363s, 101.35mph/163.10km/h.
Lap record: T. Sykes, 1m 37.864s, 100.82mph/162.26km/h (2016).

Points

1, Rea 470; 2, Davies 335; 3, Van der Mark 309; 4, Sykes 273; 5, Melandri 250; 6, Lowes 213; 7, Fores 194; 8, Laverty 134; 9, Savadori 125; 10, Razgatlioglu 120; 11, Baz 115; 12, Camier 102; 13, Torres 98; 14, Rinaldi 77; 15, Mercado 62; 16, Ramos 56; 17, Gagne 51; 18, Hernandez 28; 19, Jacobsen 21; 20, Haslam 14; 21, Giugliano 11; 22, Canepa 7; 23, Hanika 5; 24, Ray 3; 25, Mossey 2; 26, Jezek 2; 27, Andreozzi 1.

WORLD SUPERBIKE CHAMPIONSHIP · 2018

Round 12 SAN JUAN VILLICUM, Argentina · 13-14 October, 2018 · 2.657-mile/4.276km circuit · WEATHER: Race 1 · Dry · Track 35°C · Air 21°C; Race 2 · Dry · Track 43°C · Air 24°C

Race 1: 21 laps, 55.797mi/89.796km
Time of race: 34m 55.037s · **Average speed:** 95.878mph/154.301km/h

Pos.	Rider	Nat.	No.	Entrant	Machine	Tyres	Time & Gap	Laps
1	**Jonathan Rea**	GBR	1	Kawasaki Racing Team WorldSBK	Kawasaki ZX-10RR	P		21
2	**Marco Melandri**	ITA	33	Aruba.it Racing - Ducati	Ducati Panigale R	P	9.163s	21
3	**Toprak Razgatlioglu**	TUR	54	Kawasaki Puccetti Racing	Kawasaki ZX-10RR	P	11.410s	21
4	**Xavi Fores**	ESP	12	Barni Racing Team	Ducati Panigale R	P	11.796s	21
5	**Eugene Laverty**	IRL	50	Milwaukee Aprilia	Aprilia RSV4 RF	P	12.441s	21
6	**Tom Sykes**	GBR	66	Kawasaki Racing Team WorldSBK	Kawasaki ZX-10RR	P	12.690s	21
7	**Alex Lowes**	GBR	22	Pata Yamaha Official WorldSBK Team	Yamaha YZF R1	P	15.597s	21
8	**Michael van der Mark**	NED	60	Pata Yamaha Official WorldSBK Team	Yamaha YZF R1	P	16.846s	21
9	**Loris Baz**	FRA	76	GULF ALTHEA BMW Racing Team	BMW S 1000 RR	P	28.117s	21
10	**Leon Camier**	GBR	2	Red Bull Honda World Superbike Team	Honda CBR1000RR	P	28.164s	21
11	**Florian Marino**	FRA	51	TripleM Honda World Superbike Team	Honda CBR1000RR	P	41.449s	21
12	**Roman Ramos**	ESP	40	Team GoEleven Kawasaki	Kawasaki ZX-10RR	P	41.783s	21
13	**Maximiliam Scheib**	CHI	77	MV Agusta Reparto Corse	MV Agusta 1000 F4	P	47.736s	21
14	**Gabriele Ruiu**	ITA	16	Team Pedercini Racing	Kawasaki ZX-10RR	P	55.986s	21
	Lorenzo Savadori	ITA	32	Milwaukee Aprilia	Aprilia RSV4 RF	P	DNF	15
	Chaz Davies	GBR	7	Aruba.it Racing - Ducati	Ducati Panigale R	P	DNF	12
	Jake Gagne	USA	45	Red Bull Honda World Superbike Team	Honda CBR1000RR	P	DNF	6
	Leandro Mercado	ARG	36	Orelac Racing VerdNatura	Kawasaki ZX-10RR	P	DNF	4
	Jakub Smrz	CZE	96	Guandalini Racing	Yamaha YZF R1	P	DNS	0

Fastest race lap: J. Rea on lap 11, 1m 39.175s, 96.45mph/155.22km/h.

Race 2: 21 laps, 55.797mi/89.796km
Time of race: 35m 13.668s, · **Average speed:** 95.033mph/152.941km/h

Pos.	Rider	Time & Gap	Laps
1	**Jonathan Rea**		21
2	**Xavi Fores**	3.273s	21
3	**Marco Melandri**	4.660s	21
4	**Chaz Davies**	6.838s	21
5	**Tom Sykes**	9.377s	21
6	**Alex Lowes**	10.945s	21
7	**Toprak Razgatlioglu**	12.638s	21
8	**Lorenzo Savadori**	13.958s	21
9	**Michael van der Mark**	15.715s	21
10	**Jake Gagne**	20.861s	21
11	**Loris Baz**	25.595s	21
12	**Leandro Mercado**	33.171s	21
13	**Roman Ramos**	47.254s	21
14	**Gabriele Ruiu**	55.140s	21
	Maximiliam Scheib	DNF	12
	Leon Camier	DNF	7
	Eugene Laverty	DNF	2
	Florian Marino	DNF	1
	Jakub Smrz	DNF	1

Superpole		
1	Melandri	1m 39.012s
2	Rea	1m 39.452s
3	Laverty	1m 39.530s
4	Sykes	1m 39.558s
5	Fores	1m 39.590s
6	Lowes	1m 39.730s
7	Razgatlioglu	1m 40.070s
8	Savadori	1m 40.083s
9	Davies	1m 40.094s
10	Camier	1m 40.189s
11	Van der Mark	1m 40.343s
12	Mercado	1m 40.349s
13	Baz	1m 40.352s
14	Gagne	1m 40.718s
15	Marino	1m 41.484s
16	Scheib	1m 41.714s
17	Ramos	1m 41.893s
18	Smrz	1m 42.041s
19	Ruiu	1m 42.093s

Fastest race lap: J. Rea on lap 14, 1m 39.807s, 95.83mph/154.23km/h.
Lap record: New Circuit.

Points

1, Rea 520; 2, Davies 348; 3, Van der Mark 324; 4, Sykes 294; 5, Melandri 286; 6, Lowes 232; 7, Fores 227; 8, Razgatlioglu 145; 9, Laverty 145; 10, Savadori 133; 11, Baz 127; 12, Camier 108; 13, Torres 98; 14, Rinaldi 77; 15, Mercado 66; 16, Ramos 63; 17, Gagne 57; 18, Hernandez 28; 19, Jacobsen 21; 20, Haslam 14; 21, Giugliano 11; 22, Canepa 7; 23, Marino 5; 24, Hanika 5; 25, Ruiu 4; 26, Scheib 3; 27, Ray 3; 28, Mossey 2; 29, Jezek 2; 30, Andreozzi 1.

Round 13 LOSAIL, Qatar · 26-27 October, 2018 · 3.343-mile/5.380km circuit · WEATHER: Race 1 · Dry · Track 30°C · Air 30°C

Race 1: 17 laps, 56.831 miles/91.460km
Time of race: 33m 34.913s · **Average speed:** 101.538mph/163.410km/h

Pos.	Rider	Nat.	No.	Entrant	Machine	Tyres	Time & Gap	Laps
1	**Jonathan Rea**	GBR	1	Kawasaki Racing Team WorldSBK	Kawasaki ZX-10RR	P		17
2	**Tom Sykes**	GBR	66	Kawasaki Racing Team WorldSBK	Kawasaki ZX-10RR	P	1.424s	17
3	**Alex Lowes**	GBR	22	Pata Yamaha Official WorldSBK Team	Yamaha YZF R1	P	3.705s	17
4	**Eugene Laverty**	IRL	50	Milwaukee Aprilia	Aprilia RSV4 RF	P	4.723s	17
5	**Marco Melandri**	ITA	33	Aruba.it Racing - Ducati	Ducati Panigale R	P	10.579s	17
6	**Loris Baz**	FRA	76	GULF ALTHEA BMW Racing Team	BMW S 1000 RR	P	13.173s	17
7	**Michael van der Mark**	NED	60	Pata Yamaha Official WorldSBK Team	Yamaha YZF R1	P	14.557s	17
8	**Chaz Davies**	GBR	7	Aruba.it Racing - Ducati	Ducati Panigale R	P	17.216s	17
9	**Jake Gagne**	USA	45	Red Bull Honda World Superbike Team	Honda CBR1000RR	P	17.277s	17
10	**Toprak Razgatlioglu**	TUR	54	Kawasaki Puccetti Racing	Kawasaki ZX-10RR	P	18.179s	17
11	**Lorenzo Savadori**	ITA	32	Milwaukee Aprilia	Aprilia RSV4 RF	P	24.924s	17
12	**Leandro Mercado**	ARG	36	Orelac Racing VerdNatura	Kawasaki ZX-10RR	P	30.183s	17
13	**Xavi Fores**	ESP	12	Barni Racing Team	Ducati Panigale R	P	34.931s	17
14	**Roman Ramos**	ESP	40	Team GoEleven Kawasaki	Kawasaki ZX-10RR	P	46.851s	17
15	**Gabriele Ruiu**	ITA	16	Team Pedercini Racing	Kawasaki ZX-10RR	P	58.890s	17
	Maximillian Scheib	CHI	77	MV Agusta Reparto Corse	MV Agusta 1000 F4	P	DNF	8
	Leon Camier	GBR	2	Red Bull Honda World Superbike Team	Honda CBR1000RR	P	DNF	7

Fastest race lap: J. Rea on lap 2, 1m 57.284s, 102.61mph/165.14km/h.
Lap record: J. Rea, 1m 56.974s, 102.89mph/165.58km/h (2016).

Race 2: Cancelled due to track conditions.

Superpole		
1	Sykes	1m 56.124s
2	Rea	1m 56.255s
3	Lowes	1m 56.355s
4	Laverty	1m 56.534s
5	Savadori	1m 56.959s
6	Fores	1m 57.281s
7	Baz	1m 57.347s
8	Van der Mark	1m 57.362s
9	Melandri	1m 57.407s
10	Camier	1m 57.682s
11	Razgatlioglu	1m 57.695s
12	Davies	1m 57.867s
13	Mercado	1m 58.440s
14	Gagne	1m 58.559s
15	Ruiu	1m 58.956s
16	Ramos	1m 59.300s
17	Scheib	1m 59.390s

Points

1, Rea 545; 2, Davies 356; 3, Van der Mark333; 4, Sykes 314; 5, Melandri 297; 6, Lowes 248; 7, Fores 230; 8, Laverty 158; 9, Razgatlioglu 151; 10, Savadori 138; 11, Baz 137; 12, Camier 108; 13, Torres 98; 14, Rinaldi 77; 15, Mercado 70; 16, Ramos 65; 17, Gagne 64; 18, Hernandez 28; 19, Jacobsen 21; 20, Haslam 14; 21, Giugliano 11; 22, Canepa 7; 23, Marino 5; 24, Hanika 5; 25, Ruiu 5; 26, Scheib 3; 27, Ray 3; 28, Mossey 2; 29, Jezek 2; 30, Andreozzi 1.

2018 FINAL POINTS TABLE

Position	Rider	Nationality	Machine	Phillip Island/1	Phillip Island/2	Buriram/1	Buriram/2	Aragon/1	Aragon/2	Assen/1	Assen/2	Imola/1	Imola/2	Donington/1	Donington/2	Brno/1	Brno/2	Laguna Seca/1	Laguna Seca/2	Misano/1	Misano/2	Portimao/1	Portimao/2	Magny-Cours/1	Magny-Cours/2	San Juan Villicum/1	San Juan Villicum/2	Losail/1	Losai/2l	Total Points
1	**Jonathan Rea**	GBR	Kawasaki	11	20	25	13	25	20	25	20	25	25	20	16	25	-	25	25	25	25	25	25	25	25	25	25	25	-	**545**
2	**Chaz Davies**	GBR	Ducati	16	-	16	25	20	25	16	11	13	20	8	11	8	16	20	20	20	13	13	13	11	20	-	13	8	-	**356**
3	**Michael van der Mark**	NED	Yamaha	7	9	9	20	11	11	20	16	10	-	25	25	13	20	8	11	13	20	16	20	9	16	8	7	9	-	**333**
4	**Tom Sykes**	GBR	Kawasaki	20	13	10	-	10	10	13	25	20	16	16	10	16	-	9	8	11	11	11	11	20	13	10	11	20	-	**314**
5	**Marco Melandri**	ITA	Ducati	25	25	8	9	13	16	10	9	16	-	-	5	20	1	11	-	9	16	20	16	10	11	20	16	11	-	**297**
6	**Alex Lowes**	GBR	Yamaha	10	11	11	16	9	13	4	2	6	10	13	13	11	25	16	13	-	10	6	5	-	9	9	10	16	-	**248**
7	**Xavi Fores**	SPA	Ducati	13	16	20	11	16	-	11	13	11	13	-	-	2	8	10	10	10	-	-	6	16	8	13	20	3	-	**230**
8	**Eugene Laverty**	IRL	Aprilia	8	1	7	-	-	-	-	-	4	7	10	-	10	13	13	16	16	8	-	9	7	5	11	-	13	-	**158**
9	**Toprak Razgatlioglu**	TUR	Kawasaki	3	6	1	8	7	7	6	7	5	8	-	20	6	7	-	-	5	4	8	-	8	4	16	9	6	-	**151**
10	**Lorenzo Savadori**	ITA	Aprilia	-	-	4	7	1	6	1	6	8	-	11	9	9	11	2	-	8	9	-	10	13	10	-	8	5	-	**138**
11	**Loris Baz**	FRA	BMW	5	7	5	4	5	1	9	8	3	5	9	6	-	5	1	6	-	7	10	7	6	6	7	5	10	-	**137**
12	**Leon Camier**	GBR	Honda	9	10	13	10	-	-	-	-	-	-	6	8	7	9	-	3	7	6	-	2	5	7	6	-	-	-	**108**
13	**Jordi Torres**	SPA	MV Agusta	-	8	6	-	-	8	7	10	2	11	5	7	-	-	7	9	-	-	9	3	4	2	-	-	-	-	**98**
14	**Michael Ruben Rinaldi**	ITA	Ducati	-	-	-	-	8	9	-	4	9	9	4	-	1	10	-	-	-	5	7	8	-	3	-	-	-	-	**77**
15	**Leandro Mercado**	ARG	Kawasaki	6	4	3	-	-	3	8	-	1	6	3	4	4	-	-	5	6	-	5	1	2	1	-	4	4	-	**70**
16	**Roman Ramos**	SPA	Kawasaki	2	5	2	3	6	5	5	-	-	4	-	-	3	6	4	4	3	1	2	-	1	-	4	3	2	-	**65**
17	**Jake Gagne**	USA	Honda	4	3	-	2	4	4	-	-	-	-	-	3	-	4	6	7	2	2	3	4	3	-	-	6	7	-	**64**
18	**Yonny Hernandez**	COL	Kawasaki	-	-	-	5	2	-	1	-	3	-	5	2	5	1	-	-	4	-	-	-	-	-	-	-	-	-	**28**
19	**PJ Jacobsen**	USA	Honda	-	2	-	6	-	2	2	3	-	2	1	-	-	3	-	-	-	-	-	-	-	-	-	-	-	-	**21**
20	**Leon Haslam**	GBR	Kawasaki	-	-	-	-	-	-	-	-	7	-	7	-	-	-	-	-	-	-	-	-	-	-	-	-	-	-	**14**
21	**Davide Giugliano**	ITA	Aprilia	-	-	-	-	3	-	3	5	-	-	-	-	-	-	-	-	-	-	-	-	-	-	-	-	-	-	**11**
22	**Niccolo Canepa**	ITA	Yamaha	-	-	-	-	-	-	-	-	-	-	-	-	-	-	-	-	4	3	-	-	-	-	-	-	-	-	**7**
23	**Florian Marino**	FRA	Honda	-	-	-	-	-	-	-	-	-	-	-	-	-	-	-	-	-	-	-	-	-	-	5	-	-	-	**5**
24	**Karel Hanika**	CZE	Yamaha	-	-	-	-	-	-	-	-	-	-	-	-	-	-	3	2	-	-	-	-	-	-	-	-	-	-	**5**
25	**Gabriele Ruiu**	ITA	Kawasaki	-	-	-	-	-	-	-	-	-	-	-	-	-	-	-	-	-	-	-	-	-	-	2	2	1	-	**5**
26	**Maximilian Scheib**	CHI	MV Agusta	-	-	-	-	-	-	-	-	-	-	-	-	-	-	-	-	-	-	-	-	-	-	3	-	-	-	**3**
27	**Bradley Ray**	GBR	Suzuki	-	-	-	-	-	-	-	-	-	-	2	1	-	-	-	-	-	-	-	-	-	-	-	-	-	-	**3**
28	**Luke Mossey**	GBR	Kawasaki	-	-	-	-	-	-	-	-	-	-	-	2	-	-	-	-	-	-	-	-	-	-	-	-	-	-	**2**
29	**Ondrej Jezek**	CZE	Yamaha	1	-	-	-	-	-	-	-	-	1	-	-	-	-	-	-	-	-	-	-	-	-	-	-	-	-	**2**
30	**Alessandro Andreozzi**	ITA	Yamaha	-	-	-	-	-	-	-	-	-	-	-	-	-	-	-	-	1	-	-	-	-	-	-	-	-	-	**1**

MAKING HISTORY

By GORDON RITCHIE

Main: French trio Corentin Perolari (6), Jules Cluzel (16) and Lucas Mahias (144) splash away in the Qatar finale. The subsequent Superbike race was cancelled.

Inset, left: Sandro Cortese celebrates his championship.
Photos: Gold & Goose

Above: The Supersport title was a career saver for former Moto3 champion Sandro Cortese.

Top right: Defending champion Lucas Mahias surrendered his crown, but narrowly pipped compatriot Cluzel to second.

Above right: Jules Cluzel battled Cortese all year.

Right: Another of the dominant Yamaha riders, Federico Caricasulo took a home win at Misano.

Below right: Randy Krummenacher started strong, but faded somewhat later in the year.

Below far right: After 125 races and 43 wins, injury forced all-time Supersport superstar Kenan Sofuoglu into retirement.

Photos: Gold & Goose

YAMAHA riders might have dominated it, but the FIM Supersport World Championship of 2018 proved to be competitive, unpredictable and historic in all other ways. There was also a brand-new champion in the form of class rookie Sandro Cortese (Kallio Racing Yamaha), who added the title to his status as Moto3 champion. Kallio Racing is a Finnish privateer team, which brought another underdog twist to the compelling action across all 12 rounds.

Some threads of WorldSSP history were wound up, too.

After five world championship wins and enough trophies to block the Bosphorus, Turkish legend Kenan Sofuoglu finally retired. His title quintet, 43 race wins, 85 podium places and 34 poles are all record scores, which came in the course of 126 race starts. He had been the World Supersport gold standard for years: if a rider could beat him over the season, then almost invariably he would become world champion.

Sofuoglu was a reluctant retiree, but serious pelvic injuries in 2017 and another big hit in round one of the 2018 season were deciding factors.

The first round at Phillip Island was plagued by the usual tyre blistering, and worse. Modern WorldSSP machines are just too much for grooved DOT tyres over a (supposed) full race distance at the mercilessly left-handed circuit.

Sofuoglu's fast crash in FP3 re-rattled his pelvis, which was still healing, hurt both hands and caused some serious soft tissue impacts. Being Sofuoglu, he raced anyway.

A planned two-part 15-lap race was red-flagged, then abandoned in favour of a single nine-lap sprint. Sofuoglu was up to third at one stage, but dropped to an eventual 13th, feeling a vibration and worrying that his tyres were going to fail again.

Mahias was the clear winner, having also taken Superpole, with Randy Krummenacher (Bardahl Evan Bros Racing Yamaha) second and Cortese outfoxing Mahias' GRT Yamaha team-mate, Federico Caricasulo, for third place in his very first WorldSSP race. The top four riders were covered by 1.556 seconds.

Next came a very different circuit in Thailand, where Krummenacher took the prize. Five riders fought it out, but when Jules Cluzel (NRT Yamaha) fell, it was down to four.

A last-corner gladiatorial clash between Krummenacher and Mahias resulted in the Swiss winning by just 0.041 of a second, with Caricasulo getting the better of Cortese for third. There was no Sofuoglu; he had been diagnosed with more damage to his pelvis after his big Aussie off.

At Aragon, we saw a novelty in the class, as Cortese took his first pole and then his first win. In the wastelands in the winter, he had been rescued by the talented, but taciturn Finns of the Kallio Racing Team.

His payback began in earnest at this round, after a fight with the other podium men, Caricasulo and Cluzel, turned into victory by 1.426 seconds, with his rivals locked in a close fight for second. Mahias was five seconds from the win, in fourth.

Assen provided one of those races that had everything, and dramas before, during and after. In many ways, it was a leveller, and great rolling theatre was laid on for the large local crowd.

Anthony West (EAB antwest Racing Kawasaki) had injured his wrist, and in a season that was darkening after his early high hopes, he missed the Assen round.

Krummenacher had to return to the pits for more fuel and started from the very back. That made his run to second, behind the resurgent Cluzel, all the more remarkable to watch.

Cluzel won by 0.291 of a second, from Krummenacher, with competitive MV Agusta Reparto Corse by Vamag rider Raffaele De Rosa right in the slipstream for third. Mahias was fourth, and Luke Stapleford (Profile Racing Triumph) fifth, still less than a second down on the win. Cortese was sixth, just 1.112 seconds back.

Then Stapleford was hit with a post-race ride-through time penalty following a collision with Caricasulo, but subsequently he was exonerated.

There was still no Sofuoglu at Assen, and rumours of re-

tirement were building. Against medical advice, he tried to ride at his Kawasaki Puccetti Racing squad's home round at Imola. He took part in practice, but realised that the race would be beyond him. Bowing to pressure from family and friends, he withdrew.

Cluzel was on top again, from Caricasulo, De Rosa and Cortese, the top four all inside the same second once more.

Donington was next up, and again the Yamaha hegemony was infiltrated by De Rosa and his MV. Cortese won from Cluzel, with De Rosa third; then Krummenacher fourth, Mahias fifth and Caricasulo sixth.

A return to Brno, and the two riders who eventually would duel for the championship slugged it out between the trees that hug the magnificent circuit. Cluzel triumphed by 0.148 of a second, with De Rosa just over three seconds back.

Before the start of an obscenely long summer break, there was virtually a mini summer break of a month between Brno and Misano.

Races at the seaside track are always popular, but in 2018 it was particularly special for the fans, who watched Caricasulo win the race by 1.4 seconds from another Italian, De Rosa, with a German of Italian extraction, Cortese, third.

At Portimao, when the season resumed for a rush of four races, Mahias was so potent on his Yamaha that he beat Caricasulo by nearly three seconds, with Kyle Smith (CIA Landlord Insurance) completing the first Honda top-three finish of the year. But not before dramas that lifted the tension to the point of being almost unbearable.

Mahias had been leading until a cruel puncture, and shortly after, a crash for two riders brought out the red flag. Sniffing a finish after all, Mahias got back on and rode slowly back on a completely flat tyre. He fell off more than once, and then reached the pit lane from the alternate entry reserved for marshals and rescue vehicles.

He lost his points, as did Cluzel when Cortese crashed

in front for him and both went down. Cortese remounted to take sixth place.

Two weeks later, it was France, and another immaculate win for Cluzel, now closing in on points leader Cortese. Sandro was second, however, having won out in a final battle with Mahias.

The brilliant, but not quite complete, Argentine circuit of Villicum produced some problems, but they were overcome most effectively by the top three riders of the current season, Cluzel, Cortese and Mahias, who repeated their finishing order in France.

The finale, in the desert of Qatar, was simply mind blowing, both before and during the race.

After the scene had been set for a bumper race-day, a gigantic sandstorm, a rainstorm and finally a track that was flooded in some key areas produced the trickiest of conditions for Cortese and Cluzel to determine who would become the champion.

With Mahias' points for his flat-tyre 'win' at Portimao having been restored, his opportunity to finish second overall would have a bearing on the final outcome.

Cluzel and Cortese fought it out for the win, in race and championship. Instead of the six-point advantage Cortese had had over Cluzel entering Qatar, however, the difference had been cut to five after Mahias' surprise reinstatement of points. So if Cluzel won and Cortese was second, Cluzel would end up champion after all, equal on points, but with more wins in the locker.

In an epic race for all manner of reasons between Cortese and Cluzel, the Frenchman eventually tried too hard, after Mahias – sensing another victory – had overtaken the long-time leading duo. Now Cluzel would not have enough points just by beating Cortese. He tried the impossible – and fell. He restarted, but fell again, much more heavily, and Cortese was already champion.

Mahias, Cortese and Caricasulo filled the final podium places of the year, and to add insult to another nasty ankle injury for Cluzel, he dropped to third overall. It was a savage end to his season. But it was career redemption for Cortese and vindication for the privateer Kallio Racing team.

The European Supersport Championship-within-a-champi-

Above: Markus Reiterberger stepped down from WorldSBK to win the Superstock 1000 title for BMW.

Left: Mika Perez lost out to Carrasco by a single point in the Supersport 300 championship.

Far left: Ecstatic Cortese and his Kallio Racing crew share the moment at Losail.

Centre row, from left: Raffaele De Rosa took five podiums for MV Agusta; it was win or bust for Cluzel in Qatar; Rob Hartog claimed the European Championship class on his Kawasaki.

Below left: Honda's Kyle Smith struggled against the Yamahas, scoring just a single podium at Portimao.

Below: Supersport 300 champion Ana Carrasco celebrates the result of riding like a girl.

Photos: Gold & Goose

onship, conceived for riders who only competed in the European races, was won by Rob Hartog (Team Hartog Against Cancer Kawasaki).

FIM Supersport 300 World Championship

Leading lady Ana Carrasco (21, DS Junior Team Kawasaki) starred in her own truly, madly, deeply historic world championship-winning epic in eight parts. It was a European motorbike drama with a climax so tense and unpredictable that Hollywood producers would have thrown it out after a first reading. Too fantastical – a woman world champion?

With some newly homologated bikes in 2018, like the KTM RC390R and the Kawasaki Ninja 400, there was a great deal of pre-season performance equalisation by the regulators, and too much mid-season rule modifying – however necessary – to keep things in balance. Yamaha, with a 300 not a 400, were so much on the back foot that the original handicapping rules were given the boot after one round. The true nature of competitiveness in this class is a matter of a few revs, a few cubic centimetres or a few kilograms, from each bike or each rider.

Seven riders won races and 14 stood on the podium, so the races were statistically and entertainingly close.

After the first rule fiddling, it became obvious that such a talent as Carrasco, allied to her tiny frame and commensurately light weight, would run away with it. After two consecutive clear wins, the minimum weight rules were tweaked again, closing things up all the more.

In the Magny-Cours finale, Carrasco finished a lowly 13th, but was champion all the same. Potential champion Scott Deroue (MRM Kawasaki) had suffered a technical failure, and Mika Perez (ParkinGO Kawasaki) had lost the lead of the race – and championship – two corners from the end.

Carrasco might have won the title by a single point, a margin that seemed thinner than her bike's paintwork, but she performed a determined feat that many had said simply could not be done – beating the men and big boys at their own game. 'Ride Like A Girl', as her own championship T-shirt proclaimed during her victory lap.

Superstock 1000 European Championship

With Dorna's philosophy, STK1000 had to go sooner or later. Already downgraded from an FIM cup to a European championship, the series received its death sentence at the end of 2017 and the *coup de grace* in autumn, 2018.

With 2017 champion Michael Ruben Rinaldi and his main rival, Toprak Razgatlioglu, having gone to WorldSBK for 2018 (following many previous top Stock riders of the past), one big name joined the class, tipped for success.

BMW's favourite Bavarian son, Markus Reiterberger (alpha Racing Van Zon BMW), recovered from the disappointments of recent WorldSBK reversals with a sometimes dominant and sometimes workmanlike season for Superstock's last hurrah.

Roberto Tamburini (Berclaz Racing Team BMW) pushed Reiterberger hardest, while others such as Maximilian Scheib (Aprilia Racing Team) and final-round winner Federico Sandi (Motocorsa Racing Ducati) made sure everybody stayed honest over all eight races.

BMW, Ducati and Aprilia fielded race-winning bikes, and eight riders made it to the podium. The championship fight went to the final round, as had been common since 1999, this time at Magny-Cours.

Reiterberger was well clear on points, but catchable if he suffered a real disaster. And he nearly blew it. He recovered from a fast off-track excursion while chasing a final win, however, and third place gave him an unassailable lead from Tamburini and Scheib.

Reiterberger won four races; Matteo Ferrari (Barni Racing Ducati) took a local victory at Imola as a wild-card; while Tamburini, Scheib and Sandi claimed a win apiece.

ISLE OF MAN TT

ALL SHOOK UP!

By OLI RUSHBY

Above: Tucked in and flying. Peter Hickman en route to his second win of the week in the Senior.
Photo: David Collister/photocycles.com

Right: Another BMW in the air. Michael Dunlop triumphed in the opening Superbike race.
Photo: Monster Energy

THE Isle of Man TT was thrown into the unknown in 2018, with one of the biggest grid shake-ups in recent years. The absence of a number of key players opened the way for some different names at the top of the timing sheets, but that didn't make for slower speeds around the notorious mountain course, and lap records were broken in every class.

The intense rivalry between Michael Dunlop and Ian Hutchinson had characterised the 2016 and 2017 TT races, when they had shared victories across the five main solo classes. With two victories each in 2017 (Hutchinson, Superbike and Superstock; Dunlop, the sole Supersport race and the Senior), they were the men to beat around the 37.73-mile course.

Their rivalry would be put on hold for 2018, however, with Hutchinson having to recover from injuries sustained when he crashed out of the lead of the Senior TT in 2017. After rebreaking the left leg he had almost lost after his 2010 Silverstone crash, the Bingley Bullet had endured an agonising ten-month fight-back to achieve his goal of being back on the grid for the TT, having signed a deal to replace John McGuinness in the Honda Racing squad.

But when Hutchinson appeared at the annual pre-TT press conference in March still wearing the external fixator cage, which held his leg together as the bone regrew, doubts were cast over whether he'd make it to the start line.

An X-ray taken towards the end of April revealed that his leg was strong enough for the cage to be removed and, determined as ever, he was back on a bike getting his first taste of the CBR1000RR Fireblade at Mallory Park just days after the operation. Two weeks later, he was on the grid at the North West 200, where a couple of top-ten finishes suggested that he was fit for the TT, but he had already admitted that his return was more a case of preparing the Honda for 2019 than fighting for wins.

Miraculously, he made the grid, but 23-times TT winner John McGuinness, also recovering from a broken leg, wasn't so lucky. Initially, things had gone well, and his plans to be back at the TT appeared to be on track. A new deal with Norton Racing seemed to have reinvigorated the most successful living TT rider. Having had his external fixator cage removed in March, he made a point of walking on to the stage at the press launch without crutches. Then it all went wrong. He returned to hospital, following a family holiday, to be told that he'd rebroken the leg at the site of the original fracture.

Doctors forecast that it would only take eight weeks before he was back on his feet, meaning that there was a slight possibility of him lining up in the number-one spot. In agreement with the TT organisers and Norton team, however, he decided that it wasn't worth the risk, which ruled him out of a second successive TT.

Bruce Anstey was another big name who was absent from proceedings. The 13-times TT winner had been set to race the MotoGP-inspired RC213V-S for the Padgetts Racing squad once again in 2018, but in April, his partner Anny announced that racing would have to take a back seat after the 49-year-old had been diagnosed with cancer for a second time. Ever the fighter, Anstey did a parade lap on the RCV and was planning to return to race at the TT in 2019.

That turned all attention towards one man – Michael Dunlop. Still the outright lap record holder after becoming the first rider to lap the course in under 17 minutes with a 133.962mph average speed in 2016, he was undoubtedly the main target heading into the 2018 event.

Dunlop's pre-season hadn't been without dramas. After he'd arrived in Spain to test with the Hawk Suzuki team,

with whom he'd won the 2017 Senior, it appeared that the 15-times TT winner would continue with the GSX-R1000 for another year. It soon became clear, however, that all wasn't rosy between Dunlop and the Hawk team. The 2017 TT had not been easy for the Suzuki squad. An engine problem had ruled Dunlop out of the Superbike race, and had it not been for a red flag in the Senior, which enabled them to change the rear shock, he wouldn't have been in contention for the blue riband outing either.

Dunlop had told Hawk that he'd be happy to stay for 2018 provided the bike took a step forward, with more help from Suzuki. When that help and development did not materialise, however, an amicable split was announced at the end of March.

At this point, just months before the roads season began, Dunlop's options were limited. It was clear that he wanted to be back on the BMW machinery that had taken him to five 1000cc TT wins since 2014. And that led him to join TAS Racing Tyco BMW, who had been left without a team-mate for upcoming Manxman Dan Kneen following Hutchinson's defection to Honda.

No love had been lost between Dunlop and the TAS team in the past, but he and Philip and Hector Neill decided to let bygones be bygones and give it a go. Thus one of the strongest teams on the grid joined forces with arguably the strongest rider – an ominous prospect.

Peter Hickman had finished on the podium in each of the five TTs he'd started in 2017, and he was favourite to challenge Dunlop in 2018. He'd taken the TT by storm as fastest-ever newcomer on his 2014 debut and had risen through the ranks year by year, culminating in his 2017 podium lockout. The Lincolnshireman came to the TT with one goal, to take his first mountain-course win, and lining up once again with the Smiths BMW squad, he appeared to be in a strong position to do so.

Weather so often dictates events for TT fortnight, but not in 2018, with Mona's Isle basking in sunshine for the entire two-week festival. Every practice session went ahead without disruption, allowing riders to put in plenty of laps before racing even began, and with a decent amount of rubber laid on the track after just a few nights, the times were frightening from the off.

On only the second night of Superbike practice, Dean Harrison was below the lap record for the class with an average speed of 133.462mph. It was the quickest practice-week lap in history, the Yorkshireman having been on fire out of the blocks and able to set the pace from a standing start. Remaining with the Silicone Engineering Kawasaki squad, he had the benefit of running a full-spec Superbike engine for the first time in his career.

With Hickman's hopes of a first win, and Harrison seeking to add to his 2014 Lightweight TT victory, it was becoming apparent that the 2018 TT might not be all about Dunlop domination. The Ulsterman qualified second in the Superbike class for Tyco BMW with a quickest lap of 132.983mph, while Hickman was third at 132.806mph.

The elation and excitement generated by a potentially fast TT series disappeared during Wednesday evening practice, when the dreaded red-flag call was made shortly after the session got under way. Manx rider Dan Kneen had come off his Tyco BMW through the fast Churchtown section and had succumbed to his injuries at the scene.

Having secured his first TT podium in the 2017 Superstock race, Kneen had been on the up in 2018 and had signed for the factory-backed Tyco squad. His quickest lap on Tuesday evening, 132.258mph, was his fastest ever, and it put him fourth on the combined practice time sheets.

Shortly after Kneen's fatal crash, Steve Mercer and three other riders were caught up in a bizarre incident involving a course car. Sent back around the circuit in reverse direction to return to the paddock, they collided with the car as it was en route to the scene of the accident. Mercer was taken to hospital with serious injuries, where he remained as MOTOCOURSE went to press. The ACU launched an independent investigation into the circumstances surrounding the crash.

The paddock was left numb, and practice pace dropped off towards the end of the week, leaving Harrison unbeaten at the top of the time sheets.

Peter Hickman led the way in the Superstock class with a quickest lap of 130.829mph, while Harrison was fastest on the 600s. Ben and Tom Birchall appeared to be in a strong position to continue their domination of the sidecar class, topping the three-wheeled qualifying. Michael Dunlop's Paton led the way in the Lightweight class after obliterating the existing 650-twin lap record on the opening night of practice with an average speed of 120.87mph.

RST SUPERBIKE TT

Qualifying had shown that three men had the edge: Harrison, able to lap incredibly quickly from a standing start, current lap record holder Dunlop and Hickman. Given the lightning speeds in practice, anticipation was high as to what we'd see over the next six days.

However, a number of questions remained. In previous years, Dunlop rubber had been far superior to opponent Metzeler in the Superbike class, and Dunlop-shod bikes had won every Superbike and Senior TT since 2008. In 2018, a number of Dunlop riders, including Michael Dunlop and Hickman, had complained about a lack of feeling from the Dunlop rear. Could this give Harrison the extra push he needed to take Metzeler's first big-bike win in ten years?

After a sublime start, the Kawasaki rider shattered the sector record from the start line to Glen Helen on the opening lap. Then, over the entire 37.73 miles, the Yorkshireman set a new outright lap record of 134.432mph. The blistering opening lap gave him a strong lead of 11.3 seconds over Dunlop, the Tyco BMW rider appearing to be the only man able to challenge the Kawasaki, following Peter Hickman's retirement at the Grandstand with an engine issue.

After another 134mph lap (134.180mph), Harrison extended his lead to 16.3 seconds as they slowed for the pits

Above: James Hillier's Kawasaki disturbs the peace at Black Dub on his way to third in the Superbike race.
Photo: David Collister/photocycles.com

Top right: Peter Hickman defeated Dunlop to win the Superstock TT.
Photo: BMW Press Club

Above right: Michael Dunlop dedicated his Superbike win to fallen Tyco BMW comrade Dan Kneen.
Photo: Monster Energy

Right: Dean Harrison (Kawasaki) took a comfortable win in the second Supersport race.
Photo: David Purves

on lap two, but a slick pit stop from the Tyco BMW crew allowed Dunlop to begin to close on the early race leader.

The gap was back down to 11 seconds at the end of lap three, but it was over the next two sectors where Dunlop gained most ground, and he more than halved Harrison's lead. It was shaping up to be a TT classic over the final two laps, but it came to a premature end when Harrison retired at the Sulby Crossroads with a clutch problem on lap four.

That left Dunlop in the clear at the front, with Padgetts Honda's Conor Cummins slotting into second place and the JG Speedfit Kawasaki of James Hillier moving up to third.

David Johnson took a strong fourth for the Shaun Muir Gulf BMW outfit, ahead of veteran Michael Rutter, while Honda's Lee Johnston took a firm sixth. Martin Jessopp was seventh on the Rider's BMW, ahead of Ivan Lintin, while privateer Phil Crowe enjoyed his best ever TT result in ninth. Josh Brookes rounded out the top ten on the booming V4 Norton.

The victory moved Dunlop to joint fourth on the all-time win list, level with arch rival Hutchinson. Dedicating the victory to fallen team-mate Dan Kneen, Dunlop said, "It's hard to celebrate this week. We can't say or do anything, but that is for Dan and his family."

With no last-lap battle, Dunlop backed off in the closing stages, so Harrison's 134.432mph opening lap stood as the new outright lap record. But with the weather forecast positive, the question was just how much quicker could they go?

RL360 SUPERSTOCK TT

It wasn't long before Harrison's status as the fastest man around the mountain course came under threat, with a record-shattering Superstock race on Monday.

In previous years, Hutchinson and Dunlop had shown that the more basic-specification Superstock bikes, which are as close as you can get to showroom models, could lap as quickly as the high-tech superbikes. Hutchinson had set the class lap record at 133.098mph in 2016, but that would be obliterated during 2018's four-lap race as eventual winner Peter Hickman fought back from a lap-one mistake.

The Smiths BMW rider had lost almost 20 seconds after overshooting at Braddan Bridge and being forced to make a U-turn to regain the course. With time in hand, he put his head down to recover the loss.

Another strong start by Dean Harrison resulted in him leading Michael Dunlop by five seconds at the end of the opening lap; Hickman had slotted into third.

Hickman's new record, an average speed of 134.077mph, came on lap two, making him the second quickest man in TT history. It was enough for him to take the lead at the end of that lap, but it was short-lived, as he lost time in the pits to both Dunlop and Harrison, the Smiths BMW squad's fumble handing Dunlop the lead at Glen Helen on lap three. Just half a second separated Dunlop and Harrison, with Hickman a further 0.7 of a second back.

Hickman was back in the lead by Ramsey on the third lap, but he and Michael Dunlop were inseparable on sector times, with just 0.1 of a second between the duelling BMWs halfway around the final lap. Then an astonishing run over the mountain, combined with Dunlop being held up by backmarkers, allowed Hickman to pull four seconds on the Ulsterman to take his first TT win.

Another class record of 134.403mph on the final lap meant that Hickman narrowly missed out on the outright record. It was, he admitted later, the hardest he'd ever ridden a bike around the TT course.

Harrison crossed the line a comfortable third, a minute ahead of Gulf BMW's David Johnson, who held off a hard challenge from JG Speedfit Kawasaki's James Hillier. Michael Rutter completed the top six, while newcomer Davey Todd produced a standout performance for Burrows Suzuki to take an impressive tenth place.

MONSTER ENERGY SUPERSPORT
Races One & Two

While there was nothing between the leading trio in the 1000cc classes, Michael Dunlop seemed to have an advantage in the Supersport category, having set the fastest lap by over 11 seconds in practice.

Hickman's larger stature and the underpowered Triumph 675 all but ruled him out of contention for the win. That left only Dean Harrison's Kawasaki to challenge the Ulsterman, who had switched back to a PTR-prepared Honda CBR600RR under the MD Racing banner. His last outing on Honda machinery had been in 2013, when he had set the lap record at 128.666mph, an impressive benchmark that would stand for five years. In the end, the man to break it was the man who set it.

After yet another lightning start, Dean Harrison led at Glen Helen on the opening lap, with the duo split by just 0.2 of a second, but Dunlop had taken control by the end of the 37.73 miles.

The Ballymoney man took the race by the scruff of the neck on the second lap, annihilating his own lap record with a speed of 129.197mph, despite slowing into the pits. That record helped Dunlop stretch out a six-second lead by the end of lap three, and having caught Harrison on the road, he tucked in behind his rival for the final lap. Harrison moved over on Glencrutchery Road to allow the victor to cross the line first.

Thirty seconds behind the leaders, there was an intense battle for third between Peter Hickman and James Hillier. They were separated by just 0.098 of a second at Ballaugh on the final lap, but Hickman secured the final rostrum spot with a strong run over the mountain. Conor Cummins finished fifth for Padgetts Honda, ahead of the Monster McAMS Yamaha of Josh Brookes.

After the race, Dunlop quipped that he could do a 130mph Supersport lap, and with Dean Harrison having had no answer to the now 17-times TT winner in race one, race two looked like a foregone conclusion. But it's never that simple at the Isle of Man TT.

Bolting out of the blocks again, Harrison led at Glen Helen by an impressive two seconds. This time, it appeared that Dunlop couldn't run with the Silicone Engineering Kawasaki in the early stages of the race, and Harrison stretched the gap sector by sector.

The Yorkshireman's lead became more comfortable after the second-lap pit stops, Dunlop having been slapped with a 30-second penalty for speeding in the pit lane. That elevated Hickman to second, with James Hillier inheriting third.

Harrison crossed the line to take his second TT win and first of the week by a comfortable margin. Conor Cummins finished fourth for Padgetts Honda, while a gutted Dunlop was left just fifth after his penalty was applied. Josh Brookes equalled his best ever TT finish with sixth place for Monster McAMS Yamaha.

Locate.im SIDECAR – Races One & Two

Ben and Tom Birchall continued their Isle of Man domination. Having won the previous three sidecar TT races, they were favourites for Saturday's opening encounter, and they stormed to the win in style, shattering their existing lap record.

The race was not without complication, however, being red-flagged following an incident on the opening lap. Both riders involved were reported to be conscious and were taken to Nobles hospital for treatment, later being discharged.

Upon the restart, the Birchalls were flying, shattering their own lap record from a standing start with an average speed of 117.702mph on the opening lap, but they didn't stop there. They went on to annihilate it with the first ever 118mph sidecar lap at an average speed of 118.69mph.

Dominating from start to finish, the Birchalls crossed the line 47 seconds ahead of John Holden and Lee Cain, who also set their quickest ever lap. Tim Reeves and Mark Wilkes completed the podium.

The Mansfield pair upped the ante further in Friday's second race, blasting to 119.25mph on the second of the three laps to dominate en route to their fifth consecutive TT win.

Holden and Cain finished second again, 22 seconds behind, with Tim Reeves and Mark Wilkes taking their second rostrum of the week in third.

BENNETTS LIGHTWEIGHT

Lap records were falling left, right and centre, and the Lightweight class was no exception. With Michael Dunlop having already broken the class record on the opening night of practice, it was clear from the off that the four-lap battle would be a quick one. But the Ulsterman didn't have an easy time on the ultra-fast Paton.

Twice Lightweight TT winner Ivan Lintin and IEG Kawasaki's Derek McGee joined Dunlop in shattering the existing record on the opening lap. However, drama would shortly strike for Dafabet Devitt Kawasaki's Lintin, who retired at Bedstead on the second lap, handing Dunlop the lead.

Time lost in the pits resulted in the Paton rider losing it to McGee on the penultimate lap, and while he was able to retake the lead, the Irishman remained in tow. However, Dunlop would further shatter the existing lap record of 120.848mph with a stunning 122.750mph on the final lap to take his third win of the week. McGee was second, and 2017 winner Michael Rutter third.

It was Dunlop's 18th victory around the mountain course, and it moved him ahead of Dave Molyneux and into third place on the all-time winners' list, behind 23-times winner John McGuinness and Michael's uncle, Joey Dunlop, who had 26.

Above: **Unbeatable, unbeaten – the Birchall brothers charge through Kirk Michael.**

Above left: **More for the family cabinet. Tom and Ben Birchall claimed their fourth and fifth consecutive Sidecar wins.**

Photos: Mark Walters

Top left: **Michael Dunlop took an emphatic 18th TT win on the Paton in the Lightweight TT.**

Right: **Quids in – Michael Rutter picked up the big prize for the first all-electric 120mph lap in the sparsely populated TT Zero race.**

Photos: Bernd Fischer

SES TT ZERO

Since John McGuinness hit 119.279mph to set the TT Zero lap record in 2015, the Mugen squad had been determined to break 120mph. However, with McGuinness having retired from 2016's race and Bruce Anstey having suffered a problem with the bike on his way to the 2017 win, the magic figure had eluded the Japanese firm.

For 2018, with both McGuinness and Anstey absent, Mugen were forced to revise their entire line-up. Former double TT Zero winner Michael Rutter and Honda rider Lee Johnston took over.

Mugen having offered a hefty bonus for a 120mph lap, Rutter charged off the line, but found himself with little competition after team-mate Johnston had to make an unscheduled stop on track, his chain having jumped the sprockets. Rutter made the target at 121.824mph, taking his sixth TT win in the process.

The University of Nottingham team's Daley Mathison crossed the line after recording a lap of 119.294mph, beating McGuinness's previous record and taking the runner-up spot. Johnston finished third after putting his chain back on and continuing.

Once again, the class failed to attract a large number of entries, with just five machines finishing.

POKERSTARS SENIOR TT

After the quickest race week in TT history, the island was buzzing ahead of the biggest event of them all. Lap records had been shattered in every class, and with Michael Dunlop, Dean Harrison and Peter Hickman set to go head to head for one final time, it was a question of when, not if, Harrison's outright lap record would be bettered.

In response to the issues suffered earlier in the week, Dunlop flew in a new batch of rubber for Michael Dunlop and Hickman. They were able to test the new rear tyre in a practice session on Wednesday and were said to be happy with the progress.

As in every other race that week, the Silicone Engineering Kawasaki of Harrison bolted off the line to take an early lead, just over a second ahead of Hickman, with Dunlop slotting into third.

Waved flags at Barregarrow, prompted by an oil leak from James Hillier's Kawasaki, meant that the opening laps were a little slower than Saturday's superbike race.

Harrison's lead was still just over a second at the end of the first lap, but another blinding opening few sectors resulted in the Yorkshireman pulling out a 5.5-second lead as they slowed for the pits on lap two.

A slower pit stop by Hickman and another strong opening sector from Harrison led to the lead stretching to its greatest extent at Ramsey, with 8.2 seconds splitting the pair. As Hickman hit his strongest part of the course over the mountain, however, he brought it back down to a second on his way to a new outright lap record with an average speed of 134.456mph.

Harrison was back in control once more on lap five, with the lead back up to five seconds, but Hickman was on a charge towards the end. Less than two seconds separated them going into the final lap, and with Harrison losing time between Ballaugh and Ramsey, Hickman took the lead for the first time.

From there, the Lincolnshireman didn't look back, crossing the line two seconds ahead of his rival. In the process, he obliterated the outright lap record with the first ever 135mph lap in history at an average speed of 135.452mph.

Conor Cummins gained his second podium of the week for Padgetts Honda, ahead of a desolate Michael Dunlop, who had dropped off the pace significantly after a strong start. Josh Brookes took both his and Norton's best ever TT finish in fifth, while Gary Johnson completed the top six.

Above: Butterly time: Michael Dunlop waits in line before the start of the Senior.

Left: Clutching his first Senior trophy, Peter Hickman proudly displays his record 135.452mph lap speed.
Photos: David Collister/photocycles.com

Top right: Nearly, but not quite. Dean Harrison was just a couple of seconds adrift.

Above right: Josh Brookes took fifth on the Norton.

Right: Conor Cummins (Padgetts Honda) was a distant third, his second podium of the week.
Photos: Bernd Fischer

Photo: BMW Press Club

WILLIAM DUNLOP 1985–2018

William Dunlop (*above*) died after crashing during practice for the Skerries 100 road races in Northern Ireland. He had been making a return to the roads after deciding to withdraw from the 2018 Isle of Man TT to be with his pregnant partner.

The 32-year-old was a regular on the international road-racing scene, following in the footsteps of his father, Robert, and uncle, Joey. He had started racing at the age of 17, going on to win at both national and international level. He made his debut at the Isle of Man TT in 2006 and went on to achieve five podiums around the mountain course, with a best result of second place.

ADAM LYON 1991–2018

Adam Lyon died after an incident at Casey's, just after the 28th Milestone, during the opening Supersport race.

The 26-year-old was making his debut at the TT and had qualified 24th for the Supersport race with a fastest lap of 122.261mph. He had set his fastest lap of the course during Superbike qualifying with an average speed of 123.443mph.

JAMES COWTON 1992–2018

James Cowton died during the Southern 100 races on the Isle of Man. The McAdoo Kawasaki rider was involved in a four-bike incident during the 600 challenge race.

The 25-year-old had been enjoying a successful Southern 100, recording a string of podium finishes. Earlier in the year, he had taken his debut international victory with a win in the North West 200 Supertwin race.

Photo: BMW Press Club

DAN KNEEN 1987–2018

Thirty-year-old Dan Kneen (*above*) lost his life after an incident at Churchtown during Wednesday evening's practice session.

Having achieved his debut podium at TT 2017, the Manxman without doubt was a rising star. He had set his quickest ever lap of the mountain course, at 132.258mph, just 24 hours before his death and had appeared to be a potentially strong challenger for the following week's races.

2018 BENNETTS BRITISH SUPERBIKE CHAMPIONSHIP REVIEW

IT'S HASLAM, AT LAST!

By OLLIE BARSTOW

TO call Leon Haslam's long-awaited Bennetts British Superbike Championship win in 2018 'belated' is quite an understatement. After several near misses, he was finally unbeatable in a fast and varied series.

Haslam needed no reminding of his unwitting reputation as the nearly-man of two-wheel motor sport. Three times runner-up in BSB, his lengthy tenure at the forefront of Superbike racing – both domestically and internationally – had earned him elite status. But he came into 2018 without having won a championship title in a career that stretched back to the 1990s.

So if his title success was to be 'better late than never', it was just as well that it was achieved in epic style. And it should be remembered just how far he had had to bounce back from his most painful near-miss yet, both physically and mentally, having suffered a terrifying 173mph crash in the 2017 Brands Hatch finale. It had shattered his ankle and his title hopes, paving the way for Shane Byrne to take an unprecedented sixth BSB championship.

Despite having finished 2017 dejected, bruised and battered, Haslam kicked off the new season fighting fit and more focused than ever, again riding the JG Speedfit Kawasaki. Twenty-six races later and finally he could pull on a '#1 Champion'-emblazoned T-shirt, taking his rightful place alongside Byrne, Ryuichi Kiyonari, Niall Mackenzie and others on the BSB roll call.

Cynics inevitably will point out the absence of Haslam's most ubiquitous adversary, Shane Byrne, who had suffered a brutal neck injury that cruelly ended his season at the half-way point. However while it may be insincere to make this just a footnote, Haslam's 17 wins, 21 podiums, five pole positions and not a single DNF tell their own story. In short, his performance was flawless in 2018.

That's not to say he had it easy, as he came up against stern opposition from familiar foes and a new wave of exciting fresh talent. But none of them could sustain the pressure over the entire season

It was mostly a case of 'as you were' across the 2018 grid, with many teams fielding unchanged line-ups in the hope that familiarity and consistency would give them the edge in a championship where even minor errors can make a significant difference.

Haslam was joined again at JG Speedfit by Luke Mossey. Byrne – chasing a third successive and seventh overall BSB title – continued to lead the Paul Bird Motorsport-helmed Be Wiser Ducati team, with Glenn Irwin alongside.

Having been runner-up to Byrne in 2017, Josh Brookes, 2015 British Superbike Champion, stuck with Yamaha machinery, but switched from Anvil Hire TAG Racing to the McAMS team, alongside exciting youngster Tarran Mackenzie. The experienced James Ellison went the other way in a straight swap.

Hoping for an injury-free campaign to unlock the full potential of the new Fireblade, Dan Linfoot and James O'Halloran paired up once more in the official Honda Racing team. Hawk Racing-run Buildbase Suzuki, meanwhile, shuffled its riders to charge 2017 rookie standout Bradley Ray and experienced National Superstock 1000 runner-up Richard Cooper with building on a promising first season on the new GSX-R1000.

Despite its age relative to rivals, the BMW S1000RR remained well represented. Smiths Racing retained its 2017 Showdown contender, Peter Hickman, and signed former European Superstock champion Sylvain Barrier, while Tyco BMW welcomed back Michael Laverty to ride alongside Christian Iddon.

Following his eye-catching run to the 2017 Showdown, Jake Dixon continued with RAF Regular & Reserves on a Kawasaki ZX-10R. Other standout entries included 2017 National Superstock 1000 champion Danny Buchan with FS-3 Kawasaki, Taylor Mackenzie lining up on the Moto Rapido Ducati and ex-Moto2 rider Gino Rea making his BSB debut with new team OMG Suzuki.

As ever, the series played out over 26 races and 12 rounds, including seven races and three events to determine the title through the Showdown.

Donington Park kicked off with an unexpected double triumph by Ray. The 20-year-old's promotion to the official factory-backed Suzuki team had been anticipated, following his eye-catching rookie turn on a satellite variant, but few had expected a brace of wins straight out of the box.

His success was achieved with aplomb, too, having resisted the attentions of more experienced rivals. It also proved that Suzuki's still developing 'Gixxer' was now up to the task of going with the front-runners.

Ray passed for the lead on lap six of race one, then controlled the pace to defeat Byrne and Ellison. He repeated the feat in race two, despite patches of wet threatening to catch out the less wary. Beating Haslam and Linfoot across the line, his maximum haul of 50 points set him nicely on course for the Showdown, even at such an early stage.

However, the same could not be said of two of his podium fellows. Neither Ellison nor Linfoot – two fancied contenders pre-season – would set foot on the rostrum for the remainder

Above: A year after brake failure had dashed Leon Haslam's title hopes at Brands Hatch, he tied up the title in style at the same circuit.

Right: Before his accident, 'Shakey' Byrne's single win had come at the April Brands Hatch round.

Left: Haslam got to display the No. 1 plate at last.

Far left: 'Pocket Rocket' and 'Rocket Ron', father and son, with JG Speedfit Kawasaki team chief Jack Valentine.

Photos: Clive Challinor Motorsport Photography

of the season. Ellison was inconsistent; Linfoot's progress was tempered by two periods out with injury.

In round two at Brands Hatch, BSB's stalwarts powered to the top, with Shane Byrne and Leon Haslam sharing a win apiece. At his home track, Byrne was made to work hard for victory in race one, tailing the on-form Ray, who did a mighty job of soaking up the pressure before a minor error at Paddock Hill Bend, three laps from the flag, invited the Ducati man through to snatch victory.

A damp second race allowed Haslam to come to the fore, but only after outlasting his rivals in a thrilling encounter that resulted in a number of riders hitting the front at various points as conditions evolved. The defining moment came on the penultimate lap, when Haslam dived past Irwin's Ducati for a lead he'd retain to the flag, while Laverty made a welcome return to the rostrum, although it would be his and Tyco BMW's only podium success in 2018.

On to the crests and troughs of Oulton Park, where Haslam began to demonstrate the rhythm that ultimately would set the tone for his championship. In a year that didn't often see him on pole – round one being the sole occasion during the season when he topped Saturday qualifying – his consistent race pace often told come Sunday. (His four other pole starts had come as the result of victories in earlier races of double- or triple-headers.)

Nowhere was this more evident than at Oulton, where he worked his way to the front in both races. In race one, he beat Dixon, with Byrne completing the podium. Then he rebuffed Australian O'Halloran on the Honda and Dixon again.

With Ray off the podium in both races, Haslam swept to the championship summit for the first time.

Above: Suzuki's Bradley Ray was a surprise double winner at the Donington Park season-opener.
Photo: www.suzuki-racing.com

Left: An injury-hit season for Tyco BMW's Christian Iddon kept him out of the Showdown.
Photo: BMW Press Club

Above right: Peter Hickman (fresh from success at the Isle of Man TT), Josh Brookes and Jake Dixon sport the silverware after the second race at Thruxton.

Top right: Jason O'Halloran displays spectacular style on his Honda – sideways at 130mph through Silverstone's Woodcote corner.
Photos: Clive Challinor Motorsport Photography

However, the season was dealt a blow away from the cameras during the short hiatus that followed, when it was reported that Byrne had suffered a horrific accident while testing at Snetterton. Details of the extent of his injuries emerged slowly. He had suffered a broken neck and back in the crash. Alarmingly – albeit mercifully – it was revealed that he had undergone major surgery to prevent him from being left paralysed.

He was required to wear a brace and neck 'halo' after leaving hospital to prevent any movement and improve natural healing. Not only was his season over, but also there remained concern over whether the illustrious champion would ever ride another race bike again.

Byrne's accident cast a shadow when the season resumed at the same circuit a couple of weeks later, but nonetheless the racing was back in the headlines following a pair of thrilling contests around the Norfolk track.

Once again, Haslam called upon his experience to take the double. Ray led from pole – one of six of the season – only to low-side into retirement, allowing Irwin to take over. The Northern Irishman was stalked by a fast-approaching Haslam, however, who pulled off the move he needed to make it four wins in a row.

In race two, Haslam went head to head with Brookes, the wily Australian producing his best ride of the season thus far. It culminated in a decidedly boisterous final lap. Brookes dived for the win into the last corner, but the loss of momentum allowed the LG Speedfit rider to pull alongside on the drag to the line.

They made elbow contact as Brookes attempted to stifle Haslam's progress, but it was not enough to prevent the latter from taking the win. In addition, the closely-following Dixon was able to sneak into second place for his fourth successive podium.

Dixon's stealthy progress had taken him to third overall – once Byrne was removed from the equation – reminiscent of his cumulative charge to a surprise Showdown spot in 2017 on the ZX-10R. Back then, it had been a breakthrough weekend at Knockhill that had set him on a course for the upper echelons. Twelve months later, it would do the same as once again Dixon mastered the tricky Scottish venue to firmly establish his title credentials.

Dixon squared up against Haslam from pole, and though the more experienced of the ZX-10R riders moved into the lead midway through the race, Dixon's unrelenting pressure and sheer gumption on the brakes into the final corner forced a mistake from Haslam five laps from home, and he pulled away for victory.

Haslam was classified second from Danny Buchan, whose third place marked a maiden podium finish for FS-3 Racing, one of BSB's newer teams. It was a welcome boost in confidence for Buchan, whose two dominant National Superstock 1000 titles were at odds with his recent sporadic BSB results.

Buchan doubled up in race two with another rostrum from pole; the 25-year-old was now well into Showdown contention. Up at the front, Dixon and Haslam resumed their tussle, with the latter eventually taking advantage of a wobble from Dixon to grab the lead for a sixth win in seven races.

With round six at Brands Hatch marking the mid-point of the season, Brookes and McAMS Yamaha's burgeoning title ambitions came to life in formidable fashion with a double

95
McAMS
YAMAHA
RACEWAYS

25
McAMS
DAMS

91
OXFORD
Speedfit
QUATTRO
ROYAL AIRFORCE
SHOEI

victory. After falling just short at Snetterton, Brookes barely saw a single bike ahead of him come race-day. With the McAMS machine resplendent in its retro red and white livery to celebrate 20 years of the Yamaha R1, he led two corners into the first race before romping on to victory, a feat he'd repeat from pole position in race two.

The scraps behind provided the entertainment, with Irwin doing his utmost to go with Brookes, but in both races the Ulsterman's Ducati followed the Yamaha across the finish line in second. Back at the circuit where his 2017 title challenge had ended so abruptly, Haslam played it cool in both races to notch up a brace of third places.

After a career that had spanned so many years, there weren't many 'firsts' remaining in Haslam's BSB repertoire. At Thruxton, however, he had the pleasure of ticking off his first career win around the UK's fastest circuit, having come out on top of a fierce scrap in race one to strengthen his already substantial title-favourite status.

By contrast, Josh Brookes had a superb record at Thruxton. The Australian topped the podium there for an eighth time in race two, his third win in four races raising his championship profile.

Podium honours were shared by the consistent Dixon and the heroic Peter Hickman, who had spent the night in hospital with a virus. He produced one of the strongest rides of his career to scythe towards the front of the field on the Smiths BMW.

This catapulted Hickman right back into Showdown contention, with only two rounds and five races to come before the top-six cut-off would be activated. Up front, Haslam was already guaranteed to go through, while the presence of Dixon, Brookes and Irwin seemed a formality.

However, six riders had a genuine shot at the remaining two spots, headed by Ray, the only 2018 race winner in the group. Buchan was sixth, but just a few digits clear of Hickman. Having notched up solid points if not podiums, Iddon flew the flag for Tyco BMW, ahead of Cooper on the second of the Buildbase Suzukis and O'Halloran, whose Honda Racing team were facing the real possibility of not reaching the Showdown for the first time.

Two became one when Ray confirmed his entry ticket with a return to form in round eight at Cadwell Park. A pair of composed second places at the technical and tricky venue put him clear enough to be the first Suzuki rider in the final six since 2013.

Haslam delivered a third double victory – wins 11 and 12 overall – with two hard-fought successes, defeating Ray in the first race, before prevailing in an entertaining scrap with Dixon in the second, when his rival ran off and dropped back.

With a triple-header at Silverstone standing between the riders and the Title Showdown, the final spot appeared to be going one of three ways, with Hickman now in prime position on 128 points, from Buchan on 119 and Iddon with 111.

Despite the tiny margins for error, with no one rider enjoying a strong weekend at the Northamptonshire venue, Hickman's eighth in race one was enough to guarantee his route into the Showdown for a second successive year, in spite of two subsequent DNFs.

Out front, it was Haslam yet again, adding his first trio of victories. Having stalked his way to the front each time, he had got the better of Irwin in race one, before enjoying a fun fight with Dixon in race two, which ended with the Kawasaki man low-siding dramatically on the final lap at Brooklands.

In race three, Haslam came up against an unfamiliar foe

Above: Ulsterman Glen Irwin secured third overall by winning the opener at Brands Hatch's season finale.

Top left: Another son of a famous father, McAMS Yamaha rookie Tarran Mackenzie claimed a maiden BSB podium at Silverstone.

Above left: Although Josh Brookes struggled to find a set-up to his liking on the works-backed Yamaha, he managed three wins.

Left: Haslam and Dixon, locked in combat. This was at Silverstone, but it could have been almost anywhere else during the season.

Photos: Clive Challinor Motorsport Photography

Above: **Jake Dixon powers to victory in the opening Showdown race at Oulton Park.**

Top right: **Dan Linfoot podium-bound in the opening round at Donington – his season was scuppered by crashes and injuries.**

Top far right: **Kawasaki-mounted 2017 British Superstock 1000cc Champion Danny Buchan narrowly missed his Showdown chance after a qualifying crash at Oulton Park.**
Photos: Clive Challinor Motorsport Photography

Above right: **Peter Hickman divided his time between road and track, and was fifth overall in BSB.**

Above far right: **Michael Laverty (Tyco BMW) had good pace at times, but lacked consistency.**
Photos: BMW Press Club

Right: **The BSB Showdown contenders – Irwin, Dixon, Haslam, Ray, Brookes and Hickman.**
Photo: Clive Challinor Motorsport Photography

in Tarran Mackenzie – son of BSB legend Niall – who was in the midst of a fantastic weekend. He had finished third in race one and had been on course for the same result in race two, only to crash with Dixon on the final lap. The 25-year-old saved his best until last, though, battling to the line with Haslam in race three, only to be denied his first win by the wiliness of his vastly more experienced rival.

Introduced in 2010, the Title Showdown's equalising points format had been created to prevent any championship from becoming a foregone conclusion, citing Leon Camier's record-breaking 2009 title run as a prime example. Indeed, with 12 wins and a 147-point lead by the conclusion of Silverstone, it would have been a case of 'when' and not 'if' for Haslam by this point…

Nevertheless, despite seeing his lead shrink, with those valuable wins translating to podium credits – five points per win – Haslam still retained a comfortable margin over his rivals on 568 points. He was 45 points clear of Dixon on 523. The remaining four qualifiers followed – Brookes (519), Ray (519), Irwin (516) and Hickman (504).

It would take something particularly special for anyone to turn the tide of Haslam's unrelenting momentum. But that is exactly what happened in the first Showdown round at Oulton Park, where Dixon stormed to a brilliant double win.

In a treacherously wet first race, Dixon started from pole, but gave way to fast-starting Tommy Bridewell, who romped into the lead on the Moto Rapido Ducati. The Devizes-man had begun the season on the Halsall Suzuki, but after being dropped four rounds into the season, he had re-emerged for round six on the Panigale vacated by Taylor Mackenzie, quickly looking at home on the twin-cylinder machine.

Although Dixon grabbed back the lead on lap eight, Bridewell chased the Kawasaki home for his and his team's first podium of the season. He went on to take third in race two as well.

Haslam brought his bike home in third, a damage-limiting reward for his super charge from 24th on the grid, after technical issues had plagued qualifying. Even so, despite his more advantageous front-row start in race two, he still had no answer to Dixon, and with the margin between them trimmed to 31 points, there were hopes of a genuine head-to-head for the title.

BSB's annual jaunt to mainland Europe and magnificent Assen set the scene for the penultimate round, the battle for honours once more between Haslam and Dixon. Mackenzie led initially in race one, but both riders stalked their way through the order, before Haslam snatched the lead from the McAMS Yamaha rider after some exhilaratingly side-by-side action. It was decisive, and while Dixon also got the better of Mackenzie, it improved Haslam's championship advantage.

With more of the same in race two, Dixon ran second ahead of Haslam for much of the encounter. His title hopes were dealt an all but critical blow, however, when his Kawasaki ZX-10R slowed on lap ten. A technical fault led to a DNF, and at this stage of the season, he would struggle to recover.

Haslam compounded Dixon's woes by reeling off the Assen double, ahead of Brookes and Hickman. His timely 14th win of the year tightened a vice-like grip on the crown.

Haslam came to the season finale at Brands Hatch as the man to beat for the second year in succession. In 2017, his margin had stood at 32 points. This time, it was almost double that, 61 points over Dixon. Even if Dixon won all three races, Haslam needed just 14 points – a single podium finish – to take the spoils.

As it happened, Haslam wasted no time in getting it out of the way, producing a tactical and tentative ride to sixth in race one. Coupled with Dixon's determined ride to second, it proved more than enough to complete the inevitable.

Brushing off the anguish of missing out in 2017, an emotional Haslam revelled in a title glory that, while long awaited, was superseded by the manner in which it had been achieved. Victory in race two brought his tally to a magnificent 15 victories, and he celebrated in style on top of the podium. Surely his season will be remembered as one of BSB's most immaculate on record.

With two more podiums at Brands Hatch to put towards his season record, Dixon's gutsy performance turned many heads in 2018. He was Haslam's shadow for much of the

SHOEI
4

83

Bennetts
60

tyco
OXFORD

Bennetts
Bennetts
hager
ROYAL AIRFORCE
BUILDBASE
SUZUKI
McAMS
SMITHS
60

Right: Richard Cooper was largely overshadowed by Hawk Racing team-mate Bradley Ray, but scored a dominant victory in the final race of the year at Brands Hatch.
Photo: www.suzuki-racing.com

Below: 'Shakey' Byrne – a horrendous crash in testing put the five-times champion out for the season, and perhaps permanently.

Bottom: Tommy Bridewell salutes his Riders Cup triumph, for those who didn't make the Showdown top six.
Photos: Clive Challinor Motorsport Photography

year, and the final margin disguises a fight that was physically a lot closer. Either way, Dixon's stock soared on the back of the season, and an international stage beckoned for the youngster…

The ever consistent Irwin left his best until last, claiming his first win of the year at Brands Hatch, a success that contributed towards his third place in the standings. It was a positive way to end a tough year for the Be Wiser Ducati team. While it remained to be seen whether Byrne would ever line up on a BSB grid again, Irwin had stepped up to the role of team leader with aplomb. Moreover, PBM had signed his younger brother, Andrew, to deputise for Byrne, and the second of the Irwin clan certainly showed that talent ran in the family.

A Showdown stalwart, Brookes couldn't quite make inroads on the top three, and he ended another lucrative season in fourth place; while Hickman's unlikely run to the Showdown culminated in another top-five result for the plucky Smiths BMW team. Despite an indifferent end to the season that was the antithesis of his stunning curtain-raising double, Ray and Buildbase Suzuki were still a very exciting – if inconsistent – combination in 2018, one that many predicted would simply get better and better.

Despite having missed two rounds and been forced to switch teams, Bridewell claimed the BSB Riders Cup as the top contender outside the Showdown, following a tremendous run in the latter stages that yielded four podiums from seven races, which allowed him to leapfrog from 13th to seventh overall.

At the end of a very tough season for Honda, O'Halloran was the best placed of its riders, in eighth, ahead of Iddon, who had a podium-free run to ninth overall. The ever improving Mackenzie rounded out the top ten from Buchan and Cooper, the Buildbase Suzuki rider having demonstrated his experience in difficult conditions to take victory in the final race of the year.

As the sun set on the 2018 season, attention was already turning towards an enticing 2019 campaign. The No. 1 plate wouldn't be seen, however, with Haslam returning to the world stage in the multiple-title-winning Kawasaki Racing factory Superbike squad. Dixon was also moving on, to the Moto2 World Championship.

However, the season would herald the Superbike debut of Scott Redding, set to swap MotoGP for something a little closer to home with PBM Ducati. With a question mark hanging over Byrne's participation, the time was right for new legends to make themselves known…

Above: Supersport champion Jack Kennedy battles with title rival Ben Currie at Oulton Park.

Top right: Eunan McGlinchey took the Junior Supersport Championship.

Top far right: British Sidecar Champions Steve Kershaw and Stuart Clarke.

Above right: Ryan Vickers clinched the National Superstock 600cc title.

Above far right: Josh Owens was the inaugural GP2 champion, running with the BSB class.

Right: HEL Motostar Champion Jake Archer (2) battles with rival Storm Stacey at Oulton Park.

Below right: Rob Guiver claimed ten victories in his successful Ducati TriOptions campaign.

Far right: Keith Farmer on his way to the Pirelli National Superstock championship.

Photos: Clive Challinor Motorsport Photography

Dickies British Supersport Championship

As ever, the British Superbike Championship support series delivered action often befitting a headline act. But while the Dickies British Supersport Championship had become known for its down-to-the-wire racing in the past, there would be no mistaking 2018's deserving title-winner.

A Supersport stalwart, Ireland's Jack Kennedy reeled off a dominant campaign against a tough field to wrap up the title on the Integro Yamaha. With 11 wins to his name – including a devastating run of eight in a row early in the year – even an injury sustained out of competition, which forced him to miss an entire event, couldn't halt his momentum.

That's not to say Kennedy didn't have pressure, with Ben Currie often the man on top of the podium when he wasn't. Riding the Gearlink Kawasaki, Currie took seven race wins to keep the title battle alive until the final round, but he couldn't do anything to prevent the Irishman from wrapping up victory.

James Westmoreland made it two Gearlink Kawasaki riders in the top three overall, while James Rispoli (Everquip Yamaha), Bradley Jones (Integro Yamaha) and David Allingham (EHA Yamaha) completed the top six, the last named one of only four riders to top the podium in 2018. The other was Alastair Seeley, the former champion who joined the series mid-season on the EHA Yamaha and won four times en route to ninth.

In the Dickies Junior Supersport Championship, Eunan McGlinchey took the honours on the Team #109 Kawasaki, his eight wins having put him comfortably clear of runner-up Brian Hart (KTM) and Elliot Pinson (Pinson Kawasaki).

Pirelli National Superstock 1000 Championship

Despite an indifferent season at Superbike level, Tyco BMW enjoyed title-winning success in the Pirelli National Superstock 1000 Championship with Keith Farmer, who in turn added another notable championship to his repertoire.

After winning the British Supersport title in 2017, Farmer claimed a second Superstock 1000 success – six years after the first – after prevailing in a season-long tussle with Billy McConnell (Buildbase Suzuki) and Joe Collier (EHA/In Competition Aprilia).

In a tightly-contested season that went down to the wire, Farmer's four wins – anchored by a double success at Knockhill – ultimately made the difference in edging out his Australian rival by 10.5 points.

In the Pirelli National Superstock 600 Championship, there was no stopping Ryan Vickers, who swept to title glory by winning all but two races in 2018. Indeed, riding the Mototechniks Yamaha YZF-6, Vickers won every race he finished, to end the year well clear of runner-up Joe Sheldon-Shaw and Aaron Clarke. Aaron Clifford and Korie McGreevy were the only riders other than the title winner to top the podium, at Donington Park and Knockhill respectively.

Other Championships

In its third year with Honda Moto3 machines, the immensely competitive HEL Motostar British Championship was won by Jake Archer, whose remarkable form out of the box – seven wins from the first eight races – set him well on course for title success.

Though Archer was never headed in the standings, Jack Scott and Storm Stacey pushed hard to keep him honest by regularly joining him on the podium, but 11 victories for the 18-year-old suggested that he would be one to watch in future.

New for the 2018 season, the British Talent Cup had been created from Dorna's ambitious 'Road to MotoGP' programme, and was aimed at riders between the ages of 12 and 17. The races supported three BSB events, plus the British rounds of World Superbikes and MotoGP, with a finale at the last grand prix in Valencia. Rory Skinner was twice second, to be crowned inaugural champion.

Despite a lacklustre start to the season, Rob Guiver was the class of the field in the 2018 Ducati TriOptions Cup, with ten wins from 16 races putting him well clear of his rivals. Lewis Rollo and Sean Neary followed up in second and third positions overall.

Runners-up in 2017, Steve Kershaw and Stuart Clarke romped to title success in the Hyundai Construction Equipment British Sidecar Championship with 17 victories – including a dominant 12 in a row – that put them well clear of their nearest opposition.

YAMAHA
21
YAMAHA

65

Premier
DUCATI ROMFORD
13

tyco
OXFORD
tyco
OXFORD

SIDECAR WORLD CHAMPIONSHIP

NEVER GIVE UP!

By JOHN McKENZIE

THE 2018 championship was eagerly anticipated, with the return of five-times champion Tim Reeves to challenge 2017 champion Ben Birchall. Reeves had skipped the previous season to race his 1000cc outfit in the British Championship, where he had won all 20 races.

Reeves was accompanied by a new passenger, the experienced Mark Wilkes, who had been third in 2017 with John Holden. Meanwhile, Tom and Ben Birchall had totally dominated the first 600cc season, winning every race bar the last.

Finnish five-times champion Pekka Paivarinta had a new passenger in Jussi Veravainen, replacing Kirsi Kainulainen, who'd gone solo racing.

There was quality in depth. Add 2015 champion Bennie Streuer, and the top four drivers between them had won the previous 13 world titles, and 109 of the previous 126 world championship races. Amazingly, it was the first season since 2012 that the triumvirate of Reeves, Birchall and Paivarinta had competed together. A veritable battle of giants loomed. "It's going to be close this year..." said defending champion Birchall wryly. Little did he know.

Eleven races – the highest number since 2007 – across seven circuits beckoned, leading to a nail-biting cliffhanger of a finish.

Round 1 – Le Mans, France

The Birchall brothers, on their Mitchells of Mansfield LCR Yamaha, posted a pole time that was half a second quicker than second man Reeves. The hard work was undone, however, when they fluffed the start, losing five places.

Reeves and Wilkes set a furious pace on the Carl Cox Motorsport RS Adolf Yamaha, while Birchall, fighting through the pack, almost left the track on the first lap. By lap two, Birchall was at Reeves's heels; by lap five, less than a second covered Reeves, Birchall and Streuer. Then Streuer's tyres faded, handing third to Paivarinta as the leaders pulled clear.

Reeves was able to defend against repeated challenges and claimed his sixth Le Mans victory by just over a second.

Paivarinta was third, 15 seconds adrift; Streuer flipped while dicing with Holden.

Reeves was ecstatic: "They said it would take us half a season to get going on the 600!" He won on his new Adolf RS chassis; remarkably, it was the first World Championship race in 15 years that had not been won by an LCR.

Round 2 – Slovakiaring, Slovakia

The nine-year-old Slovakiaring, near Bratislava, was a new venue, and the round was the first two-race 50-point weekend. The challenging 5.922km track, one of the longest in Europe, gave plenty of options for slipstreaming on the fast straights.

Birchall took pole position from Reeves by a mere thousandth. Paivarinta completed the front row, a second down.

Saturday's seven-lap Sprint was eventful; Paivarinta (44-Racing LCR Honda) quickest away, but Reeves ahead by the third corner. Third-placed Birchall shuddered to a halt and had to reset the engine ECU, dropping a lap. Then he had to pit to repair wheel-arch damage, sustained while fighting past Grabmuller. The brothers rejoined and posted fastest lap, taking three points for 13th.

Reeves and Paivarinta swapped the lead back and forth, until the former was forced off track, crunching his wheel-arch. That allowed Holden to make an attempt for second, but he skidded off, flipping the outfit and taking Streuer with him. Reeves managed to miss the debris to regain a distant second, 12 seconds down, with the consistent Alan Founds and Tom Christie taking third and their first rostrum. Streuer got back on track, 30 seconds down, for his first points of the season.

The sun shone for Sunday's 13-lap Gold Race.

Paivarinta led away again, but Reeves took over directly, while Birchall was also ahead on the first lap. Reeves and Birchall skirmished for the lead, Paivarinta and Streuer for third; a second covered all four after six laps.

Birchall managed to get back ahead briefly on lap 13, but Reeves had the upper hand, winning by 0.401 of a second. Just behind, Streuer kept Paivarinta at bay by the same margin. Less than two seconds covered the first four, a breathtaking classic race.

"Fantastic," said Reeves. "It was qualifying laps every lap!"

Round 3 – Sachsenring, Germany

After a month's break, the season was approaching its fulcrum, with four races over eight days, starting at the Sachsenring for the first time in four years.

Rain marred practice and the Sprint Race. Poleman Reeves took an early lead, followed by Paivarinta, who pressed, but couldn't find a passing point. Reeves won by a second; Birchall struggled on the damp track, finishing an unaccustomed 20 seconds behind. Although he liked the result, Reeves was not happy about the track or the conditions: "It was no fun at all."

New boys Sam and Adam Christie came home a very respectable fourth.

It was dry for the first time all weekend for the 19-lap Gold Race, but as a result, no one had any tyre or machinery settings.

Again, Reeves and Paivarinta led away, but were stalked by the Birchalls, who took the lead on the sixth lap, never to be headed. They claimed their first win of the year by ten seconds.

Reeves was looking comfortable on 115 points, 25 more than Paivarinta and 31 ahead of Birchall.

Round 4 – Pannoniaring, Hungary

On to the next double-header, and the halfway point. Birchall, who had won both races at this track in 2017, set his third pole, but only by two-hundredths over Reeves.

Birchall was quick away, but soon was demoted to third by Reeves and Paivarinta. With a clear track, Reeves was away, and a sequence of fast laps earned a defendable margin over Paivarinta, to win by almost four seconds. Birchall was third.

In the Gold Race, the Birchalls' hopes for better were dashed when they retired on lap two. They'd

Left: Pekka Paivarinta and Jussi Veravainen at Assen; they snatched second overall.

Below left: World champions again – the Birchall Brothers, Ben and Tom.

Far left: The Birchalls lead Reeves (77), Streuer (4) and Paivarinta, who fought all year long.

Below: Tucked in. Tim Reeves and Mark Wilkes ran out of luck.

Photos: Mark Walters

barely made the grid, plagued with electrical problems that had dogged them all year.

Paivarinta piled the pressure on Reeves, the two outfits swapping the lead. On lap seven, Reeves made a lunge into Turn Ten, but spun off. The half minute it took to get the outfit out of the gravel put him last, but eventually he made tenth. Paivarinta won by almost 40 seconds from Streuer, whose best result so far had come when he passed Lewis Blackstock on the last lap. Blackstock's third was his first podium of 2018.

Reeves's points lead at the top was cut to 11 from Paivarinta, while Birchall, some 46 points down, was watching his title slip away.

Round 5 – Assen, Netherlands

Just before Assen, the FIM retrospectively disqualified Paivarinta, Lukas Wyssen and Jacob Rutz from the May Sachsenring races, for fuel infringements. Paivarinta lost 36 points, while Birchall gained four. Reeves was still some 42 points ahead going into the biggest meeting of the year.

Birchall claimed a fourth pole in five meetings, but Reeves had to consider the championship. Three thirds would be enough, but he had never been the type to choose safety when a race was to be had.

A huge crowd watched a superb battle over 17 laps. Birchall led away, then Paivarinta scythed through for a few corners, but Birchall took it back. At the start of lap two, he seemed set to get clear, but Reeves had passed the Finn and reeled in the two-second deficit. It took five more laps, then a tremendous race ensued.

The two British teams, both identically powered by Yamaha, were to and fro. On lap ten, hurtling into the famous chicane, Birchall outbraked Reeves on the outside, only for Reeves to nudge him amidships, almost putting both out. Birchall seemed to have an advantage. Then suddenly his engine cut – the return of the electrical problem.

He managed to keep going, but Paivarinta took second as he limped home third.

Reeves's fifth win in eight races put him into a seemingly unassailable 51-point lead with just three races to go. Twenty-five points from 75 was all that would be needed.

What could possibly go wrong?

Well, pretty much everything as it turned out…

Round 6 – Rijeka, Croatia

Arriving at the newly resurfaced Rijeka, the Birchalls stuck by their "Never give up" mantra and took another pole, almost a second clear of Reeves. Streuer made his second front-row start of the season.

Reeves led away, but Birchall squeezed through at Turn Four, and then the race was red-flagged after Blackstock and Wyssen collided. With no injuries, both teams made the restart.

This time, Birchall got the jump. Then a cruel run of luck began for Reeves. Going into Turn Five, his engine blew spectacularly, punching a hole in the cases. As he steered off the track, the machine caught fire. It was his first DNF of the year, but sadly not the last.

Birchall by now was alone, and he won by 11 seconds from Paivarinta. It was a crucial morale booster, and it cut Reeves's points lead to 26. "We're right back in it now and just have to make sure everything is perfect for tomorrow," said Birchall.

Reeves and his team worked through the night repairing the fire-damaged outfit, and made it satisfactorily through eight laps of warm-up. Though wary, he still seemed to be in a comfortable position.

Nerves were jangling for Sunday's 18-lap Gold Race. If Birchall beat Reeves, he would have one more title chance at the final round, but if Reeves won, he'd be champion.

Reeves shot away at the start, but on lap two, Birchall took him around the outside at Turn Two. Reeves ran off to avoid a collision, dropping several places. He fought back through the field to fifth, but the engine had been damaged in the excursion, forcing a second retirement of the weekend.

Birchall won by almost 30 seconds, leaving Paivarinta and Streuer to scrap for second.

Reeves's 51-point cushion had dropped to one point in two days.

Round 7 – Oschersleben, Germany

The entire season depended on the result of one 21-lap race, and each team had only one real option. They had to finish in front of the other.

Birchall led the usual front row: Reeves second, Paivarinta third, ruing his disqualification, but still in with a title chance if both Reeves and Birchall failed to finish.

Despite a close challenge from Reeves, Birchall scorched away, managing to pull enough of a gap to break the tow. He seemed in control. Then, on lap six, the season reached a climax. Passing the flag, Reeves's passenger Wilkes put up his hand as the machine slowed – a collapsed sidecar wheel bearing. That put the title squarely into Birchall's hands; he took the flag with a comfortable 20-second margin.

To compound Reeves's despair, Paivarinta shook off Streuer's challenge, for second in the race and the championship.

With three wins in a row, the Birchall brothers were astounded at the turn in fortunes: "We didn't think we'd do it, but it shows what we keep saying, never ever give in."

The best season for several years went down to the wire. As ever, we can ponder the what-ifs: what if disqualification hadn't cost Paivarinta 36 points; what if Birchall's electrical problems hadn't slowed him in Slovakia, Hungary and at Assen; what if Reeves's phenomenal bad luck at the last three rounds hadn't wiped out months of hard work. Any one of them could have taken the title.

Bennie Streuer, 2015 champion, had a slow start to the season, but found pace to challenge as the year progressed. With spirited showings from Holden, Blackstock, Founds and Wyssen, the level was close, despite thinning grids towards the end of the year. There was a notable result from new boys Sam and Adam Christie from East Yorkshire, whose consistency gave them fifth overall.

It's not a old man's game at the top, but the enthusiasm of Birchall, Paivarinta and Reeves showed no sign of diminishing. We could look forward to their battle resuming in 2019.

US RACING REVIEW

BEAUBIER STRIKES BACK

By LARRY LAWRENCE

Above: **Consistent Cameron Beaubier regained the MotoAmerica crown for Yamaha with a mid-season surge.**
Photo: Gold & Goose

Above right: **Yoshimura Suzuki's defending champion, Toni Elias, won the most races, but lost his title.**

Right: **Suzuki's Roger Hayden called time on his long, illustrious career.**
Photos: MotoAmerica/Brian J. Nelson

THE 2018 MotoAmerica AMA/FIM North American Road Racing Championship featured a number of milestones to take its place nicely in the 43-year history of the one-time AMA Superbike Championship.

The biggest news of 2018 was the strong comeback by Cameron Beaubier and Yamaha, after they had lost the title to Toni Elias and Yoshimura Suzuki in 2017. Both Beaubier and Elias marched up the ranks on the all-time wins list, and Suzuki became the first manufacturer in series history to reach the 200-win mark.

For long-time observers, the series appeared to continue to grow at a steady rate, in terms of race attendance. But there were challenges, most noticeably in respect of TV coverage as a result of an impasse with beIN Sports and several of its cable providers. Also, despite the team's achievements, rumours circulated late in the season that Yamaha would reduce its MotoAmerica racing budget for 2019, with its incredibly successful Supersport programme expected to bear the brunt of the downsizing.

Yoshimura Suzuki had dominated 2017, with Roger Hayden second to Elias. Yamaha rallied and gave Beaubier a consistently potent R1 Superbike. He was good rain or shine and was solid from circuit to circuit. At 25, he was entering the prime of his racing career, and it would have been tough to pick anyone but him as favourite for 2019.

Beaubier's season started slowly, but then came a mid-season rush, and he won seven of eight races from June to August. With Elias having suffered costly crashes, he was able to clinch the championship at the penultimate race weekend at New Jersey Motorsports Park, in a wet race two on Sunday. The win was the 32nd of his AMA Superbike career, a mark that put him equal third on the all-time win list with Miguel Duhamel.

The Beaubier/Elias rivalry seemed certain to continue in 2019. The Monster Energy Yamaha R1 and Yoshimura Suzuki GSX-R1000 appeared to be evenly matched, so it would probably come down to rider consistency. The pattern appeared set: Beaubier slightly more reliable over a variety of tracks and conditions, but Elias mostly better in any head-to-head late-race battle.

It also seemed more certain than ever that Beaubier would spend his entire career racing in MotoAmerica. In many ways, his position was similar to that of Mat Mladin 20 years before, when no world championship seat that might have been available was a title contender, and he would not be able to make anywhere near the money.

With that in mind, it was at least conceivable that Beaubier could go on to rack up Mladin-type all-time career numbers. Beaubier had 32 Superbike wins after five years in the series. At that same point in his career, Mladin had had 18. With 82 wins and seven titles when he retired at 37, Mladin hadn't had the advantage of regular double-header rounds during those first five years, while Beaubier had time on his side. If he were to race until the age of 35, at an average of eight wins per year, that would be 80 more wins, combined with his existing 32. He could easily obliterate all previous win and championship records, and become the first 100-win rider in MotoAmerica/AMA Superbike history.

MotoAmerica cannot be faulted for trying new things. In 2018, it signed a new branding and sponsorship agreement, and brought in big-name attractions at some rounds in an attempt to attract younger fans (skateboarder Tony Hawk and Friends at Road Atlanta, a country music concert at VIR). It also stepped up with a very aggressive push on social media.

You have to interact with younger fans where they live, but it takes time to see if these types of effort pay dividends.

There were good signs, with slightly bigger crowds than in 2017, but were the numbers good enough to sustain the series long term? Officials spoke privately of getting to a financial break-even, but the numbers had to continue to improve to attract major sponsorship and additional factory support, something that could place the series on a more stable footing.

In terms of team participation, once again there was no question that the championship would eventually go to either the factory Yamaha or Suzuki team, but things headed in the right direction for the rest of the MotoAmerica Superbike paddock. The Honda-supported squad fielded two riders for much of the season, a step up from its one-rider 2017 effort. The new Attack Performance Yamaha squad, with Josh Herrin, was instantly competitive and won a pair of races. Yamalube/Westby Racing's Mathew Scholtz also broke the four-rider factory stranglehold on the series with a high-profile win in the rain at the Circuit of The Americas. Suzuki also

had a strong satellite effort with M4 ECSTAR Suzuki's Jake Lewis; and Scheibe Racing/Hayes Brakes BMW was well represented with the always exciting Danny Eslick.

MotoAmerica was fully aware of the difficulties fans faced from mid-season, with local cable and/or satellite providers turning off beIN SPORTS due to the broadcast company's ongoing negotiations with its distributors. Despite what MotoAmerica described as "temporary issues", it claimed that interest and viewership of the series rose dramatically in 2018, saying that it had moved ahead of World Superbike and approached MotoGP numbers. Total viewership (television and digital) for the season had been up 50 per cent, year on year.

It boiled down to beIN being aware of the value of MotoGP and MotoAmerica, given that the outfit wanted to be a regular cable sports channel across the board, like ESPN and Fox Sports. The cable systems heard loud and clear motorcycle racing fans' displeasure about cutting off beIN. The silver lining was that the broadcaster was likely to be in a stronger position once the issue was finally resolved.

Roger Hayden retired at the end of the season, bringing to an end the era of the Hayden brothers, which had begun over 20 years before in AMA Pro Racing. He was the last rider to have experienced the big-money period of American road racing, which had lasted for about a decade from the mid-1990s. None of today's riders enjoys the million-dollar-plus annual contracts of that time Today, the salaries of the top riders are half, or perhaps even a quarter, of those paid in the salad days of American road racing.

Above: **Elias leads Beaubier, Hayden and Gerloff on his way to a second win in a wet Wisconsin.**

Top right: **More rain at CoTA gave Mathew Scholtz the chance for a second Superbike win.**

Photos: MotoAmerica/Brian J. Nelson

Above right: **While Roger Hayden couldn't conjure a final win in 2018, he did score two podium places at Laguna Seca.**

Above far right: **Elias took nine wins in the 20 races.**

Photos: www.suzuki-racing.com

Right: **Yamaha's JD Beach (95) was the convincing winner of the Supersport championship ahead of Hayden Gillim (69).**

Photo: MotoAmerica/Brian J. Nelson

Road Atlanta – 13–15 April

MotoAmerica wisely changed its series opener from supporting the MotoGP weekend at Austin, Texas, to its own event at Road Atlanta in mid-April. Suzuki's Toni Elias continued his tradition of sweeping the opening weekend, as he'd done the previous two years at Circuit of The Americas.

On the heels of his dry win in Saturday's race, the defending champion came back on Sunday in the rain and hunted down Beaubier, stalking the double MotoAmerica champion and passing him on the inside into Turn One to start the 17th of 18 laps. Then he put his head down and rode a perfect lap to win by 1.639 seconds. It was his 18th Superbike victory.

It had been "a perfect weekend. I didn't expect to win a wet race," said Elias. "The bike was good at the beginning, but I needed more confidence. Cameron [Beaubier] and Roger [Hayden] helped me to find my pace, and at the end of the race, I was able to go a little bit more. My team did a really great job, in the wet and dry, during this winter, and I am happy. There are a lot of fast guys, and we will have to fight a lot, but we will be consistent."

It was a great opening for Yoshimura Suzuki, celebrating the 40th anniversary of being the factory entry. Suzuki brought back its first AMA Superbike champion, Wes Cooley, as special guest, much to the delight of veteran fans.

Elias left the Peach State with a perfect 50 points – 14 more than Yamalube/Westby Racing's Mathew Scholtz. Beaubier was third with 27 points, four better than his new Yamaha team-mate, Garret Gerloff, and Kyle Wyman, tied for fourth on 23.

Circuit of The Americas – 20–22 April

Again, Scholtz showed during the combined MotoGP/MotoAmerica weekend that when it rains, he pours it on. The South African won his second career MotoAmerica race and, like the first at the end of 2017 in Alabama, on a wet track.

Under sunny skies on Sunday, Elias turned in a flawless performance, 10.068 seconds clear of Beaubier, who took a second podium in two days. In spite of not winning, Beaubier was upbeat, knowing that he'd survived two up-and-down weekends to start his championship bid. He'd crashed out of second place in the rain on Saturday, but was able to remount to salvage third.

Elias now led Scholtz 88–71, with Beaubier 25 points behind. Herrin and Gerloff filled the championship top five.

Virginia International Raceway – 4–6 May

Elias continued to demonstrate his uncanny knack of being able to win close races in the closing laps. He stalked race-long leader Beaubier before taking the lead and ultimately the win with two laps to go in Saturday's 20-lap race one. It was a milestone 20th win, the Spaniard becoming the fastest rider in AMA Superbike history to reach that total.

Beaubier was a frustrated second, just 0.114 of a second from victory.

There was a massive crash when Garrett Gerloff went down, setting off a chain reaction. Bobby Fong and Roger Hayden also fell trying to avoid him, the latter flipping dramatically over the handlebars of his Suzuki. The crash prompted Hayden to seriously consider retiring, given the number of concussions he'd suffered during his 20 years of pro racing and the effects they might have later in life.

Elias continued his momentum on Sunday, winning his fifth race in six starts. The victory moved him past Fred Merkel and into sixth on the all-time AMA Superbike win list. At this stage, already with a commanding 35-point lead, it appeared almost inevitable that Elias would roll to his second consecutive MotoAmerica title. But that was about to change dramatically.

Road America – 1–3 June

In a race that ranked among the best in series history, Beaubier beat Josh Herrin by just 0.002 of a second (in other words, a few inches) in the Dunlop Championship race one, after a dramatic last lap in which points leader Elias crashed out with just a handful of corners to go.

These three fought for the duration, not always cleanly, and they were summoned to Race Direction afterwards. It started in Turn One on the final lap, when Elias ran his Suzuki into Beaubier's Yamaha, forcing him wide. Seeing red, Beaubier fought back and went for an inside pass at Canada

Corner, as Elias was closing the door. They collided and Elias went down, sliding into the gravel trap.

A long meeting between those involved after the race resulted in no sanction against Beaubier, leaving the Suzuki camp furious.

On Sunday, Beaubier won again, over Herrin and Roger Hayden, while rival Elias ran wide and had to settle for fourth. The result was a sudden turnaround in the championship. Beaubier had arrived at Elkhart Lake trailing by 35 points. He left with pole position, two Superbike wins and a two-point lead.

Notable at Road America was the introduction of a new version of Dunlop's KR451 N-Tek rear slick race tyre, which was larger in circumference than the previous version. Elias appeared to struggle to find comfortable settings on his Suzuki for the new rubber. It was an issue the team would chase throughout the mid-season.

Weathertech Raceway Laguna Seca – 22–24 June

At the combined World Superbike/MotoAmerica weekend at Laguna Seca, Beaubier opened a gap over rival Elias and the rest of the competition. The Californian had a perfect weekend, racing in front of his friends and family to complete a two-race sweep.

On both days, he battled with Herrin's Attack Performance Yamaha. In Saturday's race one, he gradually pulled away to a 5.403-second victory from his exhausted rival. Hayden was third. In Sunday's race, Beaubier and Herrin ran in tandem up front for the first 19 of 24 laps. Beaubier took over from Herrin on the 16th, and the Georgian was keeping him honest when he crashed out at Rainey Curve.

Interestingly, Herrin did double duty racing as a wild-card in World Superbike. He qualified 15th, retired from race one and was 16th in race two, just outside the points.

Beaubier had completely turned the tables on the competition, going from 35 points behind to 29 ahead in the span of just four races.

Utah Motorsports Campus – 20–22 July

At the desert course in Utah, it appeared that Elias and Suzuki had turned it around, with the prospect that he could chase down Beaubier. The Suzuki rider pounced on the Yamaha late in race one, taking the lead with three laps to go and holding off his rival by 0.494 of a second on a hot sunny day on the outskirts of Salt Lake City.

Elias accomplished the feat after an earlier crash that had burned his factory Suzuki beyond repair. His win was historic, for it marked Suzuki's 200th victory in AMA Superbike racing.

Suzuki's celebration evaporated on Sunday, however. Beaubier had the pace and was pulling away when Elias crashed out on the sixth lap. That put him 49 points behind Beaubier with four rounds (eight races) remaining.

Sonoma Raceway – 10–12 August

It was at his home track, Sonoma Raceway in California's wine country, that Beaubier all but put the 2018 championship in the bag. He raced his Yamaha to a clean sweep of the Sonoma weekend, increasing his winning streak at the scenic circuit to four in a row.

He won Saturday's race by a colossal 7.2 seconds after breaking the track record en route to pole position during Superpole. On Sunday, he won by 6.5 seconds, after breaking away early and leading by 1.1 seconds on the first lap.

"We've had a really good string lately," Beaubier said. "I just want to keep the momentum going into the last three rounds. I'm really just enjoying my bike and enjoying racing right now. Last year, when I kept crashing and trying to come up with something, and trying to race Toni and Roger [Hayden], it was tough because I found myself on the ground

LUCAS OIL
LUCAS OIL

DUNLOP
AMA
2018
TWINS CUP
CHAMPION
SHOEI

Attack
PERFORMANCE
YAMAHA
DUNLOP

Above: Elias (1), Beaubier (6), Hayden (95), Gerloff (31) and Lewis (85) fan out at the start of the race in Utah.

Far left: Alex Dumas won the Liqui Moly Junior Cup Championship on his KTM.

Left: Andrew Lee celebrates clinching the Stock 1000 title in the rain at New Jersey.

Below far left: Chris Parrish took the Twins Cup for Suzuki after a close battle with Jason Madama.

Below left: Josh Herrin took two wins for Yamaha, including this one in the wet at New Jersey.

Photos: MotoAmerica/Brian J. Nelson

at least once a weekend. I'm just happy right now, and I just want to keep going."

At this stage, he led Elias 298–235; Herrin was third with 187 points.

Pittsburgh Int'l Race Complex – 24–26 August

The paddock was subdued during the Pittsburg weekend, having learned that Brian Drebber, the MotoAmerica announcer, had succumbed to injuries sustained in a motorcycle accident on his way to the airport to fly to the race.

Josh Herrin won his first Superbike race in five years, the Attack Performance/Herrin Compound Yamaha rider having mastered wet/dry conditions to take the first of two Motul Superbike races of the Championship of Pittsburgh.

A feature of Sunday's race was one of the all-time great last-lap battles in series history. The Superbike final came down to the very last lap of the 2.78-mile PittRace course and featured several close passes by both riders. In the end, though, victory went to Elias and his Yoshimura Suzuki – by just 0.046 of a second from Monster Energy/Yamalube/Yamaha Factory Racing's Beaubier. It was Elias's seventh win of the season and the 23rd of his MotoAmerica Superbike career, and he dedicated the victory to Drebber.

New Jersey Motorsports Park – 7–9 September

Josh Herrin mastered the conditions on Saturday during a very wet Championship of New Jersey at New Jersey Motorsports Park, the Georgian reinforcing his victory of a few weeks before in Pittsburgh with a textbook display of wet-weather riding that earned him a second Motul Superbike victory of the season. It was the sixth win of his AMA Superbike career and his first in the rain.

Herrin beat Yamalube/Westby Racing's Mathew Scholtz by 37.1 seconds, the South African having backed off the pace at the end of the race when he saw the gap he had on Monster Energy/Yamalube/Yamaha Factory Racing's Beaubier. Herrin's margin of victory was one of the largest in the 42-year history of the championship.

Beaubier clinched his third MotoAmerica Superbike Championship in style during Sunday's race two, when the 25-year-old Californian took his eighth Motul Superbike win of the year on a wet and dreary day.

He had led from the start and never put a wheel wrong in harrowing conditions on the 2.25-mile Thunderbolt Raceway. At the end of the shortened 18-lap race, Beaubier was 13.65 seconds ahead of Yoshimura Suzuki's Roger Hayden.

Barber Motorsports Park – 21–23 September

Although Beaubier had already clinched the title, Elias could still score some bragging rights if he could win both races of the final round. A victory on Saturday at the scenic Barber Motorsports Park tied him with the newly crowned champion. They had eight victories apiece heading into Sunday's season finale in the Championship of Alabama.

With all the top championship positions decided, Sunday's race was a go-for-broke battle, and it was Elias, Beaubier and Herrin who put on one of the best races of the season in an epic three-way tussle.

Elias had his hands full for the duration – with Herrin early on, then Beaubier as the trio diced it up. Beaubier made a mistake in Turn Five with two laps to go, which allowed Elias to pull out a lead. But the new champion put his head down and turned in two stellar laps to reel the Spaniard back in. It was too little, too late, however, and Beaubier was forced to settle for his 16th podium finish of the year. A ninth win of the season made Elias the series wins leader for 2018.

In the final standings, Beaubier had 390 points, 51 more than Elias. Herrin ended the season third, 50 points clear of Mathew Scholtz, while Superbike rookie Garrett Gerloff rounded out the top five, just one point ahead of Jake Lewis.

Supersport

Monster Energy/Yamaha Extended Service/Graves/Yamaha's JD Beach was so dominant that he clinched the 2018 MotoAmerica Supersport Championship with three races to go. With his second-place finish in race one at New Jersey Motorsports Park, the well-like Kentuckian scored the second MotoAmerica Supersport Championship of his career.

"I've been working my butt off this year," Beach said, reflecting on his season. "It's been really good. We've been lucky at times and good at times. We put the whole year together."

Hayden Gillim, Beach's friend and training partner, finished second in the series on a Rickdiculous Racing Yamaha, while Frenchman Valentin Debise was third on an M4 ECSTAR Suzuki. Those three were the only riders to win in Supersport in 2018, and in most races they split away quickly from the rest of the field – unusual for this normally close class.

Beach won 11 races, Gillim four and Debise two.

Stock 1000

The new-for-2018 Stock 1000 class replaced the Superstock 1000 class that had raced alongside Motul Superbike for the previous three years. It was intended for up-and-coming riders looking to display their talents at national level. For the most part, it drew sparse entries.

RiderzLaw Racings' Andrew Lee wrapped up the title early by virtue of a fifth-place result aboard his Kawasaki ZX-10R in a wet race at New Jersey Motorsports Park in early September. By the end of the season, Californian Lee had earned a series-leading three wins in the eight-race championship.

"Leading into the opening weekend of the series, we weren't even too sure if we were going to make the first round," Lee said. "So doing my first full season as a pro, it's fantastic. Couldn't have asked for anything more."

Two-times race winner Travis Wyman finished second on a BMW, while Chad Lewin was third on a Yamaha after winning one round.

Twins Cup

The Twins Cup was another new class, and it became a two-rider battle that went down to the wire. At the finale at Barber Motorsports Park, the championship came down to a battle between Ghetto Customs Suzuki rider Chris Parrish and Syndicate/AP MotoArts Yamaha's Jason Madama.

The two riders had arrived separated by just two points. Parrish finished eighth, while Madama was ninth, giving Parrish the title by a scant three points.

The most competitive bikes in the new class were Suzuki SV650s and Yamaha FZ-07s, popular machines in American club road racing, and the series had been devised to give those club riders an easy entry into MotoAmerica. There were good numbers throughout the season, and with six different winners in nine rounds, it was also very competitive.

Liqui Moly Junior Cup

A third new category in MotoAmerica was the Junior Cup class for aspiring young racers. It expanded on the old KTM RC Cup, allowing additional manufacturers. The series was modelled on the FIM Supersport 300 World Championship.

The prime machines were KTM RC390s, Yamaha R3s and Kawasaki Ninja 300s. MotoAmerica incorporated a couple of balancing regulations during the series to level the playing field between brands.

French Canadian Alex Dumas won the championship convincingly on his KTM Orange Brigade/JP43 Training RC390, having scored a class-leading ten wins. Yamaha R3 riders Cory Ventura and Jay Newton were second and third respectively. In total, there were six different winners in the 17-round series.

MAJOR RESULTS

OTHER CHAMPIONSHIP RACING SERIES WORLDWIDE

Compiled by PETER McLAREN

MOTOAMERICA/AMA North American Road Race Championship

Road Atlanta, Braselton, Georgia, 13-15 April, 2018, 21 laps, 53.55 miles/86.18km.
Race 1
1 Toni Elias (Suzuki); **2** Mathew Scholtz (Yamaha); **3** Garrett Gerloff (Yamaha); **4** Bobby Fong (Yamaha); **5** Jake Lewis (Suzuki); **6** Kyle Wyman (Yamaha); **7** Danny Eslick (BMW); **8** David Anthony (Kawasaki); **9** Cameron Beaubier (Yamaha); **10** Josh Herrin (Yamaha).

Race 2 (18 laps, 45.90 miles/73.87km, shortened due to rain)
1 Toni Elias (Suzuki); **2** Cameron Beaubier (Yamaha); **3** Mathew Scholtz (Yamaha); **4** Kyle Wyman (Yamaha); **5** Roger Hayden (Suzuki); **6** Josh Herrin (Yamaha); **7** Sebastiao Ferreira (Yamaha); **8** Bruno Silva (Kawasaki); **9** Garrett Gerloff (Yamaha); **10** Danny Eslick (BMW).

Circuit of the Americas, Austin, Texas, 20-22 April, 2018, 15 laps, 51.40 miles/82.72km.
Race 1
1 Mathew Scholtz (Yamaha); **2** Josh Herrin (Yamaha); **3** Cameron Beaubier (Yamaha); **4** Toni Elias (Suzuki); **5** Jake Lewis (Suzuki); **6** Kyle Wyman (Yamaha); **7** Garrett Gerloff (Yamaha); **8** David Anthony (Kawasaki); **9** Bobby Fong (Yamaha); **10** Barrett Long (Yamaha).

Race 2
1 Toni Elias (Suzuki); **2** Cameron Beaubier (Yamaha); **3** Garrett Gerloff (Yamaha); **4** Josh Herrin (Yamaha); **5** Jake Lewis (Suzuki); **6** Mathew Scholtz (Yamaha); **7** Roger Hayden (Suzuki); **8** Danny Eslick (BMW); **9** David Anthony (Kawasaki); **10** Cameron Petersen (Honda).

Virginia International Raceway, Danville, Virginia, 4-6 May, 2018, 23 laps, 51.75 miles/83.28km.
Race 1 (20 laps, 45.00 miles/72.42km, shortened due to red flag)
1 Toni Elias (Suzuki); **2** Cameron Beaubier (Yamaha); **3** Mathew Scholtz (Yamaha); **4** Josh Herrin (Yamaha); **5** Jake Lewis (Suzuki); **6** David Anthony (Kawasaki); **7** Kyle Wyman (Yamaha); **8** Danny Eslick (BMW); **9** Sebastiao Ferreira (Yamaha); **10** Max Flinders (Yamaha).

Race 2
1 Toni Elias (Suzuki); **2** Cameron Beaubier (Yamaha); **3** Mathew Scholtz (Yamaha); **4** Josh Herrin (Yamaha); **5** Jake Lewis (Suzuki); **6** Kyle Wyman (Yamaha); **7** Danny Eslick (BMW); **8** Bobby Fong (Yamaha); **9** Cameron Petersen (Honda); **10** David Anthony (Kawasaki).

Road America, Elkhart Lake, Wisconsin, 1-3 June, 2018, 13 laps, 52.00 miles/83.69km.
Race 1
1 Cameron Beaubier (Yamaha); **2** Josh Herrin (Yamaha); **3** Garrett Gerloff (Yamaha); **4** Jake Lewis (Suzuki); **5** Roger Hayden (Suzuki); **6** Danny Eslick (BMW); **7** Bobby Fong (Yamaha); **8** Kyle Wyman (Yamaha); **9** Cameron Petersen (Honda); **10** David Anthony (Kawasaki).

Race 2 (8 laps, 32.00 miles/51.50km, shortened due to red flag)
1 Cameron Beaubier (Yamaha); **2** Josh Herrin (Yamaha); **3** Roger Hayden (Suzuki); **4** Toni Elias (Suzuki); **5** Bobby Fong (Yamaha); **6** Garrett Gerloff (Yamaha); **7** Jake Lewis (Suzuki); **8** Danny Eslick (BMW); **9** Cameron Petersen (Honda); 10. Kyle Wyman (Yamaha).

Laguna Seca Raceway, Monterey, California, 22-24 July, 2018, 23 laps, 51.47 miles/82.84km.
Race 1
1 Cameron Beaubier (Yamaha); **2** Josh Herrin (Yamaha); **3** Roger Hayden (Suzuki); **4** Garrett Gerloff (Yamaha); **5** Mathew Scholtz (Yamaha); **6** Danny Eslick (BMW); **7** Cameron Petersen (Honda); **8** Jake Lewis (Suzuki); **9** Kyle Wyman (Yamaha); **10** David Anthony (Kawasaki).

Race 2
1 Cameron Beaubier (Yamaha); **2** Toni Elias (Suzuki); **3** Roger Hayden (Suzuki); **4** Mathew Scholtz (Yamaha); **5** Garrett Gerloff (Yamaha); **6** Jake Lewis (Suzuki); **7** Kyle Wyman (Yamaha); **8** Danny Eslick (BMW); **9** David Anthony (Kawasaki); **10** Cameron Petersen (Honda).

Utah Motorsports Campus, Tooele, Utah, 20-22 June, 2018, 17 laps, 51.87 miles/83.39km.
Race 1
1 Toni Elias (Suzuki); **2** Cameron Beaubier (Yamaha); **3** Josh Herrin (Yamaha); **4** Garrett Gerloff (Yamaha); **5** Jake Lewis (Suzuki); **6** Mathew Scholtz (Yamaha); **7** Kyle Wyman (Yamaha); **8** Danny Eslick (BMW); **9** Cameron Petersen (Honda); **10** Geoff May (Yamaha).

Race 2
1 Cameron Beaubier (Yamaha); **2** Garrett Gerloff (Yamaha); **3** Jake Lewis (Suzuki); **4** Mathew Scholtz (Yamaha); **5** Roger Hayden (Suzuki); **6** Kyle Wyman (Yamaha); **7** Danny Eslick (BMW); **8** Cameron Petersen (Honda); **9** Jayson Uribe (Honda); **10** Bruno Silva (Kawasaki).

Sonoma Raceway, Sonoma, California, 10-12 August, 2018, 22 laps, 48.84 miles/78.60km.
Race 1
1 Cameron Beaubier (Yamaha); **2** Josh Herrin (Yamaha); **3** Toni Elias (Suzuki); **4** Garrett Gerloff (Yamaha); **5** Jake Lewis (Suzuki); **6** Roger Hayden (Suzuki); **7** Danny Eslick (BMW); **8** Kyle Wyman (Yamaha); **9** Geoff May (Yamaha); **10** Jayson Uribe (Honda).

Race 2
1 Cameron Beaubier (Yamaha); **2** Toni Elias (Suzuki); **3** Josh Herrin (Yamaha); **4** Garrett Gerloff (Yamaha); **5** Mathew Scholtz (Yamaha); **6** Jake Lewis (Suzuki); **7** Roger Hayden (Suzuki); **8** Danny Eslick (BMW); **9** Kyle Wyman (Yamaha); **10** Jayson Uribe (Honda).

Pittsburgh Intl Race Complex, Wampum, Pennsylvania, 24-26 August, 2018, 18 laps, 50.04 miles/80.53km.
Race 1 (15 laps, 41.70 miles/67.11km, shortened due to track conditions)
1 Josh Herrin (Yamaha); **2** Garrett Gerloff (Yamaha); **3** Mathew Scholtz (Yamaha); **4** Toni Elias (Suzuki); **5** Cameron Beaubier (Yamaha); **6** Jake Lewis (Suzuki); **7** Roger Hayden (Suzuki); **8** Bobby Fong (Honda); **9** David Anthony (Kawasaki); **10** Kyle Wyman (Yamaha).

Race 2
1 Toni Elias (Suzuki); **2** Cameron Beaubier (Yamaha); **3** Josh Herrin (Yamaha); **4** Jake Lewis (Suzuki); **5** Mathew Scholtz (Yamaha); **6** Bobby Fong (Honda); **7** Danny Eslick (BMW); **8** Kyle Wyman (Yamaha); **9** David Anthony (Kawasaki); **10** Max Flinders (Yamaha).

New Jersey Motorsports Park, Millville, New Jersey, 7-9 September, 2018, 23 laps, 51.75 miles/83.28km.
Race 1
1 Josh Herrin (Yamaha); **2** Mathew Scholtz (Yamaha); **3** Cameron Beaubier (Yamaha); **4** Roger Hayden (Suzuki); **5** Cameron Petersen (Honda); **6** Kyle Wyman (Yamaha); **7** Garrett Gerloff (Yamaha); **8** Jake Lewis (Suzuki); **9** Max Flinders (Yamaha); **10** Danny Eslick (BMW).

Race 2 (18 laps, 40.50 miles/65.18km, shortened due to rain)
1 Cameron Beaubier (Yamaha); **2** Roger Hayden (Suzuki); **3** Toni Elias (Suzuki); **4** Garrett Gerloff (Yamaha); **5** Jake Lewis (Suzuki); **6** David Anthony (Kawasaki); **7** Kyle Wyman (Yamaha); **8** Danny Eslick (BMW); **9** Max Flinders (Yamaha); **10** Sam Verderico (Yamaha).

Barber Motorsports Park, Birmingham, Alabama, 21-23 September, 2018, 21 laps, 49.98 miles/80.45km.
Race 1
1 Toni Elias (Suzuki); **2** Josh Herrin (Yamaha); **3** Mathew Scholtz (Yamaha); **4** Roger Hayden (Suzuki); **5** Jake Lewis (Suzuki); **6** Danny Eslick (BMW); **7** Garrett Gerloff (Yamaha); **8** Bobby Fong (Honda); **9** Cameron Petersen (Honda); **10** Kyle Wyman (Yamaha).

Race 2
1 Toni Elias (Suzuki); **2** Cameron Beaubier (Yamaha); **3** Josh Herrin (Yamaha); **4** Mathew Scholtz (Yamaha); **5** Jake Lewis (Suzuki); **6** Danny Eslick (BMW); **7** Bobby Fong (Honda); **8** Roger Hayden (Suzuki); **9** Geoff May (BMW); **10** Ben Young (BMW).

Final Motul Superbike Championship points:

1	Cameron Beaubier	390
2	Toni Elias	339
3	Josh Herrin	289
4	Mathew Scholtz	239
5	Garrett Gerloff	208
6	Jake Lewis	207

7 Roger Hayden, 172; **8** Kyle Wyman, 157; **9** Danny Eslick, 152; **10** David Anthony, 97.

Final Stock 1000 Championship points:

1	Andrew Lee	166
2	Travis Wyman	119
3	Chad Lewin	91
4	Shane Richardson Jr	74
5	Stephen Incledon	48
6	Melissa Paris	43

7 Roi Holster, 37; **8** Timothy Bemisderfer, 34; **9** Andy DiBrino, 29; **10** Tawfik Khalil, 26.

Final Supersport Championship points:

1	JD Beach	388
2	Hayden Gillim	300
3	Valentin Debise	182
4	Bryce Prince	174
5	Nick McFadden	170
6	Richie Escalante	148

7 Anthony Mazziotto, 137; **8** Cory West, 129; **9** Braeden Ortt, 126; **10** Jason Aguilar, 117.

Final Twins Championship points:

1	Chris Parrish	147
2	Jason Madama	144
3	Kris Turner	65
4	Curtis Murray	48
5	Ryan Roth	44
6	Justin Filice	40

7 Danielle Diaz, 33; **8** Brian McGlade, 31; **9** Aaron Tulchinsky, 31; **10** Shane Perry, 26.

Final Liqui Moly Junior Cup Championship points:

1	Alex Dumas	295
2	Cory Ventura	221
3	Jay Newton	196
4	Ashton Yates	172
5	Sean Ungvarsky	134
6	Jackson Blackmon	134

7 Gavin Anthony, 126; **8** Kevin Olmedo, 118; **9** Jamie Astudillo, 116; **10** Renzo Ferreira, 91.

Endurance World Championship

BOL D'OR, Paul Ricard Circuit, France, 14-17 September, 2017.
FIM Endurance World Championship, Round 1.
683 laps of the 3.598-mile/5.791km circuit, 2457.7 miles/3955.3km
1 GMT94 YAMAHA (David Checa, Niccolò Canepa, Mike Di Meglio), 24h 0m 52.472s.
2 WEPOL BMW Motorrad Team by penz13.com, 674 laps; **3** Honda Endurance Racing, 673 laps; **4** Voelpker NRT48 Schubert-Motors by ERC, 673 laps; **5** IVRacing BMW CSEU, 671 laps; **6** F.C.C. TSR Honda France, 670 laps; **7** Suzuki Endurance Racing Team, 670 laps; **8** Tati Team Beaujolais Racing, 670 laps; **9** Team 33 Accessoires - Louit Moto, 667 laps; **10** Junior Team LMS Suzuki, 663 laps; **11** sarazin motorsport by hall moto 02, 662 laps; **12** No Limits Motor Team, 650 laps; **13** Aviobike, 648 laps; **14** AMSS-TRB VIDRA TEAM SERBIA, 647 laps; **15** Team R2CL - MKS - Partelya, 646 laps.
Fastest lap: TEAM SRC KAWASAKI, 1m 58.386s, 109.36mph/176.0km/h, on lap 2.
Championship points: 1 GMT94 YAMAHA, 60; **2** WEPOL BMW Motorrad Team by penz13.com, 43; **3** Honda Endurance Racing, 42; **4** F.C.C. TSR Honda, 37; **5** Suzuki Endurance Racing Team, 33; **6** Team NRT48 - BMW Motorrad, 32.

24 HEURES MOTOS, Le Mans Bugatti Circuit, France, 19-22 April, 2018.
FIM Endurance World Championship, Round 2.
843 laps of the 2.600-mile/4.185km circuit, 2192.2 miles/3528.0km
1 F.C.C. TSR Honda France (Freddy Foray, Alan Techer, Josh Hook), 24h 1m 4.008s.
2 Honda Endurance Racing, 842 laps; **3** Wepol Racing by penz13.com, 840 laps; **4** Bolliger Team Switzerland, 838 laps; **5** Team SRC Kawasaki, 833 laps; **6** 3ART- Moto Team 95, 833 laps; **7** Moto Ain, 833 laps; **8** Junior Team LMS Suzuki, 828 laps; **9** Mercury Racing, 824 laps; **10** GMT94 Yamaha, 823 laps; **11** Tati Team Beaujolais Racing, 817 laps; **12** Team R2CL, 815 laps; **13** WSB-Endurance, 814 laps; **14** Gert56 German Endurance Racing Team, 814 laps; **15** Team 18 Sapeurs Pompiers, 814 laps.
Fastest lap: YART - Yamaha, 1m 37.426s, 96.06mph/154.6km/h, on lap 110.
Championship points: 1 F.C.C. TSR Honda France, 95; **2** GMT94 YAMAHA, 91; **3** Honda Endurance Racing, 82; **4** WEPOL Racing by penz13.com, 81; **5** MERCURY RACING, 48; **6** Suzuki Endurance Racing Team, 41.

8 HOURS EWC SLOVAKIA RING, Slovakia Ring, Slovakia, 10-12 May, 2018.
FIM Endurance World Championship, Round 3.
224 laps of the 3.680-mile/5.922km circuit, 824.3 miles/1326.5km
1 YART - YAMAHA (Broc Parkes, Marvin Fritz, Max Neukirchner), 8h 1m 37.659s.
2 GMT94 YAMAHA, 224 laps; **3** F.C.C. TSR Honda France, 224 laps; **4** Honda Endurance Racing, 223 laps; **5** NRT48, 222 laps; **6** MERCURY RACING, 221 laps; **7** Suzuki Endurance Racing Team, 221 laps; **8** Bolliger Team Switzerland, 220 laps; **9** TEAM SRC KAWASAKI, 219 laps; **10** Yamaha Viltaïs Experiences, 218 laps; **11** ATOMIC 68, 218 laps; **12** Wójcik Racing Team, 218 laps; **13** Gert56 German Endurance Racing Team, 217 laps; **14** WSB-Endurance, 216 laps; **15** No Limits Motor Team, 216 laps.
Fastest lap: F.C.C. TSR Honda France, 2m 4.185s, 106.63mph/171.6km/h, on lap 211.
Championship points: 1 F.C.C. TSR Honda France, 116; **2** GMT94 YAMAHA, 115; **3** Honda Endurance Racing, 101; **4** WEPOL Racing by penz13.com, 81; **5** MERCURY RACING, 63; **6** Suzuki Endurance Racing Team, 55.

8 HOURS EWC OSCHERSLEBEN, Oschersleben, Germany, 7-10 June, 2018.
FIM Endurance World Championship, Round 4.
312 laps of the 2.279-mile/3.667km circuit, 710.9 miles/1144.1km
1 F.C.C. TSR Honda France (Freddy Foray, Alan Techer, Josh Hook), 8h 0m 49.802s.
2 TEAM SRC KAWASAKI, 312 laps; **3** GMT94 YAMAHA, 312 laps; **4** NRT48, 311 laps; **5** MACO RACING Team, 307 laps; **6** MOTO AIN, 306 laps; **7** Junior Team LMS Suzuki,: 305 laps; **8** Tati Team Beaujolais Racing, 305 laps; **9** No Limits Motor Team, 305 laps; **10** Suzuki Endurance Racing Team, 304 laps; **11** Yamaha Viltaïs Experiences, 304 laps; **12** Motobox Kremer Racing #65, 303 laps; **13** Honda Endurance Racing, 303 laps; **14** MERCURY RACING, 301 laps; **15** Aviobike, 301 laps.
Fastest lap: F.C.C. TSR Honda France, 1m 27.149s, 94.08mph/151.4km/h, on lap 244.
Championship points: 1 F.C.C. TSR Honda France, 146; **2** GMT94 YAMAHA, 136; **3** Honda Endurance Racing, 109; **4** WEPOL Racing by penz13.com, 81; **5** MERCURY RACING, 70; **6** NRT48, 68.

SUZUKA 8 HOURS, Suzuka, Japan, 26-29 July, 2018.
FIM Endurance World Championship, Round 5.
199 laps of the 3.617-mile/5.821km circuit, 719.8 miles/1158.4km
1 YAMAHA FACTORY RACING TEAM (Alex Lowes, Michael van der Mark, Katsuyuki Nakasuga), 8h 0m 1.728s.
2 Red Bull Honda with Japan Post, 199 laps; **3** Kawasaki Team GREEN, 198 laps; **4** S-PULSE DREAM RACING IAI, 196 laps; **5** F.C.C. TSR Honda France, 196 laps; **6** GMT94 YAMAHA, 196 laps; **7** Honda Asia-Dream Racing, 195 laps; **8** KYB MORIWAKI MOTUL RACING, 195 laps; **9** Honda Endurance Racing, 194 laps; **10** YOSHIMURA SUZUKI MOTUL RACING, 194 laps; **11** Team KAGAYAMA U.S.A., 194 laps; **12** Suzuki Endurance Racing Team, 193 laps; **13** BMW Motorrad39, 193 laps; **14** MERCURY RACING, 192 laps; **15** BMW Financial Services 135, 191 laps.
Fastest lap: Kawasaki Team GREEN, 2m 7.527s, 102.09mph/164.3km/h, on lap 77.

FIM Teams' Endurance World Championship points:

1	F.C.C. TSR Honda France	171.5
2	GMT94 YAMAHA	158.5
3	Honda Endurance Racing	127
4	WEPOL Racing by penz13.com	81
5	MERCURY RACING	80.5
6	Suzuki Endurance Racing Team	79.5

7 NRT48, 71; **8** TEAM SRC KAWASAKI FRANCE, 63; **9** Bolliger Team Switzerland, 53; **10** Tati Team Beaujolais Racing, 49; **11** YAMAHA FACTORY RACING TEAM, 45; **12** Junior Team LMS Suzuki, 43; **13** MOTO AIN, 41; **14** Red Bull Honda with Japan Post, 36; **15** Kawasaki Team GREEN, 31.5.

Isle of Man Tourist Trophy Races

ISLE OF MAN TOURIST TROPHY COURSE, 2-8 June, 2018, 37.73-mile/60.72km circuit.

RST Superbike TT (6 laps, 226.38 miles/364.32km)
1 Michael Dunlop (BMW), 1h 44m 13.398s, 130.324mph/209.736km/h.
2 Conor Cummins (Honda), 1h 45m 4.259s; **3** James Hillier (Kawasaki), 1h 45m 25.919s; **4** David Johnson (BMW), 1h 45m 58.637s; **5** Michael Rutter (BMW), 1h 47m 27.374s; **6** Lee Johnston (Honda), 1h 47m 42.014s; **7** Martin Jessopp (BMW), 1h 48m 4.898s; **8** Ivan Lintin (Kawasaki), 1h 48m 7.017s; **9** Philip Crowe (BMW), 1h 48m 12.101s; **10** Joshua Brookes (Norton), 1h 48m 14.276s; **11** Sam West (BMW), 1h 48m 16.964s; **12** Jamie Coward (BMW), 1h 48m 21.999s; **13** Shaun Anderson (Suzuki), 1h 48m 31.783s; **14** Derek Sheils (BMW), 1h 49m 8.054s; **15** Derek McGee (Kawasaki), 1h 49m 42.533s.
Fastest lap: Dean Harrison (Kawasaki), 16m 50.384s, 134.432mph/216.347km/h, on lap 1 (record).
Previous Superbike TT lap record: Michael Dunlop (BMW), 16m 58.254s, 133.393mph/214.675km/h (2016).

Locate.im Sidecar TT Race 1 (3 laps, 113.19 miles/182.16km)
1 Ben Birchall/Tom Birchall (Honda), 57m 33.635s, 117.987mph/189.882km/h.
2 John Holden/Lee Cain (Honda), 58m 20.767s; **3** Tim Reeves/Mark Wilkes (Honda), 58m 42.668s; **4** Peter Founds/Jevan Walmsley (DDM), 59m 30.256s; **5** Alan Founds/Jake Lowther (Yamaha), 1h 1m 16.994s; **6** Conrad Harrison/Andrew Winkle (Honda), 1h 1m 33.593s; **7** Darren Hope/Lenny Bumfrey (Suzuki), 1h 2m 14.600s; **8** Gary Gibson/Daryl Gibson (Suzuki), 1h 2m 33.444s; **9** Gary Bryan/Philip Hyde (Baker), 1h 3m 3.297s; **10** Gregory Lambert/Julie Canipa (Honda), 1h 3m 15.195s; **11** Gordon Shand/Frank Claeys (Shand), 1h 3m 30.104s; **12** Steve Ramsden/Matty Ramsden (LCR), 1h 3m 58.243s; **13** Mike Roscher/Shaun Parker (LCR Suzuki), 1h 4m 2.997s; **14** Andy King/Alun Thomas (Lumley/Ireson), 1h 4m 25.987s; **15** Craig Melvin/Stuart Christian (Suzuki), 1h 4m 36.775s.
Fastest lap: Ben Birchall/Tom Birchall (Honda), 19m 13.320s, 117.771mph/189.534km/h, on lap 3.
Sidecar lap record: Ben Birchall/Tom Birchall (LCR), 19m 19.746s, 117.119mph/188.485km/h, (2017).

Monster Energy Supersport TT Race 1 (4 laps, 150.92 miles/242.88km)
1 Michael Dunlop (Honda), 1h 11m 51.072s, 126.027mph/202.821km/h.
2 Dean Harrison (Kawasaki), 1h 12m 1.350s; **3** Peter Hickman (Triumph), 1h 12m 1.608s; **4** James Hillier (Kawasaki), 1h 12m 3.414s; **5** Conor Cummins (Honda), 1h 12m 44.356s; **6** Joshua Brookes (Yamaha), 1h 12m 57.357s; **7** Gary Johnson (Triumph), 1h 13m 6.152s; **8** Lee Johnston (Honda), 1h 13m 12.190s; **9** James Cowton (Kawasaki), 1h 13m 45.145s; **10** Ivan Lintin (Kawasaki), 1h 13m 54.952s; **11** Derek McGee (Kawasaki), 1h 13m 56.472s; **12** Davey Todd (Honda), 1h 14m 19.574s; **13** Martin Jessopp (Triumph), 1h 14m 19.987s; **14** Dominic Herbertson (Triumph), 1h 14m 26.256s; **15** Sam West (Kawasaki), 1h 14m 30.746s.
Fastest lap: Michael Dunlop (Honda), 17m 31.328s, 129.197mph/207.922km/h, on lap **2** (record).
Previous Supersport lap record: Michael Dunlop (Honda), 17m 35.659s, 128.666mph/207.069km/h (2013).

RL360 Superstock TT (4 laps, 150.92 miles/242.88km)
1 Peter Hickman (BMW), 1h 8m 49.976s, 131.553mph/211.714km/h.
2 Michael Dunlop (BMW), 1h 8m 54.428s; **3** Dean Harrison (Kawasaki), 1h 9m 3.579s; **4** David Johnson (BMW), 1h 10m 16.337s; **5** James Hillier (Kawasaki), 1h 10m 21.259s; **6** Michael Rutter (BMW), 1h 10m 51.480s; **7** Martin Jessopp (BMW), 1h 11m 43.806s; **8** Sam West (BMW), 1h 11m 47.242s; **9** Ivan Lintin (Kawasaki), 1h 11m 49.149s; **10** Davey Todd (Suzuki), 1h 11m 50.396s; **11** Daley Mathison (BMW), 1h 12m 15.059s; **12** Dominic Herbertson (BMW), 1h 12m 21.654s; **13** Brian McCormack (BMW), 1h 12m 23.183s; **14** Craig Neve (BMW), 1h 12m 23.370s; **15** James Cowton (Kawasaki), 1h 12m 25.373s.
Fastest lap: Peter Hickman (BMW), 16m 50.601s, 134.403mph/216.301km/h, on lap **4** (record).
Previous Superstock lap record: Ian Hutchinson (BMW), 17m 0.510s, 133.098mph/214.200km/h (2016).

Monster Energy Supersport TT Race 2 (4 laps, 150.92 miles/242.88km)
1 Dean Harrison (Kawasaki), 1h 11m 28.059s, 126.703mph/203.909km/h.
2 Peter Hickman (Triumph), 1h 11m 46.730s, **3** James Hillier (Kawasaki), 1h 11m 58.508s, **4** Conor Cummins (Honda), 1h 12m 8.333s, **5** Michael Dunlop (Honda), 1h 12m 14.160s, **6** Joshua Brookes (Yamaha), 1h 12m 51.195s, **7** Lee Johnston (Honda), 1h 13m 5.465s, **8** Gary Johnson (Triumph), 1h 13m 25.657s, **9** James Cowton (Kawasaki), 1h 13m 28.648s, **10** Ivan Lintin (Kawasaki), 1h 13m 39.852s, **11** Ian Hutchinson (Honda), 1h 14m 1.328s, **12** Davey Todd (Honda), 1h 14m 4.899s, **13** Sam West (Kawasaki), 1h 14m 15.534s, **14** Dominic Herbertson (Triumph), 1h 14m 21.429s, **15** Daniel Cooper (Honda), 1h 14m 30.423s.
Fastest lap: Dean Harrison (Kawasaki), 17m 32.124s, 129.099mph/207.765km/h, on lap 2.
Supersport TT lap record: Michael Dunlop (Honda, 17m 31.328s, 129.197mph/207.922km/h (2018).

Bennetts Lightweight TT (4 laps, 150.92 miles/242.88km)
1 Michael Dunlop (Paton), 1h 15m 5.032s, 120.601mph/194.088km/h.
2 Derek McGee (Kawasaki), 1h 15m 19.633s; **3** Michael Rutter (Paton), 1h 16m 30.242s; **4** Stefano Bonetti (Paton), 1h 16m 40.194s; **5** Joey Thompson (Paton), 1h 18m 13.175s; **6** Ian Lougher (Paton), 1h 18m 26.857s; **7** Michael Sweeney (Kawasaki), 1h 18m 27.273s; **8** Adam Mclean (Kawasaki), 1h 18m 38.044s; **9** Julian Trummer (Kawasaki), 1h 19m 4.182s; **10** Dominic Herbertson (Kawasaki), 1h 19m 12.721s; **11** John Barton (Kawasaki), 1h 20m 7.063s; **12** Barry Furber (Suzuki), 1h 20m 17.207s; **13** Andrew Dudgeon (Kawasaki), 1h 20m 25.295s; **14** Darren Cooper (Kawasaki), 1h 20m 34.557s; **15** Forest Dunn (Kawasaki), 1h 20m 45.787s.
Fastest lap: Michael Dunlop (Paton), 18m 26.543s 122.750mph/197.547km/h, on lap **4** (record).
Previous Lightweight TT record: James Hillier (Kawasaki), 18m 43.955s, 120.848mph/194.486km/h (2015)

SES TT Zero (1 lap, 37.73 miles/60.72km)
1 Michael Rutter (Mugen), 18m 34.956s; 121.824mph/196.057km/h.
2 Daley Mathison (University of Nottingham), 18m 58.600s; **3** Lee Johnston (Mugen), 21m 26.668s; **4** James Cowton (Brunel), 23m 14.934s; **5** Adam Child (Moto Corsa), 27m 50.042s; **6** Shaun Anderson (Brammo), 30m 16.155s.
Previous TT Zero lap record: John McGuinness (Mugen), 18m 58.743s, 119.279mph/191.961km/h (2015).

Locate.im Sidecar TT Race 2 (3 laps, 113.19 miles/182.16km)
1 Ben Birchall/Tom Birchall (Honda), 57m 25.040s, 118.281mph/190.355km/h.
2 John Holden/Lee Cain (Honda), 57m 47.960s; **3** Tim Reeves/Mark Wilkes (Honda), 58m 3.738s; **4** Alan Founds/Jake Lowther (Yamaha), 59m 20.730s; **5** Lewis Blackstock/Patrick Rosney (Honda), 1h 0m 21.459s; **6** Conrad Harrison/Andrew Winkle (Honda), 1h 0m 37.918s; **7** Gary Bryan/Philip Hyde (Baker), 1h 0m 48.452s; **8** Steve Ramsden/Matty Ramsden (LCR), 1h 0m 58.064s; **9** Estelle Leblond/Melanie Farnier (SGR Suzuki), 1h 1m 36.707s; **10** Gary Gibson/Daryl Gibson (Suzuki), 1h 2m 13.039s; **11** Karl Bennett/Maxime Vasseur (Suzuki), 1h 2m 26.992s; **12** Michael Jackson/Harry Payne (Suzuki), 1h 2m 31.853s; **13** Gary Knight/Daniel Evans (Kawasaki), 1h 2m 51.386s; **14** Gordon Shand/Frank Claeys (Shand), 1h 3m 23.450s; **15** Mike Roscher/Shaun Park (LCR Suzuki), 1h 4m 29.802s,
Fastest lap: Ben Birchall/Tom Birchall (Honda), 18m 59.018s, 119.250mph/191.914km/h, on lap **2** (record).
Previous Sidecar lap record: Ben Birchall/Tom Birchall (LCR), 19m 19.746s, 117.119mph/191.703km/h (2017).

PokerStars Senior TT (6 laps, 226.38 miles/364.32km)
1 Peter Hickman (BMW), 1h 43m 8.065s, 131.700mph/211.951km/h.
2 Dean Harrison (Kawasaki), 1h 43m 10.126s; **3** Conor Cummins (Honda), 1h 44m 50.559s; **4** Michael Dunlop (BMW), 1h 45m 45.315s; **5** Joshua Brookes (Norton), 1h 46m 9.904s; **6** Gary Johnson (Kawasaki), 1h 47m 6.818s; **7** Martin Jessopp (BMW), 1h 47m 58.408s; **8** Jamie Coward (BMW), 1h 48m 27.787s; **9** Davey Todd (Suzuki), 1h 49m 0.059s; **10** Brian McCormack (BMW), 1h 49m 4.383s; **11** Craig Neve (BMW), 1h 49m 34.789s; **12** Michael Sweeney (BMW), 1h 50m 10.011s; **13** Daley Mathison (BMW), 1h 50m 21.707s; **14** Rob Hodson (BMW), 1h 50m 30.453s; **15** Danny Webb (BMW), 1h 50m 40.735s.
Fastest lap: Peter Hickman (BMW), 16m 42.778s, 135.452mph/217.989km/h, on lap **6** (record)
Previous Superbike TT and Outright lap record: Michael Dunlop (BMW), 16m 53.929s, 133.962mph/215.591km/h (2016).

British Championships

DONINGTON PARK, 1-2 April, 2018, 2.487-mile/4.002km circuit.
Bennetts British Superbike Championship, Round 1
Race 1 (18 laps 44.784 miles/72.073km)
1 Bradley Ray (Suzuki), 27m 12.977s, 98.61mph/158.7km/h.
2 Shane Byrne (Ducati); **3** James Ellison (Yamaha); **4** Dan Linfoot (Honda); **5** Luke Mossey (Kawasaki); **6** Glenn Irwin (Ducati); **7** Jason O'Halloran (Honda); **8** Peter Hickman (BMW); **9** Leon Haslam (Kawasaki); **10** Michael Laverty (BMW); **11** Jake Dixon (Kawasaki); **12** Josh Brookes (Yamaha); **13** Danny Buchan (Kawasaki); **14** Christian Iddon (BMW); **15** Taylor Mackenzie (Ducati).
Fastest lap: Ray, 1m 29.949s, 99.55mph/160.21km/h.

Race 2 (18 laps 44.784 miles/72.073km)
1 Bradley Ray (Suzuki), 28m 0.955s, 95.80mph/154.18km/h.
2 Leon Haslam (Kawasaki); **3** Dan Linfoot (Honda); **4** Danny Buchan (Kawasaki); **5** Shane Byrne (Ducati); **6** Christian Iddon (BMW); **7** Glenn Irwin (Ducati); **8** Luke Mossey (Kawasaki); **9** Jason O'Halloran (Honda); **10** Michael Laverty (BMW); **11** Josh Brookes (Yamaha); **12** Jake Dixon (Kawasaki); **13** Richard Cooper (Suzuki); **14** Tommy Bridewell (Suzuki); **15** Gino Rea (Suzuki).
Fastest lap: Haslam, 1m 31.709s, 97.63mph/157.13km/h.
Championship points: **1** Bradley Ray, 50; **2** Shane Byrne, 31; **3** Dan Linfoot, 29; **4** Leon Haslam, 27; **5** Luke Mossey, 19; **6** Glenn Irwin, 19.

Dickies British Supersport Championship, Round 1
Race 1 (8 laps 19.904 miles/32.032km)
1 Benjamin Currie (Kawasaki), 12m 30.235s, 95.30mph/153.37km/h.
2 Jack Kennedy (Yamaha); **3** Ross Twyman (Yamaha); **4** Tom Oliver (Yamaha); **5** James Westmoreland (Kawasaki); **6** Tommy Philp (Yamaha); **7** David Allingham (Yamaha); **8** Danny Booth (Yamaha); **9** Robert Kennedy (Yamaha); **10** Tim Neave (Yamaha); **11** Bradley Perie (Yamaha); **12** Joey Thompson (Kawasaki); **13** Sam Wilford (Yamaha); **14** Dan Stamper (Yamaha); **15** Daniel Drayton (Kawasaki).
Fastest lap: Currie, 1m 32.017s, 97.31mph/156.61km/h.

Race 2 (16 laps 39.808 miles/64.065km)
1 Benjamin Currie (Kawasaki), 26m 54.031s, 88.68mph/142.72km/h.
2 Jack Kennedy (Yamaha); **3** Tom Oliver (Yamaha); **4** James Rispoli (Yamaha); **5** David Allingham (Yamaha); **6** James Westmoreland (Kawasaki); **7** Tommy Philp (Yamaha); **8** Ross Twyman (Yamaha); **9** Tim Neave (Yamaha); **10** Bradley Perie (Yamaha); **11** Bjorn Estment (Yamaha); **12** Bradley Jones (Yamaha); **13** Harry Truelove (MV Agusta); **14** Daniel Drayton (Kawasaki); **15** Matthew Wigley (Yamaha).
Fastest lap: Currie, 1m 39.942s, 89.59mph/144.19km/h.
Championship points: **1** Benjamin Currie, 50; **2** Jack Kennedy, 40; **3** Tom Oliver, 29; **4** Ross Twyman, 24; **5** James Westmoreland, 21; **6** David Allingham, 20.

BRANDS HATCH INDY, 15 April, 2018, 1.208-mile/1.944km circuit. Bennetts British Superbike Championship, Round 2
Race 1 (30 laps 36.237 miles/58.318km)
1 Shane Byrne (Ducati), 22m 58.754s, 94.62mph/152.28km/h.
2 Bradley Ray (Suzuki); **3** Jason O'Halloran (Honda); **4** Leon Haslam (Kawasaki); **5** Christian Iddon (BMW); **6** Jake Dixon (Kawasaki); **7** Glenn Irwin (Ducati); **8** Michael Laverty (BMW); **9** Tommy Bridewell (Suzuki); **10** Peter Hickman (BMW); **11** Tarran Mackenzie (Yamaha); **12** Danny Buchan (Kawasaki); **13** Josh Brookes (Yamaha); **14** Jakub Smrz (BMW); **15** Luke Mossey (Kawasaki).
Fastest lap: Ray, 45.201s, 96.20mph/154.82km/h.

Race 2 (22 laps 26.574 miles/42.767km)
1 Leon Haslam (Kawasaki), 19m 41.564s, 80.96mph/130.29km/h.
2 Glenn Irwin (Ducati); **3** Michael Laverty (BMW); **4** Shane Byrne (Ducati); **5** Josh Brookes (Yamaha); **6** Christian Iddon (BMW); **7** Bradley Ray (Suzuki); **8** Tommy Bridewell (Suzuki); **9** Tarran Mackenzie (Yamaha); **10** Carl Phillips (Kawasaki); **11** James Ellison (Yamaha); **12** Danny Buchan (Kawasaki); **13** Luke Mossey (Kawasaki); **14** Peter Hickman (BMW); **15** Taylor Mackenzie (Ducati).
Fastest lap: Haslam, 52.730s, 82.46mph/132.72km/h.
Championship points: 1 Bradley Ray, 79; **2** Shane Byrne, 69; **3** Leon Haslam, 65; **4** Glenn Irwin, 48; **5** Michael Laverty, 36; **6** Christian Iddon, 33.

Dickies British Supersport Championship, Round 2
Race 1 (16 laps 19.326 miles/31.102km)
1 Jack Kennedy (Yamaha), 12m 36.769s, 91.94mph/147.96km/h.
2 Benjamin Currie (Kawasaki); **3** Jamie Perrin (Yamaha); **4** Joe Francis (MV Agusta); **5** Bradley Jones (Yamaha); **6** Ross Twyman (Yamaha); **7** Tom Oliver (Yamaha); **8** David Allingham (Yamaha); **9** James Rispoli (Yamaha); **10** Dan Stamper (Yamaha); **11** James Westmoreland (Kawasaki); **12** Kurt Wigley (Yamaha); **13** Robert Kennedy (Yamaha); **14** Bradley Perie (Yamaha); **15** Tommy Philp (Yamaha).
Fastest lap: Currie, 46.819s, 92.88mph/149.47km/h.

Race 2 (12 laps 14.495 miles/23.327km)
1 Jack Kennedy (Yamaha), 9m 36.624s, 90.49mph/145.63km/h.
2 James Rispoli (Yamaha); **3** Benjamin Currie (Kawasaki); **4** Ross Twyman (Yamaha); **5** Robert Kennedy (Yamaha); **6** Bradley Perie (Yamaha); **7** James Westmoreland (Kawasaki); **8** Bradley Jones (Yamaha); **9** Ryan Dixon (Yamaha); **10** Josh Owens (Kalex); **11** Tim Neave (Yamaha); **12** David Allingham (Yamaha); **13** Dan Stamper (Yamaha); **14** Ryan Vickers (Yamaha); **15** Jamie Perrin (Yamaha).
Fastest lap: Currie, 47.079s, 92.36mph/148.65km/h.
Championship points: **1** Jack Kennedy, 90; **2** Benjamin Currie, 86; **3** Ross Twyman, 47; **4** James Rispoli, 40; **5** Tom Oliver, 38; **6** James Westmoreland, 35.

HEL Performance British Motostar Championship, Round 1
Race 1 (18 laps 21.742 miles/34.99km)
1 Jake Archer (KTM), 14m 57.433s, 87.22mph/140.37km/h.
2 Asher Durham (Mahindra); **3** Storm Stacey (KTM); **4** Edward Rendell (KTM FTR); **5** Jack Scott (KTM); **6** Elliot Lodge (FTR); **7** Brandon Paasch (Mahindra); **8** Edmund Best (KTM); **9** Liam Delves (DR-Moto); **10** Jack Nixon (KTM); **11** Chris Taylor (Mahindra); **12** Victor Rodriguez (Honda); **13** Lee Hindle (KTM); **14** Max Cook (Honda); **15** Cameron Horsman (Honda).
Fastest lap: Paasch, 49.092s, 88.58mph/142.55km/h.

Race 2 (20 laps 24.158 miles/38.879km)
1 Jack Scott (KTM), 16m 39.626s, 87.00mph/140.01km/h.
2 Jake Archer (KTM); **3** Brandon Paasch (Mahindra); **4** Asher Durham (Mahindra); **5** Edward Rendell (KTM FTR); **6** Eugene McManus (KTM); **7** Jack Nixon (KTM); **8** Storm Stacey (KTM); **9** Taz Taylor (Kalex KTM); **10** Lee Hindle (KTM); **11** Victor Rodriguez (Honda); **12** Max Cook (Honda); **13** Fenton Seabright (Honda); **14** Liam Delves (DR-Moto); **15** Cameron Horsman (Honda).
Fastest lap: Archer, 48.921s, 88.89mph/143.05km/h.
Championship points: **1** Jake Archer, 45; **2** Jack Scott, 36; **3** Asher Durham, 33; **4** Brandon Paasch, 25; **5** Storm Stacey, 24; **6** Edward Rendell, 24.

OULTON PARK, 7 May, 2018, 2.692-mile/4.332km circuit.
Bennetts British Superbike Championship, Round 3
Race 1 (18 laps 48.456 miles/77.982km)
1 Leon Haslam (Kawasaki), 28m 41.418s, 101.33mph/163.07km/h.
2 Jake Dixon (Kawasaki); **3** Shane Byrne (Ducati); **4** Bradley Ray (Suzuki); **5** Jason O'Halloran (Honda); **6** Josh Brookes (Yamaha); **7** Danny Buchan (Kawasaki); **8** Tommy Bridewell (Suzuki); **9** Tarran Mackenzie (Yamaha); **10** Richard Cooper (Suzuki); **11** James Ellison (Yamaha); **12** Ryuichi Kiyonari (Honda); **13** Gino Rea (Suzuki); **14** Jakub Smrz (BMW); **15** Mason Law (Kawasaki).
Fastest lap: Haslam, 1m 34.972s, 102.04mph/164.22km/h.

Race 2 (18 laps 48.456 miles/77.982km)
1 Leon Haslam (Kawasaki), 28m 40.954s, 101.36mph/163.12km/h.
2 Jason O'Halloran (Honda); **3** Jake Dixon (Kawasaki);**4** Shane Byrne (Ducati); **5** Glenn Irwin (Ducati); **6** Josh Brookes (Yamaha); **7** Bradley Ray (Suzuki); **8** Danny Buchan (Kawasaki);9 Richard Cooper (Suzuki); **10** Tommy Bridewell (Suzuki); **11** Peter Hickman (BMW); **12** James Ellison (Yamaha); **13** Michael Laverty (BMW); **14** Taylor Mackenzie (Ducati); **15** Ryuichi Ki-

yonari (Honda). **Fastest lap:** Haslam, 1m 34.857s, 102.16mph/164.42km/h.
Championship points: 1 Leon Haslam, 115; 2 Bradley Ray, 101; **3** Shane Byrne, 98; **4** Jason O'Halloran, 63; **5** Glenn Irwin, 59; **6** Jake Dixon, 55.

Dickies British Supersport Championship, Round 3
Race 1 (12 laps 32.304 miles/51.988km)
1 Jack Kennedy (Yamaha), 19m 41.652s, 98.41mph/158.38km/h.
2 Benjamin Currie (Kawasaki); **3** Jamie Perrin (Yamaha); **4** James Rispoli (Yamaha); **5** James Westmoreland (Kawasaki); **6** Bradley Jones (Yamaha); **7** David Allingham (Yamaha); **8** Tom Oliver (Yamaha); **9** Josh Owens (Kalex); **10** Ross Twyman (Yamaha); **11** Bradley Perie (Yamaha); **12** Tommy Philp (Yamaha); **13** Bjorn Estment (Yamaha); **14** Joey Thompson (Kawasaki); **15** Danny Booth (Yamaha).
Fastest lap: Kennedy, 1m 37.718s, 99.17mph/ 159.60km/h.

Race 2 (16 laps 43.072 miles/69.318km)
1 Jack Kennedy (Yamaha), 26m 17.555s, 98.29mph/158.18km/h.
2 Benjamin Currie (Kawasaki); **3** James Rispoli (Yamaha); **4** James Westmoreland (Kawasaki); **5** Bradley Jones (Yamaha); **6** Ross Twyman (Yamaha); **7** Bradley Perie (Yamaha); **8** Tom Oliver (Yamaha); **9** Tommy Philp (Yamaha); **10** Sam Wilford (Yamaha); **11** Joey Thompson (Kawasaki); **12** Danny Booth (Yamaha); **13** Robert Kennedy (Yamaha); **14** Daniel Drayton (Kawasaki); **15** Richard Kerr (Triumph).
Fastest lap: Currie, 1m 37.890s, 99.00mph/ 159.32km/h.
Championship points: 1 Jack Kennedy, 140; **2** Benjamin Currie, 126; **3** James Rispoli, 69; **4** Ross Twyman, 64; **5** James Westmoreland, 59; **6** Tom Oliver, 54.

HEL Performance British Motostar Championship, Round 2
Race 1 (10 laps 26.920 miles/43.324km)
1 Jake Archer (KTM), 17m 36.126s, 91.76mph/147.67km/h.
2 Storm Stacey (KTM); **3** Asher Durham (Mahindra); **4** Edward Rendell (KTM); **5** Elliot Lodge (FTR); **6** Jack Scott (KTM); **7** Eugene McManus (KTM); **8** Taz Taylor (Kalex KTM); **9** Liam Delves (DR-Moto); **10** Edmund Best (KTM); **11** Jack Nixon (KTM); **12** Victor Rodriguez (Honda); **13** Lee Hindle (KTM); **14** Fenton Seabright (Honda); **15** Cameron Horsman (Honda).
Fastest lap: Archer, 1m 44.400s, 92.82mph/ 149.39km/h.

Race 2 (14 laps 37.688 miles/60.653km)
1 Jake Archer (KTM), 24m 36.486s, 91.89mph/ 147.88km/h.
2 Storm Stacey (KTM); **3** Jack Scott (KTM); **4** Edward Rendell (KTM); **5** Asher Durham (Mahindra); **6** Brandon Paasch (Mahindra); **7** Eugene McManus (KTM); **8** Taz Taylor (Kalex KTM); **9** Elliot Lodge (FTR); **10** Liam Delves (DR-Moto); **11** Edmund Best (KTM); **12** Chris Taylor (Mahindra); **13** Lee Hindle (KTM); **14** Fenton Seabright (Honda); **15** Scott Ogden (Honda).
Fastest lap: Stacey, 1m 44.270s, 92.94mph/ 149.57km/h.
Championship points: 1 Jake Archer, 95; **2** Storm Stacey, 64; **3** Jack Scott, 62; **4** Asher Durham, 60; **5** Edward Rendell, 50; **6** Brandon Paasch, 35.

SNETTERTON, 17 June, 2018, 2.969-mile/ 4.778km circuit.
Bennetts British Superbike Championship, Round 4
Race 1 (16 laps 47.502 miles/76.447km)
1 Leon Haslam (Kawasaki), 30m 10.370s, 94.46mph/152.02km/h.
2 Glenn Irwin (Ducati); **3** Jake Dixon (Kawasaki); **4** Josh Brookes (Yamaha); **5** Danny Buchan (Kawasaki); **6** Tarran Mackenzie (Yamaha); **7** Peter Hickman (BMW); **8** James Ellison (Yamaha); **9** Christian Iddon (BMW); **10** Richard Cooper (Suzuki); **11** Taylor Mackenzie (Ducati); **12** Mason Law (Kawasaki); **13** Sylvain Barrier (BMW); **14** Gino Rea (Suzuki); **15** Shaun Winfield (Yamaha).
Fastest lap: Irwin, 1m 47.351s, 99.56mph/ 160.22km/h.

Race 2 (16 laps 47.502 miles/76.447km)
1 Leon Haslam (Kawasaki), 29m 1.207s, 98.21mph/158.05km/h.
2 Jake Dixon (Kawasaki); **3** Josh Brookes (Yamaha); **4** Dan Linfoot (Honda); **5** Danny Buchan (Kawasaki); **6** Peter Hickman (BMW); **7** Richard Cooper (Suzuki); **8** Christian Iddon (BMW); **9** Michael Laverty (BMW); **10** Andrew Irwin (Ducati); **11** Gino Rea (Suzuki); **12** Taylor Mackenzie (Ducati); **13** Mason Law (Kawasaki); **14** Sylvain Barrier (BMW); **15** Shaun Winfield (Yamaha).
Fastest lap: Haslam, 1m 47.660s, 99.27mph/ 159.76km/h.
Championship points: 1 Leon Haslam, 165; **2** Bradley Ray, 101; **3** Shane Byrne, 98; **4** Jake Dixon, 91; **5** Glenn Irwin, 79; **6** Josh Brookes, 72.

Dickies British Supersport Championship, Round 4
Race 1 (9 laps 26.720 miles/43.002km)
1 Jack Kennedy (Yamaha), 17m 59.430s, 89.11mph/143.41km/h.
2 Benjamin Currie (Kawasaki); **3** James Westmoreland (Kawasaki); **4** Ross Twyman (Yamaha); **5** Bradley Jones (Yamaha); **6** Sam Wilford (Yamaha); **7** Tommy Philp (Yamaha); **8** Ryan Dixon (Yamaha); **9** Danny Booth (Yamaha); **10** Daniel Drayton (Kawasaki); **11** Mike Brouwers (Honda); **12** Ross Patterson (Kawasaki); **13** Jorel Boerboom (Kalex); **14** Harry Truelove (Yamaha); **15** Matthew Wigley (Yamaha).
Fastest lap: Kennedy, 1m 50.929s, 96.35mph/ 155.06km/h.

Race 2 (15 laps 44.534 miles/71.671km)
1 Jack Kennedy (Yamaha), 28m 15.800s, 94.54mph/152.15km/h.
2 Ross Twyman (Yamaha); **3** James Rispoli (Yamaha); **4** Bradley Jones (Yamaha); **5** Tommy Philp (Yamaha); **6** Sam Wilford (Yamaha); **7** Josh Owens (Kalex); **8** David Allingham (Yamaha); **9** Tim Neave (Yamaha); **10** Danny Booth (Yamaha); **11** Kurt Wigley (Yamaha); **12** Bjorn Estment (Yamaha); **13** Ryan Dixon (Yamaha); **14** Jorel Boerboom (Kalex); **15** Eugene McManus (Kalex).
Fastest lap: Kennedy, 1m 51.732s, 95.65mph/ 153.94km/h.
Championship points: 1 Jack Kennedy, 190; **2** Benjamin Currie, 146; **3** Ross Twyman, 97; **4** James Rispoli, 85; **5** James Westmoreland, 75; **6** Bradley Jones, 68.

KNOCKHILL, 8 July, 2018, 1.267-mile/ 2.039km circuit.
Bennetts British Superbike Championship, Round 5
Race 1 (30 laps 38.007 miles/61.166km)
1 Jake Dixon (Kawasaki), 24m 2.179s, 94.87mph/152.68km/h.
2 Leon Haslam (Kawasaki); **3** Danny Buchan (Kawasaki); **4** Glenn Irwin (Ducati); **5** Bradley Ray (Suzuki); **6** Michael Laverty (BMW); **7** Christian Iddon (BMW); **8** Josh Brookes (Yamaha); **9** Richard Cooper (Suzuki); **10** Peter Hickman (BMW); **11** Andrew Irwin (Ducati); **12** Luke Mossey (Kawasaki); **13** James Ellison (Yamaha); **14** Tarran Mackenzie (Yamaha); **15** Mason Law (Kawasaki).
Fastest lap: Buchan, 47.644s, 95.73mph/ 154.06km/h.

Race 2 (30 laps 38.007 miles/61.166km)
1 Leon Haslam (Kawasaki), 23m 57.841s, 95.16mph/153.15km/h.
2 Jake Dixon (Kawasaki); **3** Danny Buchan (Kawasaki); **4** Glenn Irwin (Ducati); **5** Michael Laverty (BMW); **6** Christian Iddon (BMW); **7** Richard Cooper (Suzuki); **8** Andrew Irwin (Ducati); **9** James Ellison (Yamaha); **10** Peter Hickman (BMW); **11** Tarran Mackenzie (Yamaha); **12** Luke Mossey (Kawasaki); **13** Dan Linfoot (Honda); **14** Mason Law (Kawasaki); **15** Gino Rea (Suzuki).
Fastest lap: Haslam, 47.462s, 96.10mph/ 154.65km/h.
Championship points: 1 Leon Haslam, 210; **2** Jake Dixon, 136; **3** Bradley Ray, 112; **4** Glenn Irwin, 105; **5** Shane Byrne, 98; **6** Danny Buchan, 95.

Dickies British Supersport Championship, Round 5
Race 1 (18 laps 22.804 miles/36.699km)
1 Jack Kennedy (Yamaha), 14m 53.145s, 91.92mph/147.93km/h.
2 Benjamin Currie (Kawasaki); **3** James Westmoreland (Kawasaki); **4** David Allingham (Yamaha); **5** James Rispoli (Yamaha); **6** Ross Twyman (Yamaha); **7** Bradley Jones (Yamaha); **8** Bjorn Estment (Yamaha); **9** Sam Wilford (Yamaha); **10** Josh Owens (Kalex); **11** Jamie Perrin (Yamaha); **12** Tom Oliver (Yamaha); **13** Dan Stamper (Yamaha); **14** Bradley Perie (Yamaha); **15** Tim Neave (Yamaha).
Fastest lap: Kennedy, 49.179s, 92.74mph/ 149.25km/h.

Race 2 (26 laps 32.939 miles/53.01km)
1 Jack Kennedy (Yamaha), 21m 32.049s, 91.78mph/147.71km/h.
2 Benjamin Currie (Kawasaki); **3** James Westmoreland (Kawasaki); **4** David Allingham (Yamaha); **5** Ross Twyman (Yamaha); **6** James Rispoli (Yamaha); **7** Josh Owens (Kalex); **8** Bjorn Estment (Yamaha); **9** Tim Neave (Yamaha); **10** Sam Wilford (Yamaha); **11** Dan Stamper (Yamaha); **12** Bradley Perie (Yamaha); **13** Rory Skinner (Kawasaki); **14** Richard Kerr (Triumph); **15** Tom Oliver (Yamaha).
Fastest lap: Kennedy, 49.227s, 92.65mph/ 149.11km/h.
Championship points: 1 Jack Kennedy, 240; **2** Benjamin Currie, 186; **3** Ross Twyman, 118; **4** James Westmoreland, 107; **5** James Rispoli, 106; **6** Bradley Jones, 77.

HEL Performance British Motostar Championship, Round 3
Race 1 (18 laps 22.804 miles/36.699km)
1 Jake Archer (KTM), 15m 47.753s, 86.62mph/ 139.40km/h.
2 Jack Scott (KTM); **3** Storm Stacey (KTM); **4** Eugene McManus (KTM); **5** Asher Durham (Mahindra); **6** Chris Taylor (Mahindra); **7** Brandon Paasch (Mahindra); **8** Edmund Best (KTM); **9** Liam Delves (DR-Moto); **10** Elliot Lodge (FTR); **11** Victor Rodriguez (Honda); **12** Thomas Strudwick (Honda); **13** Taylor Moreton (Honda); **14** Rhys Irwin (Honda); **15** Charlie Atkins (Honda).
Fastest lap: Stacey, 51.993s, 87.72mph/ 141.18km/h.

Race 2 (22 laps 27.872 miles/44.856km)
1 Jake Archer (KTM), 19m 19.566s, 86.53mph/ 139.26km/h.
2 Storm Stacey (KTM); **3** Asher Durham (Mahindra); **4** Jack Nixon (KTM); **5** Chris Taylor (Mahindra); **6** Edmund Best (KTM); **7** Liam Delves (DR-Moto); **8** Edward Rendell (KTM FTR); **9** Brandon Paasch (Mahindra); **10** Elliot Lodge (FTR); **11** Lee Hindle (KTM); **12** Thomas Strudwick (Honda); **13** Victor Rodriguez (Honda); **14** Taylor Moreton (Honda); **15** Scott Ogden (Honda).
Fastest lap: Archer, 52.072s, 87.59mph/ 140.96km/h.
Championship points: 1 Jake Archer, 145; **2** Storm Stacey, 100; **3** Asher Durham, 87; **4** Jack Scott, 82; **5** Edward Rendell, 58; **6** Brandon Paasch, 51.

BRANDS HATCH GP, 22 July, 2018, 2.433-mile/ 3.916km circuit.
Bennetts British Superbike Championship, Round 6
Race 1 (20 laps 48.664 miles/78.317km)
1 Josh Brookes (Yamaha), 28m 49.695s, 101.28mph/162.99km/h.
2 Glenn Irwin (Ducati); **3** Leon Haslam (Kawasaki); **4** Jake Dixon (Kawasaki); **5** Christian Iddon (BMW); **6** Peter Hickman (BMW); **7** Richard Cooper (Suzuki); **8** Danny Buchan (Kawasaki); **9** Andrew Irwin (Ducati); **10** Michael Laverty (BMW); **11** Chrissy Rouse (Suzuki); **12** Tommy Bridewell (Ducati); **13** Bradley Ray (Suzuki); **14** Jason O'Halloran (Honda); **15** Mason Law (Kawasaki).
Fastest lap: Brookes, 1m 25.883s, 101.99mph/ 164.14km/h.

Race 2 (20 laps 48.664 miles/78.317km)
1 Josh Brookes (Yamaha), 28m 40.671s, 101.81mph/163.85km/h.
2 Glenn Irwin (Ducati); **3** Leon Haslam (Kawasaki); **4** Jake Dixon (Kawasaki); **5** Tarran Mackenzie (Yamaha); **6** Christian Iddon (BMW); **7** Tommy Bridewell (Ducati); **8** Danny Buchan (Kawasaki); **9** James Ellison (Yamaha); **10** Peter Hickman (BMW); **11** Michael Laverty (BMW); **12** Andrew Irwin (Ducati); **13** Luke Mossey (Kawasaki); **14** Chrissy Rouse (Suzuki); **15** Jason O'Halloran (Honda).
Fastest lap: Haslam, 1m 25.498s, 102.45mph/ 164.88km/h.
Championship points: 1 Leon Haslam, 242; **2** Jake Dixon, 162; **3** Glenn Irwin, 145; **4** Josh Brookes, 130; **5** Bradley Ray, 115; **6** Danny Buchan, 111.

Dickies British Supersport Championship, Round 6
Race 1 (11 laps 26.765 miles/43.074km)
1 Benjamin Currie (Kawasaki), 16m 19.659s, 98.35mph/158.28km/h.
2 David Allingham (Yamaha); **3** Ross Twyman (Yamaha); **4** Jamie Perrin (Yamaha); **5** Kyle Ryde (Kalex); **6** Josh Owens (Kalex); **7** James Rispoli (Yamaha); **8** James Westmoreland (Kawasaki); **9** Sam Wilford (Yamaha); **10** Bradley Jones (Yamaha); **11** Tim Neave (Yamaha); **12** Bradley Perie (Yamaha); **13** Bjorn Estment (Yamaha); **14** Tom Oliver (Yamaha); **15** Harry Truelove (Yamaha).
Fastest lap: Allingham, 1m 28.409s, 99.08mph/ 159.45km/h.

Race 2 (18 laps 43.798 miles/70.486km)
1 Kyle Ryde (Kalex), 26m 44.868s, 98.24mph/ 158.1km/h.
2 Josh Owens (Kalex); **3** David Allingham (Yamaha); **4** Sam Wilford (Yamaha); **5** James Westmoreland (Kawasaki); **6** Benjamin Currie (Kawasaki); **7** Alastair Seeley (MV Agusta); **8** Bradley Jones (Yamaha); **9** James Rispoli (Yamaha); **10** Bjorn Estment (Yamaha); **11** Bradley Perie (Yamaha); **12** Tim Neave (Yamaha); **13** Harry Truelove (Yamaha); **14** Tom Oliver (Yamaha); **15** Ryan Dixon (Yamaha).
Fastest lap: Currie, 1m 28.238s, 99.27mph/ 159.76km/h.
Championship points: 1 Jack Kennedy, 240; **2** Benjamin Currie, 224; **3** Ross Twyman, 134; **4** James Westmoreland, 133; **5** James Rispoli, 126; **6** David Allingham, 122.

HEL Performance British Motostar Championship, Round 4
Race 1 (9 laps 21.899 miles/35.243km)
1 Jake Archer (KTM), 14m 4.713s, 93.33mph/ 150.2km/h.
2 Storm Stacey (KTM); **3** Asher Durham (Mahindra); **4** Jack Scott (KTM); **5** Brandon Paasch (Mahindra); **6** Elliot Lodge (FTR); **7** Edward Rendell (KTM FTR); **8** Edmund Best (KTM); **9** Jack Nixon (KTM); **10** Scott Ogden (Honda); **11** Thomas Strudwick (Honda); **12** Victor Rodriguez (Honda); **13** Taylor Moreton (Honda); **14** Cameron Horsman (Honda); **15** Charlie Atkins (Honda).
Fastest lap: Stacey, 1m 32.657s, 94.54mph/ 152.14km/h.

Race 2 (14 laps 34.065 miles/54.822km)
1 Jake Archer (KTM), 21m 53.168s, 93.39mph/ 150.3km/h.
2 Asher Durham (Mahindra); **3** Storm Stacey (KTM); **4** Brandon Paasch (Mahindra); **5** Edward Rendell (KTM FTR); **6** Edmund Best (KTM); **7** Eugene McManus (KTM); **8** Liam Delves (DR-Moto); **9** Jack Nixon (KTM); **10** Victor Rodriguez (Honda); **11** Thomas Strudwick (Honda); **12** Max Cook (Honda); **13** Scott Ogden (Honda); **14** Elliot Pinson (KTM); **15** Jerry Van De Bunt (Honda).
Fastest lap: Archer, 1m 32.670s, 94.52mph/ 152.12km/h.
Championship points: 1 Jake Archer, 195; **2** Storm Stacey, 136; **3** Asher Durham, 123; **4** Jack Scott, 95; **5** Edward Rendell, 78; **6** Brandon Paasch, 75.

THRUXTON, 5 August, 2018, 2.356-mile/ 3.792km circuit.
Bennetts British Superbike Championship, Round 7
Race 1 (20 laps 47.120 miles/75.832km)
1 Leon Haslam (Kawasaki), 25m 33.822s, 110.59mph/177.98km/h.
2 Jake Dixon (Kawasaki); **3** Peter Hickman (BMW); **4** Josh Brookes (Yamaha); **5** Glenn Irwin (Ducati); **6** Jason O'Halloran (Honda); **7** Luke Mossey (Kawasaki); **8** Mason Law (Kawasaki); **9** Tarran Mackenzie (Yamaha); **10** Chrissy Rouse (Suzuki); **11** Tommy Bridewell (Ducati); **12** James Ellison (Yamaha); **13** Christian Iddon (BMW); **14** Sylvain Barrier (BMW); **15** Martin Jessopp (BMW).
Fastest lap: Mossey, 1m 15.758s, 111.95mph/ 180.17km/h.

Race 2 (20 laps 47.120 miles/75.832km)
1 Josh Brookes (Yamaha), 25m 30.686s, 110.82mph/178.35km/h.
2 Peter Hickman (BMW); **3** Jake Dixon (Kawasaki); **4** Leon Haslam (Kawasaki); **5** Tarran Mackenzie (Yamaha); **6** Jason O'Halloran (Honda); **7** Tommy Bridewell (Ducati); **8** Luke Mossey (Kawasaki); **9** Glenn Irwin (Ducati); **10** Mason Law (Kawasaki); **11** Andrew Irwin (Ducati); **12** Bradley Ray (Suzuki); **13** Michael Laverty (BMW); **14** Richard Cooper (Suzuki); **15** James Ellison (Yamaha).
Fastest lap: Mossey, 1m 15.448s, 112.41mph/ 180.91km/h.
Championship points: 1 Leon Haslam, 280; **2** Jake Dixon, 198; **3** Josh Brookes, 168; **4** Glenn Irwin, 163; **5** Bradley Ray, 119; **6** Danny Buchan, 111.

Dickies British Supersport Championship, Round 7
Race 1 (12 laps 28.272 miles/45.499km)
1 Kyle Ryde (Kalex), 15m 44.279s, 107.78mph/ 173.46km/h.
2 Josh Owens (Kalex); **3** Benjamin Currie (Kawasaki); **4** Jack Kennedy (Yamaha); **5** James Rispoli (Yamaha); **6** Jamie Perrin (Yamaha); **7** David Allingham (Yamaha); **8** Sam Wilford (Yamaha); **9** Ross Twyman (Yamaha); **10** Tim Neave (Yamaha); **11** Tom Oliver (Yamaha); **12** Bradley Jones (Yamaha); **13** Mike Brouwers (Honda); **14** Jorel Boerboom (Kalex); **15** Bradley Perie (Yamaha).
Fastest lap: Perrin, 1m 17.681s, 109.18mph/ 175.71km/h.

Race 2 (16 laps 37.696 miles/60.666km)
1 Josh Owens (Kalex), 20m 45.326s, 108.97mph/ 175.37km/h.
2 Jack Kennedy (Yamaha); **3** James Rispoli (Yamaha); **4** Jamie Perrin (Yamaha); **5** James Westmoreland (Kawasaki); **6** Sam Wilford (Yamaha); **7** Tom Oliver (Yamaha); **8** Mike Brouwers (Honda); **9** Jorel Boerboom (Kalex); **10** Bradley Perie (Yamaha); **11** Tim Neave (Yamaha); **12** Bradley Jones (Yamaha); **13** Bjorn Estment (Yamaha); **14** Richard Kerr (Triumph); **15** Kurt Wigley (Yamaha).
Fastest lap: Owens, 1m 17.057s, 110.06mph/ 177.13km/h.
Championship points: 1 Jack Kennedy, 285; **2** Benjamin Currie, 249; **3** James Rispoli, 162; **4** James Westmoreland, 146; **5** Ross Twyman, 143; **6** David Allingham, 133.

HEL Performance British Motostar Championship, Round 5
Race 1 (12 laps 28.272 miles/45.499km)
1 Storm Stacey (KTM), 16m 19.578s, 103.90mph/167.21km/h.
2 Jack Scott (KTM); **3** Edmund Best (KTM); **4** Asher Durham (Mahindra); **5** Edward Rendell (KTM FTR); **6** Chris Taylor (Mahindra); **7** Brandon Paasch (Mahindra); **8** Jack Nixon (KTM); **9** Taylor Moreton (Honda); **10** Eugene McManus (KTM); **11** Victor Rodriguez (Honda); **12** Sharni Pinfold (KTM); **13** Fenton Seabright (Honda); **14** Cameron Horsman (Honda); **15** Shane Faber (KTM).
Fastest lap: Archer, 1m 19.842s, 106.22mph/ 170.96km/h.

Race 2 (14 laps 32.984 miles/53.083km)
1 Jack Scott (KTM), 18m 53.555s, 104.75mph/168.58km/h.
2 Asher Durham (Mahindra); **3** Jake Archer (KTM); **4** Storm Stacey (KTM); **5** Edward Rendell (KTM FTR); **6** Edmund Best (KTM); **7** Jack Nixon (KTM); **8** Brandon Paasch (Mahindra); **9** Chris Taylor (Mahindra); **10** Eugene McManus (KTM); **11** Taylor Moreton (Honda); **12** Victor Rodriguez (Honda); **13** Thomas Strudwick (Honda); **14** Scott Ogden (Honda); **15** Fenton Seabright (Honda).
Fastest lap: Archer, 1m 19.795s, 106.29mph/171.06km/h.
Championship points: 1 Jake Archer, 211; **2** Storm Stacey, 174; **3** Asher Durham, 156; **4** Jack Scott, 140; **5** Edward Rendell, 100; **6** Brandon Paasch, 92.

CADWELL PARK, 19 August, 2018, 2.180-mile/3.508km circuit.
Bennetts British Superbike Championship, Round 8
Race 1 (18 laps 39.240 miles/63.151km)
1 Leon Haslam (Kawasaki), 27m 56.169s, 84.27mph/135.62km/h.
2 Bradley Ray (Suzuki); **3** Jake Dixon (Kawasaki); **4** Glenn Irwin (Ducati); **5** Tommy Bridewell (Ducati); **6** Christian Iddon (BMW); **7** Peter Hickman (BMW); **8** Tarran Mackenzie (Yamaha); **9** James Ellison (Yamaha); **10** Josh Brookes (Yamaha); **11** Richard Cooper (Suzuki); **12** Luke Mossey (Kawasaki); **13** Jason O'Halloran (Honda); **14** Michael Laverty (BMW); **15** Tom Neave (Honda).
Fastest lap: Haslam, 1m 26.691s, 90.52mph/145.69km/h.

Race 2 (18 laps 39.240 miles/63.151km)
1 Leon Haslam (Kawasaki), 26m 12.279s, 89.84mph/144.58km/h.
2 Bradley Ray (Suzuki); **3** Jake Dixon (Kawasaki); **4** Peter Hickman (BMW); **5** Glenn Irwin (Ducati); **6** Christian Iddon (BMW); **7** Michael Laverty (BMW); **8** Danny Buchan (Kawasaki); **9** Richard Cooper (Suzuki); **10** Luke Mossey (Kawasaki); **11** Jason O'Halloran (Honda); **12** Tom Neave (Honda); **13** Martin Jessopp (BMW); **14** Sylvain Barrier (BMW); **15** Shaun Winfield (Yamaha).
Fastest lap: Dixon, 1m 26.514s, 90.71mph/145.99km/h.
Championship points: 1 Leon Haslam, 330; **2** Jake Dixon, 230; **3** Glenn Irwin, 187; **4** Josh Brookes, 174; **5** Bradley Ray, 159; **6** Peter Hickman, 126.

Dickies British Supersport Championship, Round 8
Race 1 (11 laps 23.980 miles/38.592km)
1 Jack Kennedy (Yamaha), 16m 29.407s, 87.25mph/140.42km/h.
2 Benjamin Currie (Kawasaki); **3** Bradley Jones (Yamaha); **4** Tom Oliver (Yamaha); **5** Jamie Perrin (Yamaha); **6** James Westmoreland (Kawasaki); **7** Sam Wilford (Yamaha); **8** Tim Neave (Yamaha); **9** Kyle Ryde (Kalex); **10** Josh Owens (Kalex); **11** Keenan Armstrong (Kawasaki); **12** Daniel Drayton (Kawasaki); **13** Bjorn Estment (Yamaha); **14** Bradley Perie (Yamaha); **15** Harry Truelove (Yamaha).
Fastest lap: Kennedy, 1m 29.055s, 88.12mph/141.82km/h.

Race 2 (16 laps 34.880 miles/56.134km)
1 Benjamin Currie (Kawasaki), 24m 6.019s, 86.83mph/139.74km/h.
2 Jack Kennedy (Yamaha); **3** Josh Owens (Kalex); **4** James Rispoli (Yamaha); **5** Bradley Jones (Yamaha); **6** Tom Oliver (Yamaha); **7** Jamie Perrin (Yamaha); **8** James Westmoreland (Kawasaki); **9** Sam Wilford (Yamaha); **10** Tim Neave (Yamaha); **11** Kyle Ryde (Kalex); **12** Bjorn Estment (Yamaha); **13** Keenan Armstrong (Kawasaki); **14** Richard Kerr (Triumph); **15** Tommy Philp (Yamaha).
Fastest lap: Owens, 1m 29.681s, 87.51mph/140.83km/h.
Championship points: 1 Jack Kennedy, 330; **2** Benjamin Currie, 294; **3** James Rispoli, 178; **4** James Westmoreland, 165; **5** Ross Twyman, 143; **6** Bradley Jones, 137.

HEL Performance British Motostar Championship, Round 6
Race 1 (9 laps 19.620 miles/31.575km)
1 Jack Scott (KTM), 14m 6.490s, 83.44mph/134.28km/h.
2 Jake Archer (KTM); **3** Storm Stacey (KTM); **4** Asher Durham (Mahindra); **5** Brandon Paasch (Mahindra); **6** Eugene McManus (KTM); **7** Chris Taylor (Mahindra); **8** Jack Nixon (KTM); **9** Elliot Lodge (FTR); **10** Sam Burman (KTM); **11** Sharni Pinfold (KTM); **12** Victor Rodriguez (Honda); **13** Thomas Strudwick (Honda); **14** Scott Swann (Honda); **15** Cameron Horsman (Honda).
Fastest lap: Stacey, 1m 33.047s, 84.34mph/135.74km/h.

Race 2 (8 laps 17.440 miles/28.067km)
1 Jake Archer (KTM), 12m 31.600s, 83.53mph/134.43km/h.
2 Jack Scott (KTM); **3** Storm Stacey (KTM); **4** Asher Durham (Mahindra); **5** Brandon Paasch (Mahindra); **6** Eugene McManus (KTM); **7** Jack Nixon (KTM); **8** Elliot Lodge (FTR); **9** Sam Burman (KTM); **10** Sharni Pinfold (KTM); **11** Victor Rodriguez (Honda); **12** Scott Swann (Honda); **13** Thomas Strudwick (Honda); **14** Scott Ogden (Honda); **15** Cameron Horsman (Honda).
Fastest lap: Archer, 1m 32.838s, 84.53mph/136.04km/h.
Championship points: 1 Jake Archer, 256; **2** Storm Stacey, 206; **3** Jack Scott, 185; **4** Asher Durham, 182; **5** Brandon Paasch, 114; **6** Edward Rendell, 100.

SILVERSTONE, 8-9 September, 2018, 1.640-mile/2.640km circuit.
Bennetts British Superbike Championship, Round 9
Race 1 (30 laps 49.212 miles/79.199km)
1 Leon Haslam (Kawasaki), 27m 25.739s, 107.65mph/173.25km/h.
2 Glenn Irwin (Ducati); **3** Tarran Mackenzie (Yamaha); **4** Josh Brookes (Yamaha); **5** Jake Dixon (Kawasaki); **6** Jason O'Halloran (Honda); **7** Luke Mossey (Kawasaki); **8** Peter Hickman (BMW); **9** Gino Rea (Suzuki); **10** Tommy Bridewell (Ducati); **11** Andrew Irwin (Ducati); **12** Dan Linfoot (Honda); **13** Danny Buchan (Kawasaki); **14** Michael Laverty (BMW); **15** Christian Iddon (BMW).
Fastest lap: Dixon, 54.109s, 109.14mph/175.65km/h.

Race 2 (30 laps 49.212 miles/79.199km)
1 Leon Haslam (Kawasaki), 27m 23.270s, 107.81mph/173.5km/h.
2 Josh Brookes (Yamaha) **3** Glenn Irwin (Ducati); **4** Jason O'Halloran (Honda); **5** Christian Iddon (BMW); **6** Tommy Bridewell (Ducati); **7** Gino Rea (Suzuki); **8** Luke Mossey (Kawasaki); **9** Andrew Irwin (Ducati); **10** Richard Cooper (Suzuki); **11** Dan Linfoot (Honda); **12** Danny Buchan (Kawasaki); **13** James Ellison (Yamaha); **14** Bradley Ray (Suzuki); **15** Mason Law (Kawasaki).
Fastest lap: Haslam, 54.256s, 108.84mph/175.17km/h.

Race 3 (26 laps 42.650 miles/68.639km)
1 Leon Haslam (Kawasaki), 23m 42.398s, 107.94mph/173.71km/h.
2 Tarran Mackenzie (Yamaha); **3** Jake Dixon (Kawasaki); **4** Glenn Irwin (Ducati); **5** Jason O'Halloran (Honda); **6** Josh Brookes (Yamaha); **7** Bradley Ray (Suzuki); **8** Richard Cooper (Suzuki); **9** Tommy Bridewell (Ducati); **10** Christian Iddon (BMW); **11** James Ellison (Yamaha); **12** Danny Buchan (Kawasaki); **13** Mason Law (Kawasaki); **14** Gino Rea (Suzuki); **15** Sylvain Barrier (BMW).
Fastest lap: Mackenzie, 54.177s, 109.00mph/175.42km/h.
Championship points (Start of Showdown): 1 Leon Haslam, 568; **2** Jake Dixon, 523; **3** Josh Brookes, 519; **4** Bradley Ray, 519; **5** Glenn Irwin, 516 **6** Peter Hickman, 504.

Dickies British Supersport Championship, Round 9
Race 1 (18 laps 29.527 miles/47.519km)
1 Alastair Seeley (Yamaha), 17m 7.168s, 103.49mph/166.55km/h.
2 Jack Kennedy (Yamaha); **3** Benjamin Currie (Kawasaki); **4** Josh Owens (Kalex); **5** James Rispoli (Yamaha); **6** James Westmoreland (Kawasaki); **7** Kyle Ryde (Kalex); **8** Sam Wilford (Yamaha); **9** Kurt Wigley (Yamaha); **10** David Allingham (Yamaha) **11** Jamie Perrin (Yamaha); **12** Tom Oliver (Yamaha); **13** Tommy Philp (Yamaha); **14** Bjorn Estment (Yamaha); **15** Richard Kerr (Triumph).
Fastest lap: Kennedy, 56.290s, 104.91mph/168.84km/h.

Race 2 (26 laps 42.650 miles/68.639km)
1 Benjamin Currie (Kawasaki), 24m 3.323s, 103.51mph/166.58km/h.
2 Sam Wilford (Yamaha); **3** Josh Owens (Kalex); **4** Jack Kennedy (Yamaha); **5** Alastair Seeley (Yamaha); **6** Kyle Ryde (Kalex); **7** David Allingham (Yamaha); **8** Kurt Wigley (Yamaha); **9** Bjorn Estment (Yamaha); **10** Bradley Jones (Yamaha); **11** Tom Oliver (Yamaha); **12** Bradley Perie (Yamaha); **13** James Westmoreland (Kawasaki); **14** Robert Kennedy (Yamaha); **15** Richard Kerr (Triumph).
Fastest lap: Kennedy, 56.249s, 104.99mph/168.96km/h.
Championship points: 1 Jack Kennedy, 366; **2** Benjamin Currie, 335; **3** James Rispoli, 191; **4** James Westmoreland, 181; **5** David Allingham, 152 **6** Bradley Jones, 145.

HEL Performance British Motostar Championship, Round 7
Race 1 (18 laps 29.527 miles/47.519km)
1 Jake Archer (KTM), 18m 16.443s, 96.95mph/156.02km/h.
2 Storm Stacey (KTM); **3** Jack Scott (KTM); **4** Asher Durham (Mahindra); **5** Brandon Paasch (Mahindra); **6** Eugene McManus (KTM); **7** Chris Taylor (Mahindra); **8** Edward Rendell (KTM FTR); **9** Sharni Pinfold (KTM); **10** Elliot Lodge (FTR); **11** Sam Burman (KTM); **12** Josh Whatley (Honda); **13** Victor Rodriguez (Honda); **14** Thomas Strudwick (Honda); **15** Cameron Horsman (Honda).
Fastest lap: Stacey, 1m 0.078s, 98.30mph/158.19km/h.

Race 2 (22 laps 36.089 miles/58.08km)
1 Jake Archer (KTM), 22m 13.918s, 97.40mph/156.75km/h.
2 Storm Stacey (KTM); **3** Jack Scott (KTM); **4** Brandon Paasch (Mahindra); **5** Asher Durham (Mahindra); **6** Edward Rendell (KTM FTR); **7** Eugene McManus (KTM); **8** Elliot Lodge (FTR); **9** Sharni Pinfold (KTM); **10** Scott Swann (Honda); **11** Victor Rodriguez (Honda); **12** Sam Burman (KTM); **13** Scott Ogden (Honda); **14** Josh Whatley (Honda); **15** Thomas Strudwick (Honda).
Fastest lap: Stacey, 59.973s, 98.47mph/158.47km/h.
Championship points: 1 Jake Archer, 306; **2** Storm Stacey, 246; **3** Jack Scott, 217; **4** Asher Durham, 206; **5** Brandon Paasch, 138; **6** Edward Rendell, 118.

Bennetts British Superbike Championship, Round 10
OULTON PARK, 16 September, 2018, 2.692-mile/4.332km circuit.
Race 1 (16 laps 43.072 miles/69.318km)
1 Jake Dixon (Kawasaki), 28m 37.789s, 90.26mph/145.26km/h.
2 Tommy Bridewell (Ducati); **3** Leon Haslam (Kawasaki); **4** Andrew Irwin (Ducati); **5** Michael Laverty (BMW); **6** Jason O'Halloran (Honda); **7** Tarran Mackenzie (Yamaha); **8** Peter Hickman (BMW); **9** James Ellison (Yamaha); **10** Dan Linfoot (Honda); **11** Bradley Ray (Suzuki); **12** Glenn Irwin (Ducati); **13** Richard Cooper (Suzuki); **14** Gino Rea (Suzuki); **15** Fraser Rogers (Kawasaki).
Fastest lap: Dixon, 1m 45.778s, 91.61mph/147.44km/h.

Race 2 (18 laps 48.456 miles/77.976km)
1 Jake Dixon (Kawasaki), 28m 42.530s, 101.27mph/162.9km/h.
2 Leon Haslam (Kawasaki); **3** Tommy Bridewell (Ducati); **4** Tarran Mackenzie (Yamaha); **5** Josh Brookes (Yamaha); **6** Glenn Irwin (Ducati); **7** Luke Mossey (Kawasaki); **8** Peter Hickman (BMW); **9** Andrew Irwin (Ducati); **10** James Ellison (Yamaha); **11** Dan Linfoot (Honda); **12** Dean Harrison (Kawasaki); **13** Mason Law (Kawasaki); **14** Gino Rea (Suzuki); **15** Fraser Rogers (Kawasaki).
Fastest lap: Dixon, 1m 34.749s, 102.28mph/164.61km/h.
Championship points: 1 Leon Haslam, 604; **2** Jake Dixon, 573; **3** Josh Brookes, 530; **4** Glenn Irwin, 530; **5** Bradley Ray, 524; **6** Peter Hickman, 520.

Dickies British Supersport Championship, Round 10
Race 1 (12 laps 32.304 miles/51.988km)
1 Alastair Seeley (Yamaha), 19m 48.268s, 97.86mph/157.49km/h.
2 Jack Kennedy (Yamaha); **3** Benjamin Currie (Kawasaki); **4** James Rispoli (Yamaha); **5** Bradley Jones (Yamaha); **6** James Westmoreland (Kawasaki); **7** Jamie Perrin (Yamaha); **8** David Allingham (Yamaha); **9** Josh Owens (Kalex); **10** Harry Truelove (Yamaha); **11** Tom Oliver (Yamaha); **12** Sam Wilford (Yamaha); **13** Kyle Ryde (Yamaha); **14** Keenan Armstrong (Kawasaki); **15** Kurt Wigley (Yamaha).
Fastest lap: Kennedy, 1m 38.218s, 98.67mph/158.79km/h.

Race 2 (15 laps 40.380 miles/64.985km)
1 Benjamin Currie (Kawasaki), 27m 59.507s, 86.55mph/139.29km/h.
2 Jack Kennedy (Yamaha); **3** Alastair Seeley (Yamaha); **4** James Westmoreland (Kawasaki); **5** Josh Owens (Kalex); **6** Bradley Jones (Yamaha); **7** James Rispoli (Yamaha); **8** Bjorn Estment (Yamaha); **9** Keenan Armstrong (Kawasaki); **10** David Allingham (Yamaha); **11** Tom Oliver (Yamaha); **12** Kyle Ryde (Yamaha); **13** Richard Kerr (Triumph); **14** Kurt Wigley (Yamaha); **15** Tommy Philp (Yamaha).
Fastest lap: Kennedy, 1m 46.482s, 91.01mph/146.47km/h.
Championship points: 1 Jack Kennedy, 406; **2** Benjamin Currie, 376; **3** James Rispoli, 214; **4** James Westmoreland, 204; **5** David Allingham, 167; **6** Bradley Jones, 167.

HEL Performance British Motostar Championship, Round 8
Race 1 (10 laps 26.920 miles/43.324km)
1 Jack Scott (KTM), 18m 49.084s, 85.83mph/138.13km/h.
2 Dan Jones (KTM); **3** Storm Stacey (KTM); **4** Brandon Paasch (Mahindra); **5** Jake Archer (KTM); **6** Jack Nixon (KTM); **7** Chris Taylor (Mahindra); **8** Asher Durham (Mahindra); **9** Scott Swann (Honda); **10** Scott Ogden (Honda); **11** Sharni Pinfold (KTM); **12** Elliot Lodge (FTR); **13** Taylor Moreton (Honda); **14** Connor Sellors (Mahindra); **15** Victor Rodriguez (Honda).
Fastest lap: Nixon, 1m 49.688s, 88.35mph/142.19km/h.
Race 2 (10 laps 26.920 miles/43.324km)
1 Jack Scott (KTM), 17m 53.805s, 90.25mph/145.24km/h.
2 Jack Nixon (KTM); **3** Storm Stacey (KTM); **4** Jake Archer (KTM); **5** Chris Taylor (Mahindra); **6** Eugene McManus (KTM); **7** Edward Rendell (KTM FTR); **8** Elliot Lodge (FTR); **9** Scott Swann (Honda); **10** Scott Ogden (Honda); **11** Thomas Strudwick (Honda); **12** Victor Rodriguez (Honda); **13** Cameron Horsman (Honda); **14** Charlie Atkins (Honda); **15** Taylor Moreton (Honda).
Fastest lap: Scott, 1m 45.064s, 92.24mph/148.44km/h.
Championship points: 1 Jake Archer, 330; **2** Storm Stacey, 278; **3** Jack Scott, 267; **4** Asher Durham, 214; **5** Brandon Paasch, 151; **6** Edward Rendell, 127.

Bennetts British Superbike Championship, Round 11
ASSEN, 30 September, 2018, 2.822-mile/4.452km circuit.
Race 1 (18 laps 50.800 miles/81.755km)
1 Leon Haslam (Kawasaki), 29m 11.271s, 104.42mph/168.05km/h.
2 Jake Dixon (Kawasaki); **3** Tarran Mackenzie (Yamaha); **4** Peter Hickman (BMW); **5** Glenn Irwin (Ducati); **6** Tommy Bridewell (Ducati); **7** Jason O'Halloran (Honda); **8** Christian Iddon (BMW); **9** Josh Brookes (Yamaha); **10** James Ellison (Yamaha); **11** Michael Laverty (BMW); **12** Richard Cooper (Suzuki); **13** Danny Buchan (Kawasaki); **14** Luke Mossey (Kawasaki); **15** Dan Linfoot (Honda).
Fastest lap: Hickman, 1m 36.435s, 105.35mph/169.55km/h.

Race 2 (18 laps 50.800 miles/81.755km)
1 Leon Haslam (Kawasaki), 30m 13.891s, 100.82mph/162.25km/h.
2 Josh Brookes (Yamaha); **3** Peter Hickman (BMW); **4** Glenn Irwin (Ducati); **5** Richard Cooper (Suzuki); **6** Andrew Irwin (Ducati); **7** Bradley Ray (Suzuki); **8** James Ellison (Yamaha); **9** Danny Buchan (Kawasaki); **10** Christian Iddon (BMW); **11** Jason O'Halloran (Honda); **12** Dean Harrison (Kawasaki); **13** Sylvain Barrier (BMW); **14** Fraser Rogers (Kawasaki); **15** Luke Mossey (Kawasaki).
Fastest lap: Haslam, 1m 36.330s, 105.47mph/169.74km/h.
Championship points: 1 Leon Haslam, 654; **2** Jake Dixon, 593; **3** Josh Brookes, 557; **4** Glenn Irwin, 554; **5** Peter Hickman, 549; **6** Bradley Ray, 533.

Dickies British Supersport Championship, Round 11
Race 1 (12 laps 33.866 miles/54.502km)
1 Alastair Seeley (Yamaha), 20m 11.901s, 100.60mph/161.9km/h.
2 Jack Kennedy (Yamaha); **3** James Rispoli (Yamaha); **4** Benjamin Currie (Kawasaki); **5** Josh Owens (Kalex); **6** James Westmoreland (Kawasaki); **7** David Allingham (Yamaha); **8** Sam Wilford (Yamaha); **9** Kyle Ryde (Yamaha); **10** Jamie Perrin (Yamaha); **11** Tom Oliver (Yamaha); **12** Bradley Jones (Yamaha); **13** Harry Truelove (Yamaha); **14** Guus Boes (Suzuki); **15** Bjorn Estment (Yamaha).
Fastest lap: Currie, 1m 39.743s, 101.86mph/163.93km/h.

Race 2 (16 laps 45.152 miles/71.232 km)
1 Alastair Seeley (Yamaha), 26m 44.142s, 101.33mph/163.07km/h.
2 Jack Kennedy (Yamaha); **3** Benjamin Currie (Kawasaki); **4** David Allingham (Yamaha); **5** Jamie Perrin (Yamaha); **6** James Rispoli (Yamaha); **7** James Westmoreland (Kawasaki); **8** Sam Wilford (Yamaha); **9** Tom Oliver (Yamaha); **10** Kyle Ryde (Yamaha); **11** Bradley Jones (Yamaha); **12** Harry Truelove (Yamaha); **13** Bjorn Estment (Yamaha); **14** Guus Boes (Suzuki); **15** Richard Kerr (Triumph).
Fastest lap: Seeley, 1m 39.383s, 102.23mph/164.52km/h.
Championship points: 1 Jack Kennedy, 446; **2** Benjamin Currie, 405; **3** James Rispoli, 240; **4** James Westmoreland, 224; **5** David Allingham, 190; **6** Bradley Jones, 177.

BRANDS HATCH GP, 14-15 October, 2018, 2.822-mile/4.452km circuit.
Bennetts British Superbike Championship, Round 12
Race 1 (20 laps 48.660 miles/78.311km)
1 Glenn Irwin (Ducati), 28m 43.077s, 101.67mph/163.62km/h.
2 Jake Dixon (Kawasaki); **3** Tarran Mackenzie (Yamaha); **4** Andrew Irwin (Ducati); **5** Peter Hickman (BMW); **6** Leon Haslam (Kawasaki); **7** Josh Brookes (Yamaha); **8** James Ellison (Yamaha); **9** Danny Buchan (Kawasaki); **10** Michael Laverty (BMW); **11** Bradley Ray (Suzuki); **12** Luke Mossey (Kawasaki); **13** Gino Rea (Suzuki); **14** Dean Harrison (Kawasaki); **15** Josh Elliott (Suzuki).
Fastest lap: Dixon, 1m 25.578s, 102.36mph/164.73km/h.

Race 2 (20 laps 48.660 miles/78.311km)
1 Leon Haslam (Kawasaki), 33m 0.140s, 88.47mph/142.38km/h.
2 Tommy Bridewell (Ducati); **3** Jason O'Halloran (Honda); **4** Richard Cooper (Suzuki); **5** Christian Iddon (BMW); **6** Peter Hickman (BMW); **7** Glenn Irwin (Ducati); **8** Bradley Ray (Suzuki); **9** Josh Brookes (Yamaha); **10** Josh Elliott (Suzuki); **11** Luke Mossey (Kawasaki); **12** Mason Law (Kawasaki); **13** Shaun Winfield (Yamaha); **14** Aaron Zanotti (Kawasaki); **15** N/A.
Fastest lap: Haslam, 1m 37.058s, 90.25mph/145.24km/h.

Race 3 (20 laps 48.660 miles/78.311km)
1 Richard Cooper (Suzuki), 33m 34.093s, 86.98mph/139.98km/h.
2 Tommy Bridewell (Ducati); **3** Jake Dixon (Kawasaki); **4** Christian Iddon (BMW); **5** Josh Brookes (Yamaha); **6** Leon Haslam (Kawasaki); **7** Gino Rea (Suzuki); **8** Jason O'Halloran (Honda); **9** Peter Hickman (BMW); **10** Sylvain Barrier (BMW); **11** Bradley Ray (Suzuki); **12** Danny Kent (Suzuki); **13** Mason Law (Kawasaki); **14** Shaun Winfield (Yamaha); **15** Aaron Zanotti (Kawasaki).
Fastest lap: Cooper, 1m 39.034s, 88.45mph/142.35km/h.

Dickies British Supersport Championship, Round 12
Race 1 (8 laps 19.464 miles/31.324km)
1 Jack Kennedy (Yamaha), 11m 53.918s, 98.16mph/157.97km/h.
2 Alastair Seeley (Yamaha); **3** Jamie Perrin (Yamaha); **4** James Westmoreland (Kawasaki); **5** Sam Wilford (Yamaha); **6** Bradley Jones (Yamaha); **7** David Allingham (Yamaha); **8** Bjorn Estment (Yamaha); **9** James Rispoli (Yamaha); **10** Tom Oliver (Yamaha); **11** Kyle Ryde (Triumph); **12** Tommy Philp (Yamaha); **13** Richard Kerr (Triumph); **14** Bradley Perie (Yamaha); **15** Kurt Wigley (Yamaha).
Fastest lap: Seeley, 1m 28.205s, 99.31mph/159.82km/h.

Race 2 (18 laps 43.794 miles/70.48km)
1 James Westmoreland (Kawasaki), 30m 45.735s, 85.42mph/137.47km/h.
2 Jack Kennedy (Yamaha); **3** Bradley Jones (Yamaha); **4** James Rispoli (Yamaha); **5** Tom Oliver (Yamaha); **6** Josh Owens (Kalex); **7** Richard Kerr (Triumph); **8** Sam Wilford (Yamaha); **9** Charlie Nesbitt (Yamaha); **10** Tommy Philp (Yamaha); **11** Bradley Perie (Yamaha); **12** Robert Childs (Yamaha); **13** Aaron Ridewood (Kawasaki); **14** Mike Brouwers (Honda); **15** Jorel Boerboom (Kalex).
Fastest lap: Westmoreland, 1m 40.988s, 86.74mph/139.59km/h.

HEL Performance British Motostar Championship, Round 9
Race 1 (10 laps 24.330 miles/39.155km)
1 Jack Scott (KTM), 15m 41.488s, 93.04mph/149.73km/h.
2 Jake Archer (KTM); **3** Edward Rendell (KTM FTR); **4** Storm Stacey (KTM); **5** Jack Nixon (KTM); **6** Dan Jones (KTM); **7** Eugene McManus (KTM); **8** Elliot Lodge (FTR); **9** Edmund Best (KTM); **10** Max Cook (Honda); **11** Scott Ogden (Honda); **12** Connor Sellors (Mahindra); **13** Sharni Pinfold (KTM); **14** Sam Burman (KTM); **15** Thomas Strudwick (Honda).
Fastest lap: Archer, 1m 33.062s, 94.12mph/151.48km/h.

Race 2 (12 laps 29.196 miles/46.986 km)
1 Jake Archer (KTM), 21m 30.232s, 81.47mph/131.11km/h.
2 Jack Scott (KTM); **3** Storm Stacey (KTM); **4** Asher Durham (Mahindra); **5** Taylor Moreton (Honda); **6** Elliot Lodge (FTR); **7** Sharni Pinfold (KTM); **8** Cameron Horsman (Honda); **9** Rhys Irwin (Honda); **10** Sam Burman (KTM); **11** Jack Hart (Honda); **12** Ross Turner (Honda); **13** Osian Jones (Honda); **14** Harvey Claridge (Honda); **15** Charlie Atkins (Honda).
Fastest lap: Archer, 1m 45.246s, 83.23mph/133.94km/h.

Final British Superbike Championship points:

1	Leon Haslam,	699
2	Jake Dixon,	629
3	Glenn Irwin,	588
4	Josh Brookes,	584
5	Peter Hickman,	577
6	Bradley Ray,	551

7 Tommy Bridewell, 178; **8** Jason O'Halloran, 176; **9** Christian Iddon, 167; **10** Tarran Mackenzie, 163; **11** Danny Buchan, 147; **12** Richard Cooper, 140; **13** Michael Laverty, 116; **14** James Ellison, 110; **15** Luke Mossey, 99.

Final British Supersport Championship points:

1	Jack Kennedy	491
2	Benjamin Currie	405
3	James Westmoreland	262
4	James Rispoli	260
5	Bradley Jones	203
6	David Allingham	199

7 Sam Wilford, 182; **8** Tom Oliver, 166; **9** Alastair Seeley, 160; **10** Jamie Perrin, 154; **11** Ross Twyman, 143; **12** Bjorn Estment, 96; **13** Bradley Perie, 94; **14** Tim Neave, 81; **15** Tommy Philp, 78.

Final British Motostar Moto3 Championship points:

1	Jake Archer	375
2	Jack Scott	312
3	Storm Stacey	307
4	Asher Durham	227
5	Brandon Paasch	151
6	Edward Rendell	143

7 Jack Nixon, 122; **8** Eugene McManus 121; **9** Elliot Lodge, 112; **10** Edmund Best, 88; **11** Chris Taylor, 85; **12** Sharni Pinfold, 79; **13** Sam Burman, 79; **14** Liam DeLves, 49; **15** Dan Jones, 30.

Supersport World Championship

Round 1 • PHILLIP ISLAND, Australia • 25 February, 2018 • 2.762mile/4.445km circuit • (9 laps, 24.858 miles/40.005km)
1 Lucas Mahias, FRA (Yamaha) 14m 7.811s, 105.552mph/169.870km/h.
2 Randy Krummenacher, SUI (Yamaha); **3** Sandro Cortese, GER (Yamaha); **4** Federico Caricasulo, ITA (Yamaha); **5** Luke Stapleford GBR (Triumph); **6** Raffaele De Rosa, ITA (MV Agusta); **7** Jules Cluzel, FRA (Yamaha); **8** Kyle Smith, GBR (Honda); **9** Ayrton Badovini, ITA (MV Agusta); **10** Thomas Gradinger, AUT (Yamaha); **11** Niki Tuuli, FIN (Honda); **12** Loris Cresson, BEL (Yamaha); **13** Kenan Sofuoglu, TUR (Kawasaki); **14** Hikari Okubo, JPN (Kawasaki); **15** Tom Toparis, AUS (Kawasaki).
Fastest lap: Cortese, GER (Yamaha), 1m 33.072s, 106.832mph/171.930km/h (record).
Championship points: 1 Mahias, 25; **2** Krummenacher, 20; **3** Cortese, 16; **4** Caricasulo, 13; **5** Stapleford, 11; **6** De Rosa, 10.

Round 2 • BURIRAM, Thailand • 25 March, 2018 • 2.830mile/4.554km circuit • (17 laps, 48.105 miles/77.418km)
1 Randy Krummenacher, SUI (Yamaha), 27m 49.852s, 103.709mph/166.904km/h.
2 Lucas Mahias, FRA (Yamaha); **3** Federico Caricasulo, ITA (Yamaha); **4** Sandro Cortese, GER (Yamaha); **5** Thitipong Warokorn, THA (Kawasaki); **6** Anthony West, AUS (Kawasaki); **7** Raffaele De Rosa, ITA (MV Agusta); **8** Ratthapark Wilairot, THA (Yamaha); **9** Niki Tuuli, FIN (Honda); **10** Luke Stapleford, GBR (Triumph); **11** Thomas Gradinger, AUT (Yamaha); **12** Jack Kennedy, IRL (Triumph); **13** Loris Cresson, BEL (Yamaha); **14** Decha Kraisart, THA (Yamaha); **15** Ayrton Badovini, ITA (MV Agusta).
Fastest lap: Krummenacher, SUI (Yamaha), 1m 37.620s, 106.832mph/171.930km/h (record).
Championship points: 1 Krummenacher, 45; **2** Mahias, 45; **3** Caricasulo, 29; **4** Cortese, 29; **5** De Rosa, 19; **6** Stapleford, 17.

Round 3 • ARAGON, Spain • 15 April, 2018 • 3.155-mile/5.077km circuit • (16 laps, 50.475 miles/81.232km)
1 Sandro Cortese, GER (Yamaha), 30m 47.791s, 98.339mph/158.262km/h.
2 Federico Caricasulo, ITA (Yamaha); **3** Jules Cluzel, FRA (Yamaha); **4** Lucas Mahias, FRA (Yamaha); **5** Kyle Smith, GBR (Honda); **6** Luke Stapleford, GBR (Triumph); **7** Sheridan Morais, POR (Kawasaki); **8** Niki Tuuli, FIN (Honda); **9** Anthony West, AUS (Kawasaki); **10** Rob Hartog, NED (Kawasaki); **11** Randy Krummenacher, SUI (Yamaha); **12** Loris Cresson, BEL (Yamaha); **13** Eemeli Lahti, FIN (Suzuki); **14** Michael Canducci, ITA (Kawasaki); **15** Stefan Hill, GBR (Triumph).
Fastest lap: Cortese, GER (Yamaha), 1m 54.644s, 99.065mph/159.430km/h.
Championship points: 1 Mahias, 58; **2** Cortese, 54; **3** Krummenacher, 50; **4** Caricasulo, 49; **5** Stapleford, 27; **6** Cluzel, 25.

Round 4 • ASSEN, Holland • 22 April, 2018 • 2.822mile/4.542km circuit • (18 laps, 50.801 miles/81.756km)
1 Jules Cluzel, FRA (Yamaha), 29m 49.168s, 102.217mph/164.502km/h.
2 Randy Krummenacher, SUI (Yamaha); **3** Raffaele De Rosa, ITA (MV Agusta); **4** Lucas Mahias, FRA (Yamaha); **5** Luke Stapleford, GBR (Triumph); **6** Sandro Cortese, GER (Yamaha); **7** Niki Tuuli, FIN (Honda); **8** Rob Hartog, NED (Kawasaki); **9** Thomas Gradinger, AUT (Yamaha); **10** Loris Cresson, BEL (Yamaha); **11** Hannes Soomer, EST (Honda); **12** Ayrton Badovini, ITA (MV Agusta); **13** Andrew Irwin, GBR (Honda); **14** Wayne Tessels, NED (Kawasaki); **15** Eemeli Lahti, FIN (Suzuki).
Fastest lap: Krummenacher, SWI (Yamaha), 1m 38.108s, 103.564mph/166.670km/h (record).
Championship points: 1 Mahias, 71; **2** Krummenacher, 70; **3** Cortese, 64; **4** Cluzel, 50; **5** Caricasulo, 49; **6** Stapleford, 38.

Round 5 • IMOLA, Italy • 13 May, 2018 • 3.067mile/4.936km circuit • (17 laps, 52.140 miles/83.912km)
1 Jules Cluzel, FRA (Yamaha), 31m 53.653s, 98.088mph/157.857km/h.
2 Federico Caricasulo, ITA (Yamaha); **3** Raffaele De Rosa, ITA (MV Agusta); **4** Sandro Cortese, GER (Yamaha); **5** Randy Krummenacher, SUI (Yamaha); **6** Anthony West, AUS (Kawasaki); **7** Niki Tuuli, FIN (Honda); **8** Lucas Mahias, FRA (Yamaha); **9** Luke Stapleford, GBR (Triumph); **10** Hikari Okubo, JPN (Kawasaki); **11** Rob Hartog, NED (Kawasaki); **12** Thomas Gradinger, AUT (Yamaha); **13** Loris Cresson, BEL (Yamaha); **14** Andrew Irwin, GBR (Honda); **15** Nicola Morrentino, ITA (Kawasaki).
Fastest lap: Mahias, FRA (Yamaha), 1m 51.529s, 99.003mph/159.330km/h.
Championship points: 1 Krummenacher, 81; **2** Mahias, 79; **3** Cortese, 77; **4** Cluzel, 75; **5** Caricasulo, 69; **6** De Rosa, 51.

Round 6 • DONINGTON PARK, Great Britain • 27 May, 2018 • 2.500mile/4.023km circuit • (20 laps, 49.996 miles/80.460km)
1 Sandro Cortese, GER (Yamaha), 30m 30.800s, 98.309mph/158.213km/h.
2 Jules Cluzel, FRA (Yamaha); **3** Raffaele De Rosa, ITA (MV Agusta); **4** Randy Krummenacher, SUI (Yamaha); **5** Lucas Mahias, FRA (Yamaha); **6** Federico Caricasulo, ITA (Yamaha); **7** Ayrton Badovini, ITA (MV Agusta); **8** Thomas Gradinger, AUT (Yamaha); **9** Sheridan Morais, POR (Kawasaki); **10** Andrew Irwin, GBR (Honda); **11** Anthony West, AUS (Kawasaki); **12** Loris Cresson, BEL (Yamaha); **13** Kyle Smith, GBR (Honda); **14** Hannes Soomer, EST (Honda); **15** Corentin Perolari, FRA (Yamaha).
Fastest lap: Cortese, GER (Yamaha), 1m 30.913s, 98.984mph/159.300km/h.
Championship points: 1 Cortese, 102; **2** Cluzel, 95; **3** Krummenacher, 94; **4** Mahias, 90; **5** Caricasulo, 79; **6** De Rosa, 67.

Round 7 • BRNO, Czech Republic • 10 June, 2018 • 3.360mile/5.403km circuit • (16 laps, 53.716 miles/86.448km)
1 Jules Cluzel, FRA (Yamaha), 33m 15.783s, 96.894mph/155.935km/h.
2 Sandro Cortese, GER (Yamaha); **3** Raffaele De Rosa, ITA (MV Agusta); **4** Lucas Mahias, FRA (Yamaha); **5** Randy Krummenacher, SUI (Yamaha); **6** Thomas Gradinger, AUT (Yamaha); **7** Anthony West, AUS (Kawasaki); **8** Kyle Smith, GBR (Honda); **9** Eemeli Lahti, FIN (Suzuki); **10** Loris Cresson, BEL (Yamaha); **11** Rob Hartog, NED (Kawasaki); **12** Hannes Soomer, EST (Honda); **13** Hikari Okubo, JPN (Kawasaki); **14** Alfonso Coppola, ITA (Yamaha); **15** Alex Baldolini, ITA (Honda).
Fastest lap: Mahias, FRA (Yamaha), 2m 3.886s, 97.561mph/157.010km/h.
Championship points: 1 Cortese, 122; **2** Cluzel, 120; **3** Krummenacher, 105; **4** Mahias, 103; **5** De Rosa, 83; **6** Caricasulo, 79.

Round 8 • MISANO, Italy • 8 July, 2018 • 2.626mile/4.226km circuit • (19 laps, 49.892 miles/80.294km)
1 Federico Caricasulo, ITA (Yamaha), 31m 20.416s, 95.517mph/153.720km/h.
2 Raffaele De Rosa, ITA (MV Agusta); **3** Sandro Cortese, GER (Yamaha); **4** Jules Cluzel, FRA (Yamaha); **5** Randy Krummenacher, SUI (Yamaha); **6** Anthony West, AUS (Kawasaki); **7** Kyle Smith, GBR (Honda); **8** Lorenzo Gabellini, ITA (Yamaha); **9** Hikari Okubo, JPN (Kawasaki); **10** Ayrton Badovini, ITA (MV Agusta); **11** Marco Bussolotti, ITA (Yamaha); **12** Corentin Perolari, FRA (Yamaha); **13** Rob Hartog, NED (Kawasaki); **14** Luke Stapleford, GBR (Yamaha); **15** Hannes Soomer, EST (Honda).
Fastest lap: Cortese, GER (Yamaha), 1m 38.193s, 96.275mph/154.940km/h (record).
Championship points: 1 Cortese, 138; **2** Cluzel, 133; **3** Krummenacher, 116; **4** Caricasulo, 104; **5** Mahias, 103; **6** De Rosa, 103.

Round 9 • PORTIMAO, Portugal • 16 September, 2018 • 2.853mile/4.592km circuit • (16 laps, 45.653 miles/73.472km)
1 Lucas Mahias, FRA (Yamaha), 33m 7.991s, 91.418mph/147.123km/h.
2 Federico Caricasulo, ITA (Yamaha); **3** Kyle Smith, GBR (Honda); **4** Raffaele De Rosa, ITA (MV Agusta); **5** Randy Krummenacher, SUI (Yamaha); **6** Sandro Cortese, GER (Yamaha); **7** Hannes Soomer, EST (Honda); **8** Ayrton Badovini, ITA (MV Agusta); **9** Thomas Gradinger, AUT (Yamaha); **10** Hikari Okubo, JPN (Kawasaki); **11** Hector Barbera, ESP (Kawasaki); **12** Luke Stapleford, GBR (Yamaha); **13** Miquel Pons, ESP (Kawasaki); **14** Jaimie Van Sikkelerus, NED (Honda); **15** Christian Stange, GER (Kawasaki).
Fastest lap: Mahias, FRA (Yamaha), 1m 45.220s, 96.620mph/157.110km/h.
Championship points: 1 Cortese, 148; **2** Cluzel, 133;**3** Mahias, 128;**4** Krummenacher, 127;**5** Caricasulo, 124;**6** De Rosa, 116.

Round 10 • MAGNY-COURS, France • 30 September, 2018 • 2.741mile/4.411km circuit •(19 laps, 52.076 miles/83.809km)
1 Jules Cluzel, FRA (Yamaha), 32m 11.633s, 97.056mph/156.196km/h.
2 Sandro Cortese, GER (Yamaha); **3** Lucas Mahias, FRA (Yamaha); **4** Thomas Gradinger, AUT (Yamaha); **5** Randy Krummenacher, SUI (Yamaha); **6** Corentin Perolari, FRA (Yamaha); **7** Raffaele De Rosa, ITA (MV Agusta); **8** Kyle Smith, GBR (Honda); **9** Hikari Okubo, JPN (Kawasaki); **10** Hector Barbera, ESP (Kawasaki); **11** Hannes Soomer, EST (Honda); **12** Ayrton Badovini, ITA (MV Agusta); **13** Federico Caricasulo, ITA (Yamaha); **14** Peter Sebestyen, HUN (Honda); **15** Luke Stapleford, GBR (Yamaha).
Fastest lap: Cortese, GER (Yamaha), 1m 41.185s, 97.518mph/156.940km/h (record).
Championship points: 1 Cortese, 168; **2** Cluzel, 158; **3** Mahias, 144; **4** Krummenacher, 138; **5** Caricasulo, 127; **6** De Rosa, 125.

Round 11 • SAN JUAN VILLICUM, Argentina • 14 October, 2018 • 2.657mile/4.276km circuit • (19 laps, 50.483 miles/81.244km)
1 Jules Cluzel, FRA (Yamaha), 33m 7.991s, 91.418mph/147.123km/h.
2 Sandro Cortese, GER (Yamaha); **3** Lucas Mahias, FRA (Yamaha); **4** Thomas Gradinger, AUT (Yamaha); **5** Corentin Perolari, FRA (Yamaha); **6** Randy Krummenacher, SUI (Yamaha); **7** Kyle Smith, GBR (Honda); **8** Hikari Okubo, JPN (Kawasaki); **9** Hector Barbera, ESP (Kawasaki); **10** Loris Cresson, BEL (Yamaha); **11** Ayrton Badovini, ITA (MV Agusta); **12** Luke Stapleford, GBR (Yamaha); **13** Hannes Soomer, EST (Honda); **14** Christian Stange, GER (Kawasaki); **15** Peter Sebestyen, HUN (Honda).
Fastest lap: Cortese, GER (Yamaha), 1m 43.818s, 92.131mph/148.270km/h (record).
Championship points: 1 Cortese, 188; **2** Cluzel, 183; **3** Mahias, 160; **4** Krummenacher, 148; **5** Caricasulo, 127; **6** De Rosa, 125.

Round 12 • LOSAIL, Qatar • 27 October, 2018 • 3.343mile/5.380km circuit • (12 laps, 40.116 miles/64.560km)
1 Lucas Mahias, FRA (Yamaha), 24m 49.552s, 96.953mph/156.031km/h.
2 Sandro Cortese, GER (Yamaha); **3** Federico Caricasulo, ITA (Yamaha); **4** Thomas Gradinger, AUT (Yamaha); **5** Randy Krummenacher, SUI (Yamaha); **6** Corentin Perolari, FRA (Yamaha); **7** Hector Barbera, ESP (Kawasaki); **8** Raffaele De Rosa, ITA (MV Agusta); **9** Hannes Soomer, EST (Honda); **10** Peter Sebestyen, HUN (Honda); **11** Ayrton Badovini, ITA (MV Agusta); **12** Loris Cresson, BEL (Yamaha); **13** Jaimie Van Sikkelerus, NED (Honda); **14** Christian Stange, GER (Kawasaki); **15** Nacho Calero, ESP (Kawasaki).
Fastest lap: Cortese, GER (Yamaha), 2m 2.873s, 97.947mph/157.630km/h.

Final World Supersport Championship points:

1	Sandro Cortese, GER	208
2	Lucas Mahias, FRA	185
3	Jules Cluzel, FRA	183
4	Randy Krummenacher, SUI	159
5	Federico Caricasulo, ITA	143
6	Raffaele De Rosa, ITA	133

7 Thomas Gradinger, AUT, 86; **8** Kyle Smith, GBR, 72; **9** Luke Stapleford, GBR, 56; **10** Anthony West, AUS, 51; **11** Ayrton Badovini, ITA, 49; **12** Loris Cresson, BEL, 40; **13** Hikari Okubo, JPN, 39; **14** Niki Tuuli, FIN, 38; **15** Corentin Perolari, FRA, 36.